New Perspectives
on Our Lives with
Companion Animals

Aaron Honori Katcher
Alan M. Beck

E D I T O R S

New Perspectives on Our Lives with Companion Animals

UNIVERSITY OF PENNSYLVANIA PRESS *Philadelphia*

Library of Congress Cataloging in Publication Data
Main entry under title:
New perspectives on our lives with companion animals.
Bibliography: p.
    1. Pets—Social aspects—Congresses. 2. Pets—
Therapeutic use—Congresses. 3. Pet owners—
Psychology—Congresses. 4. Pets—Behavior—Congresses.
I. Katcher, Aaron Honori. II. Beck, Alan M.
SF411.5.N48   1983   155.9'2   82-40484
ISBN 0-8122-7877-1

Designed by ADRIANNE ONDERDONK DUDDEN

There is a similarity between poetic and scientific imagination. The resemblance is greatest when a new area of research begins to command attention. Without research support, recognition in journals and scientific meetings, and a place in a curriculum, ideas are very much like "airy nothing." It is necessary for people of both vision and resource to give them "habitation and a name." Research and teaching about the bond between people and companion animals was given such a habitation within veterinary medicine by Dean Leo K. Bustad of Washington State University, College of Veterinary Medicine, and by Dean Robert R. Marshak of the University of Pennsylvania School of Veterinary Medicine. Dean Bustad has, through enormous persuasive effort, generated national and international interest and support for work in this area, bringing veterinarians, health care professionals, and the humane community into a working relationship with each other. The fruits of that working relationship included this conference, the international network of societies fostering an interest in human beings and companion animals, and the model People-Pet Partnership Programs at Washington State University. Dean Marshak worked within his university to create the Center for the Interaction of Animals and Society, the first interdisciplinary center devoted to the study of social and psychological relationships between human beings and animals.

Contents

P A R T   O N E
Animals and People: The Tie Between

P A R T   T W O

A Social Predator for a Companion

PART THREE
Society with Animals

PART FOUR
Companion Animals and Human Health

PART SEVEN
Context for Companion Animal Studies

Acknowledgments

Funding for the preparation of this manuscript was provided by a grant from the EXXON Foundation.

Compilation of the manuscript and the bibliography was the work of Nancy Shriver Hahn with the assistance of Frances Paone and Barbara Dixon.

Editing this manuscript was made easier and more pleasurable by the continuing evidence of interest in the conference reflected in the regular appearance of information about animals and their human companions in the print and electronic media. The source for most of this information was the work described at the conference and contained in this volume. The dissemination of information was facilitated by the dedicated work of the staff of Golin Harris, Inc.

The success of the conference as a whole and much of the modification of the manuscripts that took place between the conference and the publication of this volume were the result of the animated discussions both at the scientific sessions and at the workshops. The session chairpersons and the workshop leaders made a large contribution to the success of the conference and the quality of the papers in the proceedings.

Contributors

Robert K. Anderson, D.V.M., M.P.H. *Professor and Director, Program in Veterinary Medicine, University of Minnesota, Minneapolis, Minnesota*

Edward Baker, V.M.D. *Englewood, New Jersey*

Pat Baxter, *Edwin Schlossberg, Inc., New York, New York*

Nora Beahl, B.S., M.T. *Interdisciplinary Studies, School of Public Health, University of Minnesota, Minneapolis, Minnesota*

Alan M. Beck, Sc.D. Director, *Center for Interaction of Animals and Society, School of Veterinary Medicine, University of Pennsylvania, Philadelphia, Pennsylvania*

Natalie Bieber, M.S., C.A.G.S. *Adjunct Lecturer, Southern Connecticut State College, New Haven, Connecticut*

Peter L. Borchelt, Ph.D. Director, *Animal Behavior Therapy Clinic, Animal Medical Center, New York, New York*

Leo K. Bustad, D.V.M., Ph.D. *Dean and Professor, School of Veterinary Medicine, Washington State University, Pullman, Washington*

Ann Ottney Cain, Ph.D. *Professor of Psychiatric Nursing, School of Nursing, University of Maryland, Baltimore, Maryland*

Ange Condoret, D.V.M. *Veterinarian, Bordeaux, France*

Cathleen Connell *College of Human Development, Pennsylvania State University, University Park, Pennsylvania*

Bernadine Cruz, *Veterinary Student, School of Veterinary Medicine, University of California at Davis, Davis, California*

Maxine P. Fisher, Ph.D. *Research Associate, Department of Anthropology, Queens College, Forest Hills, New York*

Archie I. Flowers, D.V.M., M.S. *Professor of Veterinary Public Health, College of Veterinary Medicine, Texas A&M University, College Station, Texas*

Erika Freidmann, Ph.D. *Assistant Professor, Health Science, Brooklyn College, Brooklyn, New York*

Lawrence Glickman, V.M.D., Dr.Ph. *Associate Professor, Chief Epidemiologist, Clinical Studies, School of Veterinary Medicine, University of Pennsylvania, Philadelphia, Pennsylvania*

Evelyn L. Goldberg, Sc.D. *Department of Epidemiology, School of Hygiene and Public Health, John Hopkins University, Baltimore, Maryland*

Margaret Hahs, *Veterinary Student, School of Veterinary Medicine, University of California at Davis, Davis, California*

James Harris, D.V.M. *Montclair Veterinary Hospital, Oakland, California*

Benjamin L. Hart, D.V.M., Ph.D. *Professor, Neurological Biology and Behavior, Department of Physiological Sciences, School of Veterinary Medicine, University of California at Davis, Davis, California*

Norman D. Heidelbaugh, V.M.D., M.P.H., S.M., Ph.D. *Professor and Head, Department of Veterinary Public Health, College of Veterinary Medicine, Texas A&M University, College Station, Texas*

Linda M. Hines, M.A. *Director, People-Pet Partnership Program, College of Veterinary Medicine, Washington State University, Pullman, Washington*

Katherine A. Houpt, V.M.D., Ph.D. *Assistant Professor of Physiology, New York State College of Veterinary Medicine, Cornell University, Ithaca, New York*

John A. Hoyt, D.Div. *President, Humane Society of the United States, Washington, D.C.*

James S. Hutton *Hertfordshire, United Kingdom*

Sue Igou, R.N. *Veterans Administration Medical Center, Coatesville, Pennsylvania*

Barbara Jones, Ph.D. *Anthropologist, Center for the Interaction of Animals and Society, School of Veterinary Medicine, University of Pennsylvania, Philadelphia, Pennsylvania*

Eileen B. Karsh, Ph.D. *Associate Professor of Psychology, Department of Psychology, Temple University, Philadelphia, Pennsylvania*

Aaron H. Katcher, M.D. *Associate Professor of Psychiatry, University of Pennsylvania, Philadelphia, Pennsylvania*

Robert W. Kennedy, Ph.D. *Staff Psychologist, Veterans Administration Medical Center, Coatesville, Pennsylvania*

Barbara Knight, M.P.S.S. *College of Human Development, Pennsylvania State University, University Park, Pennsylvania*

James A. Knight, M.D. *Department of Psychiatry, Louisiana State University of Medicine, New Orleans, Louisiana*

Dan J. Lago, Ph.D. *Assistant Professor of Human Development, College of Human Development, Pennsylvania State University, University Park, Pennsylvania*

Elizabeth Atwood Lawrence, V.M.D., Ph.D. *School of Veterinary Medicine, Tufts University, Westport, Massachusetts*

Boris M. Levinson, Ph.D. *Professor Emeritus of Psychology, Yeshiva University, Elmhurst, New York*

Randall Lockwood, Ph.D. *Assistant Professor, Department of Psychology, State University of New York, Stony Brook, New York*

James Lynch, Ph.D. *Professor of Psychiatry, School of Medicine, University of Maryland, Baltimore, Maryland*

Aubrey Manning, D.Phil., F.R.S.E., *Department of Zoology, University of Edinburgh, Edinburgh, United Kingdom*

William A. Mason, Ph.D. *Professor of Psychology, California Primate Research Center, University of California at Davis, Davis, California*

Deborah Meislich *Student, University of Pennsylvania Medical School, Philadelphia, Pennsylvania*

Peter R. Messent, M.A., D.Phil. *Animal Behaviourist, Animal Studies Centre, Leicestershire, United Kingdom*

Michael F. Miller, Ph.D. *Statistical Laboratory, University of California at Davis, Davis, California*

Roger A. Mugford, B.Sc., Ph.D. *Clinical Animal Behaviourist, Ottershaw, Chertsey, Surrey, United Kingdom*

Sybil R. J. Murray *Veterinary Student, School of Veterinary Medicine, University of California at Davis, Davis, California*

Michael J. McCulloch, M.D. *Northwest Psychiatric Association, Portland, Oregon*

William F. McCulloch, D.V.M., M.P.H. *Professor of Veterinary Public Health, Director, Center for Comparative Medicine, College of Veterinary Medicine, Texas A&M University, College Station, Texas*

Geary Olsen, D.V.M. *Division of Epidemiology, School of Public Health, University of Minnesota, Minneapolis, Minnesota*

Marcia G. Ory, Ph.D., M.P.H. *Behavioral Sciences Research, National Institute on Aging, National Institute of Health, Bethesda, Maryland*

James Quackenbush, M.S.W., A.C.S.W. *Instructor, School of Veterinary Medicine, Center for the Interaction of Animals and Society, University of Pennsylvania, Philadelphia, Pennsylvania*

Joseph S. Quigley, D.V.M. *Instructor, Department of Veterinary Health, School of Public Health, University of Minnesota, Minneapolis, Minnesota*

Susanne S. Robb, R.N., Ph.D. *Associate Chief, Nursing Service for Research, Veterans Administration Medical Center, Pittsburgh, Pennsylvania*

Michael Robin, M.S.W. *Maternal and Child Health, School of Public Health, University of Minnesota, Minneapolis, Minnesota*

Bernard E. Rollin, Ph.D. *Professor of Philosophy, School of Veterinary Medicine, Colorado State University, Colorado Springs, Colorado*

Jay Ruby, Ph.D. *Associate Professor of Anthropology, Department of Anthropology, Temple University, Philadelphia, Pennsylvania*

Ingrid Salmon *Salmon & Bock, Consulting Psychologists, Surrey Hills, Victoria, Australia*

Peter Salmon, Ph.D. *Salmon & Bock, Consulting Psychologists, Surrey Hills, Victoria, Australia*

Joel S. Savishinsky, Ph.D. *Associate Professor and Chairman, Department of Anthropology, Ithaca College, Ithaca, New York*

Edwin Schlossberg, Ph.D. *Author and Designer, New York, New York*

James A. Serpell, Ph.D. *Zoologist, Department of Zoology, University of Cambridge, Cambridge, United Kingdom*

Robert S. Shurtleff *College of Veterinary Medicine, Washington State University, Pullman, Washington*

Betsy A. Smith, Ph.D. *Associate Professor, Social Work Department, Florida International University, Tamiami Campus, Miami, Florida*

Sharon L. Smith, Ph.D. *Ethologist, Center for the Interaction of Animals and Society, School of Veterinary Medicine, University of Pennsylvania, Philadelphia, Pennsylvania*

Mary Stewart, D.V.M., M.R.C.V.S. *Department of Animal Husbandry, Veterinary Hospital, Glasgow University, Glasgow, Scotland*

Jane Tate, Ph.D. *Research Associate Program in Ecology, University of Tennessee, Knoxville, Tennessee*

Robert ten Bensel, M.D., M.P.H. *Professor and Director, Maternal and Child Health, School of Public Health, University of Minnesota, Minneapolis, Minnesota*

Mary Thompson, R.N., M.S. *Gerontological Clinical Specialist, Veterans Administration Medical Center, Coatesville, Pennsylvania*

Robert L. Van de Castle, Ph.D. *Director, Sleep and Dream Laboratory, University of Virginia Hospital, School of Medicine, Charlottesville, Virginia*

Lyle Vogel, D.V.M., M.P.H. *U.S. Army, San Diego, California*

Victoria L. Voith, D.V.M. *Director, Animal Behavior Clinic, Center for the Interaction of Animals and Society, School of Veterinary Medicine, University of Pennsylvania, Philadelphia, Pennsylvania*

Alyse Zee, M.S.W. *Doctoral Student, School of Social Work, University of Pennsylvania, Philadelphia, Pennsylvania*

Introduction

Interest in how human beings interact with companion animals was not stimulated by the observations of Darwin, or by the basic biological studies of the critical periods for socialization by John Paul Scott and John Fuller and by Fox. The scientific fuel for the current interest in human-animal relationships was provided by the work of Samuel Corson and Boris Levinson, which seemed to indicate that animals could have therapeutic value for disturbed children and adults. The works of these authors are those most frequently cited in this and previous volumes on human-animal relationships. Levinson recognized the value of animals for normal child development, but his audience was more excited about their therapeutic potential. One immediate consequence of this interest in the therapeutic use of animals was the recognition of how little information we had about the events that pass between all of those millions of relatively normal pet owners and their pets: pets who do not rescue anyone from wells or from mental illness. There are six other published proceedings of meetings that centered around the social roles of companion animals. But these six volumes contain only a small number of observational studies of human-animal interaction. This book contains the greatest volume of material about interaction between people and animals brought together in any single work.

The history of the organization of the conference is described briefly by Bruce Fogle following this general introduction. The social context for the meeting was formed by the Group for the Study of the Companion Animal Bond (now the Society for Companion Animal Studies), which originated in a 1979 meeting in Dundee, and the Delta Society, which was founded in the United States in 1977. The Center on Interactions of Animals and Society at the Veterinary School of the University of Pennsylvania was chosen to host the meeting because, at the time, it was the only university center with both a commitment to companion animal studies and a diverse collection of scholars actively pursuing research in this area. The center was established in 1977 to further a comprehensive understanding of the way in which people and animals share their lives. During its first two years, the center was funded by grants from the Marilyn M. Simpson Charitable trusts and a training grant from the National Institutes of Mental Health (NIMH). In 1979 the Geraldine R. Dodge Foundation provided funds for an expansion of the center's research and establishment of a full-time core staff. The center developed in three major areas: research programs to improve understandiing and use of the bond between people and animals; clinical services for animals and their owners; and programs that expanded the curriculum for veterinary students while also reaching out to the entire university and the surrounding community. The conference was a logical extension of the center's commitment to education.

Fortunately the meeting attracted a wide variety of people with diverse interests, and the audience far outnumbered the membership of the organizing societies. The mix of people contributing to the conference was critical to the success of the conference. Ethologists, animal and human psychologists, psychiatrists, sociologists, anthropologists, and epidemiologists discussed people and animals with their own particular instruments of observation. Veterinarians, psychologists, psychiatrists, nurses, and social workers also provided clinical studies of human-animal interaction. But the contrast between animal and man, culture and nature, is too great a dialectic, too important a system of contrasting symbols, to be left to the scientists alone. It is important to understand how the symbolic meanings of animals interact with both our behavior toward animals and our thoughts and dreams about animals. As Jane Tate describes in Part Two of this volume, our experience with teddy bears has unfortunate influences on our interaction with black bears. It is not enough, however, to see animals in a context of symbols to explain our behavior toward them; they must be seen in a context of value as well. Both the conference and this volume profited from the presence of philosophers and humanists who were concerned with the value of animals in an ethical sense and raised questions about how we ought to treat animals as well as the more familiar questions about how we do treat animals. Since animals are important metaphors for the expression of ethical ideas (the lamb, the jackal, and the dove being three cases in point), it is not possible to study man's behavior toward animals without understanding the ethical systems that govern these day-to-day encounters.

The conference was more than a discussion of research. There was too much advocacy in the air to pretend that people were there just to present and evaluate evidence about how people interact with cats, dogs, horses, and other pets. The organizers and supporters of humane organizations were well represented. Their interest was in the enhancement of the social value placed on animals, particularly cats and dogs, and the placement of animals from shelters that would otherwise have to be killed. People from animal control organizations were convinced that advocacy of the health and psychological values of animals would make their jobs easier and less destructive. Veterinarians were there to learn something about clinical problems with animal behavior and to learn more about their clients. Some were there to learn how to act as consultants to animal therapy programs, thus adding a new arena to veterinary practice. Social workers and psychiatrists were anxious to add the use of animals to their therapeutic armory and to share in some of the therapeutic optimism that combining people and pets seems to generate. The conference was supported in part by corporations that profit from animal ownership, because they were anxious to develop information to justify animal ownership in the face of increasing economic and social restrictions.

This volume includes perspectives from a wide range of disciplines reflecting both the intent to study and, in some instances, to advocate animal ownership. Widely differing modes of presenting argument and evidence are employed. Even the chapters that present factual observations and use the rhetoric of behavioral science have a wide range of style. Accounts of single happenings when a person and an animal were brought together, personal reminiscences about the author's experience, case reports, small surveys in which the population was obtained by convenience, well-constructed large surveys of a defined sample, and true experiments with defined protocols are all represented. The citations used by the authors and the authors' definition of a relevant domain also vary. Some use only the traditional rhetoric of their science; others appeal to both poetic sensibility and a canon of scientific fact. Others cite no literature at all but dwell only on their own experience or analysis. This mix of method is appropriate for a field with so little research and so great a complexity. It is also appropriate for a field in which the business at hand is the generation of hypotheses and the formulation of a method for the testing of those hypotheses.

No attempt was made to reduce this exuberant variety or to edit the papers into a single style. The design of the symposium was to create a mix of people to start the process of serious thinking about human-animal relationships. In order for people to think creatively they need to be exposed to material that is still inchoate enough to force the listener to think a bit before he files the information. The conference was exciting because people who usually do not speak together spent three days in intense dialogue that continued through the scientific sessions, spilled into the hallways, knotted people at the lunches, dinners, and less formal gatherings, and continued again at the workshops. This volume represents only the most formal and organized portion of that conference. We hope it will also have the same catalytic effect and encourage people to lift the veil a little farther from their own consciousness of how people interact with animals.

The organization of a volume as diverse as this one has to be somewhat arbitrary. The first part is in concept a map for the study of human animal relationships with the cartographer being an ethologist with an eclectic appreciation of the tools that must be used to study behavior, particularly behavior as complex as interaction between people and animals. His excellent map is complemented by papers discussing the interaction between real people and animals and values and images of animals within particular cultural contexts. It is not possible to limit a study of a man patting a dog to their mutual behavior even when the observers are paying attention to word, gesture, and movement, and even when the history of the participant's life with the other species is known. It is necessary to consider the meaning of dog within the man's culture, the methaphorical means of dogs and the acts of petting a dog, and in a wider sense the system of values, images, metaphors, and narratives that instruct us how to use real and imaginary animals.

The section on the study of conventional relationships between pets and people was placed first because it has been generally neglected. The primary emphasis has been given to the study of the therapeutic potential of animals, not the role of animals in normal human families. The editors feel that the study of human-animal relationships is not only interesting in its own right but is a particularly important tool for the study of problems in human behavior such as the meaning of touch at different stages of the human life cycle.

Part Two emphasizes a darker side of our relationship with dogs: the inevitable consequences of having a gregarious predator as a favorite pet. The control of aggressive behavior and the problems created when a pack animal is left alone for considerable portions of the day are of concern to the veternarian who must treat these problems on a day-to-day basis. These clinical problems are also an interesting window into the animal nature of dogs, as the chapter on fatal dog bite illustrates. The study of conflicts in our relationships with animals that result from the animals' normal behavioral repertoire is also in the domain of the program of research sketched out by Aubrey Manning: the extension of ethological and experimental methods to the study of interaction.

Part Three considers the social implications of keeping animals and the problems posed in an urbanized society. This process is complicated by the rise in energy prices, making central dens and multiple-level dwellings more necessary, and by the entry of so many women into the work force that housing is empty of caretakers during the day. Dr. Alan Beck's paper is complemented by two excellent surveys of attitudes of owners and those who do not own animals. These surveys are useful in understanding what will be necessary if we are to preserve cities as havens for people and animals alike. The two surveys (Joseph S.

Quigley et al. and Peter Salmon) could also have been included in the first section as part of the methodology for understanding the role of animals in human life.

Part Four asks the question: To what extent are animals good for us in some real and concrete sense? The chapters discussing animals and health attempt to determine if there are health gains for normal people from animal ownership. The problems inherent in this investigation of social influences on health and the delicate balance between hope and fact that sustains interest in the hypothesis that animals are good for people's health are well illustrated. One major contribution emerging from the research is the suggestion that both animal ownership and the degree of attachment between owner and animal must be taken into account if the influence of pets on health and well-being is to be studied. If attachment to animals brings with it some psychological or health benefit, it must follow that loss of an animal companion can be a threat to our equilibrium. Part Five explores the problem of grief following loss of an animal and its relationship to the grief experienced after loss of a human companion.

Part Six on therapeutic uses of animals explores the potential benefit of animals for very specialized populations. This area of investigation, aside from the prosthetic use of animals like seeing eye or hearing ear dogs, is very difficult to evaluate. It is difficult to evaluate any kind of psychotherapy, even after millions of dollars worth of research efforts, and there has been very little organized study of the value of pets as a psychotherapeutic aid. The concluding section of the book examines the context for a study of social relations with animals. William F. McCulloch, Bernard Rollin, and Robert S. Shurtleff, all of whom teach at veterinary schools, look at relationships between people and animals in veterinary medicine and in a context of values. This orientation is shared by John Hoyt's contribution on moral constraints on the use of animals. Aaron Katcher and Boris Levinson try to integrate insights from both science and humanities, the first to explore why animals may have peculiar importance to human beings, and the second to chart out a future for the field, or, in essence, to predict the contents of the next proceedings volume.

This introduction began with Darwin's description of the behavior of a dog greeting his master. It has been a long time since the publication of that work, and few have continued to study dogs and people in that fashion. This volume is a small extension of Darwin's description of man and dog. The contributions to this volume ask questions and make suggestions for future research. One wishes that at least some of the generations of scientists who have observed behavior since Darwin had watched how animals and people operated upon each other instead of isolating animals from people by encasing them in machines and seeing how they operated the machinery. Sadly, those scientists who did not wish to observe animals operating machinery tended to flee civilization altogether and observe wild animals in the wilderness. Neither a skinner box nor a forest is the natural environment for a dog, a cat, or a budgie. The natural environment for companion animals is a family and home, and it is time that we sat down, perhaps even in our own homes, and started seeing these companions in their natural habitat.

As we have already indicated, before this publication there were very few empirical studies of human-animal interaction. As a result, the participants in the symposium were compelled to cite and describe a small number of studies very frequently. To reduce the size of this volume, and to spare the reader who wishes to read the volume or parts of it as a unit, we have eliminated as much redundant citation or discussion of the literature as we could without doing violence to the authors' arguments. We have also removed sections of papers designed to justify an interest in relationships between human beings and animals. We assume that the reader accepts the relevance of such studies, and if he remains unconvinced upon reading the material in this volume, it is doubtful that multiple recitations of statistics of animal ownership or allusions to the family status of animals will convince him. We apologize both to the authors of the papers that were altered by these elisions and to the often cited authors whose already large citation index was diminished.

Because of the same redundancies we have chosen to present one composite bibliography at the end of the volume. This should have the additional advantage of discouraging duplication of large portions of this work with the xerox machine.

Bruce Fogle

How Did We Find Our Way Here?

During the past decade, in various disciplines and from different vantage points, science has been looking more closely at the relationship between pet animals and their owners. This interest began in the early 1970s, when in Britain and in Canada symposia were held which examined the role of pet animals in society. In the meantime, two exciting things were happening in the United States. Boris Levinson and Sam Corson were investigating the therapeutic roles that small animals could fill in therapy for the young and the old and publishing their observations and suppositions. At the same time, Victoria Voith and Ben Hart were examining pet animal behavior from a fresh and logical perspective: that of the animal's relationship with its owner and family. Others, in their respective fields, were publishing articles whose central theme was the bond between companion animals and their owners. By the end of the 1970s, articles were appearing by psychologists, psychiatrists, sociologists, veterinarians, and ethologists on this subject. The topic was ripe for a cohesive force.

That cohesion took place at the University of Dundee in March 1979, when thirteen psychologists, psychiatrists, behaviorists, and veterinarians met for two days to discuss the pet-owner bond.

At the end of this meeting a study group was created. It set for itself the following objectives:

1. To study the nature of the emotional and psychological bond between people and companion animals.
2. To study the consequences of this bonding on the emotional well-being and physical and mental health of pet owners.
3. To consider other roles that companion animals serve within society.
4. To study the roles of various health and social care professions in relation to the above and to establish an interdisciplinary approach in dealing with human–companion animal interactions.
5. To collect information and encourage research on human–companion animal interactions and to disseminate such information to produce practical benefit.

The first concrete result was a symposium entitled "The Human–Companion Animal Bond," sponsored by the British Small Animal Veterinary Association and held in London in January 1980. Two hundred people participated in this symposium and, adhering to the original objectives, the information that was presented was expanded upon and published a year later. Other projects, such as the Royal National Institute for the Deaf's Hearing Dogs for the Deaf scheme developed as a direct consequence of that meeting.

This meeting, the first major American symposium on the Human–Companion Animal Bond, should take us further in our quest for a greater understanding of why so many people in Western society keep pets and treat them as they do. It is an exciting quest because it is from its very roots interdisciplinary and international, holistic in the best possible way. But there is a problem.

Science likes fact. Science likes its fact compartmentalized. The endocrinologist, for example, studies hormones and their function and dysfunction in the body. But the endocrinologist does not study that body's consequent actions in society because of those hormones. The study of the bond between people and pets suffers from this compartmentalization of science. Because it is a study of a bond between two social species, it must, by its very nature, be an interdisciplinary work. It defies compartmentalization. It is the study of a social interaction that cannot be scientifically controlled. The bond or interaction may involve such nonscientific things as affection or pride. And worst of all for the compartmentalist, it seems trivial. Pet animals are thought of as aberrations of mankind, misguided dead-end consequences of our interfering with the natural order. In addition, our response to pets is, to the scientist, banal and cloying.

If you love them, open log fires and Barry Manilow's voice create a backdrop. If you hate them, odious piles of feces and contagious microorganisms complete the picture.

The fact that to me indicates that we must learn more about the relationship between people and pets is the simple one that over one-half of all households in the English-speaking world keep them. It is a majority phenomenon, yet compared to other majority phenomena so little has so far been scientifically explained. That is what is so intriguing about the human–companion animal bond, and that is what this volume begins to answer.

PART ONE

Animals and People:
The Tie Between

Introduction

This section should be read as a program for the study of social relationships between people and animals. Aubrey Manning is a highly able guide, and his proposition that ethology should be central to the program of study is credible because companion animals do not usually use words or attend to our words in the same way that we do. Fortunately, the ethological method he describes is exceptionally broad, admitting the utility of experimental studies, observations and analysis of language, historical accounts of the development of individual relationships, and the exploration of the existence of thought in both people and their animal companions. Once the ethologist realizes that the home, the yard, and the park are the natural habitat of the dog, he can sit down on a bench (Peter Messent) or cross the threshold and park near the television set (Sharon Smith) and begin observing.

The descriptions of experiments extend the field of their observations into yards and homes. William Mason and Eileen Karsh use experimental methods to look at the biological basis of relationships with pets. William Mason's exploration of the dog as a surrogate mother for primate infants suggests that the ability to form a bond with another species may have a very long history in human evolution. Eileen Karsh's demonstration that exposing kittens to early contact with humans makes the mature cat more sociable with humans provides more evidence of the plasticity of social behavior in mammals and the important long-term consequences of interaction with humans during the socialization period. These two discussions of the biology of keeping a pet and being a pet complement the review of the anthropological evidence about pets and domestication of animals that follows later in this section.

The ethologist does not usually question his subjects about their behavior, and he usually uses relatively small sample sizes. Sociologists are fond of questioning their subjects because it permits the use of relatively large sample sizes. But it leaves them with the problem of relating a response to a questionnaire to important areas of behavior other than responses to questionnaires. In this section Ben Hart and his associates question veterinarians and obedience show judges to obtain profiles of behavior for individual breeds of dogs. Unfortunately, it is not possible to determine if the profiles represent cultural conventions about breeds or accurate perceptions of behavioral differences. James Serpell uses a questionnaire to compare owners' profiles of their own dog and an "ideal" animal and uses the data to derive groups of adjectives that describe what people expect from a dog. It would be of interest to know the stability of these expectancies, both within and between individual societies. Ann Cain uses questionnaires to describe the human response to an animal and, in particular, the position of the animal within the family. It is important to continue to describe exactly what people mean when they say a pet is "a member of the family" because such investigation should shed light on expectancies, met and unmet, from human family members. Much of the information in Joel Savishinsky's paper touches on cultural variation in the animal's status as a member of the family. These three studies asked their questions about people and animals overtly. Randall Lockwood uses an indirect projective technique: response to an ambiguous picture to describe how animals modify the social image of the people they are associated with. Pairing a person with an animal resulted in a more favorable response to the person. These results confirmed the physiological findings of Aaron Katcher et al. reported in Part Four, which indicated that children felt safer in the presence of an experimenter accompanied by a dog than they did when faced with an unaccompanied experimenter. Thus an animal is not only a member of a social unit, the family, it can also be an important means of altering personal identity.

Five of the chapters in this section are by cultural anthropologists. Anthropologists have long recognized the singular importance of animals in the myth, ritual, and social process of nonindustrialized societies. Most of that interest has been directed toward the symbolic or ritual significance of animals or the relationships between people and animals that were economically significant, like pigs, cows, or game. Even in the accounts of relatively primitive cultures, little attention was paid to the actual interactions between people and pet animals. Joel Savishinsky provides a general review of the anthropological and historical literature describing emotional bonds between people and animals we recognize as pets. His work is particularly significant because it emphasizes the high order of contradiction that can occur in our attitudes and behavior toward animals. These contradictions also exist in our own society and were described by Perin (1981) and Katcher (1982). This review makes an important method-ological contribution by suggesting that when a pet is considered to be like a child, it is necessary to compare attitudes and behaviors toward children and toward the pet in order to learn more about each kind of relationship. Maxine Fisher illustrates the conflicts that arise when people learn to love animals they also eat. Her article should also remind us of the dangers of an anthropocentric vision. If the pig can be as lovable as the dog and the dog as tasty as the pig, then we must be careful about attributing to much of our special feelings about pigs and dogs to the innate characteristics of these animals. The dangers of overgener-alization are also illustrated in Barbara Jones's paper on horseback riding in our society. Her analysis of the symbolic and actual roles of the horse exposes the banality of the commonly held explanations for why horseback riding is a more important sport for young women than for young men. Elizabeth Lawrence looks at the role of pet horses in modern Crow Indian life and shows how actual pet horses perform the important symbolic function of keeping the Crow in touch with their past. Jay Ruby's contribution on the way animals appear in home photographs illustrates the way pets are used to construct a personal rather than a cultural past. The collection of family photographs is the only biography that almost all Americans possess, and most of the photographs in those collec-tions have a significance as keys to historical narratives of family. The salient presence of pets in those collections of photographs both illustrates and provides a means of studying the family role of pets. It complements more conventional means of studying the roles that animals have in families.

Animals real and unreal have a life in our dreams and waking thoughts that may be only partially dependent upon the dreamer's or thinker's acquaintance with real animals. Robert Van de Castle explores what has been written about the appearance of animals in dreams and in responses to psychological tests. His analysis, which includes all animals, is complemented by Barbara Jones's discus-sion of the symbolic role of the horse. This review of animals in dream life again illustrates the high order of complexity in our feelings about animals by describ-ing how animals are associated with fear in dreams, just as they seem to be associated with affection in our waking lives. Van de Castle's observation that dreams about animals are frequent in childhood and decline with age comple-ments two important recurrent themes in this volume: the identity of animals with children and the belief that animals have a particular significance in the lives of children.

The work of this section is complemented by papers in the other parts of the volume. In Part Two, Jane Tate's ethological study of how tourists interact with begging black bears is a vivid illustration of how the bear embodied in the soft toys and stories of childhood can condition behavior toward very real and dangerous wild animals. Tate reminds us again of the importance of social signals in the lives of animals. Even under very trying circumstances, the bears use aggressive gestures as a display or signal, with very little physical contact with the tourists. The chapter on severe or fatal dog bite is an excellent example of what could be called "reconstructive ethology." The conditions that triggered the predatory attack of the two dog packs were experimentally reconstructed by the authors. This is an important methodological tool for the analysis of events which are, fortunately, highly infrequent. The survey studies of Peter Salmon, Joseph Quigley et al., Michael Robin et al., Marcia Ory and Evelyn Goldberg, and Dan Lago and Barbara Knight all provide data on how people perceive animals in the context of their lives. Finally, Aaron Katcher and Boris Levinson in the concluding part illustrate the importance of relating the symbolic context surrounding animals to our actual behavior with animals.

Aubrey Manning

1

Ethological Approaches to the Human–Companion Animal Bond

Ethologists used to be fairly easily recognized. They had a zoological background and were strongly influenced by, if not actually derived from, the groups that developed around Konrad Lorenz, Niko Tinbergen, and their students. Now, rather than a distinct body of work or workers, there exists a distinctive ethological approach to behavior studies shared by people of diverse origins and with diverse aims. This approach starts with the recognition that because all animals have evolved to match the demands and constraints of their natural environment, both physical and social, their behavior cannot be fully understood without reference to that environment.

As a consequence of this attitude, the ethological approach often includes attempts to understand the adaptive function of the behavior in question and how it may have evolved. It is perfectly valid to study animals in the laboratory (or the home) or to abstract certain features—such as an operant conditioning response—which may be shared by diverse animals. The ethological view, however, is that on their own, such studies yield an incomplete and possibly misleading picture of an animal's behavioral capacities. For example, numerous

studies of learning ability which have gone beyond prescribed laboratory conditions and have allowed animals to perform under more natural circumstances
have shown that so-called "laws of learning" derived solely from the methods of
experimental psychology are of very limited application (Seligman and Hager,
1972; Hinde and Stevenson-Hinde, 1973; Manning, 1976). Ethology, then, is
not concerned only with instinctive behavior but with the totality of how animals
respond in their natural environments. The ethological approach to learning is
becoming important, and we find psychologists using ethological methods to
study it. Conversely, we find zoologists using operant conditioning techniques to
study the reproductive behavior of sticklebacks (Sevenster, 1973).

Because of their accent upon the behavior of wild animals in their natural
environment, ethologists have, until recently, devoted relatively few studies to
domestic animals and pets. This omission is surprising, for Konrad Lorenz, who
greatly influenced the emergence of modern ethology following World War II,
always kept numerous pet animals and wrote about them with characteristic
perceptiveness (Lorenz, 1952; 1964). He recognized that absolute tameness did
not mean an animal's natural behavioral repertoire was reduced but that it might
be rendered all the more accessible to an acute observer.

The neglect of domestic animals is fast being reversed. There is a flourishing
Society for Veterinary Ethology in Europe, and the increasing concern for
animal welfare among both scientists and lay public has led to much new
research. The symposium on the human–companion animal bond is a further
example of the same trend, but its scope goes further because it focuses our
attention on the interactions between people and the animals that live with
them. The study of this interspecies relationship will force us to extend our
concepts and our approach. We must certainly include the ethology of the
human owners as well as that of their pets. Human ethology has begun to
flourish almost as a discipline of its own (von Cranach, Foppa, Lepennies, and
Ploog, 1979), although there has been little attention to our relationships with
animals.

I can best illustrate the ethological concepts I regard as most valuable for this
purpose by relating them to the original approach of what is sometimes called
classical ethology.

THE BEHAVIORAL REPERTOIRE AND ITS DEVELOPMENT

Formerly, the study of instinctive behavior concentrated upon pattern of movement, posture, and response to stimuli, which were highly species-specific.
Tinbergen's group, for example, studied the reproductive behavior repertoire of
gulls. All members of this group possess homologous patterns of display, but in
each species they have a particular form. Similarly, the situations eliciting the
displays, though broadly comparable, show characteristic divergences between

species, as do the frequencies with which the patterns are performed (Tinbergen, 1959). Studies such as Tinbergen's gave relatively little attention to the development of behavior within the individual and to variation between individuals. Many of the earlier studies concentrated on birds and fish, which show more limited individual variation than mammals. The owner of a pet dog or cat has no difficulty discerning its species-specific behavior patterns. For instance, one of the most striking features of the domesticated dog is the way it retains, through all the panoply of morphological types, a common repertoire derived from its wild ancestor. Nevertheless, for most owners it is not this repertoire that best describes the behavior of their pets. They concentrate upon the individual characteristics that make up their pet's own personality and stress its capacity to modify its behavior through experience.

The study of behavioral development is now one of the central issues in ethology. It has progressed far beyond the sterile misunderstandings of the instinct *or* learning, nature *or* nurture controversy, and provides us with a framework for studying the way in which genetic and environmental factors interact in the developing animals (see, for example, Bateson, 1976).

In further studies, we shall attempt to discover the strategies or patterning of such interactional developmental processes. For example, "sensitive periods" may be found; times during which the young animal is open to particular influences so that some input from its environment produces a marked change in its behavior or at least in its behavioral potential. Thus several elegant studies on bird song development (see Manning, 1979, for a short review) have revealed in some species sensitive periods for hearing the song of neighboring adults. If the young bird does not hear song during this time, earlier or later experience is ineffective. The timing and extent of such periods are not necessarily under direct genetic control but may be determined by what has gone before; that is, the animal becomes sensitive to an environmental factor once its behavior has reached a certain stage. Such a developmental "program" must also involve genetic controlling factors. It is the task of developmental ethologists to investigate the operation of such programs and not to be satisfied with applying simplified labels such as "innate" or "acquired."

The human pet owner is in a particularly good position to observe how genetically based predispositions can be shaped through varied experience. The pioneering work of Scott and Fuller (1965) has provided a systematic survey of the behavioral development of different dog breeds. We can discern how the contrasting personalities of fox terriers and cocker spaniels are derived from an interplay between genetic and environmental factors and how far individual experience can affect breed characteristics. In fact, the breed differences are very comparable to the variation between species found in gulls. Species differences in the overall levels of fear and aggressiveness affect the performance thresholds and the form of alarm calls and threat postures, for example. Tinbergen could plausibly interpret these differences as a result of natural selection operating on the gulls in their different breeding habitats. Terriers and spaniels, products of artificial selection, show similar differences in thresholds for barking and aggressive approaches.

COMMUNICATION

Classical ethology was much concerned with analyzing intraspecific communication. One of its great contributions was to provide evidence that many of the most conspicuous features of animals—crests, bright colors, scent glands, songs—evolved for a signal function. Furthermore, a number of studies demonstrated that animals commonly show extreme responsiveness to these features in conspecifics. Ethology helped us to understand the origins and function of some of the astonishing diversity of animal adornments and displays. This early work concentrated on relatively short-term interactions between mates or territorial rivals and concerned the communication of tendencies to attack, flee, or mate. More recently has come the recognition that other response tendencies are often communicated and that interactions reflect sequences of events and take place over a much longer time span. (Smith [1977] has provided an influential modern review.) We can see that in social animals communication within a group can be based on very subtle cues which take into account, not just current events, but the past history of interactions between the individuals.

At a relatively simple level, some long-term studies of kittiwakes—monogamous cliff-nesting gulls—have shown that pairs which keep the same mate from one breeding season to the next begin incubation a day or two earlier than newly mated birds (young birds breeding for the first time or divorced birds that are remating with a new partner). The period of intense mutual courtship display which is essential to cement the pair bond and bring both birds, particularly the female, into full reproduction condition is shorter in birds that know each other (Coulson, 1966). Lorenz's remarkable lifetime study of greylag geese—another species that usually mates for life—also provides numerous examples of the way in which communication varies between individuals and pairs as they gain experience together (see Lorenz, 1978).

Given such complexities in bird communities, the extraordinarily subtle communication systems within some mammalian societies, particularly the primates, are not surprising. Communication is the behavioral basis of their social structure. Consider the remarkable results obtained by Kummer's group (1974), who studied the bonding between a male hamadryas baboon and an unattached female. A few minutes of uninterrupted contact is often enough to establish a bond with communication by sexual presentation and mutual grooming. What is so extraordinary is the manner in which other males immediately recognize and accept that this bonding has occurred. They do not try to lure or steal females away from other males, even though they are dominant over them in other circumstances and could easily defeat them. The new social relationship, communicated by the patterns of movement and interaction between the male and female, is treated almost as sacrosanct, and other males stay clear. They appear ill at ease and look away from the pair if they are forced to stay close to them in a cage.

The social carnivores also have a highly developed communication system for conveying relationships within a group. We must expect to find such finely tuned communication between pets, especially dogs, and their human companions. All of us have seen how sensitive dogs are to transgression of the social norms, for example, showing patterns of behavior that may be described as "jealousy" if undue attention is given to new individuals. Years of experience of each other's signals and responses clearly bring to each partner in this relationship an acute sensitivity to the mood and intentions of the other as indicated by tiny behavioral changes, which may be unconscious on the human side.

SOCIAL ORGANIZATION

In its early stages, ethology concentrated on studying relatively simple dyadic interactions, often in monogamous animals. It quickly became clear that ethological concepts would have to be extended and developed to cope with much more complex interactions between animals and with other types of social organization. First, it was necessary to consider the extension of communication which is possible between members of a society who have spent months or years in each other's company. Second, ethologists had to bring their own contribution to such concepts as "relationships," "dominance," "role," and "social structure" derived from the social sciences. One contribution that has proved most fruitful is the study of social organization as a further level of adaptation to the environment. Social organization can vary dramatically between close relatives, for example, territorial, monogamous red grouse versus lek-forming, polygynous black grouse, or one-male groups of *hamadryas* baboon versus multimale groups of *cynocephalus* baboons. It can also vary according to season of the year, as, for example, many monogamous birds form flocks in winter. In all such cases a close study of the ecology and behavior of the species has enabled construction of plausible hypotheses to account for the differences observed. Sometimes it is possible to verify a hypothesis from natural experiments, for example, bird species that are monogamous or polygynous depending on the richness of the local habitat. Much of this work, aiming to reconstruct and, if possible, measure the selective forces operating upon the individual animal through its social life, has become part of the subject matter now included within the blanket name "sociobiology." Crook (1970, 1980) was, in my view, one of the most innovative workers in this area. Most recently Hinde (1979) has provided a full discussion of an ethological approach to relationships which takes account of the social and physical environment acting upon individuals.

All this may seem rather remote from the human–companion animal bond, but social organization is important because the ethological approach has given us new insights into the nature and adaptiveness of the social behavior of, for example, cats and dogs, which has helped us to understand the way these animals interact with us.

COGNITIVE ETHOLOGY

This aspect of ethology has not been formally considered until recently. It is concerned with the nature of the mind and consciousness of animals. For some people such concepts are anathema. They feel not only that cognitive ethology is a nonsubject but that it will always remain so. They point out that the consciousness even of other human beings can never be observed directly but only inferred by comparison. Thus in the absence of any possible means of proof for animals, it is best to apply Morgan's canon—"In no case may we interpret an action as the outcome of the exercise of a higher psychical faculty, if it can be interpreted as the outcome of the exercise of one which stands lower in the psychological scale."

In contrast, there are many ethologists—and I count myself among them—who feel convinced that some animals, certainly carnivores, ungulates, whales, and primates, exhibit some of the attributes of a mind. The alternatives required to explain simple memory and response to stimuli and reinforcement are sometimes tortuous in the extreme. Although we accept that formal proof will be impossible, we think that animals should be given the benefit of the doubt. This is not a feeling which is inspired by considerations of animal welfare and certainly does *not* imply that scientists who do not share our view are any less concerned with the welfare of the animals they study. We feel that it is worthwhile trying systematically to collect evidence bearing on this question from a diverse range of species, even if such evidence is largely circumstantial.

The serious reopening of this topic is due to the courageous influence of Donald Griffin, whose book *The Question of Animal Awareness* has just gone into a second edition (1981). The title suggests the approach. Griffin is trying to draw attention to a large number of cases, many of them anecdotal, in which animals appear to be aware of the potential outcome of their activities. He suggests that they are capable of forming mental images of some kind. Since their brains are smaller and less elaborate than ours, these images would not necessarily resemble those we form, but they would nevertheless give animals some extra degree of experience of and control over their behavior.

There can be little doubt that any form of mental imagery and "awareness" would impart a considerable advantage to animals possessing them. Natural selection should operate upon emerging minds, and ethologists are naturally concerned with the evolution of the behavior they study. Cognitive ethology, if it can get off the ground, is bound to consider the evolution of mind and consciousness. Although it is possible that the very rapid increase in brain size occurred during the later evolution of *Homo sapiens* and was accompanied by a sudden emergence of novel cognitive processes, it is hard to believe that some forms of such cognition are not represented in animals with smaller brains. Indeed, this is another strong circumstantial argument for refusing to dismiss cognitive ethology out of hand.

SUGGESTIONS FOR FUTURE RESEARCH

COGNITIVE ETHOLOGY

Humans with companion animals are in a unique position to make valuable observations, although they are often ill suited to be objective while doing so because of the bond of affection they share with their pet. They are almost certain to take the consciousness of their dog or cat companion for granted. But, because the animal is frequently interacting with a human being in a complex environment, it is likely to be intellectually stretched on many occasions, even if it has a materially easy existence as far as food and shelter are concerned.

It will be valuable to watch for occasions when dogs or cats try to manipulate the behavior of their human companions. Are there ever signs that animals try to deceive by giving false signals? Griffin (1981) cites examples which suggest that chimpanzees are capable of deception, but we know of no other convincing cases.

Highly trained animals such as sheep dogs and guide dogs for the blind are likely to be placed in situations that demand initiative. Anecdotes abound in such cases. Vines (1981), in a fascinating account of the methods used to train sheep dogs, gives examples of the cognitive skills of the dogs, which strongly suggest that, faced with a novel situation, they can apply to advantage their past experience with the rigid response patterns of sheep. "Dogs experience particular difficulty when faced with recalcitrant ewes with lambs; one such ewe which had split off from the main flock refused to be moved and faced the dog square on, stamping its hooves. The dog returned to the main flock, cut off several sheep, and brought them over to the stubborn ewe. The ewe promptly joined this group and the dog was able to move them all back to the main flock."

If such observations can be gathered systematically with adequate knowledge of the animal's previous experience in such situations, we may be able to make a reasonable assessment of the various alternative explanations for such remarkable behavior. I suggest that for this, and indeed for all work on human-animal interactions, it will be valuable to have experienced ethologists observe the interactions rather than relying entirely on reports from the human member of the pair. Sharon Smith's contribution to this volume reports on some studies of this nature which are essential if we are to learn the range and detail of possible behavioral responses.

Ethologists should also try to gather more systematic evidence on animals dreaming. All dog owners are familiar with this phenomenon, which is at least external prima facie evidence of internal mental imagery. Such information as we have is almost entirely ancedotal, and regular observations, backed up with video records for further analysis, will be valuable. There are fewer accounts of cats dreaming. Is this a genuine difference? Does it merely reflect greater internalization in cats or is it possible that the slow, stealthy stalking of the cat's hunting behavior is less easily discerned in a sleeping animal than the obvious yelping dream chases of dogs? The work of Jouvet (1979) suggests that there may be a difference between the normal control of dreaming in these two species. Specific brain lesions in cats (in the *locus caeruleus*) release them from the normal relaxed posture they adopt during their paradoxical or rapid-eye-movement sleep. They then show conspicuous movements in their sleep which suggest dreams of hunting just as dogs do.

SOCIAL BEHAVIOR AND DEVELOPMENT OF THE BOND

The basic ethology of animal domestication is well known, although several questions on the earliest states remain (see Messent and Serpell, 1981, for a good review). For example, we can understand how the social organization of wolves predisposed them to form a stable bond with humans. The great majority of a wolf's life is spent as a subordinate member of a small pack. Its social bonding is sufficiently open in its programming that human beings are accepted as dominants provided that exposure to them comes early enough. Scott and Fuller's (1965) work has shown the sensitive period for social imprinting to be waning at about twelve weeks of age. There is some evidence that young wolves born in the wild can bond to humans and that domestic dogs kept isolated beyond twelve weeks remain very wild. The remarkable feature of normal development in dogs (and cats) is that although they incorporate humans into their social group they retain conspecifics there also.

It would be interesting to look in more detail at social bonding in young dogs and cats in the human family situation. There seems no doubt that some dogs relate almost entirely to one person and are ill at ease or even hostile to others. (I am not referring here to guard dogs, which may be specifically trained to respond in this way.) Is the specialized bonding of such dogs related to events in the early history of introduction to the family? Are there consistent differences among breeds? Are these differences in the extent of the sensitive period or to the degree of generalization to a range of human companions or both?

Far less studied in this respect, cats show a wider range of social organization than dogs and appear to be more opportunistic. There are now a number of studies of feral cats, which show strong signs of matrilineal groups. It would be interesting to compare bonding to humans by single kittens of both sexes and by groups of kittens.

Finally, I suggest it will be worthwhile to look at the processes involved in training dogs. The study of sheep dogs shows clearly that the shepherd has to integrate his words of command to match the natural movements of the young dog, which certainly have some genetic component in their development and relate to the hunting of wolf packs. Other trainers must try to prepare their dogs—guide dogs, for example—for less natural situations. Consistent breed differences in these respects would be interesting to explore because it might be possible to relate them to different levels of compatible or noncompatible inherited tendencies.

THE HUMAN RESPONSE TO ANIMAL COMPANIONS

The general nature of the human response to pets is familiar. The majority of humans get pleasure from contact with animals which is not obviously a form of substitution or sublimation—animals are nice to have around. Many people treat them like a special child. Several psychologists have recorded that the language and inflection of voice used when speaking to animals resembles that used when adults address young children. In many cases animals *are* used as substitutes for children or human companions. There is particular interest in the role animal companions can play in helping physically or mentally handicapped children. I think that there is great ethological interest in the way such relationships develop.

One of the most flourishing areas of human ethology is work with young children. It is obviously attractive for certain types of study to take human beings who are as little affected by culture and experience as possible. Even a two-year-old is already a highly cultural person, but nevertheless interactions in kindergartens or nursery schools are amenable to direct observation in a way that is impossible later.

Some of the pioneer observational studies (see Blurton-Jones, 1972) used description of movement alone—treating the children very much as a field worker studying primates would do. The emphasis was on nonverbal communication to the exclusion of speech. Other human ethologists have tried to combine both elements of communication (Manning and Herrmann, 1981). They point out that, even by nursery-school age, children are highly verbal and the interpretation of interactions is hampered without records of what children say. Through careful and detailed observation of posture and expression it has been possible to learn a great deal about the processes involved in the early development of children, especially their formation of social bonds with family and friends and the role of aggressive behavior. One of the most striking examples has been the Tinbergens' application of ethological techniques to the study of childhood autism (1972, 1976).

I know of no systematic studies of the behavior of children with animals, and I suggest they will be important. It will be particularly worthwhile to compare the behavior of normal children toward their pets with that of children who are known to have problems in their social relationships with others. Such studies should not be confined to children with severe mental illness; Manning and

Herrmann report that children commonly have problems in establishing good relationships in peer groups. Sometimes these problems can be related to problems at home. Children sometimes treat animals as toys, handling them as if they were inanimate objects; at other times they treat them as friends or companions, perhaps conveniently subordinate companions. How do these responses differ between children well and less well socially adjusted? I suggest that the early stages of the introduction of a pet to a family will be of special interest. How does the behavior of children change as the pet becomes familiar and bonded into the family?

Such studies will require a close knowledge of the normal behavioral repertoire of children. For example, it will be essential to record the subtleties of hand positions and facial expressions. These can indicate small changes in underlying tendencies to approach or avoid, tendencies to behave aggressively, and so on. Children exhibit several types of smiles, which differ in their context (Brannigan and Humphries, 1972). For instance, the so-called simple smile in which the closed mouth turns up at the corners is typically shown in nonsocial interactions—playing alone with toys. Upper smile and broad smile are seen in greetings and social interactions. They can be partially "faked," that is, assumed without the underlying pleasant feelings; but if they are faked, a small pouch below the eyes resulting from the muscle contractions that help to move up the corners of the mouth usually fails to appear. Without attention to such detail we shall be failing to exploit the advantages of the ethological approach. Good ethologists become totally familiar with the total behavior of the animals they study. The close observation of subtle changes in facial expressions, vocalizations, and postures will offer us the means for a sensitive monitoring of how a child is responding to a new or familiar animal and will help us to chart the progress of the relationship. Of course, we shall not want to ignore the animal's responses, and it will be very interesting to observe its direction of gaze and its disposition to approach and initiate contact. Do animals respond differently toward children whose own tendencies to approach and whose gaze differs?

I have tried to make a few suggestions as to directions for research concerning this fascinating human-animal relationship. Investigators studying the human–companion animal bond will undoubtedly have more ideas. I think it is very important to bring those studies into the field of comparative ethology. There is much to be gained by keeping the study of human-animal interactions in touch with and in resonance with ethological concepts of investigation.

William A. Mason

2

Dogs as Monkey Companions

Ebony has liquid brown eyes and winning ways, and she has long been a favorite of the students working in my laboratory. Ebony is a mongrel, very much like countless other nondescript dogs wandering on the streets of any large city every day. What makes Ebony different from the others is that she has spent most of her life with a monkey as her constant companion. Ebony has lived with several monkeys. The last one, Samson, is nearly two years old and is now a fine looking young male. Samson and Ebony have lived together from the time he was a small infant. They are together always. They sleep together, eat together, play together. Samson, who never knew his real mother, accepts Ebony as if she were his own mother. And Ebony has done nothing to spoil the illusion.

For more than twenty years, my associates and I have been investigating the social development of monkeys, hoping to find out what experiences these animals need to develop normally. Everyone knows that social influences play a very important part in the development of the human infant. We now know that this is also true of monkeys and apes. Nevertheless, it is not easy to say precisely what elements are important and what are not. For example, how much of our behavior as parents has any lasting influence on our children, and what effects does it produce? How much of the adult's personality is determined by childhood experiences? Every parent at one time or another has pondered such questions and has finally despaired of arriving at any definite answers. Although experiments, such as the one currently under way with Ebony and Samson, can never give complete answers to questions about human development, they can provide important clues.

Our research is based on rhesus monkeys, a species that is native to India but has been born and bred in captivity for many years. We have learned a great deal about its physiology, its behavior, and its early development. Although the newborn rhesus monkey is more advanced physiologically and behaviorally than the human infant, it shares many of the same needs and shows similar developmental patterns. For example, the newborn monkey and the human infant both have well-developed sucking reflexes at birth and both require frequent feedings. Another similarity between newborn monkey and human infant is that the regulation of body temperature is not very efficient. Ordinarily, this presents no problem to the infant monkey, for it is held or carried constantly by its mother and derives the warmth it needs from her body. If the baby monkey is separated from its mother, however, it must be kept warm. This is usually done by placing it on a heating pad and giving it a small blanket that it can wrap itself in and cling to.

When a monkey is separated from its mother and given a heating pad and a blanket, within a few weeks it develops a strong emotional attachment to the blanket. It is usually to be found clinging to its blanket and becomes frantic when separated from it. When it is in a frightening situation, it is much more calm and emotionally secure if the blanket is there. Although human infants sometimes develop a similar emotional attachment to something soft and cuddly, such as a furry toy or a blanket, the attachment is not nearly so strong and dramatic as it is in monkeys. In many ways, the monkey seems to treat its blanket as though it were its mother. For this reason, some scientists have concluded that rhesus monkeys show something very much like the imprinting phenomenon that the famous Austrian ethologist Konrad Lorenz described in chickens and geese.

We have taken advantage of this tendency of the infant rhesus monkey to form an emotional bond to any soft and furry object, and to treat it as its mother, as a means of investigating how the characteristics of the mother influence the monkey's psychological development. We cannot make the monkey form an emotional attachment; it must do that on its own. But knowing the kind of object to which it is likely to become attached, we are able to give the object particular properties that are of interest to us because of their potential effects on development. For example, one of our experiments was concerned with the mobility of the mother. Infant monkeys are carried everywhere by their mothers, which means that they receive a great deal of varied stimulation as she goes about her daily activities of feeding, moving along with her group, and interacting with its members. Is this movement stimulation important in the normal development of the rhesus monkey? To answer this question, we raised monkeys with artificial mothers made from plastic cylinders covered with artificial fur. One group of monkeys had mothers that were mechanized to simulate the movements of a real mother as she carries her infant. Another group had artificial mothers identical to those of the first group, except that they were fixed in one place and did not move. One of the most interesting findings of this experiment was that the monkeys whose mothers did not move habitually rocked their bodies back and forth in a rigid and stereotyped fashion—particularly when they were upset—in a pattern similar to that shown by severely retarded humans, by blind children, and by some children with psychiatric disorders. Not one of the monkeys raised with the moving mothers developed this stereotyped rocking (Mason and Berkson, 1975). So it seems that the movement stimulation that the monkey mother provides her infant as she carries it with her during the early months of its life fulfills an important need. We cannot conclude from this, of course, that human children develop rocking for exactly the same reasons as the infant monkey does, but the results do suggest that movement stimulation, such as parents give when they carry a baby or swing it gently, may also be meeting an important need of the human child. In fact, it has been shown since our findings were first reported that if special care is taken to give congenitally blind children this stimulation, they do not develop rocking or show the other forms of repetitive stereotyped activities that are so common in such children.

That brings us to Ebony and Samson, who are part of our most recent series of experiments in which we are comparing the development of monkeys raised with dogs or with plastic animals covered with artificial fur. A monkey with each type of substitute mother is shown in Figure 2.1. We used dogs rather than the monkeys' real mothers because we wanted the monkeys to have a true social companion, but one that did not show the specialized instinctive behaviors and complex caretaking patterns of the natural mother. We thought this would give us a clearer idea of some of the features of early social experience that were of general importance to the infant monkey. We have found that dogs are ideal for this purpose. Although they do not attempt to mother the baby monkeys, they are remarkably tolerant and gentle with them and extremely sociable (Mason and Kenney, 1974). We want all of our monkeys to have many opportunities for varied experience, so we raise them in spacious outdoor cages where they can see the normal activities around a busy laboratory. In addition, we give them regular play periods in a large outdoor enclosure.

How do the two groups of monkeys differ? One might guess that the monkeys raised with dogs are more content or happier than the monkeys raised with plastic horses. No one knows how to measure happiness in a monkey, but, from all the evidence available to us, it does not seem that monkeys raised with hobby horses are unhappy. They seem content. They eat well, grow normally, and are in the same generally excellent physical condition as the monkeys raised with dogs. Another guess might be that monkeys raised with dogs develop a much stronger emotional attachment to their substitute mothers than do monkeys raised with plastic horses. This also appears not to be true. We have measured the strength of the monkey's emotional attachment to its substitute mother in various ways, and in most tests we found little if any difference between the two groups.

The most interesting differences between our two groups appeared when we began to look away from the monkey's reactions to its substitute mother and to examine its reactions toward the rest of the world. We looked at these from two points of view (Mason, 1978).

First, we looked at how the environment affected the monkey's emotional responses. We knew that young monkeys are upset when they are in a place that is strange to them, and we compared the emotional reactions of our two groups to such unfamiliar situations. We measured vocal activity and heart rate, two good indicators of emotional arousal. To our surprise, monkeys raised with dogs were more aroused in these situations than monkeys raised with plastic horses: they vocalized more, had higher heart rates, and in general seemed more agitated. Some of these findings are presented in Figures 2.2 and 2.3.

Our second concern was with how the monkeys acted on the environment. Apart from their emotional responses, how did they react to new situations? We examined this question by putting the monkeys in different settings in which they could make something of interest to them happen by their own efforts. In one experiment, we put the monkey in a room where, by climbing up a pole, it could get a piece of food or candy suspended overhead. Monkeys raised with dogs solved this problem easily, but most of the monkeys raised with plastic horses did not even try. Contacts with such problems and percentage of solutions are presented in Figures 2.4 and 2.5.

In another experiment, we gave the monkeys an opportunity to look at colored slides projected on a screen and found that the monkeys raised with dogs were much more interested in looking at the pictures than were the monkeys raised with the toy horses. These results are presented in Figure 2.6 (Wood, Mason, and Kenney, 1979).

What is most exciting about these findings is the clear suggestion that the kind of mother a monkey is raised with has a generalized effect on the way it approaches and deals with the world. Even though the monkeys in both our groups had plenty of stimulation from the environment and many opportunities to explore and to learn, monkeys raised with dogs seem much more curious, alert, outgoing, and engaged with the environment than do monkeys raised with plastic horses. It is as though for each group, the substitute mother served as a model to the monkey of what the world is like and how to cope with it. Monkeys raised with fur-covered plastic toys, substitute mothers that are obviously not responsive to the monkeys or to the environment, tend to be passive and unresponsive, just as their mothers are; monkeys raised with dogs also resemble their mothers in being active, alert, and outgoing. These differences in patterns of coping with the environment suggest some of the ways in which the behavior of parents could affect the development of human personality traits. It is even possible that the individual's susceptibility to certain psychosomatic disorders, such as cardiovascular disease, may be heavily influenced by the kind of parental "model" it has experienced. We are exploring this possibility in our current research.

With respect to the primary theme of this volume, I believe our results support two important conclusions that have emerged in many of the other contributions. First, our findings demonstrate the profound importance to primates of a close and ongoing relationship with another social being. The effects of such a relationship are pervasive. They are manifest in behavior, in physiology, and indeed seem to be reflected in the individual's basic stance toward the world, its habitual ways of dealing with challenges and changes. Second, our results show that these effects do not require that the companion be a member of one's own species, or even a near phylogenetic relative. We have long known that the dog is an effective companion animal for man, and we have, indeed, selectively bred it to some extent for this purpose. We now know that its efficacy as a social companion is not limited to man but extends to the nonhuman primates as well.

Figure 2.1A. Rhesus monkey infant with canine substitute mother

Figure 2.1B. Rhesus monkey infant with inanimate substitute mother

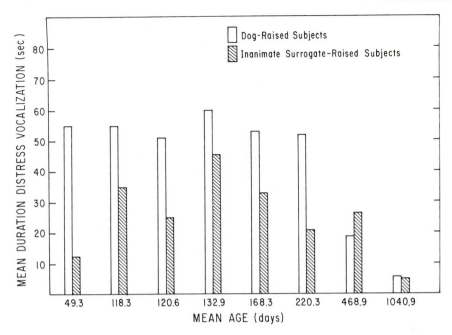

Figure 2.2. Mean distress vocalizations (coo, scream) of monkeys raised with canine and inanimate substitute mothers (Mason, 1978)

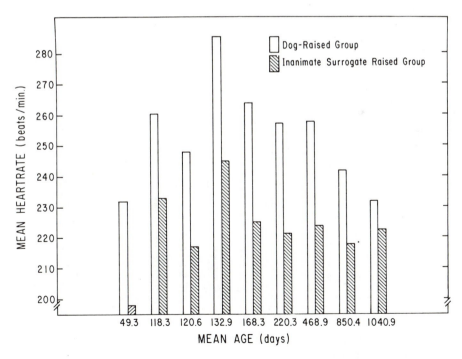

Figure 2.3. Mean heart rate of monkeys raised with canine and inanimate substitute mothers (Mason, 1978)

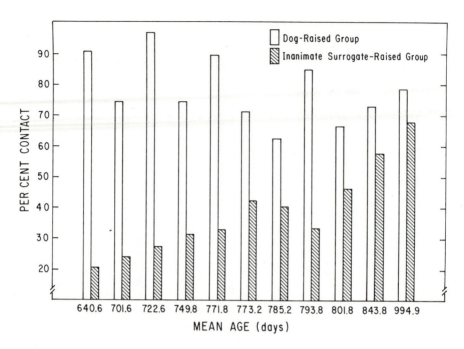

Figure 2.4. Percentage of trials in which problems were contacted by monkeys raised with canine and inanimate substitute mothers (Mason, 1978)

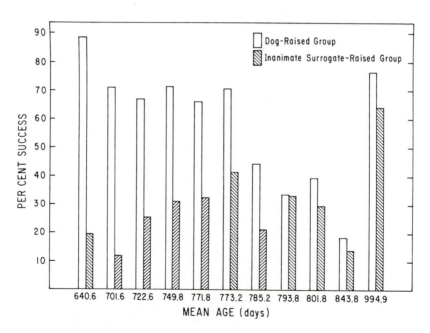

Figure 2.5. Percentage of problems solved by monkeys raised with canine and inanimate mother substitutes (Mason, 1978)

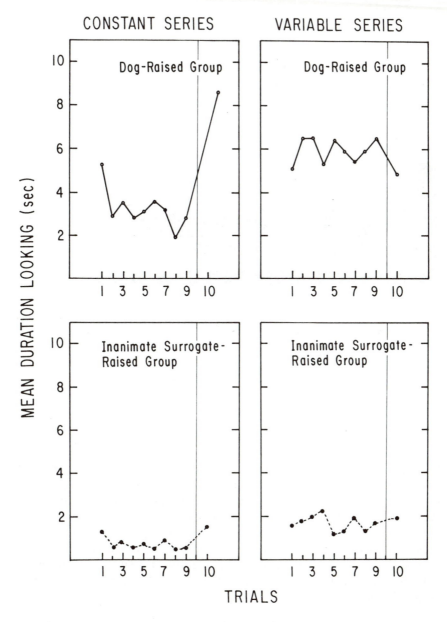

Figure. 2.6. Duration of looking at projected color slides by monkeys raised with canine and inanimate mother substitutes. Constant series: The same slide was presented on trials 1–9, and on trial 10 a novel slide was introduced. Variable series: A different slide was presented on each trial (Wood, Mason, and Kenney, 1979).

Eileen B. Karsh

3

The Effects of Early Handling on the Development of Social Bonds Between Cats and People

During the past few years I have made observations on cats reared in my research colony and in my home that have convinced me that the attachment between cats and people can be profoundly altered by experiences early in the cat's life. In the laboratory, we have found that cats that had been exposed to people but had not been handled very much when they were young became hard to catch, difficult to handle, and actively avoided people when they were mature. At home we had a kitten that my son handled, starting when the kitten was three weeks old. This kitten has grown up to be an extremely friendly cat who clearly prefers people to other cats.

REVIEW OF THE LITERATURE

Studies have shown the strong effect of an animal's exposure early in life to members of its own species, to members of another species, or to no other living organism (social isolation). Most of this work has been done on dogs and monkeys. Harlow and his associates (Harlow and Harlow, 1962; Harlow, Harlow, and Suomi, 1971), for example, found that total isolation during the first six to twelve months of life produced asocial monkeys that exhibited bizarre behavior and no social, sexual, or defensive behavior that is typical of the species. Scott (1962) described a socialization period in dogs (from three to twelve weeks) when primary social bonds are formed. Puppies isolated during this socialization period did not develop attachments to dogs or people (Fuller, 1977). Litters of puppies raised without any human contact for fourteen weeks developed normal relations with dogs but not with people (Freedman, King, and Elliot, 1961). Conversely, puppies that were reared by people and had no contact with other dogs during the socialization period became closely attached to humans but not to other dogs (Scott, 1980). Both dogs and monkeys are social species. Very minimal exposure to a person, such as the sight of a person leaving food, was enough to socialize puppies to humans (Scott and Fuller, 1965). Adult cats, on the other hand, are in nature relatively asocial, leading solitary lives except for the purposes of mating and rearing the young (Leyhausen, 1979). The typical domesticated cat has been characterized as aloof and much less friendly than the typical domesticated dog. Therefore, it was a challenge to try to alter the friendliness or attachment of the cat by manipulating its experiences during the socialization period.

Fox is the only investigator who has described the socialization period in cats. He characterized it as beginning at seventeen days of age (compared to twenty-three days for the dog), when increased sensory abilities and improved locomotor abilities enable the kitten to interact with the environment and with littermates (Fox, 1970). He said nothing about the end of the socialization period in cats other than that the "socialization processes underlying the development of emotional attachments in the cat clearly need more investigation" (ibid., p. 566). In a later, popular book, Fox stated, "As in the dog, there seems to be a critical period early in life (ranging from four to eight weeks) when kittens are most easily socialized with people. This attachment can be enhanced by giving the kitten a lot of handling" (Fox, 1974:139). No published experiments were cited in support of this statement. More recently, Beaver (1980:83), in a book on feline behavior, stated that the socialization period in cats "probably ranges from three to nine weeks of age." She refers to Scott's (1962) work with puppies and also to the Fox (1974) book, so there appears to be no published data on the socialization period in cats.

Relatively few studies have been done on the socialization of cats to their own or other species. A well-known study by Kuo (1930) showed that cats that had been reared with rats did not kill rats as adults. In a later study, Kuo (1960) found that a kitten or puppy brought up with both its own species and another species became attached only to the conspecifics (same species). A kitten or puppy reared with only an alien species became attached to members of other species (even to birds) as measured by indexes of distress. Fox (1969) found that kittens raised with a Chihuahua pup from four weeks of age played with other pups without showing fear at twelve weeks. Kittens that had no experience with pups until twelve weeks, however, avoided them and behaved defensively when approached. Kuo (1960) also found that cats isolated for a long period (birth to ten months) behaved peculiarly and did not relate well to people or other cats. Seitz (1959) found similar behavior in isolated cats. All of these studies deal with socializing cats to their own species or to other animals. There has been little scientific focus upon the socializing of cats to people.

In the late 1950s, investigations of early experience focused on the increased stimulation provided by handling infant animals. Although this handling experience was somewhat stressful to the young animal, it seemed to have beneficial effects. The handled animals showed accelerated development in maturation of the central nervous system and in physical development. They also showed less fear in an open field test of emotionality and were generally more resistant to stress (Levine, 1960). Several studies investigated the effect of handling on cats. Meier (1961) found that handling Siamese kittens for twenty minutes daily during the first thirty days of life increased their rate of development. Handled kittens opened their eyes one day earlier, they emerged from the nesting box 2.6 days earlier, and they developed Siamese coloration earlier. In another study Meier and Stuart (1959) found that kittens handled for ten minutes daily from birth until ninety days tended to learn a discrimination and reversal task better than nonhandled kittens did; they also developed coloration earlier. In a large study that involved forty kittens, Wilson, Warren, and Abbott (1965) found that the twenty kittens that were handled (for five minutes daily from birth to forty-five days) approached a person (sitting on a chair in the middle of a 3.6 x 3.6 meter enclosure) sooner (35 seconds for handled versus 105 seconds for nonhandled) and contacted the person more frequently than the nonhandled kittens did. Handling, however, did not facilitate learning a Hebb-Williams maze or a discrimination reversal.

Collard (1967) was interested in the effects of handling on fear of strangers and on play behavior. Kittens from five and a half to nine and a half weeks of age were handled by one person, by five different people, or by no person. During the first week of the experiment, the kittens were carried for one minute and held in the lap and stroked for three minutes. For the next three weeks, the kittens were carried or held for only one minute and then were called by the experimenter or were enticed to play with a string. Collard found that the five-person kittens showed the least fear of strangers, but the one-person kittens played more and showed more social behavior, particularly toward the person who had handled them. They purred, played with the familiar person's hands or clothing, and made more than twice as many playful or affectionate contacts (climbing on, rubbing against, mouthing, and so on) as the other kittens. These are striking findings considering the small amount of handling. In a pilot study for the present experiment, we also found that a kitten handled by one person for only five minutes daily, from three to seven weeks of age, became extremely friendly to people, while the nonhandled littermate remained distinctly aloof.

Most of the studies cited have looked at the effects of handling from birth to weaning on precocious development, tolerance to stress, and facilitation of learning. The present experiment is concerned with the effect of handling during the socialization period on the attachment of cats to people.

THE EXPERIMENT

The study reported here is the first part of a larger project. The first experiment involved twelve experimental cats (seven female, five male), each of which was handled by three or four people during the entire socialization period (three to fourteen weeks). These were compared to seven control cats (four female, three male) that were not handled during the socialization period. Eight of the twelve experimental cats and all seven control cats were born in the laboratory and continue to live there in a free environment (not caged). Four of the experimental cats were born and handled at home. Two of these were brought in to live in the laboratory at fourteen weeks af age, and the other two continue to live in the home environment with two cats and three people. The two cats living at home spent time being acclimated to the laboratory and were brought in weekly to be tested. All of the above cats were reared by their mothers with siblings and continue to live with siblings and other cats. All the cats, both handled and nonhandled, had daily exposure to people.

Two additional cats were taken from their mother at four weeks, and both were brought up by a student in a home setting (two one-person cats with littermate). This arrangement was made to find out whether separation from the mother during the socialization period increased attachment to a person. These kittens were given supplementary food before being separated from their mother (Borden's kitten replacement milk and baby food cereal) and were fed by hand for about two weeks before they learned to eat from a dish at five to six weeks of age.

The handling procedure consisted of holding a kitten in the arms or on the lap and stroking or petting it for five minutes. Three of the experimental kittens were handled once daily and the rest were handled three times daily.

MEASURES

We have used four main measures of cats' attraction to, or friendliness toward, people. The first measure, *separation distress*, is the most frequently used index of attachment for children and young animals (Gewirtz, 1972). It has been used to measure attachment in cats by Kuo (1938, 1960) and by Rheingold and Eckerman (1971). The Rheingold and Eckerman procedure consisted of putting a kitten in a strange room alone for three minutes and recording the number of distress cries. During a second three-minute test period the kitten was put in the strange room in contact with a littermate or with its mother, who was caged to prevent nursing. The presence of either family member reduced crying substantially at two and four weeks of age and eliminated crying at six and eight weeks. We modified the Rheingold and Eckerman procedure. We exposed each kitten (at different times) to the mother (not caged), to a littermate, and to a person, and we also tested the kitten alone. Because we did not start to use this measure at the beginning of the study, we have data for only five handled and two control kittens from five to ten weeks of age. These data show that, at five weeks of age, the presence of a person reduced crying from 44 cries (alone) to 1.2 cries (with person) for the handled kittens and from 61 cries (alone) to 3 cries (with person) for the control kittens. With their mother present, the handled kittens averaged 1.4 cries, the controls 1.5 cries; with a littermate, the handled kittens made .4 cries and the controls made 2.5 cries. These data suggest that for both handled and nonhandled (control) kittens, the presence of a person reduces distress crying as much as the presence of the mother does. The behavior of the handled and control kittens differed in the amount of time spent in direct contact with the person; the handled kittens spent more time with the person. We are currently collecting more extensive separation distress data. The detailed results presented here are from six kittens, three handled and three nonhandled controls. We found that at two weeks of age, before the kittens were handled, they emitted almost as many distress cries in the presence of a person (77) as they did when they were alone (88), but they cried much less frequently when a littermate was present (17 cries). The 88 cries made in our alone condition is comparable to the 84 cries found by Rheingold and Eckerman (1971) for thirty two-week-old kittens when alone. We found that when the handled kittens were four weeks old (and had been handled for ten days) the presence of one of the handlers reduced the number of cries to less than 4, while the littermate reduced crying to 3 cries. The presence of a person also reduced crying for the nonhandled kittens from 89 cries when alone to 28 cries with a person present. These data suggest that the presence of a familiar person reduces crying more for the handled than for the nonhandled kittens. The presence of the person reduces crying substantially for all kittens at four weeks of age and usually eliminates crying for most kittens by six to eight weeks of age.

A second measure, which we developed, involved the *preference* for a person or for a cat in a testing room (1.8 x 1.8 meters). We started testing preference when the cats were four months old and continued testing at least once a month until age one year. In this test, the person and the object cat were each contained within a separate enclosure made of a wooden frame covered with two-inch chicken wire. The cat to be tested was placed in the test room for a six-minute period. We measured the amount of time that was spent on top of or near (within 15 centimeters) the person and the object cat. We also noted other responses, such as putting a paw through the wire enclosure and the amount of interaction with the person or object cat. We found that the handled cats spent more time with the person (137 seconds) than with the cat (95 seconds) while the control cats spent less time with the person (103 seconds) than with the cat (165 seconds). The handled cats spent significantly more time with the person (137 seconds) than the control cats did (103 seconds), $t(17) = 5.14$, p $<$ .001.

The two one-person kittens spent a greater amount of time with the handler (235 seconds) than with their sibling, who was the object cat (32 seconds), but they still preferred another person (121 seconds) to the sibling (67 seconds), showing about the same preference that other handled cats did for a person. These data are very similar to Collard's (1967) findings. Her one-person kittens showed 50 percent more play responses to the handler than to a stranger, but they showed about the same number of play responses to a stranger that the five-person kittens did.

A third measure, also developed in our laboratory, involved *approach* to a person in the same testing room (1.8 x 1.8 meters). This measure was used after all the cats were mature (at least seven months old). First, the cat was adapted to the test room for a three-minute period, and during that time the number of distress cries was recorded. Then the cat was removed and a familiar person was seated at the far corner of the test room, on the floor, with a line drawn at a distance of 15 cm. around the person. The cat was then reintroduced through an opening in the wall, and the time taken to reach the person (latency) was recorded. Time spent with the person during the three-minute test period was recorded as well as other responses such as the number of friendly head and flank rubs and friendly approach sounds (called "mhrn" by Moelk, 1979). We found that the handled cats took significantly less time to reach the person (32 seconds) than the controls did (128 seconds), $t\,(17) = 2.20$, $p < .05$. These results are in striking agreement with those of Wilson, Warren, and Abbott (1965), who found that handled cats took about 35 seconds to reach a person seated on a chair in a larger test room, while nonhandled cats took 105 seconds. Our handled cats spent significantly more time with the person (66 seconds) than the control cats did (16 seconds), $t\,(17) = 2.23$, $p < .05$. The two one-person kittens took less time to reach the handler (11 seconds) than to reach another person (22 seconds), and they spent more time with the handler (89 seconds) than with another person (23 seconds).

The fourth and last measure involved a person *holding* a cat while an experimenter recorded how long the cat stayed with the person. The person did not actively restrain the cat. In *holding while standing*, the person was in a standing position and held the cat, ventral side up, cradled in her/his arms. In *holding while sitting*, the person sat on a wooden chair and held the cat in her/his lap, while stroking the cat and talking to it. For holding while standing, the handled cats stayed over twice as long (33 seconds) as the control cats (12 seconds). This difference was significant, $t\,(17) = 3.43$, $p < .01$. For holding while sitting, the handled cats again stayed much longer (62 seconds) than the controls (34 seconds). The two one-person kittens stayed much longer with the handler for holding while standing (77 seconds) than with another person (41 seconds.)

In addition to these objective measures, we have observed in the laboratory that the handled cats seem to approach people more frequently and to be generally friendlier. If someone sits on a chair, handled cats will come up to her, rub against her, sit in her lap, on her shoulder, or next to her on the floor. When they are young, handled kittens invariably climb up one's leg to get closer. Visitors are sometimes surprised by this behavior.

Handled cats living in homes have even more opportunity to exhibit their preference for people. All of these cats will sleep next to a person instead of another cat, when given the opportunity. They follow and sit near people frequently. And if one is not paying attention to them, they like to come and sit on the book or paper that one is reading.

CONCLUSIONS

The experiments done thus far clearly show that the handled cats are friendlier and better companions to people than are the nonhandled cats, even though all of the cats have had exposure to people. The only treatment difference between the experimental and control cats was in handling during the socialization period. We are planning to use the friendly, handled cats as companion animals in a pet-facilitated therapy program.

In further studies on this project, we are evaluating the effect of the presence (or separation from) the mother and/or littermates on the attachment of cats to people. We are also looking at the effect of handling by one versus several people on friendliness toward the handler and toward other people. We will investigate the effect of different amounts of handling and the effect of the timing of the handling from birth to six months. There is some previous literature on this last issue. Scott (1962) has found that four to eight weeks is the optimal time to socialize puppies to persons. Fox (1974b) has suggested that this is also the best time for kittens, but there are no published confirming data. In addition, we will look at other procedures such as handling and feeding (suggested by Wenzel, 1959) and handling and talking to kittens (Moelk, 1979) to see whether they will increase attachment.

In a current study, we are using single kittens or littermate pairs separated from the mother and brought up in close contact with persons in a home setting, like the two one-person kittens already described. When the first of these kittens returned for testing two weeks later (at age six weeks), the contrast between her and the two nonhandled littermates (who remained in the laboratory with their mother) was dramatic. The person-reared kitten had gained more weight and was much larger than the two littermates. She was much calmer: she hardly cried in the separation distress tests, averaging 2 cries when alone compared to 22 cries for her littermates. And she was obviously much friendlier, not only to her handler but also to other people, including strangers.

From our preliminary work, we can be certain that early handling has profound effects on the socialization of cats to people. The specific details, however, remain to be investigated.

Sharon L. Smith

4

Interactions Between Pet Dog and Family Members: An Ethological Study

The research reported here contributes to the understanding of the human–companion animal bond from an ethological perspective. Ethology is the study of the behavior of animals in their natural environment. Many people seek answers to the same basic questions about the human–companion animal bond. For example, what is it about companion animals that is satisfying and beneficial to humans, and what happens between humans and companion animals that results in attachment or in abandonment? These questions are directed at a complex system, and answers exist on many different, interacting psychological, social, and medical levels. The more levels that are explored, the more complete the understanding of the system.

I employed ethological methods to study interactions between humans and their pet dogs. In the initial descriptive phase of the study, I directly observed family members and the dog in the home. The dog was well integrated in the ten families observed, and the families were satisfied with and attached to the dog. The first objective was to describe behaviorally the nature of their actions and interactions: form, sequence, and context. The second objective was to examine these descriptions for common patterns. The results of the second objective are discussed here.

METHODS

I recruited ten white families among dog owners waiting to see a veterinarian. The families all lived in middle-class suburbs and consisted of at least two adults who were not retired. Five families were composed of couples with children. Three families consisted of couples with no children living at home but in one, children and grandchildren frequently visited. One family was composed of a couple and her mother. The last family consisted of a single parent, her children, and her parents. Seven families had children living at home or frequently visiting. In three of the families an adult member was not especially attached to the dog.

Each dog was the only pet dog in the household, had been in residence at least one year, was healthy, and was not pregnant. The dogs varied from one and one-half years to seven and one-half years old, weighed from four to eighty pounds, and were both mixed and purebred. The smallest was a Yorkshire terrier and the largest a Shepherd-Doberman mix. Four were female, and six were male. During the first visit to each home I interviewed the family, primarily asking questions about the dog.

I observed the dog and family members in and around the home for a total of twenty to thirty hours, three hours per session, in the late afternoon and early evening within a three-week period. I instructed the people to go about their usual activities and to refrain from talking to me. While observing I did not talk or get up and follow the dog closely because these actions attracted the dog's attention. To lessen further the dog's attention toward me, I ignored the dog, even on arrival. Occasionally the dog still approached. Then I held up a clipboard between us and blocked eye contact, in order to stop the dog. I recorded behavioral data by writing a running commentary in a personally devised shorthand. The commentary followed simultaneously the behavior of both dog and family members, especially behavior each directed toward the other. I videotaped only the last one or two sessions, following the same procedures. At the end of the last observation session I asked about the effect of my presence on everyone's behavior.

I analyzed the information for recurrent patterns at two levels: structural and external variable. The structural level concerned descriptions or classes of behavioral acts and interactions, that is, their form and movements over time. The external variable level concerned variations in behavioral acts and interactions as a function of such external variables as the dog's size, person's sex, or family's composition (see Duncan and Fiske, 1977, for a discussion of these levels of analysis).

RESULTS

STRUCTURAL FEATURES

A prominent structural feature of the behavior of dogs and people in the home was the asymmetry in directed attention. In each family the dog was more attentive to the people than the people were to the dog. The dog watched, approached, or followed one or more individuals; when it rested, it often faced people in the same or the next room. When the dog focused its attention elsewhere, such as standing by the door and looking out, it still turned its attention to family members by approaching or watching. At least at this time of day, the dog's location, orientation, and direction of movement were greatly influenced by the location of one or more family members, regardless of the person's focus of attention. In contradistinction, people did not interrupt their activity to seek out the dog when the dog was not present.

I examined the structures of two common types of interactions, hand contacts and play. Hand contacts were any form of touching the dog by hand. They were either any of various intergrading motions (stroke, rub, and scratch) or motionless contact (resting hand on dog). Hand contacts shared a fundamental structural characteristic. They were often cooperative interactions: both participants cooperated in coordinating their locations to achieve and sometimes maintain proximity. Even though it was the person who touched the dog, the dog participated consistently by remaining within reach and sometimes participated actively by nosing or pawing when the person's contact lapsed. Although the person often looked at the dog at the time, hand contacts did not require a person's complete attention. The person sometimes attended elsewhere while engaged in hand contact (for example, watched television or another person). Hand contacts were often performed in sequence, a nonrandom sequence for at least one type of contact, the "sound pat." The "sound pat" was defined as the action of hitting the dog with the palm of the hand with enough force to be heard. "Sound pat" did not occur at just any point in the sequence of hand contacts. It usually occurred at the middle or end of the series. The few times it occurred at the beginning of a series or alone, the dog and person were engaged in some other interaction immediately or shortly before.

Play varied in structure and often centered around a toy. Play was not a prerogative of children; adults readily played with the dog. Several different types of play were identified: fetch, keep-away, tug, chase, and wrestle. Most play bouts incorporated more than one type and many included hand contact. Underlying this variation was a structure all play interactions shared. The participants coordinated their actions with respect to each other in such a way that the interaction continued. It appeared as if the purpose of playing was to keep playing. This was especially evident during toy play. For example, during fetch and keep-away, the participants cooperated in alternating possession of the toy. During tug, the participants shared possession of the toy. If one pulled the toy away from the other, that one either returned the toy for further tugging or retained it and played keep-away. Even during chase and wrestle the participants coordinated their actions so that the interaction continued, even though one could outdistance, immobilize, or injure the other.

No special signal was apparent that consistently initiated a play bout. (The play bow seems to serve this function among dogs.) To start playing, a person or the dog performed an action typical of ongoing play. For example, a person might pick up a toy and make it obvious by shaking it; the dog then would go after the toy.

Given the efforts expended to continue play interactions, the procedures for terminating play were of particular interest. To stop the play interaction a participant refrained from performing play behavior (for example, ignoring the ball after the dog fetched it) and sometimes also performed actions incompatible with play behavior (such as leaving the room). When the person stopped toy play, he or she did so when the dog had the toy. When the dog stopped toy play, it did so when the person did not have the toy. The dog might or might not have it. When either stopped playing, the other sometimes continued performing play behavior, but, unless the first joined in, the play interaction was considered terminated.

During play the participants performed a series of actions. In many cases the action of one participant appeared to be in response to the previous action by the other. Play bouts were not the only occasions for such series of responses. The dog and person sometimes engaged in complex nonplay interactions with each responding to the other at least twice without interruption. At this level of analysis the unit being examined was the series of actions, alternating participants, and uninterrupted by a lapse in attention. Hand contacts were often a part of these interactions. The following example of this complex, nonplay interaction was taken from field notes: Dog approaches person, person talks to dog, dog sits, person praises dog and holds out hand, dog lifts paw, person shakes paw, paw shake is repeated, dog puts paw on chair, person pushes fist against dog's mouth, dog grooms himself. Each act appeared to be a response to the previous one, although there was no way to be certain.

Routine daily maintenance of the dog such as feeding the dog was often accompanied by social interactions. One or two family members were usually present when the dog was fed and while the dog ate. If not, the dog sometimes carried food to the room with people and ate there. In all the families someone usually talked to the dog at meal time. In some families someone, not always the feeder, routinely interacted with the dog. The following are some examples. One dog was told to stay away when its dish was put on the floor; then the dog barked, the feeder said, "O.K.," and the dog started eating. People interacted with the dog in a variety of ways to encourage the dog to eat. One person commanded and pointed to the dish, and the dog returned to its dish. Another moved her hand along the dog's back toward its head and talked about taking the food while the dog was at its dish; the dog bared its teeth. Another person pretended to eat milk bones with elaborate verbal and visual actions; the dog then tried to get at the food, but the person prevented this before letting the dog have the food.

EXTERNAL VARIABLES

When the behavior of the dog and family members was considered in relation to variables present among the participants, variations in behavior were found. The structural features described above were characteristic only of those participants who were attached to the dog. Three of the families stated that one of them, the husband in each case, was not attached to the dog. These husbands associated and interacted with the dog much less often than did other family members, and the dog seldom watched or followed them. When they did interact, the interactions were very brief, inattentive, or atypical in structure. Two were never observed playing with the dog, and the third played but atypically. For example, when the man played keep-away, he retained possession of the toy and seldom allowed the dog a turn. When the dog did get the toy, immediately the man picked up another toy. Instead of attempting to take the original toy from the dog, he teased the dog with the second toy. In other words, he refused to cooperate in alternating possession of the toy, a rule followed by those attached to the dog.

The association and interaction between dog and adult family members differed by degree in families with children compared to families without children. In childless families the people and dog interacted more readily, more frequently, and more complexly. The dog spent relatively more time very close to someone (within three feet). People were likely to interact with the dog at any time, interrupting their own activity. They also interacted more frequently, five or more bouts per hour per person, compared with one or two in families with children. Before hand contacts the person was more likely to approach the dog (35 percent to 65 percent of approaches), compared with a person in a family with children (20 percent or less of approaches). Nonplay interactions were complex more often; they involved alternation of actions between the participants that continued uninterrupted for two or more complete cycles. Approximately two per hour per person occurred compared with one every two or more hours per person in families with children.

In contrast, in families with children this degree of closeness, interaction rate, and complexity seldom occurred even when children were not physically present. Most adults interacted with the dog at a rate of one or two bouts per hour; several interacted three times per hour. The dog regularly monitored the people but usually from many feet away or from the next room. Before hand contacts the dog approached the person in most cases. When the person approached, usually it was while on the way somewhere or before feeding or grooming the dog and rarely only for the purpose of touching the dog. Hand contacts occurred under certain circumstances; these were times when people's hands were unoccupied. Unlike childless families, people did not interrupt activities involving hands, such as eating and preparing dinner, to touch the dog.

Male and female adults were on the whole similar in their interactions with the dog. One difference had an interesting correlation. Some men had a higher rate of hand contact and/or play with the dog than did their wives (at least twice the rate). These men were away from home for longer periods than their wives. When a man was home as much as his wife, interaction rates were similar.

When differences among the dogs were examined, one difference, size, correlated with interactional differences. Three dogs were small (four to eighteen pounds) and lived in families with and without children. These dogs were more likely to contact a person actively—to stand up with paws on a person's leg or to jump onto a lap. Larger dogs were seldom or never observed to do this with one exception: a medium-sized dog that interacted at a very low rate. Yet these dogs' active contact did not reliably result in interacting or in eye contact with the person. Another interactional difference correlated with the dog's size: small dogs were seldom given sound pats compared with larger dogs.

Undoubtedly, my presence as an observer had some effect on the subjects, but the following evidence suggests that the effect was not large on the activities seen. The dog ignored me, especially after the first session, and when the dog did approach, blocking with the clipboard consistently resulted in the dog stopping and wandering away. The dog and person interacted easily and smoothly, as if enacting a very familiar routine. The people seldom looked at me, and at one time or another they actively disagreed among themselves, cleaned house, slept, and yelled at the children. I have also observed people playing with the dog in a park, where the subjects were unaware of being observed. Play under the two circumstances could not be distinguished. In response to being questioned about the effect of my presence, the people said that they had gone about their usual activities for the time of day and that in my presence their's and the dog's behavior differed, if at all, only in a few respects. For example, one family did not roughhouse together as usual. In short, I probably did not see all the different interactions the subjects engage in. But those seen were performed in the usual manner with possible changes only in duration and frequency.

DISCUSSION

This study has begun to document the nature of the attachment relationship between human and dog by examining their actions and interactions with respect to each other. The following structural features of their behavior were thought to be salient because of their frequency in every family. (1) Family members allowed the dog free access to them and the dog focused its attention on them. (2) Family members exercised considerable choice in behavior in relation to the dog at a given moment, including ignoring the dog, and the dog accepted this behavior. (3) Interactions were cooperative in structure. (4) Tactile contact was a common way of interacting.

Evidence that these features were related to attachment was presented from two sources. (1) Family members expressing a lack of attachment to the dog did not interact with the dog or did so briefly or uncooperatively. Seldom did either direct attention toward the other. (2) Family members attached to but absent from the dog for periods longer than other family members seemed to make up for lost time and interacted with the dog more frequently.

Since people and dogs overlap ecologically, interactions between them are not remarkable per se. What is remarkable is the nature of the interactions when the dogs are pets in the home. Despite belonging to different evolutionary orders, these dogs and people cooperated in coordinating their interactions so that the interaction continued at least momentarily. They responded to each other behaviorally in a variety of ways. Yet it appeared that at any given moment their behavior was not random. They appeared to interact for the purpose of interacting; no material outcomes were apparent, such as access to a limited resource like food. In this way the interactions of these people and their dogs resembled those of members of the same species.

Interactions between dog and family members contrasted with those between the two people in ways that probably reinforced attachment to the dog. The person had more flexibility and less complexity to deal with when interacting with a dog than with a person. Procedures for initiating, maintaining, and terminating an interaction were relatively simple. Human interactions, such as greetings and conversations, prescribe a greater number of rules on verbal and nonverbal levels (Duncan, 1975; Kendon and Ferber, 1973). When a dog and person came together and interacted, nothing about their behavior or situation mandated how they were to interact within a broad range, or, indeed, whether they interacted. They had considerable choice in behavior. No dog was observed to inflict negative consequences on a person following their association. When not interacting, the dog frequently directed its orientation, location, and movements so that it remained near or repeatedly returned to family members. The dog was in effect signaling its availability and increasing the probability of an encounter, and yet the person at any particular time could choose to ignore this signal without jeopardizing their relationship. Small dogs were more obtrusive by actively contacting the person, yet the person might ignore this signal.

Certain interactions might be more permissible in public with a dog than they would be with another person. Hand contacts with the dog were common and varied. Men, in particular, touched the dog repeatedly; in this society public touching by men is acceptable only when confined to narrowly defined structures and contexts. Another example is play. Adults played with the dog, sometimes vigorously and extensively. Seldom was hand contact or play observed between adults during the study, but such interactions might have been suppressed in the presence of an observer.

The presence of children may reduce interactions of adults with other family members, including the dog. Families with children interacted with the dog less often than those without children. Another study examined the interactions between adults as a function of a child's presence. When heterosexual couples accompanied and unaccompanied by children were observed in public places, the adults were observed to touch and talk to each other significantly less often when accompanied by children (Rosenblatt, 1974). If this reduction in interaction between adults is pervasive, a dog may give license to adults with children to engage in more interactions than adults with children but no dog.

This study noted common patterns in behavior among the families observed. The degree that these patterns reflected characteristics of these families unrelated to the dog was unknown. For example, some of the patterns might reflect characteristics of these families associated with volunteering for such a study. Any study requiring the subjects' informed consent is potentially biased by factors inherent in volunteering. At least the consistent differences found within this group of families were likely to reflect the relationship between the dog and family members.

As more families are observed, behavioral patterns between people and their dogs will become better defined and perhaps more varied in conjunction with greater variation between families. Then these behavioral patterns can be the foundation for hypotheses about the cause, development, or effects of the bond between humans and dogs. One hypothesis might be that when individuals consistently interact cooperatively with the dog, they are unlikely to abandon the dog and are likely to mourn its loss and to benefit physically and psychologically from its presence. Identifying behavioral parameters for the human–companion animal bond opens up exciting possibilities for prediction, prevention, intervention, and stimulation of outcomes concerning people and their companion animals.

Peter R. Messent

5

Social Facilitation of Contact with Other People by Pet Dogs

Pets are said to facilitate interactions between their owners and other people. Mugford and M'Comisky (1975) used the term "social lubricant" to describe this phenomenon, which they reported from a study of elderly people who were given a pet budgerigar (parakeet). They found that the birds became a focal point for communication with friends, family, and neighbors who came to visit.

This phenomenon had been referred to by Levinson (1969a, 1972). He was particularly concerned with the use of pets for child psychotherapy but also considered the effect of pets on dynamics within the family. He pointed out that in some situations, the pet could act as a major sourcefor discussion or as an emotional clearing house for the family members. He also pointed out that pets could have a psychotherapeutic role with withdrawn children. Children who would not communicate with adults would attempt to talk to pets, and in several cases this led to more normal relationships with people. Condoret (1977) has described some clinical cases of this nature from his studies in France.

Corson and co-workers have published several papers on pet-facilitated therapy (Corson et al., 1975a, 1977; Corson and Corson, 1981) which supported the views of Levinson on a pet's facilitation of interhuman social relationships.

Corson and Corson (1981) used the term "bonding catalyst" to describe how in geriatric institutions pets facilitated interaction with other patients, residents, and staff. Brickel (1979) reported results with cats in a hospital geriatric ward that supported those of Corson et al.

Apart from the suggestions of Levinson on the role of pets in family social dynamics, all the studies reported above have concentrated on special situations or psychotherapy and not on the normal pet owner. It is clear, however, that the "social lubricant" effect of pets is much in evidence for this group as well. Mugford (1980) found a dramatic increase in unsolicited friendly contacts between himself and strangers when he was accompanied by a good-looking dog. The prevalence of this opinion among a group of dog owners was measured in a survey done in Sweden by Adell-Bath et al. (1979). They asked a series of questions to a sample of 259 people. Two of these questions have particular relevance. To the statement, "The dog makes friends for me," 57 percent of the respondents agreed, and 22 percent agreed with doubt. To the statement, "The dog gives me the opportunity of talking with other people," the comparable figures were 63 percent and 20 percent. These responses indicate the possible importance of dogs in increasing contact with others, at least if the owner wishes that to happen.

Of comparative interest in this context was a report by Coelho (1980) describing guardian behavior by baboons toward felines. He observed a group of baboons in a primate colony where one individual on two separate occasions, one lasting two months, adopted a feral juvenile cat. The adopting baboon was able to use the adopted cat as a social facilitator in her interaction with other baboons and in eliciting male protective responses. Perhaps even pet ownership is not a wholly human preserve.

The purpose of the study described here was to investigate the role of pet dogs in facilitating social interactions between their owners and other people. People were observed while they were walking with their dogs. This provides an occasion for objective study of the interactions between dogs and people away from all the difficulties inherent in studying pets in the home. It was possible to make observations not only on the social lubricant role of dogs but also on various behavioral interactions between dog and owner such as play, touching, and talking to the dog. Play in dog-owner relationships has received relatively little attention, although Mugford (1980) discussed the possible benefits of play with pets both to children and adults. The importance of touching and talking to pets and how people do these activities under certain conditions are described by Katcher (1981). Observational data on play, touching, and talking to pets are still very limited, and this study gave the opportunity of adding to these data.

METHOD

The study took place in two parts. The first part was at and near Hyde Park, London, in August 1979. Eight volunteers who were dog owners were recruited and asked to do two similar walks through part of Hyde Park and some of the surrounding streets, once with their dog and once without. Walks started from a veterinary surgery near Hyde Park, and half the owners walked first with their dog and half without.

The walks were followed by the observer at a distance of about 50 yards with specific instructions that there should be no interactions between the walker and observer. A record was made of the responses of all people who passed within five feet of the walker or his/her dog. The following categories of response were scored by the "contacts," although some categories were lumped together in later analysis: 1. No response; 2. Looked at dog; 3. Looked at owner; 4. Slowed/turned; 5. Stopped; 6. Talked to dog; 7. Touched dog; 8. Talked to owner.

If a response at the end of the list was scored, this meant that some or all of the response categories above also occurred. The sex and approximate age of these "contacts" were also recorded. It was agreed with one of the eight subjects to walk in Regent's Park, not Hyde Park, to keep to their normal routine. For the remaining 7 subjects, the route in Hyde Park was not in the normal area for walking their dog.

In the second part of the study, all walks took place over the normal route for dog and owner at a routine time of day. Eighty-eight walks in total were observed, all with the dog present. Forty walkers took part in the study and between one and six walks were observed for each.

Three different sites were included in the study—Chellaston, Nottingham, and Fulham. Chellaston is a semirural village in the Midlands, Nottingham is a medium-sized city also in the Midlands, and Fulham is an inner suburb of London. The following technique of observation was similar to the earlier study except that behaviors were recorded by a microphone and cassette recorder system rather than with pen and paper.

Responses of "contacts" were noted according to the same list of categories used previously, but "no" responses were not recorded in this part of the study. Several additional factors were measured, however. These were timing of contacts, length of walk, length of contacts, touching, talking and play interactions between the owner and dog, and similar behaviors with other dogs met on the walk.

RESULTS

Table 5.1 shows the responses generated by the seven subjects.

Although the number of subjects used was small, the overall number of contacts observed was large. A simple chi-squared analysis was done on the results, lumping together all the categories where any response was observed into a single grouping. Using 2 X 2 chi-squared analysis, there was a significantly higher number of responses when walking with the dog than when walking without the dog ($p < 0.001$). The data for walking with the dog showed differences depending on the area being walked. Three areas were covered, the

Table 5.1. RESPONSES BY CONTACTS TO SEVEN SUBJECTS WALKING WITH OR WITHOUT DOG (percent)

Contact behavior	Without Dog		With Dog		
	all walks	all walks	parks only	street only	subway only
No response	98	78	49	86	76
Looked at dog	0	11	19	7	17*
Looked at owner	1	2	6	0	5*
Slowed/stopped	1	6	15	5	1*
Owner slowed/stopped	0	3	8	1	1*
Talked to owner	0	1	3	0	0*
Observation (n)	290	392	68	237	87

*Added together as "any response" for chi-squared analysis.

park, the streets, and the subway area, which is extensive and connects Hyde Park to Oxford Street under Marble Arch. There were significantly more responses in the park than either in the subway or on the street ($p < 0.001$), and there were significantly more responses in the subway than on the street ($p < 0.05$).

A final result from this part of the study was the mean time for the walk in the presence or absence of the dog (Table 5.2), a result that includes the walker who used Regents' Park. The duration of the walk was significantly longer when the dog was present, usually because a longer route was taken or the person walked more slowly with the dog present.

The single walker who walked her dogs along their normal daily route in Regents' Park stopped and spoke to several friends. She did this both when she was with and without her dogs. Therefore, the second part of the study concentrated on owners walking their dogs over their normal route and examined interactions in more detail. A secondary consideration was that it is difficult to persuade people to go on walks without their dog!

Since the number of walks per walker varied between one and six, the analysis of results was difficult. For some of the data, results are presented for the total number of walks (88). For other data, averages where appropriate were first calculated for each walker, and analysis was then done on these values (n = 40). This latter measure is a fairer way of presenting much of the data because otherwise there is a distortion in favor of the few subjects who were observed on several walks.

Table 5.2. MEAN WALK DURATION (minutes), LONDON PARK STUDY

With dog	25.3	n = 8
Without dog	19.6	n = 8

Difference significant ($p < 0.05$), Wilcoxon Matched Pairs Test.

First, however, some of the results are better looked at overall, such as those relating to the proportion of walks where certain activities occurred. On 69 percent of all walks, at least one spoken interaction took place, and the overall mean number of speaking interactions per walk was 2.8. On 75 percent of walks, a contact looked at the dog at least once, and the percentage of walks where any interaction took place was even higher at 78 percent. Someone waved at the owner from a house or passing car on 13 percent of walks. The dog was touched by a contact on 15 percent of walks and talked to on 8 percent of walks. A game of any type with the dog was seen on 36 percent of walks, and a fetch game on 18 percent.

The spoken interactions were analyzed in some detail. For all of the walks, there was an average of 2.8 spoken interactions per walk. Table 5.3 analyzes these further with the length of conversation being broken down into categories cross-tabulated against four categories of contacts or interactants.

About 60 percent of the spoken interactions took the form of a single word greeting, such as "Hello." In the other 40 percent a genuine conversation took place, meaning that overall there was on average more than one conversation per dog walk (Table 5.3). The length of conversation was further broken down by Messent whether or not the interactant was with a dog and by whether the interactant was male or female. For statistical analysis, some grouping of values was done to give sufficiently high figures in results cells to perform a 3 x 2 table chi-squared analysis. This analysis showed that there were significantly more long conversations when the interactant was also with a dog ($p < 0.001$). There was an indication of a similar trend for female interactants versus male ones, but this result was only significant at $p < 0.1$.

Length of conversation was also analyzed for some categories of the dogs and

Table 5.3. LENGTH OF CONVERSATIONS AT CHANCE MEETINGS OF DOG OWNERS WHILE WALKING THEIR DOGS (walk number is 88)

Length of Conversation	Category of Interactant (percent)				
	All	No Dog*	With Dog*	Male†	Female†
Greeting only	60.2	71.1	43.2	65.7	55.9
>30 seconds	17.2	14.1	22.1	13.0	20.6††
30 seconds–1 minute	9.4	7.4	12.6	12.0	7.4††
1–3 minutes	8.2	2.7	16.8	6.5	9.6§
3–5 minutes	2.0	2.0	2.1	2.0	1.5§
5–10 minutes	0.8	0.7	1.1	0	1.5§
> ten minutes	2.0	2.0	2.1	0	3.7§
Total number	244	149	95	108	136

*No dog versus with dog interactant conversation lengths significantly different by chi-squared analysis $p < 0.001$, using 3 x 2 table.
†Male versus female interactant conversation lengths different at $p < 0.1$ (chi-squared tests).
††Grouped for chi-squared analysis.
§Grouped for chi-squared analysis.

Table 5.4. LENGTH OF CONVERSATIONS AND INFLUENCE OF REGION, DOG PEDIGREE, AND SEX OF OWNER (walker n = 40)

Length of Conversation	Walker with Pedigree Dog*	Walker with Nonpedigree Dog	Notting-ham	London*	Chellaston	Male Walker†	Female Walker
Greeting only	56.5	62.1	56.1	58.7	61.5	59.9	57.0
> 30 seconds†	22.0	15.5	15.9	20.0	25.0	20.4	19.2
30 seconds–1 minute†	7.0	11.7	9.8	9.3	6.3	10.5	6.6
1–3 minutes§	10.0	5.8	11.4	6.7	6.3	5.9	11.3
3–5 minutes§	1.5	1.9	1.5	2.7	1.0	0	3.3
5–10 minutes§	0.5	1.9	1.5	1.3	0	2.0	0
10+ minutes§	2.5	1.0	3.8	1.3	0	1.3	2.6

*Difference not significant by chi-squared analysis.
† Difference significant at $p < 0.1$.
§ Combined for chi-squared analysis.

their owners (Table 5.4). There was no difference in length of conversation based on whether the dog walked was a pedigree breed or on the region where the walk occurred.

There was, however, a trend for female walkers to hold longer conversations than male walkers, although this was only significant at the 10 percent level. The sex of the walker was analyzed against the sex of the interactant in terms of the number of spoken interactions with each sex, as shown in Table 5.5, which showed that walkers were significantly more likely to speak to people of their own sex.

To analyze the number of times certain activities occurred on walks and to make statistical comparisons between subgroups, the data were later changed to a per walker basis. Some of the mean results per walker for various behaviors are shown in Table 5.6.

The results from various subgroups were then calculated. First, factors were considered relating to the dog being walked—pedigree/nonpedigree, small/medium/large, male/female, and neutered/entire. Second, the three regions of study were compared, and finally male versus female walkers were compared.

Table 5.5. COMPARISON OF NUMBER OF SPOKEN INTERACTIONS OF ANY LENGTH BY SEX OF WALKERS AND SEX OF INTERACTANTS

Sex of Interactant	Sex of Walker	
	Male	Female
Male	63	46
Female	61	74

Probability of result by chi-squared test was $p = 0.05$.

Table 5.6. MEAN VALUES PER WALKER (n = 40) FOR PARAMETERS RECORDED PER DOG WALK

Parameter	Mean Result
Length of walk	25.4 min.
Times walker touched own dog	2.8
Times walker touched other dog	0.3
Times walker played fetch game	1.3
Times walker played any game	3.5
Times walker talked to dog	1.1
Times walker commanded dog	1.3
Times other person looked at dog or owner	5.9
Times other person talked to owner	1.9
Times other person waved at owner	0.2
Times other person touched dog	0.2
Times other person talked to dog	0.1

Because numbers of these subgroups were small, and variance of results was high, differences in values needed to be large to give statistically significant results. Significances were calculated using Mann-Whitney U-test for comparing two variables and the Kruskall Wallis test for three or four variables.

Tables 5.7–5.10 show some of the results selected either because differences were significant or because results can be compared with other published studies. The results in Table 5.7 showed a directional trend toward pedigree dogs' increasing interactions, but no difference was significant. A few pedigree dog walkers had very high scores, but in general there was no difference between the groups.

Table 5.8 shows that there was a trend for female walkers to talk to and command their dogs more often than male walkers. There was no difference for touching dogs, however, or on other parameters. The apparent difference between men and women for playing any game was entirely accounted for by one individual who played a very large number of games with her dog.

Table 5.7. COMPARISON OF WALKERS WITH PEDIGREE AND NONPEDIGREE DOGS ON SELECTED PARAMETERS

Walker Group	n	Mean Number of Times Behavior Observed		
		Other Person Looked at Dog	Other Person Talked to Owner	Any Interaction
Pedigree	19	3.2	2.5	3.6
Nonpedigree	21	1.8	1.4	1.9

None of these differences were significant (Mann-Whitney U-test, 2-tailed).

Table 5.8. COMPARISONS OF MALE AND FEMALE WALKERS ON SELECTED PARAMETERS

Walker group	n	Mean Walk Length (min.)	Mean Number of Times Behavior Observed				
			Touched Dog	Talked to Dog	Commanded Dog	Any Interaction with Other Person	Played Any Game
Male	17	28.3	3.2	0.5*	1.6*	2.3	2.0
Female	23	23.2	2.7	1.5*	2.9*	1.7	4.6

*Male/female difference significant p < 0.1 (Mann-Whitney U-Test, 2-tailed).

With size of dog, as Table 5.9 shows, there were significantly more fetch games with larger dogs at the 10 percent level. This difference was not significant if all games were taken into account.

For the region where the walk occurred, the results are shown in Table 5.10 for fetch games, commanding dog, and other people talking to the owner.

There was a significant regional difference for fetch games and for commanding dog at the 10 percent probability level. There was no significant difference between regions for spoken interactions.

Table 5.9. SIZE OF DOG AND FREQUENCY OF PLAY BEHAVIOR

Dog Size	Mean Number of Times Played	
	Fetch Game	Any Game
Small	0	0.4
Medium	1.3*	7.7
Large	1.9*	2.4

* Difference significant by Kruskal-Wallis 1-way Anova test, p < 0.1 (2-tailed).

Table 5.10. COMPARISON OF REGIONS FOR SELECTED WALK PARAMETERS

	Mean Number of Times Behavior Observed per Walk		
	Played Fetch Game	Other Person Talked to Owner	Owner Commanded Dog
Nottingham	0.9*	2.2	2.9†
London	1.2*	1.6	1.8†
Chellaston	2.2*	1.9	2.5†

*Regional difference significant p < 0.05 Kruskal-Wallis 1-way Anova Test, (2-tailed).
†Regional difference significant p < 0.1 Kruskal-Wallis 1-way Anova test, (2-tailed).
Other difference not significant.

The sex of the dog was intitially analyzed by four groups—entire male, castrate male, entire female, spayed female. But because the group sizes were very small, male/female differences alone were also calculated. There were no significant differences by sex of dog, although mean walk length was longer for male dogs at 28.4 minutes against 20.3 minutes for female dogs.

DISCUSSION

These results provide clear evidence to support the view that pets have a function as "social lubricants" for typical dog owners. The first part of the study showed that even when walking in a new locality, the presence of a dog significantly increased the likelihood of contact between a stranger and the subjects. The presence of the dog was not the only factor; the area being walked also had a significant effect. The contact rate in the park was especially high compared with that in the street. It appeared that people were much more friendly in the park and so were more likely to interact with the person, but only if the dog were present. Nevertheless, it is not possible to say exactly what it was about the dog that was appealing to people in the "social lubricant" context. It is likely that other factors, such as the presence of a child in a pram, might equally have facilitated social interactions. In the absence of any such controls in the study described here, however, it is not possible to speculate further.

The increase in walk length when the dog was present is also of interest because it supports the view that dogs can benefit owners by an increase in exercise. Even on a walk over the same route both with and without the dog, as should have occurred here, the presence of the dog made the walks longer either because of added diversions while walking or increased time to travel a given distance.

The study of owners with their dogs on their routine walk suggested that friendships soon develop with others using the same area. This supports the questionnaire findings of Adell-Bath et al. (1979). The results also suggest that other dog owners are especially likely to become friends since on average the conversations with this group lasted for longer than those with people without dogs.

The benefits of an increased number of friends through walking the dog are obvious, especially for people who are likely not to have many friends, such as the elderly. There was no evidence from this study that the elderly walker was less likely to talk to others than the younger walker; if anything, the opposite was true. It is clear from earlier surveys, such as that of Adell-Bath et al., that the dog owners appreciate the friendly contact that results from walking the dog.

The data from the second part of the study were also interesting from the viewpoint of owners' interaction with their own and other dogs. Touching the dog and talking to the dog were very common behaviors. These two behaviors have been discussed by Katcher (1981), and the present study confirms the high degree of touch contact between owner and pet even in an outdoor situation where it could be argued that there is less need for it than indoors. Many of the people met on walks touched or talked to the dog in addition to talking to the owner, which emphasizes both the significance of the dog in the interaction and the strength of the touch and talk response to the dog by owner and nonowner alike.

The comparison of subgroups such as male versus female owner and the three study regions was made difficult by the small numbers in these subgroups and the great variation in the results.

Nevertheless, some trends emerged which could usefully be followed up in future studies. There was a suggestion that pedigree dogs were more likely to elicit interest and contact from others than nonpedigree dogs. This could reflect the type of owner as much as the dog. The sex of the owner seemed to have no effect on touching dogs, confirming results of Katcher (1981), but it did relate to the sex of people they interacted with most, the length of conversations, and talking to or commanding their dog. More data are required to substantiate these findings, which may relate more to cultural and social factors than to any direct effect of the dog.

One important area that has not been discussed is that of play, which has received little attention with respect to the dog-owner relationship except for reviews such as that of Mugford (1980). Adell-Bath et al. (1979) did ask about play in their questionnaire study. To the statement, "The dog gives me an outlet for playfulness," 51 percent of the respondents agreed completely and 29 percent agreed with doubt. The observations reported here showed that a game of any type occurred in 36 percent of the walks observed, with several play bouts, that is, fetch games or tag games, often occurring on those walks. Play is, therefore, a significant activity, and it was also very general since sex of dog, sex of owner, and region walked did not affect its frequency. Smaller dogs were played with less, but this might not be true in other situations outside the present study, such as in the home or garden.

This research has shown several ways in which walking the dog can be of benefit to the owner in addition to the traditional view of the walk as providing exercise for the dog. Even in a study with the limitations of this one, the role of dogs in increasing social contacts has been very clearly demonstrated.

Such a result would have been predicted by almost any dog owner, but some quantification on its extent is a valuable addition to the literature. This finding should also be seen in the overall context of dog ownership in the community. The benefit of dogs through the social contacts they help generate for their owners must be a major consideration in any discussion on the role of pets in communities if, for example, certain negative viewpoints on dogs are put forward.

Benjamin L. Hart, Sybil R. J. Murray,
Margaret Hahs, Bernadine Cruz, and
Michael F. Miller

6

Breed-Specific Behavioral Profiles of Dogs: Model for a Quantitative Analysis

Current interest in the behavioral interactions between dogs and their owners must take into account behavioral patterns and predispositions of both the dog and the owner. Matching certain breeds of dogs with certain types of people or examining the behavioral effects of different types of dogs on people requires a reliable, unbiased approach to determining breed characteristics of canine behavior.

The current popular literature contains statements about breed differences in behavior such as trainability, activity level, aggressiveness, watchdog behavior, and mellowness with children. The perspectives obtained are from breeders and breed associations, however, and are likely to reflect self-interest and personal biases.

The purpose of the project described here was to develop data-based breed profiles of behavioral predispositions that are of importance to people wanting a dog as a pet. People who want a dog live in a variety of environments ranging from small apartments to houses with large grounds. The human environment may range from that of a single man or woman to a large family with young children. Some people wanting a pet may be more concerned about watchdog behavior than about the dog's behavior toward children. A family with young children may have the opposite concern. To some people, ease of training and absence of destructive tendencies may be of paramount importance.

The growing interest in using dogs in psychotherapy and institutional settings brings up the issue of matching a dog's behavior to a particular relationship with people. Several social programs are available to promote the use of pets as companions for the elderly, the lonely, persons in nursing homes and prisons, and students in dormitories (Bustad, 1980). Such programs include the People-Pet Partnership Council of the Washington State College of Veterinary Medicine and the Pet-A-Care program of the San Francisco Society for the Prevention of Cruelty to Animals. The Humane Society of Hennepin County in Minnesota initiated a Pets by Prescription program with the intention of offering physicians in the Twin City area an opportunity to use pets with particular characteristics for specific companionship needs of their patients.

Dogs are usually chosen as the most appropriate pet for therapeutic programs. Often the selection is approached on the basis of size and hair type. But information about specific behavioral attributes and disadvantages of various breeds of dogs is essential for the success of pet-people matching programs as well as for the selection of a dog as a family or personal pet. A general guideline of basic behavioral characteristics of breeds is needed to help prospective pet owners and professionals offering advice to narrow down their choices. Information of this nature was sought by the project. With a general guideline in hand, one can go to local authorities such as dog breeders and trainers for information about behavioral characteristics of particular lines within breeds to decide upon an individual dog.

In this chapter we describe the rationale and experimental design of our program to develop data-based objective breed profiles of the fifty-six most popular breeds. A few examples of the results obtained are also presented.

RATIONALE

ADVANTAGES OF PUREBREDS

The main advantage of selecting a purebred rather than a mixed breed as a "prescription dog" for therapeutic purposes or as a family pet is that one has more success in predicting what the dog will be like as an adult. For example, one can predict with utmost accuracy the ways in which a collie puppy will differ, morphologically, from a German Shepherd puppy when the dogs reach maturity. Presumably, this same concept holds for behavior. The magnitude of genetic influences over behavior has already been established in the specialty of behavioral genetics. Any behavioral trait that can be measured can be affected by genetic manipulation. The main difference between genetic control of morphology and genetic control of behavior is that in the latter instance environment has a more pronounced effect.

BREED-SPECIFIC BEHAVIOR

Breeds of dogs have been maintained along rigid morphological lines for hundreds of years. In some instances there has been a concerted effort to enhance and maintain behavioral traits as well. Thus it is recognized that it is easier to train hunting breeds than nonhunting breeds to carry out certain maneuvers in the field. Sheep dogs are easier to train to herd livestock than are other breeds.

There is reason to believe that breeds of dogs differ in many behavioral characteristics that have not necessarily received attention in a breeding program as well as in behavioral traits intentionally selected. The work of Scott and Fuller (1965) documents that when exacting laboratory tests are conducted on various breeds, behavioral differences are apparent. These workers studied five breeds and tested trainability, emotionality, and problem-solving ability. The number of breeds studied and the type of tests administered were limited in applicability to the needs of a pet owner, but the work demonstrates that one could expect to find reliable breed differences in a variety of behavioral traits.

PROJECT DESIGN

It is financially impossible to study many dogs in the laboratory, and the characteristics that concern a pet owner are not easily examined in a laboratory setting. The alternative is to tap a resource of information about dog breeds that is a step removed from the laboratory. The approach of this study was to survey groups of authorities about dogs for a consensus regarding breed differences in behavior and to assume that the consensus approximates differences that would be apparent in theoretical laboratory studies.

The approach is predicated upon three principles: (1) Many behavioral characteristics differ significantly among breeds of dogs, and the magnitude of differences and within-breed variability differ from trait to trait and between breeds. (2) The behavioral differences are known by people who have extensive experience with dog breeds and dog-owner relationships. (3) The behavioral information that exists in the minds of dog authorities can be obtained by interviewing large numbers of different authorities, with an interview format that minimizes the opportunity for the informants to talk about dogs in which they may have vested personal interests. The goal of the approach was to acquire data that would yield percentile rankings of behavioral traits.

METHOD

INFORMANTS

Four categories of informants were considered: obedience judges, dog show judges, professional handlers of dogs at shows, and veterinarians in small animal practice. For all groups a directory is available. Each group was considered large enough to produce the required number of telephone contacts. Members of each group probably view dogs from different perspectives. On the basis of preliminary interviews we selected obedience judges and small animal veterinarians as informants. Forty-eight informants in each group were interviewed. These people were randomly selected from the directories so as to represent male and female informants and eastern, central, and western states equally.

BEHAVIORAL CHARACTERISTICS

Thirteen types of behavior were felt to be of primary interest to prospective pet owners. The behavioral characteristics were expressed specifically in a question that asked the informants to rank a list of seven dogs with regard to the trait in question. The informant was also asked to compare male with female dogs in general. The list of characteristics is outlined in Table 6.1. Each characteristic was asked about in a way that illustrated the usefulness of the behavior. For example, excitability was explored in the following question: "A dog may normally be quite calm but can become very excitable when set off by such things as a ringing doorbell or an owner's movement toward the door. This characteristic may be very annoying to some men and women. Rank these breeds from least excitable to most excitable."

EXPERIMENTAL DESIGN

The 56 breeds represented the 55 most frequently registered breeds of the American Kennel Club, as of 1978, plus the Australian shepherd, which was

Table 6.I. BEHAVIORAL CHARACTERISTICS RANKED IN ORDER OF DECREASING MAGNITUDE OF F RATIO

| Behavioral Characteristic | F Ratio | Number of Breeds on which Informants Differed Significantly ($p < .01$) | | |
		Region	Informant Type	Informant Sex
1. Excitability	9.6	0	3	0
2. Activity	9.5	0	2	1
3. Tendency to bite children	7.2	2	1	1
4. Objectionable barking	6.9	0	1	0
5. Playfulness	6.7	1	0	1
6. Ease of training	6.6	0	0	0
7. Value as watchdog	5.1	1	2	2
8. Aggression toward dogs	5.0	1	0	0
9. Tendency to dominate people	4.3	1	1	0
10. Territorial guarding	4.1	1	2	0
11. Demand for affection	3.6	0	2	1
12. Destructiveness	2.6	1	4	1
13. Ease of housebreaking	1.8	0	0	1

fairly popular in 1978 but was not recognized as a breed until 1980. The 56 breeds were divided into 24 working breeds, 16 hound/hunting breeds, and 16 miscellaneous/terrier breeds (Table 6.2.).

Preliminary interviews indicated that if informants were asked to rank more than about 8 breeds on 13 questions they tended to tire during the interview. In the official interviews informants were given a list of 7 breeds to rank for all 13 questions. These 7 breeds for each interviewer were arranged to include 2 dogs from the working group, 2 from the hound/hunting group, and 3 from the miscellaneous/terrier group. The selection of breeds for each interview was randomized.

A set of 8 interviews, with 7 dogs per interview, thus included all 56 breeds. A total of 96 interviews yielded 12 sets of interviews about each of the 56 breeds divided equally across geographical location, type, and sex of informant. Three interviewers divided equally the telephone interviews.

Ranking of the dogs was recorded from one to seven when a straight ranking was given by an informant. A mean rank was assigned for dogs given a tie. For example, if two breeds were given a first-place rank by an informant, each breed

Table 6.2. DOG BREEDS EVALUATED

Breed	Group	AKC Rank	Breed	Group	AKC Rank
Afghan hound	Hound	31	Irish setter	Hunt	10
Airedale	Terr	33	Keeshond	Misc	41
Akita	Work	53	Labrador retriever	Hunt	5
Alaskan Malam.	Work	32	Lhasa Apso	Misc	12
Austral. shepherd	Work		Maltese	Terr	34
Basset hound	Hound	23	Newfoundland	Work	49
Beagle	Hound	6	Norwegian elkhound	Hound	38
Bichon frises	Misc.	51	Old English sheepdog	Work	25
Bloodhound	Hound	52	Pekingese	Misc	17
Boston terrier	Misc.	27	Pomeranian	Misc	20
Boxer	Work	24	Poodle—miniature	Misc	1
Brittany spaniel	Hunt	18	Poodle—standard	Misc	1
Cairn terrier	Terr	37	Poodle—toy	Misc	1
Chesap. Bay retriever	Hunt	45	Pug	Misc	42
Chihauhua	Misc.	21	Rottweiler	Work	47
Chow chow	Misc.	29	Samoyed	Work	30
Cocker spaniel	Hunt	4	Saint Bernard	Work	28
Collie	Work	13	Schnauzer—miniature	Terr	9
Dachshund	Hound	8	Scottish terrier	Terr	35
Dalmatian	Misc	40	Shetland sheepdog	Work	11
Doberman pinscher	Work	2	Shi Tzu	Misc	22
English bulldog	Misc	36	Siberian husky	Work	15
English springer spaniel	Hunt	16	Silky terrier	Misc	46
Fox terrier	Terr	44	Vizla	Hunt	50
German short point	Hunt	26	Weimaraner	Hunt	43
German shepherd	Work	3	Welsh corgi	Work	48
Golden retriever	Hunt	7	West Highland terrier	Terr	39
Great dane	Work	19	Yorkshire terrier	Misc	14

would be assigned a score of 1.5 and the third-ranked dog a score of 3. If all dogs were considered equal, a rank of 4 was assigned to all dogs. If the informant did not know anything about a dog breed it was assigned the rank of "m." All other ranks were mathematically adjusted to use the full 1–7 scale.

All information about geographical location, type, and sex of informant and name of interviewer was recorded on a coding sheet for use in punching computer cards. Responses about male versus female dogs for each of the thirteen questions were also coded.

INTERVIEWING FORMAT

A letter had been sent previously to each potential informant about the project. In the initial telephone contact a more convenient time was arranged if necessary. Most calls required thirty to forty-five minutes, but some lasted more than one hour. Some introductory comments were informally made during the first part of the interview, but the content of the introduction was the same for all. Friendly comments on the weather, value of dogs, and queries about the informant's background were interjected throughout the interview. The thirteen questions were read in a conversational manner. If the informant had difficulty ranking breeds, the interviewer would follow once with a prompting statement such as: "So what you are saying is that goldens are as active as bassets." This often induced the informant to come up with a rank. Prompting was used no more than once per breed per question. If a question had to be illustrated by an example, the interviewer gave no fewer than two examples so as to avoid situation-specific judgment. At the end of each interview the informant was asked to volunteer information.

RESULTS AND DISCUSSION

On all behavioral characteristics there were significant differences among breeds (F ratio range, 1.84 to 9.56, df. 55). The range in F ratio, however, revealed that some characteristics provided a more reliable basis for distinguishing among breeds than other characteristics. Dog breeds would appear to differ more reliably in excitability and general activity than in ease of house-training or tendency to be destructive (Table 1). This result confirms a behavioral judgment that excitability and general activity are characteristics that are more closely tied to genetic background than are destructiveness and house-training, which are more readily influenced by a dog's environment.

Examples of the ranking of breeds on the different behavioral characteristics are illustrated in Tables 6.3–6.5 for the traits of excitability, value as a watchdog, and ease of house-training. These traits are chosen as examples because they represent the best, middle, and least reliable distinguishing traits as indicated by F ratio. Consistent with the differences in F ratio, there is a smaller spread in mean scores in going from excitability to house-training.

Table 6.3. RANKING ON EXCITABILITY: MOST TO LEAST (F Ratio, 9.5) FOR THE TOP FIVE AND BOTTOM FIVE RANKED DOGS

Rank	Breed	Mean Score	Standard Error
1.	Fox terrier	6.32	0.213
2.	West Highland terrier	6.10	0.334
3.	Schnauzer	6.09	0.329
4.	Silky terrier	5.97	0.359
5.	Yorkshire terrier	5.93	0.266
52.	Chesapeake Bay retriever	2.25	0.350
53.	Australian shepherd	2.17	0.500
54.	Newfoundland	1.69	0.301
55.	Basset hound	1.51	0.272
56.	Bloodhound	1.24	0.122

Table 6.4. RANKING ON VALUE AS WATCHDOG: MOST TO LEAST (F Ratio, 5.1) FOR THE TOP FIVE AND BOTTOM FIVE RANKED DOGS

Rank	Breed	Mean Score	Standard Error
1.	Schnauzer	5.89	0.347
2.	West Highland terrier	5.88	0.345
3.	Scottish terrier	5.69	0.290
4.	Doberman pinscher	5.66	0.534
5.	German shepherd	5.54	0.392
52.	Vizla	2.40	0.377
53.	Basset hound	2.39	0.304
54.	Saint Bernard	2.26	0.358
55.	Newfoundland	2.22	0.382
56.	Bloodhound	1.77	0.267

Table 6.5. RANKING FOR EASE OF HOUSE-TRAINING: MOST TO LEAST EASILY TRAINED (F Ratio, 1.8) FOR THE TOP FIVE AND BOTTOM FIVE RANKED DOGS

Rank	Breed	Mean Score	Standard Error
1.	Doberman pinscher	5.57	0.343
2.	Australian shepherd	5.33	0.583
3.	Welsh corgi	5.19	0.537
4.	Poodle standard	5.09	0.552
5.	Poodle miniature	4.91	0.607
52.	Pekingese	3.34	0.390
53.	Dalmatian	3.26	0.399
54.	Fox terrier	3.18	0.544
55.	Dachshund	2.98	0.491
56.	Basset hound	2.93	0.446

On all behavioral characteristics there were instances in which the informants significantly (p < .01) differed in the ranking of a few breeds as a function of their geographical location, whether the informant was an obedience judge or a small animal veterinarian, or a man or a woman. In overall excitability ranking, for example, the German shepherd breed was ranked 25 with a score of 3.62. If left to obedience judges alone, this breed would have ranked 7 with a score of 2.30, but if left to the veterinarians, German shepherds would have slipped to a rank of 41 with a score of 4.95. Obviously, a veterinarian in small animal practice finds German shepherds much more excitable than do obedience judges. The Chesapeake Bay retriever ranked 36 overall on being a good watchdog. The score given to this breed by women informants, however, would have put it at the bottom rank, whereas the score given by men informants would have moved it up to a rank of 24. The differences in the ranking by men and women may reflect a personal bias.

A percentile ranking for each behavioral trait on five popular breeds of dogs (golden retriever, cocker spaniel, Doberman pinscher, German shepherd, and standard poodle) are presented in Tables 6.6–6.10. These tables illustrate one manner in which these data may be used. If one were interested in the dog with the least tendency to bite children, the golden retriever would be best because it ranks in the tenth percentile in tendency to bite (Table 6.6). As a bonus, one would also get a dog that was one of the least aggressive toward other dogs, easily dominated, and had little tendency to be destructive as an adult. If being a good watchdog were about as important as a low tendency to bite children, however, the golden would be a poor choice. The cocker spaniel would be a poor choice on both accounts (Table 6.7). The Doberman pinscher (Table 6.8) and German shepherd (Table 6.9) breeds excel as watchdogs and guard dogs but are not easily dominated and have a higher probability of being destructive. The standard poodle might be considered a compromise (Table 6.10). It ranks better than half of all the breeds surveyed in having a low tendency to bite, and it is one of the more easily dominated and easily trained breeds. Its value as a watchdog is in the upper eightieth percentile, which makes it a much better bet than the golden

Table 6.6.   BREED PROFILE OF GOLDEN RETRIEVER

Characteristic (Most–Least)	Percentile	Characteristic (Most–Least)	Percentile
Excitability	20	Aggression to dogs	10
Activity	40	Tendency to dominate	10
Tendency to bite	10	Territorial guarding	10
Objectionable barking	10	Demand for affection	70
Playfulness	80	Destructiveness	10
Ease of training	80	Ease of house-training	90
Watchdog	20		

from this standpoint. Small animal veterinarians gave this breed a significantly higher score as a watchdog than did obedience judges. If one considered the latter group of informants a better source of information about watchdogs, the score as a watchdog should be adjusted down for poodles.

The analysis of our data is not complete. We have developed a method of presenting behavioral characteristics that is more honest than that available in

Table 6.7. BREED PROFILE OF COCKER SPANIEL

Characteristic (Most–Least)	Percentile	Characteristic (Most–Least)	Percentile
Excitability	60	Aggression to dogs	30
Activity	50	Ease of dominating	50
Tendency to bite	80	Territorial guarding	20
Objectionable barking	60	Demand for affection	90
Playfulness	50	Destructiveness	60
Ease of training	60	Ease of house-training	50
Watchdog	20		

Table 6.8. BREED PROFILE OF DOBERMAN PINSCHER

Characteristic (Most–Least)	Percentile	Characteristic (Most–Least)	Percentile
Excitability	30	Aggression to dogs	80
Activity	40	Tendency to dominate	60
Tendency to bite	40	Territorial guarding	90
Objectionable barking	30	Demand for affection	60
Playfulness	30	Destructiveness	60
Ease of training	90	Ease of house-training	90
Watchdog	90		

Table 6.9. BREED PROFILE OF GERMAN SHEPHERD

Characteristic (Most–Least)	Percentile	Characteristic (Most–Least)	Percentile
Excitability*	50	Aggression to dogs	90
Activity	40	Tendency to dominate	70
Tendency to bite	50	Territorial guarding	90
Objectionable barking	60	Demand for affection	30
Playfulness	60	Destructiveness*	90
Ease of training	90	Ease of house-training	70
Watchdog	90		

*Obedience judges gave lower scores than veterinarians.

Table 6.10.   BREED PROFILE OF STANDARD POODLE

Characteristic (Most–Least)	Percentile	Characteristic (Most–Least)	Percentile
Excitability*	50	Aggression to dogs	30
Activity	60	Tendency to dominate	20
Tendency to bite	40	Territorial guarding	60
Objectionable barking	50	Demand for affection	70
Playfulness	90	Destructiveness	40
Ease of training	90	Ease of house-training	90
Watchdog*	80		

*Obedience judges gave lower scores than veterinarians.

the popular literature and that allows a person systematically to go about choosing a breed of dog most suited to a particular need. Percentile ranks on different behavioral measures can be compared among those breeds in which a person is most interested. Usually a compromise will be struck because of several behavioral characteristics that are of concern. We have provided evidence that some behavioral traits are better discriminators among dog breeds than others. The evaluation of a breed may, in some instances, be influenced by the type, sex, or geographical location of the informant. The information yielded by this study is intended to be an aid in choosing breeds; the decision can be made only by the prospective dog owner.

James A. Serpell

7

The Personality of the Dog and Its Influence on the Pet-Owner Bond

In recent years it has become apparent that there is more to the relationship between people and pets than meets the eye. It is now clear that during and as a consequence of interactions with pets many people experience beneficial changes in physiology (Katcher, 1981) and psychology (Brown, Shaw, and Kirkland, 1972; Mugford and M'Comisky, 1975; Delafield, 1976; Kidd and Feldmann, 1981). It is also clear that these beneficial changes have a practical application in the treatment of the mentally and physically disabled (Levinson, 1972; Corson and Corson, 1980a). But we still do not fully understand exactly how pets produce these effects. In short, the fundamental mechanism of the human–companion animal bond remains a partial mystery.

It is reasonable to assume that some special attributes of pets and their behavior toward their owners are essential to the maintenance of their unique bond. These special attributes can be investigated in two ways. Either one can conduct a detailed observational study of pets and their owners interacting under controlled experimental conditions, or one can ask the owners what aspects of their pet they most appreciate. There are pros and cons to both methods. The former has the advantage that it provides objective quantitative information in the form of an inventory of behavioral interactions, but it has the disadvantages that it is relatively costly in time and equipment and at the end of the study the problem remains of deciding which of the many interactions that have been recorded are most important in maintaining the relationship. The latter technique has the advantage that it is easy to perform and generates large amounts of data in a relatively short time, but it suffers from the serious drawback that it relies on the subjective, inexact, and potentially unreliable statements made by experimental subjects. To overcome this problem social psychologists have devised a number of ingenious, sometimes devious, methods of questioning human subjects which aim to reduce the subjectivity (and the unreliability) of the resulting data. The study reported here adopted a modified version of one such method (Rubin, 1974) as a means of questioning pet owners about their pets. For various reasons—primarily to simplify the collection and analysis of data—all the subjects used were dog owners.

METHODS

The study began with a series of semistructured interviews with twenty-five dog owners living in and around Cambridge in England. Subjects were contacted through veterinary surgeries, dog-training schools, and an advertisement placed in a local newspaper. Each interview lasted approximately one and one-half hours and aimed to explore every possible aspect of each owner's relationship with his or her pet. The interviews were recorded and later examined for salient recurring themes such as qualities of the pet or the aspects of the pet's behavior to which the majority of owners attached particular significance as judged by the intensity and quality of the owners' comments about particular items. The following list of canine attributes emerged as important to the majority of owners:
 1. Playfulness
 2. Reaction to separation (day)
 3. Nervousness
 4. Attachment (to one person)
 5. Excitability
 6. Friendliness to strangers
 7. Territorial barking
 8. Friendliness to other dogs
 9. Attitude to walks
10. Obedience on walks
11. Obedience at home
12. Intelligence or aptitude
13. Protectiveness
14. Possessiveness
15. Loyalty/affection

16. Sensitivity to owner's moods
17. Attentiveness
18. Reaction to owner's homecoming
19. Reaction to separation (night)
20. Attitude to food
21. Sense of humor
22. Expressiveness

A simple questionnaire was designed in which each of the twenty-two attributes was expressed as a linear scale with each end representing opposite dimensions of that particular attribute and with a midpoint representing the average or intermediate position between the two extremes. Thus the scale for, say, "playfulness" took the following form:

Never or   **Very playful**
rarely plays_____ **always enjoys games**

A second group of fifty-seven dog owners completed this questionnaire, first, by marking a cross (X) on each line or scale where they considered their dog lay between each pair of extremes, and second, by marking a circle (O) where their "ideal" dog would lie on the same scales. All the scales were the same length so it was possible to measure (in millimeters) the positions of the two marks relative to each other and to one end of the scale. Subjective statements such as "Rover is a bit too nervous" or "My dog is very affectionate" could then be converted into quantifiable numerical data-points that could be handled statistically. An example of a page of a completed questionnaire is shown in Figure 7.1. In this case the dog in question was ideal with respect to separation distress, attachment, excitability, and friendliness to strangers but was less playful and more nervous than the owner would have liked. Finally, at the end of the same questionnaire owners were asked directly to state which characteristics of their dog they found most and least appealing and to provide basic background information about themselves and their pet.

RESULTS

A histogram showing the medians and interquartile ranges of the "actual" and "ideal" scores for each variable is provided in Figure 7.2. The "actual" scores are represented by the left-hand columns in each pair and the "ideal" by the right-hand columns. Wilcoxon's matched-pairs signed-ranks test was used to calculate the significance of the differences between "actual" and "ideal" scores for each variable. The results of this analysis are expressed graphically in Figure 7.3. (Wilcoxon's test produces a statistic "z," which is a measure of the difference between the paired samples that are being compared. In this case, the higher the value of "z" the greater the probability that the difference for each variable is statistically significant.) In Figure 7.3, five canine attributes are listed between the $p < 0.05$ and the $p < 0.001$ lines which appear to be minor sources of dissatisfaction for this sample of Cambridge dog owners: overexcitability, lack of intelligence, separation anxiety both during the daytime and at night, and oversensitivity to the owners' moods. Above the $p < 0.001$ line and isolated by a distinct gap are another five attributes which seem to be the principal sources of dissatisfaction for this sample of dog owners: lack of protectiveness (perhaps a sign of the times), disobedience both on walks and in the home, nervousness, and possessiveness. More interesting from the point of view of insights into the nature of the human–companion animal bond are the twelve items below the $p < 0.05$ line, because these represent aspects of canine personality for which there is no significant difference between "actual" and "ideal" scores.

Referring to Figure 7.2 and comparing these twelve characteristics, it is apparent that they fall roughly into two groups. Seven of them—playfulness, attachment to one person, friendliness to other people, territoriality, friendliness to other dogs, attitude to food, and sense of humor—have medians fairly close to the midpoint or average and relatively large interquartile ranges (for both "actual" and "ideal").

In other words, the dogs were relatively variable with respect to these characteristics, and their owners were relatively variable about what they preferred. This finding could be interpreted as implying that this sample of owners did not attach major importance to how their dogs rated on these particular personality scales (for example, an owner may appreciate his dog's playfulness, but his relationship with the pet is not seriously impaired if the dog is not playful). It is unlikely that owners would have such variable attitudes to these characteristics if they were of crucial importance in maintaining the relationship. In contrast, the remaining five characteristics—expressiveness, enjoyment of walks, loyalty/affection, welcoming behavior, and attentiveness—have medians close to the maximum and relatively narrow interquartile ranges. Moreover, each of these extremes of canine personality concurs closely with the owner's ideal. It would appear that these items lie closer to the heart of the relationship than the rest.

Another important difference between "actual" and "ideal" that is not immediately apparent from these data emerges if one examines correlations between the variables. Spearman's rank-correlation coefficients were calculated between the scores for all the "ideal" variables, and a relatively simple geometrical pattern of associations was found (Figure 7.4). This patttern contains a ringlike structure of positive correlations between the dimensions intelligence, loyalty/affection, welcoming behavior, enjoyment of walks, obedience, and expressiveness, and two side branches made up of sense of humor and attentiveness and protectiveness. This nexus of positive correlations is in turn negatively correlated with a second group of variables consisting of separation anxiety, nervousness, and possessiveness (the correlations between intelligence and obedience, nervousness and separation anxiety may help to explain why intelligence—or lack of it—occurs as a minor source of dissatisfaction in Figure 7.3, since it may have been displaced higher up the graph than expected through its association with these other variables).

The pattern of correlations between "ideal" variables contrasts markedly with the larger and more complex profile that emerges when "actual" variables are compared (Figure 7.5). In this case, four distinct groups or clusters of variables can be detected (demarcated by dotted lines). A striking feature of this pattern is the lower right-hand cluster, which includes the five variables previously found to be most important in the dog-owner relationship (expressiveness, enjoyment of walks, loyalty/affection, welcoming behavior, and attentiveness) and which also closely resembles the ringlike structure of positive correlations described in Figure 7.4. The major differences are the more central position of attentiveness, the presence of sensitivity (a minor source of dissatisfaction in Figure 7.3), and the complete absence of obedience, which, in this case, is negatively correlated with the dog's age and has little or nothing to do with its intelligence, expressiveness, or enjoyment of walks.

Another important aspect of this cluster is that it is the only one of the four which is unlikely to give rise to serious conflicts with the owner's expectations of the dog, the only possible source of dissatisfaction arising from the association between sensitivity and possessiveness. In contrast, the other clusters could all produce significant conflicts. The two upper groups associated with youthfulness are potentially in direct conflict with each other from the owner's viewpoint: while owners clearly appreciate the energy, playfulness, friendliness, and sense of humor of young dogs, they are also significantly dissatisfied with the disobedience and separation anxiety shown by dogs in the same age group. The reverse would apply to older dogs. Similarly, in the lower left-hand cluster, owners tend to value the protectiveness and territoriality of dogs but do not appreciate the nervousness and possessiveness with which these attributes are often associated. As before, these results indicate that a relatively small group of attributes are involved in maintaining the relationship.

DISCUSSION

The main aim of this study was to disentangle from the complex network of interactions between dogs and their owners the particular attributes of pet animals which contribute most to the formation and maintenance of the human-animal bond. Thus far, the study has been a partial success in that it has incriminated a relatively small and closely related group of variables and has eliminated many others. But there still remain problems of interpretation. Clearly, it would be unwise to attach equal significance to all the variables within this group. Enjoyment of walks, for example, is evidently important to dog owners but is unlikely to play a major part in the relationship between people and cats or people and parakeets. Likewise, a certain amount of ambivalence appears to be attached to the attribute sensitivity, and the attribute intelligence seems to owe its importance chiefly to its associations with attentiveness and expressiveness.

One of the more valuable insights provided by the variables in this group arises from the positive associations between affection—a nebulous and poorly defined concept at best, although clearly of central importance for good pet-owner relations—and welcoming behavior, attentiveness, expressiveness, and sensitivity (Figure 7.5). This association suggests that it may be possible to define loyalty and affection in terms of these other variables, two of which (attentiveness and welcoming behavior) could in practice be measured by direct behavioral observation. In other words, behavioral attributes such as these may provide a key for unlocking at least some of the secrets of the human–companion animal bond.

There are also theoretical and experimental grounds for believing that welcoming behavior and attentiveness may be of particular importance in pet-owner relationships. The functional significance of greeting behavior in humans has not been studied in any detail, but elaborate and energetic greeting rituals have evolved in many other animal species, and ethologists believe that these displays serve to cement social and sexual bonds (Tinbergen, 1959; Lorenz, 1965; Nelson, 1978; Serpell, 1981). The importance of attentiveness, or more specifically patterns of eye contact and mutual eye contact, in human relationships has been recognized by psychologists for some time (Argyle and Dean, 1965; Exline and Winters, 1965; Kendon, 1967). Argyle (1975) states: "There have been a number of decoding experiments showing that gaze is perceived as a signal for liking. . . . if an experimenter interviewed two subjects, the subject who was looked at most inferred that she was preferred. Direction of gaze was found to be a more effective signal than bodily orientation in this experiment. Other experiments have shown that if A looks at B, not only does B perceive A as liking him, but he in turn likes A more."

Finally, the results of this study suggest a reason why the domestic dog is universally the most popular pet animal and was the first species to be domesticated by man. It is among the most intelligent of domestic species, and for morphological reasons it is also the most expressive (Bolwig, 1962). Its wild ancestor, the wolf, is a highly social animal. It lives in hierarchical societies in which elaborate greeting displays, patterns of gaze, and extreme sensitivity to the emotional states of other individuals play a major part in maintaining the stability of social relationships within the group (Mech, 1970). In short, the dog is almost human, but, owing to its subordinate status, it displays few of the signals which people perceive as competitive or threatening in their interactions with each other.

Inevitably, there are objections to drawing such generalized inferences from this type of data. First, the original questionnaire may have ignored aspects of the pet-owner relationship that may be just as important as the aspects detected in this study. Second, the results do not expose the true personality of the domestic dog; rather, they illustrate the way a certain group of Cambridge dog owners view their pets and their pets' behavior. This limitation may not be a serious problem because the way people perceive their pets must ultimately be responsible for maintaining the human–companion animal bond.

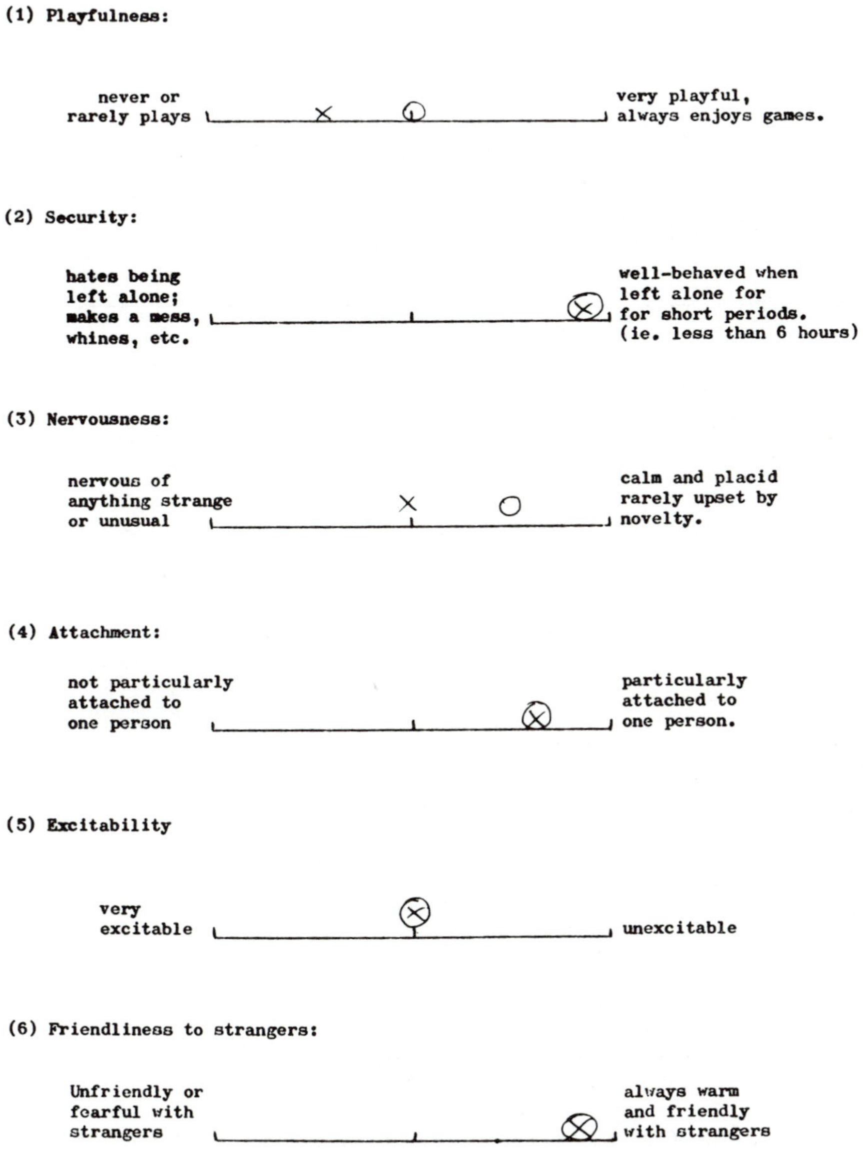

(1) Playfulness:

never or
rarely plays |————— X ——— Ⓛ ——————————| very playful,
always enjoys games.

(2) Security:

hates being
left alone;
makes a mess, |——————————————————⊗| well–behaved when
left alone for
for short periods.
whines, etc. (ie. less than 6 hours)

(3) Nervousness:

nervous of
anything strange
or unusual |——————————— X —— O ———————| calm and placid
rarely upset by
novelty.

(4) Attachment:

not particularly
attached to
one person |———————————————⊗—| particularly
attached to
one person.

(5) Excitability

very
excitable |———————⊗———————| unexcitable

(6) Friendliness to strangers:

Unfriendly or
fearful with
strangers |——————————————⊗| always warm
and friendly
with strangers

Figure 7.1. Sample of completed page of dog owner questionnaire.

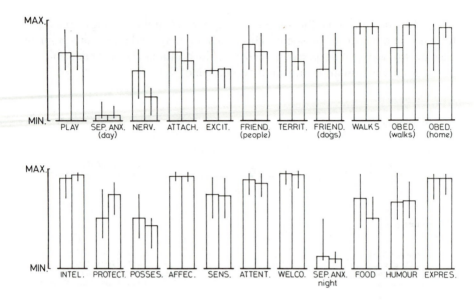

Figure 7.2. Medians and interquartile ranges of "actual" (left-hand columns) and "ideal" (right-hand columns) for 22 different personality variables (N = 57).

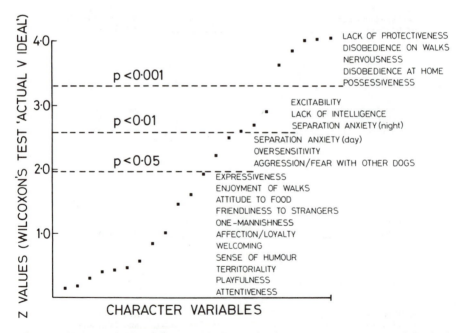

Figure 7.3. Values of "z" (Wilcoxon's matched-pairs signed-ranks test, N = 42) for paired comparison of "actual" and "ideal" scores for the 22 personality variables.

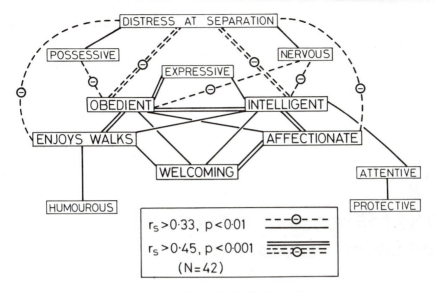

Figure 7.4. Diagrammatic representation of statistically significant positive and negative associations (Spearman's rank correlations) between "ideal" variables. The two measures of separation anxiety and obedience were so highly correlated as to be included under single headings.

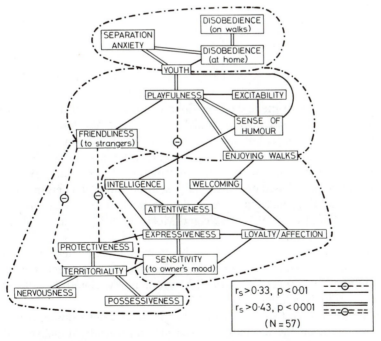

Figure 7.5. Diagrammatic representation of correlations (Spearman's) between actual variables. The two measures of separation anxiety and the two measures of friendliness were so closely correlated as to be included under single headings.

Randall Lockwood

8

The Influence of Animals
on Social Perception

We continue to live in the age of the "lonely crowd" described by sociologists thirty years ago (Riesman, Glazer, and Denny, 1950). We have frequent encounters with many people but limit more prolonged interactions to a select few. The decision to make the transition from an encounter to an interaction is often made quickly on the basis of very little information. Far-reaching social judgments are often made based on superficial first impressions of a person's physical appearance, clothing, makeup, perceived warmth, and other cues (Thornton, 1943; Asch, 1946; Kelly, 1950; Argyle and McHenry, 1971; Zunin and Zunin, 1972; Reis and Nezlek, 1980).

Many authors have commented on the dramatic effectiveness of animals as bridges to social interaction. Often these observations have been made in a clinical setting (Levinson, 1969a, 1972; Mugford and M'Cominsky, 1975; Corson et al., 1977b; McCulloch, 1981b; Messent, 1981).

There are at least two explanations for the phenomena observed in these studies. One is that the animals involved are intrinsically attractive and the humans associated with them become interesting (or at least tolerated) by association. Once the doorway to interaction has opened a bit, the person can be evaluated on his own merits. This seems to be the case in some reports of animals used in a therapeutic setting. Levinson (1969a) noted that patients often began conversations with his canine "co-therapist," then addressed him and the dog together, and finally initiated conversation with human therapists.

A second process that may also be at work when animals facilitate social interaction is that people may form impressions or "dispositional attributions" concerning others on the basis of their association with animals. Perceived relationships with animals clearly enter into our opinions of public figures, particularly politicians. Franklin Roosevelt, when accused of sending a destroyer to the Aleutian Islands to retrieve his Scottish terrier Fala, managed to use the charges to his advantage and ingratiate himself with the nation's dog lovers by declaring: "These Republican leaders have not been content with attacks on me, or my wife, or my sons. No, not content with that, they now include my little dog Fala. Well . . . I don't resent these attacks . . . but Fala does resent them. . . . I think I have a right to resent, to object to libelous statements about my dog." The issue was promptly dropped.

Richard Nixon forestalled his political demise for thirty years by invoking the image of that "little cocker spaniel . . . black and white spotted . . . named Checkers." Lyndon Johnson received protest mail rivaling antiwar mail in quantity when he was pictured lifting his beagles by the ears. Politicians, movie stars, and other celebrities are routinely portrayed in the presence of animals to accentuate their positive traits.

We decided to attempt to document objectively the effect of the presence of an animal on the perception of people and social interactions. It was hypothesized that adding an animal to a social scene should alter both the perception of the people in the scene and the overall mood of the interaction.

To test this idea, we constructed a set of five scenes modeled after the Thematic Apperception Test (TAT). These scenes depicted ambiguous situations involving one or two people. The scenes were chosen so as to be meaningful either with or without the animal present. The animals were not pictured as being directly involved in the interaction but were simply present.

METHOD

SUBJECTS

The subjects were sixty-eight undergraduate psychology students recruited from introductory classes at Stony Brook. Each received $2 and course extra credit for participating. A second group of subjects was recruited from the general community around the University of Pennsylvania, School of Veterinary Medicine, by way of poster announcements. Data from these subjects are not included in this analysis.

PROCEDURE

Subjects were tested in groups of two or three in our laboratory. Each was given a package of five sealed folders. Each folder contained a line drawing, a semantic differential form to be used to rate the people in the pictures, and a form for rating the mood or tone of the scene. Packages contained either two, three, or no folders featuring a version of a picture containing an animal. The order of appearance of the five pictures was randomized across subjects.

> This package contains 5 folders. Starting with folder number 1 open the folder and look at the picture for a minute or two. Ask youself the following questions: Who are the people in the picture? What is the relationship between them? What has been happening in the picture? What will happen next?
> When you have an idea about what the picture represents, complete one rating sheet for each person in the picture, then answer the questions about the mood or tone of the scene.
> When you have finished with a picture, put the rating sheets back in the folder, set it aside and proceed with the next one. Please go through the folders in the order they are arranged. Do not go back to a folder after you have set it aside.
> Thank you.

Figures 8.1–8.5 depict the five scenes with the animals present (pictures 1A–5A). The alternate scenes (10–50) are identical except the animal is missing. A second animal version of picture 5 (5B, Figure 8.6) was prepared in which only the direction of the leash was changed.

The semantic differential scales were presented as a set of adjective pairs arranged in the following fashion:

strong I_____I _____ I_____ 0 _____ I_____ I_____I weak
        very   moderate   slight   slight   moderate   very

Subjects were given the following instructions for each adult in the scene:

> Based on what you think is going on in the picture, please rate the _____ on the following characteristics. Circle the point which you feel represents where this person would fit on each scale. Circle O if you have no opinion or if you think the person would be in the middle of the two characteristics.

Two versions of the scales were prepared to control for possible directional bias in responding. In both versions the adjectives were presented in the same order but the adjective pairs were reversed, that is, one scale would read weak _____ strong and the other, strong _____ weak. The form used was varied across subjects, but to avoid confusion each subject used the same version of the semantic differential for all evaluations. The scale for rating people contained twenty adjective pairs (Table 8.1). The scale for evaluating the tone of the scene had eleven pairs (Table 8.2).

Table 8.1.   ADJECTIVE PAIRS ON THE SEMANTIC DIFFERENTIAL SCALE FOR PEOPLE

unhealthy-healthy	stingy-generous
confident-worried	dependent-independent
curious-disinterested	unsatisfied-satisfied
intelligent-unintelligent	happy-sad
aggressive-nonaggressive	bold-timid
weak-strong	gentle-rough
industrious-lazy	apathetic-involved
harmless-dangerous	comfortable-uncomfortable
unfriendly-friendly	unsympathetic-sympathetic
trustworthy-untrustworthy	wealthy-poor

Table 8.2.   ADJECTIVE PAIRS ON THE SEMANTIC DIFFERENTIAL SCALE FOR MOOD OR TONE OF SCENE

friendly-hostile	tense-relaxed
important-unimportant	humorous-serious
destructive-constructive	formal-casual
unromantic-romantic	expected-unexpected
cooperative-uncooperative	pleasant-unpleasant
dangerous-safe	

When subjects had completed all five folders (thirty to forty-five minutes) they were asked to complete a questionnaire giving personal information and descriptions of past experiences with animals (Table 8.3).

Table 8.3.   EXPERIENCE WITH ANIMALS QUESTIONNAIRE

Age _____   Sex _____   Marital status _____   # children_____
Brothers and sisters _____   Occupation _____
In what country were you born? _____
1. Is there a pet in your home? (Students—Is there a pet in your family's home?)
2. If so, please list all pets:
3. Do any of the above animals belong to you?
4. Do you consider any of the above animals important to you?
5. Please list any pets you had in the past that were important to you:
   Type of animal   How long you had it

6. Are you afraid of any kinds of pet animals? If so, please explain:
7. Have you ever been bitten or injured by any kind of animal? If so, please explain:
8. Were you ever prohibited from having pets when you were growing up? If so, please explain:

Data from the semantic differential forms and questionnaires were coded and entered into a CBM microcomputer for cross-tabulation. This system allowed us to compare the distribution of ratings of people in the two versions of each picture for the entire subject population or in specific subpopulations defined by the demographic data (for example, male versus female, pet owners versus nonowners).

RESULTS

SUBJECT DEMOGRAPHICS

Our population contained 20 men (29 percent) and 48 women (71 percent). Of these, 36 (53 percent) presently had a pet in their household. This proportion is consistent with the pattern of dog and cat ownership (58 percent) in the general U.S. population (Purvis and Otto, 1976). One-half of the study population considered at least one animal in the household to be important to them. Nearly all of the subjects (82 percent) listed at least one animal as having been important to them at some point in their lives. Surprisingly, 28 subjects (41 percent) reported having had some negative experience with animals, including dog bite, serious cat scratch, cat-scratch fever, or severe allergy. Seventeen (25 percent) had been bitten by a dog.

RESPONSE TO PICTURES

Pictures 10 and 1A (N = 33 and 35)   The presence of the dog had little effect on the interpretation of this scene, apparently in part because of the overwhelmingly negative evaluations of the older woman. People viewing either picture characterized her as being less happy, healthy, intelligent, friendly, and confident than the younger woman. This negative stereotyping of scenes involving the aged by college students has been reported in gerontological studies.

Two significant differences in the distribution of ratings of the women were observed. Without the dog present (10), 27 percent rated the younger woman as slightly to very happy and 55 percent saw her as slightly to very sad. With the dog in the scene (1A) these figures were reversed, 51 percent saw her as happy and 29 percent as sad ($X^2 = 12.34$, p = .05). The older woman was viewed as lazy by 15 percent and industrious by 33 percent in the absence of the dog. With the dog there was an overall positive shift in the distribution, with 43 percent seeing her as industrious ($X^2 = 12.68$, p < .05).

The overall mood of this scene was viewed as tense and formal by all subjects, but the addition of the dog made it significantly less formal ($X^2 = 12.36$, p = .05). There were no significant differences in the ratings provided by men versus women or owners versus nonowners.

Pictures 20 and 2A (N = 39 and 29)   Across all subjects, the woman in this scene was viewed as slightly to very strong by 72 percent when the dog was not present. With the dog, all subjects (100 percent) rated her in this way (X^2 = 12.5, p < .05). Without the dog, 82 percent viewed her as sad; with the dog only 41 percent saw her as sad (X^2 = 16.55, p < .01). In addition, 56 percent of the viewers of 10 described the woman as bold. With the dog present 83 percent described her in this way (X^2 = 14.67, p < .02). Among subjects who had not reported bad experiences with animals, 75 percent said the woman was slightly to very worried without the dog, but only 40 percent saw her as worried with the dog present (X^2 = 11.5, p = .07). There was no such trend among those who had had negative experiences.

The overall mood of the scene was rated the same in both 20 and 2A, with the exception that the subjects with no negative animal experiences viewed it as significantly less tense with the dog present. There were no sex differences or nonowner versus owner differences in the ratings of either the woman or the mood of the scene.

Pictures 30 and 3A (N = 43 and 25)   Viewers of the scene with and without the cat responded significantly differently on only one adjective; 37 percent scored the man as moderately to very comfortable without the cat while 52 percent rated him in this way with the cat present (X^2 = 14.76, p = .02). This is consistent with the findings of Katcher (1981) that a large proportion of pet owners allow their pets to sleep in their bedroom or on the bed. There were no significant differences in the ratings associated with sex or pet ownership.

Pictures 40 and 4A (N = 41 and 27)   Several attributes of the man in this scene were distributed significantly differently in the ratings of the two versions. In picture 40, 22 percent scored him as slightly to very generous and 27 percent as slightly to very stingy. Among viewers of the scene with the animals, 44 percent rated him as generous and only 2 percent as stingy (X^2 = 19.1, p < .01). Similarly, 49 percent of those viewing the scene with animals rated him as friendly compared to 11 percent without animals (X^2 = 13.6, p = .03).

The tone of the scene was also rated significantly more constructive in 4A (X^2 = 13.16, p < .05) and safer (X^2 = 15.7, p < .02). People who had had negative experiences with animals did not show this effect. Pet owners responded in the same way as nonowners, with the addition that they also rated the scene as significantly less tense with animals present.

Pictures 50, 5A, and 5B (N = 29, 21, and 18)   This scene produced the most interesting variety of responses. The man in the picture was rated as slightly to very intelligent by 55 percent without the dog present but by 83 percent when he held the leash (X^2 = 15.3, p < .02). This effect was even more pronounced among subjects with no reported bad experiences with animals, and was lacking in those that had had such experiences. The man holding the leash was also seen as being significantly more satisfied, friendly, industrious, and wealthy (all p < .05). A possible negative connotation of his association with the dog is that he was judged as being significantly more aggressive in that scene ($X^2 = 13.0$, p = .04). This interpretation does not seem to imply physical aggressiveness or threat to the woman, since she was judged to be safer in this scene than when she held the leash ($X^2 = 12.5$, p = .05) or when no dog was present ($X^2 = 15.3$, p = .02).

The woman in the scene was also perceived to be wealthier when associated with the dog in 5A ($X^2 = 15.97$, p = .01) as well as friendlier ($X^2 = 13.1$, p < .04). There were no other differences associated with sex or pet ownership of the viewers.

DISCUSSION

Overall there was a general tendency to interpret people associated with pets or wild animals in TAT-style scenes in a more positive light than when the pictures lacked the animals. With the possible exception of the aggressiveness rating of the man in picture 5B, the presence of animals never had a negative effect on ratings of people in these scenes, even among non–pet owners or people who had had negative experiences. There were few sex differences in the responses, which may indicate a homogeneity across sex in attitudes and behavior to animals consistent with the finding of Katcher (1981) that men and women were nearly identical in their interactions with animals in veterinary clinic waiting rooms.

The general lack of difference between the responses of subjects who presently had a pet and those who did not may mean that pet owners do not differ dramatically from nonowners, as suggested by Guttmann (1981). Another possible explanation is that our nonowner population was not "pure" in the sense that 80 percent of them had at one time owned at least one animal they considered to be important to them.

An important variable in determining the presence or absence of a positive effect of having an animal in the scene was whether or not the subject had had a negative experience with animals in the past. Although this group did not show a negative shift in ratings of people associated with animals, they often failed to show the positive changes characteristic of the rest of the population. This suggests that events such as dog bite, which have often been considered to be trivial, might have long-range effects on the way one perceives another human being who is associated with animals.

What is the significance of the positive influence of the presence of animals on social perception? One possibility is that it reflects a correlation of attitude similarity with attraction to others (Byrne and Nelson, 1965). Most of our subjects (82 percent) had been pet owners at some time and thus might share some attitudes with people portrayed as associated with animals.

A second possibility is that this effect reflects a valid difference between people associated with animals and those that are not. Our subjects' judgments of these people as happier, friendlier, wealthier, and more relaxed may be rooted in their actual past interactions with others.

The literature dealing with personality differences between pet owners and nonowners is sparse and sometimes inconsistent. Since pet ownership is not included in the census or in most sociological surveys, there is little information on such variables as crime, divorce, or suicide rates in owners versus nonowners. In addition, as we have indicated, nonownership need not imply negative attitudes toward animals, and pet owners might possess animals for reasons other than affection.

Our study indicated that people associated with animals in TAT scenes were often judged to be friendlier, happier, bolder, and less tense. Brown, Shaw, and Kirkland (1972) reported that low affection for dogs was associated with low affection for people and, in males, low desire for such affection. Guttmann (1981) found that the only significant difference between owners and nonowners was that owners showed a higher permanent acceptance of commitment and toleration of possible burdens and a greater tendency to avoid loneliness. In a study of elderly owners versus nonowners, Kidd and Feldmann (1981) found owners to be more optimistic, confident, and helpful. In addition, pet owners are exposed to psychological benefits described by Bossard (1944) and Katcher (1981) including having an outlet for affection, the challenge of responsibility, something to keep them busy, something to talk to, something that makes them feel safe, and a stimulus for exercise. These findings from real populations are consistent with the ratings given to the characters in our pictures.

This study also indicated that people associated with animals were perceived as less dangerous both in the sense of being in less danger from others and being less of a threat to others. There is, as yet, little documentation of the latter view, but there is evidence that cruelty to animals may be associated with adult crime (Hellman and Blackman, 1966).

The perception of people associated with animals as being wealthier is also valid. Several surveys have indicated higher average income among pet owners. These people may also be potentially more interesting as social contacts since other surveys have indicated that owners are more likely to attend concerts and read poetry than nonowners (Ordish, 1981).

In summary, people can make use of perceived relationships to animals in forming preliminary social judgments. These judgments have some basis in fact and are at least as valid as impressions based on superficial cues of appearance and attire. Thus animals, particularly in an urban environment, can provide powerful links to other people and to the natural world.

Figure 8.1 1A

Figure 8.2 2A

Figure 8.1 10

Figure 8.2 20

Figure 8.3 3A

Figure 8.4 4A

Figure 8.3 30

Figure 8.4 40

Figure 8.5 5A

Figure 8.6 5B

Figure 8.5 50

Ann Ottney Cain

9

A Study of Pets in the Family System

My interest in the study of pets in the family came as a result of my observations over a number of years. I was intrigued with pets—my own and other people's. As a psychiatric nurse, educator, and clinician, I have a very special interest in family therapy and particularly in family therapy that is based on the theoretical orientation of Dr. Murray Bowen. Dr. Bowen, in his work with families, has conceptualized the family as a system; that is, family members are all interrelated and comprise, by their relationships as well as by their individual existences, a system or a larger whole.

In 1965, Dr. Bowen wrote that this family emotional system "at . . . times . . . may include members of the extended family network and even nonrelatives and pets" (p. 219). It has been very evident to me in my clinical work with families and in my supervision of graduate students' clinical work with families that pets do have a significant role in the family system.

Students frequently report that family members answered the question, "Who do you feel closest to in your family?" by naming the dog or the cat or another pet. It happened too many times not to have some significance in terms of family relationships.

My observations were further supported by a conversation with Linda Bell, a psychologist at the University of Chicago, who had been conducting a research project using paper sculpting as a means of describing families. She asked family members to arrange all the members of the family on a flannelboard in a way that represented the interpersonal relationships in the group. She found that family members very often included their pet and either placed the pet in a central position or put the pet on the board several times so that he was close to each family member.

Dr. Boris Levinson, a professor of psychology at Yeshiva University in New York, has spent many years studying the role of the pet with children and in families. He has commented, "The role of the pet in the family will depend upon the family structure, the emotional and physical strengths, and weaknesses of each of its members, the emotional undercurrents, and the social climate" (Levinson, 1968b:511).

In 1972, Elaine Apostoles interviewed ten families and wrote a seminar paper at the University of Maryland in which she discussed the subject of pets and applied some of the concepts of the Bowen theory to five of these families. She recognized the importance of pets in the family system and recommended further studies.

RESEARCH STUDY

This study was designed to answer the research question, What is the role of the pet in the family system? Veterinarians have described significant pet-human interactions, as have some psychotherapists, but knowledge of pet-human relationships is heavily based on anecdotal evidence. Families had not been asked, in any formal way, questions that would provide a description of the role of their pet in their family. The goal of this research study was to acquire that information by means of a questionnaire.

The design of the study was a combination of both exploratory and descriptive research. Data were collected by means of a sixty-one-item questionnaire, which was designed to ask family system questions that would provide an accurate description of the pet's role in the family.

Operational definitions used were:

Role: A part or function assumed by someone.

Pet: An animal that is tamed, kept as a companion, or to which one forms an emotional attachment.

Family: A household; all the people living in the same house. They may or may not be related by ancestry or marriage.

System: A set of interrelated elements that have a boundary; a set of persisting interrelationships between parts of a whole.

Family system: This term reflected the principle that family members are all interrelated and comprise, by their relationships as well as by their individual existences, a system or larger whole.

The sample was a convenience sample. Anyone with a pet and living in a family or household who wanted to participate in the study was eligible to fill out the questionnaire. One psychiatrist and one social worker from New York, one social worker from New Jersey, and three psychiatric nurses, one each from Alabama, California, and Texas, collaborated with me by distributing the questionnaires to appropriate families.

Data were collected from families in eleven states. The sample size was 62 and represented 60 different family units. Data were collected in 4 months (May to September, 1977). There was a 73 percent return on the distributed questionnaires. Eighty-five questionnaires were sent out and 62 returned—an excellent response, which could reflect a very high interest in the subject. Participation in the study was purely voluntary. No names were solicited, and the questionnaires were mailed directly back to the researcher.

Initially, a pilot test of five subjects was conducted and several changes were made in the questionnaire. The questionnaire was developed by the researcher and had not been used before, thus no previous test of validity existed. Another research associate and a family systems therapist reviewed the questionnaire to increase the content validity before its use.

The data were analyzed using content analysis; this was the most appropriate method for handling the data from this questionnaire. Categories were formulated and answers were classified under appropriate categories. A previously uninvolved person was asked to review these categories for inter-rater reliability.

The persons who participated in this study had a variety of pets: dogs, cats, fish, hamsters, chickens, birds, rabbits, horses, squirrel monkeys, a lamb, a sheep, a goat, a pigeon, a skunk, and a tarantula (spider). Eighty-nine percent of the respondents had pets while growing up.

The number of pets in the families ranged from one to thirty-seven. The respondent listing thirty-seven pets had two cats, two dogs, a goat, a lamb, a sheep, and thirty chickens; most of these pets had names. The next highest number of pets in a family was nine: one dog, six cats, and two fish. Another family had five cats and three dogs, a total of eight pets.

The length of time the respondents had had their pets ranged from two months (bird) to twenty-one years (cat). The next longest time period was thirteen and one-half years (dog).

Sixty-two respondents gave eight-nine reasons for choosing their pets; 49 percent fell within the combined category of pleasure and companionship. This finding validates previous reports in the literature of the primary motives for pet ownership. The other 51 percent fell in the following categories:

Rescue of an abandoned pet: 11 percent.

Educational function for children: 11 percent. This included learning to play with and care for a pet, learning responsibility, and learning not to be afraid of animals. Mention was made of learning about life events such as birth and death. One participant commented: "The death of our cat gave me an opportunity to role-model grieving for my children and to encourage them to express their feelings." Another said: "Sometimes I think our household revolves around the animals. They seem to bring out the best in the kids as far as responsibility, kindness, affection, first aid, and concern for another living thing. We have all developed a much deeper respect for life in general due to our dealings with our pets."

Replacement of a person or pet: 10 percent. This included child substitutes and the "empty nest" situation. One respondent referred to her pet as her "change of life" baby and another commented: "If there were children in our family, I don't think the dog would have the same status."

Protection: Environmental and personal: 10 percent.

Gifts: 7 percent.

Sport and breeding: 2 percent.

No mention was made of the pet being a vehicle of prestige and status, although this reason for having pedigree pets has been frequently mentioned in the pet literature.

Respondents listed 138 names for their pets. Forty-nine percent of these were people names and 51 percent were pet names. Examples of people names were Heidi, Joshua, Ashley, Scarlett, Samantha, Stephanie, Elizabeth, Arnold, Herbie, Ethel, Fred, Fletcher, and Timothy. Examples of pet names were Tiger, Brownie, Snoopy, Lady, Brandy, Peanut, Puddles, Fudgie, Tigger, and Fat Cat.

Of the one hundred reasons given for selecting their pet's name, thirty named their pet after its physical characteristics such as Fat Cat, Tiny, Coco, Midget, and Blackie. Twenty-two named them after TV shows, movies, cartoon characters, book characters, flowers, and songs such as Scarlett, Ashley, Snoopy, Tigger, Lacey, and Midnight Confession. Fifteen named their pets after specific persons such as Freud, Martin Luther, Sarey Gamp, a German ski instructor, a veterinarian and his wife, chairman of a company, and the president of the United States. Thirteen obtained pets who were already named, and these names were maintained. Ten named their pets after objects or places in countries of their heritage such as Shamrock, Shannon, and Tara. Five named them for a previous pet. Three named them for the season of the year such as Holly, Pinecomb, and Passover. Two named them because they liked the sound of the name, and one named his pet after a college mascot (Ralphie, the Colorado Buffalo).

Respondents reported spending an average of approximately $10 monthly or $120 yearly on their pets in addition to food. They spent money for items such as collars, chains, rawhide, leashes, kitty litter, sweaters, shampoo, licenses, veterinarians, medicine, boarding, grooming, dog-sitting, and toys.

Eighty-seven percent of the respondents reported that they had established rules for their pets. Seventy-eight percent of those said that family members enforced these rules. Of the 9 percent that did not enforce the rules, either children or one adult member was more permissive and allowed breakage of rules, usually causing dissension in the family.

The question about what family members disagreed on in regard to their pets was answered by 82 percent of respondents. Of these, 22 percent (14) said there were no disagreements, 60 percent (37) reported three major areas of disagreement: 46 percent (17) disagreed over the disciplining of their pets; 32 percent (12) disagreed over the care of their pets; and 22 percent (8) disagreed over the space used by their pets.

Parents did not like the pets sleeping with the kids or being taken every time the family went somewhere; there were arguments about whether the pets would stay in the bedroom or out at night; there were arguments about whether the pet should stay inside or outside and about who was going to clean the fish tank, clean up after the dog, or empty the cat's litter box; one family member would be too lenient with the pet and another too harsh, which often led to arguments; one respondent wrote: "We've had many fights about the dog. My husband said that I really cared more about the dog than about him. I agreed. It took quite a while for things to get back to 'normal' between us."

In answer to the question, "Was there any change in your family after you got your pet?" 66 percent of the respondents said "No," and 32 percent reported 24 changes in two categories, positive and negative. Of the positive changes, 14 or 58 percent of the reported changes were increased closeness expressed around the care of the pet; more time spent together playing with the pet; more happiness of family members; and less arguing. Of the negative changes, 10 or 42 percent of the reported changes were more arguing and problems over rules and care of the pet and less time spent with other family members; for example, children spent less time with their parents and husbands spent less time with their wives.

One respondent said that solving arguments between family members had changed since they got their pet. She said that now, whenever there is a family argument her favorite comment is, "Stop fighting—you're upsetting the dog," or "Get quiet—the dog is upset." She commented that this is always more effective than saying, "Don't hit your brother."

Another respondent described a change in self and wrote: "In interacting with my dog I am confronted with myself—my faults, my stubbornness, my giving in, my feeling sorry for. It's more of a confrontation with my dog than with my sons because the results show up more quickly. I am forced to acknowledge my part in what goes on." When asked how important their pet was to the family, the respondents gave the following ratings: extremely important, 7 percent; very important, 55 percent; important, 10 percent; moderately important, 8 percent. Sixteen percent listed pets as family members, using words such as fairly, quite, and pretty important. Four percent did not answer this question.

When asked to identify the periods of their lives in which their pets were most important, participants responded as follows: 16 percent did not respond; 26 percent said when they were sad, lonely, or depressed; 15 percent said during an illness and after the death of a significant other; 11 percent considered the pet equally important in all periods of life; 10 percent said during crises such as job crises, moving, separation, and divorce; 6 percent listed childhood; 6 percent listed a period of temporary absence of spouse or children; 5 percent said when their marriage was without children; 1.5 percent listed the teenage period; 1.5 percent said during a time when unemployed; 1.5 percent said the pet had never been important.

When asked if anything unusual or significant was happening in their family just before or at the time they got their pets, 66 percent (forty-one) of the respondents listed forty-eight significant happenings. Of these forty-one respondents, sixteen (39 percent) had recently made geographic moves; fourteen (34 percent) were experiencing a loss because of separation, divorce, death, or an important family member moving away; five (12 percent) said a previous pet had recently died; four (10 percent) had recently married; three (7 percent) had recently had a child; three (7 percent) reported their spouses as just beginning graduate school; two (5 percent) got their pet when other family members were away on a trip; one (2 percent) reported getting the pet during a crisis at work. In 82 percent of these forty-eight significant happenings, pets could be viewed as a substitute in an experience of loss.

One of the most significant findings of the study is that 87 percent of all respondents considered their pet a member of their family. Only 10 percent did not, and 3 percent said both yes and no. These answers clearly support the concept that the pet is an actual member of the family system.

Fifty-six percent said they thought of their pet as an animal, 36 percent said they thought of their pet as a person, and 8 percent considered their pets somewhere in between an animal and a person.

When asked who they felt closest to in the family, 71 percent named another significant adult, 11 percent listed children, 8 percent said the pet, and 5 percent said it varied at different times.

When asked who gets the most strokes (in Transactional Analysis terms) in the family, 44 percent said pets, 18 percent said children, 18 percent said family members got equal strokes, and 13 percent named the other significant adult in the family. This is the finding that got the most attention in the Associated Press release, which reported that an overwhelming majority of pet owners admit that they find it easier to focus attention and affection on their animals than on other family members. Articles carried headlines like, "Pets Out-Class Family Members as Objects of Affection" and "Pets Found with Most of Attention in Family." This is not exactly how the participants in this study phrased it, but it is pretty close.

Eighty-one percent of the respondents described their pets as "tuned in" to the feelings of family members. They gave many examples such as pets were sensitive to illness, depression, anger, tension, turmoil, happiness, and excitement. They reported that pets had experienced diarrhea, stomach upsets, and epileptic attacks when times were tense in the family. I believe that during these times, pets could be described as the barometers of anxiety in the family and that they often indicate family tensions and conflicts.

When asked what their pets did when other family members were affectionate, 92 percent (57) of all respondents answered the question. Of those, 19 percent (11) reported that the pet showed no change or did nothing; 16 percent (9) reported passive responses such as being quiet, sleeping, and waiting; 65 percent (37) reported active responses such as jumps up and tries to get between people, tries to "muzzle in"—comes to be petted; acts jealous—tries to join us; tries to interfere—wedges in between people; demands attention; tries to be included—"We're like the Three Musketeers." The following question was applicable to only 61 percent (38) of the respondents because many had only one pet. When asked what they did when their pets fought with each other, of those 61 percent, 24 percent (15) said their pets did not fight; 18 percent (11) said they did nothing when fighting occurred; 19 percent (12) had specific responses such as seven separated their pets; five yelled at the aggressor or verbally reprimanded pets. Sixty percent of the respondents said that pets did not "act out" feelings of family members; 36 percent stated that they did and listed examples such as frisky when others are happy; quiet when someone is sick; fight with each other when tension is high; act depressed when family members are sad.

When asked how their pets behave when there is a crisis or high anxiety in the family, fifty-three participants responded. Of these, 19 percent reported their pet had no reaction. Twenty-eight percent reported reactions described as independent, including behaviors such as hyperactivity, restlessness, anxiety, barking, running, inability to eat or sleep, soiling on the floor, and developing illnesses that required medication. Fifty-three percent reported reactions described as interactions with the family, including 32 percent who reported movements toward family members such as staying close, seeking more attention, and protecting family members. Twenty-one percent reported movements away from family members such as hiding, withdrawing, and distancing.

The question about their pet's reaction to a new family member or a birth was relevant to only 31 percent (19) of all respondents. Of those nineteen respondents, twenty reactions of pets were described. Eleven of those reactions were positive such as the pet was happy with the new family member—either adult or baby—or the pet was more attached to the new baby than to others. Nine of those reactions were negative such as the pet withdrew at the birth of the baby, the pet ignored the new member, or the pet reacted with disgust, cried a lot, or demanded additional attention. One respondent reported that her pet became sick within 8 hours and had a gastric hemorrhage within 3 days when she kept a three-month-old baby for 5 days. Another respondent wrote: "I was closer to my pet before the birth of our child. I prepared the dog to anticipate the baby—to reduce his jealous reactions, I placed a baby doll in the crib and taught him not to jump on the crib. It worked!"

Thirty-seven percent of all respondents reported that they had made friends, increased their social contacts, or maintained social relationships by means of their pets. Examples given were that some started conversations with people over pets; some made friends through obedience training classes; children met other children in their new neighborhood via their pets; one respondent began dating her veterinarian; and another met her husband while walking her dog.

Dr. Murray Bowen considers the triangle to be the basic building block of any emotional system. A triangle is formed when the tension within a two-person emotional system exceeds a certain level. Triangles are patterned ways of dealing with intense feeling states. These triangles can consist of three people or two people and an issue (or pet) within the family system. Increased closeness between any two family members results in increased distance from the third member of the triangle. Pets, like humans, can be triangled into a family system to relieve an uncomfortable situation. Triangles involving pets usually provide a display of affection, anger, or distancing. Triangling was described in the questionnaire as a process in which two persons (or pets) transfer the tension or intense feeling between them onto a third person (or pet). Respondents were asked to give an example of triangling that they thought involved pets in their family. Forty-eight percent (30) of the respondents gave the following examples: fourteen described situations in which they yelled or expressed anger or tension at the pet instead of at another family member. Five described situations in which family members argued over the pets, for example, taking sides in discipline situations and when family members rebelled by breaking pet rules. Three said they talked to their pet instead of to other family members but so that these other family members could hear. Others reported that their pets would fight each other and get upset when family members were upset and that the pet would interfere when family members showed affection or fought with each other.

The following specific examples of triangling behavior were given.

1. Husband sweet-talks the dog instead of his wife (husband and dog are in a close, togetherness position, and the wife is in the outside, distant position).

2. Mother is angry with daughter but yells at the dog instead (conflict moves and then is between mother and dog, and the daughter maintains the more comfortable, outside position).

3. The pets become the subject of observation and conversation between husband and wife. Warmth, concern, and affection are shown for the pets rather than for one another. This works particularly well in a pursuer-distancer relationship. It provides the pursuer a nonthreatening place to pursue (the pet) and allows more space for the distancer while this is occurring.

4. Mother talks to the cat instead of to her daughter and says things she would not say directly to her daughter, so that the daughter hears her.

5. Tension or fighting erupts between the pets when family members are distancing or reactive. Pets fight if the silent treatment is going on between the husband and the wife.

6. Father is friendlier to the dog than to his son (father and dog are in a close, togetherness position, and the son is in the outside, distant position).

7. Mother spends more time grooming and talking to the dog than talking to her daughter (mother and dog are in the close position, and the daughter is on the outside).

8. One respondent said that whenever any anger or tension was present in family members and they were uncomfortable, the focus always went to the dog. She observed that it was "safer."

9. The husband complains about the cat so the wife becomes stricter. Then the husband takes sides with the cat and reacts to the wife's strictness. The wife then gets angry with husband for "butting in," and so the triangle goes.

10. Sometimes an example of triangles was given in answer to another question. For example, when asked what the pet is doing when family members are affectionate, one respondent commented: "That is why my husband hates the dog! The dog barks and growls during love-making and proceeds to chew up anything that he can find—clothing, bedding, and so on. Locking him out of the bedroom creates an even bigger scene—it *is* a problem!" She went on to describe the sequence of the triangle: the dog becomes jealous of the husband and the wife in bed and tries to get in the middle. The husband kicks the dog. The wife becomes upset and angry with the husband and comforts the dog. The wife's final comment was, "It took a long time to forgive him for kicking 'my' dog."

When asked if they had ever had a pet who was lost permanently, died, or was killed, 81 percent (50) of the respondents had and described their reactions vividly.

All but two of the fifty respondents described the loss as a time of sadness, grieving, crying, mourning, and loss for the family. Some descriptive words used were supergrief, crushed, sobbed, and heartbroken. Two families said everyone but the father was sad.

Of the fifty respondents who had lost a pet, eighteen (36 percent) did not obtain another pet; thirty-two (64 percent) did and gave the following reasons for replacing the original pet: their love of pets or to get comfort from their loss.

In answer to the question, "Have you ever not liked a pet and wanted to get rid of him?" 65 percent of the respondents said "no"; 35 percent said "yes." Of the 35 percent of total respondents who said "yes," only 45 percent actually had gotten rid of their pets. They gave the following reasons: unable to housebreak, the pet was aggressive, the pet had a nasty disposition, unable to manage, too big to handle, fear of the pet, and the pet was too ill to be treated.

The other 55 percent of the respondents that wanted to get rid of their pets only thought about it but never actually did. They gave almost the same reasons for wanting to do this with the additional reasons that the pet was also an inconvenience and too much trouble. One might hypothesize that once you have a pet, even if you do not like it, you can get "hooked" and have great difficulty deciding to get rid of it. One study respondent put this in perspective by writing, "Yes, I wanted to get rid of them—and I've felt the same way about my husband and my kids! But it passes—and they are eventually loved the same as always."

CONCLUSION

I believe that the sixty-two respondents in this study answered the questions very openly, but it is important to note that this was a small, convenience sample and not a random one and, therefore, care must be taken in generalizing. The study group was, however, a cross-section of people who shared their thoughts and ideas about their pets in their families—and the majority indicated that pets are considered family members and described their role in the family as very important. The pet *is* a significant member of the family.

Elizabeth Atwood Lawrence

10

The Human-Horse Bond in Crow Indian Life and Culture

There are many different types of human bonds with various species of companion animals. The nature of these bonds is in many cases determined not only by personal traits but by the particular culture or society to which an individual belongs. Though certain people within a society may differ in their personal interactions with animals, nevertheless there often exists a general culturally sanctioned mode of regarding a certain species of animal. This outlook imbues the species with specific meaning within that group—meaning that is linked to the historical and cultural context.

This chapter focuses on the interaction between contemporary Crow Indians and their horses. My observations result from anthropological field research carried out among this Plains tribe of southeastern Montana over a period of several years. Though it is generally assumed that the importance of human-horse interactions in Plains Indian life virtually ceased with the end of the tribes' free-roving era and the beginning of the reservation period, such has not always been the case. For in my field studies I found that the horse still plays a highly significant and dynamic part in contemporary life on the Crow Indian Reservation.

As a background for the understanding of the horse as a companion animal within the present-day culture of one particular Plains group—the Crow people—I will briefly summarize the salient points concerning the influential part played by the horse during the flowering of the Plains Indian horse culture in the eighteenth and nineteenth centuries. Although horses have been closely interwoven with human history and culture in many different times and places, perhaps no human-horse relationship is more dramatic than that exemplified by the Indians of the North American Plains, whose life and culture were profoundly transformed by their acquisition of the horse. Indeed, the way of life that developed among the Plains tribes as a result of becoming mounted peoples became their society's most distinctive feature. It is this period of tribal history between the introduction of the horse and the end of nomadic life by which Plains Indians are still characterized, not only by many scholars and the general public but the natives themselves. Even today, Plains Indians like the Crows continue to look back to the horse era with nostalgia and enduring pride.

For such peoples as the Crows, of course, the coming of the horse vastly improved the quality of life in innumerable ways. The equine animal revolutionized transportation, making it faster, easier, and more comfortable. The power of the horse made possible the building of larger and more comfortable lodges and the possession of more material goods because horses could carry far heavier loads than dogs or human beings. Bison hunting, formerly carried out on foot, was transformed into a glorious and thrilling equestrian pursuit as well as a quicker way to obtain meat. Plains Indian warfare took on new dimensions of intensity because braves were infinitely more powerful and mobile as mounted warriors. Plains Indian horsemen became legendary among the world's most skillful riders. Through their close partnership with the animals they seemed to become as one with their horses. Certain Plains tribes earned a reputation among the United States soldiers who were sent to fight against them as the greatest "light cavalry" in the world. Intertribal horse raiding became a major exploit for the warriors. Capturing prized horses from an enemy was considered an honorable occupation. It was a feat that required reckless courage and could lead to advanced status within a society where fortitude was required for survival.

Because horses were involved in almost every aspect of Plains Indian society, there developed a relationship with the animals which went beyond the utilitarian and was ultimately crystallized into a new value system. Horses became the tribe's most treasured possessions. Abundance and quality in ownership of horses were synonymous with prestige and wealth. Horses were the medium of exchange in trade, comprised payment for a bride, and were given away at ceremonies and celebrations to express kinship ties and to bestow honor.

From time immemorial Plains Indian world-view had encompassed a belief in the unity of all forms of life and a respect for animals as partners. Thus it was natural that horses became part of the human spiritual and aesthetic spheres, as well as the pragmatic. The horse was not only a co-worker but could also act as intermediary between the human and the supernatural force and was able to communicate with certain individuals. Plains people, out of admiration, turned to horses for artistic expression, depicting them on important items of culture such as war shields, lodgeskins, and religious objects.

One of the most tragic aspects of the Plains natives' lives after they were placed upon reservations was the cessation of active participation in the horse-related activities they had formerly enjoyed as mounted nomads. For the Crows, adverse reaction to this loss was a significant factor contributing to the difficult adjustment to a sedentary existence. The glories of past times were to remain in their memory. Horses, above all else, had given their life meaning and their culture its distinctiveness, making them a proud and respected people. Without horses, the native Americans were dispirited, and tribal pride was at low ebb. Forced removal by the government of large numbers of Crow horses during the early 1900s caused deep and lasting sorrow within Crow society and contributed to cultural disintegration.

In recent times, however, the Crows were fortunate in being able to bring about a return of horses to their reservation, and the people of the tribe have experienced renewed involvement with the animals. Initially, this return of horses was due to the efforts of a native Crow Reservation superintendent, who knew firsthand the great importance of horses in his people's culture. He set up a program to revitalize reservation life by bringing back horses and improving their quality. In so doing he helped immeasurably in reviving Crow spirit and pride.

From my field work it became evident that this revitalization of the Crow relationship with horses not only represents for these people an important link to the glorious past of their tribe but also brings pleasure and a sense of purpose to the present.

On the reservation today horses continue to be part of virtually every Crow ritual. Valued mounts are still given away during special ceremonies like adoptions and during important celebrations. Horses have retained their status as the most treasured of gifts, and their bestowal cements significant social relationships such as that between brothers-in-law.

The Crow horse comeback was intensified at the time of World War II and is traceable to several influences. The coming of war revived old customs and rituals relating to warriors for those Crow Indians entering military service. Such traditions from the past naturally involved the Plains warrior's former partner in battle—the horse—and so drew increased attention to the animal. Another factor that served to increase the popularity and abundance of horses on the Crow Reservation in recent times was the production of the annual Custer Battle Reenactment. This was a restaging of the famous cavalry versus Indian battle, presented by the Crow people, and taking place very near the area where the actual Battle of the Little Big Horn was fought. Through their participation in this drama, playing the role of the Cheyenne and Sioux (though the Crows were in reality allied with the United States government in this battle), the natives were once again reminded of their own proud history as free-roving nomads and mounted warriors.

A third important influence in the intensification of horse interest for the

Crows was the rise of the rodeo as a popular national sport in the United States. The Crows, like some of the other Plains Indian groups, readily adopted this horse-centered activity into their tribal life. No doubt the most significant event serving to revitalize and perpetuate Crow interactions with horses was the postwar revival of the annual Crow Fair. This event continues to be the highlight of the year on the reservation. In this festival, whose stated purpose is to preserve and give continuity to Crow traditions of the past, the horse plays a starring role. People camp in teepees, and many of their mounts are taken with them to the campground. In addition to featuring a week-long all-Indian rodeo, there is horse racing, another favorite Crow sport with roots in the past. Horse parades are also very popular events in which awards are presented for the finest horses, costumes, and accoutrements. Throughout all of these contests, intense ethnic pride is expressed, as riders try to outdo each other in proving that Crow Indians are still the finest of horsemen.

During my close association with the Crow people I found that almost everyone on the reservation is concerned in some way with horses. This does not mean that every person interacts with the animals closely or individually—as by riding them or participating in horse-related contests—though a large majority do. For many other people, there is a deep satisfaction in just having horses on Crow lands. The natives are comforted by seeing large horse herds grazing on their ancestral homelands. They feel this is the way life ought to be for the Crow people, as it was in the past and must continue to be in the future. Absence of horses often means loss of identity. For many Crows, including those who do interact physically with horses, their relationships are typically oriented toward many horses rather than focusing on a personal one-to-one relationship. But their bonds to horses are still highly meaningful and intimately related to Crow perceptions of themselves and their cultural context.

Neighboring white ranchers often criticize the Crows for what non-Indians perceive of as harshness to their horses. The Crows view it otherwise. They respect hardihood in all living creatures, including themselves. For the native Plainsmen, a "coddled" horse would not be worthy or desirable. Traditionally, a Crow Indian would not want a pet horse according to my terms. But to be without horses, for almost any Crow, would be a sad plight indeed.

Thus horses remain an integral part of modern Crow Indian life and culture, not an outdated relic from the vividly remembered past. For the equine animal has now been well adapted to activities that are compatible with reservation existence. Adaptability is a Crow trait that has favored tribal survival into modern times with a good share of the native culture intact. And it is to a considerable degree by means of the horse as a companion animal that it has been possible to combine preservation of the old ways with meeting the challenges of the present day. Now the Crow Indians' interactions with their horses rest not upon utility, as in the past, but on an affective bond that grew out of historic relationships but has been transformed and given fresh meaning by changing conditions.

Horses, then, continue to have deep significance for the Crow people. For these native Americans, an Indian, most particularly a Crow Indian, is by nature a horseman. The horse activities that have been so successfully established on the reservation give direction and purpose to life. The satisfaction derived from the prevalence of horses on tribal lands serves as a source of encouragement in facing the difficult problems of daily existence which Crows feel are imposed upon them by the dominant white society. Horses, too, seem to represent for the Indians the antithesis of the mechanized age, which to them is the hallmark of Anglo-European conquest in the New World and the force behind the subjugation of the American natives. Horses, to the Crows, are uniquely Indian; their particular interaction with horses differentiates them from other ethnic groups. Other people have horses, but Crow horses are the finest; others ride, but Crows are the real and most natural horsebacks. For contemporary Crows the bond to horses remains strong—a valued part of their culture and society and a vital force in the preservation of their rich Plains heritage into the future.

Barbara Jones

11

Just Crazy About Horses:
The Fact Behind the Fiction

The bond between people and horses is enigmatic. Though there are many stereotyped conceptions of this bond, there is almost no evidence or research to justify the assumptions. Affection for horses has been discussed as if everyone rode and liked horses for the same reason. Actually the reasons are varied and dependent upon many factors. The goal of this chapter is to shed light on this complex phenomenon.

Three topics will occupy our attention: the differences between owning a horse and owning other pets; the affectional and instrumental dimensions of owning horses; and differences in the way men and women relate to their horses. These topics were investigated by studying data on horse ownership and the general popularity of the horse; cultural stereotypes about riding and riders including the horse's image in film; psychological and psychiatric speculation about the meaning of the horse to individuals; and some results of my own research with horse owners. This research involved interviews with members of an English-riding Pony Club in the East, questionnaire responses from this group and other horse owners and lovers in the area, and a questionnaire published in a midwestern horse magazine, which included people who rode English, Western, and both styles.

The data clearly indicate that there are significant variations among groups of horse owners engaged in different horse activities. Generalizations from this research cannot be made to all horse owners. The research subjects did not include people who love horses but do not own them, and these individuals should be regarded as a distinctly different population.

THE DIMENSIONS OF THE HORSE PHENOMENON

The horse is one of the most popular animals in America. Kellert (1980a) found that it ranks second behind dogs in popularity among the segment of the American public over eighteen years of age. Freed (1965) asked more than 3,800 East coast elementary schoolchildren what animal they would like to be and noted that the horse was the second choice, behind dogs, for boys and third, behind dogs and cats, for girls. Americans are not the only ones who regard horses highly. Morris (1967) found that the horse was the third choice for British children, who responded to requests by a TV zoo program for names of most and least liked animals.

A study done by the Heritage Conservation and Recreation Service showed that twenty-six million people over the age of twelve rode at least once in 1979 and fourteen million rode more than five times. The age of riders decreased steadily from 30 percent in the twelve to seventeen age bracket to about 3 percent in the over fifty-five group ("Popularity of Horseback Riding," 1980). Children under twelve were not considered, so it must be assumed that the riding public is larger than stated.

There is no census of horses in the United States and consequently are no accurate figures on horse ownership. Estimates of the horse population generally agree that there are about eight million of them in the country at present (Otto and Purvis, 1978). The *U.S. News and World Report* ("Again the Cry, 'Get a Horse'") stated in 1973 that the horse sector supported an annual $13 billion industry. But it is extremely difficult to gather data on the sales of horses except in the racing industry, which makes up only about 3 percent of the 1.9 million horse-owning households in the United States (Lawrence, 1981). A 1977 Gallup poll determined that one out of five Americans either now owns or has owned a horse, with an equal number of men and women now owning them (4 percent each in the total population). More men than women, however, previously owned them: 22 percent and 12 percent respectively. According to this poll, the most popular purebred horse is the quarter horse, linked significantly with Western riding, though draft horses are owned by an equal percentage of men and women (4 percent each) ("Quarter Horse: Most Popular Breed," 1978).

People become horse owners in various ways. The magazine *Horseman*, which caters primarily to Western riders, noted in a 1979–80 readership poll that

36 percent of subscribers bought their first horse for children, 30 percent for an adult, and 34 percent were raised around horses. My own magazine survey of predominantly Arabian horse owners found that 18 percent bought their first horse for a child, 26 percent for an adult, 30 percent always had had them, and 23 percent had them when young and resumed their horse activities when older.

The *U.S. News* survey and the Gallup poll disagree on the age of horse owners. The latter lists more than 70 percent of owners as being over 30 while the *U.S. News* report states that 40 percent are under 20, a contradiction possibly explained because the *News* survey may have counted horses owned by parents of children under 20.

An examination of sex ratios and ages of some equine magazine subscribers shows that the average age is above thirty, and that men and women and different age groups are attracted to different horse activities.

Even though most owners seem to be over twenty, my own research indicates that many owners developed a liking for horses at a very early age. In the midwestern survey significant differences appeared between men and women: 52 percent of the women and 20 percent of the men were interested by age five (the difference is significant at .01 level), and 85 percent of the women and 46 percent of the men by age ten (significant at .001 level). The East coast survey showed 45 percent and 89 percent of women interested by ages five and ten and 25 percent and 83 percent of the men (not significant).

We have almost no data on the ratio of men and women riders. There seem to be more girl than boy riders at the lower ages and more men than women professionals. For example, the United States Pony Clubs, in which English riding is the norm, have approximately 10,000 members nationwide, and only about 10 percent are boys (Helwig, 1980). But the following analysis of the percentage of men to women judges shows that men still are the majority, though the relative numbers of women are increasing.

The percentage of women judges certified by the American Horse Show Association has risen from 25 percent in 1958 to 43 percent in 1980. The higher percentages are found in the equitation divisions (where riding ability rather that

Table 11.1

	MALE	FEMALE	MR. & MRS.	AVERAGE AGE
Horseman's Journal (Thoroughbred)	90.8%	9.2%		40.5
Western Horseman	49.3%	50.7%		38
Horseman (Primarily Western)	40.9%	48.7%	10.4%	21–36 Median
Practical Horseman (Primarily English)	11%	89%		31
The Arabians Show Horse { Most ride both	23.2%	76.8%		⎰ Avg. 35.5
English and Western styles	26.8%	73.2%		⎱ Male 43 Female 33

the horse itself is judged) and in the English riding categories. In 1958, in the twenty-six categories of judging officials, women numbered 33 percent in hunter equitation and 41.9 percent in saddleseat equitation, though only 16.7 percent in the stockseat (Western) equitation. In 1980 the following divisions, out of twenty-three categories, had 50 percent or more women judges: technical delegates for dressage (50 percent), dressage (66.7 percent), hunter (51.6 percent), and hunter equitation (52.3 percent). Stockseat still had only 25.7 percent women judges. These figures were compiled from the approved lists of judges in the 1980 American Horse Show Association *Rule Book* and Self, 1958 and probably bear only a very loose relationship to the ratio of male to female riders.

Women were allowed to compete in the equestrian events in the Olympics only after 1955 and in international eventing championships in 1953. The first women's European competition for show jumping was introduced in 1957, though all international jumping competitions were open to women only in 1975 (Edwards, 1977). Until recently, the Olympic equestrian events have been dominated by the military. Now, some of the most successful riders in the world are women.

A history of women's participation in the riding arena cannot be given here. One historian notes, however, that "throughout recorded history, woman's role in the hunting field has accurately represented her status in the world. Huntresses have come and gone, as has female emancipation in a larger sense. When women have ridden, driven, or walked to hounds, then they have been dominant in the family, influential in society, and powerful in politics" (Longrigg, 1979:90).

The Gallup poll statistics indicate that women are increasingly entering the riding world, but in what capacity it is impossible to tell. And the statistics presented above indicate that teenage girls are not the most active in horse activities, as is popularly believed. In fact, one Minnesota study reported that, though 80 percent of the households engaged in horse activities had dependent children, in only 26 percent of the families were teenage girls the most interested in horses. In over half of the households, adults were the most interested: mothers, 21.6 percent; fathers, 20.5 percent; adult female children, 11.1 percent; and adult male children, .6 percent (Otto and Purvis, 1978).

STATUS AND THE HORSE

English riding has always been associated with the British upper classes, as has horse racing until this century. Two British queens, Elizabeth I and Victoria, were avid devotees of riding and helped make the sport acceptable for the ladies of their age. Hunting horses were considered fashionable luxury items for the seventeenth-century woman (Camden, 1975), as they are now.

The popular image of the horse owner continues to be associated with status and money. *Town and Country* has regular articles on horse activities: hunting, polo, including women's polo, saddlebred horses, and, of course, racing (Arnold, 1979; Insinger, 1981; and the entire July 1981 issue). The upper classes are still shown in pictures with their horses, though now Arabians and Appaloosas also rank with hunters, Thoroughbreds, and open jumpers. According to one *Town and Country* article, campaigning a hunter or jumper costs on average $30,000–$40,000 per year, "roughly twice the price of keeping a Thoroughbred in race training" (Insinger, 1981:101), and there is little chance to recoup even a small fraction of this or the purchase price of the horse in winnings.

Horse shows are big business in the United States and are often the raison d'etre for owning horses. The American Horse Council discovered that, in 1979, there were almost thirty-seven thousand horse shows in the country, grossing over $317.6 million ("Study on the Economic Impact of Horse Shows," 1980). This figure does not include racing or rodeo.

It is evident that certain horse activities, such as polo, can be maintained only by the wealthy. For the vast majority of horse owners, however, the economic facts are very different. Both the *U.S. News and World Report* and the Gallup poll are in agreement that more than half of the horse owners are in the under $10,000 income range, and the Gallup poll notes that only about a fifth are in the over $20,000 range. [2]

THE HORSE IN FILM

Although "status" is one of the symbolic loadings the horse carries in our culture, the animal's image in film usually emphasizes different concerns. This image has been consistent over the years. Certain relationships between the horse and human characters and the explicit symbolic values linked to horses can be discerned in many films.

Though many western films focus on a stallion, the standard symbol of masculinity, a curious inversion appears in many situations: the stallion sometimes takes on explicit feminine characteristics, especially when domesticated. For example, the love of a man for a particular horse may be likened to that for a woman, the position of horse vis-a-vis a character may be as wife or captive heroine, and the taming of the horse is likened to the winning of a woman. Conversely, a less common theme is that of a horse being the male symbol to woman. Zane Grey's books were explicit in their equation of heroine and wild stallion, for example, *Wild Horse Mesa* (1924), though the movie versions were less overt. The situation is often complicated because the horse is usually closely identified with both hero and heroine in many ways, so that the animal has both male and female aspects. In earlier movies, the emphasis in the relationship between horse and protagonist was on mutual aid, complementarity, and equality and often involved statements about the distribution of power. Few other animals are used in quite the same way in film, primarily because the horse is consciously used as a symbol of the human spirit and freedom. Plots often revolve around threats to such freedom and in balancing freedom and domestication in a partnership with a human.

There have been a few changes in the way the horse has been presented over the years. In earlier, silent movies, the animal was heavily anthropomorphized: horses often thought and talked in subtitles. More recently, the horse has been presented as much more dependent and passive and hardly humanized. The emphasis is much more on the instrumental uses of the horse. Instead of being equated with righteous adults, the horse is equated with children or an abused adult, and more horse films are aimed only at children now, with child protagonists. In adult-oriented films, where the horse is used in an almost purely symbolic vein, freedom and the spirit are the qualities emphasized.

The number of TV shows and movies about horses, especially westerns, has declined drastically from the early 1960s. Children, therefore, do not have the media role models that were popular in earlier times, in which riding was essentially an adult male activity and the horse played a much more active, personalized part in the action, other than winning the race or horse show.

This complicated cultural imagery of the horse in film suggests a consideration of what the horse means to individuals as personal symbols. There are parallels between the cinematic use of horses and how they are interpreted in the psychological literature.

THE PSYCHIATRIC AND PSYCHOLOGICAL VIEWPOINTS

Most psychological professionals tend to focus on the meaning that the abstract concept or image of "horse" has to an individual rather than on the relationship between a particular person and a particular animal. Though the popularity of the horse is tremendous, most people do not own one, and their relationship to the animal should be described as symbolic.

The popular interpretations of psychoanalytic theory tend to assume that the horse is a masculine, penis symbol. Some, but not all, Freudian theorists make this assumption. For example, Foulkes (1978:220–22), in discussing guidelines for dream interpretations, directs analysts to consider horses and snakes "male, and thus impermissible ego-identification figures for female dreamers . . . unless there is some specific indication to the contrary. The basis for these conventions is fairly obvious, and supporting evidence has been discussed by Morris (1967)." Morris's "evidence," however, is equivocal because he bases his conclusions on the equation of the "mounting" of a horse with sexual mounting, the facts that more girls than boys in his British survey liked the animal, that the "powerful, muscular and dominant animal is more suited to the male role,"[3] that the act of riding involves postures similar to those of sexual intercourse, and that the popularity of the animal peaked at about puberty. A number of these observations might also point to the conclusion that the horse is female since the rider is on top and dominating the animal, and thus the equation of horse only with "male" may be incomplete. Morris hedges his bets, however, when he notes that those who own and ride horses "quickly learn the many more varied rewards that go with this activity. If, as a result, they become addicted to horse-riding, this is not, of course, necessarily significant in the context we have been discussing" (Morris, 1967:231–232). Freud was not so quick to assume a universal meaning in the image of the horse. In the case of Little Hans, who had a severe horse phobia, "the falling horse was not only his dying father but also his mother in childbirth" (Freud, 1963:164).

Jungians tend to go to the opposite extremes when discussing the horse: it is interpreted predominantly as a libido and mother symbol, part of the collective unconscious (Jung, 1956, 1959). But Jung also saw the horse as representing phallic sexuality in certain situations. It would seem that horse symbols are open to varied sexual interpretations, as in the film use of the animal.

Comments by Levy and Levy (1958) offer some of the more enlightened guidelines for the investigations of animal symbolism, and they recognize that it is a very intricate phenomenon. In analyzing more than 7,000 drawings of animals plus accompanying stories, gathered from an entire school district population in the East, they found that the horse "relatively infrequently represents either the essential male or female principle. The structure and activities of the horse are apparently sexually ambiguous to permit its frequent use by those who are themselves ambiguous" (Levy and Levy, 1958:339). This last statement is directed toward research by Schwartz and Rosenberg (1955), which concluded that drawings of horses indicate the presence of cross-sex drives in the artist (the horse represents the sex opposite to that of the artist), a conflict which Levy and Levy found in only a substantial minority of their horse-drawing subjects. One cannot, of course, generalize to all who drew horses. In addition, horses can stand for other things. For example, in a study of disturbed children by Bender and Rapoport (1944), horse and bird drawings represented movement, the getting out of an unpleasant home environment. Levy and Levy note (1958:339), "The chief generic meaning of the horse . . . relates to ego characteristics of action, work, service, help and so on. In fewer cases it represents the unconscious and danger (wild horses, nightmares). Less frequently it represents the mother principle. . . . In our experience, a secondary psychodynamic explanation is that the horse represents the harmonious relationship between the ego and the id." In a study on the borderline between the public and private symbolic realms, Gill (1967) attempted to discover whether there were any consistent trends in assigning sex roles to animals, which would throw light on standard preceptions in the Rorschach test. He noted that horses, in the abstract, are stereotyped as male by 95 percent of adult females, 90 percent of adult males, and 58 percent and 60 percent by boys and girls, respectively, reflecting his finding that preadolescents consistently showed a lower tendency to assign sex roles to animals than did adults. He mentioned that "boys and girls who deviate from the average in assigning sex role show a dominance of negative feelings toward both sexes" (1967:55), which suggests "their own insecurity and frustration in sex-role acceptance." But there is no overwhelming tendency among children to characterize the horse as one sex or another since 60 percent is rather low in comparison with other animals such as the dog, beaver, ape, and wolf, which for all groups (> 82 percent) was male, and the butterfly, which was female. In addition, he found that individuals tended to assign those animals whose qualities they did not value to the opposite sex.

This study also leads us to suspect any analysis of individual perception or symbolization of an animal derived solely from popular media presentations of that animal (including myth, which Jung used almost exclusively in his investigations). Although dogs are regarded as male by all the groups Gill studied, *Lassie* was the longest running TV animal show: seventeen years plus reruns. This review tends to support the view that horses carry a variety of symbolic meanings, depending upon the needs of the individual. My own research supports this theory.

PONY CLUBBERS AND OTHER HORSE OWNERS

The individuals I studied attached a wide range of meanings and emotions to horses they owned, but there are similarities among individuals and groups, which have their roots in the requirements inherent in owning a horse, the nature of the horse, and the uses to which it is put.

METHODOLOGY

I interviewed forty-six members and former members of a Pony Club, thirty-four girls and twelve boys from thirty-two families, about their attitudes toward horses and related subjects. With one exception, the families of these children, who ranged in age from eight to twenty, owned their own horses. None rode Western style, and two families did competitive trail riding. Though there was a wide variation in levels of participation in the club, most engaged in showing and eventing (a combination of dressage, cross-country, and stadium jumping skills). I spent time with them at lessons, shows, and occasionally at home though all interviews but one were conducted in their homes. I also talked to parents, instructors, professionals, and semiprofessionals in the area. The interviews with the children, though open-ended, were structured around a list of questions, and they have not been totally analyzed.

THE PONY CLUB

Pony[4] Clubs started in England and are becoming increasingly popular in this country. The group with which I was involved met regularly, with and without horses, conducted shows, events, and study groups and held dances, dinners, ski trips, and other structured or informal activities. Parents are officers, though there is a committee of the children which plans some activities. The clubs are strictly structured to advance the members through nine levels of ability, and the riders must pass stiff tests of general knowledge and riding ability to pass from one level to the next. There are yearly "rallies" on the local and regional level (which may include clubs from several states), divided so that children of the same general level of competence compete against each other.

In this club, children and families help each other in traveling to shows, in competition, lending horses and equipment, offering advice about professional horse services, giving lessons, and so on. There are also contacts with other clubs and their members. In short, Pony Clubs offer overlapping networks of information, mutual aid, and opportunities for socializing, rather than each member being isolated in his or her fondness for horses and riding.

Because of this atmosphere, it is difficult to say how much of the attitudes of the children are influenced by parents, instructors or other individuals active in the club, rather than developing from individual reading and emotional needs. The children also learn other ways people can relate to horses and have, therefore, many different role models from which to pick and choose. For example, the highest level riders often attract a coterie of younger riders.

PARENTAL INFLUENCES

Some generalizations can be made about the influence of family members on young riders. They are often crucial in the development of the liking for riding and for horses. For instance, 91 percent of the Pony Club boys and 70 percent of the girls became interested in horses through family members. Though none of the results are significant, more men than women in all the samples (East Coast questionnaire and magazine) were influenced by their relatives, and more women than men got themselves interested. In fact, in the Pony Club none of the boys did so (Table 11.2). In the Pony Club sample, mothers had the greatest impact: 39 percent of the girls and 33.3 percent of the boys had mothers who started them riding. It is obvious that parental support, especially financial, is necessary for a child to obtain and maintain a horse.

Parents in the sample generally insisted that the children do all of the caring for their horses themselves, though they helped out financially and in other capacities such as grooming at shows, building stables and fencing, being on Pony Club committees, and officiating at shows and events. A number of parents also insisted that their children engage in other sports in addition to riding so that they would be "well rounded."

Parents often looked at competition as a quasi-"proof of accomplishment," as indicating that the children are taking their horses and riding seriously and not wasting time and money, which can be considerable. Though most parents do not insist upon their children's success in such endeavors, the club includes a few of what can only be termed "Little League parents" who put undue pressure on their offspring. Such characters are a standard topic for cartoons and columns in horse publications, and most members are aware of the problems they cause.

The fact that parents usually required the children to do most of the work with the horses, combined with the stringent requirements of the club, might

Table 11.2.   WHO GOT YOU INTERESTED IN HORSES? (percent)
Questionnaire Sample from East Coast (open-ended question)

| | Pony Club | | Horse Owners not in Pony Club | | Nonowners |
	Female(33)	Male(12)	Female(102)	Male(11)	Female(49)
No answer	—	—	48.0	54.5	53.1
Self	21.2	—	20.6	9.1	26.5
Friend	—	—	5.9	9.1	12.3
Neighbor	9.1	8.3	1.0	—	4.1
Spouse	—	—	1.0	—	—
Mother	39.4	33.3	4.9	9.1	—
Father	—	16.7	1.9	—	—
Sister	64.7 { 12.1	16.7 } 91.7	4.9 } 23.5	9.1 } 27.3	2.0 } 4.0
Parents	6.1	25.0	11.8	9.1	2.0
Grandparents	12.1	—	—	—	—
	100	100	100	100	100

Magazine Sample (forced choices)

	Female (142)	Male (43)
No answer	4.9	—
Self*	24.6	16.3
Neighbor	7.8	—
Children	4.9	18.6
Parents	29.6	18.6
Sibling	5.6 } 47.9	7.0 } 60.5
Other relative	7.8	16.3
Other	14.8	23.2
	100	100

*Not included in list of forced choices; "other" category probably includes "self" choice.

help to explain the finding that, compared to the other East Coast respondents, the Pony Clubbers scored significantly lower when rating their interest on a 1 to 10 scale (see Table 11.3). Interest is still high, however, with an average of 9 for girls and 8.4 for boys.

Not everybody who rides or has a horse is necessarily crazy about it. The Pony Club children rode for different reasons: some because the horses were there already and riding looked like fun; some because parents pushed them; others because they loved to compete and if they could not do so, would not have the horses; and, of course, some because they loved horses and persuaded parents to buy one. There were cases of sibling rivalry—"If she can do it so can I"—as well as parents or other relatives buying a pony for a previously uninterested child. There were accusations that some children rode only for status reasons,

Table 11.3. HOW WOULD YOU RATE YOUR INTEREST ON A 1–10 SCALE, WITH 10 BEING EXTREME INTEREST AND 1 BEING NO INTEREST AT ALL? (percent)

| | Owners not in Pony Club | | Nonowners | Pony Club | |
	Female (102)	Male (11)	Female (49)	Female (33)	Male (12)
No answer	—	2.9	—	2.0	—
5	8.3	—	9.1	—	—
6	8.3	2.0	9.1	4.1	3.0
7	8.3	2.9	9.1	2.0	6.1
8	16.7	4.9	9.1	14.3	18.2
9	25.0	15.7	9.1	18.4	27.3
10	33.3	71.6	54.5	59.2	45.4
Average:	8.4	9.6	8.6	9.3	9.0

In comparing interest between groups, the ratings were divided into 9–10 and 5–8 to form contrasting categories. The results were as follows:

Owners not in Pony Club compared to Pony Clubbers: sig. = .01 (X^2) Female owners not in Pony Club compared to female Pony Clubbers: sig. = .05 (X^2)

Male owners not in Pony Club compared to male Pony Clubbers: not significant (Fisher's exact probability).

and, though nobody admitted that that was the sole reason he or she rode, a few pointed out that a person was special if he or she had the opportunity to ride.

We must keep in mind that riding a horse is only one of the many activities that people do with the animal. The children groomed them, braided their manes and tails, fed them, gave them baths, doctored them, talked to them, simply watched them, went swimming with them, a few read to them, and, last but not least, all cleaned up after them. Although riding horses was all that interested some of the children, for others it was not the most important aspect of keeping a horse. Just being able to look out of a window and see horses grazing in a pasture satisfied some, including adults.

SEX RATIO AMONG YOUNG RIDERS

In discussing the uneven sex ratio among young riders, it is more fruitful to ask why boys do not ride rather than why so many girls do ride.

My interviews gave me a clue to one of the possible reasons. Quite a few girls and one or two boys mentioned that they had been teased and given a hard time by school classmates about their riding activites. Some of them noted that they had been called "rich snobs" simply because they had horses and thought that their critics were jealous. Most said that the critics considered riding a sissy, easy activity, a girls' sport. There was no appreciation of the hard work and skill involved; the implication was that one needed only to hang on, pull on the reins, and kick. A few of the children solved their problem by bringing troublemakers home to ride, and this usually put an end to criticism. But many suffered in silence. Significantly, most members did not discuss their riding activities with classmates.

In general, boys are much less prone to engage in cross-sex activities than girls (Hetherington and Parke, 1979), and since English riding seems to be classified as a girls' sport, the pressure on boys not to ride is probably great. But what about the boys in a Pony Club? As we have seen, most of them became involved through their family and knew from experience that riding is challenging, a high-risk sport, and certainly not easy. Where else can one win blue ribbons, have parents cheering, and meet girls? They also had good role models in the international caliber male riders in the area.

What do boys like about riding? Most approached it as an interesting sport rather than a grand passion, and the more common responses included the challenge and unpredictability of riding and the differences between horses they have ridden. The possibility of injury was not stressed, though one boy who had a prominent scar from a riding accident admitted with a laugh that he enjoyed the attention it received. The element of danger does seem to add a certain relish, however, especially when parents are squeamish about watching them jump. Riding did not prevent them from being interested in other, more traditional male pastimes such as sports, cars, science pursuits, and so forth.

Another factor explaining the uneven sex ratio may be differences in skills. Professional horse people have commented, both to me and in print (Chenevix-Trench, 1970), that girls make better riders than boys. The skill differences may be due to the earlier physical maturity of girls relative to boys, but a more important element may be personality differences. Riding, especially such activities as dressage, is often cited as being more of an art than a test of wills between rider and horse. Indeed, too much aggressiveness and the use of brute strength may be counterproductive in dressage. The ideal is for the horse and rider to be in such subtle communication that they become as one, like ballet partners. For people who do not ride or who do so casually, it is often difficult to comprehend that the goal in skilled riding, Western or English, is to channel the natural energy, balance, and movements of the horse into flowing, graceful, yet powerful patterns. This involves using almost imperceptible cues such as shifting the center of balance in the saddle ever so slightly, or using as little pressure on the reins as is necessary. It would seem that the traditional personality characteristics of girls are better for this influence and teamwork: empathy, communicative skills, and the use of subtle manipulation. The horse has to be listened to, through hands, legs, and the whole body, as one male instructor persistently shouted during lessons. Instructors have commented that boys have to learn these skills and that they are often initially too rough and bossy and must learn that a horse has to be outwitted rather than overpowered.

Boys can and do perform as well as girls once they learn these lessons. It is often assumed that competing with girls tends to demoralize boys, but none of the boys I interviewed felt uncomfortable competing with girls—or being beaten by them, or even learning from them. Their attitude is that good riders are good riders, whatever their sex.

It has also been widely speculated that girls like horses until they discover boys, whereupon they drop the horses. Horses are considered to be transitional objects, used initially as "substitutes" to fill certain needs which are fulfilled later by people or other activities. The horse is not such a "substitute" for the Pony Clubbers I interviewed, both male and female. Many of the girls had boyfriends or crushes on a young man, and not a few adolescent romances sprouted in the club. The boys had the normal, ambivalent attitudes toward girls and enjoyed the attention they received.

Most of the members had outside interests, and in some cases I wondered how they could juggle them all: other sports, school clubs and committees, and so on. There were conflicts about the allocation of time, and their other activities were chosen carefully. A conflict often mentioned by older children determined to become excellent riders was the lack of time for socializing, either with the opposite sex or with friends, some of whom complained openly to them. A few have solved their problem by enlisting the aid of friends or boyfriends in their horse activities, but most find it a dilemma. I do not think that this situation is peculiar to riding, since some who had friends in other sports noted that these other athletes felt similar conflicts, especially if they were aiming toward sports scholarships.

It is true that as the children get older they tend to drop out of riding or cease hoping to be professionals. They grow to realize that the goal of being a professional is practically unattainable unless they have an outside source of income to support their money-draining avocation. But the cessation of horse activities is more often the result of more pragmatic concerns: time, space, and money. This population is, on the whole, college-bound and thus the horses are often sold or handed down to siblings when the child leaves for school. Another important factor is that above the age of eighteen, riders are no longer considered juniors under horse show rules and fewer classes are open to adult amateurs. After this age, the competition becomes extremely intense, and one must ride against professionals or the wealthy, who can afford exceptional horses. They either have to become exceptional riders themselves or give up the hope of competing successfully, something many very much enjoy.

It would seem, then, that the lack of participation in riding by boys has several causes, and one cannot approach the problem by concentrating on female psychology. English riding, especially showing, is an appropriate feminine activity now, and most girls asked did not consider themselves "tomboys."

Perhaps the growing popularity of the more challenging eventing will draw more boys into the fold.

DIFFERENCES BETWEEN HORSES AND OTHER ANIMALS AS COMPANIONS

Horses are not the ordinary "pet." Besides the fact that horses are usually bought to be ridden (and shown)—a specific instrumental goal—and not just for company, they are more expensive to keep. They also demand more time and care than other animals kept as companions.

An important consideration is that though dogs and cats are, ideally, often kept by one family for their entire lifetimes (and, except for barn cats, the families in the study kept to this ideal), horses and ponies are not. Because it is necessary to match the size and ability of a mount to that of a child, it is normal for a child to "go through" several ponies or horses. Some of the animals are passed down to siblings, but most are sold.

The serial ownership of equines seems to produce a distancing effect on the relationship between horse and rider. Many of those interviewed felt closer to their first horse or pony than to later mounts. The distancing is probably a defense against the probable future loss of the animals and related to the scrutiny of the animals with an eye toward instrumental goals. One of the more interesting aspects of the interviews was the often extreme objectivity children had about their horses' personalities, abilities, and quirks. A goodly number expressed the cynical but joking opinion that the horses liked them only when they wanted to be fed. And, if a horse is unsuitable because it does not fit expectations, it is sold, as is a continually lame animal.

There are some significant differences between information on attitudes of horse owners toward their animals and data gathered by Katcher (1980) and his colleagues from adult dog owners. Despite the distancing caused by the instrumental motives for owning horses, these horse owners expressed feelings that linked the horses more closely to themselves than did the dog owners. A total of 76.9 percent of the adult and child owners in the East Coast sample and 84.2 percent of the predominantly adult magazine survey respondents considered all or one of their horses members of the family (80.9 percent of all owners), but only 48 percent of the other animal owners did so. There was a significant (.025) difference between male (54.5 percent) and female (81.39 percent) horse owners in the East Coast sample, though the sex differences in the magazine sample did not reach significance.[5] Of the East Coast owners, 89.8 percent talked to their horses as persons[6] as did 88 percent of the dog owners. But 53.8 percent of the under-twenty East Coast respondents (including nonowners) and 41 percent of the adults confided in their horses (57.7 percent of owners overall did so), whereas only 28 percent of the adult dog owners did so. Despite their lower interest ratings, Pony Clubbers scored higher on all the above points (Tables 11.4 and 11.5).

That "pet" is not synonymous with "family member" is indicated by the fact that only 62.2 percent of the East Coast owners considered one or more horses as pets, compared to the 76.9 percent who regarded them as family members. The magazine survey did not show a difference. Both sets of data show that the more people rode only for pleasure, that is, the less showing and fewer other structured activities, the more likely they were to consider their horses pets. The people who did more with their horses considered them closer (confiding, family members, and so on) than this other group (and were more likely to have been injured in horse-related activities).

The majority of Pony Clubbers (87.5 percent of the girls and 91.7 percent of the boys) think of their horse as their friend, though more girls than boys (56 percent versus 33 percent) think of them as best friends. Of the children I asked, most stated that they were closer to their horses than to friends and siblings, and several noted that they were closer to them than to their parents. There is one major difference between having a human friend or confidant to turn to and having an animal friend, as has been noted by other researchers. The children were explicit and often echoed each other's words: the horse never talks back, never gives you advice or tells you things you do not want to hear, and it does not pass along everything you tell it to all and sundry, a peculiar failing of human friends.

These data are difficult to reconcile with the distancing perceived in the relationship between horse and owner that is reflected in and caused by the high turnover of animals. Several mechanisms are probably at work. First, as was pointed out to me by one Pony Club mother, this distancing was not surprising because horses require much more work than do other pets. Second, because horses do not usually form as strong bonds with people as do dogs and cats[7] (compounded by the owner turnover rate), they are "hard to get" emotionally. The owner may be trying to make the relationship closer than it actually is on the part of the horse, or be trying constantly to "woo" the animal, a tactic less necessary with dogs and cats. The children recognized that horses are not as affectionate as these other animals: a fourteen-year-old boy, an excellent rider, stated, "You can't relate to a horse. Horses aren't friendly. They don't come up to you like a cat and sit in your lap and want to get petted . . . so you have to . . . make them like you, I guess." A few children even expressed distaste for the emotional "begging" of their family dogs and cats. This "fictive kinship" with the horse may be explained in two ways: first, by the theory of cognitive dissonance, wherein an individual reduces dissonance between what is wished and what is experienced by minimizing the negative or emphasizing the positive aspects of a dissonant situation (Festinger, 1957); or second, by what psychologists call "intermittent conditioning" or "partial conditioning" (Kimble and Garmezy, 1963), which is not mutually exclusive with the first process. If an individual's efforts receive only sporadic positive feedback, he or she becomes more strongly conditioned than if the feedback is consistently positive. Behavior reinforced in this manner is much harder to extinguish. Since owners do not get constant positive feedback from their horses, and in some cases very little, they may be trying to reduce the "distance" between them by imputing "familial" qualities to the animal or they may strive harder and longer for positive feedback.

Another, perhaps more important, factor that enters the picture is riding lessons. It is probable that riders who regularly take lessons and who strive for excellence, or at least competence, go through various stages in their relationship with the horse. First, they simply feel a romantic kinship with the horse, reflected in interviews when children talk fondly about their first pony. They feel a thrill at being able to ride at all. Then, because they are beginning to concentrate on improving their riding (and horse), they tend to become "separated" from the animal and realize that this is difficult work, self-conscious and intellectual, entailing a recognition of the horse's abilities and faults as well as their own. The horse and rider are not yet working well together, and the rider may feel alienated and frustrated. As the team matures and gains competence and experience, the rider regains a feeling of unity with the horse because they are working together more or less smoothly. But this is a never-ending spiral; as one goal is reached, another takes its place. Sometimes the horse is incapable of reaching the goal and is traded in for another mount. This series of stages is not experienced with other pets but may be common in other sports and the learning of new skills. One Pony Club–related complication for the rider is that it is usually deemed necessary for him or her to ride a variety of horses and not get too used to or dependent upon any one animal. The thought is that the riders are not learning anything new or how to ride in the abstract (able to ride any horse) if they insulate themselves in a specific relationship with one animal.

These stages may explain why during interviews I noticed a rough differentiation between types of riders. The first type was mainly concerned with becoming an excellent rider (the achiever), the second with the personal relationship with the animal (the relater). A third type was more interested in riding as an exciting sport, and this attitude was more prevalent in boys. The differences are more dynamic than absolute; the third type may, over the years, change into the first or second type, and the stages or types may be found all at once in the same individual in his or her relationships to different horses or riding goals. Because of individual emotional needs, or even a real or imagined belief in their own incompetence at riding, the "relater" may feel threatened by the loss of the initial feeling of undifferentiated closeness with the horse. The achiever feels another conflict, which one girl put succinctly when she said that if you love your horse too much, you cannot ask it to do what is necessary for training and competition. The relaters may mention this kind of work in talking about what they do not want to do with their horses, and they give many examples of horses breaking down under the pressure.

The primarily utility value of the horse for the achievers does not mean that they do not love their animals. In fact, they might experience relationships with their horses which are closer than those the relaters experience. The bond is based on training hard together and becoming attuned to each other, in achieving a standard of communication attained by very few casual riders or by few people with other pets. In such cases, "fictive" kinship with the horse may be an inappropriate way of labeling the relationship, because it is based upon "real" closeness. Taking lessons and working hard and sometimes painfully toward excellence might also produce cognitive dissonance, however. It is known that the experience of discomfort in being accepted in a group makes the individual value that group more highly than if he or she did not have to work so hard to be accepted (Aronson and Mills, 1959).

Returning to a consideration of horses as "family," when we review what kinds of "people" horses are considered, we find great complexity. In classifying horses as family members, 22.1 percent of East Coast owners considered them to be about the same age as they were, adjusting answers with ages of respondents. These owners include 15.6 percent child categories and 5.2 percent adult or older categories (Table 11.4). Women tended to look at horses as children (44 percent versus 22.5 percent for men), with a secondary emphasis on "older" or adult categories (11.2 percent). Men, on the other hand, tended to view horses more as adults or older (32 percent), though child was the second largest perception (22.5 percent). Katcher found that 35 percent of his dog owners considered their pets children. In the magazine sample, answers were less oriented toward the subjects' ages: about 20 percent of the over twenty-year-old subscribers considered their horses children; almost none considered them adults. Women again led in seeing horses as children, 26 percent as opposed to 18 percent of the men.

The fact that different groups of people perceived their horses in dissimilar ways is illustrated in the magazine survey when we compare men and women engaged in riding English, Western, and both styles. More people who rode both styles tended to regard one or more horses as family members: women in 90.6 percent of the cases and men in 84.1 percent of the cases. Men who rode English style were last with 50 percent, and the other groups had almost identical scores, 76 percent. These same men led the others in seeing their horses as children, 62.5 percent; and women who rode English style were last with 15.4 percent child responses.

When we turn to how the East Coast owner sample talked to their horses, as opposed to thinking about them as family members, we find a different story. There are many more adjusted "same age" responses, 57.8 percent, with "same age" being the largest category (40.4 percent), and "child" second (13.6 percent) (Table 11.5).

For both questions there were "mixed" answers, and about 13 percent of respondents showed marked divergences in how they regarded their horses in the abstract and how they talked to them, that is, adult versus baby. This response reflected more the findings from interviews, since most children noted that they thought of and talked to their horses in various ways. For example, a horse might

TABLE 11.4.   EAST COAST SAMPLE
Do you consider your horse a member of the family? If so, what kind of member (baby, child, adult, etc.)? (percent)

A	Owners and Nonowners	Owners	Owners Female	Owners Male	Owners under 21	Owners 21+
Total	208	156	134	22	101	53
Yes	64.4	76.9	81.3	54.5	77.2	75.5
No	15.9	17.3	12.7	40.9	11.9	24.5
Other	2.4	2.6	3.0	—	5.9	—
No response	17.3	3.2	3.0	4.5	5.0	—
	100.0	100.0	100.0	100.0	100.0	100.0

B Category of Member

Baby/child	35.6	41.0	44.0	22.5	43.6	34.0
Adult/older	12.0	14.0	11.2	32.0	13.8	15.1
Same age	1.0	1.0	1.5	—	2.0	—
Sibling	5.8	7.0	7.5	4.5	8.9	3.8
Mixed answer	1.4	2.0	2.2	—	1.0	3.8
Misc.	9.6	11.0	11.2	9.0	12.9	7.5
No response	34.6	24.0	22.4	32.0	17.8	35.8
	100.0	100.0	100.0	100.0	100.0	100.0

C Similar age responses (number)

	Under 21	21 and over	
Child*	24		
Adult/older		8	T = 34 or approximately
Same age	2		22.1% of the total of 154

*Does not include "baby" responses, all of which occurred in the female under 21 group, especially in the 11–15-year-old bracket.

remind them of the grandparent who gave it to them, but they treated it as a child or adult as the occasion warranted. "Objective" grounds were used to categorize certain types of horses; a young or inexperienced horse was a child, an experienced horse an adult, a broodmare an "old lady."

Why there are differences in how the sexes perceive the horse is difficult to explain at this point, aside from any "obvious" linking of women and children. Men also see horses as children. But does this mean that men and women are expressing nurturant, authoritarian, or both impulses? Interviewees, male and female, stated that the horse is a "child" both when it is acting up and when it is in need. Perhaps boys who see horses as adults are reflecting their own need to feel adult, or they feel more dependent upon the animal, or they need to see the

TABLE 11.5. EAST COAST SAMPLE
Do you ever talk to your horse as you would a person? If so, how old a person (baby/child, same age, adult, etc.)? (percent)

A	Owners and nonowners	Owners	Owners female	Owners male	Owners under 21	Owners 21+
Total	208	156	134	22	101	53
Yes	83.7	89.8	91.1	81.8	94.1	83.0
No	5.8	3.7	3.7	13.6	1.0	11.3
No response	10.0	5.2	5.2	4.6	4.9	5.7
	100.0	100.0	100.0	100.0	100.0	100.0
B Category of person						
Baby/child	24.5	27.6	29.1	18.2	24.8	34.0
Adult/older	7.7	9.0	8.2	13.6	8.9	37.7
Same age	37.0	40.4	39.6	45.0	47.5	28.3
Mixed	4.3	4.5	4.5	4.5	3.0	7.5
Misc.	.5	.6	.7	—	—	1.9
No response	26.0	17.9	17.9	18.2	15.8	18.9
	100.0	100.0	100.0	100.0	100.0	100.0

C Similar age responses

	under 21	21 and over	
Child*	21		
Adult/older		5	T = 89 or 57.8% of the
Same Age	48	15	total of 154

*Does not include the "baby" category, all of which occurred in the female under 21 age group.

activity as an adult one. Cuddling or babying horses may reinforce their critical peers' view of riding.

PONY CLUBBERS' FEELINGS TOWARD HORSES AND RIDING

On this subject the interview material illuminates some of the complexities of the situation not to be found in questionnaire data.

The theme that was the most strongly expressed during the interviews was "mutual dependence." On the one hand, most children had the opinion that their horses were totally dependent—"totally helpless" was a common phrase—and this view was based on the great deal of care that goes into keeping the horse healthy. This dependent quality came out most strongly in the children when I asked them what they would be if they had to turn into horses. The vast majority described a domestic horse that was well taken care of and was not passive—living off daisies—but working. Curiously, almost none mentioned the love of an owner in their fantasies; they were sublimely self-contained as horses, and only occasionally did a child hope to have a good master. They wanted not a loving master, but one who looked after their needs.

Not only did the children mention the helplessness of the horse; they also stressed their own dependence upon the animal. One young girl put it succinctly when she said that her horse was like her "sick mother: the horse takes care of me, but I have to take care of the horse." (She also noted that her horse would make a great boy friend—"He's cute"—but this was a very rare response with other children even when I persisted). The children's dependence is obviously based in reality; they must trust the horse to carry them over dangerous courses and jumps. They often cite times when their horse, after throwing them inadvertently, did not run but stayed with them, which they considered an expression of caring and loyalty. Horse and rider learn together, and many children stressed not only what they teach the horse but what it has taught them. It is usual, and infinitely safer, for an inexperienced rider to be given an experienced horse (the opposite of the common practice of giving a young dog or cat to a child). The horse knows its business and will not shy at every new thing. In addition, its proper responses to correct body aids teaches the child how to ride.

It is obvious that the children are melding their own feelings of nurturance and dependency into their feelings for their horse. The animal is both child and caretaker for them, as they are for the horse.

The impression that the girls gave of boys who rode, and the boys gave of each other, was that boys in general cared less about their horses than did the girls. I have, however, seen boys kissing their horses and otherwise expressing affection for them even in such public situations as shows, even though the traditional male demeanor precludes such demonstrations. Katcher (1981) notes that it seems culturally acceptable for men to express affection for pets in public, and this is probably true for horses also. Boys often stated to me, without the slightest hint of embarrassment, that they loved their horses but that most other boys were not as close to their horses as they themselves were. There is probably little verbalization of feelings about this between boys, as there is between girls. The interviews might have been one of the few times where they felt they could express these emotions. Nevertheless, they usually concentrated on the nonrelationship aspect of horse owning, and I was surprised when the mother of the boy who gave me the quote about horses not being friendly told me that she overheard him telling his new horse, "I love you so much. I want you to be with me forever and ever."

In attempting to learn what qualities were most appealing about horses in general, I found the children inarticulate. One very young man immediately described the soft coat of his pony; others stated simply that the horse was beautiful. When we look at the various posters, models, or magazine pictures kept by children and parents in their homes, however, we find a number of standard themes. Mares and foals are very popular, as are horse heads and horses grazing or running in fields. Riders are few or nonexistent, and the atmosphere is of freedom and peacefulness. But when we turn to home photographs, the child riding the horse is most prevalent, especially going over jumps in shows, accepting ribbons, and so forth. These pictures are the parental image of the horse situation because they have taken the pictures in most cases.

The large proportion of "same age" responses in the questionnaires points to the fact that there might be a significant degree of identification with the horse on many levels. This is probably because of the necessity for the horse and rider to act as a team, to be on the same "wavelength" as much as possible.

Another reflection of the identification aspect of the relationship lies in the fact that most people believe that the horse picks up nervousness or other emotions from its rider, especially in competition. The belief probably has a basis in fact since an apprehensive rider's reflexes are thrown off, upsetting the usually more relaxed dialogue to which the horse is accustomed.

Riding is, in an important sense, the incorporation of the power and abilities of the horse. The rider is doing something that he or she could not ordinarily do as a mere human. But, I do not think that we should get carried away with the implications of this romantic image of the horse-rider bond touted in literature and art. Incorporation of power may be difficult. Horses are "human" too; they have bad days, have quirks of mood and personality, differ in ability and willingness, and may be bad-tempered or lazy. They are frustratingly prone to breaking down the day before the big show or in the middle of it. In the interviews little was said of the feeling of power that is alleged to come from riding. In fact, the opposite seemed to be more common: the frustration and feelings of powerlessness that come when the horse does not do as expected or wanted, or when one is training long, hard hours and things are not meshing.

This brings us to the subject of control over a horse. One of the goals of riding is to be "aggressive," but this primarily means to be assertive, self-confident, and goal-oriented rather than gratuitously pushing the horse around, which is disapproved. Many horses need a "masterful" rider because they may be fearful, stubborn, or too spirited. An aggressive rider brings out the spirit and best capabilities of the horse and channels its energies to the task at hand, rather than smothering it or wearing it down in a needless power struggle.[8] The rider must also trust his animal and know its limitations and quirks as well as its strengths. Advice sometimes heard during shows is, "Let the horse do it," which is not a command to let the horse run wild but to believe that it is capable of doing what it is asked to do. Young riders with experienced ponies are usually given this advice, and it teaches them self-confidence.

It must also be pointed out that a mismatch of horse and rider may cause a variety of problems such as boredom and lack of interest, extreme frustration, fear, or other worries. One of the prime ways of reviving flagging interest in a youngster, especially a boy, is to provide a more challenging but not unmanageable horse.

Though a number of adult riders and former riders mentioned to me that they enjoyed the feeling of control they had over the animal, and some instructors stated that certain individuals have difficulty in suppressing their domineering urges and letting the horse be half of the team effort, I think that one of the most important dimensions of control the rider must acquire is that of the rider over him or herself. Many children said that one of the most difficult things to learn is to control one's temper while riding. A novice rider is learning to control his body, emotions, and, in the process, his horse.

When aggressive feelings were expressed in interviews, they were usually in the context of competing rather than simply riding and training the horse. Some of the children were highly competitive, a few only in riding, others in many areas of their lives. A number commented that the goal of a show was all that kept them riding each week.

It may well be that horses represent for both boys and girls the independence and freedom they do not experience in other areas of life. Love of wild horses may express this desire more, and the relative isolation and independence of the act of riding may satisfy these needs. Nevertheless, this group of Pony Clubbers seems rather "domesticized" compared to the standard cowboy image. None of the boys and very few of the girls wished to be wild in their fantasies about being horses. One girl thought she wanted to be wild because she felt "bossed around" at home. Significantly, she described horses as "totally helpless—except when they kill people." The barns and pastures also offered many of the children havens from pressures and conflicts at home, school, and with friends.

There is a sense of freedom that comes from doing a cross-country course, and most of the children liked eventing more than showing. It was seen as less pressured, more challenging, and more equitably judged. Eventing is not liked because the children are worry-free, since it is on cross-country courses that the animals give them the most trouble. Spills and injuries are common. But many treat the situation as training and the gaining of experience rather than a must-win situation. For the same reasons, hunting is another enjoyable activity for many riders.

Other factors might be involved in riding enjoyment. Stemming from his own experiences in fox hunting, Rosenthal has been investigating "risk sports," those that entail a high degree of danger (1968, 1980). He noted that there was a feeling of euphoria, of floating, after completing a successful hunt, and he now believes this state might be linked to the production of beta endorphins by the body (1982). These substances reduce pain sensitivity and create euphoria, slow the heart rate and reduce blood pressure, lift depression, and can be addicting. Dr. Leroy Berk (1981, 1982), who is conducting research on the production of beta endorphins in athletes and nonathletes, informs me that people who exercise regularly can produce endorphins not only while exercising but in anticipation of exercise and can do so more easily than nonathletes in other stressful situations.

Dr. Rosenthal produces some findings that have relevance to the previously discussed stages that riders go through. He points out that the feelings of elation and euphoria primarily occur when the participant in a risk exercise was in the "good-to-expert" competency category and that inexperienced people might feel "dejected and depressed" (1980). This might explain why many of the young riders expressed frustration when discussing their riding. Lack of progress in lessons and failures at showing may exacerbate feelings of relative incompetence.

The feeling of unity experienced in riding may also be another common reaction to activities that require great concentration and skill. Csikszentmihalyi (1975) discusses intrinsic rewards some individuals feel in what he calls "flow experiences," which include sports, games, rituals, and creative endeavors such as composing music. Characteristics of such experiences include the "merging of action and awareness" and a loss of the sense of a separate ego, of consciousness of self. There is a sense of total participation in, of unity with, the task at hand. If a mountain climber can feel a sense of unity with the "piece of rock as well as the weather and scenery," then how much more can a rider feel a sense of identity with another living being, the horse, when successfully performing a dangerous and highly refined activity together.

Csikszentmihalyi notes that a sense of danger can heighten the sense of flow in an activity, and both Rosenthal and Csikszentmihalyi state that individuals, to continue to feel the euphoric state or flow, often "up the stakes" by participating in increasingly "riskier" and more challenging activities as their competency grows.

SEX AND THE SINGLE RIDER

I have deliberately left a vexing problem until last, after I have presented the complexities of the horse-human bond. It can be summed up by the frequent response by men to my research: "Don't women ride because of sex?" It is difficult to understand just what is meant by such statements, especially when they refer to all women who ride, young or old. Does it mean that women are getting sexual satisfaction from the act of riding and this is the only reason they ride? Does it mean that all women who ride have serious sexual conflicts? Are they promiscuous, frigid, hysterical, afraid of real men? Do they want a mobile penis or a feeling of masculine power? All of these theories have been proposed to me.

Stereotypes about women riding have a long history. Fox hunting used to be connected with sexuality because assignations could be easily arranged: it was difficult to chaperone women in the field. Chenevix-Trench (1970) noted that John Adams, in 1805, believed "it was no longer considered bold, masculine, and indelicate for ladies to enjoy a recreation which invigorates the body, amuses the mind, gratifies the eye, and contributes so much to the felicity of the gentlemen who are honored with the care and attendance of our fair country-women in these salutary exercises" (p. 287). But negative images still existed. A famous British jockey notes that the English stereotype of the fox-hunting woman during World War I was of "a hard boiled, leathery faced hunting woman who swears and drinks like a man and is completely devoid of any feminine appeal. Happily this species is more often conjured up in the imagination of non-hunting people than actually met with in real life" (Brown, 1952:99). Now, however, not only women, but men, are the focus of stereotypes. English riding is considered effeminate, and some forms of Western riding are taken as indicating conflicts over masculinity—the overly macho cowboy image, for instance.

The previously mentioned narrowly focused beliefs about women riders persist because these beliefs ignore the realities of women's enjoyment in riding. These judgments totally ignore men's enjoyment of riding and the satisfaction they derive from it. None of the theorists assume that men ride for sexual satisfaction. Obviously something other than sex is appealing about riding. The orgasmic theory does not recognize the fact that a state of overt sexual stimulation is a very dangerous condition to be in when hunting, jumping, or doing other dangerous riding activities. In addition, riding and training horses are not always pleasurable activities. Since there are so many other ways to get subliminal or overt sexual stimulation, why would someone choose riding when it is dangerous, painful, hard work, and generally inconvenient on several counts (mucking out stalls every day, veterinary bills, and the like)? The theories ignore all the other work done on the great general popularity of the horse for young and old and men and women, the varied meaning horses have to individuals, their importance as a status symbol, and so on.

Of course, there are individuals who are working out sexual conflicts with their riding activities and love of horses, but this is found in other activities as well and cannot be used to generalize to all in those activities. As Levy and Levy (1958) point out, the horse may be important to people who need to work out sexual conflicts because it is sexually ambiguous itself. Since children are still grappling with their sexual identities, the animal may help them "try out" various emotional needs, seeing it as baby and adult, as mother or boy friend, as needing authority or nurturance, as being powerful or helpless, and so on. These needs may be normal or pathological, depending upon the individual. And, as Morris (1967) notes, the sexual element of riding may be totally eclipsed by the other "varied rewards" of riding.

Increased sexual enhancement is sometimes cited as being a consequence of physical exercise and sporting activity. Rosenthal (1968) notes that he has been told that risk exercise "appreciably enhances" a person's sex life. It would be unusual if a person who is getting satisfaction from performing a difficult, sometimes dangerous physical activity did not feel increased self-esteem and contact with his or her body and thus more sexual in a general sense. These are consequences of activity and certain situations, not motivations for engaging in them. Besides, all this applies to both sexes and cannot be used as an explanation of why women ride.

Most animals that can be petted allow people to obtain sensual gratification from them, but we must not assume that this is overt sexual satisfaction. The sense of touch, which allows us to express nonsexual affection, to feel physically secure, to feel grounded and calm, is extremely important to us (Katcher, 1981; Montagu, 1971). All the gratifications and rewards that come from having a companion animal are satisfied in the horse-person relationship, and because they have been excellently covered elsewhere I will not discuss them. But horses offer something else also: the opportunity for types of physical exercise not usual with other pets.

Riding offers certain satisfactions from the special nature of the human–companion animal bond. Does a racing car greet one in the morning? Can one confide in a parachute? Can one feel nurturant toward a mountain? A combination of factors makes riding appealing to both men and women, and concentrating on one of them is doing injustice to both the sport and its participants.

NOTES

1. The western spotted horses, not pintos, developed by the Nez Perce Indians.

2. I have serious doubts about a survey that places half of Arabian horse owners in the under $3,000 income range with no explanations. This breed of horse is possibly one of the most expensive to buy and is one of the newest forms of investment for the wealthy. Either the poll contains serious errors or the owners of the putative Arabians are romanticizing their animals. My own magazine survey showed that half of the Arab owners lie in the over $20,000 income range.

3. Just because an animal is big, powerful, or even unequivocally masculine does not necessarily mean that it will be used only as a male symbol. Douglas (1981) points out that while the bull used in the Spanish bullfight is by definition male, it is used as a symbol of the female in popular Spanish slang about sexual intercourse and relations with the feminine in general.

4. The word "pony" does not have here its usual definition of horses under 58″ high at the shoulder at maturity but simply refers to a child's mount.

5. An interesting fact is that 28.8 percent of the female nonowners regarded horses as family members. There were only two male nonowners, neither of whom answered the question.

6. This question was not asked of the magazine subscribers.

7. Some owners have disputed this idea and often tout the virtues of their favorite breed. I have also seen and have been told of various situations when the horse has shown affection and extreme loyalty, but this is more usual when the animal and person have been together for years.

8. Some horses must be exercised before training or showing to get their energy level down to a productive level. This is not the kind of "wearing down" I am talking about, which is an assertion of dominance for its own sake.

Joel S. Savishinsky

12

Pet Ideas:
The Domestication of Animals, Human
Behavior, and Human Emotions

The concept of domestication has literally a homely origin. To domesticate means not only to tame or bring under human control but to attach to the home, and it is traceable to *domus* and *domesticus*, the Latin words for home or house. A domestic, be it a domestic beast, servant, or slave, is a creature that belongs to the household, and a domestic animal is a tame beast that lives in or near a human domicile.

The verb to domesticate also has, among its dictionary meanings, the ideas of civilizing and naturalizing. This meaning is significant in view of the fact that anthropologists tend to see nature and civilization as opposed concepts. But to naturalize here means not only to admit an alien person into the citizenship of another country but also to introduce a plant or animal to a place where it is not indigenous so that it may flourish there under the same conditions as native species (Oxford Universal Dictionary, 1955:1312). It suggests allowing a creature to feel at home and to prosper in an alien land, rendering its cultured state into second nature.

When looked at from a cultural rather than a purely literal viewpoint, however, we find that most domesticated animals are not actually domestic, that is, they are not of the household. Pets are different because they are the only animals that are both domesticated and domestic. They are distinctive not only because they are often kept within the home but because they are retained there as favorite animals and treated with special fondness and affection. Pets are exceptional because they alone, of all the animals over which people exercise dominion, share intimacy as well as proximity with their keepers.

Pets, however, often seem incidental to social scientists. They and their owners are often viewed as curiosities or as enjoying a relationship that is an adjunct to a farming or herding way of life. Sometimes pet keeping is used to illustrate the aberrations or obsessions of which people are capable, or it is benignly presented as a small, warm light illuminating the more humane side of being human. At best, pet keeping is usually relegated to a footnote upon the larger dimensions of domesticity.

I would like to argue that pet keeping is a much more significant dimension of culture than it is usually perceived to be. A study of the role of pet keeping in different societies reveals important relationships between pets and key social and historical processes. Specifically, pet-keeping patterns illuminate aspects of the history of domestication, the ethological training of hunters, the nature of status systems, the dynamics of child socialization, the processes of human bonding, and the roots of cultural symbols and metaphors. In this chapter, I will examine each of these relationships and draw from them a set of cross-cultural comparisons.

THE HYPOTHESIZED INFLUENCE OF PET KEEPING ON THE ORIGINS OF EARLY ANIMAL DOMESTICATION

The relationship between the domestication of animals, the hunting of them for food, and the adoption of them as pets is uncertain and open to contradictory interpretations. It has been hypothesized that the casual adoption of wild animals as pets may have contributed to the domestication of the dog and various herd animals. Young animals were presumably the most likely candidates for such adoption, and their presence in a community could have facilitated domestication either by attracting other wild members of the same species to enter the human orbit or by the formation of a breeding population once a sufficient number of pet animals from the same species became attached to human masters (Zeuner, 1963).

One source of support for this idea is the prevalence of pets in primitive communities which lack significant domestic animals other than the dog. Examples can be found among Australian aborigines, who keep tame wallabies, possums, dingoes, bandicoots, and cassowaries in their camps; among Arctic peoples, who adopt bear cubs, foxes, porcupines, birds, wolves, and baby seals; and among South American jungle tribes, who take on agoutis, pacas, parrots, boa constrictors, and capuchin monkeys as pets (Zeuner, 1963; Briggs, 1970; Henriksen, 1973; Laughlin, 1980; Durrell, 1964; Henry, 1964; Goldman, 1963).

The Cubeo of lowland Colombia, for example, domesticate animals of almost every variety as household pets in their attempt to communicate and maintain social relations with the animal world (Goldman, 1963). Pet boa constrictors in Guiana help to control vermin around jungle households (Durrell, 1964), and the Gilyak of Siberia domesticated ermine to catch rats (Knox, 1870). The dingoes of the aborigines serve as warm blankets against the nighttime cold (Meggitt, 1965). New Guinea people, who keep pet cassowaries, use these birds as a source of feathers for decoration, bride price payments, and status (R. Rappaport, 1968).

Although a relationship between such pet-keeping patterns and the origins of animal domestication is plausible, it is thrown into question by the actual treatment that such adopted pet animals receive. Pet keeping in which animals are kept as curiosities or as useful aids for minor purposes differs from the practice in settled or so-called civilized societies. In the latter cases, pets have become enduring, humanized members of the family. In contrast, the pets of hunters and foragers are often ephemeral members of their communities. They are frequently treated like disposable if animated toys, subjected to physical abuse and neglect, insufficiently fed, and either killed or allowed to die when their amusement value declines. Pets are often left in the care of children, whose fickle commitment to them commonly presages an early death (Briggs, 1970). Such practices would not and do not lead to ongoing relationships and a fixed pattern of incorporating specific animals into the human community. Furthermore, some foraging societies specifically forbid the adoption of wild animal pets (de Laguna, 1969–70).

When we indiscriminately apply the term "pet keeping" to both foraging and modern societies, then, we are implying a similarity of intent and behavior that may not exist. Both types of societies keep pets, but these superficially similar patterns mask underlying differences of attitude and treatment. Pets in preagricultural societies were probably not sufficiently fed because of a lack of adequate food to maintain them. Poorly fed animals do not breed well in captivity and are thus poor candidates for domestication (Messent and Serpell, 1981). The ephemeral presence of pets among contemporary "primitive" peoples suggests that in earlier, prehistoric societies, they were not enduring companions whom people made lifelong "members of the family." Some of the prime attributes of Western pet-keeping practices were therefore lacking. Other features of the Western pet complex, including the animals' use as status symbols and sources of pride, their owners' emotional and financial investment in them, and the pets' provision of companionship and aesthetic satisfaction all seem to have come about after humans became more deeply involved in domesticating animals for utilitarian needs (Fox, 1981).

Considering, then, the range of treatments and taboos applied to adopted wild animals in preagricultural societies, it seems equally plausible to argue that pet keeping is an outgrowth of domestication rather than a prelude to it. This interpretation would view pet keeping as developing from the proximity, constancy, and intimacy with animals that domestication allowed.

The issue admittedly has something of the "Which came first: the chicken or the egg?" about it. Intimacy and association go together. But while intimacy presupposes some form of association, creatures can associate on bases other than intimate interest and affection. Models of the domestication process, which outline a sequence of human-animal relationships going from parasitism and scavenging by animals through their exploitation and domestication by man, do not necessarily include pet keeping as a stage on the way. That pet animals were involved in the process is humanly possible, logically unnecessary, and culturally uncertain, and it therefore leaves open the idea that one can achieve domesticity without first engaging in petting.

THE ROLE OF TAMED WILD ANIMALS IN THE ETHOLOGICAL TRAINING OF HUNTING PEOPLES

In foraging societies, wild animals that have been adopted as pets may have served to sensitize hunters to the behavior of their prey as well as to the ethology of wild animals in general. By enhancing the ethological sensitivity of hunters, pets would have allowed such people to be more adept at stalking and hunting.[2] This argument has credibility because one need not maintain an animal for a long time or breed it in order to learn about its behavior. A few days or weeks of interaction and observation may be sufficient to pick up important behavioral clues about a species, including the ways in which its members respond to their prey and predators. From adopted predators, such as wolves and wild dogs, people could learn about their strengths and weaknesses, their stalking and sensory abilities, and their patterns of social and emotional response. The hunter who can imitate or mimic relevant animals, be they predators or prey, is himself likely to be a much more accomplished stalker.

This argument suggests that pet keeping, to the extent it existed among foragers, would have made them better hunters rather than necessarily leading them on to become herders and domesticators of wild breeds. This may help to explain why such animal adoptions are common in many societies that possess either no animals or only the dog as a domesticate. The Naskapi of northeastern Canada adopt pet animals from many of the species they hunt, including young foxes and porcupine (Henriksen, 1973). The Aleutian Islanders, another hunting people, take on geese, ducks, seals, and other of their prey as pets (Laughlin, 1980). Siberian tribes tamed wild reindeer and bear cubs to study their behavior, to employ them as sacrifices, and to use them as decoys in hunting other members of their species (Levin and Potapov, 1964; Zeuner, 1963). Such predatory animals as Arctic wolves and Australian dingoes occur as pets, respectively, among the Naskapi and the Australian aborigines.

In such societies, social interest, playfulness, and human curiosity as motives for taming animals would be reinforced by the value of such pets as teachers. The semidomesticated pet dingoes of some aborigines, for example, might have been more valuable as teaching aids than as actual hunting aids (Meggitt, 1965; Fisher, this volume). It is significant that the Cree of subarctic Canada consider a wild animal species to be the "pet" of a hunter if that man consistently succeeds in killing large numbers of that animal during his lifetime. The hunter's "pet" species is believed to mourn for the man upon his death (Tanner, 1979). Even the sadistic behavior to which adopted pets are subjected in foraging societies may be part of the cultural training children receive for dominance, aggression, and displacement toward animals—traits they can later apply when they become adult hunters and trappers of wild game.

THE POSITION OF PETS AS SYMBOLS OF STATUS, CLASS, AND POWER IN STRATIFIED SOCIETIES

In cultures with established patterns of domestication, pets are often used as symbols of status, class, and power. This phenomenon is particularly notable in stratified societies. People of position use exotic or luxury pets and noble sports as emblems of personal power and class privilege. This has been true of nobility and royalty in Mycenean, Egyptian, Roman, Polynesian, and European societies. It has also been a feature of emerging class systems and of the rise of the nouveau riche in Western societies and Plains Indian cultures. On some Polynesian islands, royalty monopolized the possession of scarce dogs: they appropriated the canine pets given away as gifts by Europeans; and they included their pets within the taboo systems that protected their privileged status (Luomala, 1960). Mycenean royalty, Egyptian pharoahs, and Roman rulers all imported dangerous, costly, and dramatic beasts as pets, using their possession as a display of both their power and their exceptional, sometimes sacred ability to tame and control the created world (Szasz, 1969).

The European tradition of pet keeping has a long history that bears out George Orwell's assertion in *Animal Farm* (1946) that while all animals are equal, some are more equal than others. The European nobility, for example, had the exclusive right to own certain types of hunting dogs (such as greyhounds) during the medieval period; they thus hunted "noble" game with noble pets, leaving the lower social orders to hunt ignoble animals with their own breeds of terriers and mongrels (Scott, 1968).

Exotic pets were also linked with European status systems. During the period of the Crusades, exotic animals were reintroduced to Europe by soldiers and merchants; the ownership of strange beasts as pet possessions became a mark or reaffirmation of people's elevated rank. Royal menageries flourished (Carson, 1972). As a sign of political favor, diplomats bestowed exotic pet animals as gifts on their patrons and clients (Byrne, 1981). Following the discovery of the Americas, exotic New World animals imported as royal pets included pumas, cougars, and jaguars (Szasz, 1969).

One of the most striking features of this symbolic system was the political identity of certain types of pets and certain types of people. The practice of keeping exotic pets, for example, was similar to the way in which members of the European nobility historically advertised their exceptional privileges by surrounding themselves with human as well as nonhuman "freaks," including giants and dwarfs. The court paintings of Velazquez provide a visual record of such strange menages. In *Las Meninas* (The Maids of Honor, 1656), for example, Velazquez shows us the Spanish Infanta surrounded by a retinue of both adult humans and the Infanta's pets: the latter include the angelic child's personal dwarf, her pet midget, and her large mastiff. The presence of human and canine pets sets off the size, power, and normality of the girl as well as the pets' dependency on and fidelity to their mistress (Kahr, 1976). Such art also reveals the symbolic equivalence of pets and slaves: in Renaissance and baroque portraits of European royalty, their canine pets, dwarf retainers, and Negro slaves are all pictured as possessions, props, and political emblems who reflect the power and wealth of their owners.

The social critic Leslie Fiedler has observed that the ownership of human freaks and freakish pets—dwarfs and lap dogs, lions and giants—has historically been one way that people of rank and wealth flaunt and advertise their position. Those with the power and the financial means can afford to possess the extraordinary, including creatures from the mysterious realm on the fringes of culture; ownership of the extraordinary implies their godlike power to possess and control the esoteric parts of creation (Fiedler, 1978). The medieval historian Johan Huizinga (1924) reports that when the female dwarfs became fashionable objects of amusement in fifteenth-century Europe, a French duchess had a locksmith furnish her with two iron collars, one to hold fast her pet dwarf girl and the other to put around the neck of the her pet monkey. The duchess' sense of style shows the symbolic identity of exotic pets and human freaks. It reflects the wider truth that luxury pets and humans mirrored one another's exceptional qualities: only a rare person would have the wit, the style, and the means to have a rare pet.

The concept of noble sports is another aspect of the relationship between rank and pet ownership. Animals that are employed in sports and entertainment are usually highly trained, but in the pampering and special treatment they receive, and in the attention given to their names and pedigrees, they share many of the qualities of the pet. Furthermore, the sporting events that prized animals are involved in are usually associated with specific social classes and ranks, and so the degree of nobility of the animal and the sport tend to be correlated. Fox hunting, show jumping, polo, falconry, and Thoroughbred horse racing have traditionally been royal or upper-class sports. The use of pet animals in cockfighting, dog-fighting, bear-baiting, and bull-baiting, by contrast, has historically been a hallmark of other ethnic and class populations (Carson, 1972).

People who have achieved or aspire to higher status have been known to acquire the pet animals that allow them to participate in the sporting activities of the upper class. This was true among various Plains Indian groups when the new equestrian way of life in the eighteenth and nineteenth centuries created novel types of wealth and distinctions of social rank among them. Upwardly mobile Blackfoot Indians tried to obtain the best race horses in their community—animals who were both esteemed status items and whose racing profits further bolstered their wealthy position (Ewers, 1980). In Western cultures, the ownership of show horses and show dogs, polo ponies, and hunting hounds and horses has long marked the old and the nouveau riche in the United States and Great Britain. The untitled landed gentry of eighteenth-century English society achieved a degree of nobility through acquisition of such prized canines and equines; prestige pets were both a means to status and a reward for having achieved it. Such people were also careful to advertise these possessions through commissioned portraits of their most valuable pets. Some of the best-known animal painters of the period (such as George Stubbs) largely supported themselves through such work (Taylor, 1975).

These examples from Egyptian, Roman, medieval, English, American, Plains Indian, and Polynesian cultures show how pets become a kind of living heraldry, an animated, almost totemic symbol of class and group identity. Although there are many other cultural status symbols, pets are especially potent because they can simultaneously symbolize sensibility, taste, domesticity, nurturance, and other virtues. Furthermore, whereas other symbols can be owned and displayed, pets can parade and do tricks. Not only can they be shown off, together with their owners they can actively show off. To the pets' status value are added the dimensions of participation and performance. In some cultures, their display renders them into totem animals who advertise the privileges and ancestry of class rather than clan. When valued pets are conscientiously bred and reared over several generations within a family or social class, human kinship and pet pedigrees become enmeshed and inseparable. The nobility of certain sports and entertainments, and the careful attention to the breeding of both participating animals and their owners, create a caste system and an etiquette that embrace the lives of both humans and pets (Scott, 1968).

THE PSYCHOLOGICAL AND THERAPEUTIC SIGNIFICANCE OF PETS IN THE EMOTIONAL REPERTOIRES OF INDIVIDUALS AND FAMILIES

At a more democratic level, pets provide people with many therapeutic benefits: companionship, love, humor, play, exercise, a sense of power, and outlets for displacement, projection, and nurturance—only some of which may be consciously recognized by owners. Pet keeping, particularly talking to animals and the tactile experience of petting, have been shown to reduce stress, promote feelings of reverie and comfort, and enhance longevity and physical health (Katcher, 1981).

Regarding nurturance, pets can function as child substitutes at various phases of the life cycle. They fill this role for the unmarried, for those who are married but childless, and for those whose children are grown and gone. It is significant that the modern therapeutic jargon for the latter situation, "the empty nest syndrome," is itself a faunal metaphor: the cure is to adopt a pet and become a born-again parent. Psychologically, the quality of pets as "perpetual infants," eternally innocent and dependent, underscores their childlike identity. The emotional bonding with the pet-as-child can be very subtle. The pets who are child substitutes not only stand in for the children we do not have, they also stand—as our own children do—for the children we ourselves once were. By parenting the pets who represent us as we once were, we relive our own childhoods. The pet is simultaneously an animal, a child, and our own infantile selves.[3]

Such indentifications can be found in the pet-keeping patterns of other societies. The Andamanese Islanders speak of their pet dogs as "children"; the Kaingang of Brazil speak of their children as "pets" (Man, 1932; Henry, 1964). Among the Hare Indians, a nomadic hunting-fishing-trapping people in the subartic regions of Canada's Northwest Territories, people keep large numbers of sled dogs for transportation purposes. One Hare Indian man whom I lived with for part of an Arctic winter adopted one of his half-grown sled dogs as if it were a child to ease the loneliness of his bachelor life. He was a rejected suitor, aged thirty-five, who singled out this one animal for exceptional treatment. The rest of his dogs received the usual mixture of care, regard, and aggressive displacement that other Hare meted out to their canines. But this six-month-old animal, now large enough to be trained to pull a sled and kept chained up to an outside stake, was allowed free run of the man's tent and cabin, fed by hand, sung and spoken to, and never harnessed up (Savishinsky, 1974a). Among the Utku Eskimo of the central Arctic, a people who habitually treat both pups and adult dogs abusively, childless adults behave differently. They are the only people who pamper pups, giving them the "overflow of the desire to protect and nurture" and lovingly treating them as babies. Like children, pups become the object of what the Utku call *niviug* feelings, which include demonstrativeness, tenderness, kissing, and cuddling (Briggs, 1970:70).

The Hare are one of several societies that also include pet animals within their system of teknonymy—a cultural naming pattern in which adults are named after one of their children rather than, as we do in the West, naming a child after one of its parents. Among the Land Dayaks of Borneo and among the Hare and other subarctic Indians, adults whose children are grown and gone, or who have had no children, are sometimes addressed by names that identify them as the parent of their favorite pet. The animal's name becomes a part of the person's social identity, substituting for the name of the absent child (Geertz and Geertz, 1968; Savishinsky, 1975).[4] The Hare sometimes name a pup after a recently deceased dog whom it resembles in the same way that they name an infant after a dead relative whom it resembles (Sue, 1964). Both pup and child are believed to be reincarnations of their namesake. Human and canine naming patterns thus extend spiritual beliefs to the young of both species.

Among pastoral African peoples such as the cattle-herding Nuer, a man is named after his favorite ox or the bull calf of the cow that he and his mother milked. The man's ox-name becomes a special part of his identity and is the preferred term for addressing him among his age-mates (Evans-Pritchard, 1940). Western pet names reflect individual and class values and are statements about how owners wish to be identified and perceived (Levi-Strauss, 1966; Levinson, 1972). Pet names that are aggressive, pedigreed, aesthetic, humorous, deprecating, or literary in content are acts of self-revelation. In naming their pets, people indirectly label themselves.

One of the most intense forms of intimacy between humans and pets is the actual breastfeeding of young animals by human females, which has been reported, for example, for Melanesian peoples and their pigs, Australian aborigines and pet dingoes, Spanish peasants and pups, the Andemanese Islanders and their dogs, sixteenth-century English wetnurses and the spaniel pups of noblewomen, and Polynesian peoples with both dogs and pigs (Simons, 1961; Meggitt, 1965; Cipriani, 1966; Bustad, 1980a; Luomala, 1960; Kuhn, 1955; Fisher, this volume). Suckling in these cases is sometimes a pragmatic measure to keep a rejected or orphaned animal alive, but it also has an emotional basis and a firm dimension of human-animal bonding. To describe such breastfed animals as child substitutes may be an understatement, considering the primal, nurturant quality of the relationship.

These practices, and the emotional bonds that develop between a Hare Indian man and his lead dog, a Blackfoot Indian and his prized war horse, and a Nuer and his namesake ox, reflect that profound degree of psychological identification between owners and pets. Many Western pet owners identify with their animals' sexuality and freedom and so resist obeying leash laws or having their pets neutered (Carson, 1972; Levinson, 1972; Fox, 1975a). In divorce cases, American pet owners sometimes fight over their animals as bitterly as they do over issues of child custody (Levinson, 1972; Amon, 1979). These varied behaviors demonstrate that pets extend the individual ego by becoming part of both public and self-image. The animals' special abilities, their beauty, their names, their accomplishments, and their possession reflect like mirrors on their owners' competence, taste, training, and care-giving abilities.

To the extent that pets are ego extensions, a person's choice of an animal is an act of self-definition. Pets can be as much of a personal signature as hair style or clothing. One exercise in Gestalt therapy is to ask people to picture themselves as an animal and then paint or act out the beast who has arisen from their unconscious. This imaginative identification with a personal totem offers important insights into the individual's self-image and its animal counterpart.[5] In the more mundane choices that make up Western culture, we say a lot about ourselves by choosing a dog rather than a cat and by picking a poodle rather than a Doberman as our real-life companion animal. Since people have been noted to pick pets who mirror their personalities, their appearance, and their behavior, this pattern reinforces the cultural perception that what dogs and cats are like as animals is reflected in what dog owners and cat-lovers are like as people.[6]

Therapeutically, pets have been used in the treatment of autistic children, psychotic adults, and disturbed families. People have learned to recognize that their behavior with pets reflects core features of their personae. Pet abuse can be a clue or a precursor to the abusive treatment of a child or spouse. On the positive side, companion animals enhance the ego development and social skills of regressive clients, and they defuse hostilities and provide a shared source of social interest in families whose members have established pathological patterns of relating to one another. Pets have been found to improve the health and behavior of the isolated and institutionalized elderly, of inmates in penal institutions, and of handicapped, retarded, postcoronary, lonely, and hospitalized individuals.[7]

The benefits are less structured but no less discernible in non-Western cultures. In the abusive treatment of dogs among the Hare, the Utku Eskimo, and the central African pygmy, and in the aggressive behavior toward cattle among the Fulani and other African pastoralists, the redirection of hostility toward pet animals is a crucial part of a restricted emotional repertoire (Savishinsky, 1974a; Briggs, 1970; Singer, 1978; Lott and Hart, 1977). In these societies, people who are expected to exercise considerable emotional control in their dealings with kin and neighbors are allowed to displace their rage and anger onto pets, sled dogs, cattle, and other domesticated beasts. It is the presence of pets in the pecking order—living members of the household who are alternately loved and abused—which allows people to live with one another in relative peace. Families are, in a sense, held together by the domestic victims, enemies, and animals that they harbor.

The use of pet animals in therapy—with children, geriatric and mental patients, alcoholics, criminals, and families—is a reversal of the process of domestication. It was the human domestication of animals and plants that made our modern civilization possible. Nowadays, when confronted with a patient who cannot function in daily life, we place him in therapy in order to civilize him—make him capable of functioning in our culture. When a pet animal becomes the vehicle by which this socialization occurs, then it is the animal who domesticates the man, rather than the reverse. The appropriateness of animals for this purpose rests partly on the fact that they are less challenging than people and can thereby enhance a client's relationship skills in a nonthreatening way. They are "transitional objects" through which patients can overcome insecurity, create ego boundaries, and go on to develop a widening circle of warmth, approval, and social interaction.[8] But, as Carl Jung (1964), Rollo May (1974), and others suggest, such creatures may represent the demonic and animalistic parts of the self which most people have trouble integrating into their personae. From this perspective, pet keeping can be an ongoing dialogue with the animal underside of the psyche and thus be a way for people to make themselves whole.

THE ROLE OF PETS AS AGENTS OF CHILD SOCIALIZATION

In societies where domesticated animals are economically significant, pet keeping is a part of the process by which children learn important technical skills and a sense of nurturance and economic responsibility. Children may shepherd a flock, herd cattle or pigs, or feed and care for dogs, and they are usually given young animals of important species to raise as pets. Raising single animals as pets allows children to develop a personalized and manageable relationship with domesticated beasts, which can then be transferred to larger numbers of animals in a herd, flock, or team.

Many studies have emphasized the role of childhood pets in the learning of nurturance and responsibility among pastoral people. Some of the same processes occur in foraging societies. Among the Hare of subarctic Canada, for example, pups are placed in the care of young children who not only care for and feed these pet animals but learn to harness and drive them by using miniaturized sled equipment. Children learn to take pride not only in their dogs' strength and appearance but in their own competence as sled drivers. By watching and mimicking their elders, children learn both technical tasks and the use of dogs as appropriate outlets for displaced anger and tension. Childhood experiences with pet pups thus provide significant opportunities for establishing cultural patterns of responsibility, nurturance, emotional expression, displacement, discipline, and motor skills (Savishinsky, 1974a).

The bond between pet and child is further reinforced by the fact that they are both treated in similar ways by Hare adults. Neither pup nor child receives guided instruction in learning new tasks. They learn instead by trial and error, observation, modeling, and vicarious reinforcement. The young of both species are indulgently treated when infants but find that affection is abruptly withdrawn at the age of five or six months for pups and about five or six years for children. It is at these ages that canines first learn to pull in a dog team and that children experience parental demands to carry out domestic chores and responsibilities. Furthermore, in childhood and puppyhood, the males of both species receive somewhat preferential treatment when compared to that given females. Boys are allowed to avoid economic responsibilities and to indulge in displays of anger and rebellion until a later age than their sisters. Young males sometimes receive better food and clothing than young females, perhaps echoing the historic practice of selective female infanticide among the Hare and other Arctic peoples. Similarly, female pups are more likely to be killed at birth than their male siblings, reflecting the cultural value placed on the size, strength, and speed of male canines. Growing up thus has some of the same emotional discontinuities and educational problems for children and pups when they are being put in harness for adult life (Savishinsky, 1974b, 1975).

The relationship between Western urban children and their pets is different. It tends to be divorced from the acquisition of economically relevant skills because few children or adults are involved in occupations in which domesticated animals are important. Rather, the family and its pets serve other purposes. As modern life has become more urbanized and alienated, and as family size has decreased, we have moved away from the earlier, idealized image of the rural extended family and its farmyard beasts. The only animals left in most people's lives are their economically marginal pets, who now complete the modern image of the bourgeois nuclear family and its domestic sensibilities (Mugford, 1980).

The pets of Western children are consequently pictured in a different functional light. They are seen as instruments for enhancing childrens' psychological development, for improving their social skills, for conveying a broad sense of moral responsibility to others, and for teaching such basic facts of biology as the nature of birth, sex, anatomy, excretion, and death. Pets replace absent parents and siblings and provide opportunities for children to play out their fantasies, express feelings, and act out conflicts and dreams. They are thus part of the child's imaginative and projective world (Levinson, 1972, 1975; Bettelheim, 1977). Desmond Morris has argued that young children prefer large pets because they are protective, parental figures; older children prefer smaller animals as pets because they represent infants toward whom the older child can act as a parent. Morris refers to the latter type of pet keeping as "infantile parentalism," suggesting that this is one way in which young people cope with both parental identification and the loss of their own childhood (1967).

Anthropologists, who emphasize the multiple roles that people play in various societies, might be equally impressed by the complex of roles into which pets are cast: they can be child substitutes and surrogate spouses for adults, and parent substitutes, surrogate siblings, creatures of myth, and stand-in friends for the young. One can perhaps feel some compassion for the poor neurotic pet who may have to be, for its owners, a mother, father, husband, wife, son, daughter, brother, sister, therapist, playmate, and lover—an all-purpose person—all within a single household and a single lifetime.

THE USE OF PETS AS A PROJECTIVE MEDIUM IN ART, METAPHOR, AND LITERARY IMAGERY

Animals as intimately involved in human life as pets often bear the burden of symbolizing cultural aesthetics and domesticity. Among adults, the fantasy world of children is matched by the seriously playful images that pets take on in art, metaphor, literature, and belief systems. In art, portraiture provides an especially rich set of insights into how people perceive both their pets and themselves.

During the eighteenth and nineteenth centuries in both the United States and Great Britain, family and individual portraiture often incorporated pets as part of personal and domestic imagery. In the works of Gainsborough, Reynolds, Stubbs, and lesser known folk artists, the presence of a pet dog, cat, or horse serves to demonstrate both the human sensibilities of its owner and the way in which the pet comprises an important extension of the person's public image (Clark, 1977). The inclusion of pets in family portraiture mirrors the emergence of the nuclear family—and its appendages—as a bourgeois domestic ideal in the eighteenth century. Domesticity expresses itself not only in marriage, children, and the family estate but in the animals that are an intimate part of daily life.

The American mystique of rural life and small town domesticity, which has been both captured and partly created by artists such as Norman Rockwell, also paints the pet as a ubiquitous part of the scene. The aesthetic identity of pets and people also occurs in non-Western societies. Before embarking on a raiding party, Plains Indian warriors painted and dressed both themselves and their prized war horses, dancing together with them in what the Blackfoot called "the riding big dance" (Ewers, 1980). Hare Indian sled drivers dress themselves and their dogs in their finest parkas and dog blankets before entering town after a long stay in the bush. Some of the blankets are fixed with bells, so men and dogs often make their entrance both in costume and in concert with one another (Savishinsky, 1974a).

The linguistic creation of pet animal metaphors and epithets reflects the central (albeit ambiguous) place of such animals in cognitive and expressive realms. The anthropologist Edmund Leach (1964) has observed that pets do not fit neatly into the cultural categories that people use to classify the creatures of their world. They ambiguously fall between humans and livestock, being partly human and partly animal at one and the same time. Using examples from British and American English, and from the Kachin of Burma, Leach demonstrates that pets, because they fall into an intermediate category, share some of the same taboos and verbal treatment that people apply to their human intimates and close kin. People and animals are classified in similar ways, the crucial factor being their distance from and degree of intimacy with the community doing the classifying. As close but ambiguous creatures, pets are classified as inedible in the same way that close relatives are tabooed as sex partners. Like certain types of blood kin and in-laws, pets become the subject of cultural taboos in killing, and they provide the content for verbal epithets and sexual innuendo: pets such as the dog, cat, and goat become terms of abuse when applied to human beings whom people wish to label as also being taboo, anomalous, or deviant.

Such emotion and ambiguity seem to be inextricably bound up with the nature of the pet. Polynesians, who esteem and often revere their dogs, also used the dog as a linguistic symbol of the social outcast (Luomala, 1960). Hare Indians both value and abuse their dogs but adamantly resist killing their own animals. They ask—and even pay—for other people to shoot their old or seriously injured dogs, stating that they cannot bear to destroy an animal who has served them for so many years. Polynesian, New Guinea, and Asian peoples, who consider pet species—such as pigs and dogs—to be edible, nevertheless refrain from eating their own animals (Simoons, 1961; Fisher, this volume).

The emotional ambiguity of the pet bond is also expressed on a spiritual plane. Primitive and premodern societies linked pet keeping and taming with holiness. In the bear cult of various Siberian tribes, wild bear cubs were tamed, cared for, and fed for years by a "bear master" before being ritually slaughtered at an important clan ceremony (Levin and Potapov, 1964). It was primarily the marginal, ambiguous, but sacred figure—the saint, shaman, or medicine man—who could communicate with and tame animal spirits. Specialized relations with particular species are found in the "antelope shaman" of the Shoshoni, the "jaguar shamans" of South American jungle tribes, the Siberian bear masters, and the Australian aborigine shamans, who tamed reptiles to demonstrate their totemic powers (Goldman, 1963; Steward, 1955; Levi-Strauss, 1963). In the Western spiritual tradition we have the sanctifying powers of Elijah with the ravens, Daniel with the lions, and St. Francis of Assisi with birds and other species. In all these cases, taming is an attribute of holiness. The spirit companion is a holy pet.

For modern Western people devoted to obedience, show, and sporting events, the sense of power that comes from training a prized animal may substitute for the spiritually more primal act of taming a wild beast. But many writers on pet keeping and dog training emphasize the spiritual qualities of having a companion animal. A number of monastic orders in the East and West have centered their religious life around the raising and training of dogs, valuing the animals both as a source of income and as a means to spiritual growth (Monks of New Skete, 1978).

In some societies, however, tamed animals have paid for the privilege of human companionship with the loss of their own spirituality. Such peoples as the Atna of Alaska, the Yukon Indians, and the Kaingang of Brazil regard the dog as the only animal in the world without spiritual qualities because it has fallen under human control (de Laguna, 1969–70; McClellan, 1970; Henry, 1964). In such groups, domestication is a transactional event. The shaman or saint who tames an animal gains the spirituality that other animals lose in the very act of being tamed.

Cultures ambiguously combine themes of heroism and abuse in their treatment of pets. Western folklore is replete with tales of heroic pets—dogs who save families from household fires and rescue drowning children—and our media mythology of Lassie and Rin-Tin-Tin immortalizes the exploits of such creatures.[9] On the other hand, people in the field of animal welfare are painfully aware of the abuse, hostility, neglect, and abandonment to which we also subject our pets and laboratory animals. The Hare are similarly ambiguous in their canine imagery. They tell many stories of alert dogs who have saved their drivers from a cold winter's death by detecting a break in the river ice or by navigating through a blinding, midwinter whiteout to the haven of an encampment (Savishinsky, 1975). Yet the Hare displace much of their anger and frustration onto their dogs, occasionally abandoning them, often subjecting them to considerable physical and verbal abuse.

The dangers of human intimacy for the pet are manifest in the way many cultures associate domestic animals with witches. Witchcraft beliefs usually include the concept of a witch familiar, a creature who acts as a witch's accomplice or into whom the witch is actually transformed in order to accomplish evil. Witch familiars may assume human or fantastic shape, but they are most often conceived of as animals; whether in medieval Europe, colonial Salem, or among the contemporary Navaho, witches most commonly assume the form of domestic beasts and pets (Harris, 1975; Starkey, 1963; Kluckhohn, 1967). The emphatically European association of cats with witches (and witches with women) may simply reflect the commonness of cats as household pets and pest destroyers, but a symbolic explanation may also be in order. The image of cats as unsociable animals may have prompted their association with witches and the devil. Secular leaders, churchmen, and the laity, with their interests in social control and scapegoating, may have unwittingly taken advantage of the symbolic similarity between independent cats, vulnerable and uncontrollable (i.e., deviant) people, and society's other archenemy, the devil. Cats could thus have served as a symbolic bridge linking together the malicious and antisocial creatures of the animal world, human society, and the satanic realm.

American and British English are languages especially rich in pet metaphors. In phrases like teacher's pet, pet idea, pet peeve, and pet hate, and in the notion of a loved person as one's pet, we domesticate both our passions and our poisons by binding them to our household animals. The same metaphoric style is at work when we describe sexual foreplay as a particularly enjoyable kind of petting. Foreplay, consummation, or any other exciting event used to be the cat's pajamas or the cat's meow. Philandering has an agricultural metaphor, "to sow one's wild oats," but it is also referred to as the quintessentially catlike activity of "going over the fence."

The cultural denigration of both women and cats makes their metaphoric association understandable. In the revered tradition of male chauvinist piggery (again a faunal metaphor), we often link prurient or illicit sex with female and feline qualities: when they cannot be satisfied elsewhere, men go to a cat house to get some pussy. An unappealing woman, by contrast, is a dog, though she may be found objectionable or unobtainable because she is a bitch or acts catty in her behavior. Unimaginative children and people who ape one another are copycats. A winning individual is top dog; a handicapped or underrated person an underdog. Pathetic individuals lead a dog's life in a dog-eat-dog world. They suffer through the dog days of August, and when they confuse their priorities or do things in an inverted way, we think of it as the tail wagging the dog. A person who hogs resources which he himself cannot use is a dog in the manger. A damaged book is dog-eared, lousy poetry is doggerel, and a pathetic look is a hang-dog expression. The best we can say about a dutiful but uninspired worker is that he is dogged.

Besides our modern metaphors, pets have long served as symbols for Western sex roles. The medieval historian Eileen Power (1954) notes the prevalence of household pets among English nuns and wealthy French housewives in the Middle Ages. She quotes the written advice that a Parisian husband gave to his wife, urging her to take their pet dogs as a model for her own behavior:

> Of the domestic animals you see how a greyhound, or a mastiff, or a little dog, whether on the road or at table, or in bed, always keeps near to the person from whom he takes his food, and leaves and is shy and fierce with all others; and if the dog is afar off, he always has his heart and his eye upon his master; even if his master whip him and throw stones at him, the dog follows, wagging his tail and lying down before his master, seeks to mollify him, and through rivers, through woods, through thieves and through battles follows him. . . . Wherefore for a better and stronger reason women, to whom God has given natural sense and who are responsible, ought to have a perfect and solemn love for their husbands; and so I pray you to be very loving and privy with your husband (106–7).

The link between pets and sexual politics is clear. As Power observes, "The simile of the little dog was selected with care, for the medieval wife, like the dog, was expected to lick the hand that smote her" (107).

In Western culture especially, pets are also used as literary devices. They enhance characterization and appear as biographical subjects. Pets are used more than wild animals as literary subjects in the West because they are the only animals most Westerners and writers come in contact with. Wild animals figure more prominently in primitive myth because of the paucity of domestic animals there and because primitive myth tries to mediate between the realms of culture and nature (Levi-Strauss, 1966). But for Western people, domestication is the border zone between the cultural and natural realms, and so we observe its most cultured inhabitants—our pets—with as great attention as preliterate people observed the creatures of nature. Children's literature makes extensive use of pet animal figures as instruments for conveying moral and political messages: as characters in their own right or through their relationship with their owners, literary pets demonstrate the social responsibility and the economic values of thrift and hard work that underlie the ethos of Judaeo-Christianity and modern capitalism (Kramnick, 1980). Bruno Bettelheim has argued that children vicariously identify with animals they encounter in their fairy tales and that it is through such unconscious identification that children are helped to work out the psychological problems that surround their growth and maturation (1977).

Pets can be equally potent in adult literature. Western novelists, such as Colette in her book *The Cat* (1958), use people's reactions to pets as a way of encapsulating their entire personalities. In *The Cat*, Colette pairs an extremely narcissistic man and his feline pet, each of whom supports the other's total indifference to all other intimate attachments. In a marvelous, four-page short story, "A Cat in the Rain," Ernest Hemingway (an avid pet keeper throughout his life) dissects an entire marriage by contrasting how a disaffected husband and wife respond to a stranded animal (1930).

Fictional characters are commonly described by the use of pet metaphors. Jane Austen, who denotes the infantile behavior of a man in *Sense and Sensibility* as "the puppyism of his manner," has a female character complain of a boring party: "Lord! we shall sit and gape at one another as dull as two cats" (1906). Writers as varied as T. S. Eliot (1968), James Thurber (1963), and Virginia Woolf (1933) have made pet dogs and cats the subjects of memoirs, poems, and biographies.

Finally, pets have been elevated to the level of political symbols and allegorical figures. George Orwell's *Animal Farm* (1946) turns household pets and barnyard beasts into revolutionary figures: as these animals act out the totalitarian terror of our times, we are reminded of how easily domestication can serve as a prelude to slavery. Jack London's works (1965), especially *Call of the Wild* and *White Fang*, are particularly fascinating because London takes the phenomenon of pet keeping and enlarges upon it to explore the themes of culture versus nature, domestication and wildness, bonding and intimacy. *Call of the Wild* and *White Fang* are, in fact, two sides of the same allegorical coin. In the first book, Buck—a pampered California house dog—is kidnapped to the Yukon, where his experiences as a sled dog and his encounters with savage people lead him to a rediscovery of his wolf origins and his ineradicable wild nature. It is, in the end, a parable of de-domestication. White Fang, by contrast, is an Arctic wolf who is drawn into human society, tamed, bonded to his human keepers, and finally domesticated to a petted life of household and family loyalty. These works show that London saw the boundary between culture and nature to be permeable, with a state of domestication being a tenuous condition for both animals and men. Since pets are the creatures in our modern world who most clearly straddle these two realms, their lives become an allegory for our human condition.

CONCLUSION

Pets shed light on the ways different societies try to work out the relationship between culture and nature. It can be argued that Western people, who are more alienated from nature by their culture than most other people, employ their pets to reestablish that connection. In some non-Western societies people live surrounded by nature, but civilized peoples live surrounded by culture (Hughes, 1981). The pieces of nature we retain—the amusement park jungles and zoos, the deer parks and royal forests, the national parks and game preserves—are all cultural artifacts. Like the biblical Eden and the Persian paradises of antiquity, they are attempts to recreate the peaceable kingdom of mankind's precultural condition. But as parts of culture encased in our cultural shell, we surround these places with fences, boundaries, and "no trespassing" signs. The pets of non-Western peoples are elements of their outside which have been taken inside. But Western pets are more like strangers in a strange land, naturalized citizens cut off from their own roots and rooted instead in our own needs.

That is why Western pet keeping—with its pet cemeteries and hotels, its canine psychiatrists and beauticians, its gourmet foods and fashions, and its pet insurance policies and retirement homes—often becomes a parody of domestication, turning people into the servants of their beasts. The invitation to parody has been commercially exploited: the faddish "pet rocks" and the "dogless leash" of recent years have allowed non–pet owners to dress up their domestic image in the emperor's new clothes.

But the sources of such parody cannot easily be dismissed. Animal domestication, which began as a process of extending human mastery over the members of other species, has culminated in those species controlling many of their putative masters. Our clinical literature and personal observations are filled with many individuals who are far more adept at loving their pets than they are at dealing with people (Levinson, 1972). There are also individuals whose pathological ties to humans are carried over into, or are compensated for by, their bonds to their animals. An extremely neurotic "need to be needed" leads some people to turn their pets into "emotioinal slaves" (Fox, 1975a). Pet loss in such cases can cause debilitating grief and mourning (Fogle, 1981a). While such behaviors provide psychologists with important insights into the psyches of their clients, one can only guess at how small are the number of such cases that actually come to clinical attention. The social conflict and stress caused by irresponsible pet owners whose animals pollute the environment and threaten the lives of people and other creatures undermines the argument that pet keeping necessarily promotes a sense of social responsibility (Beck, 1973; Perin, 1981). When we confront the image of Nazi concentration camp officers who pampered their pets while they simultaneously bayoneted babies, we are forced to question the inherently humanizing benefits of the human–companion animal bond (Reznikoff, 1975; Styron, 1980). The dominance of culture over nature has here been reversed.

The contrast between culture and nature is recognized in all societies, but the gap between them is emphasized more by some people than by others. Totems, rituals, and myths mediate between culture and nature, and cultural categories keep these two ideas distinct and in their place (Levi-Strauss, 1966). But pets actually bridge and embody both of these realms. My pet theory about pets is that their ambiguity as cultured, nonhuman creatures who share our intimate lives allows them to mediate in this manner. In keeping pets, we combine the conscious and the unconscious in the same way that we do when observing rituals, telling myths, and respecting categories. The bonding and reconciliation of culture with nature that pets symbolize is one of the most important of these meanings, and it is not less effective for the subtle way it works on us. We are not only the sole species that makes symbols: we are also the only creatures who keep other animals as pets.

The bonding of people with animals, like all emotional and intimate ties, has both positive and negative valences. It is one item on a list of cultural contradictions whose terms cannot easily be reconciled. The relationship between domestication and slavery is another such case. The reclassification of human slaves as domestic animals, and the perception of both human and animal possessions as pets, show Western society's attempt at a cognitive solution to the moral dilemma of human bondage. Contradictory cultural responses to nonhuman companion animals—abuse and love, reverence and neglect—constitute another ambiguity. The ambivalence here stems from two sources: one is the dual origins of pets in nature and culture; the second is the ambivalence of people who themselves feel torn between these two realms. Such individuals project their dilemma onto their pets, bestowing on them the commensurate meanings and contradictory treatments.

Sometimes a perceptive intelligence can voice the experiences that others cannot name. The poet May Sarton has described the presence of a pet inside a house as a kind of wildness within, a counterpoint to the balance and order of culture (1977). The wild part of the pet is that piece of ourselves which looks at culture from without, questioning whether it is worth joining the human scene and accepting its restrictions. In Jungian terms, pets are an embodiment of the "shadow," the half-tamed demon of our persona that we all have to live with and try to integrate into ourselves if we are to be whole (Jung, 1964). These qualities of the pet may be part of the challenge and curiosity that impel both civilized and primitive people to invite in strays, adopt wild beasts, and tame them: in this way, we capture their wildness but, instead of eradicating it, we make it part of our all-too-cultured and orderly lives. Taming and relating to such pets and incorporating them into our lives are therefore not simply ways of "getting back in touch with nature." They are ways of reconnecting to our own natures, making our peace with culture, and making ourselves more complete as people. Since the ability to tame wild animals is a quality often associated with shamans, saints, and other holy persons, pet keepers may enjoy not only a sense of power in their ties to their animals but a sense of sacredness as well.

NOTES

1. The research on which this paper is based was made possible by a Post-Doctoral Fellowship for Independent Research from the National Endowment for the Humanities (1979–80). Additional work was facilitated by a Dana Fellowship Award from Ithaca College in 1981. The Arctic data were collected during 1967, 1968, and 1971 under research grants from the National Science Foundation and the National Museums of Canada. I would like to thank Susan Savishinsky for helpful comments on an earlier draft of this essay.

2. This argument has been proposed by William Laughlin (1968: 304–5, 310, 320), who supports it with data on Aleut pet keeping and the way hunters use pets to learn about animal behavior (Laughlin, 1980). Henriksen (1973) has made the same observation on pet keeping among Naskapi Indians.

3. Almost all students of pet keeping have noted the position of pet animals as child surrogates; see Lorenz (1964), Morris (1967), Szasz (1969), Levinson (1969a, 1972) and Corson and Corson (1981). The idea that pets—and dogs in particular—are child

substitutes is indirectly supported by the fact that humans have selectively bred dogs for juvenile or pedomorphic qualities of small size, flat face, and large eyes and for such infantile behaviors as playfulness, docility, and submissiveness (Lorenz, 1964; Messent and Serpell, 1981). Toy breeds of dogs are the genetic outcome of extreme selection for infantilism and dependency in pets (Fox, 1975a). From an evolutionary perspective, the domestication of both humans and other animals has emphasized the phenomenon of neoteny or fetalization; that is, the process by which the modern members of a species grow up to resemble more closely the infant members of earlier forms of their species (Montagu, 1962). Fetalized pets thus constitute an extension of this trend.

4. Features of totemism also enter into the naming process. Writing of certain Australian and American Indian tribes, Levi-Strauss (1966) notes that in some cases personal names are derived from the features of a clan's totem animal; in other groups, it is the totem animals who are named after members of the totemic kin group.

5. Certain projective tests in psychology, in which people are asked to identify an animal they would most or least like to be, offer comparable insights (Levinson, 1972). The animal content of personal dreams is similarly revealing (Cf. Van De Castle, this volume).

6. The physical and behavioral resemblances between pets and their owners have been noted by Lorenz (1964), Levinson (1975), Fox (1975a), and the Monks of New Skete (1978).

7. Much of the literature on the therapeutic uses of pets is summarized in the works of Levinson, Condoret, Bustad, and Corson. See Levinson (1969a, 1972), Condoret (1973), Bustad (1980b), and the essays in Anderson (ed., 1975), Corson and Corson (eds., 1980), and Fogle (ed., 1981).

8. Cf. Levinson (1972), Corson and Corson (1981); the concept of "transitional object" used by these authors is taken from the work of Winnicott (1957).

9. In Stith Thompson's monumental *Motif-Index of Folk Literature* (1955), he identifies a large number of folklore plots from many societies involving heroic dogs, including one that he titles "dog defends master's child against animal assailant." In folklore concerning the heroism of certain Christian saints such as Saint Guinefort and Saint Christopher, these figures are identified with dogs. In the Dombes region of France in the thirteenth century, local lore transformed a greyhound who had saved his master's son into a saint (Saint Guinefort), whose cult was still being followed in that area in the twentieth century. St. Guinefort's special dispensation was his capacity to minister to sick infants (Little, 1981). The image of Saint Christopher may also be cited. St. Christopher's name means "Christ-bearer," and he is described in legend as a brutish giant with a doglike face. His features were transformed into a more human appearance after he carried the Christ child across a river. In the iconography of the Eastern church, St. Christopher is often pictured as having the head of a dog (Monks of New Skete, 1978).

Maxine P. Fisher

13

Of Pigs and Dogs:
Pets as Produce in Three Societies

Several years ago, the renowned British cultural anthropologist Edmund Leach put forward the half-baked but delectable idea that there is a parallel between the kinds of people we are encouraged by society to marry (or even to have sexual relations with) and the kinds of animals we are encouraged to acquire a taste for (Leach, 1964). He pointed out that just as bedding and wedding our closest kin are taboo, likewise marriage with people who look, sound, or behave far differently than those of our in-group is never considered proper etiquette.

We choose our foods, said Leach, in much the same way. As we taboo sex and marriage with nuclear family members and regard the violation of this taboo as incestuous, so we taboo as food those animals most familiar to us because of our regular and intimate relations with them and regard their consumption as cannibalistic. Leach claimed that we also tend to eschew as food those animals that are highly exotic to us, just as people look askance at a marriage between individuals of widely divergent social groups. We are, according to this theory, a middle-of-the-road species, veering away from the very foreign and familiar when mating or eating.

I have called this idea delectable because it suggests a relationship which, though not immediately obvious, appears upon reflection to be satisfying. It has been used to explain why the English and Americans are horrified at the notion of eating cats or dogs. I have called it "half-baked" because in studying the relationship between canines and people around the world, I have found this idea to be culture-bound and in need of emendation. The success of such porcine personalities as Porky Pig and, more recently, Miss Piggy notwithstanding, I think it is safe to say that few Americans have regular and intimate relations with live pigs. For most of us, pigs fall squarely into Leach's middle, edible, nonpet category. But in some other cultures the pig-human bond is comparable to that between dogs and people in our own. For this reason, it seems worthwhile to explore attitudes and treatment relating to dogs and pigs cross-culturally in examining Leach's hypothesis about what can and cannot be eaten with impunity.

In the 1930s Margaret Mead observed that in New Guinea "pigs are so petted and cossetted that they assume all of the characteristics of dogs—hang their heads under rebuke, snuggle up to regain favor, and so on" (Mead, 1977). In the highlands of New Guinea women have traditionally been responsible for tending the pigs. In this part of the world, men and women have not been getting on for years. The mutual antagonism between the sexes here—enshrined in cultural beliefs and practices—stems partly from the custom of men to import their wives from distant, often hostile, villages. "We marry our enemies" is a New Guinea highland proverbial saying (Meggitt, 1980). Consequently, men do not fully trust their wives. They feel safer living together in the men's longhouse, surrounded by the familiar faces of the men they grew up with, their weapons, and the paraphernalia for their rituals than they do in a lonely dwelling shared by an alien wife. In fact, the less physical contact the men have with women in general, the greater their sense of well-being. Too much contact with women is believed to cause everything from premature balding to serious brain damage. Not surprisingly, therefore, a wife, who lives alone in a hut with her young children and the half dozen or so pigs entrusted to her, is likely to develop strong attachments to the animals. The women suckle the piglets as they do their own infants and carry them to the distant garden areas, where each day they work cultivating the yam and sweet potato crops. When the pigs are somewhat older, the women hand feed them and continue to fondle them, groom them, decorate them, and care for them when they become sick. At night, the pigs sleep with the women in their huts; the larger ones may stay in a partitioned section of the house. After being fed breakfast, the older animals leave for the day to forage in the open areas surrounding the villages, returning to their mistresses at night.

Paula Brown mentions that the women of the Chimbu tribe name each of their pigs. Typical names, she says, "are those of locations, colors, physical characteristics, what was given for them. . . . Clearly. . . . pigs are recognized as having their own individual habits and peculiarities" (Brown, 1978). "The theft of a cherished beast," notes another female anthropologist who has worked in the highlands, "may make a woman distraught with anxiety or grief" (Strathern, 1972).

Yet the purpose of domesticated pig production in New Guinea is to provide needed animal protein for human consumption. Pig feasts are "part of a total ecological-economic-social-political-religious system" in which the quantity of pigs that each village can raise for consumption—mostly by others—is an indicator of political and economic status, as well as being an appeal to the all-powerful ancestral spirits to provide continued fertility (Brown, 1978).

Pork is therefore not a staple in New Guinea village diet. On the contrary, pigs are slaughtered infrequently and only for important ritual occasions. These, however, sometimes require massive killings. In November of 1963, for example, Roy Rappaport observed one clan kill ninety-six of its pigs. These villagers distributed the meat to an estimated two thousand people—mostly potential political allies, who had come from distant areas to attend the ritual. The hosting villages "kept 2500 pounds of pork and fat for themselves, or 12 pounds for each man, woman, and child, a quantity which they consumed in five consecutive days of unrestrained gluttony" (Harris, 1978).

Though no ethnography of traditional New Guinea highland agricultural village life would be possible without a discussion of the role of pigs, few anthropologists make even passing reference to the presence of dogs in these pig-raising communities. Only among the very few groups that still rely on hunting for their subsistence is the dog regarded as being at all significant. There is, however, a much richer literature on the hunting groups of native Australia. In fact, there has been a long and lively debate among anthropologists concerning the historical relationship between aborigines and the dingo, the native dog of Australia.

Unique to dogdom, the dingo is a testament to the fact that the dog-human bond is not irreversible. The dingo was once thought to be indigenous to the Australian continent, but we now know that it arrived there only about three thousand years ago as the domesticated dog of one of the later waves of people who migrated there. We do not know exactly when or why, but once in Australia, the dog escaped to the bush and once again became a feral animal. The aborigines have tried to make a go of their relationship with the dingo a second time, though how long they have been trying is impossible to know. Since the nineteenth century, at least, aborigines have sought wild dingo pups born in the hollows of trees and brought them back to their camps with the idea of taming them. In this effort they succeed, even today, but when the mating urge comes, the camp dingo usually hightails it to the bush, typically never to make a reappearance. In captivity, the reproductive rate of these animals invariably suffers. To what extent dingoes helped the aborigines of the past to hunt game is a controversial question.

Nearly half the writers on the subject extol the dingo's tracking and hunting abilities; the others present cogent evidence to the contrary, including the remarks of tribesmen who say they leave their tame dingoes home when they go out hunting. The dingoes, they claim, are too slow to be useful; they prefer to take a dog of European breed instead. A nineteenth-century observer similarly wrote that "a dingo sometimes refuses to go any farther, and its owner has to carry it on its shoulder, a luxury of which it is very fond" (Lumholz, 1889).

If dingoes were and are such abject failures as hunting partners, and they disappear into the bush upon reaching sexual maturity, why were the aborigines eager to obtain them, as many experts assert?

One answer is their function as an ersatz blanket. In 1915, a visitor to the Everard Ranges reported that many of the women there "carried live wild dogs round their waists—the forepaws grasped in one hand, while the hind paws and tail are in the other; the extremities of the dogs in some cases almost meeting in front" (White, 1915). More than sixty years later, anthropologists still find aborigine women wearing these live canine stoles. One woman explained that they toted dingoes in this manner "so as to save their tender paws from prickles and burrs" (Hamilton, 1972). She went on to say, parenthetically, that the dogs also kept their backs warm. Some anthropologists feel that historically, the blanket function of the dingoes was the most important one to the aborigines (Meggitt). A nineteenth-century traveler, chancing upon three women asleep in a desert shelter, discovered that "sleeping with them, and under the same blanket, were no fewer than fourteen dogs" (Basedow, 1903–4). And indeed, the expression "five dog night" originated in the Australian outback.

Whether or not it was because dingoes were valued as blankets, the aborigines seem to have a history of being fond of them. For at least the last hundred years, dingoes have been regarded and treated by them as pets. A nineteenth-century traveler to Western Queensland wrote, for example, that the aborigines he met treated their dingoes "with greater care than they bestow on their own children. The dingo is an important member of the family. . . . Its master never strikes, but merely threatens it. He caresses it like a child, eats the fleas of it, then kisses it on the snout. . . . The dingo will follow nobody else but its owner" (Lumholz, 1889).

Another early observer writes: "Adult men may be seen kissing the muzzles of the pups, murmuring endearments to them" (White, 1915). More recently, an anthropologist wrote: "Idly, while talking, a man may soothe a tired dog by fingering its penis" (Berndt and Berndt, 1942). Aborigine women suckle pups, as do New Guinea women piglets, sometimes one at each breast.

Nevertheless, dingoes are included on a list of foods typically eaten by aborigines that was compiled by a European naturalist as early as 1841. And recently, during the six-month stay of an anthropologist at an aborigine camp, dog meat was served twice. "On one occasion the dog was a dingo which came near the camp, and on the other, it was an unknown mongrel chanced upon by the hunting party" (Hamilton, 1972).

For all their differences in our eyes, pigs and dogs were seen by the early inhabitants of Polynesia as similar orders of being; the two types of animals received much the same treatment on these islands. Here, too, the women were responsible for their care and often formed strong emotional attachments to them. The women suckled, named, and canoodled the pups and piglets alike. Sometimes a mother would select a puppy to be the companion and protector of her baby. From then on if the woman or child was ever a victim of sorcery, the dog was thought to ward off the evil power. Even after the death of the animal, its spirit would remain strong enough to exert a beneficial influence over its living owner, who would keep in touch by wearing a necklace of the dog's teeth. Upon their death, favorite dogs were mourned and buried amid tears and eulogies. Some islanders requested that their dog be buried with them when they died. If a child died, its dog was invariably killed and buried with it, the idea being that the child should have a companion in death. Particular dogs, as well as the species in general, were memorialized in Polynesian legend and poetry. There were, for example, the famous dogmen of Hawaii, "hairless and human-looking, but dog-tailed or dog-headed demi-gods who lived in dunes and formed the armies of their masters" (Luomala, 1960). And in Hawaii, there was Ku-ilio-loa, once an ordinary dog, but in ancient times transmogrified by a powerful god into a divinity.

Nevertheless, in precontact Polynesia, the principal reason for having dogs—or pigs—was to give them away, for these animals were among the most important media of exchange. Becoming too attached to one's pigs and dogs was like becoming too attached to one's money today. Everything from rent for land to tolls collected for river crossings was payable in pig and dog. People also used these animals as a medium of exchange for needed goods. We have on record the grief of one woman whose husband purchased a nail with her favorite dog! Men, too, were capable of showing great deference to particular dogs. For example, Chief Tu, an important early Tahitian ruler, requested the naturalist aboard Captain Cook's ship to yield his pet spaniel. The naturalist's son, also on board, objected violently because he was greatly attached to the animal. But the protocol of the situation was ineluctable, and the transfer took place with great ceremony. The chief, enthralled with the "gift," issued a command that the dog's welfare be henceforth entrusted to a special lord-in-waiting, who must forever after carry the spaniel behind his royal owner.

Polynesian magicians had their own special use for dogs. With the aid of canines, they were able to interpret signals sent from the spirit world. Sometimes spirits communicated through the movements of a living dog. In such cases the magician simply had to observe the animal. But in other cases, he ordered a dog to be butchered so that he could examine its entrails. These, it was believed, contained supernaturally sent messages, which it was the magician's job to decode.

Dogs also figured in Polynesian curing ceremonies. If a person became ill, the family (if it were wealthy) would call in a specialist, who would reach his prognosis by disemboweling a dog, then placing the carcass on a fire near the invalid's bedside where he could study the broiled remains for clues. Next the magician would eat some of the dog meat, which was expected to produce a dream that would reveal who (not what) caused the patient to become ill.

But it was not only the magicians who ate dog. On the eve of its discovery by the Western world, Polynesia was one of the dog-eating capitals of the world. On Hawaii, dogs were sacrificed regularly at important royal functions. Mementos of deceased canines were to be seen all about: the religious idols with their double row of dog teeth; the tufts of dog hair worn on the wands of the dancers, on the weapons of the chiefs, and on the breastplates of the warrior; the dog-teeth necklaces, anklets, and leggings worn by the spectators. The wife of an early missionary wrote that she witnessed between one and two hundred dogs in confinement awaiting slaughter for the feast commemorating the death of King Kamehamela. During the 1840s, the royal chefs competed with one another in dog bake-offs.

On first glance, it would seem that the three cases presented here—the pig breeders of the New Guinea highlands, the aborigines and their dingoes, and the early Polynesian islanders—argue against Leach's theory that humans taboo as food those species of animals they view and treat as pets. Yet on closer inspection, the hypothesis seems more likely to be proved valid if we amend it to say that societies do not generally encourage their members to eat those particular animals they have raised as pets. People in the New Guinea highlands relish the pork they consume at their feasts. But as Margaret Mead noted half a century ago, "your own pigs you do not eat" is an axiom of redistribution there. Similarly, while munching on the stray dingo that wandered into their camp, aborigines were adamant in telling Annette Hamilton that they would never eat their own dogs, no matter how hungry they were. Someone else's dog, on the other hand, was different. And in early Polynesia, dog meat and pork were foods that were taboo to the women of all classes. Highly prized items, they were eaten almost exclusively by the men of royal or very high social rank. And these men ate not their own animals but those that entered the chiefly or sacerdotal corrals in the form of rent, tribute, or gifts.

Jay Ruby

14

Images of the Family: The Symbolic Implications of Animal Photography

This chapter is a preliminary report on research designed to augment ethnographic descriptions of the sociopsychological roles of pets by examination of pet photographs: both their content and the social acts that surround their production and consumption. The research objective is to generate and field test an interview survey instrument and visual checklist. This instrument will be incorporated into the more comprehensive study of pets and owners and will also be applicable to the study of photography's role in the American family. The work is in its beginning stages, so the report is more speculative and programmatic than conclusive.

The study will explore the following questions: Who takes pictures of their pets and under what circumstances? How are the photographs displayed or used? How is the pet imaged and with whom? Is there any consistency within and between families in their pet picture-taking and using habits?

A variety of research techniques are employed in producing this ethnographic description in order to create complementary perspectives on the research questions. A central technique is an extended interview schedule ranging from initial demographic and cultural data about the family to participant-observation sessions such as discussing the photo album with the family. The interview schedule is based upon schedules already in use in other studies (Musello, 1977, and Chalfen, 1977). Interviews and life histories will be combined to produce a general ethnographic description of the family's involvement with pets and photography. An inventory of the household's image collection, combined with description by the family, will provide the organizing principles implicit in the photo collection, supplying further insight into the place of pets in the photographically constructed family history. An analysis of the content and composition of photos and the frequency of pet images within the collection will be noted and their comparison with images of other members of the household undertaken.

These techniques will be employed in Phase I of the research in twenty-four Philadelphia households, a sample to be stratified by age, presence or absence of children, ethnicity (Anglo- or Afro-American), and socioeconomic (working or middle) class. In Phase II of the study, a survey instrument will be constructed and tested which will provide quantitative data about the same basic set of questions answered qualitatively in the first phase. A visual checklist will also be constructed to allow sampling of a larger number of households within a short time period. In Phase III, a general ethnographic description of the relationship of pets to owners will be generated and used as the basis for a survey instrument that can be incorporated into a larger study. Finally, data generated through this instrument will be analyzed for comparison with the original ethnographic description and other study results.

The study is designed to produce three results: first, an ethnographic description of the role of pets as revealed in the family photographs and the social activities that surround the photographs; second, a survey instrument based upon ethnographic description, which could be used with a larger or numerically significant sample of households within the Philadelphia study area; and third, a methodology that employs qualitative and quantitative techniques for the study of the sociocultural role of photography in families.

As an anthropologist, I am primarily interested in learning why people make pictures—those that are painted, those that come out of the camera ready to use, those that hang on gallery walls, appear in newspapers, photo albums, and monographs on Peruvian Indians. My curiosity is inclusive, nonjudgmental, and cross-cultural. I wish to study everything that people make to be seen—all people, everywhere. I wish to construct an anthropology of visual communication.

Our search for understanding of the world in which we live has evolved from studies of the physical world through studies of the biological and social contexts in which we find ourselves. A fourth major environment is now apparent—the symbolic. This environment is composed of modes, codes, media, and structures through which we communicate, create cultures, and organize the world. The delineation of the various symbolic systems and the contexts in which they are employed and of their relationship to each other and ultimately to the physical, biological, and social environments is the most exciting exploration of the twentieth century.

Visual mass media are becoming more and more influential in the formation and stabilization of culture. Yet our knowledge of the visual domains and their interrelationships is sparse. In fact, the visual/pictorial are the most pervasive and least understood symbolic modes. We do not understand what impact the mass-mediated messages, which we consume daily in ever increasing quantities, have on the quality of our lives—from the New Guinea native who sees "Sesame Street" to the small town American child who sees the New Guinea native on a PBS documentary.

For most of Western history our visual world has been examined from one vantage point—that of "art" or "high culture." Not only have we concentrated on examining the "masterpieces" of art, but these masterpieces have been analyzed and interpreted through the eyes of the critic, professor, and connoisseur. The visual world in general has been the world of the "elite" artifact studied and admired by elites and the analysis of the popular arts of film, photography, and television using aesthetic concepts derived from the study of these masterpieces (Worth, 1981).

As an anthropologist, I am less interested in a critical analysis of "important" photographs than in the everyday use of photography by ordinary people. To paraphrase a Bertolt Brecht poem, I don't care which emperor built the Great Wall of China; I want to know where the bricklayers went the night they finished the construction.

My research involvement with the pictures people make of animals is first with the information they yield about imaging as a social process and secondarily about what they reveal about animal-human bonding. Since one cannot separate a study of imaging from the meaning and significance of the images for their makers and users, my research produces information relevant to an understanding of both photographs and pets.

Given the initial survey findings—that the owners consider their pets as members of the family and have photographs of them—it seems reasonable to hypothesize that a study of pet images may reveal dimensions of animal-human relationships possibly unavailable through more common research approaches. There appears to be a greater "plasticity" in the form and function of pet-human relationships than in any other human relationship. Norms regulating parent-child, sibling, and other familial relationships are more fully developed and codified than are pet-human relationships. Durkheim has suggested that in areas of "anomie," the absence of norms, emotions are strong and expectations often unrealistic. Therefore, a nontraditional approach to the study of these relationships may prove particularly rewarding.

It is further suggested that a systematic examination of the relationship between picture taking and pet ownership will reveal something of the sociopsychological role or function they both play in people's lives, that is, it will teach us something about pets and about photography that might not be discovered by studying the two phenomena separately.

Given these expectations, our work has developed along two related lines: a general examination of the pet as a visual symbol and an ethnographic investigation of pet photography among families. This report concentrates upon the latter.

The pictorial representation of animals is as old as art itself and is found in virtually every medium and technology for the last fifty thousand years. Animal images occur in all image-producing cultures of the world. The production and consumption of images of household and other domesticated animals is equally ancient and widespread. People have sculpted them, painted their pictures, and, for the last 140 years, taken their photographs. Animal companions serve as props in the advertising of products; in the selling of a particular lifestyle; as objects to be merchandized in every conceivable way; and, most important for this study, photographs of pets constitute a regular part of the picture-taking habits of virtually every pet owner in America. As mentioned earlier, the University of Pennsylvania survey indicated that 100 percent of the pet owners have photographs of their pets.

Pets and other family members have not often been the subjects of serious fine art photography. They constitute an appropriate subject for the family photographer and the serious amateur who enters contests. Although there has been a recent increase in autobiographical, self-referential, and family images among some photographic artists, such as Richard Avedon's study of his father, pets have not figured greatly in this movement. With the exception of Elliot Erwitt's *Son of a Bitch* (1979), a somewhat tongue-in-cheek series of dog pictures, no major photographic artist has made pets the subject of art.

The ubiquitous nature of these phenomena makes it essential to place limits upon the universe to be examined. All types of pets and all varieties of pictorial representation could be fruitfully explored. Preliminary study indicates, however, that although some people take home movies and some procure the services of professional portrait painters and photographers, the vast majority of people take their own pictures of their pets. People take more pictures of their dogs, cats, and horses than of their snakes, hamsters, or goldfish. There are no serious technical reasons for this tendency, so it may be that animals like dogs, cats, and horses who are more likely to be anthropomorphized are the most likely to be photographed. In any case, the project has concentrated upon the photographs people take of their dogs, cats, or horses and upon the social processes involved in the making and displaying of these images.

The study deals with one aspect of the most ubiquitous visual form—the family photograph of ordinary people. The approach to these images is not that of the folklorist or art historian, who might dwell upon the aesthetic qualities of the images, but rather, as Stanley Milgram suggests, as "a technology that extends two psychological functions: perception and memory. It can thus teach us a good deal about how we see, and how we remember" (1977:50).

The theoretical orientation of this research is ethnographic and founded on the application of several tendencies in anthropology, linguistics, and communication. Scholars interested in the systematic investigation of the human condition have for a long time concentrated on the study of the artifacts of human consciousness—the material manifestations of humanness. The archaeologist looked at pottery and projectile points. The folklorist collected the text of the tale. The linguist studied transcribed speech. And the visual scholar examined the picture, the film, the painting, and the television program. These artifacts were weighed, measured, and counted. Their distribution through time, space, and culture was plotted. Some unique human products were admired as works of art, and the genius of their maker was appreciated. Finally, in recent years, these objects—both unique and commonplace—were studied for the hidden messages or codes contained in their texts.

Although the textual-artifactual approach to studying human beings produces remarkable insights and important understandings, it tends to separate the artifacts from the stream of human behavior that produces and uses them. The text needs to be studied as a unified whole. The human process should be the object of the study. A movement in this direction can be traced through several thinkers and researchers. The two most directly relevant are Dell Hymes for the concept of the ethnography of communication (1964) and Sol Worth for the study of visual forms as culturally structured communicative systems (1981).

Hymes's work represents a shift in linguistics away from an emphasis on the text of language to a study of the sociocultural processes of speaking as a social act. Some linguists became interested not only in the product but also in the process and the producer. In 1964, Hymes saw the possibility of expanding his "ethnography of speaking" model into a more inclusive "ethnography of communication." It was to include all modes, media, and codes in all possible contexts, thus allowing for the possibility of exploring the relationship beween culture and communication—an anthropology of communication (Hymes, 1964).

While Hymes and other linguists were dealing with the problem of studying language in society, Sol Worth was grappling with the development of a systematic means for studying visual forms. Using film as an example, Worth examined the adequacy of the two most common approaches—film as art and film as language. By 1966 he had contextualized the aesthetic model as one aspect of the communicative process. He suggested that film will be better understood as a sign system analogous to but different from verbal language (Worth, 1966), a semiological approach to the study of film as a culturally structured communicative system (Worth, 1981).

With the Navaho project (Worth and Adair, 1972), in which he and anthropologist John Adair taught Navaho Indians to make movies and then studied the films and the social processes that surrounded their production, Worth moved from the textual to the sociocultural, contextual study of film. Shortly before his untimely death, Worth delivered a paper entitled "Ethnographic Semiotics" (Worth, 1981) in which he suggested that scholars interested in the study of meaning through sign systems should turn their attention away from their personal analysis of cultural texts to the ethnographic study of how people create meaning in their everyday lives. Ethnographic semiotics is predicated upon an approach to semiotics that advocates a theory of sign that is less dependent upon structural linguistic paradigms and more concerned with the inclusive and general science of sign systems and upon the assumption that support for any semiotic analysis lies in the information generated from field research rather than the elegance of the researcher's argument. The research discussed here was designed to explore, elaborate, and operationalize the concept of ethnographic semiotics for the study of pet photography.

It is a taken-for-granted assumption that human beings create and share symbolic codes that permit them to organize their experiences and ultimately their world into meaningful categories. To share codes is to share a culture. Because these codes and the context in which they are used are patterned, structured, and often out of the awareness of the user, they lend themselves to sociocultural scientific study. Codes such as speaking have received much attention, but visual or pictorial codes have been less frequently studied from a communication perspective (see Worth, 1981; Musello, 1977; and Moniot, 1979, for a review of the research approaches to the study of photography and other pictorial forms).

Most social science approaches to the visual form, beginning with Bateson and Mead's Balinese work in the 1930s (1941), see the camera as a data-collecting device or photographs as an elicitation technique in interviewing or as a publishable illustration (see Collier, 1966, for a survey of those uses of photography). Our work employs another approach, examining photographs as artifacts of culture. We assume that the social process surrounding photography is an ethnographic situation which is revealing of culture (see Worth, 1981; Chalfen, 1977; Ruby, 1975, 1976).

Previous studies of photography as a culturally structured representation of everyday life indicate the following generalizations about the purposes served by photography. First, a family regards its collection of images as an important historical document of significant events and people (Musello, 1977; Kotkin, 1978; Chalfen, 1977). Musello found in his 1977 study that "in its use the image was seen to evoke the extended present. In fact, through its use and interpretation it might be suggested that the photo serves . . . both as document and as 'communion'—serving as testimony of strong family ties, feelings, and values" (Musello, 1977:6). Because our preliminary study indicates that people regard pets as members of their family, an exploration of the place of pet photographs in a family as a way of understanding the symbolic relationship between people and their animal companions seems reasonable. Second, the meaning and significance of snapshots in general may lie more in the social act of taking photographs and in the subsequent act of display (that is, placing them in albums, on the wall, in a slide show, or simply passing around loose photos among family and friends in the living room) than in the observable content of the photograph itself. It is therefore assumed that a content or formal analysis of pet photographs or of any family photo is necessary but not sufficient if one wishes to understand the meaning of the image and that the analysis would have to be supplemented with participant observation in order to learn about the social processes that surround the production and consumption of these images. Finally, people, especially children, are most frequently the subject of these pictures. Families tend to take more pictures of their firstborn and more pictures of their children when they are young. There appears to be a middle-aged hiatus in family photography. The fewest pictures are taken from the time the children reach maturity until grandchildren appear or the couple begins to travel during retirement. Since pet pictures stylistically resemble baby and child photos, it is interesting to speculate about whether the pet photography also follows the cycle seen with the photographs of children. Will a family's collection of pet photographs have more pictures of puppies than of mature dogs? Is the first pet imaged more than subsequent ones?

Our study of pet photography touches upon the questions concerned with the role of family photography in our society and the role of photography in general in our lives. These questions have recently captured the popular imagination and have produced such interesting although speculative literature as Susan Sontag's *On Photography* (1977). In 1974 the Wolfman report estimated that more than seven billion photographs are taken annually by Americans; the majority of them are snapshots. No other medium or technology of communication is used by so many so often.

Based upon previous work, three hypotheses present themselves as the most probable explanation for the popularity of family photography. Though not designed solely to examine pet photography, these hypotheses are useful as a preliminary means of thinking about the problem and as a way of contextualizing this particular study within a general set of concerns. They are not mutually exclusive; rather they are culturally sanctioned tendencies. Preliminary findings indicate that one of the three tends to dominate a family's photographic habits.

First, the social event of taking a photograph of certain people, places, events, and objects can bestow on them a place of importance, significance, and noteworthiness in the history of a family. What the photograph actually looks like or what one does with the photograph afterward is secondary. When this condition prevails, photos are not elaborately displayed on the walls or in albums or even organized into slide shows. Instead they are found in the envelopes from the processing labs, in dresser drawers, closets, attics, and basements. When family members are asked to discuss their photographs, memories of the event where the photo was taken are evoked. Few comments about the exact content of the image are made. Second, if the photograph is seen as a historically significant document or aesthetic object, the family pays particular attention to its preservation, organization, and display. As Milgram points out, "Photography allowed anyone to freeze a moment of visual experience and thus to augment his memory, to preserve it beyond his own lifetime, and to show others what he saw. . . . this new capacity to fix and externalize visual experience immediately raises the question of what people choose to render into permanent photographic images" (1977:50). When a family regards its photographs in this fashion, they are prominently displayed on the wall or organized into slide shows or albums. When people are asked to discuss their family pictures, the conversation will include comments about the technical and aesthetic abilities of the photographer, the way the collection is organized, and the importance of the images. This tendency is more likely to occur among upper-middle-class, urban, college-educated families who seem to regard photography as an art form and who purchase expensive cameras. Third, if the photograph is primarily seen as a memory aid, conversation elicited by the photo will only superficially deal with the specific content of the image and will mainly serve as a springboard for a string of narratives. For example, the photograph of my dog Sam, taken in front of our summer cottage in 1954 by Uncle Fred, will cause me to tell you about Sam, our summer cottage, the summer of 1954, Uncle Fred, and his inability ever to take a picture in focus, but I will say little about the actual photograph. When this tendency predominates, family photographs function as a means to construct a particular kind of history. As Milgram suggests, "Most photographs show people during rapid change and growth thus explaining the preponderance of photographs of children and the concentration of those photos during the first few years. Their families construct a fairy tale in photo albums. They record only the happy moments: birthdays, bar mitzvahs, weddings, and vacations. The resulting pseudo-narrative highlights all that is life affirming and pleasurable, while it systematically suppresses life's pains. For most contemporary families, this album is the only narrative of its history, having supplanted the family Bible, which in earlier times contained a record of births, deaths, and marriages" (1977:108).

The third tendency is most likely to produce useful verbal data about the emotional importance of pets for their owners. Pet photos make excellent elicitation devices when interviewing owners about their emotional attachment to the animal. The image presents irrefutable evidence of the relationship and can cause the owner candidly and openly to admit to strong feelings that might be disavowed without the image.

The physical existence of the photographs make it virtually impossible for someone to deny or avoid emotional attachment to pets. A public admission of a strong emotional attachment to an animal may not be considered socially normative, so these photographs take on a special significance for the general study of human-pet relationships. They may provide the researcher with a unique opportunity to elicit information perhaps unobtainable in any other way (see Collier, 1966, for a discussion of photo interviewing techniques).

"The snapshot has become in truth, a folk art, spontaneous, almost effortless, yet deeply expressive. It is an honest art, partly because it doesn't occur to the average snapshooter to look beyond reality, partly because the natural domain of the camera is in the world of things as they are, and partly because it is simply more trouble to make an untrue than a true picture. Above all, the folk art of the camera is unselfconsciousness. It may be a significant form of self-expression, but the snapshooter doesn't think of it that way. He takes pictures merely because he likes to" (Morgan, 1974:28).

Family photographs provide a means of measuring the emotional significance or degree of bonding between people and their pets because the photos are revealing of two types of emotional attachments—the relationship between the photographer and the subject imaged and the relationships among those in the photo. In this study, photographs are being examined as a means of understanding and measuring the degree of attachment demonstrated by the photographer for what he or she photographed. People photograph what they feel positive about; for example, one takes pictures at weddings, not divorces.

These images constitute a pleasant, uncomplicated moral universe of parties, weddings, births, picnics, and vacations. Family photographs show smiling faces living in a world as it should be. By systematically studying these photographs, we can discover how pets fit into this idealized world. Their importance can be measured by the frequency of their appearance, the place they have in the collection (for example, are pet photographs more likely to be displayed or stored than other types of family photographs?), by the style or "look" of the photographs (preliminary findings indicate pet photographs resemble baby and child photographs and can be differentiated from photographs of adults and of animals that are not household pets), and by the stories they elicit when people talk about their pictures.

In addition to the relationship between the photographer and the photographed, family photographs reveal something about the relationship among the people, places, and events in the pictures. Although "on-camera" behavior is stylized and idealized and often controlled by the photographer, these images provide some insights into the network of emotional attachments within the family. (Although it is an attempt to popularize before we have sufficient knowledge to do so, Akeret's book [1973] on photoanalysis is a preliminary exploration of the relationships between people in a photograph [see Chalfen (1974) for a critique on Akeret]). For this study, the photographs will be examined to see with whom the pets are photographed. Alone? Primarily with babies and children? When they are photographed with adults, are pets frequently held as if they were infants? Our preliminary investigations seem to indicate a hierarchical relationship of adult-child-pet. Pets may be regarded as infants who never grow up, and at least photographically they occupy the position of preverbal infants in family pictures.

Photographs are valued objects, a part of the ongoing lives of people and not something especially created for or by the study. "When you take a picture of the present, you take it into the future and you have something from the past. I have hundreds of pictures of my mother and she is no longer here. *But I have these pictures to remind me, and you know, I think I have a treasure"* (John Clomax of

Washington, D.C., at the Smithsonian Folklife Festival, in Cutting-Baker et al., 1976; emphasis added).

A recent study entitled "The Meaning of Cherished Personal Possessions for the Elderly" (Sherman and Newman, 1977–78) suggests that family photographs are among the most cherished objects of the elderly. Family photographs along with other souvenirs are a means of fixing memories. They may provide the stimulus for certain narratives that are not retrievable through other techniques.

Photographs constitute "a stylized reality. Depicting certain kinds of events in certain ways, family photographs are an expression of American values and lifestyles, a form of family folklore. Oftentimes, the pictures work back upon the viewers, *forcing them to remember in certain ways. As one festival goer (The Smithsonian Folklife Festival) told us, 'You tend to form your memories around the pictures you have taken'*" (Martha Ross in Cutting-Baker et al., 1976:69; emphasis added).

In some ways the role of pets and the role of snapshots in our lives are similar. They are both so common and ordinary that they are often overlooked as topics for "important" research. They are a part of the taken for granted of our everyday lives, and they are almost invincible. Nearly everyone either takes or appears in snapshots. Yet "no one to my knowledge has suggested an ethnography of picture taking, of photography or of snapshot communication" (Chalfen, 1977:3).

Michael Lesy (1978) has stated the problem: "Because snapshots are private documents, badly reproduced, they are very difficult for a stranger to understand or a scholar to study. They often appear to be conventional pictures of conventional rituals in which the camera has become part of the celebration. Further examination reveals a more profound complexity: in such pictures, the flow of profane time has been stopped and a sacred interval of self-conscious revelation has been cut from it by the edge of the picture frame and the light of the sun or the flash. Figures, gestures in tableaux, juxtaposed with objects, centered in mandalas—actors in psychodramas." We are in the process of locating a set of measures of how household pets are embedded in family life through a study of how pets are photographically treated. Gaining an understanding of the pet pictures will provide us with unique insights into the social and emotional role played by our animal companions. We stop time and record our own personalized versions of history with our cameras. Our dogs, cats, and horses have become part of that record. The pictures are important because they help us to remember. We wish to study these documents and the social processes that surround them so that we may better understand the emotional bond between humans and their animal companions.

Robert L. Van de Castle

15

Animal Figures in Fantasy and Dreams

Unlike the other contributions to this volume, which deal with the relationships between people and the external animals who reside in their homes and zoos or who roam the streets and forests, this chapter focuses upon the internal animals who dwell in our waking imagination or our nocturnal dreams. If we are to increase our understanding of the role that companion animals can play in our everyday lives, we need to be more aware of the ways that animal figures are viewed in our fantasy lives.

Menninger (1951) provides a good survey of how attitudes toward animals can vary from culture to culture. Menninger reminds us that sexual contact with animals was reported by 8 percent of the male population in Kinsey's sample and offers some detailed case histories of such zoophiliac practices. In an article entitled "Zoophily and Zooerasty," Rappaport (1968) reviews the roles of animals in the expression of both love and hatred. Another excellent bibliographic source of people's ambivalent relationship to animals can be found in Carson's book, *Men, Beasts and Gods: A History of Cruelty and Kindness to Animals* (1972). Should we need a more recent reminder that animals, in this case cats, can be viewed in very negative ways, the September 21, 1981, issue of *Time* magazine reports that a 1981 book entitled *101 Uses for a Dead Cat* sold 600,000 copies in just a few months and that there were 575,000 copies in print of the *The Second Official I Hate Cats Book* and an earlier *I Hate Cats Book*. The latest book along these lines is the *The Cat Hater's Handbook*.

Why do we react so strongly to animals? The reason is not likely to be rational; the intensity of zoophily-zooerasty responses suggests deeper, more irrational forces. Carl Jung suggested that "animals are the expressions of the unconscious components of self" (1959:187). If this is so, it should prove fruitful to explore the manner in which animals appear in imaginative productions that are under the sway of unconscious factors. With this goal in mind, a brief review will be undertaken to explore the frequency and form in which animal characters materialize in various fantasy situations.

ANIMALS IN FANTASY

STORYTELLING AND ASSOCIATION TECHNIQUES

Pitcher and Prelinger (1963) obtained free-fantasy stories from 137 nursery school and kindergarten children and found that approximately one-third of the characters were animals. Different animals were portrayed at different age levels of the children, and boys and girls portrayed different animals. Girls used small domestic animals more often than did boys and frequently gave them proper names; if they used a wild animal, it had a friendly quality and was given a home in the farmyard or house. Boys, on the other hand, used more wild animals whose home was in the jungle, and they were portrayed as ferocious opponents with much biting, devouring, and killing occurring. These authors feel the animal characters serve as carriers of the child's own wishes, worries, and concerns. They theorize that the friendly animals that often behave in a human-like manner may represent the acceptable aspects of the child, whereas the wild, aggressive animals may serve as a convenient representation of the child's consciously not acceptable hostile wishes to harm and destroy.

A more structured form of storytelling involves asking a child to answer certain questions about fables (Fine, 1948; Kramer, 1968). Several of these fables involve animal characters.

In a study by Freed (1965), 3,863 children aged eight to sixteen years were asked in a "projective question" to indicate the animal they would most like to be and the one they would least like to be. Boys made 100 different choices of animals they would like to be, but girls made only 58 choices. The animals boys would most prefer to be are a dog (32 percent), horse (9 percent), bird (9 percent), cat (7 percent), lion (6 percent), and monkey (5 percent). To be a dog was also the most popular choice for girls (34 percent) with the next most desired animals being cat (18 percent), horse (17 percent), bird (10 percent), and monkey (3 percent). For the animal they would least like to be, boys made 116 choices and girls made 89 choices. Pig (13 percent) was the most frequent negative choice for boys. The frequency figure for snake was 8 percent, and it was approximately 7 percent each for cat, rat, skunk, and elephant. The order of negative choices for girls was pig (15 percent), snake (9 percent), elephant (9 percent), lion (8 percent), skunk (7 percent) and cat (5 percent). The sex differences for both the positive and negative animal choices were significant, and there was also a significant difference between the animal choices made at different age levels. There was a general trend toward greater individuality of choice as age increased. It is interesting, in view of the recent popularity of the cat-hating books, that cats were frequently chosen by both sexes as being both the animal they would most and least like to be.

Kaplan and Calden (1967) extended Freed's "projective question" by asking which type of dog, bird, fish, wild, and domestic animal the child would most and least like to be as well as which animal was most and least like themselves. The reasons for all of these choices were also requested. These reasons were classified into fourteen categories including physical characteristics, abilities, temperament, and interpersonal characteristics. Test-retest reliability for the reasons was .72 after four months for a group of twelve emotionally disturbed adolescent boys. In an initial validation study, six judges were able to match with statistically significant success the animal test responses with class play data that reflected the self-perceptions and perceptions of others by sixth-grade students.

Goldfarb (1945), using an animal association test, asked twenty-five adolescents to name an animal in response to persons (father, mother, and so on) and to characteristics of persons (kind, cruel, and so on). He found that large animals were associated with adults, baby animals and fish with human babies, domestic animals with kind adults, and aggressive animals with cruel adults. Gorillas were associated with males, and cats, cows, and winged creatures were associated with females.

Gill (1967) gave a list of fifty animals to forty-two sixth graders and thirty-nine adults to check whether they usually considered that animal to be male or female. On another part of the test, subjects were asked to provide an adjective or descriptive characteristic for each of these fifty animals. Although most animals (73 percent) were judged to be male, the only animals considered as male by at least 82 percent of both age and sex groups were ape, dog, wolf, and beaver, and the only similarly checked as female was butterfly. The majority of subjects saw deer as female, but adult males, probably because of hunting associations, checked deer as being male. Men and boys considered skunks as female, but women and girls considered skunks male. The majority of girls rated crab and cockroach as male, but the majority of boys did not. With the exception of bee, all of the aggressive animals were considered male. Most of the female animals were seen as positive and passive. Preadolescents showed less tendency to assign sex roles to animals than did adults. The animal qualities considered valuable by the subjects in this study included passive attributes such as softness and peacefulness as well as aggressive features such as strength and industry.

ANIMAL DRAWINGS

In an early British study by Ballard (1913), twenty thousand drawings were collected from London children aged six to sixteen and ten thousand drawings from country children in Wales. The three-page report mentioned that country children drew more animals.

Several drawing studies have been carried out in which the interpretive significance of specific animals or the class of animals has been assessed through the use of case history material, psychological test data, or both. Brick (1944) obtained drawings from two hundred schoolchildren aged three to fifteen and observed that large, powerful animals were drawn by children with disturbed social relations manifested in feelings of inferiority. Bender and Rapoport (1944) secured animal drawings from problem children aged seven to thirteen years and reported that the children with mild behavior problems drew nonaggressive looking animals and the neurotic children drew aggressive animals. Children whose difficulty was primarily mother-centered drew ducks, and those who were escaping by truancy or vagrancy from broken homes drew birds or horses.

Schwartz and Rosenberg (1955) discuss a large number of animal figures and the presumed problem evidenced by the more than eight hundred patients who drew them. Some examples of their interpretations are that drawings of waterfowl were made by persons who had a wish for a never-experienced warm home life; birds were drawn by people who wished to get away from an unpleasant environment or who feared desertion by a loved one; chickens were drawn by individuals too dependent to leave home; horses were associated with "some greater-than-average component of opposite sex drives"; elephants indicated oedipal struggles; pigs and rodents were drawn by individuals with low popular esteem and guilt about self-worth; those who drew cows were orally fixated individuals with addictive predilections.

The most extensive examination of animal drawings was reported by Levy and Levy (1958). They present normative data based upon 7,346 drawings secured from seven groups: adult males; adult females; male prisoners; male institutionalized psychotics; female institutionalized psychotics; male adolescents; and female adolescents. More than one thousand animal drawings were obtained from each of these seven groups. The most common of the nearly seventy animals listed were dog (1,540), cat (1,275), horse (1,184), and bird (738). The first three animals (dog, cat, horse) were drawn significantly more often by normal adults, birds were drawn significantly more often by adolescents and institutionalized males. Cats were drawn significantly more often by females; horses were drawn more often by males. Although the authors propose some generic interpretations for a few animal figures, such as birds, they emphasize the importance of considering intraspecies differences such as between an eagle and a canary or between a peacock and a vulture.

Koocher and Simmonds recommend that after a subject has drawn an animal, the request be made to "draw the animal which is the opposite of the one you just drew." Their rationale for this technique is that "while the first drawn animal may be viewed in terms of self-image, the animal-opposite presents the opportunity to examine the perceived un-self; the complementary roles, denied or repressed aspects of the client's personality" (1971:9).

Waehner (1946) asked fifty-five female college students to make a series of free drawings. Rather than focusing on the species involved, she evaluated the significance of whether animals did or did not appear in the artwork. None of the academically superior students produced any animal drawings, 25 percent of those in the satisfactory academic group did, 41 percent of the group with unsatisfactory academic work drew animals. Using other data, it was possible to evaluate the women's personal adjustment. Only 13 percent of the well adjusted had drawn any animals, but 51 percent of the poorly adjusted had. The author observed that the adjusted students who represented animals drew them in good movement whereas most of the unadjusted made their animals stiff or static and very primitive.

ANIMALS AS EXCLUSIVE CHARACTERS IN PROJECTIVE TESTS

Several projective tests have been developed involving animals as the only characters appearing on the cards about which the subject makes up a story. On the Children's Apperception Test (CAT), developed by Bellak and Bellak (1949), several animals are portrayed on a series of ten cards containing scenes dealing with important situations and problems in a child's life (feeding, rivalry, aggression, loneliness, interactions with parental figures). The test developers felt that animal figures would be more culture-free and less structured with regard to sex and age than human figures and would allow for easier projection of negative sentiments and unacceptable wishes. A supplementary set of ten cards (CAT-S) designed to elicit reactions to less common situations such as injury, illness, or mother's pregnancy was later added (Bellak and Bellak, 1957). An extensive survey of the literature pertaining to the CAT along with illustrations of how the test is used in clinical practice can be found in Haworth (1966).

When Bills (1950) employed ten cards containing colored pictures of rabbits, he found that children told longer stories to the animal pictures than they did to human pictures.

The Blacky Test developed by Blum (1949) consists of a family of four dog figures, and the person taking the test is assumed to identify with Blacky the pup, the one figure that appears on all eleven cards. The question has been raised as to whether women can identify as readily as males with the name Blacky and with dogs (King and King, 1964). This test attempts to evaluate the status of a subject's psychosexual development in terms of such specific psychoanalytic variables as oral eroticism, anal retentiveness, and castration anxiety.

Blum's rationale in choosing animal cartoons was that they "would appeal to the residues of childish, pre-logical thinking in adults and facilitate freedom of personal expression in situations where human figures might provoke an unduly inhibiting resistance" (Blum, 1949:16). A discussion of the test's validity is given by Blum (1962), and an annotated bibliography has been provided by Taulbee and Stenmark (1968).

ANIMALS AS POTENTIAL CHARACTERS IN PROJECTIVE TESTS

The Make-A-Picture Story (MAPS) introduced by Shneidman (1949) uses cut-out figures that can be placed against various background pictures. Two of the sixty-seven figures are animals: a cocker spaniel pup and a snake. The use and placement of these animal figures has been reported to be a useful diagnostic clue (Shneidman, 1960). With a group of fifty disturbed adolescents, Joel (1948) found the most frequently selected figure was the cocker spaniel pup, and the pup was also a frequent choice for hospitalized neurotic adults (Goldenberg, 1951).

In the Kahn Test of Symbol Arrangement (Kahn, 1957), the subject arranges sixteen plastic objects on a numbered felt strip under five different conditions. Three of the objects are dogs varying in color and size, two are butterflies differing in color and size, and one is green and resembles a parrot. Kahn claims that the way the animal figures are placed and described gives valuable insights into the subjects' ego-defense mechanisms and other facets of personality.

ANIMALS IN THE RORSCHACH TEST

The most widely used of all projective tests, the Rorschach Inkblot Test, consists of a series of ten cards containing inkblots. The subject is asked to report what images are seen as the inkblots are examined. Animals are the most frequently reported content, and on several cards they are the "popular" or expected percept. It is more difficult to discern human forms in the inkblots because the form requirements are specific: a slightly elongated torso with a head on top and two arms and two legs. Animals, by contrast, can be somewhat round and headless (clam), extremely elongated without appendages (snake), or possess unusual appendages (tentacles, wings, fins, tails), and animals appear in a wide variety of sizes, shapes, colors, and textures.

Draguns, Haley, and Phillips (1968) reviewed a large number of Rorschach studies bearing upon interpretations that might be placed upon a high percentage of animal content (A percent). Among the studies they cite are that a high A percent has been found in the protocols of the mentally deficient (Sarason, 1950), the aged (Ames, 1960), and depressed patients (Kottenhoff, 1964). A high A percent has also been associated with academic nonlearning (Boyer et al., 1967), low ratings of promotion potential (Dulsky and Crout, 1950), poor work efficiency (Kottenhoff, 1964), and lack of movement in psychotherapy (Davids and Talmadge, 1963).

The interpretation that would seem to follow from these findings is that a high A percent is related to stereotyped thinking, an impoverishment of interests, emotional constriction, and a lack of curiosity or adaptability to novel and unstructured situations. In summary, such persons seem to possess a lower level of cognitive functioning in response to complex intellectual and emotional tasks.

Some theorists have suggested that the broad category of animal content should be subdivided into groups consisting of classes of animals. Bochner and Halpern (1945) advance the hypothesis that persons reporting mild, timid animals will show an insecure, passive attitude and that those reporting aggressive, fighting animals reflect strong feelings of hostility and aggression. These authors indicate that the direction of this aggression, inward or outward, must be determined by other factors in the protocol. Townsend (1967) did not find aggressive animals to be reported significantly more often than tame animals by institutionalized boys rated as being aggressive.

Piotrowski (1957) quotes a lecture by Reiti, who had worked with juvenile delinquents, in which the claim was made that the type of animal figure reflected attitudes toward parental discipline. In Reiti's classification, the production of small animals discloses the subject's acceptance of the notion that the parents possess superior power, whereas the production of large animals is a sign that the subject sees himself as equal in power to the parents. The size of the animal is combined with the aggressiveness of the animal to make the following proposals: small, nonaggressive animals indicate ineffectual rebellion manifested in secretive, indirect, and disguised rebellious activities; large, aggressive animals indicate open defiance and criticism of parents when displeased with them; large, nonaggressive animals indicate the parent is treated as a comrade. Phillips and Smith (1953) claim that small animals are reported by neurasthenics and individuals who display a marked restriction of behavior. Alcock (1963) found that in comparison to a normal group, asthmatic children reported notably smaller and more restrained animals.

Booth (1948) contrasted the differences in the types of animal responses given by patients experiencing tension in the vascular system (arterial hypertension) with those experiencing tension in the locomotor system (chronic arthritis and Parkinsonism). The vascular group (V) had a significantly higher A percent than the locomotor group (L), and the groups also differed in the proportion of warm- blooded and cold-blooded animals they reported when location, but not total number, of these responses was considered. Booth offered the hypothesis that since cold-blooded animals (nonmammals) have greater functional dependence on the environment, persons who report such percepts see initiative as residing in the forces of the environment rather than in themselves. Since warm-blooded animals (mammals) have more independence from the environment, people giving these responses are more likely to take the initiative in dealing with the environment.

The above interpretations are contingent upon where in the inkblot the animals are seen. Booth hypothesizes that responses given to the center axis of the inkblot reflect central concerns, whereas peripheral responses are less self-directed. Booth found that the L group reported warm-blooded animals centered in the axis and the V group reported warm-blooded animals in the periphery.

Some confirmation for Booth's contention that dependence upon the environment was associated with cold-blooded animals while independence was associated with warm-blooded animals was found in a study by Linton (1954). She conducted an autokinetic experiment and classified male undergraduates as "changers" or "nonchangers" on the basis of whether they modified their judgments after being given erroneous information by a confederate working for the experimenter. Although the two groups did not differ on their overall A percent, the changers reported significantly more nonmammals, and the nonchangers, who resisted efforts to change their judgments, responded with mammal content on the Rorschach. Whereas Booth had stressed the biological properties of adaptation that mammals possess, Linton focused upon their psychological characteristics and suggested that "human-like animals reflect relative acceptance of one's own emotions, while a high proportion of distant animals reflects a tendency to depersonalize such feeling" (p. 78). Mammals, in Linton's view, thus lend themselves more readily to the projection of human affects and provide a measure of emotional self-acceptance and confidence.

Some workers have carried the analysis of animal figures down to its lowest common denominator—the individual species. By far the most detailed enumeration of animal figures and their assumed personality correlates has been provided by Phillips and Smith (1953). They list approximately fifty animals along with interpretations involving the manner in which maternal and paternal relationships, immaturity, hostility, and passivity are linked with these animal figures. Unfortunately, these authors do not provide any normative data or frequency tables for these animal figures. Systematic efforts to establish normative frequencies for several species of animals on the Rorschach have been carried out by the Swiss investigator Kuhn (1963) with a variety of populations differing in age and sex. Illustrative of his findings is the observation that snakes are given more often by prepubescent boys than girls but that the difference is markedly reversed in adolescence.

Ames et al. (1952) have investigated the animal content given by normal children at specified levels from age two to ten years. They reported that at age two domestic animals prevailed, at ages three to five wild animals were most frequent, and from ages five and one-half to ten the butterfly-bird category was the most numerous. As age increased, there was an almost steady increase in the number of different animals reported, with dogs, bears, rabbits, and elephants being among the most common. Boys reported a greater variety of different animals as well as more total animals. At the earlier ages, girls gave more domestic animals, but the distribution of small wild animals was about even between the sexes. Boys gave more wild animals, particularly large wild animals, and also gave more nonmammals such as flying and water animals, snakes, and worms.

Ford (1946) has studied the responses of 126 young children, ranging from three to seven years old, and provided a table that indicated how many children reported various animal figures. The most frequent animals (given by 25 or more children) were butterfly, bird, dog, bear, rabbit, and monkey. Responses of bug, spider, lion, mouse, cat, and frog were given by 15 to 24 children. Although Ames, Metraux, and Walker (1959) investigated the protocols of children aged 10 to 16 years, they did not provide the same detailed breakdown of animal figures for this adolescent group as they had for the group of younger children. They mentioned an increase of bird responses for this age level and that A percent was the highest for girls at age 10 to 11 and for boys at age 14 to 16.

Figures for general classes of animals were reported by Ames et al. (1954) for their elderly (age over 70) group, containing 41 normals, 140 preseniles, and 19 seniles. Among normals there were proportionally more domestic animals, insects, and birds; the presenile group had proportionally more bats and butterflies; and the senile group had almost no birds but a very high proportion of sea life.

In Booth's study (1946) described earlier, he also found significant differences in the species of animals reported by members of the study group. The vascular tension group reported more sheep and cows, whereas the locomotor tension group saw more eagles, beasts of prey, and pigs. In this article, Booth mentions that he had previously found water birds to be frequently represented in the records of persons professionally engaged in church work.

Some researchers have limited their attention to specific cards of the Rorschach. Lindner (1952) claims that depressives and ruminating obsessional patients who experience strong guilt reactions and self-recrimination are likely to give a gorilla response to the whole blot of Card IV. According to Cerf (1957), people who report a bear to the D1 area of Card VIII are dreamers who have a dependent, nurturant orientation and those reporting a rat to this same area are realists who are distrustful and self-reliant.

Sapolsky (1964) compared a group of thirty-one psychiatric patients who had given a frog response to Card VII with a matched group of psychiatric patients who had not given such a percept and found that the frog responders displayed significantly more eating disturbances. It has been suggested that the frog may symbolize the breast (Eisenbud, 1964). The soft, smooth-skinned, somewhat rounded body that gradually tapers forward to where the bulging, nipplelike eyes are prominently featured has sufficient similarities of shape and texture to make possible such an association. If a frog were symbolic of the breast, it would accord very well with Sapolsky's finding that people producing such responses experience eating difficulties. Because of their assumed maternal qualities, Orr (1958) combined Cards I, VII, and X to develop a vitality index that ranged from moving human figures at one end of the continuum to inanimate man-made objects at the opposite end. Within this hierarchy, animals were divided into warm-blooded and cold-blooded groups and a higher "life coefficient" was assigned to mammals (warm-blooded) because of their greater physiological and

psychological proximity to human beings. Orr (1958) reported that institutionalized French psychiatric patients obtained low scores, and Endora (1959) found
that a group of Ecuadorean murderers and rapists had lower scores on Orr's
indexes than did normals.

ANIMALS IN DREAMS

Because we are the evolutionary products of an ancestry stretching back millions
of years to an origin in the animal kingdom, it is to be expected that traces of our
animal heritage can be found in our physiological and psychological functioning. This menagerie within us can become very lively when sleep periodically
cycles through the rapid eye movement (REM) stage of EEG activation and
results in dreaming. Several speculations have been advanced as to the possible
meanings of the animals that appear in our dreams.

In *The Interpretation of Dreams*, Freud proposes that "wild beasts are as a
rule employed by the dream-work to represent passionate impulses of which the
dreamer is afraid, whether they are his own or those of other people. . . . It might
be said that the wild beasts are used to represent the libido, a force dreaded by the
ego and combatted by means of repression" (1961:410). In a similar vein, Ernest
Jones suggests that since children often owe their first experience of sexual
activity to the sight of animal copulation, animals lend themselves to the indirect
representation of crude and unbridled wishes. "Analytical experience has shown
that the occurrence of animals in a dream regularly indicates a sexual theme,
usually an incest one, a typical example being the maiden's dream of being
pursued or attacked by rough animals" (1959:70). An interesting attempt to link
specific animal imagery with sexuality was made by Hadfield (1954). He suggested that the basis for the widespread appearance in nightmares of crab, spider, and
vampire images was because they represented visceral objectifications of the
bodily feelings associated with orgasm. The crab portrays the violent changes in
viscera and abdominal muscles which produce a gripping sensation; the flaccid
feelings following orgasm are represented by the sprawling legs and soft underbel-
ly of the spider image; the washed-out feeling of fatigue, as though the blood had
been sucked dry, is externalized by a vampire figure.

Other theorists conceive of animals as symbolic of a much broader range of
affects than the sexual ones. Jelliffe and Brink (1917) speak to the sexual issue
when they propose that animals are at first libido objects and then become libido
symbols. These authors acknowledge that animals "are symbolic of various forces
within man's nature or external to him, forces both beneficent and harmful.
They offer substitute gratification for pleasure or satisfaction denied in direct
form" (1917:255).

Jelliffe and Brink wrote their paper on the role of animals in the unconscious
after observing "the astonishing revelation in psycho-neurotic dreams of the use
of animal material and the affective importance of it in neurotic history"

(1917:253). According to Gutheil, a neurosis may be symbolized in many ways, including animals that portray the low brutal instincts in the neurosis. He states, "Very often the unconscious is represented by sinister animals; this is particularly true in cases where unconscious pressures make the patient doubt the efficacy of his repressions" (1960:163). A related interpretation is offered by Stekel, when he states, "The danger of approaching insanity expresses itself in dreams of . . . a sudden attack by a wild beast" (1943:421).

Another possible meaning for animals that Gutheil (1960) considers is that being bitten by an animal may be a symbol of "pangs of conscience." Being swallowed by a voracious animal is a portrayal of our intense fear of birth, according to Fodor (1951). In discussing dreams of preschool children, Despert comments that "animals as motives are almost always sadistic and often totally destructive, regardless of size, etc. They bite and devour the child or chase him" (1949:141).

Animals can also be used to represent family figures. Jung (1916) notes that "theriomorphic symbols, in so far as they do not symbolize merely the libido in general, have a tendency to represent father and mother, father by a bull, mother by a cow." Freud refers to dreams in which "a dreaded father is represented by a beast of prey or a dog or wild horse—form of representation recalling totemism" (1961:41). In a paragraph describing how many specific animals such as snakes, fish, and cats are used as genital symbols, Freud states, "Small animals and vermin represent small children—for instance, undesired brothers and sisters" (p. 357).

A physiological interpretation for the frequency of animal dreams was advanced by Wundt. He thought that dream images arose because of subjective excitation of the retina, and he stated, "This is no doubt also the basis of the great fondness shown by dreams for animal figures of every sort; for the immense variety of such forms can adjust itself easily to the particular form assumed by the subjective luminous images" (1874:657).

Just as Shakespeare (Yoder, 1947) used animal analogy as a technique for character portrayal, animal figures can be employed to represent various aspects of the dreamer's character. Thus Boss writes, "In subjective interpretation a dream tortoise would signify the tortoise-like and armored character of the dreamer himself"(1958:49).

It is obvious that many views regarding the significance of animal figures in dreams have been advanced. Such dream figures are frequently considered to represent the animal side of our personality—the primitive sexual or aggressive impulses which we attempt to keep inhibited and which we fear may increase in intensity and get out of control. Animals may also signify the instinctual urges of others, especially family members, about which we are apprehensive. Another manner in which animals may be employed in dreams is to portray characterological features, as when someone is seen being sly as a fox or free as a bird.

A review of the research studies that have examined the frequency or type of animal figures in dreams will now be presented.

Blanchard (1926) questioned 230 children referred to a guidance clinic about their dreams, and 189 reported at least one dream. Of the total of 315 dreams, 46 dealt primarily with animals, and a fear element was present in 36 of these dreams. Next to parents, animals were the most frequent subject of dreams. Lions, tigers, bears, apes, and snakes were reported to be the most popular animals. There was a decline in the percentage of animal dreams as children increased in age.

Despert (1949) obtained 190 dreams from 39 preschool children attending a nursery school. A total of 55 dreams dealt predominantly with animals although animals appeared in minor roles in a larger number of dreams. The animals appearing most frequently were dogs, horses, elephants, tigers, lions, wolves, monsters, alligators, and snakes. Most of these animals were engaged in chasing, biting, or devouring the child.

Foster and Anderson (1936) asked parents to keep a seven-day record of the sleep disturbances and unpleasant dreams experienced by their children. The 519 children observed were under thirteen years of age. Animals constituted the subject matter for 40 percent of the bad dreams experienced by children aged 1 to 4 years, 16 percent of those for children aged 5 to 8 years, and 9 percent of those for children aged 9 to 12 years. No sex differences were found.

Ames studied the sleeping behavior of 50 to 100 children from babyhood through the sixteenth year of life. She noted that nightmares "come in from around 5 to 7 years of age and again from 10 to 12" (1964:12). Animal figures appeared in different forms at different age levels. She reported that at age three, children dream of farm animals; at age four of flapping wings of birds; at age four and one-half of wolves; at age five, animals, especially wolves and bears, chase the child; at age five and one-half, wild animals (wolves, bears, foxes, snakes) chase or bite the child; at age six children dream of domestic animals. No mention is made of animal figures again until age ten, when she indicates that nightmares deal with dragons, "bad guys," animals, and robbers. At age eleven, dreams are about ordinary things such as homework, pets, and sports.

Gordon (1924) asked a group of orphan children, most of whom had low IQs, whether they ever dreamed at night. She recorded their responses if they answered affirmatively. Their responses were generally short, such as "about my mama." Four of the sixty-seven girls and two of the thirteen boys reported a dream in which an animal was present.

Schnell (1955), in a study carried out in Germany, asked several hundred children aged seven to fourteen years about their dreams. The most frequent topic for the 605 dreamers evaluated was parents (173), and the second most frequent category was animals (157).

The most extensive collection of children's dreams was gathered by Kimmins (1937), a British inspector of schools. He obtained 5,600 dream questionnaires from children aged 5 to 16 years. He does not provide any tables or detailed frequency figures but reports that for children aged 5 to 7 years the fear dream is very prominent and that the fear dream of animals is more common among boys than girls. For children 8 to 14 years old, "the fear of animals is practically the same in both sexes, and is the cause of about 20 percent of fear dreams. The larger animals, e.g., lions, tigers, and bulls predominate in boys and dogs, rats, mice, and snakes in girls' dreams."

In an unpublished study, Orlowitz (1971) obtained information on 25 dreams from 13 male and 25 dreams from 13 female dreamers, most of whom were 16 or 17 years old. She found that animal figures accounted for 5.4 percent of all the characters in the male dreams and 6.6 percent of the characters in the female dreams.

The most intensive study of children's dreams in a laboratory setting using EEG indicators of dreaming was carried out by David Foulkes and his colleagues. In one study (Foulkes et al., 1967), the dreams of 32 boys aged 6 to 12 years who slept two nights under laboratory conditions were compared to the dreams of young adult males who had also slept under laboratory conditions. Animals accounted for 15.6 percent of the characters in the young boys' dreams, but no animals were reported in the dreams of the young adult males. In another study, Foulkes (1971) provides a detailed table of the various dream scores obtained by 7 boys and 7 girls aged 3 to 4 years and 8 boys and 8 girls aged 9 to 10 years who were studied at regular intervals in a sleep laboratory over a year. Included in the table are scores obtained from REM awakenings, non-REM awakenings, and sleep onset awakenings. Animals were reported more frequently by the younger children for all three awakenings. Girls reported more animals at both age levels, but for the youngest girls, the percentage figure is spuriously inflated because just one girl accounted for half the animal figures reported. When these same children and a few additional children were studied two years later, Foulkes, Shepard, and Scott (1974) again found that the youngest children reported more animal figures from all three awakenings. The youngest boys had more animal characters (46 percent) than the youngest girls (20 percent) while the older girls had more animal characters (17 percent) than the older boys (9 percent).

It is clear from the preceding review that animal dreams are common among children and that their incidence becomes less frequent as children get older. Dreams containing animals are generally described as "bad" or "scary," and the child is frequently the victim of an animal attacker. The animals dreamed about may be different for boys and girls and they may also be different at different age levels.

Attention will now be directed toward studies in which it might be possible to determine whether animal figures are prominent in the dreams of adults.

Gahagan (1936) administerd a questionnaire on typical dreams to 228 male and 331 female college students. Nearly 62 percent of these students reported being pursued by an animal, approximately 50 percent reported having dreamed of reptiles, and slightly less than 4 percent experienced dreams of being an animal. No significant sex differences occurred.

A cross-cultural study of typical dreams was carried out by Griffith, Miyagi, and Tago (1958). The 223 Japanese college students had experienced dreams involving wild, violent beasts significantly more often than the 250 American college students (42 percent versus 30 percent). Approximately one-half of both national groups reported having dreamed of snakes. Although more females in both groups reported dreaming of snakes, the difference between sexes was significant only for the Japanese group.

In Kinsey et al.'s (1953) study of female sexual behavior, it was reported that about 1 percent of women had dreamed of having sexual relations with animals. In their study of male sexual behavior, the Kinsey group claimed, "Boys who have had animal contacts, or thought about having them, quite regularly dream of such experiences" (1948:526).

One of the largest dream collections in the world has been amassed by Dr. Calvin Hall. In one study, Hall and Domhoff (1963) analyzed the aggressive interactions in 3,049 dream narratives collected from 1,940 males and females ranging in age from 2 to 80 years. These dream narratives had been collected over a period of years from students in Hall's undergraduate classes at Western Reserve University in Ohio. A standard printed form was used to record the dreams. An A/C ratio was computed by dividing the number of aggressions by the number of characters. A total of 1,490 aggressions were found in these dreams. In a table listing the characters with whom the dreamer was involved aggressively, the A/C ratio for male dreamers with animals is .48 while for female dreamers, the A/C ratio is .29. This difference is statistically significant. These A/C ratios mean that male dreamers are aggressively involved with 48 percent of all the animal characters in their dreams and that females are aggressively involved with 29 percent of the animal characters in their dreams. In a later article (Hall and Domhoff, 1964), these authors report that when this same sample of 3,049 dreams was analyzed for friendly acts, a total of 711 such acts were found. Only 9 friendly acts occurred when animal characters were involved. There was thus a clear predominance of aggressive over friendly interactions when animal characters were present in dreams.

Vance, in a master's thesis at Western Reserve University (1956), used Hall's collection of dreams and from the dream series of fifty-six male and female college students found 114 references to animals. The most common animals were dogs (28 percent) and horses (25 percent). Domestic animals accounted for 59 percent of the total figures; 90 percent of the animals lived on the land; and 80 percent had four legs. Animals attacked the dreamers in 35 percent of the women's dreams and 24 percent of the men's dreams. There was no one breed that was overly aggressive. The only animal that was helpful was the horse. For 13 percent of the women and 18 percent of the men, the animal was a companion or playmate, and a dog most often fulfilled this role. There were three dreams in which sex occurred between animals and one in which a male dreamer massaged the breasts of a female ape. A considerable diversity of animal activity occurred, and the dreamer's responses to these animals also varied. Vance's conclusions regarding the significance of animal figures in dreams will be discussed later in this chapter.

THE PRESENT STUDY

Since several studies had claimed that animal dreams seemed more common in children and that sex differences were sometimes found with regard to the animal figures appearing in these dreams, the present study was carried out to examine these variables in a more systematic fashion than had been attempted previously in the literature.

The children's dreams used in the present study came from two primary sources: Calvin Hall's collection of children's dreams obtained by elementary schoolteachers in Ohio and Florida and my collection from middle school and high school students in Virginia. The younger children's dreams were verbally described to teachers who wrote them down; the older children wrote about their own dreams. Most of the children reported only one dream, and therefore it was decided to tabulate only one dream entry per child. If several dreams were reported by one child, his or her proportion of animal dreams was computed. If this figure was higher than the average proportion for his or her age group, an animal dream was recorded for that child; if the proportion was lower than that of the age group, a nonanimal dream was recorded. If an animal dream was reported, the first one occurring in the series was used. For example, if a twelve-year-old boy reported five dreams and one of these was an animal dream, no entry for an animal dream would be made because his animal percentage figure of 20 percent was below the 25 percent figure for his age group. If, however, he had reported five dreams and two of these contained animals, he would have been tabulated as producing an animal dream because his 40 percent animal figure was above the average figure for his age group. His first animal dream in the series would have been selected for tabulation. If more than one animal species appeared in a given dream, each individual species was tabulated, thereby accounting for the total number of animal figures being greater than the total number of animal dreams.

The results of the tabulations for frequency of animal figures in children's dreams is shown in Table 15.1. A general trend is toward a decrease in the frequency of animal dreams as children become older. This decrease is slightly irregular if examined on a year-to-year basis. If two-year averages are examined, however, the steady drop in percentage of animal dreams as a function of age becomes much clearer: 39.4 percent, 35.5 percent, 33.6 percent, 29.8 percent, 21.9 percent, and 13.7 percent. In Table 15.2, it is shown that the percentage figure for adults is 7.5 percent.

The overall percentage figures for frequency of animal dreams are not very different between boys (29.6) and girls (29.0). An interactive effect between age

TABLE 15.1. FREQUENCY AND TYPE OF ANIMAL FIGURES IN CHILDREN'S DREAMS ARRANGED ACCORDING TO AGE AND SEX OF DREAMER

Age	4		5		6		7		8		9	
Sex	M	F	M	F	M	F	M	F	M	F	M	F
N dreamers	14	14	39	27	32	47	26	36	35	38	34	24
N Animal dreams	8	5	14	10	14	15	8	13	12	13	9	10
% Animal dreams	57	36	36	37	44	32	31	36	34	34	26	42
Year ave. %	46.4		36.4		36.7		33.8		34.2		32.8	
2-year ave. %			39.4				35.5				33.6	
Dog			4	1	1	2	3	1		3	1	3
Horse		2		4	1		1	2	1	2	2	
Cat			1	1	2	1	1	1				2
Snake	1	1	1		2			3	1	2		
Bear	1		2	1			1	1				
Monster	1				1	1	1		1	1	1	
Lion	1	1		1			1	2	2		1	1
Bird	1	1		1	2				1b			1
Spider			1		2	2				1		
Gorilla					1	1						2
Tiger		1			1	1			1			1
Insect	1		1a					1a		1		1a
Water Animal			1c		1c	1s						
Fish			1 + 1w			1					1	1
Rabbit						1						
Wolf				1								1
Rodent						1				1		
Alligator	1				2	2						
Elephant					1			1	2			1
Fowl					1			1	1			
Cow				1				1			1	1
Bull								1				1
Monkey	1									1		1
Pig	1							1	1			
Dinosaur					2							
Dragon					1				1		1	
Miscellany				1n	1p	1q		1d			1g	
											1n	
Generic	1	1	3	2	1							
Total	9	8	13	11	22	17	12	14	14	13	12	16

a	winged insect	d	deer	h	hyena	q	squirrel	u octopus
b	bat	f	frog	n	snail	s	seal	w whale
c	crab	g	giraffe	p	possum	t	turtle	x fox

Table 15.1. THE PRESENT STUDY (Continued)

Age	10		11		12		13		14–16			Com-bined	
Sex	M	F	M	F	M	F	M	F	M	F	M	F	bined
N. dreamers	34	27	27	36	68	80	18	12	31	42	358	383	741
N. Animal dreams	11	12	5	9	17	16	4	2	4	6	106	111	217
% Animal dreams	32	44	19	25	25	20	22	17	13	14	29.6	29.0	29.3
Year ave. %	37.7		22.2		22.3		20.0		13.7				
2-year ave. %		29.8				21.9			13.7				
Dog	1		1	1	2	3	1		1	1	15	15	30
Horse		2	3	1	6			1	6	22	28		
Cat	1	1			1	2		1			6	9	15
Snake	1		2	1						9	6	15	
Bear		2		2	3	1					7	7	14
Monster	3	1				2					8	5	13
Lion	1	1							1		8	5	13
Bird		1		1	2					1b	6	6	12
Spider			1		2						7	2	9
Gorilla	1				1	1	1		1		5	4	9
Tiger					1	1					3	4	7
Insect	1a				1a						5	2	7
Water Animal				1u	1f	1f	1u				4	3	7
Fish				1							3	3	6
Rabbit	1		1	1				1		1	3	3	6
Wolf		1			1	1					1	4	5
Rodent		2							1		1	4	5
Alligator										3	2	5	
Elephant										3	2	5	
Fowl				1				1			3	2	5
Cow						1					1	4	5
Bull					1				1		4 0	4	
Monkey									1	2	2	4	
Pig										2	1	3	
Dinosaur	1										3	0	3
Dragon											3	0	3
Miscellany				1t	1t + 1x		1d				6	4	10
Generic								1			3	7	10
Total	11	11	6	11	20	19	6	2	5	6	130	128	258

*Excludes monsters and generic

Mammal*	73	91
Mammal%	61.3	78.4
Nonmammal%	46	25
Nonmammal%	38.7	21.6

$X^2 = 8.07$ p = .01

Table 15.2 TYPES OF ANIMALS IN COLLEGE STUDENTS' DREAMS

		Males	**Females**	**Total**
N Dreamers		485	316	801
N Dreams		2,000	2,000	4,000
N Animal Dreams		151	149	300
% Animal Dreams		7.5	7.5	7.5

Type	M	F	Both	Type	M	F	Both
Dog	24	42	66	Rabbit	2	2	4
Horse	21	38	59	Wolf	4	0	4
Cat	10	17	27	Squirrel	3	1	4
Bird	18	9	27	Pig	2	2	4
Snake	16	8	24	Lion	2	1	3
Fish	10	11	21	Elephant	2	1	3
Insect	8	12	20	Sheep	2	1	3
Water animal	10	6	16	Spider	1	1	2
Fowl	9	5	14	Bull	2	0	2
Rodent	2	8	10	Ox	2	0	2
Bear	8	1	9	Dinosaur	0	2	2
Cow	6	3	9	Donkey	1	1	2
Tiger	3	4	7	Fox	1	1	2
Crocodile	5	1	6	Giraffe	2	0	2
Turtle	5	0	5	Other	5*	3†	8
Deer	4	1	5	Generic	13	12	25
				TOTAL	**203**	**194**	**397**

*1 each of ape, boar, dragon, camel, mountain goat
†1 each of possum, clam, worm
Mammal†† 98 128
Nonmammal†† 92 54
$X^2 = 13.66$ p = .001
†† Excludes generic

and sex is present, however. Boys have a higher percentage of animal dreams between ages four and six (43.5 percent) than girls do (34.1 percent). This pattern is reversed from ages nine to eleven. The percentage figures for girls at this age level is 35.6 percent while that for boys is 26.3 percent. There is a slight shift back to boys at ages twelve to thirteen when the percentage of animal dreams for the boys is 24.4 percent and that for the girls is 19.6 percent.

The animals most frequently appearing in children's dreams are dogs, horses, and cats. These three species account for 28.3 percent of the total number of animal figures present in these children's dreams. The next most frequent animals are a group of wild or frightening animals, which includes snakes, bears, monsters, lions, spiders, gorillas, tigers, and insects. Monsters were tabulated only if it seemed clear that they represented some form of animal or were half animal such as wolf-man. This group of eight frightening animals, which did not include birds, accounted for 33.7 percent of the total animal figures. There were, of course, other frightening animals, such as alligators or bulls, but these were comparatively infrequent.

Some sex differences were apparent. Girls had more dreams than boys of horses and cats (24.2 percent versus 9.2 peercent) whereas boys had more dreams than girls of the eight frightening animals listed in the preceding paragraph (40.0 percent versus 27.3 percent). There was also a significant sex difference in phylogenetic level of the animal figures. More girls than boys dreamed about mammals (78.4 percent versus 61.3 percent) while more boys than girls dreamed about nonmammals (38.7 percent versus 21.6 percent).

The reader may wish to make other comparisons from Table 15.1. Some combining of similar species was occasionally necessary to keep the length of the table manageable, for example, crocodile was included with alligator, coyote with wolf, and so forth.

The next analysis involved college students' dreams. A total of four thousand dreams from 801 dreamers were examined for the presence of animal figures. Most of these dreams came from Calvin Hall's collection, but approximately 375 dreams came from my collection of dreams from Denver University students.

Table 15.2 presents the types of animals reported in these college students' dreams. The percentage of animal figures for college students was much lower (7.5 percent) than it had been for children (29.3 percent).

As they had been for children, dogs were the most common animal dreamed about by college students, followed by horses, but cats were now tied for third place with birds. Dogs, horses, and cats accounted for 38.3 percent of the animals for college students, whereas the same three animals had accounted for 28.3 percent in children's dreams. The combination of snakes, bears, monsters, lions, spiders, gorillas, tigers, and insects, which accounted for 33.7 percent of the animals in children's dreams, amounted to only 16.6 percent of the animals present in college students' dreams. These figures indicate that adults dream more often of domesticated or pet animals whereas children dream more frequently of wild, threatening animals.

Although there were no sex differences in the overall percentage of animal dreams for adults, there were significant sex differences in the phylogenetic level of the animals dreamed about. Women dreamed about mammals more often than men did, but men dreamed about nonmammals more often than women did. This was the same pattern found for children's dreams and thus represents a generalized sex difference that cuts across age levels.

What could account for this sex difference in phlyogenetic level of animal figures appearing in dreams? In reviewing the Rorschach, the work of Booth (1948) and Linton (1954) suggested that individuals who report mammals are less externally oriented and have greater acceptance of their own emotions. Since mammals are more humanlike, people who report more mammals should also be inclined to report more humans. If these assumptions are correct, it would be predictable that women should have more mammal content because they generally are considered to be more in touch with their own feelings and to be less uncomfortable in the realm of emotions than men are. In addition to dreaming of comparatively more mammals, women also have more human characters in their dreams than men do (Hall and Van de Castle, 1966). Thus women may dream more about mammals because they can more readily identify with the emotional self acceptance and social acceptance of others that seem to be symbolized by the presence of mammals in dreams. That is, mammals may represent greater emotional maturity.

An interesting confirmation for this suggestion that a higher level of animal phylogenetic development might be associated with a higher level of social and emotional maturity was found in a dream series reported by Boss (1958). The dreamer was an engineer who sought psychotherapy for depression and impotence. During his three years of treatment, he produced a total of 823 dreams. His initial dream in therapy was of being in a dungeon where the bars over the windows were shaped like mathematical formulas. He later dreamed of machinery, transportation conveyances, and bridges. He subsequently dreamed of plants, then insects, then toads, frogs, and snakes. The first mammal was a mouse disappearing down a mousehole, then pigs, and finally lions and horses. His first human form was a woman swimming under a pond of ice, and he eventually was dancing at the peasant feast with a passionate woman. Boss credits C. G. Jung with first drawing attention to "phylogenetic development" in serial dreams when there are "especially intense periods of maturing in the life of the dreamer" (Boss, 1958:115).

To pursue this topic of what meanings might be attached to animal figures in dreams, I decided to carry out a contingency analysis to discover what other elements are present when animal figures appear in dreams. Four groups of dreams from American college students were examined. The first group (human only) consisted of 907 dreams in which all the characters were humans. This group contained dreams experienced by 454 males and 453 females. There were three groups of dreams in which the predominance of animal figures varied. The first animal group consisted of dreams in which both human and animal characters appeared, but the number of human characters was greater than of animal characters in each of the 54 dreams involved. In the second animal group, an equal number of human and animal characters appeared in each of the 40 dreams. The third animal group contained 56 dreams in which only animal characters appeared or if human characters were present, they were outnumbered by animal characters. An equal number of males and females were represented in each of the three groups of animal dreams. These dreams were part of the data base used for tabulating the frequency of animal figures in adult dreams shown in Table 15.2. The assumption underlying this grouping of animal dreams was that if animal figures do represent some unusual affective or cognitive component of mentation, there should be progressive changes in dream scores as the predominance of animal figures systematically increases. Various dream scores selected from the Hall–Van de Castle (1966) system of content analysis were employed to test this assumption. The results of the comparisons between the four groups of dreams are shown in Table 15.3.

Table 15.3.   CHANGES IN SELECTED CONTENT SCORES AS ANIMAL FIGURES BECOME MORE PREDOMINANT IN DREAMS

Content Score	Types of Characters			
	Human Only	More Human than Animal	Equal Human and Animal	More Animal than Human
Average lines per dream	10.2	10.6	8.4	7.6
Aggressive dreams total dreams	43.7	59.2	72.5	78.6
Aggressive acts total characters	27.8	27.8	37.8	56.0
Aggression with animal total animals	23.8	33.3	50.5	
Misfortunes total characters	15.1	16.3	19.3	25.4
Apprehension total emotions	33.4	46.9	46.1	58.1
Unfamiliar and disturbing settings total settings	18.7	14.7	23.5	30.6
Outdoor settings total settings	33.8	49.3	58.8	77.7
Body parts total objects	10.9	11.8	15.8	20.7
Physical and movement total activities	47.0	57.8	59.3	67.2
Failure and success total characters	9.2	10.6	11.8	15.7
Male characters m & f characters	56.3	59.8	66.7	66.7

The first comparison in Table 15.3 indicates that dreams become progressively shorter as animal figures predominate. Since anxious dreams can cause premature awakenings, it is possible that there is something sufficiently threatening about animal dreams to cause the dreamer to abort or end such dreams quickly.

Since several theorists had proposed that animal figures might represent hostile or destructive impulses, the category of aggression was examined. There is a marked increase in the percentage of aggressive dreams as animal figures predominate. Not only are there more aggressive dreams but within the dreams the number of aggressive acts associated with each dream character also increases markedly. In the "human only" category, there are 27.8 aggressive acts for every 100 characters, but for the "more animal than human" category, the figure doubles to 56 aggressive acts for every 100 characters. The next analysis attempts to uncover whether the animal characters themselves might be the source of the increased aggressive activity. If the three animal groups are compared, it can be seen that for every 100 animal characters in the "more human than animal" category, 23.8 aggressive encounters occur, but the figure more than doubles to 50.5 aggressive encounters when the "more animal than human" group is examined. These analyses show that there is a definite association between animal figures in dreams and aggression; as animal figures gain increasing predominance there is a marked acceleration of aggressive activity, and this aggression is focused on the animal figures.

A misfortune is scored when some negative outcome such as death, illness, or a natural catastrophe like a tornado occurs in a dream. No personal agent is involved; an act of God or fate is responsible for the calamity. The next comparison in Table 15.3 reveals that there is a slight but steady increase in these natural disasters as the predominance of animal figures increases. As might be expected from the increase in aggressive events and misfortunes, apprehension becomes the main emotion as the predominance of animal figures increases.

The apprehension associated with animal dreams might be expected to be disruptive to the dreamer's equilibrium, and he might feel disoriented, as is suggested by the next analysis, which shows that there is an increase in the proportion of unfamiliar and distorted settings or background of the dream when animal figures clearly predominate. To clarify the nature of these settings further, the next analysis was undertaken. It shows that outdoor settings (woods, fields, beaches), away from the security of buildings and other structures associated with civilization, are the most frequently encountered ones as the predominance of animal figures increases.

Given these stresses, the dreamer may not feel very integrated, and his body image may not be secure. The next analysis deals with that consideration. There are increasing references to isolated parts of the body (head, limbs), as the predominance of animal figures increases.

Dreams in which animals appear are very active and lively. When physical (lifting or hitting) and movement (walking or running) activities are combined, it can be seen that active and strenuous activities (as opposed to talking, looking, or listening) are more likely to be involved when there is a predominance of animal figures.

The preceding analyses suggest that animals do pose problems for the dreamer. They upset him, possibly disorient him, and may make him insecure about his body imagery. Such a situation calls for efforts at solution. Failure or success is involved whenever a dreamer decides to accept a problem or challenge and attempts to solve it. Depending on the outcome, failure or success is scored. The next analysis suggests that there is some slight increase in coping efforts whenever animal figures begin to predominate. There are more failures or successes per character as animal predominance increases.

The last analysis was undertaken because of the finding by Gill (1967) that most animals (73 percent) on an association test were judged to be male. When characters are identified with regard to sex, there is a greater likelihood that dream characters will be identified as male if they are more strongly associated with the presence of animal characters. This association between males and animals is reflected in such statements as "He behaved like an animal"; seldom do we hear "She behaved like an animal." If an association between women and animals occurs, it is generally in the context of a natural maternal instinct to nourish and protect her young.

Friendly interactions were not analyzed in Table 15.3 because there were so few of them. To give the reader some idea of how aggressive and friendly interactions are distributed when only human charcters are involved, a tabulation was made as to the relative frequency of aggression and friendliness in dreams. As was listed in Table 15.3, 43 percent of the dreams contain some element of aggression in those dreams where only humans are involved, but friendliness is not far behind; 40.7 percent of the dreams where only humans are involved contain at least one expression of friendliness. A different picture emerges when the nature of the dreamer's interactions with animals is considered. On 87 occasions the dreamer was aggressively involved with animals, but on only 17 occasions the dreamer was involved in a friendly interaction with animals. A close examination of these interactions reveals that the animal attacked the dreamer on 47 occasions and acted friendly on only 2 occasions. By way of contrast, in the "human only" category, the dreamer is attacked by other humans on 258 occasions but receives friendliness from other humans on 206 occasions. Apparently, if a dreamer is going to have another character initiate some interactional pattern with him, there is a 44 percent chance that he will receive friendliness if the other character is a human but only a 4 percent chance if that character is an animal.

The dreamer also frequently behaves in an aggressive manner toward the animals he encounters in his dreams. He attacks them on 40 occasions and offers them friendliness on 15 occasions. Friendliness was initiated by 10 women dreamers and 5 male dreamers. The sex of the dreamer has some influence on how the animal is reacted to but not on how the animal reacts. Animals attack 23 males and extend friendliness to 1; they attack 24 females and extend friendliness to 1. Male dreamers attack the animal 23 times and are friendly 5 times; female dreamers, however, attack animals only 17 times and are friendly 10 times. The analyses presented in Table 15.3 clearly indicate that the presence of animal figures in dreams has a significant effect upon other features of the dream. In comparison to dreams containing only human characters, dreams with animal figures are more likely to be short, take place in an outdoor setting which is unfamiliar or distorted, have a great deal of activity, often of a violent nature, or be the scene of a calamity. The dreamer experiences apprehension, becomes more sensitized to various parts of his body, and exerts some effort to overcome a challenging problem encountered in his dream. As the emphasis upon animal figures increases and a greater predominance of animal figures occurs, all of the previous dream parameters become proportionately more intensified. Animal dreams are not exclusively negatively toned; sometimes the dreamer attempts to respond in an accepting or supportive role toward the animal figure, but almost without exception, if the animal figure intitiates any response to the dreamer, it is some form of threat or hostility.

The question of the universality of dream symbols has often been raised. Is there any possibility that the same dream animals, such as snakes, will appear in all cultures? The answer is clearly no. This answer is based upon an examination of the animal figures appearing in 246 dreams from two groups of Australian aborigines; 118 dreams from two groups of natives living on South Pacific islands; 190 dreams from two groups of North American Indians; and 448 dreams from Peruvians. Fish or other forms of aquatic animals were the most common species for groups living near water but were almost totally absent in the dreams of inland-dwelling groups (Central Australians and Hopi Indians). Snakes were reported fairly frequently (27 times) by Australian aborigines and Hopi Indians but not at all by South Pacific islanders and rarely (3 times) by Kwakiutl Indians and Peruvians. Kangaroos, wallabies, crocodiles, and sting rays were exclusive to Australian dreams, the only cats encountered were on the Truk Islands in the South Pacific, and the only exotic jungle animals (lion, tiger, elephant) were found in the dreams of Peruvian students. Some form of wild bird or fowl was present in the dreams of all the cultural groups examined. Except for the Peruvians, many of the animals were reported in the context of hunting or fishing activities although animals were often cast in an attacking role throughout all these cultural groups.

Another possible "cultural" context that might be considered is the setting in which the dream is dreamed. These has been considerable controversy within the field of dream research as to whether there are differences in content between the dreams reported at home and those reported in a laboratory setting. Without belaboring all the technical and theoretical issues involved in that controversy, I thought it would be interesting to examine whether there are any differences in the frequency of animal figures from home versus laboratory dreams.

Since there are considerable individual differences in the tendency to report animal dreams, it is obvious that the most meaningful comparison would involve dreams of the same individual under these two contrasting conditions. To carry out such an analysis, I used the dream reports obtained by Calvin Hall and me in a study we carried out to investigate home versus laboratory dreams that was reported in 1966 in an Institute of Dream Research monograph. I compared the 506 dreams obtained when the subject was awakened by a person monitoring his REM periods in a dream laboratory situated in a private home setting with 264 dreams that had been spontaneously recalled by these same subjects at their own homes. A total of 15 adult males, most of them college students, constituted the subject population.

To obtain an index of animal "density," I divided the number of animal characters by the total number of characters (human and animal combined). This "density" index was 3.9 percent for the REM-awakened laboratory dreams and 7.4 percent for the spontaneously recalled dreams at the subjects' homes.

I also made another analysis to determine whether animal figures were more likely to be associated with a particular temporal phase of the night. During one part of our study, we awakened subjects only once a night and balanced these awakenings over the first four REM periods. This condition was met in a total of

196 lab dreams. It was found that animal dreams were more likely to occur during the second or third REM periods. There has been some speculation that the dream content elicited during these REM periods is more likely to deal with incidents from an earlier phase of the subject's life. If so, the finding of more animal dreams during this phase of heightened "temporal regression" would fit nicely with the fact that more animal dreams occur during childhood than adulthood.

CONCLUSIONS

What conclusions can be drawn about the significance of animal figures in dreams from this review of previous studies in which animal figures appeared in dreams and the various analyses described here?

With regard to children's dreams, an inverse relationship exists between chronological age and the frequency of animal dreams; as a child gets older, animal dreams decrease. Why is this so? In speculating upon the results he has obtained in his longitudinal study of children's dreams, Foulkes provides some contextual observations from children's dreams and their life experiences to support the hypothesis that "animal characters predominated over parent figures because they represent the child's own impulses in relation to nuclear family members and that animal interactions represent his attempts to express or control such impulses" (1974:85). As children get older, they can become freer to express their impulses more directly, not only with regard to family members but to peer groups as well. Whenever developmental landmarks are reached which could intensify issues over the control of impulses, such as during puberty, it is possible that animal figures could be temporarily reinstituted to handle these increased instinctual drives. Such an explanation would accord well with the findings presented in Table 15.1, in which girls showed an increase in percentage of animal dreams between the ages of nine and eleven and boys did so between the ages of twelve and thirteen. It is generally accepted that girls reach puberty earlier than boys, which could account for their percentage of animal dreams increasing at a slightly earlier age than it did for boys. Why, then, do boys have a high percentage of animal dreams between ages four and six? Psycholanalytic theory claims that this would be the age for young boys to experience the various emotional complications associated with the Oedipal complex when the young boy must begin to break his close ties with his mother.

If animal figures are symbolically associated with instinctual urges or impulses, it is probable that these would be more frightening for a young child who has not yet learned suppression, rationalization, or other defensive coping mechanisms because an adult presumably has to deal with strong affective drives. Some support is found for this formulation when the animal figures appearing in children's dreams were compared with those of adults. Adults reported more familiar and domesticated animals whereas children described more threatening and wild animals.

Speculation was advanced earlier that males may feel more comfortable with the world of things and objects and feel more uncomfortable with the world of people and feelings and that the reverse may hold for females. If animals do represent emotions and impulses, then animals higher on the evolutionary scale may signify more highly developed and organized emotional patterns that are ego-syntonic while animals lower on the phylogenetic scale would represent more primitive and disorganized emotions that are ego-alien. If there is any merit to these proposals, the prediction could be made that women should therefore use more highly developed forms of animal life—mammals—in their dreams while men employ more primitive and lower forms of animals—nonmammals—in their dreams. The results shown in Tables 15.1 and 15.2 supported this hypothesis. Both young girls and women reported significantly more mammals, and young boys and men had significantly more nonmammals.

If the idea that animals may signify unacceptable emotions and instinctual urges is carried a step further, it would be expected that dreams containing animal figures should differ in substantial ways from other dreams in which animals do not appear. That is exactly what occurs. Dreams containing animal figures differ in length, types of characters, settings, objects, emotions, activities, and achievement outcomes from nonanimal dreams. The more pronounced the predominance of animals, the more marked are the departures in these various dream scores. Although dreamers may try occasionally to appease or accept the animal figures in their dreams, the animals can never be trusted because they almost always turn on the dreamer and attack him.

As Vance (1965) concluded in her thesis on animal dreams, "No all inclusive statement can be made about the significance of animal figures in dreams." Emotionality per se, is not bad, and animals may sometimes symbolize positive affects such as love or tenderness or they may represent playful aspects of a relationship or admired individual qualities such as strength or courage. Such positively toned emotions are far less common, however, and it seems that animals are more generally invoked to stand for the unacceptable and frightening impulses that reside in our personalities. The particular types we employ will be a function of what culturally shared and learned associations have been imparted to us regarding particular animal species.

PART TWO

A Social Predator for a Companion

Introduction

Domestication is a form of evolution, that is, a shift in the frequency of genes that creates change in a species. Changes occur in both morphology (form) and behavior. Nevertheless, the new form is recognizable to its wild type; the laboratory rat, the cow, and corn each resembles its wild ancestors, though all behave in ways that are clearly different. The differing traits are selected by people for their own purposes. The rat was selected for docility, the cow for meat or milk, and corn for protein and uniformity of size.

It is generally believed that domestic dogs—all of them—were domesticated from the gray wolf, *Canis lupis*, and its numerous subspecies. The reasons are all conjectural; as an assistant on the hunt, as a source of food, as a guard or at least an alarm against its undomesticated ancestor, or simply as a companion to hold and care for have all been proposed. The conscious selection for the curly tail typical of many breeds may be an attempt to distinguish the new wolf from its less docile close relatives.

The occurrence of dogs appears to coincide with the development of human villages. Dogs, and even wolves habituated to humans, were probably welcomed because they ate the refuse of human society, including the human waste that undoubtedly accumulated around new, more densely populated areas. The befriending of a predator by its potential prey may seem odd; even today this relationship is persistent and pervasive.

The answer may lie in the fact that the two species, humans and wolves (dogs), have a lot in common. Both are very social. In fact, it has been proposed that more insight into human social behavior could be deduced from the study of social carnivores than from nonhuman primates because social systems are so strongly influenced by ecological conditions (Schaller and Lowther, 1969). Ecologically and socially, we may have more in common with wolves than with apes.

Wolves are very social. Their populations consist of packs occupying adjacent and sometimes overlapping ranges. Most packs contain fewer than eight members: a mated pair, about two young from the previous year, and about four juveniles from the present year. There is a linear hierarchy within the males and within the females. Wolf "government" is both autocratic (the alpha animal always leads) and democratic (alpha takes cues from the group). Wolves use a wide variety of postures, odors, and vocalizations to communicate within the pack. Scent markings and vocalizations permit the members to communicate over time and place. All members have an interest in the young.

This predisposition for a social existence lends itself to wolves becoming the companions of people. In many ways, dogs relate to their owners as dominant members of the pack; many of the same postures and vocalizations used by wolves are seen to take place between people and their dog. The "play-bow," crouch, and whimper are all commonly understood by people as if the subordinate "wolf" were communicating with the alpha animal. When this hierarchy is not clear or the dog is an alpha animal to the person, we see problems that are often a concern to owner and animal.

Despite more than fifteen thousand years of domestication, the dog still is a predator; it still attacks animals and even people. People must learn to appreciate the history of the animal and even learn to communicate with it. Those concerned with the humane care of dogs must also appreciate the undisputable fact that dogs prefer to be part of any pack and benefit from the strict supervision and discipline of a knowledgeable leader. Human signals of communication, including good obedience training, fences, and leashes are all part of our repertoire as alpha-humans.

The first three chapters in this section address the important and relatively new concept of the treatment of animals with behavior problems. Some people question the importance of treating animals with behavior problems, but these same people are often horrified by the knowledge that more than eighteen million companion animals are delivered to animal shelters yearly to be killed. What is not always appreciated is that at least 20 percent (one in five) of these animals are no longer wanted because they have, or are perceived to have, a behavioral problem (Argus Archives, 1973). We may never know how many other "problem" animals are allowed to escape or are given away. The first chapter in this section reviews the history of the field; the author is a leading participant in that history. Dr. Victoria Voith recounts the wide variety of treatment protocols available and notes the importance of understanding the total behavioral situation: remember that an animal's problem is a behavior perceived as such by its human companion.

Peter Borchelt's "Separation-Elicited Behavior Problems in Companion Animals" is a good example of how a private behaviorist/practitioner handles the common problem of animals that "get into trouble" when left alone. In the section "Loss of a Companion Animal," it is clearly established that people grieve the separation from their animals; perhaps it is not surprising that dogs, too, react adversely when separated from their companion owners.

Katherine A. Houpt's chapter on aggressive behavior in dogs gives yet another example of the handling of a common and serious animal behavior problem. An animal's aggressiveness is probably the most common disruption of the bond between people and their animals as well as being a serious public health problem because it often involves other people (bite victims) besides family members. Unlike other behaviorists and most animal trainers, Houpt is uncomfortable with food rewards. The fact that there is no clear protocol even with this common issue indicates the newness of the field. There are no truly objective studies to evaluate the effectiveness of treatment regimes involving single treatment protocols (most behaviorists use several treatments at the same time), controlled experiments, the use of placebos, independent observations of the animal's behavior or improvement, or systematic replication of the methods.

The last two chapters in this part report on animal behavior problems that have serious social consequences from a research, rather than a treatment, point of view. Jane Tate's "Human-Bear Interactions" is an important contribution not only to our understanding of bear behavior but to understanding how important our knowledge of animals can be in determining our own behavior and why it is so very important to improve the public's general knowledge about animals.

The general public's need to see, touch, and *feed* animals (all part of our relationship with our companion animals) is in direct conflict with the National Park Service's desire (also reflecting the wishes of many people) to conserve these large animals that get more aggressive when fed by people. It is amazing that for many, the perception of these animals does not appear to include the potential danger of intimate contact: for these people, bears are "companion" animals. The reader should look ahead in this volume at Edwin Schlossberg and Pat Baxter's study of Macomber Farm for at least one attempt to improve people's understanding of animals and Alan M. Beck's "Animals in the City" for other examples of social conflict and possible solutions.

The last chapter in the section, "Dog Attack Involving Predation on Humans," may, at first, appear out of place in a volume that, for the most part, discusses, demonstrates, and evaluates the many positive roles animals play in the lives of people. But, as no drug or treatment is without side effects, so, too, with the human–companion animal bond. The fatal attacks that were studied, like all that are known to have occurred, involved owned, that is, companion dogs, not wild strays or rabid animals. Some of the studies were initiated at the request of the legal system (lawyers or medical examiners) and represent yet another aspect role of the animal behaviorist: forensic consultant. Predation on humans is not a typical behavior of the companion animal, and all the animals involved were raised in a not atypical but uncommon way. The importance of proper socialization to people cannot be overemphasized in the development of a mutually beneficial human–companion animal bond.

Victoria L. Voith

16
Animal Behavior Problems: An Overview

Animal behavior problems are behaviors of animals that owners consider a problem to themselves, other people, or the animal itself. Such problems can be normal behavior, either instinctual or learned, or abnormal behavior, either congenital or acquired primary pathophysiological disorders, or the result of early or later environmental experiences.

Man undoubtedly has always been interested in animal behavior. Initially, human-animal interactions may have been predator-prey relationships, with man sometimes being the predator, other times the prey. Later, man used knowledge of animal behavior to domesticate animals and train them for companionship or utilitarian purposes.

Application of knowledge about animal behavior began with early man and wild animals, developed further with domestication and castration to manage groups of domestic male animals, became a scientific discipline in the 1940s, and now includes the field of clinical animal behavior, which is directed to treat most of the behavior problems of primarily companion animals.

Scientific research has greatly increased man's knowledge about animal

TABLE 16.1

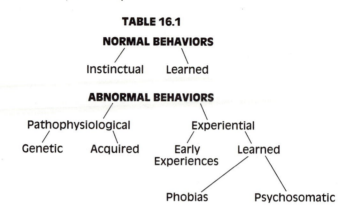

behavior and in the last thirty years has provided information that has been applied in a variety of ways. For instance, learning principles were used to train pigeons to identify and track objects on the radar screen (Skinner, 1960). Pigeons have been trained to inspect capsules or diodes and to accept suitable items and reject defective ones (Cumming, 1966; Verhave, 1966). The birds were easily trained, could work long periods of time, and had a higher accuracy rate than human inspectors.

In the 1950s, the Brelands (Breland and Breland, 1951) reported on a new area of applied animal behavior—commercial animal training. The Brelands envisioned opportunities and financial benefits for experimental psychologists in this new field. Using learning principles, they trained animals to perform a variety of interesting tasks for the amusement of the public and to aid in military operations. Intermittent schedules of reinforcement and highly motivating rewards were used to train animals to perform naturally occurring behaviors on cue and to shape naturally occurring behaviors into other forms. For example, chickens readily scratch the ground and peck at items. Chickens were trained to scratch the ground or peck at piano keys when a signal such as a light was turned on. They did these behaviors to obtain a palatable reward. The behaviors appeared to a spectator as dancing and playing the piano. Raccoons and rats were taught to play basketball. These animals naturally handle items and were shaped to deposit balls through a hoop (Breland and Breland, 1951, 1961). Pigeons have also been trained to spot downed aviators and sailors in water, to deliver messages by tracking a laser beam to a target area, and to give alarm signals when they spot people hiding in the bush (Bailey, 1981).

In the 1970s, academic animal behaviorists employed a multidisciplinary approach to understanding and treating animal behavior problems. Tuber, Hothersall, and Voith (1974) successfully used a combination of knowledge about species-typical behaviors, classical and operant conditioning, and behavior modification techniques to treat phobias, anxieties, and fear-induced aggressive behavior of companion dogs. These problems were typically not addressed by dog trainers—at least with a high rate of success. Their article introduced a new concept in the field of applied animal behavior, that of using scientific information to correct behavior problems of companion animals.

Several different approaches to treating animal behavior problems have evolved. Some therapists use home visits, others diagnose and begin treatment sessions at office visits, and some handle cases over the telephone. Behaviorists with strong backgrounds in comparative psychology and ethology tend to focus on the behavior of the animals. Owners are, of course, made aware of their own behaviors that contribute to the problem behavior of their pet and are advised to avoid such behaviors. Likewise, owners are instructed in environmental manipulations, social signals, and behavioral techniques that will facilitate appropriate behavior in their pets. Some psychologists involved in animal behavior therapy insinuate that basic personality traits or behavioral disorders of the owners usually must be addressed before any therapeutic intervention is valid or can be effective for their pet. There have been no studies to confirm this opinion, and the behaviorists whose intervention focuses only on the animal report high success rates.

Most therapists rely on the owner as the agent of change. The behaviorist carefully instructs the owner on how to effect a change, and most of the procedures are carried out by the owner at home. The majority of techniques involve manipulating the environment, using species-typical signals and counterconditioning procedures, and relying heavily on positive reinforcements and nonaversive techniques (Tuber et al., 1974; Voith, 1979). One therapist, whose approach relies heavily on aversive associations with electric shock, reports that this technique is successful in ameliorating a variety of behavior problems of companion animals (Tortora, 1981). To date, however, no independent evaluations and assessments of the outcome of any of the presently used approaches have been made by persons unassociated with the intervention techniques.

Environment, physiology, learning, and genetics all help determine an animal's behavior. For example, spraying is an "instinctive" behavior, the performance of which is influenced by several factors (Figure 16.1). The number of other cats in the vicinity and the sounds, odors, and physiological reproductive status of other cats tend to influence spraying behavior. Hormones influence spraying. Androgens facilitate spraying, and synthetic progestins inhibit spraying. Castration tends to suppress spraying (Hart and Barrett, 1973). Intact males spray more often than castrated males. Learning can also be influential—some cats learn not to spray—at least when the owner is present.

Another example of a behavior that is readily recognized as influenced by several factors is intermale aggression in dogs, which is a genetically based behavior (Figure 16.2). The presence of testosterone plays a role in intermale aggression. Castration prohibits or suppresses intermale aggression in approximately 50 percent of dogs (Hopkins et al., 1976). Progestins can suppress fighting in both intact and castrated males. A dog can learn to inhibit its aggression if it has been trained to do so. Previous fighting experience also determines whether an animal engages in aggression. Environmental factors such as the presence of a bitch in heat may stimulate fighting in males that normally get along amicably. The presence or absence of an owner who has trained the dog not to be aggressive also plays a role in whether the animal may fight.

Because there are many factors that influence behavior, it should not be surprising that there are numerous ways of intervening and altering behavior problems. Behavior can be changed by manipulating the environment, altering the physiological status of the animal via surgical techniques and drug therapy, or using learning principles such as behavior modification techniques. The multiplicity of variables explains why persons from a variety of backgrounds (practical experience, ethology, learning theory, ecology) can usually effect a change in an animal's behavior. The more one understands the variables involved in behavior, however, the more effective one can be in diagnosing and designing a treatment plan to correct behavior problems. No matter how much practical experience one has, without a theoretical base one's effectiveness is limited. Most behavior cases are unique with respect to some behavior variables. The broader one's base of knowledge, the greater the probability of accurately diagnosing and competently treating routine as well as unusual behavior problems of animals. The major areas of intervention to effect a behavior change are environmental manipulation, physiological intervention, and behavior modification.

The environment can be manipulated by reducing the number of cats in a household or prohibiting access of visiting cats to the windows and doors to reduce spraying behavior by a cat within a house. Removing a bitch who is in estrous may prevent fighting and urine marking by male dogs. Providing an appropriate scratching substrate may induce a cat to eliminate in the litterbox rather than elsewhere, and putting a litterbox in a location a cat prefers may facilitate use of the litterbox.

A major example of physiological intervention is castration, which has been used for centuries to induce general tractability and reduce intermale aggression of domestic animals. Castration eliminates or reduces masculine behaviors such as roaming, urine marking, intermale aggression between cats and dogs, and mounting behavior in dogs (Hart and Berrett, 1973; Hopkins et al., 1976).

The physiology of an animal can be altered with drug therapy. Practitioners are well aware that progestins can influence spraying behavior of male cats, urine marking and mounting behavior of dogs, and intermale aggression of dogs and cats. The psychotropic drugs that alter the mood or emotional state of an animal can be used in treating behavior problems. Hyperactivity and general restlessness can be reduced with specific drugs. Antidepressant and antianxiety agents have been reported to help dogs that are depressed and anxious (Lapras, 1977).

Neurosurgery has been used with some success in treating behavior problems in animals. Amygdalectomies have been reported to reduce aggressive behavior in fearful dogs in a laboratory setting (Andersson and Olseen, 1965). Bilateral lesions of the medial preoptic nuclei of the hypothalamus will suppress spraying behavior in male cats that have not responded to castration or progestin therapy (Hart and Voit, 1978). Side effects such as hyperphasia and a "startle" reaction during sleep may preclude acceptance of this procedure. Olfactory tractotomies have been reported to reduce spraying behavior in cats without producing side effects (Hart, 1981).

Electroconvulsive therapy has been reported to be successful in the treatment of aggressive behavior of dogs, although the mechanism by which this therapy works is not known. Remission may occur within several months to a year; however, the animals can be successfully retreated (Redding and Walker, 1976).

Disease states can also alter the physiological status of the animal and consequently its behavior. Cystitis, polydipsia and diabetes insipidus affect urination behavior patterns. Neurological and metabolic disorders can alter an animal's behavior. Often painful disorders such as panosteitis, anal sac ulitis, intervertebral disk problems, or ear infections are not directly observed by the owner, but a change in the animal's behavior is usually apparent.

Treating behavior problems of animals is rewarding because it is interesting, it often saves an animal's life, it helps people, it contributes to basic knowledge of the behavior of companion animals (particularly dogs and cats) in their natural habitat (people's homes), and it contributes to knowledge about the human–companion animal bond.

People demonstrate their attachment to their pets in a variety of ways. Pets are kept in the home, taken on trips, accompany the owner throughout the day, and sleep with the owner. Many owners keep pets despite inconveniences caused by their pets' behaviors. Owner profiles and attitudes were assessed in a series of 100 animal behavior cases seen at the University of Pennsylvania from December 1980 to March 1981 (Voith, 1982). Sixty-one involved one dog, one involved 2 dogs in a household, 31 involved a single cat, 6 involved 2 cats in a household, and 1 involved 3 cats and a dog. The majority of people who brought in a pet also had other animals—52 percent of the dog owners and 68 percent of the cat owners. Only 4 of the dog owners had not had a dog before, and only 2 of the cat owners had not had a cat before. When clients were asked why they had not gotten rid of the pet because of the behavior problem, overwhelmingly the first response (55 percent of both dog and cat owners) involved statements of affection such as, "I love him/her," "I am attached to . . . " or "another person in the household loves, likes, or is attached to. . . . " The second most common immediate response was a humanitarian reason such as, "No one else would take this animal" or "I feel I have a responsibility to a pet." Persons who gave a humanitarian reason usually also included a statement of affection. The third most immediate response was that getting rid of the animal was not a consideration.

There were no significant differences between dog and cat owners as to why they had not gotten rid of the pet, whether they had considered euthanasia as a solution to the problem, or whether they felt guilty about having caused the problem. More dog owners than cat owners (45 percent versus 34 percent) referred to the pet as a person at some time during the interview. There were no correlations between the household structure (single, 2 adults, or family) and the reasons given for having kept the pet. The 2 people (1 cat and 1 dog owner) who answered that they could not live without the animal lived alone without other pets in the household, but not all persons living alone with no other pets gave that answer. Jamie Quackenbush, a social worker on the staff at the Veterinary Hospital of the University of Pennsylvania who counsels people in crisis situations regarding illness or death of a pet, has also observed a correlation between a dependency upon the animal and a solitary living situation (Quackenbush, 1981).

Owners can recognize their attachment to a pet and at the same time acknowledge that it is causing them inconvenience, financial or social expense, or emotional stress. When owners feel that the cost or disadvantage of keeping a pet outweighs the benefits or advantages, they usually decide to get rid of the pet. But, this decision is rarely without regret or sorrow. People often acknowledge their attachment to a pet while simultaneously realizing the negative impact of the animal on their lives. It continues to be my impression, as well as that of most other animal behavior therapists who see a large number of clients, that owners of behavior-problem pets are normal, healthy individuals who have no more psychological problems, psychoses, or neuroses than the average person— pet or non–pet owner (Voith, 1981; Mugford, 1981; Borchelt, 1982). These owners, however, are clearly very attached to their pets.

Animal behavior therapy relies heavily on techniques developed for behavior modification of behavior problems in people (Wolppe, 1958, 1969). The principles used in behavior modification were developed from laboratory research with animals and successfully and broadly applied to treat behavior problems in animals—an interesting reversal of procedures, in that the techniques were first field tested on humans before being applied to animals. Animal behavior therapy demonstrates that behavior research with animals in laboratories can not only be used for the benefit of people but also for animals. Behavior modification techniques have been very effective in treating a variety of animal behavior problems. Behavior modification does not make an animal an automoton or a robot but appropriately channels behaviors into patterns that benefit both the animal and the person. Most therapists rely heavily upon positive reinforcement. Averse or noxious stimuli are counterproductive in the treatment of many animal behavior problems. Sometimes drug therapy or concurrent surgical procedures such as castration have been found to be helpful as adjunctive therapy. For example, castration, progestin therapy, and behavior modification techniques tend to work in an additive way to reduce intermale aggression in dogs (Voith, 1980).

Knowledge presently available in the scientific literature can be applied to treating animal behavior problems. More information is needed on the basic behavior of cats and dogs, particularly in a home environment. Clinical animal behavior is in an embryonic state. As more people become involved in the field, knowledge will expand. Clinical research is also needed in developing and improving diagnostic and treatment techniques.

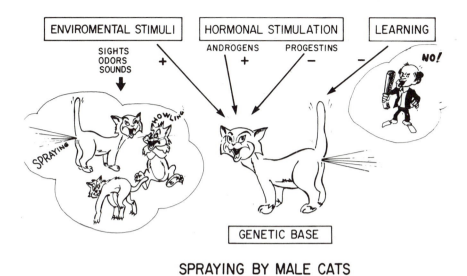

SPRAYING BY MALE CATS

Figure 16.1. Spraying by male cats is a genetically based behavior, the expression of which is influenced by many variables. (Courtesy of California Veterinarian, June 1979)

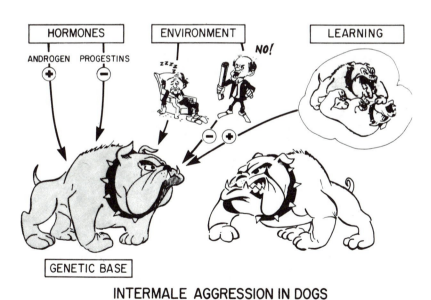

INTERMALE AGGRESSION IN DOGS

Figure 16.2. Intermale aggression in dogs is a genetically based behavior, the expression of which is influenced by a number of variables. (Courtesy of California Veterinarian, June 1979)

Peter L. Borchelt

17

Separation-Elicited Behavior Problems in Dogs

The importance of the pet-human bond is best illustrated by the fact that over one-half of the households in the United States own an average of about one and one-half pets (Allen and Westbrook, 1979). Seventy million pet owners can't be wrong! But apparently things do go wrong frequently with the pet-human relationship. Many pet owners euthanize or give their pets to adoption agencies because of difficulties with their pet's behavior.

One of the most common difficulties encountered by dog owners is the occurence of behavior problems when the dog is left alone, for instance, when the owner is at work or out of the home in the evening. The most frequent of these problems are vocalization (whining, barking, howling), elimination (urination, defecation), and destructive behavior (chewing, digging).

Historically, these problems have been viewed as neurotic, psychotic, or abnormal behavior; as "spite," that is, the dog "gets even" with the owner for leaving it alone; or as general disobedience on the part of the dog. Treatment techniques have included obedience training and a variety of punishment procedures such as leash correction, hitting with newspapers, throwing or shaking cans filled with coins or stones, and so forth.

Only recently have psychologists and animal behaviorists become interested in the behavior problems of the domestic dog. This interest has expanded the range of theories available to explain the occurence of these behavior problems and has enlarged the range of treatment techniques. For instance, the above-mentioned behavior problems are most accurately interpreted as responses to separation from an attachment person (owner).

Only during the last thirty years or so has it become general knowledge in the behavioral sciences that attachment is a behavior system of critical importance to social species. The early impetus was provided by studies of imprinting in birds (Lorenz, 1935). Studies on social attachments in dogs (Scott and Marston, 1950; Scott, Stewart, and DeGhett, 1973), monkeys (Kaufman, 1973; Harlow, 1961; Suomi, 1976; Hinde and Spencer-Booth, 1971), and humans (Bowlby, 1969, 1973) and other studies indicate that there are common features across species in the effects of lack of social attachment during development and in the behavioral effects of separation.

Although the general features of separation behavior of puppies in laboratory situations have been described (Scott, Stewart, and DeGhett, 1973), very little information is available about the separation behavior of dogs kept as companion animals in the human family. Tuber, Hothersall, and Voith (1974) and Hothersall and Tuber (1979) described some of the general features of these problems in pet dogs and discussed the theory and practice of treatment techniques. (See Voith in this section). The present chapter is based on information obtained over a three-year period (May 1978 to May 1981) from 146 cases, involving 151 dogs, that exhibited separation behavior problems. Separation-elicited problems represented 39 percent (146 of 372 cases seen) of the dog behavior problem cases seen during this time. For each case, a diagnostic interview lasting about two to three hours was conducted in the owner's home. At this time, the owner was taught the appropriate treatment techniques. In many cases, telephone follow-up totaling from a few minutes to an hour or more over a several-week to several-month period was necessary to ensure successful treatment.

In most of these cases, the behavior problems occurred when the owner was out of the home, at work, during the day. In some cases, however, the dog exhibited no problem behavior during this time but exhibited the problem(s) when the owner left the home again in the evening or on the weekend. Usually, a departure of one to several hours (or less) was sufficient to yield the problem. The problem was sometimes also exhibited at night when the owner was asleep.

SEPARATION-ELICITED BEHAVIOR IN THE DOG

Let us first consider the range of behaviors that arises from a problem with the attachment behavior system in the pet dog. I have mentioned that the most common separation-elicited behaviors are vocalization, elimination, and de-

Table 17.1. AN OVERVIEW OF SEPARATION-ELICITED BEHAVIOR PROBLEMS IN DOGS

Behavior System	Behavior Problem	Signs
Attachment	Separation Anxiety | Arrival Elation—	1. Vocalization 2. Elimination 3. Destruction 4. Behavioral depression 5. Psychosomatic response 6. Hyperactivity 7. Other (mouthing, nipping, growling, coprophagia)

struction. Although these are the most common, and certainly the most problematic for the owners, there are other adverse behaviors (Table 17.1).

It is not unusual for a dog to show a mild behavioral depression or psychosomatic sign as a result of the owner's departure. Many dogs do not eat or drink during the time the owner is absent but do so immediately upon the owner's return. Some dogs assume an obvious but difficult to describe facial or body posture of "depression," "moping," and "looking sad" when the owners leave home. Other dogs show physiological, somatic responses such as vomiting, diarrhea, bloody stool, high heart rate, or self-destructive hair chewing, pulling, or licking when the owners leave. A wide range of such psychosomatic signs may occur under these circumstances, but since they may be difficult to observe, much less measure, few data are available. Certainly, the data from separation-elicited stress responses in primates (Coe et al., 1978; Reite et al., 1978; Seiler et al., 1979; Smotherman et al., 1979), indicate that separation-elicited psychosomatic illness in the pet dog is likely. The long-range health implications of this problem are not known.

In all instances of separation-elicited problems, the return of the owner elicits a pronounced and vigorous greeting response. The dog may jump on the owner, run around in circles, wag its tail and body, lick the owner, or whine, and it continues these responses for a few minutes or more. Rarely, this "arrival elation" response continues for many hours after the owner's arrival or is restimulated by almost any attention the owner directs to the dog. In these cases, owners invariably describe the dog as "hyperactive."

In a few cases, other behaviors occurred such as coprophagia, mouthing, growling, or nipping at the owners as they walked out of the home. The two cases of coprophagia involved the dog eating cat feces when the owners were absent. Numerous cases of puppies, and some older dogs, consuming their own feces when alone have been dealt with in brief telephone consultations. In these cases, the coprophagia began as a separation-elicited problem, and no other behavior problems occurred. An appropriate punishment technique (aversive taste applied to the feces) appears to be generally effective in treating this problem. In two out of three of the cases in which mouthing, growling, and nipping the departing owners occurred, the dogs exhibited aggressive behavior problems as well as other signs of a separation problem.

INDIVIDUAL DIFFERENCES

It is clear that large individual differences exist in the expression of separation-elicited behavior. Many dogs only bark and howl when left alone; they never eliminate, become destructive, or show any indications of behavioral depression or obvious signs of psychosomatic response. Other dogs only urinate when alone. Others only chew. Others only "look sad" when the owners leave. Still others whine, urinate, and chew. Others whine, defecate sometimes, and chew at other times. Yet others had a history of eliminating but now only become destructive.

Table 17.2 illustrates this variation. The total number of each behavior problem type (excluding behavior depression) is presented, as well as the various combinations of problems that occurred. Many more instances of vocalization, elimination, and destruction occurred than psychosomatic responses or hyperactivity. Usually, only one or two behavior problem types occurred per case, although triple combinations were not infrequent. Only four cases involved four behavior problem types.

I can find no obvious correlations with other behavior systems which predict what behavior problems will occur when the dog is alone. For instance, there is no correlation between using the mouth for destructive chewing and using the mouth in other contexts such as aggression or feeding problems. Nor are dogs that vocalize when alone more likely to bark in other situations such as at strangers or other dogs. At present, the reasons why a particular dog engages in a particular separation problem are not known.

Table 17.2. RELATIVE FREQUENCY OF SEPARATION PROBLEMS AND COMBINATIONS OF PROBLEMS

	Total N	1	2	3	4
Vocalization	86	13	16	17	27	1 1 2 3	2 2
Elimination	86	17	17			1 1 1	
Destruction	100	22	2	1 5			
Psychosomatic	11	2					
Hyperactive	9	0					
Other	5	0					
Total		54	58		35		4

SHIFTS IN SEPARATION BEHAVIOR

A dog that exhibits one type of separation behavior may shift to another type ("symptom substitution"). A common cause of such shifts is the owner's use of punishment techniques. For instance, a dog that barks and howls when alone may be caught in the act of doing so by the owner and be punished. The usual punishments include suddenly coming to the door and yelling at the dog or hitting it or frightening it with a can filled with pennies or making some other loud noise.

In many cases, the dog learns to anticipate punishment for barking and ceases briefly, only to begin again a few minutes later. Owners often then wait for the barking to recur and then punish the dog again. In several cases, owners unwittingly succeeded in delaying the onset of barking for up to forty-five minutes before deciding that punishment was not likely to solve the problem. In other cases, however, appropriate punishment (that is, punishment delivered concurrently or immediately after barking) succeeded in supressing barking but did not succeed in suppressing the separation anxiety. Consequently, these dogs began displaying other signs of separation such as elimination or destruction.

Punishment that is inappropriately timed or severe may also cause shifts in the expression of separation anxiety. A common recommendation in obedience training books is to take the dog to the location of the problem (the soiled or chewed area) and deliver an aversive stimulus, usually long after the behavior has occurred. The owner's arrival and subsequent punishment of the dog may increase anxiety and thus exacerbate the separation problem. In many cases, the manifestations of separation anxiety generalized from barking only, for instance, to barking plus elimination or worse.

TEMPORAL CHARACTERISTICS OF SEPARATION BEHAVIOR

Typically, a dog begins to exhibit a separation behavior problem shortly after the owner has departed. Hothersall and Tuber (1979) present data on separation-elicited vocalization in a Llewellin setter; the latency to onset of whining was less than one minute and barking less than ten minutes after the owners left the home. In most of the cases I have observed, I ask the owners to simulate a departure by, for example, putting on their coats, turning off the lights, and taking purses, briefcases, or keys as they go out the door. I then sit quietly in the home and observe the dog for about three to five minutes until the owner returns. In the majority of cases, the dog exhibits some indication of separation behavior such as restlessness, pacing, or whining. I have seen numerous instances of urination, defecation, destructive chewing, and digging and various physiological concomitants during this period. Clearly, anxiety is elicited by the departure of the owner, and, in most instances, the dogs' behavior is not influenced by the presence of a stranger (nonattachment person).

Apparently, after the initial onset of separation behavior, the dog usually settles down and may rest or sleep most of the day until the owner returns. Some owners (or neighbors!), however, have reported the dog barking or howling for periods of time throughout the day. In a few instances, chewing and digging have apparently continued for many hours, as evidenced by the amount of damage that occurred.

ANTICIPATION OF SEPARATION

Learning involves the anticipation or prediction of stimulus-response relationships. Clearly, dogs learn to anticipate an impending departure of the owner based on the stimuli that consistently precede such a departure. For instance, some dogs learn that particular articles of clothing (for example, shoes, uniforms) or activities (putting on makeup, turning lights off) are highly correlated with the imminent prolonged absence of the owner. Thus if the prolonged absence of the owner elicits anxiety, these stimuli elicit preseparation anxiety or arousal. In many cases, dogs show a mild behavioral depression, but in other cases they exhibit overt anxiety or fear responses such as following the owner around the house, flattening of the ears, lowering or tucking of the tail, or shaking, shivering, or whining. Separation anxiety problems, like phobias, tend to be stimulus-specific and to generalize to any stimulus or along any stimulus dimension that consistently precedes the fear or anxiety-provoking event.

FACTORS THAT CONTRIBUTE TO SEPARATION ANXIETY

As mentioned above, punishment techniques often exacerbate separation anxiety problems in dogs. What factors contribute to the initial occurrence of these problems? All dogs, just as all members of any other social species, ideally form an attachment at an early age and develop or learn independence from the attachment individual(s) at a later age. This is usually accomplished through a gradual weaning process, or a period of directed exposure to the environment at an increasing distance, and for longer periods of time, away from the attachment individual. Thus the processes of attachment and separation in the species' typical environment may proceed relatively smoothly with little elicitation of extreme separation anxiety. Often the behavioral development of domestic dogs living in the human environment does not proceed smoothly; abrupt shifts in living conditions from breeder or shelter to owner, constraints on the amount of time humans may have to spend with the dog, and even lack of knowledge of the very existence or importance of attachment and separation behavior all contribute to circumstances in which the normal development of separation without anxiety does not occur.

There are many early or later experiences that can increase the likelihood of a separation problem. For instance, early weaning from the dam and subsequent human handling may lead to the puppy becoming overly attached to humans. This, of course, may be rewarding to a person who has the time to spend with a friendly and affectionate puppy. All that is required for a serious separation problem to develop is for the ever-present owner to change his or her lifestyle, for example, by taking a job or otherwise leaving the dog alone more frequently or for longer durations.

Alternately, at least in some dogs, it appears that early attachment deprivation leads to the development of overattachment and subsequent separation anxiety. For example, a puppy housed at a pet shop until the age of four to five months, well past the period of primary socialization (Scott and Fuller, 1965), may attach more strongly to its owner once it is introduced into a human household. Of course, too long or too severe a period of social deprivation leads to profound loss of attachment behavior (isolation or kennel syndrome) and the exacerbation of fear responses to humans and in general (ibid.).

A common feature in the history of severe separation problems is repeated attachment and separation. Dogs lost and then found or given up by the owners to adoption agencies and then rehomed frequently attach very strongly to the new owner and have great difficulty learning to adjust to separation.

Another factor contributing to separation anxiety problems is a change in daily routine, work schedule, or environment (for example, a move to another home). These changes can cause or potentiate separation problems in young or older dogs. In several cases, dogs that learned to adapt to day-long work-related separations, which presented no problems for many years, developed a separation problem after the owner had been home much more frequently (for example, for health reasons or unemployment) for several weeks or months and then returned to the previous schedule.

Probably the most frequent reason for separation problems is the widespread ignorance among the general public, trainers, breeders, and many veterinarians that attachment and separation behavior even exists as an important behavioral system in the dog. Of the many "dog books" on the market, few even discuss the concept of social attachment and none present a useful guide to the theory and practice of preventing or treating separation-related problems. Often the "expert" attitude is to "teach him to be obedient" or not to "spoil the dog." Thus a proper and humane respect for the psychobiology of the developing dog is absent. Early separation problems arising from the lack of proper species-typical "social weaning" plus inappropriate training or punishment techniques often culminate in severe separation behavior problems, considerable animal and human suffering, and frequently in euthanasia.

FACTORS THAT DECREASE SEPARATION ANXIETY

Continuing research in animal behavior and physiology is critical for understanding pet behavior problems in general so that more effective ways may be developed for treating them and reducing the considerable animal and human suffering that presently exists. Fortunately, the existing research literature provides a theory and supporting data with which one can interpret the myriad behaviors that occur when the pet dog is separated from its owner. The knowledge that attachment and separation occur as a widespread phenomenon among animals and that a psychobiological state, loosely described as "anxiety," is elicited by particular stimuli or stimulus sequences immediately suggests a wide range of techniques for amelioration of such behavior problems. I will briefly outline some of the most effective techniques used to treat separation problems in dogs, after a brief discussion of some techniques commonly recommended by breeders and trainers.

At the outset, it is important to note that the extreme variability in the behavioral parameters of separation problems means that several or even many techniques may be effective to some degree for each particular problem. The first "law" of animal behavior therapy is that for any problem, any technique will work some of the time. Thus there are no single and simple panaceas for behavior problems. The second "law" is that any technique has potential side effects.

As discussed earlier, punishment and correction techniques often exacerbate separation problems. Obedience training is generally irrelevant; in fact, many of the cases I have observed involved dogs that had considerable obedience experience and had done well in their training classes and at home during obedience sessions. Obedience training might be effective, however, to the degree that it reduces attachment between dog and owner and facilitates social weaning. In mild cases, the interaction between dog and owner changes in such a way that the owner provides less social contact and the dog is able to tolerate separation. In these cases, obedience training is helpful, but not because the dog is any more obedient!

Another common technique described by obedience trainers is confinement—the use of a cage or crate into which the dog is placed when it is to be separated from the owner. Often the goal is for the dog to sleep, eat, and drink in the crate so that the crate acquires positive associations. Some degree of confinement is usually essential with a puppy, if only to prevent it from injuring itself in the home and reducing the extent of damage before successful elimination training and during the stage of chewing and teething. In some cases, dogs adapt readily to confinement well into adulthood or indefinitely when separated.

In other cases, the dog's attachment to contact with or proximity to the owner develops, when it is out of the crate, to such an extent that confinement when separated is not sufficient to prevent vocalization, destruction, or even elimination behavior. In these cases, the dog may not display any obvious reluctance to enter the crate when the owner leaves (not surprising, because the stimulus context is predictable and the dog may be fed for entering the crate). But after being alone for some time, it may show overt signs of separation problems. In other cases, no obvious signs of separation anxiety are ever exhibited, but the dog may develop a behavioral depression or psychosomatic response or become hyperactive when the owner returns. Usually a crate is used which allows the dog only enough room to turn around. Thus there is considerable restriction of movement, and the dog is deprived of normal levels of exercise and exploratory behavior.

Unfortunately, the confinement technique is frequently recommended for dogs that have had no early experience with confinement and have had much experience with nonconfinement. Often these dogs are strays or have been adopted from humane agencies and exhibit the separation problem soon or immediately after being rehomed. In these cases, confinement usually exacerbates the existing problem, sometimes severely.

If, instead of focusing on the specific behaviors the dog exhibits, one focuses on the general behavioral state of the dog, then the logic of an exposure technique (Marks, 1978) for treating these problems is apparent. Separation problems have many of the characteristics of phobias (for example, specific eliciting stimuli, physiological arousal), and the vast literature on treatment of phobias can be brought to bear on this problem. Exposure (desensitization) techniques have been well formulated and documented for the treatment of phobias and can be easily adapted to separation problems (Tuber, Hothersall, and Voith, 1974; Hothersall and Tuber, 1979; Tuber, Hothersall, and Peters, 1982; Borchelt and Voith, 1982). Furthermore, the identification of the dog's behavioral state as one resembling "anxiety" immediately suggests the use of a wide range of antianxiety drugs.

The general procedure for using a desensitization (gradual exposure) technique is as follows. First, it is necessary to describe in detail the behavioral sequence the dog exhibits. Second, one must characterize in detail the stimuli associated with each response in the behavioral sequence. The functions of these stimuli may be eliciting, discriminative, reinforcing, and so on. Finally, one formulates a procedure for gradually exposing the dog to the eliciting stimulus sequence such that the responses in the sequence are kept at a low intensity and are easily habituated or counterconditioned. Counterconditioning involves rewarding the dog for a response that inhibits an identified, low-level response in the problem behavior sequence. Rewards may be food, water, play, praise, or any activity that works. The procedure involves the owner catching the dog in the act of nonanxious behavior as the dog is gradually exposed to the owner's predeparture behavior and then to longer and longer absences. Some cases progress quickly and can be solved in one or two weeks. Others progress slowly and require combinations of drug and behavior therapy over several months.

The exposure technique, if done incorrectly, will work backward and make the problem worse. If the dog is exposed too quickly to the relevant stimuli it learns to anticipate the anxiety-eliciting stimuli and thus anxiety is potentiated. To increase the chances of success the owners must be taught how to anticipate and prevent potentiation. The average person can be easily taught these techniques in a discussion-demonstration format in several hours.

In some cases, the unavoidable daily work-related departure leads to a regression in progress obtained from the exposure techniques. If the regression is not too great, one needs only to manage the behavior problem until it eventually is fully treated. This means, of course, that treatment takes longer then if the owner, or someone else, can be with the dog for most or all of the time to prevent regression while the exposure treatment is in effect. If the regression caused by work departures is severe, the use of antianxiety drugs may be required.

There are many drugs available with antianxiety properties. Animal tranquilizers approved for use in companion animals are routinely used in veterinary medicine. The minor and major tranquilizers and the tricyclic antidepressants, routinely used in human medicine for anxiety or depression-related behavior problems, may also be effective for use in companion animals. There are large individual differences in the response of dogs to these drugs as a function of drug type and dosage, and it is sometimes time-consuming to find the most effective drug for a particular animal. If, however, the appropriate drug is identified, treatment for separation problems is often easy. If the animal's response when the drug is administered is one of greatly reduced anxiety, all that is required in some cases is a gradual titration of the dose over a several-week to several-month period. Slowly decreasing the drug dosage can be equivalent to a behavioral exposure technique. In some cases, drug titration and specific behavioral exposure techniques can be combined to speed the course of treatment.

OVERVIEW

Observation and description of separation-elicited behavior problems in pet dogs in the home yields a picture of separation anxiety and separation responses remarkably congruent with laboratory data regarding separation behavior in other species. Clinical animal behavior therapy can thus add to, as well as draw from, the existing scientific literature on separation behavior. The application of research findings from the fields of behavior modification, animal learning, ethology, and psychobiology, particularly when integrated with veterinary medicine, can be fruitful in solving the vast majority of these behavior problems. Of course, there is much that is not known, and research must continue. But the number of animals presently euthanised in shelters and humane agencies could be significantly reduced with proper dissemination of currently available techniques. Much of the human and animal suffering in the home environment can be ameliorated with the proper mix of basic and applied research and public education.

Katherine A. Houpt

18

Disruption of the Human–Companion Animal Bond:
Aggressive Behavior in Dogs

The bond between pets and their owners can be strong and mutually beneficial, both physically and psychologically (Katcher and Friedmann, 1980). Unfortunately, the relationship is not always beneficial. The behavior of the pet may be such that the owner is dissatisfied with it (Wilbur, 1976) and causes the animal to be banished to an outdoor pen, to be given away, or to be killed. Many animals are kept as pets, but the species that has the closest relationship with the owner, and possibly for this reason the greatest number of behavior problems, is the dog. Dogs rarely present truly abnormal behavior. In most cases that come to the attention of animal behaviorists, dogs show normal canine behavior that is inconvenient or dangerous to the owner. The majority of behavior problems that upset the pet-human relationship involve aggression, destructiveness, house soiling, and barking.

The cases discussed here were presented over a two-year period from August 1979 to August 1981 to the behavioral consultation service of the small animal clinic at Cornell University. Our goal in consulting with the owners was to improve the pet-human relationship. The objective of this study was to determine the behavior problems most likely to be presented, to find the sex and breed incidences of aggressive behavior, and to evaluate our success in attenuating aggressive behavior.

METHODS

The behavioral consultation service of the New York State College of Veterinary Medicine at Cornell University serves two groups of pet owners: those who live within a 100 mile radius of Ithaca who can bring their animals to be seen and those who live farther away, either in New York or elsewhere. The latter group is interviewed and counseled by telephone. Almost all owners have been referred to us by their own veterinarians; very few people contact us initially. To obtain as much information as possible that may be relevant to the animal's behavior, a questionnaire is used. The owners who can bring their animals to us in Ithaca are interviewed in a conference room with the veterinarian and several students. The conference room is situated in a busy office and laboratory complex. It is, therefore, possible to observe the dog's response to strangers and to compare that response with the owner's description of the dog's behavior. The owners are often unaware that barking can be a sign of aggression and that, by encouraging barking, they have encouraged aggression. The owner's reaction to misbehavior can be ascertained. The dog's soliciting of attention from the owner can also be noted. The owner is asked to demonstrate the dog's ability to obey commands. We are careful not to make any negative comments concerning the owner's treatment of the dog until all the necessary information is obtained. If the owner is told immediately that he or she should not have let the dog run free, for example, the remaining questions may not be answered openly; the owner will try to give the "correct" answer to avoid further criticism. When the history has been taken, the proper means of disciplining the dog can be demonstrated. The owner is instructed to reprimand the dog whenever it barks or growls at a person. Proper rewarding techniques are also demonstrated. We generally do not recommend food rewards but stress that petting and praise should be given as consistently for good behavior as punishment is given for bad behavior.

Telephone consultations are handled in a similar manner, but, of course, direct observation of the dog cannot be made. Whenever possible, both members of a couple are present at the consultation or on the telephone to prevent misunderstandings that may arise when the veterinarian's advice is interpreted by one spouse to another.

Before treating the dog, we try to ensure that the dog is properly restrained so that it will not endanger the public. We insist that the dog not be allowed to run free and also ask that the dog not be given away to animal shelter or to some other individual. Treatment varies with the owner, the dog, the problem, and the amount of prior training the dog has received. One third of aggressive dogs have not been obedience trained. Because obedience training requires the dog to be submissive to the owner and because it is relatively easy for most people to find an obedience class or a private instructor, we rely heavily on this method of assisting the owner to establish dominance over an aggressive dog. Castration or ovariohysterectomy is recommended for all aggressive dogs. Castration often helps to attenuate aggression if combined with obedience training and punishment of unwanted behavior immediately after return from the hospital. Failure to institute changes in the dog's behavior immediately will lead to a regression of its behavior in a few weeks or months.

There are two reasons why we nearly always recommend castration: first, reducing the male hormone, testosterone, reduces the dog's aggressiveness; and second, the possibility that the aggressive tendencies of the dog will be passed on to his offspring is eliminated. Ovariohysterectomy is recommended for similar reasons.

The owners are instructed to spend at least fifteen minutes a day doing obedience work with the dog. At first, only the person we judge to be most dominant over the dog works with the dog, but gradually everyone in the family is told to participate. The command that we emphasize is "down" because that is a submissive posture and should be encouraged. Owners are urged not to send their dogs to be trained but instead to hire a trainer to teach them to train the dog themselves. Group obedience lessons are usually not recommended unless the dog is only mildly aggressive or small. The presence of other dogs and strangers often exacerbates aggression.

An additional exercise is given to owners of territorially aggressive dogs, that is, dogs that attack visitors. Once the dog is obeying commands well and has learned down and will stay down for several minutes, the owners are told to begin working on the dog's behavior toward visitors. They should arrange for a friend or one of the family members to come to the door at a preset time while they have the dog on a down-stay about ten feet from the front door. If the dog breaks its stay when the visitor knocks or rings the doorbell, the owner should say "No! Bad dog!," command it to lie again, and praise it for doing so. The dog should then be made to do a few other commands such as sit or heel before being commanded once again to down-stay. The owners should continue practicing with the "visitor" until the dog will stay when someone is let into the house. It may take many visits before the dog learns that a ringing bell and visitors are not excuses to break a stay. Once the visitor is inside, the dog is kept at the owner's side until everyone is seated. The dog is not allowed to walk around the room sniffing and inspecting new arrivals. The reason for instructing the owners to use practice visits and visitors is that they can concentrate on the dog's behavior without the additional stress of a social occasion.

Obedience training enables the owner to reward correct behavior, but incorrect behavior must be punished so as to decrease the dog's aggressive tendencies. The owner is advised to punish all expressions of aggression such as growling or territorial barking as well as overt biting. As soon as the dog begins to growl or snap, the owner should grab it by the scruff of the neck, lift its forefeet off the ground, look it directly in the eye, and shout "Bad dog!" If verbal punishment does not suffice to inhibit the aggressive behavior, the dog should be physically punished. The owner should strike the dog hard enough to cause pain rather than simply irritating the animal with a mild strike.

As soon as the dog has stopped growling, it should be given a command such as down. The owners should praise the dog for obeying and then continue giving commands such as heel and sit. Correct performance should be praised. The purpose of this method is not only to punish the dog quickly, firmly, and consistently for every aggressive act but also to reward good behavior so that the dog learns the difference between correct and incorrect behavior.

Owners of dogs that bite them may be understandably reluctant to attempt punishing the dog. If owners are concerned that the dog will bite them, we may suggest muzzling the dog except when it is eating. We also suggest muzzling dogs that have a history of aggression toward children. For seriously aggressive dogs we prescribe megestrol acetate, 2 mg/kg for two weeks, followed by 1 mg/kg for two weeks, and 0.5 mg/kg for a final two weeks. Although megestrol acetate does not produce a permanent reduction of aggression (Hart, 1981), it does reduce aggression sufficiently for the owner to establish or reestablish control over the dog. Progestins are not recommended for intact females, but that class of dog is rarely aggressive (see results). Progestins may be used on intact males whose owners are unwilling to have the dog castrated.

We consider euthanasia the solution to some aggressive behavior problems. If the dog is not a pet but a show or commercial dog, we recommend euthanasia so that the animal will not be used for breeding. Such a dog is not a companion animal but an economic asset. We always suggest euthanasia as an option to owners of seriously aggressive dogs. Very few owners of pet dogs are willing to consider euthanasia initially. Often, however, they decide to have the dog killed when they realize how much time and effort are necessary to rehabilitate the dog. We advise owners not to leave aggressive dogs outside in a pen or tied. Dogs in those situations can act aggressively with impunity. Even if the owner punishes all instances of aggression in other circumstances, the behavior is unlikely to extinguish when the animal is free to growl, bark, and lunge when outside by itself. When confined in the house, however, the dog may become destructive. Owners often elect to have the dog euthanized when the dog is ruining their home as well as threatening them.

All of the instructions are sent to the owner in writing as well as given verbally at the consultation. The referring veterinarian is also sent a copy of the instructions.

RESULTS

In the past two years we have treated 180 cases of which 98 were aggressive. The other major categories of behavior problems were destructiveness, house soiling, and barking (Table 18.1). Table 18.2 lists the breed incidence of aggression.

Table 18.1.   TYPES OF BEHAVIOR CASES PRESENTED TO THE NEW YORK STATE
COLLEGE OF VETERINARY MEDICINE, 1979–1981

Behavior	Number	Percent
Aggression	98	54
Destructive	23	12
House soiling	29	16
Barking	10	6
Hyperactive	7	4
Miscellaneous (phobias, coprophagia, mounting)	13	8
Total	180	100

There were 105 aggressive dogs among the 98 cases because households with
more than one aggressive dog were considered as one case. The majority of the
dogs were purebred. Only 17 percent were mixed breed dogs. The breed with the
highest incidence of aggression was the springer spaniel (16 percent). The next
highest incidence was in German shepherds (11 percent). If German shepherds
and shepherd crosses are combined, the incidence is 17 percent. Doberman
pinschers are the third most likely breed to be presented with aggressive problems.

Table 18.4 indicates that the sex ratio was 69 percent male, 31 percent
female for aggressive dogs but approximately 50 percent male for other behavior
problems. More than half the females were spayed, but less than one-third the
males were castrated. Table 18.4 indicates the age distribution. The majority of
the dogs were less than five years old; the mean age was three years.

Table 18.2.   BREEDS OF AGGRESSIVE DOGS PRESENTED TO THE NEW YORK STATE
COLLEGE OF VETERINARY MEDICINE

Breed	Number	Percent
Springer spaniel	17	16
German shepherd	12	11
Doberman	5	5
Collie	4	4
Cocker spaniel	4	4
Irish setter	3	3
Great Pyrenees	3	3
Golden retriever	3	3
Mixed breed	18	17
Other breeds	36	34
Total	105	100

Table 18.3.   SEX OF DOGS PRESENTED AS AGGRESSIVE, HOUSE SOILING, OR DESTRUCTIVE

Behavior	Number	Percent
Destructive	23 dogs	
	13 females (4 spayed)	57
	10 males (2 castrated)	43
House soiling	30 dogs	
	14 females (5 spayed)	47
	16 males (2 castrated)	53
Aggressive	105 dogs	
	33 females (18 spayed)	31
	72 males (14 castrated)	69

Table 18.4.   AGES OF AGGRESSIVE DOGS

Age	Number
< 1 yr	15
1–5 yr	68
> 5 yr	18
Unknown	4
$\bar{x} = 3 \pm 0.2$ yr	

For the purpose of this study, we defined aggression according to the victim of the aggression. Table 18.5 shows the classification of aggression by victim. Most dogs were aggressive toward people (86 percent). Aggression was directed either at the owners (57 percent) or at strangers (43 percent). Of the 98 cases, follow-up is available on only 60. Table 18.7 shows the response of the dogs to treatment. Some cases have been treated too recently to determine the outcome; in others, owners failed to respond to letters and could not be reached by telephone. The mean percentage of dogs that improved was 70 percent of those for whom follow-up is available. There was no change in 12 percent and 18

TABLE 18.5.   TYPES OF AGGRESSION PRESENTED TO THE NEW YORK STATE COLLEGE OF VETERINARY MEDICINE, 1979–81

Total aggression toward people	N = 84
owners	48
strangers	36
Total intraspecific aggression	N = 14
toward dogs in household	12
strange dogs	2

Table 18.6. OUTCOME OF AGGRESSIVE CASES

	Improved		Euthanized		No Change		No Follow-up	
	No.	Percent	No.	Percent	No.	Percent	No.	Percent
Aggression toward owner	18	(38)	8	(17)	4	(8)	18	(38)
Aggression toward stranger	18	(50)	3	(8)		0	15	(42)
Aggression toward dogs	6	(43)		0	3	(21)	5	(36)

percent were euthanized. There appeared to be more improvement in those dogs that were aggressive with strangers (86 percent) than in those who were aggressive with the owner (69 percent).

DISCUSSION

The breed distribution in this sample is somewhat skewed in favor of springer spaniels (Table 18.2). Although this may partly be the result of a letter mentioning our interest in aggression in the breed in a veterinary journal (Fisher, 1981), springer spaniels do appear to have a high incidence of aggression (Pope, 1981), which is unexpected in a breed that is not traditionally considered aggressive. Whether there is a simple genetic basis for the aggression in this breed remains to be demonstrated.

Another study found German shepherds to have the highest rate of aggression of purebred dogs (Beaver, 1983), and they were our second most numerous breed. Poodles, cocker spaniels, and Doberman pinschers are the most popular breeds in the United States today. German shepherds, collies, and miniature poodles are the breeds most frequently presented to the small animal clinic of the New York State College of Veterinary Medicine, so the position of the shepherd near the top of a list of breed incidence of aggression is not surprising. The absence of poodles from the list of aggressive dogs is more surprising.

The sex ratio of aggressive dogs reflects the effects of androgens on behavior. Numerous rodent studies have confirmed that exposure of the developing brain to androgen results in a more aggressive adult animal (Moyer, 1968). The presence of circulating testosterone in the adult male stimulates expression of the potential for aggression. Castration, as discussed above, may attenuate aggression. The high proportion of castrated dogs in this study perhaps indicates that some of the dogs were castrated in an attempt to decrease aggression. We recommend castration but find that it is effective in permanently decreasing aggression only if combined with a program of firm discipline and demonstration of dominance over the dog by the owner.

The age distribution indicates that young adult dogs are most likely to be presented as aggressive. The critical periods of dogs' development are neonatal (1 to 2 weeks), transitional (third week), socialization (4 to 13 weeks), and juvenile (12 weeks to puberty) (Scott and Marston, 1950). In our experience, social maturity in the dog is not reached at the time of physiological puberty, but rather at 18 months to 2 years. At this age dogs appear to attempt to establish themselves as the highest ranking animal in their social group. The owner may be the victim when the dog tries to become the alpha animal in the "pack" that may include humans as well as dogs.

The statistics on improvement indicate that aggression against strangers is more easily attenuated than aggression against owners. This may be true or may indicate that owners are more concerned about aggression against themselves. The treatment for aggression against strangers is prevention of the problem by not allowing the dog outside unless it is on the leash and training the dog not to rush to the door when someone comes but rather to lie quietly.

The pet-human relationship is seriously disturbed by behavior problems. We attempt to alleviate the problems, but our success is only moderate. We do reeducate the owners to prevent problems arising with the next pet.

Jane Tate

19

Human-Bear Interactions: Profile and Perspective

The increasing human population and its demands upon the environment have far-reaching effects extending beyond habitat destruction and threatened species. Of growing concern to many scientists is the modification of behavior of wildlife species as the result of human infringement upon their domain. This report focuses on interactions between black bears (*Ursus americanus*) and visitors in the Great Smoky Mountains National Park (GSMNP or park), describing not only the atypical behavior that transpires but also examining why encounters that may involve bear aggression have continued despite inherent risks to both species.

Black bears are generally shy, crepuscular animals (active during the beginning and end of the day), rarely seen by humans. They once roamed freely throughout much of the United States. Now, especially in the East, they have primarily been relegated to sanctuaries—national parks and forests. Millions of people flock annually to these same sanctuaries to escape the pressures of an urban existence, to commune with nature, and to interact with wildlife. Yet by their very numbers they have an impact upon the land, and through their littering and ignorance they often destroy what they have come to enjoy (Matthews, 1975; Curry-Lindahl, 1972). A result of this influx of visitors has been atypical behavior by some black bears. They have learned to associate people, their camping equipment, and their vehicles with food, a process that is reinforced by the willingness of many persons to offer them handouts. These bears, euphemistically known as panhandlers, forsake their usually shy and secretive ways to beg along roadsides, raid picnic tables, break into coolers, and rip open backpacks. Panhandliing behavior is not limited to bears; however, their size and strength coupled with the general naivete of many visitors creates a potentially hazardous situation. Such interactions have caused perennial problems of property damage and personal injury.

BASIS FOR PANHANDLING IN BEARS

The propensity for panhandling in bears can best be understood by examining certain facets of their natural history and evolution. During the early Miocene (about 25 million years ago) bears diverged from the Miacidae, a family of small, carnivorous, arboreal mammals (Colbert, 1955). Like their ancestors, black bears have remained forest dwellers, but their diets have changed. Though still classified as carnivores, black bears are now basically opportunistic omnivores, consuming any food item they encounter. Pruitt (1974) suggests that this transition in diet may have resulted from more stability in their environment. In the Smokies their normal diet consists primarily of vegetation with most protein coming from insects or carrion (Beeman and Peltoon, 1980); their diet is protein-deficient (Bacon, 1973).

Another relevant factor is the plasticity which they exhibit in their sociality with conspecifics. Although primarily solitary animals, bears are known to aggregate at clumped resources whether these are berry patches, fishing streams, garbage dumps, or along roadsides in national parks (Tate-Eagar and Pelton, 1979; Rogers, 1977; Egbert and Stokes, 1976; Stonorov and Stokes, 1972; Craighead and Craighead, 1971; Hornocker, 1962). Apparently this plasticity also extends to humans. Jonkel (1978) states that in interspecific interactions, bears seem to defer to humans as "super bears." Furthermore, the ecological niche of black bears is similar to that of *Homo sapiens*, and they are usually the highest ranking nonhuman species in their communities.

Finally, bears possess both a genetic and a learned ability to deal with environmental change and to use whatever resources become available (Jonkel, 1978; Burghardt and Burghardt, 1972). They have a high degree of cephalization and are presumably quite intelligent (Hemmer, 1978; Bacon, 1973). Papez (1929) reports that the brain of bears is unique among carnivores, being remarkably similar to that of the primates. Their sensory abilities are keen. Bacon (1973) states that they have excellent form discrimination as well as color vision. Such abilities likely contribute to their remarkable adaptability. Unlike other carnivores such as wolves (*Canis* spp.) and cougars (*Felis concolor*), black bears appear capable of coexisting with humans and have maintained viable and stable populations in the eastern forests of this country.

THE HUMAN ELEMENT IN PANHANDLING

These traits may make black bears amenable to becoming panhandlers, but people play an important and undeniable role in their acquisition of the habit. Basically, the contributing human behaviors fall into two categories, which I have labeled *passive neglect* and *active enticement*. Passive neglect can be viewed as the seemingly inevitable effect of people bringing food into wild areas. It is unfortunate yet true that wherever they go, people leave their trash behind. In picnic areas and campgrounds not all refuse makes its way to garbage cans. In fact, many well-meaning people consider it proper to toss apple cores and watermelon rinds to the edge of campsites. After all, they are biodegradable! Campfires are often the disposal site for paper plates, the residual odors from which permeate the surrounding area with the smell of food. Merrill (1978) reports significantly fewer bear incidents in Glacier National Park at camp-grounds allowing only self-contained stoves and prohibiting open fires. Even when everything is properly discarded in trash cans, the attractant odors remain. Furthermore, "bear-proof" garbage containers, though a definite improvement over standard models, are easily "robbed" by these strong, intelligent beasts. These problems are compounded by the design of national parks. For aesthetic and practical reasons, people congregate in the same areas, thereby increasing litter and the likelihood of attracting bears.

The more obvious avenue through which people share responsibility for panhandling is active enticement. Feeding bears in national parks is a common occurrence and can be considered a principal component of human-bear inter-actions. It occurs despite road signs, brochures, and interpretive programs attest-ing to the illegality of such activities. Indeed Bryan and Jansson (1973), in a survey conducted in Canada, reported that many respondents said that they would feed bears regardless of regulations. In a survey of visitors in the GSMNP, the most frequently given response as to why people were injured by bears was that they fed them (Burghardt et al., 1972). Similarly, most respondents in Shenandoah National Park knew that visitor carelessness caused most bear problems (Baptiste, Whelan, and Frary, 1979). Moreover, these authors reported that althhough most visitors were eager to see bears, they were unwilling to risk property damage or injury to do so. Though not an educational experience that many would advocate, Pelton, Scott, and Burghardt (1976) found that persons who had been involved in bear incidents had a more realistic view of these animals. The attitudes of people as reflected in these studies illustrate the complexity of problems encountered by National Park Service (NPS) personnel in their efforts to prevent feeding of bears. Ironically, the signs and literature advising visitors not to feed may through the power of suggestion have just the opposite effect. People are generally naive in their interactions with bears, regarding them more as household pets than as wild animals capable of inflicting injury (Tate-Eagar and Peton, 1979).

HUMAN-BEAR INTERACTIONS IN GSMNP

In an attempt to provide a scientific basis from which to approach these problems, an ethological investigation of human-bear interactions was conducted in the Great Smoky Mountains National Park from 1976 through 1978. This park has high visitor use (U.S. Department of Interior, 1976) and a high population density of black bears (Eagar, 1977; Pelton and Marcum, 1975). Objectives of the study included documenting the behavioral elements present in human-bear interactions; determining whether certain human actions were more likely to lead to ursid aggression; assessing the influence of setting factors upon the likelihood of agonistic behavior; and evaluating the effects of panhandling upon the normal behavior patterns of black bears.

PROCEDURES

Observations, using both written and photographic methods, were recorded along roadsides, in picnic areas, and in campgrounds. Data collection was concentrated during daylight hours when interactions were most likely to occur. In addition, the research team occasionally remained throughout the night at areas frequented by panhandlers to monitor activities—or lack thereof—of these animals. For each panhandling session, setting factors, types of aggression, and precipitating factors were recorded.

Bears were divided into two groups based upon the number of sessions. Group I represented those who panhandled regularly and were noted in more than fifteen sessions; Group II consisted of infrequent panhandlers. Comparisons of various parameters allowed assessment of behavioral changes as bears interacted more often with people.

RESULTS

A summary of results of different facets of the study makes possible development of a profile of human-bear interactions. Appropriate references are provided for those who may desire more details.

GENERAL RESULTS

There were 392 data observations of 33 different bears; 172 (43.9 percent) involved at least one aggressive act. Ten bears, all of whom were infrequent panhandlers, were never observed exhibiting agonistic behavior. Of 624 aggressive acts recorded, 37 involved actual physical contact and 10 resulted in injuries.

The panhandling segment of the population showed a preponderance of older females and younger males. The sex ratio was nearly equal at 16 males to 14 females (with three cubs of undetermined sex); however, from a total of 20 adults, 14 (70 percent) were females.

TYPES OF AGONISTIC BEHAVIOR

Seven categories of agonistic behavior were recorded (Table 19.1). Similar to the classifications used by Pruitt (1974), these represented varying intensities from threat postures to actions capable of inflicting injury. Each type was assigned a numeric value based upon its apparent severity, and the level of aggression for each session was obtained by summing the totals of all acts and adding two points each time physical contact was made.

Frequency tabulations showed that the blow vocalization and charge were the most likely types of aggression to occur (Table 19.1). Conversely, the bipedal swat, running toward a crowd, and low moan vocalization together accounted for less than 6 percent of the total (Tate and Pelton, 1981).

PRECIPITATING FACTORS

Rarely was an aggressive act directed toward visitors that was not apparently attributable to their inappropriate behavior (Table 19.2). Whenever more than

Table 19.1. TYPES OF AGONISTIC BEHAVIOR EXHIBITED BY PANHANDLING BLACK BEARS IN THE GREAT SMOKY MOUNTAINS NATIONAL PARK, THEIR NUMERIC VALUE BASED UPON SEVERITY, AND THEIR FREQUENCY OF OCCURRENCE

Description	Rank by Severity	Numeric Value	Frequency of Occurrence
Low moan vocalization	1	1	7
Blow vocalization	2	2	257
Running toward crowd	3	3	8
Bipedal swat	4.5	4	22
Quadripedal swat	4.5	4	45
Charge	6	5	234
Bite-snap	7	6	51
Physical contact made		2	

Table 19.2. APPARENT PRECIPITATING FACTORS FOR URSID AGGRESSION AND THEIR FREQUENCY OF OCCURRENCE, GSMNP

Precipitating Factor	Frequency of Occurrence
Crowding	244
Photographing-crowding	67
Other	49
Another bear	40
Harrassing-crowding	30
NPS personnel	29
Petting	27
Photograph kneeling-crowding	23
Petting-crowding	19
Harassing	16
No apparent reason	16
Combination of three factors	14
Handfeeding-crowding	13
Handfeeding	11
Photograph kneeling	11
Photographing	6
Cessation of feeding	3
Toss feeding	3
Toss feeding-crowding	2
Photograph with flash-crowding	1

one factor contributed, both were recorded. Although most categories are self-explanatory, a few warrant further elucidation. Since bears recognized NPS uniforms and vehicles (Tate-Eagar and Pelton, 1979; Wormser, 1966) and were frequently chased away or trapped by NPS personnel, all aggression directed toward them was included as a separate category. Intraspecific aggression occurred often when more than one bear was panhandling, and this type of aggression was cataloged under "Another Bear." Finally, all factors that were peculiar to a certain session were combined under "Other."

Frequency tabulations showed that crowding by visitors was the most common precipitator of ursid aggression (Table 19.2) accounting for nearly 40 percent of all acts. If those double factors of which crowding was a component were included, 64 percent of all ursid aggression could be attributed wholly or partially to visitors approaching too closely to the animals. Conversely, toss feeding or photographing from a distance seldom led to agonistic behavior, and less that 3 percent of the aggressive acts occurred with no apparent provocation (Tate and Pelton, 1981).

Examination of a contingency table revealed that certain visitor actions were likely to result in particular ursid responses (Table 19.3). Crowding was the most common precipitator of all aggression except the bipedal swat. Although the

Table 19.3.   FREQUENCY TABULATIONS OF TYPES OF AGGRESSION BY PRECIPITATING FACTORS FOR PANHANDLING BLACK BEARS, GSMNP

Precipitating Factors	Low moan vocali-zation	Blow vocali-zation	Running toward crowd	Bipedal swat	Quadri-pedal swat	Charge	Bite-snap
Crowding	4	96	7	1	19	102	15
Photographing-crowding		17	1		4	41	4
Other	2	29		1	1	15	1
Another bear		35			1	4	
Harassing-crowding		8		1	3	15	3
NPS personnel	1	25				3	
Petting		3		6	6	4	8
Photograph kneeling -crowding		8			4	11	
Petting-crowding		3				3	13
Harassing		8		5	1	2	
No apparent reason		8			1	7	
Three factors		2		3	2	5	2
Handfeeding-crowding		6		1	1	2	3
Handfeeding		4		2	1	3	1
Photograph kneeling		1		1		9	
Photographing		2				3	1
Cessation of feeding		1		1		1	
Toss feeding		1				2	
Toss feeding-crowding					1	1	
Photograph with flash-crowding						1	

bipedal swat occurred only 22 times, petting and harassing were its usual causes. Petting alone or in combination with crowding most often led to the bite-snap. Photographing while kneeling resulted in agonistic behavior only 11 times; yet in 9 of these the result was a charge (Tate and Pelton, 1981).

CONTACT AGGRESSION

Less than 6 pecent of all aggressive acts resulted in actual physical contact. Three types of aggression—the bipedal swat, the quadripedal swat, and the bite-snap—led to contact, with crowding, petting, and a combination thereof precipitating 78 percent of these incidents (Tate and Pelton, 1981).

DIFFERENCES IN GROUP RESPONSES

Group I bears, those on whom more than fifteen sessions were recorded, accounted for 81.4 percent of all aggression. Group II bears, however, had higher aggression indexes (mean number of aggressive acts per session). Males were more aggressive than females, with this difference being even more pronounced for Group I. None of these differences was statistically significant (Mann Whitney U test, $p > 0.02$). The mean latency (time in minutes from the initiation of the session to the performance of the first aggressive act) was significantly greater for Group I (Mann Whitney U test, $u = 29$, $p < 0.05$) (Tate-Eagar and Pelton, 1979).

SETTING FACTORS

Setting factors that may have influenced the outcome of these human-bear interactions were recorded (Tate, 1979). Sex and age of the individual bears were also used in some analyses. Multiple regression analysis showed that the duration of the session and the number of feeding incidents were the best predictors of aggression (Table 19.4). A correlation matrix was computed to facilitate interpretation of the regression results (Table 19.5).

Table 19.4. MULTIPLE REGRESSION ANALYSIS DEPICTING THE RELATIVE IMPORTANCE OF SETTING FACTORS IN PREDICTING AGGRESSION DURING HUMAN-BEAR INTERACTIONS, GSMNP*

Step	Variable Entered	R^2	F Value for Entire Model	Probability for Entire Model
1	Duration	0.178	84.33	.0001
2	Feeding incidents	0.206	50.19	.0001
3	Temperature	0.215	35.29	.0001
4	Age	0.222	29.58	.0001
	Sex (replacing temperature)	0.235	29.72	.0001
5	Temperature	0.245	24.93	.0001
6	Weather	0.247	21.05	.0001
7	Time	0.250	18.19	.0001
8	Distance	0.251	15.98	.0001
9	Number of visitors	0.251	14.22	.0001

*The F-values and probabilities of the individual variables in each of the models were not included because of space limitations; however, it should be noted that through the five-variable model, all individual variables had a significance level of $p < 0.05$.

Table 19.5. CORRELATION MATRIX (AND PROBABILITY VALUES) FOR ALL SETTING FACTORS IN PANHANDLING SESSIONS OF BLACK BEARS, GSMNP*

	Sex	Age	Date	Time	Dura-tion	Dis-tance	Temper-ature	Wea-ther	Num-ber of Visi-tors	Feed-ing Inci-dents	Level of Aggres-sion
Sex	1.00	-0.69	0.10	0.23	0.02	0.22	0.02	-0.09	0.14	-0.03	0.05
		.00	.06	.00	.75	.00	.75	.08	.00	.53	.35
Age		1.00	0.18	-0.05	0.02	-0.15	-0.01	0.14	-0.06	0.08	0.11
			.00	.31	.68	.00	.88	.01	.25	.13	.03
Date			1.00	0.44	0.11	-0.03	-0.21	0.19	-0.13	0.05	0.00
				.00	.04	.52	.00	.00	.01	.37	.97
Time				1.00	-0.05	0.30	-0.13	0.18	-0.20	-0.11	-0.05
					.36	.00	.01	.00	.00	.04	.37
Duration					1.00	0.10	0.03	-0.03	0.14	0.64	0.42
						.04	.62	.59	.01	.00	.00
Distance						1.00	-0.04	-0.04	-0.15	-0.02	-0.01
							.49	.39	.00	.61	.79
Temperature							1.00	-0.43	0.23	0.10	0.13
								.00	.00	.04	.01
Weather								1.00	-0.02	0.00	0.01
									.66	.98	.81
Number of visitors									1.00	0.31	0.18
										.00	.00
Feeding incidents										1.00	0.40
											.00
Level of aggression											1.00

*Computer coding for these setting variables can be found in Tate, 1979.

ACTIVITY PATTERNS

Panhandling bears exhibit atypical activity patterns, having become much more diurnal. Black bears are normally crepuscular with peaks of activity at 0800 and 1800 hours (Garshelis, 1978); however, the distribution of 406 observations of roadside panhandlers (excluding recorded sessions) was trimodal with peaks at 1800–1900, 1000–1100, and 1400–1500. Similar trends were reported by Barnes and Bray (1967) for panhandlers in Yellowstone National Park.

PROFILE OF INTERACTIONS

These data can now be incorporated with information from field notes and movie films to provide generalized scenarios of what transpires in typical human-bear interactions. If the number of visitors is small and there is no feeding, bears may simply lie at the edge of vegetative cover. Despite an aura of excitement and much photographing, most people maintain an appropriate distance. As word of the bear's presence travels, the crowd increases, and eventually someone tosses food. Social facilitation soon results in more feeding, and the bear approaches the crowd. The duration of the session is positively correlated with the number of visitors present and the amount of feeding. As these increase, the atmosphere changes: the noise level rises, visitors rush about, the bear is often crowded or completely surrounded, and people become bolder in their behavior. The bear may "warn" the visitors by threatening postures or vocalizations, but these usually are unheeded. The longer the session endures, the greater is the likelihood of ursid aggression. When the situation becomes too anxiety-laden, the bear retreats and terminates the interaction. How experienced the bear is at panhandling has a definite influence on the length and nature of the session. A "professional" accustomed to interacting with people is more tolerant and panhandles longer. An inexperienced bear who has not learned what to expect is more likely to behave aggressively or to cease panhandling in a shorter time.

Besides the general mood of a panhandling session, there are also specific, rather predictable responses to particular stimuli. The principal consideration is distance; anytime an activity is performed so close to bears that their individual space is violated, the result is likely to be aggression. When bears are photographed from afar, there is no apparent response. But if a visitor kneels near a bear to take a photograph, he is likely to be charged. The overwhelming desire of many people to be photographed near a bear often results in their being the target of ursid aggression. It is not the actual photographing but the crowding that accompanies such pursuits that precipitates agonistic behavior. The number of feeding incidents is a good predictor of levels of aggression yet paradoxically feeding per se rarely precipitates an aggressive act. Having offered food to bears, people often seem to expect something in return and may approach too closely or attempt to pet them. Other visitors may harass the animals, which increases the bears' anxiety level and may hasten aggression or retreat. Males are more likely to come greater distances from cover than females. Because of their more aggressive nature and larger size, they are perhaps less intimidated by humans ("the super bears"). A similar pattern is found between age and distance, with the older (presumably larger and more experienced) bears being more willing to leave the security of cover. There is, however, an inverse relationship between crowd size and distance from cover. As the crowd becomes larger, the bear is more reluctant to approach.

DISCUSSION

What transpires in a panhandling session can be considered the result of mutual conditioning, with both people and bears influencing each other's behavior. People use positive reinforcement (food) while bears rely on negative reinforcement (aggression). Yet problems result because the two species have different perceptions of the situation. To bears, panhandling represents the end; they are simply exploiting a new food resource and not seeking domestication. For visitors, feeding is merely a means of gaining closer contact with these wild animals, perhaps to satisfy a primal desire in a mechanized world. Steinhart (1980), describing how feeding has historically had symbolic meanings among men, states that modern man by offering food to wild animals may be trying to capture some of their spirit, a notion that is increasingly romanticized by an urban existence.

There is for bears an approach-avoidance conflict inherent in panhandling. This classic motivational concept provides a useful vehicle for analyzing their behavior. (The reader is referred to Cofer and Appley, [1967], for a discussion of conflict theory). Their attraction to food is countered by historic avoidance of humans, and they frequently vacillate between approaching the crowd and retreating toward cover. Such behavior is especially pronounced in infrequent panhandlers and during the initial stages of acquiring the habit. Food provides strong positive reinforcement, and bears endure much stress to obtain it. This finding is is even further substantiated by the alteration of their normal activity patterns to include those times when visitors are more likely to be present and panhandling more productive. The invasion of individual space that is so prevalent in panhandling produces anxiety and fear (terms used here in their motivational context without implying the subjective feelings that may or may not accompany them). Often a threshold is reached at which the negative aspects of the situation outweigh the positive. At this point the bear either becomes aggressive or ceases the interaction, behaviors that are consistent with the "fight or flight" theories of animal spacing (McBride, 1971). Moreover, this threshold is variable in a manner reminiscent of Huxley's (1934) "elastic disc." It is dependent upon the psychological and physiological states of the animal (Leyhausen, 1971) as well as upon what transpires in the panhandling session.

One final—and perhaps overriding—point should be made in discussing ursid behavior. It is the incredible restraint practiced by the bears. Although superficially the number of aggressive acts seems high (624), only 37 resulted in contact, and only 10 of those in injuries (scratches and bites). Analysis of movie films indicated that bears were capable of making contact whenever they chose because of their quickness and agility coupled with the temporary tonic immobility of the visitors, who were surprised at being the target of ursid aggression. Frame-by-frame analysis of films further illustrated this restraint. One bear merely rested clenched teeth against a girl's bare leg rather than biting. Another, with his paw raised into swatting position, slowly lowered it to the ground rather than scratching a man's arm.

This proof of bears' restraint is consistent with accepted ideas that animals will avoid fighting and rely upon threat postures whenever possible (Barash, 1977; Ewer, 1968), but the extent of restraint in bears' behavior is astounding. In essence they are using their entire agonistic repertoire merely to threaten—as a means of communicating to people that they are behaving inappropriately.

Kummer (1971) states that at close range social stimuli become so powerful that communication becomes compulsive, that crowding carries a constant provocation to react. Perhaps it is the frequent crowding of bears by visitors that has resulted in so many aggressive acts, especially since that is one form of communication apparently understood by humans and is effective at achieving the desired result of regaining (at least temporarily) the bear's individual space.

But what of the people? What motivates them to continue these interactions even after witnessing ursid aggression or injury? Perhaps some of the answers lie in understanding how the general public views wildlife. Debates on the inherent values of other animals are not new; they have surfaced many times throughout history from Aristotle to Descartes to Schweitzer. Petulla (1980) states that historically the dominant cultural value of wildlife in this country has been exploitive, and Matthews (1975) contends that television and the tourist trade are two of the greatest debasers of human attitudes toward wildlife today. Other authors have also recently tried to evaluate and categorize feelings prevalent in our society (Dasmann, 1981; Hendee and Schoenfeld, 1973; Curry-Lindahl, 1972). The International Union for Conservation of Nature and Natural Resources (1963) and the World Wildlife Fund (1967) have published declarations on the subject. Perhaps the most extensive study was provided by Kellert (1980b) in which he listed the attitudes toward wildlife as follows: naturalistic, ecologistic, humanistic, moralistic, scientistic, aesthetic, utilitarian, dominionistic, negativistic, and neutralistic. Certain of these attitudes were observed in the ways people interacted with bears. The most obvious was the humanistic category, defined by Kellert as "strong affection for individual animals, principally pets. Regarding wildlife, focus is on large, attractive animals with strong anthropomorphic associations" (p.33). A principal mode of interaction with bears was to regard them as pets. Visitors pictured themselves as temporary caretakers, frequently pursuing this role through one of its most basic avenues—feeding. Parents encouraged children to pose for photographs standing next to the bears as if they were family dogs. People also expressed affection by attempting to pet animals. And indeed the bears seem harmless enough, standing on the roadside eating doughnuts. Their appearance often seems so anthropomorphic that it is difficult to think of them as wild animals. There is prevalent in our society what I call the "teddy-bear syndrome." From childhood we are exposed to stuffed bears in the stories of Goldilocks, Smokey the Bear, Yogi and Boo-Boo, Gentle Ben, and Paddington. It is little wonder that these images prevail when visitors encounter panhandling bears.

The naturalistic and aesthetic attitudes, though difficult to distinguish between, were also present in human-bear interactions. Kellert (1980) states that "observation and personal involvement with wildlife are the keys to the naturalistic interest in the outdoors" (p.33) and describes the aesthetic attitude as being concerned with "the artistic merit and beauty of animals or their allegorical appeal as emblematic of particular meanings" (p.34). Besides those people who fed the bears or treated them as pets, there were others present during panhandling sessions who merely watched quietly or photographed from a distance. They seemed to realize that these bears were not pets but wild animals. One couple told me that they had been coming to the Smokies on vacation for several years just to sit quietly and watch the bears. To many people, black bears have become the symbol of the eastern wilderness, a reminder of the lifestyle of an earlier era, and an avenue through which they can temporarily or symbolically experience some of its charm.

The dominionistic attitude was most often reflected by visitors harassing bears. Kellert says this embodies "satisfactions derived from the mastery and control of animals . . . expressions of prowess, skill, strength, and not unusually, masculinity . . . the human ability to confront wildness and render it submissive" (p. 34). Abuse of the animal—either physical or psychological—is the unifying element of harassment as defined in this study. It can take many forms: holding food just out of reach and tantalizing the animals, attempting to feed nonfood items such as Polaroid backings or empty bags, tossing sticks or stones, pouring soft drinks on a bear's head or coat, or (unbelievably) trying to lassoo a bear. Visitors exhibiting such behaviors were obviously seeking to establish their dominance over these bears and thereby hoping to enhance their images among other visitors. Interestingly, most harassment was shown by males.

THE DUAL PURPOSE OF NATIONAL PARKS: A DILEMMA

At the heart of this matter is the dual purpose of our national parks; they were created not only for the recreation and enjoyment of the people but also for the conservation of the "scenery . . . and the wildlife therein, and to provide for the enjoyment of the same in such a manner . . . as will leave them unimpaired for the enjoyment of future generations" (16 USCongress 1–18[f], 1964). Often these two aims are in direct conflict, and soon the decision must be made as to which shall take priority. Swanson (1978) states that the most serious wildlife problem today may be the maintenance of large predators while accommodating an increasing number of human visitors. In Glacier National Park, an integrated management program of visitor education, temporary restriction of hiking and camping, removal of unnatural food, and direct control of bears was apparently successful in limiting grizzly-human interactions (Martinka, 1974). It is obvious that such comprehensive programs are essential if we are to limit wildlife-human encounters, but these particular management actions are not always feasible.

Most of the observations in this study were recorded at overlooks along U.S. 441, the only road that passes through the park. Obviously, the NPS cannot restrict travel there (or at least would not likely be willing to do so). Removal of panhandling bears may temporarily alleviate some of these problems, yet to do so is like treating the symptoms rather than the disease. During this study, when bears were moved from a prime panhandling site, others frequently replaced them. Traditional management techniques may no longer be effective. Creative solutions based on scientific studies are the hope for the future, and education of the general public is an essential ingredient if any program is to succeed.

Indeed human-wildlife interactions have global implications. How often have we seen pictures taken in African parks of cheetahs standing on the hood of a Land Rover curiously staring at the occupants? As the human population continues to increase and the battle for land becomes more intense, will national parks be transformed into public playgrounds or become little more than zoos without bars? Will those species that can coexist with humans lose behavioral integrity and become even more atypical while those that are unable to tolerate our presence become threatened or extinct? And what of threatened and endangered species? Are these, as Ripley and Lovejoy (1978) claim, merely the penultimate stages in a process through which genetic and behavioral pathologies of animals make their disappearance inevitable without human intervention? Wildlife biologists must take new approaches that reconcile both the needs of humans and other animals while maintaining the environment; we must manage human activites as well as wildlife populations (Dasmann, 1981; Todd, 1980). Perhaps by scientifically and philosophically addressing such problems now, we can learn how to maintain viable wildlife populations "unimpaired for the enjoyment of future generations."

Bear-human contact in national parks

Peter L. Borchelt, Randall Lockwood,
Alan M. Beck, and Victoria L. Voith

20

Dog Attack Involving Predation on Humans

Recent studies have indicated that dog bites are a major medical problem, affecting millions of people each year (Beck, 1981a; Beck, Loring, and Lockwood, 1975; Harris, Imperato, and Oken, 1974). Children are the most common victims of reported bites, with nearly 2 percent of children five to nine years of age bitten annually (Beck, 1981a). Although only a small portion of bites is reported (Beck, 1981a; Hanna and Selby, 1981), that rate among children exceeds the combined rate of all reported childhood diseases. Aggression, including severe bites, by dogs toward owners usually is not reported, but the incidence is high. The most common complaint of dog owners who consult with animal behaviorists about their pets' behavior problems is aggressive behavior toward people (Voith, 1979a; 1980a; 1981c; 1983; Borchelt, 1982; see Voith and Houpt, this volume).

The recent resurgence of dog rabies, especially along the U.S.–Mexican border, has increased public concern about dog bites. It is not often appreciated, however, that deaths caused by bites of nonrabid, owned dogs are more common in the United States than deaths from rabies transmitted by any species.

Human deaths directly attributable to dog attack (not rabies) are relatively rare. The victim profile in these cases is different from that for dog bite in general. In Winkler's (1977) survey of 11 cases of human deaths from dog attack, 9 were infants, one was an elderly woman, and one an adolescent girl.

This report describes two fatalities and one near-fatality. All three incidents involved attacks by groups of dogs. Pack attacks account for less than 1 percent of reported nonfatal bites (Beck, Loring, and Lockwood, 1975) and 18 percent of fatal attacks reported by Winkler. In all three of the cases analyzed here there was some consumption of tissue from the victim. This phenomenon has not been reported in previous surveys. The victims in two of these incidents were healthy, adolescent males, whereas the typical victim of fatal dog attacks in previous reports has been an infant. In two of these cases we were able to examine most of the animals involved in the attack and observe them under conditions simulating those that may have elicited or contributed to the attack.

CASE 1

This case involved a near-fatal attack by a group of at least eleven dogs on an eleven-year-old boy (referred to as R). Information was obtained from interviews with the boy, his parents, eyewitnesses, affidavits, and observation of the animals involved.

On the afternoon of April 24, 1980, R and another boy were playing in an open sandy area flanked by woods and fields several hundred yards from a residential area in a small town. They and other children frequently played in this area. About fifteen minutes after the boys arrived, they heard barking. The victim later described the sounds as "baying, as if the dogs were chasing something." The boys had heard reports that others had been chased by dogs in this area. The boys became frightened and climbed a tree. After a few minutes they descended and ran toward a hole they had been digging. They saw a few dogs emerge from the woods and run toward them. Both boys ran. R's companion tripped and fell while R continued to run. The dogs passed the fallen boy, who remained still, and pursued R. One animal jumped, biting him at the waist. Then the other dogs joined the attack. The second boy, who had been bypassed, observed R alternately running and being dragged by the dogs. The attack continued for an estimated three to five minutes. As R weakened, he lay still. The dogs laid down around him, growling and biting him when he moved. R said he watched one dog eat a chunk of flesh, but reported that he felt no pain.

A young man drove his car into the area and "saw a pack of dogs ripping something apart." It was not until he was closer that he realized it was a boy. The victim's clothes had been torn off, with the exception of one shoe. The young man chased the dogs away and placed R in his car, which had become stuck in sand. He sent the second boy for help. Soon R's father arrived with a truck. The dogs returned and threatened both men by growling and lunging at them. The dogs were eventually chased away, and R was taken to a hospital.

R's injuries were described as multiple, complicated, dirty, ragged lacerations all over the face, ears, neck, axilla, arms, trunk, groin, thighs, and back. Arteries and veins were exposed in the left axilla, and the skin of the arm showed multiple, almost circumferential, ragged lacerations. The right and left trunk were lacerated down to the fascia. Muscle mass was missing from several areas of his body.

Based on descriptions by witnesses of the attack and by local residents, twelve dogs living at a sixty-acre industrial site 2.7 kilometers from the site of the attack were implicated in the incident. These dogs (5 males, 7 females), predominantly German shepherd–mixed breeds, were owned by a resident of the property. The owners and some of the other residents of the area reported that sometimes some of the dogs were friendly and playful. Reports by other people indicated that the dogs had chased, growled at, and bitten people and that, as a group, they commonly roamed both on and off the property. Following impoundment at a local shelter, most of the dogs were identified by R, his father, and the young man as having participated in the attack.

CASE 2

This case involved a fatal attack by as many as eight dogs on a fourteen-year-old boy. Information about this case comes from local police and coroner's reports. The animals involved were not available to us for observation.

On December 28, 1980, the boy, K, was reported missing in a rural area in the Midwest. The next day his body was found in a brush pile about 200 meters from a road and 300 meters from the nearest house. There were no witnesses to the incident, but the condition of the body, pawprints in the area and other information led police to the conclusion that death was caused by attack by a pack of dogs.

The following events were known to have occurred. At about noon on December 28, K left home on his motorcycle to play football with his friends. On his way to town he passed the car of two local men who were driving home after hunting in the area. The men followed K until he pulled over to the side of the road near the W house. As the men drove past, they saw several dogs that had been lying in the yard near the house jump up and start barking. The owners of the dogs were not home. Around 12:25, four local residents drove by the house and observed the boy's motorcycle parked on the side of the road. They did not see him or any of the dogs. The boy was reported missing that evening, and the motorcycle was found to be out of gas. K was known to have borrowed gas previously from Mr. W. It also was known that K was afraid of the dogs. The area was searched that night and the following day.

The next day, clothing was found in a field near the W house, and the body was found in a nearby brush pile. The boy was nude except for a sock on the right foot and a shoe and sock on the left. A portion of muscle was missing from the buttocks and both sides of the legs; the bones of the ischeum, both femurs, and the left tibia and fibula were exposed. There were also multiple puncture wounds in the neck, clavical area, arms, and torso. Dog hair matching that of at least one of the W dogs was found on the body. Clothing was found in the field, and pieces of clothing were found in the yard of the W house near where the dogs were housed. Mr. W had previously reported that the dogs had K's cap.

From prints in the field, it was concluded that the boy had circled a telephone pole opposite the house in an attempt to evade the dogs and had then run to the brush pile, the only source of protection in the area. From marks in the field and the distribution of shreds of clothing, it was evident that he had been pulled to the ground at several places. He had not been dragged. The attack apparently had ceased when he crawled head first into the brush pile; no bite marks were on his feet. The cause of death was officially entered as hemorrhagic shock and cold exposure.

According to police reports, eight dogs lived at the W residence. It was later discovered that one had been traded for a sack of feed on the afternoooon following the incident. The owner said he was in the process of getting rid of the dogs because he could no longer afford to feed them. There were reports that workmen had previously been bitten on or near the W property by one or more of the dogs and that Mr. W's son had also been bitten. The dogs were reported to have chased cars and motorcycles on numerous occasions.

At the coroner's inquest, a local hunter reported that he had seen several of W's dogs chasing a deer at about 11:00 A.M., approximately one hour before the incident appeared to have taken place. He indicated that the dogs had the deer down but that it had escaped. Police reports described all of the dogs as "lean" and at least one of them as "mean."

CASE 3

This case involved a fatal attack on an eighty-one-year-old invalid woman by six dogs. Information in this case comes from police and coroner's reports, interviews with the victim's son, neighbors, SPCA officials, and our observation and examination of the animals involved (Figures 20.1 and 20.2).

On January 23, 1981, Mrs. L was attacked and severely injured by dogs that lived in her home in a large eastern city. She died from her injuries the next day.

For the previous year and a half she had been cared for by her fifty-one-year-old son, M. Mrs. L had suffered a stroke and was usually confined to one room. M had brought the dogs with him when he moved in. Because the dogs barked and growled at her, they were separated from Mrs. L by a plywood barrier separating her room from the rest of the house.

On the afternoon of January 23, M and a friend left the house for about one hour. When they returned, they found the barrier down and Mrs. L on the floor in a corner of her room. Her dress had been ripped off. She had severe multiple scalp, trunk, arm, and leg lacerations. Muscle and other tissues were missing from her right and left arms and right leg. The cause of death was multiple injuries of head, trunk, and extremities.

Six dogs (three males, three females), each weighing less than twelve kilograms, were in the house at the time of the attack. From interviews with M, police, and neighbors it was determined that the dogs typically barked at passersby and strangers entering the house. Two of the dogs were very protective of M and would threaten anyone who approached him. The smallest dog, a female who had been born in the house, often stayed in Mrs. L's room and was friendly to her. The neighbor's children sometimes played with some of the animals through the backyard fence. The police reported that the dogs barked and growled "with a threatening sound" when they arrived. The SPCA officials described all of the animals as docile and frightened when placed in the SPCA truck. The dogs were impounded at a local shelter.

INVESTIGATION OF CASES 1 AND 3 UNDER CONTROLLED CONDITIONS

After the animals in Cases 1 and 3 were impounded, questions were raised about whether these dogs were capable of such attacks and about the circumstances that had elicited or escalated the encounters. Our objectives in examining the animals were to determine the overall health of the animals; intragroup behavior; responses to people, and responses to stimuli approximating those present at the time of the attack.

CASE 1

On June 13 and 14, 1981, seven weeks after the incident, we visited the scene of the attack and obtained accounts from the victim, his father, and two witnesses.

Nine of the dogs were still present at the animal shelter, two of the original group having died. All dogs reportedly ate ravenously at the shelter.

The dogs were taken to a fenced football field. Examinations and subsequent interactions were recorded on Super 8mm sound film. Veterinary examinations revealed that all of the animals had poor, coarse hair coats and all but one were underweight. Several exhibited weak, sloping pasterns and had readily palpable tuber coxae and vertebral processes, and some had enlarged joints at the costochondral junctions. One had tapeworms protruding from the rectum.

During individual examination, all of the dogs were timid, but one animal briefly bared its teeth. A professional trainer and handler approached each dog and assessed if for previous attack training. None gave any indication of such training.

When released into the field, the dogs engaged in a variety of social behaviors including greeting, play, and dominance-subordinance. They appeared to be familiar with one another, and most stayed close together on the field. They showed no threatening or aggressive behaviors toward any people present and, when given a package of chicken parts, showed only short bouts of competition with no overt fighting.

The trainer, wearing a padded sleeve, walked among the dogs without eliciting a response from them. Running elicited a few barks but no attack. Serendipitously, several people on motorbikes appeared along a hillside road about 100 meters from the field. The dogs began barking and, in a group, ran parallel to the bikes. Most of the animals then redirected their chase to the trainer. After the bikes were stopped and he remained still, the animals moved away.

To simulate conditions that might have occurred if the dogs had encountered humans while chasing prey, the trainer stood behind a van parked in the center of the field, out of view of the dogs. A cyclist was instructed to ride outside the fence, keeping just ahead of the dogs. After the cycle had traveled about sixty meters, it stopped out of view of the dogs, and the trainer, wearing a padded suit, ran from his position. Seven of the nine dogs immediately pursued him, and five of them delivered multiple bites to his arms, legs, thighs, and buttocks. Analysis of the films showed that the first and most persistent attacks came from those animals fitting the victim's (R) description of the dogs who were most aggressive toward him.

When the trainer stopped moving, all of the dogs eventually released their grip. When he screamed, kicked, or struggled, as the victim had done, the attack escalated. Five of the dogs bit him repeatedly, and he reported that he would have been pulled to the ground had he not been holding onto the fence.

The above situations were duplicated as closely as possible about three hours later in the presence of a group of five other dogs of similar sizes and breeds from the same shelter. These animals had no previous history of interaction with each other and were not known to have been involved in any bite incidents. These dogs exhibited some play, were not competitive for food, did not chase the motorcycle or the running man, and exhibited no aggression.

The behavior of the animals involved in the attack was consistent with our hypothesis that the dogs probably had been searching for or chasing prey at the time they encountered the boys and directed their attack toward R. R's flight and struggle resulted in escalation of this behavior.

CASE 2

Although we did not have the opportunity to observe the dogs involved in this case, the events are similar to those in Case 1. Only an hour before the attack some of the dogs had caught a deer, which then escaped. The dogs routinely chased moving vehicles (cars, motorcycles) near the house. Since the attack occurred on or near the owner's property, the initiation of this attack also may have involved territorial/protective behavior.

CASE 3

In this case there was public skepticism about the ability of these small and timid dogs to inflict serious injury. The animals were examined individually at the shelter by Victoria Voith on Janauary 28, 1981, and again by the entire group of researchers three days later. The examinations and other interactions with the dogs were recorded on videotape.

All of the dogs were timid, and some remained immobile when placed in any posture. All had long toenails, indicating that they probably rarely, if ever, exercised outside of the house. Only one of the animals would walk on a leash. One female had recently been in estrus, and one was in proestrus or estrus at the time of examination. All of the dogs appeared reasonably well-fleshed with no signs of malnutrition. Most of the dogs had short hair coats, and their ribs were not visible; however, there was no palpable layer of fat under the skin.

During the second examination, the animals were introduced one at a time into a seven-by-fifteen-meter room at the shelter in the presence of our group and several SPCA officials. The first dog released hid behind a partition and was joined there by the second. The two animals huddled close together and showed no threatening behavior. When the third dog, a male terrier–mixed breed, was introduced, he began investigating the room and was soon joined by the first two dogs. This animal was one of those reported by the victim's son to have been most threatening to the victim. When all dogs were present, the group began investigating the room, usually in proximity to one another, and led by the terrier–mixed breed or an older female beagle. The dogs failed to respond to a variety of dog toys and made no attempt to solicit play from any of the people present.

The animals were left alone in the room for one hour. When a person reentered, the dogs barked and growled, and the terrier–mixed breed attempted to bite. When directly approached, the animals would retreat under a table. As the person withdrew, the dogs approached with increased barking, growling, and attempted bites. At times, the person found it necessary to fend off these bites with a broom handle.

The animals were allowed to quiet down, then a doll approximately one meter tall was suspended from a stick and moved toward them. When it was moved quickly, the dogs retreated. If the approach was slow, they barked, and if the doll was kept still they approached and bit at the legs and torso. When the doll was allowed to fall toward the dogs, as might have happened with the victim, the animals pulled on it. The dogs growled continuously and repeatedly bit and tugged at the doll's head, neck, hair, and arms. They then dragged it beneath a table, where they chewed on it for approximately three minutes.

The pattern of this group's attack on the doll was consistent with the injuries to the victim. Most of Mrs. L's wounds were on the arms, scalp, and back of the head.

Throughout this sequence, none of the animals showed any behavior typical

of canid play, such as "play-face," play vocalizations, or play-solicitation postures (Bekoff, 1972; Fox, 1971). The behaviors were clearly aggressive and
socially facilitated. The smallest of the animals, a female beagle–mixed breed,
did not participate in the attack on the doll or in any of the threats to us.

The animals were provided with fresh food and water. There was no
aggression within the group over food and no threats toward a person withdrawing the food. In fact, the animals were friendly and tried to solicit play from the
person retrieving the dog dishes.

Later that day, the same tests were conducted with a group of four other dogs
housed at the same SPCA. No aggression was exhibited toward people, the stick,
or the doll. All of the interactions with people by this group were friendly.

A few days later, the reactions of the dogs that had attacked the victim were
again assessed. When a woman approached and withdrew with jerky, abrupt
movements, waved her arms or feet, and vocalized in a high-pitched voice, the
dogs escalated their threatening behavior, biting her shoes and the stick she held
(Figure 20.3). When the woman ceased moving and vocalizing, the dogs stopped
threatening.

Our conclusion was that five of the six animals, as a group, could easily be
provoked into repeatedly biting a human, even though the individual animals
were timid and non-aggressive.

DISCUSSION

As noted earlier, these cases differ from previously described fatal dog attacks in
that all involved pack attacks on mature individuals and all involved ingestion of
tissue from the victim. Thus we should attempt to identify the factors that might
contribute to a dog's regarding humans as potential prey.

ROLE OF HUNGER

None of the twenty-five dogs involved in these cases could be described as
emaciated, although all of those for which descriptions are available were
characterized as lean, and most of the dogs involved in Case 1 were underweight.
If the dogs had attacked to satiate their appetites, however, more tissue should
have been consumed. Interestingly, a large amount of tissue was removed from
the victim in Case 3, which involved dogs that were not underweight and
appeared to have the best nutritional status of any of those discussed.

ROLE OF PRIOR PREDATION AND SOCIAL FACILITATION OF FEEDING

In Cases 1 and 2, the animals were known to have a history of hunting together
and were probably pursuing prey soon before their attacks on people. The dogs in
Case 3 did not have a history of hunting but routinely fed together without

conflict. Thus, in all cases, after one or more individuals had initiated an attack, previous group interactions could have facilitated predatory behavior by the entire pack. Once the victim was down and bleeding, the animals' previous histories of social facilitation of feeding may have influenced the ingestive behavior.

ROLE OF TERRITORIALITY

Invasion of territory by alien or subordinate conspecifics can lead to attack among wild and domestic canids. At least 45 percent of the 2,538 dog-bite cases analyzed by Beck, Loring, and Lockwood (1975) took place on or near the owner's property. All of the eleven fatal attacks described by Winkler (1977) took place on the owner's property.

Cases 2 and 3 both took place on or near the owner's property, and in both cases the dogs involved had had previous contact with the victim. In Case 3, the dogs were very familiar with the victim but had never been alone with her in the same area. In Case 1, the animals were probably on familiar ground ("home range") but were 2.7 kilometers from their main residence. Only Case 2 may fit the traditional picture of animals defending territory from intrusion by strangers.

ROLE OF SOCIAL INTERACTION WITH PEOPLE

Most of the dogs involved in these attacks were described as friendly toward some people some of the time. The majority of the dogs observed in Cases 1 and 3 were extremely variable in their behaviors toward strangers. The animals in all three cases had unusual histories of supervision and aggressive social interactions with people. The animals involved in Case 1 were reportedly kept as guard dogs and were allowed to run at large. Several witnesses reported that the animals had been encouraged to threaten workmen in the area. We do not have details of the social history of the animals involved in Case 2, but they were reportedly allowed to run at large and frequently chased cars and motorcycles. The animals involved in Case 3 were always confined to the house or a small fenced yard. They had little contact with people other than the owner. Interestingly, the small female beagle that reportedly routinely interacted with the victim did not participate in any of the group attacks in the simulated tests. We doubt that this dog was involved in the actual attack.

In all cases there was little or no evidence that the owners had made any effective attempts to inhibit their animals' aggression toward strangers, and in some instances aggression was apparently encouraged.

ROLE OF STIMULUS CONDITIONS

Canid hunting involves vision, audition, and olfaction, but at close range the main elicitor of attack behavior is the visual stimulus of moving prey. Once vulnerable prey has been identified, group members will coordinate their activities to immobilize it, usually by bites to the hindquarters (Mech, 1970). It is not unusual for wild canids to begin feeding while the prey is still alive as long as it is incapable of escape.

In Cases 1 and 2 the animals involved apparently were experienced hunters and had probably been hunting shortly before the attacks. The dogs in all cases may have been aroused by the movements and cries of the victims. In Case 1, a motionless boy escaped injury while the running boy was chased and pulled down. The victim reported that the attack escalated when he screamed or fought against the dogs. When he remained still, the dogs stopped biting. The animals responded in the same way during the test evaluations.

In Case 2, foot and pawprints suggest that the victim had run to a telephone pole and then to a brush pile. He appears to have been pulled down several times by bites on the buttocks and legs.

We have no knowledge of the behavior of the victim in Case 3 before the attack. Since she was afraid of several of the dogs, it is possible that she cried out or moved abruptly upon seeing them loose and may have attempted to escape, then fallen or been pulled down. Many of her wounds could have been received while she was flailing her arms to defend herself. In our examination of the dogs involved, movement away from them or flailing of the arms elicited chasing, growling, and barking.

ROLE OF NUMBER OF DOGS

All of the cases in this report involved attacks by packs of at least six dogs. In Winkler's survey of 11 fatalities only 2 involved more than 1 dog (3 and 7 dogs). Pack attacks have a greater probability of being serious because of the greater number of wounds that can be inflicted and the likelihood that social facilitation will prolong or escalate the attack.

ROLE OF SIZE OF DOGS

In general, serious bites are more often attributed to larger dogs (Harris, Imperato, and Oken, 1974). In Winkler's survey, only 8 out of 21 (38 percent) of the animals identified by breed could be classified as "large," that is, adult German shepherd or larger. All of the dogs we examined in Case 1 and at least 4 of the 8 dogs involved in Case 2 were the size of German shepherds or larger. All of the animals involved in Case 3 weighed less than twelve kilograms. Clearly, the danger associated with dog attack is a product of size and number of dogs and the vulnerability of the victim. Even a single small dog is capable of killing an infant.

ROLE OF ESTRUS

A popular view is that the presence of a female in heat increases the probability of dog attack. The presence of an estrus female leads to the assembly of many male dogs and can thus indirectly increase the danger of attack associated with increased number of dogs and the aggressive behavior that may occur among them. Competition for females may increase aggression within a pack of dogs that does not have an established social hierarchy. Some clinical cases involving complaints of owners regarding aggression of pet dogs have revealed that when there are female dogs in heat in the home or vicinity, a male dog may demonstrate increased aggression toward a person who places him or herself between the intact male and estrus female (Voith, unpublished data).

Estrus females were not present during the simulation tests in Case 1 in which the trainer was attacked. Moreover, the trainer was not attacked by the control group, which did include an estrus female. We do not know if there were any estrus females in the group of dogs involved in Case 2. Case 3 did involve an estrus female, but we have no way of knowing if the elderly woman had interposed herself between this animal and any of the males in that group. The simulation tests involving this group of dogs also contained an estrus female, although a different one than was in estrus at the time of the attack. At no time did any of the investigators in the simulation situation interpose themselves between the estrus female and the other dogs. The threats were initiated by a person approaching the entire group.

COMMENTS ON DOG ATTACK INVESTIGATIONS

In all three cases, there was much concern on the part of the public, the owners, and the police investigators regarding the correct identification of the actual dogs that had engaged in the attacks. Cases 1 and 3 provided a unique opportunity for detailed evaluation of whether specific animals could have been involved in the attacks and what possible contributory factors facilitated the attacks. In both simulations, the pattern of attack was consistent with eyewitness descriptions of the incidents and the nature of the injuries.

In Case 1, the boys reported that the dogs had apparently been hunting shortly before emerging from the woods and that the dogs were running as they came into the clearing. In the simulated condition, an attack could not be elicited until the dogs had first been excited by chasing a motorcycle. They then redirected their chase toward a running man and attacked him. In this case, the animals that led the attack under the controlled conditions were the same dogs reported by the boy to have initially and persistently attacked hiim.

In Case 3, the male terrier–mixed breed, which was the dog most feared by the victim, was either the first or second dog to initiate threats and attacks toward approaching humans and the doll in the simulation tests. The only animal that did not engage in group threats and attacks toward the investigators or the doll was the small female beagle–mixed-breed reported to have had much friendly contact with the victim. The distribution of bites on the doll closely paralleled that of the wounds on the victim.

In both Cases 1 and 3, flailing of arms or legs, rapid, jerky motion, and high-pitched cries increased the intensity of the attack. Moving slowly or not moving at all resulted in reduction of the intensity of attack. This observation was corroborated by the victim's report in Case 1. It is highly likely that the attacks in these cases were intensified when the victims attempted to defend themselves or call for help.

The results of our observations give us confidence in the use of behavioral analysis and simulation methods to evaluate possible factors in dog attacks when witnesses or detailed accounts are not available. This is particularly important when there is some doubt as to the cause of death, as in Cases 2 and 3, in which there was initial doubt as to whether people or dogs caused the deaths.

PREVENTION OF SEVERE DOG ATTACK

Perhaps these cases can provide some insight into the warning signs of severe dog attack. All the dogs in these cases were lean, and some were underweight. There is no indication that hunger played a part in the initiation of the attacks in Cases 1 and 2, but these dogs did have a history of hunting as a pack unit. We believe that pack-facilitated hunting behavior and previous experience working as a coordinated unit played a role in the attack and the subsequent consumption of flesh.

None of these incidents can be considered to have been intentionally provoked by the victim. It is highly likely, however, that the natural defense reactions (flailing, kicking, and screaming) of all the victims escalated the attacks.

Most of the dogs had a history of previous aggressive threats toward people. This does not necessarily mean that they were not socialized or that their socialization had been inadequate. In fact, many of these dogs, and perhaps all of them, were reported to have interacted in a friendly manner with familiar people under certain circumstances. What is common among all of the dogs is that there was no attempt by responsible adults to inhibit the threats and aggressive behavior directed toward some people. Some of these dogs were even reported to have been encouraged to act aggressively toward people.

Often people attempt to solve the problem of aggression in dogs by restraining or isolating the animals. While confined, the dogs cannot injure anyone, but if the animals escape or encounter people unfamiliar with the problem, they could inflict injuries. Such was apparently the situation in Case 3, in which the son of the elderly woman kept his dogs behind a barrier.

The past history of social interactions of dogs with people in a variety of circumstances is probably an adequate predictor of whether these dogs are inclined to bite someone. But whether an animal could be involved in a repeated, unrelenting attack resulting in the death of the victim is more difficult to determine.

All of the animals in these situations were loose or unsupervised at the time of the incident. This is true of 45.7 percent of reported bites reviewed by Beck,

Loring, and Lockwood (1975) and 92 percent of animals involved in attacks on letter carriers surveyed by Lockwood and Beck (1975). Loose pets are more aggressive when closer to their home and more aggressive than unowned strays when approached (Rubin and Beck, 1982). But most biting incidents that occur in the home are in supervised situations where other adults are present (Voith, 1979a; 1980a; 1981c; 1982; Borchelt, 1982). This information is obtained from persons presenting their pet dogs for treatment for aggressive behavior problems. These bites, which often involve the owner as the victim, are rarely reported officially, and many of the bites are not treated by a physician. In contrast, serious repeated attacks that result in maiming or death usually occur when no one except the victim is present.

Severe dog attack is a probable product of many factors including size, number, and nutritional status of dogs; their previous aggressive encounters with people; the age, size, health, and behavior of the victim; and the absence of other human beings in the vicinity. A public health program aimed at preventing such incidents could be directed to any one or all of these factors.

The most practical point of intervention is at the level of owner responsibility. Dogs, especially those with a history of threatening any human, should not be allowed to run free or interact with people unless they are under control. Ideally, companion dogs should not threaten anyone. If owners wish to keep a dog that exhibits uncontrolled aggressive tendencies, they should seek professional help to treat the aggressive problem. In our clinical experience with family dogs that are aggressive toward people, obedience training alone has often been unsuccessful in preventing or treating this problem.

A simple education program in dog-bite avoidance directed toward likely victims (children, the elderly, letter carriers, meter readers) could further reduce the incidence of such encounters.

Although such measures would be in the best interest of humane agencies, public health and law enforcement officials, and the general public, little progress may be made in such a program until the magnitude and seriousness of dog attacks on the streets and in the home are more widely recognized.

PART THREE

Society with Animals

Introduction

The human–companion animal bond takes place within a cultural, social, and ecological environment that sets many of the parameters of normal, or at least acceptable, behaviors and roles. Animal ownership is *not* a random event: ownership or rejection of such an association often requires conscious effort and energy. The chapters in "Society with Animals" and in "Animals and People" as well as others in the "Therapeutic Uses of Companion Animals" remind us of the importance of social context: this context very much influences the nature of the human–companion animal bond.

The first chapter, "Animals in the City," sets the stage by showing that animals are very much a part of our life because of their numbers and variety. The patterns of ownership vary, however, with socioeconomic status and human density. Perhaps not surprisingly, dog ownership is more common among the wealthy, but, perhaps a surprise to those who argue that dogs help us maintain some contact with nature, ownership is much higher in the rural parts of most countries. The author also notes that attitudes toward companion animals are extremely variable. On one hand, pet animals are cherished beings that are often the companions of movie stars, politicians, and others requiring social approval, and on the other hand, they are often the cause of social conflict, and their owners are depicted as social hermits who have lost faith with their fellow humans (Worth and Beck, 1981; Cameron and Mattson, 1972). Both extremes exist at the same time in the same cultures (Katcher, 1981; Perin, 1981; Katcher, 1982).

The Salmons' "Who Owns Who? Psychological Research into the Human-Pet Bond in Australia" identifies some of the parameters of animal ownership in Australia, where dogs and horses are especially important. Using an extensive questionnaire, they make two important observations: pet animal owners are remarkably uncritical about the problems caused by their animals, and it is vitally important that people chose their own animal. Animals presented as gifts are not usually the sex or breed that would be chosen, and these animals are not as appreciated. Personal involvement in choosing to share one's life with an animal is part of creating the human-animal bond.

Joseph S. Quigley, Lyle E. Vogel, and Robert K. Anderson's "A Study of Perceptions and Attitudes Toward Pet Ownership" identifies the varying attitudes that accompany animal ownership. Owners, as one might suspect, have more positive and emotional feelings for pets than do nonowners. Perhaps one task for the future is to develop the information that would allow both groups to share an honest perception, thus making it possible to develop strategies that could meet the needs of both.

Edwin Schlossberg and Pat Baxter's report on Macomber Farm is based on the premise that an understanding of animals will bring respect and concern for their welfare. Though the report has a flavor of advocacy for the humane movement, the Massachusetts Society for the Prevention of Cruelty to Animals in particular, it is an advocacy with few detractors. The minimum "take-home" message of most zoos and animal exhibits is that animals should be appreciated because, if nothing else, they are beautiful and engaging to watch. The conservation movement has undoubtedly benefited from the myriad books and movies that have given the general public insights into the lives of wild animals. The Macomber project uses exhibits and games to encourage a similiar respect and concern for farm animals.

All the chapters in this section identify a need for a better understanding of animals and, by implication, identify the lack of understanding exhibited by planners, architects, school systems, and legislators. It is time to accept the fact that at least some people will share their lives with animals and that both people and animals can benefit from the relationship if it is done well.

Alan M. Beck

21

Animals in the City

People of all ages and all walks of life consistently demonstrate some desire to have contact with the natural environment and living things. Urbanization often replaces natural areas with man-made structures and surfaces, thus posing special problems for city dwellers still longing for contact with nature's creations. In response, urban design often includes parks with grass, streets with trees, window boxes with plants, and zoological and botanical gardens with a variety of exotic animals and flowers. Many urban dwellers choose to share their homes with animals. In addition to the keeping of the smaller, more tame species of wild animals, there has been a systematic breeding of animals for traits that are compatible with the constraints of city life. In fact, the domestication of the dog began about the time people started living in villages.

Today, Americans spend more than $4 billion dollars annually to feed their more than 48 million dogs, 27 million cats, 25 million birds, 250 million fish, and 125 million assorted captive animals totaling 4.7 billion pet creatures. More than 40 percent of U.S. households own a mean number of 1.5 dogs; 20 percent own 1.7 cats; 15 percent own 2.1 birds; 12 percent own 25 fish; and 25 percent

TABLE 21.1.   PET OWNERSHIP IN THE UNITED STATES

	Households Owning (Percent)	Number Households Owning (Millions)	Average Number Per Household	Total Number of Pets (Millions)
Dogs	40	32	1.5	48.0
Cats	20	16	1.7	27.2
Birds	15	12	2.1	25.2
Fish	12	10	25.0	250.0
Other	25	20*	†	125.0
				475.4

*Including households with raccoons, 1.8; hamsters or gerbils, 1.7; rabbits, 1.5; reptiles, 1.2; rodents, 0.9; guinea pigs, 0.4. Total = 7.5.
†Variable.
Source: Frost & Sullivan, 1980.

own an unknown quantity of assorted small amphibians, reptiles, and mammals (Frost and Sullivan, 1980). (See Table 21.1)

There is evidence that the dog population is declining, especially in cities, possibly because of the increasing number of working wives, inflation, and the trend toward living in more compact accommodations (Frost and Sullivan, 1980; Purvis and Otto, 1976). Nevertheless, more than half of the families that live in U.S. cities and their surrounding suburbs have a companion animal; ownership is even greater in rural areas (Purvis and Otto, 1976).

Perhaps one of the reasons for the many controversies that surround animal ownership is the fact that nearly half the families that also occupy cities do not have a personal pet animal. With no clear majority, the issue is how owners and nonowners can coexist in ways that are acceptable to all and to the animals themselves.

The management of animals is not a new science. Long experience in the management of wild species in nonurban areas has taught us that there is little to be gained by manipulating individual animals. Wildlife management is the management of the animals' environment, not the animal per se.

Urban animal management likewise involves control of the environment or environmental forces, like people, that affect the entire population, if not every last individual member of the population. Urban animal control, that is, population control, was at first concerned with wild animal intruders like predators, capable or perceived capable of harming humans; large domestic animals like horses and cattle capable of damaging property; and rabid dogs capable of killing people and other animals. The urbanization of rural habitats naturally discouraged wild animal intrusions, which are now limited to the smaller varieties of wildlife and only rarely dangerous ones. Extensive green belts within cities, suburbanization, and the ownership of wild species of pets have resurrected some of the earlier concerns people had about wildlife as a potential source of injury and disease transmission to humans and other urban animals.

During the summer of 1981, a captive pet wolf killed a child in Detroit (Associated Press, 1981) and a wild coyote tried to carry off and killed a three-year-old girl in Los Angeles. Apparently, the coyotes in many areas of California have lost their fear of humans because people have fed them (Starr and Huck, 1981), as has happpened with bears in national parks (Tate, 1981)

As a general rule, present-day control of wild pest species focuses on habitat alteration as does wildlife management. Making building ledge space less available for pigeons to roost on (Goodwin, 1954) and decreasing harborage for rats (Barbehenn, 1970) does more to lower their respective populations than poisons and traps (Davis, 1953).

Early urban concerns with large domestic animals, mainly horses, involved trespass, waste, and cruelty. In the 1880s, Baltimore's street sweepers actively sought horse feces for its resale value as fertilizer. (The waste products of carnivores such as dogs and cats has no value as fertilizer.) Today, the care and treatment of horses used for recreation is still a concern in many urban areas.

The fact that rabies was a disease that could involve the domestic dog was recognized some two thousand years ago; today, even in the absence of dog rabies as a widespread problem, the fear of rabies still exists and dog bite is still the most common reason for requiring postexposure rabies prophylaxis (Marr and Beck, 1976; Martin, Schnurrenberger, and Rose, 1969; Steele, 1973).

When rabies does occur, it is costly. When a single rabid dog was identified on May 10, 1980, in a small county in California, the subsequent investigation, vaccination of all potential exposures, emergency animal vaccination clinics, and increased dog control cost the people $105,790, not including lost work time, patient travel, or the cost associated with the imposition of a six-month quarantine (Cusick and Humphrey, 1981).

Today, the major concern about animals in our cities involves the animals kept by people as companions, the so-called "pet animals." As with wildlife management, the most cost-effective approach would be to control and plan for the animals' habitat. In one area the individual animal, not the population or habitat, must be examined. I propose it is appropriate to discourage, or even prohibit, the keeping of certain wild species or categories of animals, even in limited numbers, as captive pets. Society should ban the so-called exotic or wild pet for the following reasons: the consequences of escape of an animal that might pose a threat to people or natural fauna; the potential for disease transmission to people or other animals; the humane implications, whether it is routinely possible to maintain the animal in a way that is inherently kind, permitting the animal to exhibit relatively normal behaviors and physiological well-being; and the conservation implications, whether the removal or attempted removal of individuals from the wild significantly affects the whole population's survival. For these reasons, most cities discourage the ownership of all nondomesticated carnivores, venomous anthropods, and reptiles and all primates, raptorial birds, and endangered species.

Most companion animals, however, are domesticated or captive-born species that thrive better in captivity than when free of human care. Nevertheless, there is considerable controversy regarding the presence of pets in cities. The most frequent complaint received by municipal leaders involves animal control, mostly dogs (Bancroft, 1974).

Replacing rabies as a source of concern is the recognition that dog bite and waste are present-day problems affecting all urban areas (Beck, 1979, 1981a; Beck, Loring, and Lockwood, 1975; Beczon et al., 1972; Glickman and Schantz, 1981; Glickman, Schantz, and Cypress, 1979; Schantz and Glickman, 1978). In the last few years the bites of dogs have killed more people than rabies from all species (Beck et al., 1981; Winkler, 1977)

Because urban dogs demand additional services—stray control and bite investigations—urban owners are often expected to pay an additional tax in the form of a license. Perhaps because people resent additional taxes and society is still unclear about the values and problems regarding dogs, there is little compliance with and endorsement of licensing regulations, and more than half of dogs go unlicensed (American Humane Association, 1972). Around the country, the median license fee for a fertile female is almost a dollar more than for a spayed female and at least a dollar more than for a male. If the differential fee is based on the concept that some dogs are a greater social burden than others, we ought to consider differentiating on the basis of size in addition to potential fecundity, especially in urban areas. Larger dogs tend to account for the more serious bites (Harris, Imperato, and Oken, 1974) and the more serious environmental insults, be they waste or noise. Perhaps the little apartment dog is entitled to differential treatment regarding taxation and even rabies vaccination, when compared to the large animal who must be walked on public property.

In addition to encouraging smaller dogs, cities should consider total number owned per family. After a certain number, perhaps two, cities should consider special kennel or breeders' licenses that would be subject to specific evaluation such as zoning or other land-use criteria.

The model dog and cat control ordinance, developed and endorsed by both national humane societies (American Humane Association and Humane Society of the United States), the American Veterinary Medical Association, and the Pet Food Institute, suggests a maximum of five dogs after which a special kennel license would be required (American Humane Association et al., 1976). The city of Baltimore, Maryland, sets the limit at three dogs and/or cats. But most cities do not have a way of discouraging the ownership of animals until there are reports of a nuisance or acts of animal cruelty (Worth and Beck, 1981).

Most urban areas require restraint of or at least direct supervision over pet dogs on public property. The data are so overwhelming that loose pets account for the major portion of the animal bite problem (Beck, 1981a; Beck, Loring, and Lockwood, 1975; Harris, Imperato, and Oken, 1974; Parrish et al., 1959;

Winkler, 1977) that anything less than strict enforcement of leashing laws would be a violation of government's mandate to protect the public's health.

There are people who believe that permitting dogs to run loose thus becoming familiar with people makes them less likely to bite; this is one reason why dog bite is not considered a problem in England, where there are few leash laws (Peter Messent, personal communication). But there are no data to support this view, and there is evidence that loose dogs account for more than 6 percent of all automobile accidents, including 1.2 percent of accidents that involve human injury or death (Carding, 1969).

A study of pet dogs in Queens, New York, showed that the degree of restraint influenced the animal's wanderings and aggressiveness. Animals that were at least occasionally restrained had an average daily maximum excursion of 257 feet (78.3 meters) when left free, compared to pet dogs that were never restrained, whose average maximum daily excursion was 1,541 feet (165.1 meters) from their owner's residence. When approached, these straying pets behaved aggressively toward an experimenter more than 65 percent of the time, compared to encounters with ownerless strays that exhibited aggression only 12 percent of the time (Rubin and Beck, 1982). This behavior may explain why the vast majority of dog bites are inflicted by owned pets loose on public property (Beck, 1981a; Beck, Loring, and Lockwood, 1975; Harris, Imperato, and Oken, 1974). Loose pets fare so poorly in the urban environment, mainly falling prey to automobiles, that leash laws should be part of the humane as well as the health codes (Carding, 1969; Humane Society of the United States, 1979).

Control over breeding is exerted by increased licensed fees for intact females, sterilization of animals adopted out of shelters, and sterilizing clinics. But, less than half of all dogs are ever licensed (American Humane Association, 1972); less than 6 percent of the standing dog population comes from shelters (Beck, 1973); and there is little evidence that people use spaying programs, so there is much ado about nothing (Beck, 1974; Modern Veterinary Practice, 1973a, 1973b). In general, less than one half of the female dog and cat population is neutered, not enough for meaningful population control.

Considering the mobility of the urban human population, dogs that are walked on public property should be vaccinated against rabies. A three-year schedule, with appropriate vaccines, is sufficient (Steele, 1973), and does not impose a major financial burden on owners, and goes a long way in alleviating victim concern after a bite.

Dog waste should be the concern of any citizen and municipal official interested in health, sanitation, and environmental quality. Management of waste has included laws that relegate the defecating animal to the curb side of the street or to a specific area in a park. More recently, larger municipalities and many suburban communities have legislated the immediate removal of dog waste from public areas (Beck, 1979, 1981b). The growing social acceptance of these so -called "scoop laws" has encouraged more cities to pass and enforce them. There is still little evidence that cities plan exercise and "dog walking" areas although landscape and building guidelines for them exist. Cities must also provide guidelines and receptacles for the collected fecal waste. Veterinarians should better inform their clients about parasite management, and deworming programs should be more rigorous and should include nursing bitches (Kornblatt and Schantz, 1980).

Another strictly urban and suburban problem associated with dogs is dog bark. The problem is usually handled by the local police following citizen complaints. The recent renewed interest in smaller dogs and the growing number of people who can help owners with such behavior problems as excessive barking may, in time, alleviate the problem.

Despite the ever-growing number of reports of the beneficial aspects of companion animals, the real problem facing animal owners in urban areas is still a pervasive distrust of animal ownership. Books like Berkeley Rice's *The Other End of the Leash* (1968), Raymond Hull's *Man's Best Friend*(1972) and Irish Nowell's *The Dog Crisis* (1978) deign to document the problems, which are genuine indiscretions of animal owners. I have numerous newspaper articles that report owners attacking people who criticize their animal and tell of animals rescued from drowning in lieu of people and of owners taking pride in their dog's biting of a letter carrier. I do not propose that these accounts are all totally true; however, the fact that they are published at all indicates that some people believe them true and, in fact, they are generally accepted by the public. The animal owner is at times portrayed as a misanthrope whose concern for animals supersedes, and perhaps replaces, a caring for people.

I suspect the popularity of such books (actually inexpensive booklets) as Bond's "101 Uses for a Dead Cat" (1981), Cole's "Cat Hater's Handbook" (1981), and Morrow's "The Second Official I Hate Cats Book" (1981) is not simply a replacement of "Polish jokes" or a true resentment of cats (*Time*, 1981), although ailurophobia does exist, but an expression of resentment against cat owners, who are often perceived to be excessively dedicated to their pets (see Quackenbush and Glickman, this volume). The 1982 Cat Hater's Calendar was too unsubtle with its photographs to be publicly acceptable, especially by the manufacturers of products that were discernible in the pictures; the calendar was withdrawn from the market (Kay, 1981).

Even in England, where pet animal ownership has a long and recognized tradition, an organization of owners, PRO DOG'S National Charity, was formed to offset increasing evidence of intolerance toward dogs and the misanthropic image of their owners (Ordish, 1981). The PRO DOG'S pamphlet *Dogs in Towns* emphasizes responsible dog ownership, specifically addressing the management of dog bark and fouling. Apparently, dedicated dog owners realize permitting their pets to pollute the environment does not enhance their image in the community.

The general belief that dogs and cats are "child substitutes," implying that owners are emotionally incapable of raising children, is pervasive even though less than 5 percent of the dog population and less than 7 percent of the cat population are owned by people who live alone and less than 9 percent of dogs and less than 14 percent of cats reside in households that have no children. More than half of families with teenage children have a dog (Purvis and Otto, 1976). This association between animal ownership and children exists in England as well; a Pedigree Petfood (1980) survey found that children were present in 51 percent of pet-owning households compared with 37 percent in nonowning households.

The industry that produces dog food has combated the negative image of pet ownership by emphasizing that pets are good for people, literally, that pets are wonderful, which misses addressing the real issue. Few people argue about the value of pet ownership; the issue is whether pet owners are wonderful when incorporating their hobby into already crowded, unclean, and noisy cities. The common expression one hears is that cities are divided between those who love dogs and those who hate those who love dogs! Few people hate, or at least admit to hating, dogs or any other companion animal. It is people, not animals, that are expected to observe licensing, leashing, and scooping laws, and it is people who are resented when they fail. To be sure, it is often the animal that is punished, usually by death, when owners disregard leash laws.

Poorly managed dogs that run loose, soil property, and bark are bad ambassadors. People who keep so many animals that they are a nuisance for the whole community (Worth and Beck, 1981) reinforce the stereotype that animal ownership is linked with misanthropy.

Owners in cities have a special responsibility to their animals and to society because of the density of housing and the limited open space. Urban owners should fully understand these responsibilities in choosing their pet animal and budgeting their time for its care. The trend to smaller, more easily cared for pet animals should be encouraged. Pets can be wonderful for many people and at least an accepted if not a welcomed part of the urban setting for most other people, if they are maintained in a wholesome and responsible way. With some extra care, people and companion animals can share the city experience together in ways beneficial for all.

Peter W. Salmon and Ingrid M. Salmon

22

Who Owns Who?
Psychological Research into
the Human-Pet Bond in Australia

If we look at our Australian history, and in particular our literature, we find that animals have played an important role in our development as a nation. Until very recently, the Australian economy has been predominantly rural, and our livestock industries, particularly sheep and cattle, have given rise to two important domestic animals, the dog and the horse. Initially, the relationship between men and their horse and dog was a working one, in which the animal was used to move livestock. But very quickly this relationship changed into a strong personal bond of friendship between man and animal, a bond that lies at the heart of much early Australian literature, poetry, ballads, and folklore. It would seem, then, that we have a rich.cultural heritage of human–companion animal bonding on which to base our studies and research in Australia.

Studies into the human-pet bond in Australia have been few, but most of those carried out have been under the direction of an organization called Pet Care Information and Advisory Service. More recently, the work of Pet Care has been given added impetus by the formation of JACOPIS (Jint Advisory Committee on Pets in Society), based on its United Kingdom counterpart of the same name. Both groups are committed to fostering the role of animals in society through education, seeking representation on public bodies, and carrying out projects involving people and animals. Projects in recent years include placement of dogs in a prison setting and in an emergency child care center, experimental uses of guide dogs for the blind with other handicapped people, and, currently, a project involving a dog in a hospital for the aged.

After carrying out this line of work for some time, however, it was felt that we did not fully understand why the use of animals in these situations was sometimes successful and at other times a failure. In an attempt to develop this understanding, Pet Care and JACOPIS commissioned us to establish a research program that would compare Britain and the United States in an attempt to throw some better light onto the subject.

We began by making a comprehensive review of the literature, using the Dialog Computer Search facility. After reviewing some 253 references we categorized them into five major areas:

1.	Psychosocial role of pets in society	137	(54%)
2.	Pets in psychotherapy (includes both hospitals and homes for the aged)	48	(19%)
3.	Children and pets (includes normal children only)	21	(8%)
4.	Ecological/environmental pet control problems	31	(12%)
5.	Veterinary practice and the human patient	16	(7%)
	Total	253	(100%)

Clearly, previous work was oriented in two directions: first, applications of companion animals to specific situations such as therapeutic work in hospitals and with the aged, children, and so forth, and second, descriptive studies that document the incidence of human-pet bonding. What still seemed to be missing were sound, empirically based theories about the nature of the bonding.

From our own research experience we knew that we had first to establish a baseline set of criteria on the incidence of human-pet bonding in Australia in order to make comparisons with overseas studies. From this point on, we could set up a research program to look specifically at thenature of the bond.

This chapter is a report on a large-scale survey we conducted in 1980 and 1981.

I: SURVEY OF PET OWNERS

Geographically, Australia is a large country in which 70 percent of the population resides in coastal regions. The two largest cities are Sydney and Melbourne, which together account for about 60 percent of the nation's population. Melbourne was therefore chosen as being representative of urban Australia. It has a population of more than three million people and 326,000 registered dogs, or an average of one dog in every three homes. The survey technique is described below.

OBJECTIVES

The objectives were to investigate the role of pets in a normal home situation; the differential role of pets for people at different stages o the life cycle; the benefits and problems associated with pet ownership; and the level of pet owners' knowledge about municipal regulations and the responsibilities of pet ownership.

DESIGN

Field work was carried out during October 1980 and January 1981 in the city of Melbourne. Personal interviews were conducted in 308 households, representing a total of 1,063 people.

The people interviewed all had at least one registered dog because the sample was drawn from municipal registers of dog owners. The total number of pets covered in the survey was 396 dogs, 197 cats, and 193 other pets.

SAMPLE

A random stratified sampling procedure was used by first creating a ratio of population to registered dogs; both these figures were readily available on a local government basis. The population figures were taken from the 1976 census, and the dog population figures were taken from the local government register of dogs. When these strata were plotted on a map of Melbourne, it was found that the high-ratio areas closely approximated the outer suburban areas, while the low-ratio closely fitted the inner suburbs. To cross-check these results, the distributions for income and age were fitted to the same maps, and a consistent picture emerged—the highest ratio of dogs per capita was in the outer regions of the city, where the highest ratios of young children and families are also found. The inner city is characterized by a large proportio of old people, low-income earners, and very low dog numbers per capita.

The sampling criterion was randomly to select local government areas from the high, medium, and low people-dog ratio strata. Because these approximated the distribution of inner, middle, and outer suburbs, care was taken to select areas in proportion to the stratification findigs. In fact, it was found that 9 percent of the areas could be classified as high ratio/outer surburban areas, a further 11 percent as low ratio/inner suburban areas, and the remaining 80 percent as medium ratio/middle suburban areas. To ensure sampling accuracy, the final selection of areas was based on two inner, two outer, and six middle suburbs. A further restriction was placed on the number of people to be interviewed. The original recommendation was for a 1 percent sample, which would have meant more than seven hundred interviews. Cost and time ruled out this sample, and eventually a .5 percent sample was selected. Table 22.1 also shows the number of dwellings (based on the assumption that rgistrations closely approximated dwellings) which were needed in each selected area to achieve statistically reliable results. Finally, the councils cooperated in the study and provided the names and addresses of a random sample of dog owners.

QUESTIONNAIRE

Questions were asked to determine the extent to which four general variables influenced the role of the pet in the family and to explore the different roles pets played for different people. These four variables were demographic, factual, attitudinal, and level of knowledge. Table 22.1 shows the structure of the questionnaire.

A variety of question constructions were used to elicit information, including Likert scales, the semantic differential, rating scales, and simple openresponse questions. All have proved reliable in research of this nature, and they make the task of data analysis relatively straightforward.

TABLE 22.1. STRUCTURE OF QUESTIONNAIRE

Variable	Question
Demographic: Person-related	Household composition Age Sex Marital status Location (inner, middle, or outer suburb)
Demographic: Pet-related	Number of pets Types of pets Breed Age Sex Whether spayed or neutered
Factual	Length of ownership Assumption of caretaking responsibilities
Attitudinal	Motivation for acquiring dog Place where dog acquired Whether dog has lived up to expectations Level of satisfaction with dog Description of dog's behavior Description of dog's characteristics Effects of ownership on the family Effects of ownership on neighbors Benefits of ownership Problems of ownership
Level of Knowledge	Knowledge of municipal regulations Knowledge of ownership responsibilities

TABLE 22.2.   DEMOGRAPHIC CHARACTERISTICS OF RESPONDENTS

CHARACTERISTICS	PERCENTAGE
Sex	
Male	10
Female	70
Marital Status	
Married/Partner	80
Single	10
Separated/Divorced	2
Widowed	5
Nationality	
Australian	70
British	10
Other	10
Area	
Inner Surburban	8
Middle Surburban	65
Outer Surburban	20
Life Cycle Stages	
Single, no children	5
Young childless couple	10
Young family	45
Adult family	20
Old childless couple	10
Widowed, separated, or divorced	10
Pet Ownership	
One dog only	30
Two or more dogs	10
Dog, cats, and other pets	60

THE RESPONDENTS

We personally interviewed 308 respondents from households totaling 1,063 people. Table 22.2 shows a breakdown of their demographic characteristics.

The life cycle index was constructed to explore the extent to which pets play a differential role for people at different stages of life and in different household compositions. The index was constructed from three variables: marital status of the respondents, number of family members, and age of all family members. Six different "types" of families were defined as follows: single, no children; young childless couple; young family; adult family; old childless couple; widowed, separated, or divorced. The most common stage of the family life cycle associated with pet ownership was young families—couples with children under fifteen years of age. Almost half the sample fell into this group.

TABLE 22.3. CHARACTERISTICS OF THE DOGS

CHARACTERISTICS	PERCENTAGE
Sex	
Male	50
Female	50
Breed	
Purebred	60
Crossbred	40
Neutered	
Neutered	53
Not neutered	47
Size	
Small	32
Medium	37
Large	31

PET OWNERSHIP

The total number of dogs belonging to the respondents was 396. Attitudes were elicited about only one dog in each household. Although there was no significant relationship between sex and breed of the dog, there was a very significant relationship between the breed of the dog and whther it had been neutered. Only 46 percent of purebreds were neutered compared with 68 percent of crossbreds; only 20 percent of male dogs wee neutered compared with 84 percent of bitches. Table 22.3 shows the characteristics of the dogs covered in the survey.

People living alone—single, widowed, separated, or divorced—had a higher proportion of bitches than married people (70 percent compared with 47 percent), and a higher proportion of their dogs were neutered (78 percent compared to 50 percent). They also tended to have smaller dogs than those who were married. As expected, women tended to have smaller dogs than men.

People living in the outer suburbs owned more dogs (46 percent owned more than one dog) and more bitches (61 percent had bitches) compared with people living in other suburbs.

Forty-six percent of respondents had owned their dogs for less than five years. As Table 22.4 shows, in almost half of the households, the dog was the "family dog" in the sense that all members were equally attached to it and all took at least some part in looking after it.

Table 22.5 shows the most popular places from which respondents acquired their dogs. A high proportion (71 percent) of dogs received as gifts were male, whereas a high proportion (62 percent) obtained from animal shelters were female. Most dogs obtained from pet stores or animal shelters were crossbreeds, and most of them had been neutered. In contrast, most of those obtained from a breeder, bred in the home, or received as a gift were purebreds and not neutered.

TABLE 22.4.   WHO OWNS THE PET?

	PERCENTAGE
Family	49
Respondent	25
Spouse	11
Children	12
Other	3

TABLE 22.5.   WHERE WAS THE PET ACQUIRED?

	PERCENTAGE
Breeder	33
Friend/Relation	28
Other	11
Animal Shelter	8
Stray	7
Pet Store	6
Gift	5
Bred in home	2

Of interest to the "stray dog problem" is the finding that almost half of the strays were purebreds and over half had been neutered. Compared with other dogs, more strays were owned or had been taken in by old childless couples than by other people.

Respondents gave a variety of responses to the question of why they had acquired a dog. Six primary motivations, however, were found to underlie these varied responses. These are presented in Table 22.6.

As well as the desire to replace a previously owned dog, feelings of sympathy evoked by an unwanted dog emerged as a major reason for pet ownership. Together they accounted for half of the sample's motivation for owning a dog.

TABLE 22.6.   WHY WAS THE PET ACQUIRED?

	PERCENTAGE
Dog was unwanted	26
To replace previous dog	25
For the children	17
Gift	15
Just wanted a dog	10
For adult Company/Protection	7

The category of "unwanted dog" includes situations in which the dog was a stray, was about to be destroyed, the owner saw it in a pet store and felt sorry for it, and a friend's dog had a litter and they were asked, or offered, to provide a home for one.

The finding that 14 percent had been given a dog as a gift may be cause for concern; it has been suggested in the literature that "gift dogs" are not totally wanted by their owners because they did not make the decision to acquire a pet. As a consequence, these gift dogs may be a certain but as yet unquantified proportion of the stray or abandoned dog population which creates problems within the community. At this stage, however, sufficient evidence has not been gathered to support this opinion.

Getting a dog to show in competitions, for breeding purposes, to go hunting with, and as company for another dog accounted for only 3 percent of the reasons.

The reason for acquiring a dog seemed to have little effect on the respondents' attitudes toward it. One significant finding, however, was that there was a tendency for people to be more dissatisfied with their dog if it had been bought for the children (24 percent compared with 15 percent for dogs bought for adults). The other interesting finding was that two thirds of the dogs bought for the children were male, purebred, and not neutered, whereas two thirds of those bought for adults were female, crossbred, and neutered.

INTERACTION BETWEEN THE FAMILY AND THE DOG

Assumption of Caretaking Responsibilities Thirty percent of respondents do not leave their dog alone for any significant amount of time during the day; 51 percent leave it for up to four hours; and 19 percent leave it for more than four hours each day. Single people and young childless couples leave their dog alone for longer periods of time than other people—probably because they work during the day.

As Table 22.7 shows, the respondent appeared to be the primary caretaker for most of the activities mentioned. The spouse and children were involved in

TABLE 22.7. ASSUMPTION OF CARETAKING RESPONSIBILITIES BY FAMILY MEMBERS (percent)

	Respondent	Spouse	Children	Combination	No one
Who feeds it?	58	15	13	13	1
Who disciplines it?	26	15	8	16	35
Who washes/grooms it?	45	18	15	20	2
Who walks it?	24	15	14	32	15
Who takes it to vet?	39	20	6	31	4

TABLE 22.8.   RESPONDENTS' VIEWS OF THEIR RESPONSIBILITIES AS PET OWNERS (percent)

Responsiblity	Responses (N = 437)
Care for or look after the dog	22
Feed it	18
Ensure it does not roam or annoy others	18
Give it exercise	10
Keep it healthy	8
Give it love and affection	7
Groom and clean it	6
Treat it as one of the family	5
Give it attention	4
Train and discipline it	2
	100

some of these roles to varying degrees, particularly in taking the dog to the vet. Their involvement depended on who owned the dog. If the spouse or the whole family owned the dog, the spouse shared this caretaking role with the respondent. If the children owned the dog, the children joined the respondent in these activities. Children also seemed to play a greater role in washing and grooming the dog and taking it for a walk if it was owned by the whole family. The different caretaking roles assumed by children were found to be related to age. Children under sixteen years of age tended to feed and walk their dog more than older children, whereas older children disciplined the dog and took it to the vet more often. Children of all ages, however, were involved in washing and grooming the dog.

In 35 percent of the households, no one disciplined the dog. This finding is confirmed by an open-ended question about the responsibilities of owning a dog in which only 2 percent specifically mentioned training the dog as a responsibility (Table 22.8).

On the positive side, an open-ended question revealed that 18 percent of respondents considered that a major responsibility of owning a dog involved ensuring that it did not roam around and chase cars and that it did not annoy people. Apart from a general response of "caring for the dog" or "looking after it," other responsibilities mentioned included feeding and exercising the dog, keeping the dog healthy, giving it love and affection, and grooming and cleaning it, in that order.

Knowledge of Municipal Bylaws   Pet owners' knowledge of the bylaws was found to be relatively poor and confused—a result that will probably not surprise educators in this field. Forty-six percent did not know that their municipality had a law against dogs chasing or worrying people, and a smaller proportion (32 percent) were unaware of the law concerning dogs roaming unattended outside a property. Sixty percent did not know of any other bylaws.

Analyses of the data were undertaken to explore the possibility of different people having different levels of knowledge of these municipal regulations. Men and women did not differ in this respect and, in fact, throughout the entire questionnaire very few sex differences emerged. People with two or more dogs, however, tended to have a greater level of knowledge than those who only had one dog or those with multiple pets.

People living in the inner suburbs tended to have less recall of the amount they paid for the registration fee and less knowledge of municipal bylaws than people living elsewhere. On the other hand, outer surburbans were more aware of the law concerning dogs roaming. With respect to a person's life cycle stage, widowed, separated, or divorced people had the best recall of the amount they paid for their dog's registration fee, followed by married people, and then singles (80 percent, 57 percent, and 17 percent respectively). Single people not only had the worst recall but were also the least aware of municipal bylaws.

Perceptions of Their Dogs   To an open-ended question, "How would you describe your dog's behavior?" only 9 percent of responses produced a negative description such as "dislikes children," "naughty," "stupid," "useless," "aggressive," "disobedient," or "nasty temper." The remaining 91 percent of responses were positive and gave a favorable image of the dog such as obedient, well-behaved, good dog, gentle, quiet, affectionate, loving, good watchdog, good with children, and intelligent.

A series of adjectives was supplied on which respondents were asked to rate their dog. Most adjectives were again positively biased. For example, most people thought that their dogs were extremely clean, loving, intelligent, warm, playful, reliable, friendly, and obedient.

One of the outstanding results of the survey was an absolutely uncritical attitude of owners toward their dogs. Their responses to this set of questions painted a glowing picture of perfection!

At the same time, the results documenting an apparent uncritical attitude regarding pets raise a serious research problem in the area of human-pet bonding.

The use of adjective rating scales is a standard psychological test procedure for examining people's attitudes about themselves, other people, and social and political issues. When used to explore the nature of the human-pet bond, however, they did not produce any useful insights other than the above-mentioned uncritical attitudes of people toward pets. To be useful, such scales need to produce a range of answers so as to enable the researcher to tease out essential differences between people's attitudes and thus be better able to understand the nature and formation of the attitude.

It may well be that the bond arises because of limitations in normal human-human relationships. Althoug psychological tests can accurately measure these inadequacies of human relationships, they fail to detect them in human-pet relationships. Hence the nature of the bond needs a different research technique, which takes into account both human-human and human-pet relationships at the same time.

In an effort to explore these rating scales further, a series of cross-tabulations were performed on the data, which showed some variation among people despite the extremely "favorable" results in the sample as a whole.

A dog seemed to have different characteristics to owners in different life stages. For example, single people tended to describe their dogs as less reliable; to young childless couples their dog was more active and rough; people with older children saw theirs as more confident; widowed, separated, and divorced people saw theirs as more aggressive; whereas old childless couples described their dog as more reliable.

Given these descriptions, one cannot help but raise the possibility that people see their dog as an extension or projecton of themselves and thus describe it according to their own self-concept. This possibility is not suprising when one considers the enormous amount of generalization that takes place in human relationships. We tend to assume rightly or wrongly that other people will feel similar emotions and react in ways similar to ourselves. Many psychological studies have shown that people seek friendship with people who are similar to themselves in many ways, and with close association this similarity tends to increase. The same mechanism could easily operate in a human-pet relationship wherein, over time, the pet comes to acquire characteristics similar to those of its owner. Heiman (1956), discusses cases in which individuals have displaced, projected, identified, or fantasized with respect to their pets and, as a result, maintained their psychological equilibrium.

A factor analysis of the data was performed on this set of descriptive adjectives to see whether an underlying pattern of relationships existed among these descriptions. This analysis yielded three major factors: acceptance/trust, love/friendship, and intelligence/obedience. This analysis showed that pet owners described their dogs according to three components or dimensions that form a conceptual image which people have about their pets. This image, in turn, governs their relationship with the pet.

Thus a pet is seen as a living creature with whom a person can share a relationship involving trust and the warm feelings of love and emotional support. This relationship also includes a recognition of intelligence on the part of the pet. These factors are also usually found in descriptions of human-human relationships. It would seem, therefore, that these are the basic ingredients for human relationships whether they be with another person or with a pet.

According to Katcher, "The bond is distinctively different from human relationships and those distinctions are essential to the nature of our bond to companion animals" (1981:65). The results of this analysis together with other findings yet to be discussed would tend to suggest otherwise, however. The basis of the human-pet bond seems to correspond with human-human bonds, involving intellectual and emotional components as well as trust.

If, as many people would agree, our society has developed to the point where it is restrictive of adequate social interaction for many people, it would seem to be a natural tendency for people to want to compensate for this loss in some way. We do not mean to suggest that dogs are in any way an "inferior" substitute for contact with other human beings. On the contrary, they seem to be substituting for or supplementing a real inadequacy of human-human relationships in present-day societies.

Human-Pet Bond Benefits   Over half the respondents felt that their dog was a help or a source of encouragement to them when they were feeling upset; half claimed that walking the dog had encouraged conversations with people; but only a quarter thought it had helped relations with their neighbors.

In an open-ended question, "What have been the main benefits or good things which have occurred as a result of owning a dog?" the following benefits emerged. These benefits are listed from the most common mentioned down to the least common (Table 22.9).

A structured series of questions on the positive aspects of dog ownership revealed a similar picture although somewhat more limited in the variety of responses. The results of these questions are listed according to the respondents' level of agreement (Table 22.10).

As with the open-ended questions, the three main needs satisfied by dogs were companionship, protection, and happiness or pleasure. It is perhaps a commentary on our ability to communicate with one another that for over 90

TABLE 22.9.   BENEFITS ASSOCIATED WITH PET OWNERSHIP

Benefit	Percent

Companionship - adult (19%)
  - children (12%)
  - unspecified (15%)
    ("someone to talk to", "someone
    to look after")
	46

Security/protection
    ("good watchdog," "makes me feel
    safe when my husband is not home
    at night")
	27

Pleasure ("enjoyment," "fun," "entertainment")	10
Affection/love	5
An interest (walks, show competitions, hunting)	4

Teaches children
    (facts of life, to be kind to
    animals, responsibility)
	4

Something for family to share	2
Prestige	1
Made new friends through dog (at shows, training clubs)	1

TABLE 22.10.   BENEFITS OF OWNERSHIP TO DIFFERENT FAMILY MEMBERS

Statement		Percent Agreement
Given much happiness	to self	92
	to spouse	81
	to child	94
Great company	to self	91
	to spouse	79
	to child	94
Good protection	to self	75
	to spouse	58
	to child	75
Like a child	to self	60
	to spouse	50
Like a close friend	to self	53
	to spouse	42
	to child	87
Gives more exercise	to self	46
	to spouse	49
	to child	55
Taught child responsibly		78
Taught child to be gentle		74
Taught child about mating		25
Taught child about birth		19
Made family more close-knit		52
Protects home from burglary		76
Like a family member		97

percent of respondents, their dog gave them "companionship" and "happiness." It is clear, therefore, that dogs are not only a comfort for the elderly or for the lonely; they also serve as companions for people with families.

Three quarters of the respondents felt a need to be physically protected by a dog. The same number of people believed that their dog protected their home from burglary. These results are consistent with a Swedish study by Adell-Bath et al. (1979) in which two thirds of the respondents reported a feeling of being protected by their dogs.

Most respondents derived happiness and companionship from their dog, but only half felt that it was like a close friend to them. In view of this result, it would be useful to explore the differences between these two needs of friendship and companionship in future studies.

A series of cross-tabulations carried out on these questions concerning the benefits of pet ownership revealed that the dog satisfied different needs in different people.

Women were more likely than men to be helped by the dog's presence when upset, to feel protected by their dog, and to think that it had made their family more close-knit. Men felt that the dog gave them an opportunity for more exercise. Men and women did not differ with respect to whether the dog was like a child to them. A dog did tend, however, to be least like a child to single people, although this finding did not reach statistical significance.

Looking at differences between people as a function of where they lived, results showed that fewer outer surburbans considered that walking their dog had encouraged conversation; in fact, 30 percent of these people do not walk their dog! Inner suburbans felt that their dog made them feel safe but that it did not act as a deterrent to burglars.

People with two or more dogs were more likely to be helped by their dog's presence when they were feeling upset. They were also more likely to feel that the dog was a close friend than were one-dog owners and multiple-pet owners. In addition, they were most likely to consider that the dog had taught their children about mating and about birth. Throughout our analyses, we found that one-dog owners and multiple-pet owners were, strangely enough, essentially similar and were different from the multiple-dog owners. Perhaps people with more than one dog are greater "dog-lovers" than those with just one dog, while those with other pets are greater "pet-lovers," attached to pets in general rather than to dogs specifically.

Given these differences, it would seem worthwhile for future studies to take this aspect of pet ownership into account and to include it as a potentially important determinant or predictor of differences among people in their attitudes toward their dogs.

With respect to family life cycle, Table 22.11 shows the effects of a person's life stage on the benefits derived from dog ownership. Looking down the columns in this table it is apparent that dogs satisfy more of the needs of widowed, separated, and divorced people than those at other stages of life. It would seem, therefore, that certain needs of these people are not being met by a normal family network, and hence the dog plays a very important part in their lives. For example, it is more of a close friend to them, more like a child, makes them feel safer, and provides them with greater opportunity for exercise than it does for people with families.

Walking the dog had encouraged old childless couples to have conversations with people with whom they would otherwise not have spoken. Indeed, 73 percent believed this to be the case compared with only 48 percent of people at other stages of life.

Looking at Table 22.11 to see which benefits are most important to each type of family, it seems that companionship is the most important benefit for single people and those with families. Childless couples and separated, widowed, and divorced people not only derive companionship from their dog but also a good deal of protection—a dog makes them feel safe.

There are differences between families with children of different ages. Young children seem to benefit the most from a relationship with a dog. Compared with people with older children, a greater proportion of those with young children felt that the dog had taught them responsibility (83 percent compared with 64 percent); about mating (26 percent compared with 19 percent);

TABLE 22.11.   HUMAN-PET BOND BENEFITS TO PEOPLE AT DIFFERENT STAGES OF LIFE

			Role of the Dog			
	Companion	**Child**	**Friend**	**Protector**	**Comforter**	**Exerciser**
Singles	88	44	63	63	50	44
Young childless couples	96	67	75	92	63	67
Young families	87	59	44	71	60	38
Adult families	91	56	47	75	54	43
Old childless couples	100	65	65	74	65	63
Widowed, separated, divorced	96	75	83	96	71	58

about birth (21 percent compared with 11 percent); to be gentle (84 percent compared with 60 percent); and that it made their children feel safe (79 percent compared with 66 percent). The age of a child, however, seemed to make little difference in the amount of exercise, companionship, friendship, and happiness the child derived from the dog.

A factor analysis performed on the set of statements contained in Table 22.10 revealed three basic types of functions or needs fulfilled by pets. One of these was a "negative" function, namely, a nonteaching role for children. These factors were protection (for all members of the household); does not teach child about birth and mating; and friendship/happiness for child, for self and spouse, and for self. These functions of friendship for different family members were independent of one another. In other words, if the dog played a friendship role for the child(ren), it appears that it did not play this role for adults within the same family, and vice versa.

Again, the factor results give us an insight into the conceptual image people have of a pet. Not only is it a source of protection, it also provides friendship and happiness. The fourth factor is interesting in that there was a definite negative feeling that a dog could be a source of learning. Perhaps the role of the dog in a human-pet relationship is one of emotional support and physical protection, but it is not raised to the level of intellectual equality that enables one to give the pet a teaching role.

Human-Pet Bond Problems   Only 15 percent of respondents felt that their dog had not lived up to their expectations, and only 6 percent were sorry to have it. These people were more likely to have bought it for their children and have acquired it from a friend or relation. An open-ended question, "What problems have occurred as a result of owning your dog?" produced only sixty-two responses. These are listed in order of importance in Table 22.12.

TABLE 22.12. PROBLEMS ASSOCIATED WITH PET OWNERSHIP

Problem	Percent (of total sample)
Going on holidays ("Can't go"; "Have to make arrangements")	6
Restrictions on travel	
Damage and mess (digs holes, hair, dirt, chews shoes)	5
Medical and health (illness or death of dog)	3
Roaming	2
Barking (problem with neighbors, friends, strangers)	2
Fighting with other dogs	1
Veterinary accounts	1
Puppies	1

A structured series of questions on the problems of dog ownership gave a somewhat different picture concerning the relative importance of different problems, but all the freely elicited responses seem to be included in this provided set of questions.

It is clear from Table 22.13 that caretaking responsibilities such as feeding, grooming, and exercising create more of a problem for owners when going on holidays. Taking the dog to the vet also appears to be a problem.

In exploring the problems that may be experienced, no differences between men and women were found. Nor did the number of pets owned make any difference to the problems of pet ownership. The area in which people lived, however, did seem to have an effect on the problems they encountered. For example, accommodation was more of a problem to those living in the inner suburbs, and other dogs being a nuisance was more of a problem to those in the outer suburbs where dogs are most likely to roam. Apart from these two problems, people living in the middle suburbs seemed to experience more problems than people living elsewhere.

Several important results emerged with respect to the family life cycle. Overall, single, widowed, separated, and divorced people considered fewer aspects of the human-pet bond to be a problem compared with married people. The major problem of widowed, separated, and divorced people tended to be the expense of owning a dog and taking it to the vet—perhaps also because of the cost factor. Accommodation seemed to be the major problem faced by young child-

TABLE 22.13.   PROBLEMS ASSOCIATED WITH PET OWNERSHIP

Problem	Percent Agreement
Death of the dog would be upsetting	88
Regular feeding	53
Regular grooming	52
Regular exercise	49
Holidays	41
Taking the dog to the vet	39
Expensive to own	33
Noisy	30
Dog frightens people	28
Escaping	25
Smelling	21
Nobody home	20
Regular discipline	20
Damage to property	15
Accommodation	9
Complaints from neighbors	6
Unplanned litter	1

less couples, presumably as a result of living in the inner suburbs, where space, particularly garden space, is limited. To couples with a young family, the dog escaping was the major problem. This could be because small children leave gates open. Unfortunately, we have no data to indicate the real reasons why the important matter of roaming dogs is more prevalent in these young families.

Old childless couples find that exercising the dog is one of their major problems, perhaps as a result of their age. They, together with couples with older children, find that regular feeding is also a major problem—undoubtedly for two very different reasons. For the old childless couples, the problem may be the time or effort to prepare a meal or its cost. To a family with older children, the problem appears to lie elsewhere. When the data were cross-tabulated by the variable "Who owned the dog?" results showed that more problems were associated with a "family dog," that is, one owned by the whole family rather than by one person. This situation most probably arises as a result of caretaking roles being less well defined if several people own the dog. The absence of a "regular feeder" could well be the reason why feeding is a problem in families with older children.

One final factor that had an effect on people's experience of problems with pet ownership was where they had acquired their pet. Escaping was more of a problem for owners of dogs that had previously been strays. And compared with people who had obtained their dog elsewhere, people who had been given their dog as a gift tended to see more problems—going on holidays, the dog escaping, and the expense of keeping it. As a reflection of these problems, a greater proportion of these "gift dog" owners would not buy another dog if their present

TABLE 22.14. REASONS WHY OTHER DOGS ARE A NUISANCE

Reason	Percent
Roaming dogs (scare people, chase children on bikes, cause accidents)	38
Straying onto property (fouling, upturning rubbish bins, and destroying garden)	37
Barking	20
Annoying own dog (when taking it for a walk or if strays onto property)	5

dog were to die. These two findings together suggest that people who have been given a dog as a gift develop less of an attachment to it than people who made a deliberate and personal decision to acquire a dog.

In constrast to the finding reported in the Swedish study by Adell-Bath et al. (1979), people who had obtained a dog for their children or who had been persuaded by their children to get one were not less interested in getting another dog. The dog had not met their expectations as much as for other people, yet this did not seem to have an effect on their desire to have another dog.

The final problem generated by pet ownership concerns the effect of other people's dogs on the respondents. A high proportion (41 percent) felt that other dogs were a nuisance to them personally. The reasons given for this situation are presented in Table 22.14.

DISCRIMINANT FUNCTION ANALYSIS

The foregoing results were obtained from frequency distribution analyses and cross-tabulation of individual variables. Two other multivariate statistical analysis techniques were used to search for patterns in the data. The first, factor analysis, has already been reported. The second technique, discriminant function analysis, was used for three variables: area, the pet index, and the family life cycle index.

This technique was used to distinguish statistically between certain groups of people in order to explore the differential role played by dogs in different people's lives. For example, the inner, middle, and outer suburbs were treated as three groups; the discriminant function analysis was then applied to the data to see which variables best predicted membership of these three groups. In this way, a pattern within the data emerged, which was not clear in the individual analyses.

ANALYSIS BY AREA

The analysis yielded two discriminant functions, that is, two sets of variables, which, when taken together, predicted significant differences between areas. The first function clearly separated the middle suburbs from the outer suburbs. The function can be described as a "mental concept" of the dog. At one extreme is the image of the dog held by those living in the outer suburbs as an independent creature, which is bound by the constraints of bylaws. At the other extreme is the image of the dog in the eyes of those living in the middle suburbs as a child, providing support and company for the family and especially a playmate for the children. This dimension, separating middle from outer suburbs, raises an important question about the human-pet bond which has been discussed earlier. Does their image of the animal in fact reflect people's own values about themselves?

Other studies on people's concepts of where they live show big differences between people living in the open, unrestricted fringe areas of a city and those who feel constrained, living within the city.

The second function adds to this interpretation in that it separates the inner suburbs from the other two on the basis of problems with the dog. Inner suburban dwellers have maintenance problems such as exercising the dog and smell, whereas people in the other suburbs have constraint problems such as the dog posing problems with holidays. Again, physical confinement of inner city living imposes pet management problems, whereas these do not occur to the same extent in other suburbs where there is more space for the dog. The concerns of middle and outer surburbans relate more to the effects of the dog on the family, particularly the children. Problems exist for all groups, but they tend to have different priorities, depending on where one lives.

ANALYSIS BY PET INDEX

The sample was divided into three groups: one-dog owners, two- or more dog owners, and multiple-pet owners. One significant discriminant function was generated which clearly predicted those variables separating the three groups. This function has been interpreted as describing, once again, the image of the dog in the eyes of its owners. Owners of two or more dogs tended to see their dog as a close friend, whereas those with only one dog and those with multiple pets see it as more like a child.

ANALYSIS BY LIFE CYCLE INDEX

For this analysis, the life cycle index was reduced to four categories because previous analyses had shown few differences between single people and widowed, separated, or divorced people and between families with young children and families with older children. This analysis was therefore performed on four groups: single people, widows, separated, and divorced people; young childless couples; young and adult families; and old childless couples.

Two significant discriminant functions were generated; the first split the sample into those with children and those without children. By means of this discriminant function, families without children may be described as seeing their dog in a more positive light than do those with children. For example, they tended to emphasize the pleasures the dog had brought them. Those with children, on the other hand, focused more on the problems associated with dog ownership (such as escaping). As discussed earlier, dogs seem to satisfy more of the needs of people without children.

The second function clearly splits the young childless group off from the rest. This function may be described as a nuisance factor and was constructed principally from problems of accommodation and the number of hours the dog is left alone. These define the young childless group who are obviously aware of the constraints that their lifestyle imposes on the dog (Figure 22.1).

FIGURE 22.1. DIFFERENCES BETWEEN LIFE STAGES

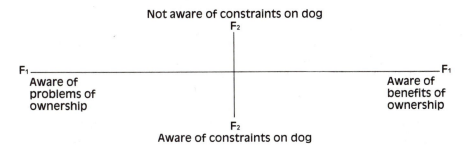

IMPLICATIONS

Results of this study have not only confirmed previous work in this area but have also revealed important findings in relation to the human-pet bond. These findings provide objective research evidence substantiating several authors' views about the differential role which pets play for people at different stages of life. It seems that pets are more important in the lives of those who are without a normal family network—childless couples both young and old and those who are widowed, separated, or divorced. A pet is more of a friend, child, protector, and comforter as well as a source of exercise for them than it is for other people.

To those with children, on the other hand, the pet seems to be another family member, acting as a playmate or friend for their children but only as company for themselves. An important exception to this finding is the case of a young couple who have recently had a baby. In this situation, the pet, who was once an integral and important part of their lives, now becomes a burden and is neglected in favor of the baby, who is as yet too small to benefit from the friendship of a pet. Finally, single people seem to lie midway between childless couples and families in the sense that their pets are not as important to them as they are to childless couples but are more important than they are to those with families. Pets are a companion to them yet not exactly a friend. They are not a child substitute, nor do they provide much comfort, protection, or exercise.

The pet ownership index was also a useful indicator of the role of the pet although its importance was far outweighed by the life cycle index. Owners of just one dog and owners of multiple pets seemed to regard their pet as more like a child whereas owners of two or more dogs regarded theirs as more of a friend.

In view of the low and confused level of knowledge about municipal regulations, there would appear to be wide scope for educators not only to inform people of the laws relating to pet ownership but also to encourage a better awareness of their responsibilities as pet owners.

The one result that tends to stand out above all others is that despite the problems generated by their pets (which were readily acknowledged) there was a remarkable tendency for people to use extreme ratings in describing their pets. For example, they were very loving, friendly, warm, intelligent, genuine, accepting, and so on. This highly uncritical attitude is a little puzzling—perhaps because we, the authors, are used to dealing with less than perfect relationships between people. Indeed, it would be surprising if a similar number of people were to describe their husbands, wives, or best friends in such glowing terms!

The final question is whether pets would be needed in an "ideal" society. Are there any needs over and above those that other humans could provide that pets do in fact fulfill? In other words, are there any components or aspects of the human-pet bond which are peculiar or specific to animals and which could not be satisfied by "perfect" people in a "perfect" world? The needs that are believed to be satisfied by pets as reported in the literature and in our study strongly suggest that there is no such thing as a human-pet bond which is distinctly different from a human-human bond. All the evidence seems to point to essentially inadequate and unsatisfactory human relationships in our present society with a consequent need to compensate for this loss with pet ownership. For example, pets are reported to satisfy needs for companionship, friendship, love, and affection—all of which have become increasingly hard to satisfy in our nuclear families living impersonal suburban lifestyles. Pets are believed to satisfy our needs for touching, playfulness, and uninhibited expression of feelings—all of which seem to be relatively prohibited in our society because people find it difficult to show their true feelings. Finally, pets are believed to be important because they give us unconditional love and are nonjudgmental or uncritical. These aspects, again, tend to remind us of the inadequacies in human relationships, and it is not surprising that they represent the ideal characteristics of a good therapist!

CONCLUSION

This study has been a beginning. It has pointed to new areas of interest as well as confirming well-known hunches. In bringing together the research evidence documented in the literature to date and the results of our own study, we hope that future work in this important area of man's relationship with companion animals will be facilitated.

Our results have shown that pets play a different role for people at different stages of their lives. As well, to each member of a family they can be something different—a companion or another child to the mother, a source of exercise for the father, a playmate or friend to the child, a grandchild to the elderly. We believe that pets give us companionship, friendship, and happiness. They also make us feel safe—especially at night and if we are alone. They make us feel important and increase our self-confidence, and sometimes, unfortunately, they relieve our hostilities by acting as our scapegoats. They also play with us and so allow expression of the eternal child inside most adults. Above all, pets allow us to love and to be loved.

Joseph S. Quigley, Lyle E. Vogel,
and Robert K. Anderson

23

A Study of Perceptions and Attitudes Toward Pet Ownership

Interactions of people and animals have been observed and recorded as an integral part of society since the earliest known history of man. These relationships have ranged from the simple to the complex in accord with evolving cultures and technology (Schwabe, 1978). Gerald Carson attributes these varying and often conflicting relationships of people and animals to "the unique ability of man to imagine and think abstractly," which, Carson says, has resulted in mankind perceiving animals in a variety of ways—as gods, slaves, subjects of art, moral examples, a source of food and fiber, and sometimes a companion and friend (1972).

Kenneth Clark (1977) has similar ideas. He also thinks man perceives animals in varying ways. These perceptions, he holds, result in a gamut of human feelings and behaviors—love, hate, fear, reverence, admiration, tenderness, and cruelty. We suggest that the human perceptions mentioned by Carson and Clark persist today and that they continue to have important consequences for people, animals, and the environment they share.

Most of us would probably agree that human feelings of love, hate, fear, reverence, admiration, tenderness, and cruelty may describe some people-pet relationships operating today. All of these words have to do with human feelings (and, some would add, animal feelings), which are constructs and cannot be quantified. This vagueness creates difficulties when attempting to analyze and explain pet ownership or, conversely, nonownership.

Some studies have attempted to describe pet ownership by creating several general classes of pet ownership. For example, a study by Wilbur (1976) categorizes pet owners as enthusiastic owners, companionship owners, status symbol owners, worried owners, and dissatisfied owners. Feldmann (1977) on the other hand, classifies the owner-pet relationship by needs which people satisfy through their pets. These are friend and partner; self-identity and self-esteem; facilitation and catalysis; and childhood development. Franti, Krause, and Borhani (1974), in a demographic study of pet owners and nonowners, suggested that the psychosocial aspects of pet ownership deserve further study.

These introductory examples indicate the complexity of animal-human relationships and some of the difficulties in fully describing such interactions. It appears that we need additional studies to add to our knowledge of those attitudes and perceptions which influence health, environment, and quality of life for both owners and nonowners of pets. We believe it is also useful to study pet-people relationships as they operate in actual community settings.

Demographic studies were conducted in a suburban city, representative of the population in northwest Hennepin County, Minnesota. This chapter reports on that portion of the studies which obtained further data to describe the perceptions and attitudes of pet owners and nonowners toward pets.

METHODS AND PROCEDURES

Since 1977, the Health Science Schools of the University of Minnesota have been working with health care consumers and providers in fourteen suburban communities in northwest Hennepin County, Minnesota, in projects which have a goal of interfacing health science teaching and service roles of the university with ongoing community health programs. For this study, one of these suburban cities was selected as being most representative of the area when census data were examined and compared for sixteen demographic factors that were thought to influence ownership of pets. This community had approximately 8,300 of the 48,000 households in northwest Hennepin County. A stratified random sample was selected from each of the eight census tracts based upon the proportionate number of households in that tract as compared to the total number of households in that city.

The selection of sample size (325) was based on such factors as the distribution (Gaussian, Binomial, Poisson) expected for the different parameters to be measured, the level of confidence desired (95 percent), the expected variability of the population, the desired length of the confidence interval, the amount of acceptable error (10 percent), the expected nonresponse rate (15 percent), and constraints of time and resources.

The individual households to be included in the sample were selected by use of a table of random numbers and the 1970 census, city block booklet, which listed the serial number of each block in every census tract and the number of housing units per block. The addresses were determined, after identification of the census number of the blocks, during an on-site visit by proceeding in a predetermined manner from a randomly predetermined corner of the block (Backstrom and Hursh, 1963). Once the address was determined, a reverse telephone directory was used to determine the individuals' names and telephone numbers.

An explanatory letter, an informed consent form, and a questionnaire were mailed to each selected household with a preaddressed, postage-prepaid return envelope. The informed consent form, the questionnaire, and the study methods received approval from the Human Subject Research Review Committee of the University of Minnesota. The letters to those households not listed in the reverse telephone directory were addressed to the current resident. The questionnaires were mailed sequentially to one census tract at a time to manage the follow-up in an expeditious manner. A period of about seven days was allowed to elapse to provide time for the households to respond by mail. If a mail response was not received in about seven days, the selected household was contacted by telephone. If the household did not have a listed telephone number or if contact was not made during three phone attempts at different times of the day, the household was contacted by a personal visit. When a person in the household was contacted, he or she given the options of completing the previously mailed questionnaire or answering the questions for the interviewer by phone or visit to the household.

Three attempts were made to contact the selected household by personal visit before classifying the household as "unable to contact." If the initially selected household was classified as "unable to contact," vacant, or a refusal, a questionnaire was mailed to the preselected alternate. If needed, a second alternate was selected by using a table of random numbers and the census block statistics booklet. All interviews, by phone and in person, were conducted by one person to avoid variations between and among interviewers.

During the follow-up by telephone, seven or eight days after mailing of the initial questionnaire, 80 of the 325 households were classified as "unable to contact," "first time refusals," and "vacant units." To replace these households, 80 additional questionnaires were mailed to the alternates to produce a total of 405 households that were mailed questionnaires. The 63 households that gave a "first refusal" to answer the questionnaires were studied further to see if they would finally complete the questionnaires or at least answer question 1 regarding ownership of a dog or cat. Of the 63 first refusals, 31 finally completed the questionnaire and 15 answered question 1 to provide data on 46 of the 63 (73 percent) "first refusals." The final summary of responses and nonresponses from the 405 households is presented in Table 23.1 as vacant units = 7 (2 percent); unable to contact units = 6 (1 percent); refusal to answer = 17 (4 percent); for a total of 30 (7 percent) sample households from which no information could be obtained. A total of 375 (93 percent) of the 405 households answered one or more of the questions to provide information for this study.

Table 23.2 presents data which indicate that the largest percentage of responders gave answers by phone; fewer by return of the mailed questionnaire; and even fewer by visit. Analysis of additional data indicated that the highest proportion of mailed questionnaires were returned by pet owners. Of these, a smaller proportion responded by phone or visits. Thus it would seem that dog and cat owners were more willing to participate by readily responding to the first mailing, whereas a greater proportion of nonowners needed follow-up phone calls and visits to achieve the 93 percent response. The nonowners apparently were less interested in providing information regarding their attitudes and perceptions of pet ownership.

RESULTS

The results reported here are part of the results of a larger study that was designed to enumerate the pet population in the representative suburban city; to identify extrinsic factors associated with ownership of pets; and to identify perceptions and

TABLE 23.1.   SUMMARY OF RESPONSES AND NONRESPONSES TO THE QUESTIONNAIRE FROM 405 HOUSEHOLDS

Classification of Household Units	No. of Units	Percent of Total Units in Sample
Vacant units	7	2
Unable to contact	6	1
Refused to answer questions	17	4
Answered one or more questions	375	93
	405	100

TABLE 23.2.   PROPORTION OF RESPONDERS THAT ANSWERED THE QUESTIONNAIRE BY MAIL, PHONE, OR VISIT

Method of Answering	Primary Sample		Sample Alternative		Total	
	No.	Percent	No.	Percent	No.	Percent
Phone	168	(56)	47	(62)	215	(57)
Mail	94	(32)	18	(24)	112	(30)
Visit	37	(12)	11	(14)	48	(13)
	289	(100)	76	(100)	375	(100)

attitudes toward pet ownership. This report concerns the latter objective. Respondents, which included only those owners or nonowners of dogs or cats or both who answered the appropriate question, were asked: "What are the major advantages of owning pet dogs, and/or cats?" Choices of companionship, love and affection, working animal, protection, sports use, breeding value, temperament and habits, pleasure, challenge, physical beauty or characteristics, education, and others were offered.

The results of this question are summarized in Table 23.3. There are very highly significant ($p < .001$) differences between the pet owners and the nonowners in the categories of love and affection, sports use, pleasure, and none. A larger percentage of the pet owners selected love and affection and pleasure as advantages when compared to the nonowners; conversely, a larger percentage of nonowners selected sports use and no advantages, when compared to pet owners. There are highly significant ($p < .01$) differences between pet owners and nonowners in their perception of the advantages of temperament and habits and of physical beauty of pets. A higher percentage of pet owners selected these characteristics as advantages for ownership when compared to nonowners.

There are significant ($p < 0.05$) differences between pet owners and nonowners in the categories of protection and challenge. A larger percentage of pet owners selected challenge as an advantage whereas a higher percentage of nonowners selected protection as an advantage.

The pet owners chose a higher number of advantages than the nonowners.

TABLE 23.3.   ADVANTAGES OF OWNING PETS: COMPARISON OF PERCEPTIONS AND ATTITUDES BETWEEN PET OWNERS AND NONOWNERS

Attributes Perceived as Advantages	By Pet Owners*		By Nonowners		
	No.	Percent†	No.	Percent†	P
Pleasure	102	58	38	21	< .001
Love and affection	119	67	67	37	< .001
Beauty	35	20	16	9	< .01
Temperament and habit	23	13	7	4	< .01
Challenge	18	10	8	5	< .05
Companionship	133	75	118	66	–
Educational	20	11	11	6	–
Breeding value	15	9	8	5	–
Just a pet	7	4	5	3	–
Others	5	3	6	3	–
Working animal	5	3	8	5	–
Protection	53	30	75	42	< .05
Sports use	9	5	22	12	< .001
No advantages	2	1	19	11	< .001
Total respondents†	177		179		
Total responses	546		409		
Responses/respondent (M)	3.1		2.3		

*Pet owners means dog and/or cat owners.
†Percent of respondents selecting an advantage (most respondents selected multiple advantages).

TABLE 23.4.   ADVANTAGES OF OWNING A PET*: COMPARATIVE RANKING OF OWNERS' AND NONOWNERS' PERCEPTIONS

Ranking of Owners	Perceptions of Advantages	Ranking of Nonowners
1	Companionship	1
2	Love and affection	3
3	Pleaure	4
†4	Protection	2†
†5	Beauty	7†
†6	Temperament	12†
7	Educational	8
8	Challenge	9
9	Breeding value	10
†10	Sports use	5†
†11	Just a pet	14†
12	Working animal	11
13	Others	13
†14	No advantages	6†

*Pet owners means dog and/or cat owners.
†Rank order of perceptions differs by two or more rankings.

The mean number of advantages chosen was 3.1 by the pet owners and 2.3 by the nonowners.

After being asked about their perceptions of advantages, the respondents were asked to select categories perceived to be a disadvantage in owning a pet. These were cost of owning a pet, physical requirement of restraint, responsibility, allergy, diseases of pets, reproduction and associated problems, noise, odor, problems with house-training, disposal of feces, overpopulation, negative temperament or habits, and other. The results of this question are summarized in Table 23.5. Again, as for the previous question, there are significant differences between pet owners and nonowners. Nonowners chose more disadvantages than did the pet owners—a mean number of 2.56 for nonowners compared with 1.80 for owners. In addition, a greater percentage of nonowners chose every disadvantage category except shedding of hair. Significantly, 15 percent of the pet owners indicated there were no disadvantages compared with only 2 percent of nonowners. A very highly significant ($p < 0.001$) difference is found in the categories of restraint problems, allergy, and overpopulation with the nonowners higher in all three cases. Some of the nonowners commented that they do not have pets because they do not believe pets should be subject to restraint. This opinion indicates an element of pet ownership concerning the rights of the pet which the questionnaire did not address.

The comparative ranking of perceptions and attitudes of owners and nonowners regarding disadvantages is shown in Table 23.6. This ranking of their perceptions indicates close agreement between owners and nonowners that the

TABLE 23.5. DISADVANTAGES OF OWNING PETS: COMPARISON OF PERCEPTIONS AND ATTITUDES BETWEEN PET OWNERS AND NONOWNERS

Attributes Perceived as Disadvantages	By Pet Owners*		By Nonowners		
	No.	Percent†	No.	Percent†	P
Restraint required	18	10	62	34	< .001
Allergy problems	9	5	38	21	< .001
Overpopulation	13	7	37	20	< .001
Diseases	8	5	23	13	< .01
Reproduction problems	10	6	25	14	< .05
Noise, odor, feces	57	32	80	44	< .05
Others	4	2	15	8	< .05
Costs of owning	39	22	48	27	–
Responsibility	104	59	109	60	–
Negative temperament	19	11	22	12	–
Shedding hair	9	5	3	2	< .05
No disadvantages	27	15	3	2	< .001
Total respondents	176		181		
Total responses	317		465		
Responses/respondents (M)	1.8		2.6		

*Pet owners means dog and/or cat owners.
†Rank order of perceptions differs by two or more rankings.

greatest disadvantages of pets are the assumed responsibility, the problems of noise, odors, and feces, and the cost of owning a dog and or cat. In contrast, this ranking indicates wide divergence in views regarding importance of negative temperament, allergy problems, and diseases as perceived disadvantages. Only three nonowners perceived no disadvantages (ranking of 12) while twenty-seven owners (ranking of 4) perceived no disadvantages in owning dogs or cats.

DISCUSSION

Feldmann (1977) and Wilbur (1976) attempted to classify pet owners into categories, but their classifications were different. An additional but also different classification was developed by Kellert(1976), who classified attitudes of people toward animals in nine categories: naturalistic, ecologistic, humanistic, moralistic, scientistic, aesthetic, utilistic, doministic, and negativistic. These previous studies attempt to categorize and emphasize the differences within the groups studied. Our study, however, indicates there are many similarities between pet owners and nonowners for some perceptions as well as widely divergent views on others.

TABLE 23.6. DISADVANTAGES OF OWNING A PET*: COMPARATIVE RANKING OF OWNERS AND NONOWNERS' PERCEPTIONS

Ranking of Owners	Perceptions of Disadvantages	Ranking of Nonowners
1	Responsibility	1
2	Noise, odor, feces	2
†6	Restraint required	3†
3	Costs of owning	4
†9	Allergy problems	5†
7	Overpopulation	6
8	Reproduction	7
†11	Diseases	8†
†5	Negative temperament	9†
12	Others	10
10	Shedding hair	11
†4	No disadvantages	12†

*Pet owners means dog and/or cat owners.
†Rank order of perceptions differs by three or more rankings.

For example, both owners (59 percent) and nonowners (60 percent) felt that responsibility for a pet was the greatest disadvantage to ownership. We are often concerned about lack of responsibility among pet owners, but these data indicate that an equal proportion of owners and nonowners recognize responsibility, and approximately 60 percent of both consider it important. Both owners (22 percent) and nonowners (27 percent) gave similar frequency to the disadvantage of cost, and this perception was ranked third as a disadvantage among pet owners and fourth by nonowners. This high ranking in frequency by both indicates relative agreement on this factor so the decision to own a pet may indicate that this disadvantage is outweighed by other perceived advantages.

In contrast to those areas of relative agreement for perceived disadvantages, there are nine areas with significant differences. Perhaps these are among the additional disadvantages which lead to decisions not to own pets. For example, required restraint of dogs or cats was considered a disadvantage very frequently (ranking 3) by nonowners (34 percent), while few owners (10 percent) considered restraint a disadvantage (ranking 6).

This finding raises several questions: Did owners have more suitable houses and yards; or were owners more aware of obedience training; or were these owners less worried about restraint; or a combination? These aspects need to be considered further.

Overpopulation and disease were also perceived with significant differences by owners and nonowners. Reasons for the differences in perceptions are not apparent, and there is a need for such understanding. The significant differences between owners (5 percent) indicating allergies as a disadvantage and nonowners (21 percent) may be the reflection of a real problem among nonowners and a primary reason why they do not have pets. On the other hand, the finding that 5 percent of owners also consider allergies a disadvantage may indicate that owners recognize the problem. In addition, as reported by Baker and McCulloch (1981), this may indicate that in spite of an allergy associated with the pet, some owners either ignore or make accommodations to deal with the problem.

As we might expect, nonowners indicated an average of 2.6 perceived disadvantages compared to 1.8 indicated by owners. In contrast, owners mentioned an average of 3.1 perceived advantages compared to 2.3 mentioned by nonowners. Thus an increased number of positive perceptions was associated with owning a pet and an increased number of negative responses was associated with status as nonowners.

Similarities and differences among owners and nonowners in their perceptions of advantages of owning pets (Table 23.3 and 23.4) illustrate the difficulties encountered when authors (Wilbur, 1976; Feldmann, 1977; Kellert, 1976) attempt to classify people and their attitudes toward pets into narrow, fixed categories. Attitudes have a complex base including personal feelings, which range from strong to weak and distinct to mixed. We often hear people say they have mixed feelings, indicating both plurality and degrees of variability. This study allowed people to indicate several responses to accommodate plurality and degrees of variability in their perceptions.

For example, among the 177 owners and 179 nonowners indicating their perceived advantages of owning pets (Table 23.3), the owners expressed more frequently the importance of feelings such as love and affection (67 percent versus 37 percent), pleasure (58 percent versus 21 percent), and beauty (20 percent versus 9 percent). On the other hand, companionship was the most frequently perceived advantage among both owners (75 percent) and nonowners (66 percent). Certainly, as is well stated by Bustad (1980a), the connotation of companionship includes the previously mentioned feelings of affection, pleasure, and so on. In this study, however, the owners appeared to be more concerned about feelings and indicated love and affection, pleasure and beauty with a significantly greater frequency than the nonowners even though perceptions of companionship were comparable for both owners and nonowners. To emphasize further the hazards of fixed categorization, it should be noted that the relative ranking (Table 23.4) of companionship, love and affection, and pleasure were very similar: rank 1-2-3 for owners and rank 1-3-4 for nonowners. To emphasize the dichotomy, these feelings had similar relative ranking within their own group, but the frequency of these feelings was significantly greater for the owners than for the nonowners.

Additional significant differences were related to perceived advantages concerned with the use of animals. Advantages of pets for protection were perceived with significantly greater frequency among nonowners (42 percent) than among owners (30 percent). Sporting use of pets was also indicated with significantly greater frequency as an advantage by nonowners (12 percent versus 5 percent). Based on these results, it appears that nonowners more frequently perceive practical, less emotional advantages of pets—protection and sporting use—while owners appear to be more sensitive to the human–companion animal bond by more frequently indicating love and affection, pleasure, and beauty as perceived advantages of owning a pet.

In summary, these data suggest that, as a group, people who own pets perceive relationships with pets with more positive and emotional feelings than people who do not own pets. Reasons for the differences and similarities between these groups were not determined in this study. But these results provide descriptive data for additional insights regarding people-pet relationships as they operate in an actual community setting representing northwest Hennepin County. We believe this and other such studies will assist in providing the information needed to deal more effectively with animal problems facing society today. As more is learned about why and how pet owners and nonowners perceive human-animal relations, this knowledge can be used to develop programs for the mutual benefit of people and animals.

Edwin Schlossberg and Pat Baxter

24

Teaching Children to Think Like Animals: The Macomber Farm Project

The exhibit program at Macomber Farm was designed by the Massachusetts Society for the Prevention of Cruelty to Animals (MSPCA) to present to the public an educational program within the context of an entertainment facility.

The essential and distinctive feature of Macomber Farm is its concern to motivate people to consider and possibly alter their thinking and behavior as they become more aware of the needs of animals. To achieve this end, Macomber Farm is "people-centered" in a way that few other learning experiences or institutions are. In most zoos and theme parks, exhibits offer information *about* animals as the central focus of the experience. Here, *the relationship of the visitors with the animals* is of paramount concern. The exhibits provide information but also structure situations to involve the active participation of visitors, so people can play games and develop feelings about the issues that are a concern rather than just passing by informational material.

A total experience here involves the farm, the animals and information about them, and the visitor in a mixture that allows a person to understand the concerns behaviorally, rather than factually, thereby stressing the importance of the animals rather than simply the facts about them. Although interest in the history, evolution, and ecology of the animals provides a context in which they can be appreciated, to stress these facts would be to stress the function of animals over being sensitive to them; it would stress their utility over their existence and would take on the tone of justification for animals rather than explanation and enhancement of sensitivity to them.

The real task, then, of both the staff and the exhibits, is to create and sustain conditions that will enable people to appreciate sensitive interactions with animals. Leading toward this understanding, the exhibit elements form a carefully planned set of clues, information, and experiences to stimulate the imagination so that people are led to gain their own insight. The ideas are not overexplained but are placed carefully throughout the exhibit program, reappearing in various configurations to rekindle the awareness of an issue. In this way visitors are brought toward a decision, but the actual thought process remains their own.

These clues can be absorbed and understood most easily when introduced through playful situations—bypassing resistance that might develop from a more direct approach. Joining activities so their behavior parallels that of an animal, people can for a brief moment "become" an animal. Through this experience, information about the lives, characteristics, and problems of the animals is clearer and of more interest.

This playful atmosphere allows the discussion of issues, concerns, and information that in more conventional representations might be considered not only offensive but tedious and frightening. The informality encourages people to assume roles they would not approach in normal life. And, in addition, visitors come to Macomber Farm to have fun, and enjoyable games and interactive situations go far to fulfill these expectations.

Visitors who pass the exhibit elements will understand a part of the intent—ranging from seeing the title to about half the total experience. But those who participate can, through their own activities and interaction with other players, gain the full measure of thought that forms the background of the design. In this sense, the exhibit program has been carefully conceived so that the visitor's participation completes the whole. Each person, whether viewer or spectator, will become aware that his or her participation matters.

Generally, it is difficult to perceive that our actions do have consequences, but here, within the context of a farm, it may be easier to detect. The notion of a farm brings to mind a self-sufficient, self-contained unit—a scaled-down model of the world. This facility is a unique and defined place where people can experience the interaction of all parts, see the importance of their own size, and grasp how a system works. Within this more comprehensible structure, the significance of one person's role is more apparent—and, understanding that, the impact of behavior in broader contexts can be more clearly seen.

THE STRUCTURE OF THE EXHIBIT PROGRAM AT MACOMBER FARM

The architecture and the animals at Macomber Farm attract the public, and the management and educational staff play an important part in reaching the public with information about animal care and the concerns of the MSPCA. But the ongoing task of translating these issues into an experience that interests a full range of visitors lies primarily with the exhibit program.

The experiential, interactive configuration that has been devised to meet the needs of this project incorporates new experiences in formats that are familiar so that people will be encouraged to participate. And it presents the exhibits with clarity so the thoughts behind the design can be easily embraced.

In many public facilities, the exhibit program often becomes an end in itself, losing and sometimes subverting the reason for its design. But here, the program works clearly toward the overall purpose for the development of Macomber Farm. Preserving the special, "people-centered" quality of the experience, the exhibits have been designed as transparencies, or frames, for the real center of the farm—people's interaction with animals—and rather than centering on themselves, the exhibits are the tools through which new experience and insight can be gained.

Through playful inventions and using a variety of physical means, the design moves in four major directions preparing visitors to be concerned with the humane issues surrounding animal care. The structural range of the design includes exhibits that orient visitors, involve them with the farm, introduce them to aspects of animal behvior, and explore the relationship that has evolved between humans and animals.

AN ORIENTATION TO THE FARM

In developing a setting where connections and experiences can lead toward a change in people's values, an essential element is to ensure that the person in whom we hope to engender the response—the visitor—feels anticipated, comfortable, and welcome. The intent is to create a shelter within which it is a natural and easy response to reconsider one's thoughts and behaviors in the company of others doing the same thing. People should feel "provided for"— there should be no sense of pressure, but rather a warm environment in which people feel at ease, and the sensitivity of the program to their needs underscores the intent to develop sensitivity between humans and animals. The activities at the farm should be clearly presented, with ample directions, so there is a ready understanding of what a visit to the farm can entail.

AN INVOLVEMENT WITH THE FARM

Some exhibits welcome visitors; others intrigue and are designed to stimulate curiosity about animals and to engage people in a discovery process that encourages questions and provides good answers. If people become so involved that they are confident and interested enough to ask questions, the goal of the farm has nearly been achieved.

Some of the exhibits create situations that encourage visitors to use their imaginations to find the "connections" so that their own thoughts and activities become a part of the answer. Granting people an important role in the exhibit program gives a sense of regard for their thoughts and for their abilities and empowers them with self-assurance about their own decision making. Although it is inappropriate to insist that people reconsider their interactions with animals, the stimulation and background to suggest this move can be provided, and the self-confidence that is an essential part of making one's own decision can be reinforced.

AN INTRODUCTION TO THE BEHAVIOR OF ANIMALS

After visitors are welcomed to the farm and their interest has been aroused, another portion of the exhibit program explores behavioral characteristics peculiar to various farm animals. This subject in itself is a rich source of material for an exhibit program, but there is a more specific reason for its use as the focal point here. To understand and be concerned with humane issues, people first have to realize and believe that animals are individual, sentient being with a particular set of needs and behaviors—and that these animals respond differently to various kinds of treatment.

Although material about animal behavior is presentd in a variety of formats, its most important manifestation is in the games that have been invented for Macomber Farm. In these playful, interactive situations, people assume new roles and can have fun participating in activities in which their behavior parallels that of an animal.

The following are some examples of the games:

The Stride Game Can you walk like a goat? Matching the length and configuration of two- and four-legged farm animals, visitors can play the six different stride games to explore how these patterns differ from one another and from human movement.

I'm Working Like a Horse Playing together to move wagons along a track, visitors can compare their strength to that of a horse.

The Motion Game Watching a videotape of a horse walking, visitors can compare a similar tape of their own movements.

The Scent Maze Pigs root underground using their acute sense of smell. Visitors can test their own abilities as they sniff their way through the scent maze.

The Sight Masks   Imagine what it is like to see like a horse. Using the sight masks, visitors can see for themselves, gazing at the world through lenses so their own vision simulates that of horses, cows, sheep, goats, chickens, or pigs.

Give the Sheep a Hand   Based on the social organization among sheep, up to twelve visitors at a time can play an electronic game, moving markers around the playing field according to the rules of sheep behavior.

Follow the Leader   Social organization among cattle is the subject of an electronic game. To move the group of markers around the gameboard, players must line up each marker in proper order for each activity.

The Chicken Gesture Game   While watching a computer-animated story, visitors can guess what the gestures of one chicken mean to another as they strive to estblish rank in the pecking order. What would vigorously flapping wings mean?

The Horse Language Game   A computer-animated story details the gestures of a horse, and visitors can guess what the animal is trying to communicate. Often the animal is "talking" to a person in the image. What would ears laid back flat against the head mean?

The Social Game   What difference does the pecking order make to a chicken? In this electronic game, players have to move their markers from perch to food to water without approaching a higher-ranking marker as the size of the playing board becomes smaller and smaller.

By playing these games, visitors learn about—and actually act out—an idiosyncrasy about an animal that marks it as a special, living being. With this information and activity incorporated into their own experience, they are better prepared to respond to the concerns of the MSPCA.

AN EXPLORATION OF THE RELATIONSHIP BETWEEN PEOPLE AND ANIMALS

Having imparted knowledge about animal behavior, the exhibit program then approaches a very complex subject: the relationship between humans and animals. Again, the material is presented through a variety of means. Sometimes text, photographs, slides, film, or the computer system provides a structure, and, in other instances, games have been devised to involve the participation of the visitor with specific issues.

This subject matter—the responsibilities incurred with the domestication of animals—speaks to the main concerns of the MSPCA. The message is serious and sometimes upsetting, and so the exhibit program introduces issues, setting the stage for a more complete explanation through programs and supplementary material available for visitors at the store.

The design of the entire exhibit program has been carefully constructed so that it can stand alone to provide a rich and stimulating experience for a visitor, but it has also been planned to serve as an adjunct to the educational programs of the MSPCA. The range of material behind the exhibits is wide, but the role of the staff is also important as a means to explore the thoughts behind the design. The exhibits provoke questions and supply answers, but they also aim to stir the visitor to ask even more—leading directly to the programs offered by educational and management personnel and the supplementary printed material prepared by them. Members of the staff contribute an enormous amount to the success of Macomber Farm through their part in the program but also because their warmth and enthusiasm about the experience can create an atmosphere that will stimulate a heightened sensitivity to animals. Because staff participate in activites at Macomber Farm, it is hoped that visitors will follow suit and be eager to do so, too.

The exhibit program has also been flexibly designed so that it can accommodate new concerns of the humane community as they might emerge over the next ten to fifteen years. This quality is often incorporated into a program so that exhibits can be changed to ensure continued public interest in visiting a facility. But because the exhibit elements are custom-made to fit all visitors who come to Macomber Farm—and fit them each time they return—the program will remain vital longer than most. The "people-centered" aspect of the design—incorporating visitors and their activities into the core of the exhibit program—ensures that each visit and each part of the day will be unique. People are the best exhibit, and the variety they bring to the experience of Macomber Farm means that any number of visits to the farm will be different, exciting, and informative for viewers and participants alike.

It seems particularly appropriate to embark on this new project—aiming to encourage people to reconsider their own actions and thoughts—in a new facility free from the history of previous experiences. The experience here will be totally new and should become a model that can extend beyond a people-to-animal transaction and reach into behavioral patterns we invoke in people-to-people situations.

A visit to Macomber Farm will provide far more than most people had expected. Here they are an important part of an experience in learning more about animals, and they are participants with the staff in the exploration. An assortment of activities are guideposts, welcoming them, stirring their curiosity, introducing them to an array of animal behavior that brings up the relationship between humans and animals. The structure of the exhibit program incorporates the visitor into the core of Macomber Farm, and through games based on animal behavior people can gain a new understanding about the issues of humane concern.

THE EXHIBIT PROGRAM AT MACOMBER FARM

The following paragraphs describe briefly what happens in each of the areas and barns at Macomber Farm.

THE RECEPTION CENTER

Greeting visitors with images that support their move from a "people" to an animal world, the exhibits welcome them and show that their visit to Macomber Farm is the reason for its development. Focusing on the human hand as an important means of communication with animals, the exhibits encourage visitors to consider how sensitively they can interact with an animal.

OUTDOOR EXHIBITS

Each of the outdoor exhibits has been developed to provide orientation to the barn that is being approached; to provide a repeating and comparative experience with the animals and activities in each barn; and, for crowded days, to offer the visitors activities outside if the barns are filled.

INDOOR EXHIBITS REPEATED IN EACH BARN

Many exhibits are repeated in each of the barns so that staff and visitors can identify the animals and learn interesting and important facts about them. These exhibits serve as adjuncts to programs, presentations, or demonstrations, and members of the host and hostess staff use them to impart understanding of why Macomber Farm has been developed and to answer questions raised by guests.

THE HORSE BARN

The exhibits at this barn engage visitors with familiar images of the horse as a beautiful and graceful animal and then explore several characteristics (strength, movement, gestural communications) as a means of introducing people to some aspects of a horse's behavioral repertoire through games where a person's activity can parallel that of the animal. Against this background, the question of human responsibility in the care of a domesticated animal is raised.

OLD NEW ENGLAND BARN

The Old New England Barn was originally built in 1808 and was dismantled and moved to Macomber Farm in 1979. It offers visitors an opportunity to compare the striking differences between a nineteenth-century barn and contemporary structures. Through this experience, visitors begin to understand the radical changes in farm life that have occurred over the past one hundred years.

The garden yields vegetables, fruits, herbs, grains, and grasses and includes information about how these crops are grown and used in a variety of ways.

THE DAIRY BARN

Most visitors to the farm are familiar with dairy cows as the major source of milk and milk products, so the dairy barn is a particularly good point from which to discuss how the biological processes of an animal enable it to produce food for our consumption. With an understanding of the normal nurturance, growth, and development of calves and the way this relates to the natural cycles of a cow, visitors will have the background they need to consider aspects of the relationship between humans and dairy cows.

THE GOAT BARN

The goat barn provides a playful environment for the animals and for the visitors, with toys included in the exhibit program for both. It also offers a context for observing some of the behavioral aspects of goats and considering their needs in relation to their living environment.

THE CATTLE AND SHEEP BARN

Variations in social dominance among groups of animals provide the subject matter for interactive electronic games in this barn. These games have been designed so that the goal and instructions for each game allow visitors to play in ways that simulate behavior patterns of sheep and cattle. Sheep move in groups, and any animal can assume the lead, whereas cattle establish a clear and rigid order of dominance.

THE SWINE BARN

In the swine barn visitors use simple devices to manipulate their learning environment and understand more about the charcteristics of swine. The pigs use similar devices to manipulate conditions in their physical environment. Through this juxtaposition, visitors will see that animals have the ability to learn certain behaviors to modify their own environment.

THE FOWL BARN

Slides and electronic games in this barn point out the wide variety of behaviors and communicative gestures that are characteristic of fowl. This information provides a context for another game that explores in more detail the ways chickens use these gestures, particularly in establishing their social order of dominance.

CONCLUSION

Macomber Farm is a tribute to the MSPCA's dedication to prevent cruelty through education. Because the facility is self-supporting and entertaining, it reaches a wide audience and will, in the future, become a model for other animal-oriented facilities.

Figure 24.1. The horse motion game

Figure 24.2. The horse language game

Figure 24.3. The scent maze

Figure 24.4. The sight masks

Figure 24.5. The stride game

PART FOUR

Companion Animals and Human Health

Introduction

Leo K. Bustad, in the first chapter in this part, marshals a variety of evidence to advocate programs bringing animals and the elderly together. He even suggests that animal ownership has the potential to reduce the cost of health care for the aged. Animals are described as one of the general goods that life has to offer, and the aged are described as a deprived group with special needs for animals. There is, however, much in common between the aged and all of us, and the ideas presented may suggest that pets could make almost everyone happier and healthier.

The material cited by Bustad as evidence of the benefit of animal ownership consists largely of a discussion of general human needs or the specific needs of the aged and the explicit suggestion that pets can, to some extent, meet those needs. The assertion that companion animals can have health value is, for the most part, highly inferential. It is based upon a chain of reasoning beginning with the recognition that human beings need social support. People with a supportive network of other people about them have been found to be healthier than people who lack social support and companionship. Because pets can act as significant others, filling certain of those important needs, it seems permissible to assume that pets can improve health. A concrete example of this reasoning is found in the review of the influence of social factors on health provided by Marcia G. Ory and Evelyn L. Goldberg. Having a human confidant has been shown to be associated with improved health status. Companion animals can act as confidants (Adell-Bath, Krook, Sandqvist, and Skantze, 1979; Katcher, 1981). Therefore, companion animals, by virtue of being confidants, should act to improve health. This line of reasoning was extensively pursued by Katcher and Friedmann (1980) in their article on the "potential" health benefits of animal ownership.

Unfortunately, very few studies have attempted directly to test the inference that pets are good for your health. They can be summarized briefly by classifying them according to the methodology used.

First, there are survey studies in which health is measured at one point in time and the health of people with pets is compared to the health of individuals of similar social characteristics without pets. The surveys of Marcia Ory and Evelyn Goldberg, Barbara Knight and Dan Lago, and Susanne S. Robb in this volume are examples of this kind of investigation. The previously reported studies of Franti et al. (1974, 1980) provide other examples.

Second, there are longitudinal studies in which an individual's health is measured over a period of time and health is defined either by objective measures such as death rate, incidence of death rates, defined organic illness, differential rates of hospitalizations, or different levels of disability (the study of Friedmann, Katcher, et al. [1980] is the only example of a study of this kind) or by subjective, less reliable measures of health such as the subject's estimation of symptom burden, morale, or other global indexes of health, emotional state, disability, morale, or quality of life (Mugford and M'Comisky's [1975] experimental study of animal placement is the one example of this kind of investigation).

Third, physiological or psychological experimental studies have been made attempting to demonstrate that pets can alter behavior, or emotional or physio-logical state, in a way that would be expected to improve health or resistance to disease. The studies of Katcher and Friedmann on pets and blood pressure, some of which are reported here, are examples of this approach.

The three survey studies in this part demonstrate that the relationship between pet ownership and health or social factors associated with health is neither large, universal, nor direct. The largest and best designed of these is Ory and Goldberg's study of the relationship between life satisfaction and pet owner-ship in one thousand one hundred rural older women. They observed that subjects who had pets but were not attached to them had lower life satisfaction scores than subjects without pets. Subjects attached to their pets resembled subjects without pets. When the influence of income on the relationship be-tween pet ownership and life satisfaction was studied, the authors observed that being attached to a pet was associated with increased morale only among subjects with relatively high incomes. Their study suggests strongly that the group least likely to be favorably affected by pet ownership is rural women who have insufficient economic means and are not attached to their pet. Lago's much smaller survey of rural residents, most of whom were women, found no relationship between morale and animal ownership even when attachment was considered. The only study indicating a positive relationship between morale and pet ownership was the one reported by Robb. Her sample was drawn from an urban patient population and was almost entirely male. The patient population studied by Friedmann, Katcher, et al. (1980), in which a positive relationship between pet ownership and survival was demonstrated, was predominantly male and urban. Certainly the results of current survey studies are compatible with the hypothesis that income, attachment, urban residence, and sex of subject play an important role in determining if the presence of an animal will result in improved morale or health. These factors must be studied as covariates in any investigation of the influence of pets on health.

Whether one considers the potential health benefits or liabilities of animal ownership, it is obvious that the owner's attachment to the animal may be the most important variable mediating the animal's influence on health or morale. Since the animal's contribution to a human being's attachment has not been identified, one can raise the question if pet dogs produce more health and happiness than pet rocks. The question is only partially ironic. Measures of how an owner feels about his animal may be as good a predictor of the effect of the animal's presence on the health or well-being of the owner as observations of their interaction. There is no generally accepted measure of attachment, and in this section Ory and Goldberg, Lago and Knight, and Friedmann, Katcher et al. all used different means of estimation. Erika Friedmann, using an attachment index derived from previous studies of human animal interaction (Katcher, 1981), demonstrated significant differences in level of attachment between black and white hospitalized patients. These differences were congruent with her previously observed differences in the health effects of animal ownership between black and white patients with coronary artery disease (Friedmann, Katcher et al., 1978).

These studies also identified a group for whom animal ownership may be a threat to health: the rural poor who are not particularly attached to animals. Allergy is another problem that threatens animal owners. Edward Baker and Michael J. McCulloch's chapter indicates that allergists differ in their response to the combination of pet ownership and allergic symptoms. Some universally recommended removal of the animals, and others were more willing to adapt treatment to the animal's presence. The latter procedure may be more realistic because many animal owners apparently ignore instructions to remove the pet. Whatever animals do for health, their value is such that owners will risk or tolerate diminished health to keep their pets. And even if pets do not affect health, they certainly have the ability to influence medical practice. Allergists who owned animals were significantly less likely to make blanket recommendations to remove all animals than were allergists without pets. Just as pets may complicate the treatment of allergies, they may also cause some people to delay hospitalization because no one is available to care for their pets. Erika Friedmann, in studying the influence of pets on their hospitalized owners, did not find pets to be a significant cause of delayed hospitalization or concern and worry to hospitalized pet owners.

The final chapter in this part discusses the physiological effects that can occur when human beings use animals as objects of contemplation. When subjects contemplate a tank full of tropical fish, the attachment between subject and fish is probably not relevant to the decrease in sympathetic nervous system activation observed. The effect is probably a specific instance of a more general phenomenon: the decrease in autonomic arousal observed when the subject's attention is turned outward and his thought patterns are interrupted. The authors do, however, raise the question of what is the relevance of the living environment to health, not only the living things we are attached to as we are attached to a pet but the living things that form the visual context for our daily lives.

Leo K. Bustad and Linda M. Hines

25

Placement of Animals with the Elderly: Benefits and Strategies

Many elderly people have discovered that animal companions satisfy some of their greatest needs. Pets restore order to their lives; provide a more secure grasp of reality; and link them to a community of caring, concern, sacrifice, and intense emotional relationships. When older people withdraw from active participation in daily human affairs, the nonhuman environment in general and animals in particular can become increasingly important. Animals have boundless capacity for acceptance, adoration, attention, forgiveness, and unconditional love. Although the potential for significant benefits to a great variety of people exists through association with companion animals, the potential seems greatest in the elderly, for whom the bond with animal companions is perhaps stronger and more profound than at any other age. Unfortunately, however, very little data exist on measurable effects of animal companionship on people, including the elderly, even though people have been associated with animals for thousands of years (see Bustad, 1980a). Strategies for current programs can be developed based on what data are available, as well as on experiences at Washington State University and many other locations. Such strategies will be suggested in this and other chapters in this volume.

DEMOGRAPHIC TRENDS FOR THE ELDERLY

On the basis of current projections, the present population of people over 65 years old in the United States will have more than doubled by the year 2030. Butler predicts that in 50 years, we will have more than fifty million people in this age group, or about 17 percent of the total population (Butler, 1980). It is within the realm of possibility that with advances in research and development, as well as significant improvements in health care, the percentage of people over 65 could go as high as 30 percent.

About one fifth of our population over 65 years old is now over 80 (4.5 million persons). By the turn of the century, it is predicted that those over 80 will total 6 million persons (Siegel, 1980). The large increase has important ramifications. From 1920 to 1960 the ratio of the number of persons over 65 to those of working age (18 to 64) doubled. In 1976 the ratio was 18 elderly per 100 persons of working age. This ratio is expected to increase to 20 per 100 by 1990 and possibly to 26 by 2020.

One related concern is that these demographic changes mean that an increasingly greater share of the national health budget, effort, and resources will go to fulfill the needs of the elderly. Not only will there be a proportionately larger number of elderly, but there will be an upward shift in the age of the elderly. And the demand for health care rises with age within the older age span. The net result is that the costs of health care will be increased remarkably, and they will be borne by relatively fewer people. Cost-saving strategies need to be developed. In this regard, studies need to be conducted to determine if animal companions can contribute to reducing the costs of health care. Research has suggested that companion animals may permit the elderly to live independently in their own homes longer and to experience better health (Katcher, 1980) or reduce their dependence on drugs (Corson and Corson, 1980a).

As we consider animals and the elderly, we also need to consider where the people live and their degree of independence. Ten years ago, about one third of the age group sixty-five or over lived in the central city, while about one fourth lived in rural areas. This proportion has probably not changed greatly (Siegel, 1980). Siegel estimates that 5 percent of the population that is over sixty-five resides in institutions. As the proportion of the older age group increases, the number of elderly institutionalized will probably increase (Brehm, 1980), which may well increase morbidity and mortality, as well as decrease life satisfaction, although the degree and quality of animal association in each situation could modify this grim prediction.

Some observation on social changes in the elderly has indicated that involuntary relocation to better housing did not seem significantly to improve their health and longevity (Kasl et al., 1980). No mention was made in this study of whether animals were involved in the relocation (for example, were they left behind?), even though it is possible that animals could affect health and well-being following involuntary or voluntary relocation.

REVIEW OF THE LITERATURE

The relative newness of the idea of carefully studying the relationship between animals and the elderly is evident from a review of the literature. It is not often that one can, by purchasing six volumes, have in hand the significant articles on a subject or bibliographies that list the important articles. This is the case, however, with studies on animals assisting the elderly. The six volumes we recommend and from which most of the review information is taken are as follows:

> R. S. Anderson, ed. *Pet Animals in Society*. New York: Macmillan, 1975.
> L. K. Bustad. *Animals, Aging, and the Aged*. Minneapolis: University of Minnesota Press, 1980.
> S. A. and E. O'L. Corson, eds. *Ethology and Nonverbal Communication in* Mental Health. Oxford: Pergamon Press, 1980.
> B. M. Fogle, ed. *Interrelations between People and Pets*. Springfield, Ill.: Charles C. Thomas, 1981.
> B. Levinson. *Pets and Human Development*. Springfield, Ill.: Charles C. Thomas, 1972.

Articles discussing the effects of animals on the elderly can be divided into two basic groups: those concerned with the noninstitutionalized elderly and those focusing on the institutionalized elderly, primarily those in nursing homes.

NONINSTITUTIONALIZED ELDERLY

A review of articles in this category must necessarily be broad. Several articles make significant comments about the adult population generally that can apply in some measure to the elderly. On the one hand, we have articles that deal with an adult population that is normal and reasonably healthy. Another group of articles deals with an adult population that is experiencing mental or physical illnesses that are in some measure debilitating.

Studies are beginning to emphasize the importance of examining the relationship between animal companions and the normal, well-adjusted segment of our population. Dr. Aaron Katcher (1981) encourages us to look at pets not as substitutes for human contact but as entities that may offer a relationship that supplements and augments human relationships. He lists a series of "somethings" that pets offer which can appeal to a wide spectrum of the adult population. According to Dr. Katcher, pets offer us something to decrease loneliness, which is a serious disease today (Lynch, 1977; Bustad, 1980a) as well as something to care for, to keep us busy, to touch and fondle, and to watch (perhaps in idle play), something that makes us feel safe, and something that provides a stimulus for exercise. He indicates the possible significance of work now under way to measure the physiological effects of pets, for example, the drop in blood pressure when people pet their animals. These studies, as well as a closer look at the "somethings" mentioned above, can provide us with critical data on the effect that pets can have on the elderly population as well as the younger adult population.

Irene Mortenson Burnside, a gerontological nurse, provides valuable insight into the general needs of the elderly, which certainly affect the relationship they have with pets. In the section, "Young Old Age through Old Old Age" in *Psychosocial Caring throughout the Lifespan* (1979), she describes the basic characteristics of the elderly and some of their most important needs, needs which to some extent could be met through relationships with an animal companion.

Pets might have a positive effect on the loneliness and emotional isolation which the elderly may experience, a feeling of being locked into oneself and unable to obtain warmth and comfort from others. Burnside also points out the impact of relocation shock and its resultant stress when the elderly are moved from home to home, room to room, or home to institution. (Could animals reduce this stress?) Life review is an important aspect of working with the elderly; encouraging reminiscence is an effective tool. (Animals can trigger reminiscences.) Therapeutic touch is also extremely important. Nonverbal communication can decrease the elderly's sensory deprivation. The sensory loss, immobility, living alone, and loss of significant others experienced by the elderly may increase the need for touching. (Touching animals, as well as being touched, could be therapeutic.) Ashley Montagu in *Touching: The Human Significance of the Skin* (1971) reviews some fascinating data with animals showing the importance of touching and gentling. Burnside reviews the very important steps one must undergo in terminating relationships with the elderly. Knowledge of these steps could be especially important in instances when persons bring pets on regular visits to the elderly and then discontinue these visits.

The Aged Person and the Nursing Process (Yurick et al., 1980) provides a comprehensive, well-referenced textbook on the "application of the nursing process as the organizing framework for nurses' efforts directed toward aged people as they experience variations in health status within the realm of 'normal.'" Dr. Susanne Robb, in her chapter "Resources in the Environment of the Aged" (1980) in the Yurick volume, describes the potential of pets as significant others for elderly people and encourages nurses to cooperate in pet therapy programs. Barbara Spier perceptively includes animals in her list of significant others in her "Guide for Assessing Developmental Tasks, Self-Concept, and Coping Mechanisms" in the same volume. Ms. Spier agrees with Robb that pets can help the elderly feel cared about and needed. One of the several sensitive pictures in the book showing animals with the elderly appears in Dr. Ann Yurick's chapter "Sensory Experiences of the Elderly Person." The photograph demonstrates the value of animals in enhancing tactile sensitivity.

In *The Broken Heart: The Medical Consequences of Loneliness* (1977), James Lynch recalled that as early as 1929 it was found that the heartbeat of dogs restrained in a Pavlovian chamber slowed dramatically in response to petting.

Katcher, Lynch, and co-workers have studied the physiological conseqences of touch in a variety of situations, with both people and animals (Lynch 1977, Katcher 1981, and Katcher et al. in this volume). The physiological response to touch may be a specific case of a more generalized mechanism described by J. I. Lacey (1959). He proposed that attention to an external task and intake of information from the environment were associated with cardiac deceleration.

Recent advances in telemetry techniques have resulted in interesting studies on mother-child and people-animal interactions. Hong, Bowden, and Kogan (1977) reviewed some of the studies of sensory stimuli on heart rate. They also conducted a study on telemetered heart rate of children during play sessions with their mothers. They found that submissive status and warm affect of the child and dominant status and warm affect of the mother were associated with low heart rate in the child. The onset of smiling was associated with cardiac deceleration in most situations.

Two studies have focused specifically on the noninstitutionalized elderly segment of the population and their relationship to pets. One of the first to call attention to this area was Dr. Boris Levinson's article, "Pets and Old Age" (1969b). He pointed out that the elderly often suffer from a loss of relatives and withdraw from active participation in human affairs. Objects and animals that provided security in early life may assume greater importance in later life. The animals may indeed be an anchor for good mental health. He also explains the fragile defense structures of the elderly and the reversal of roles they experience. In this reversal, pets can be important allies because the pets depend on the owner and offer them a measure of security. Pets can help the elderly adapt to their change in status and accept their new role. Pets do not offer competition and can lead the elderly to find new interests and move out into the environment to walk and to talk with others. Pets can also be important love objects and can be loved without fear of rejection. Levinson points out that the loss of a pet can be a great tragedy and a reminder of one's own future death. This subject is covered in great depth in the Foundation of Thanatology series Pet Loss and Human Emotion.

The classic summary of the potential benefit of pets for the elderly is given by Dr. Levinson: "A pet can provide, in boundless measure, love and unqualified approval. Many elderly and lonely people have discovered that pets satisfy vital emotional needs. They find that they can hold onto the world of reality, of cares, of human toil and sacrifice, and of intense emotional relationships by caring for an animal. Their concepts of themselves as worthwhile persons can be restored, even enhanced, by the assurance that the pets they care for love them in return" (Levinson, 1969b).

Roger Mugford and J. G. M'Comisky made a significant contribution to the literature on pets and the elderly by presenting the results of an evaluation both before and after the introduction of pets (budgerigars)into the lives of selected elderly people (Mugford and M'Comisky, 1975). They discovered that the group which received the budgies showed improvement in their attitudes toward people and in their attitudes to their own psychological health. Many formed an intimate attachment to the birds which extended far beyond the test period. The birds served as a "social lubricant" in increasing their owners' communication with others.

Information that can be relevant to the elderly who are ill is given in Dr. Michael McCulloch's article "The Pet as Prosthesis: Defining Criteria for the Adjunctive Use of Companion Animals in the Treatment of Medically Ill, Depressed Outpatients" (1981b). He points out that physical deterioration and the losses that occur in old age can increase the likelihood of depression. His study, however, does not focus on the elderly. Pets are important in helping depressed patients maintain a sense of humor and in providing valuable companionship. Dr. McCulloch lists a series of ten instances when pets might be especially helpful: chronic disability or illness; depression; a previous relationship with pets; role reversal; negative dependency; loneliness and isolation; helplessness; low self-esteem; hopelessness; and absence of humor.

He offers some very significant precautions that should be observed. When pets are introduced to the medically ill, depressed patient, those involved in the prescription should be aware of the patient's increased vulnerability to the loss of a pet; tailor the prescription of the pet to the individual; coordinate the use of prescription pets with other therapy methods; identify situations that are inappropriate for prescription pets; and be aware of the importance of timing.

He also voices a concern common among scientists active in the field of animal-facilitated therapy: "If pets are to be prescribed for human ailments, they should be subject to the same scientific indications as are surgical procedures, drug therapy, and other forms of medical and psychiatric treatment" (p. 105).

INSTITUTIONALIZED ELDERLY

A much larger body of literature deals with the importance of animals to the institutionalized elderly, whether in nursing homes or in hospitals. When nursing homes are mentioned, the image that comes to mind is that which is well documented in Bruce E. Vladeck's book, *Unloving Care: The Nursing Home Tragedy* (1980). He talks about the mountains of regulations, the administrators and nurses who spend more time with papers than with patients, the inspections that do not work, and the health providers whose interest in their work seems to be diminishing. In a review of Vladeck's book, Robert Dickman points out that health care for the elderly is much more than a provision of direct medical services: "Failure to understand and deal with loneliness, frustration, isolation, and disruptive external environment is a failure to do geriatric medicine. The therapeutic value of restoring dignity or autonomy, relieving boredom, and providing appropriate stimuli to the frail elderly is unequivocal." He points out that the measure of our society will be in the care that we give to our most debilitated elderly (p. 43).

Samuel and Elizabeth Corson also speak about the vicious cycle of debilitation, social degradation, and dehumanization which can envelope the institutionalized elderly. They delineate the psychosocial structure of a typical nursing home in their article, "Companion Animals as Bonding Catalysts in Geriatric Institutions" (1981). These structures are characterized by being a closed social group; low staff-resident ratio; highly regimented routines; mass-oriented living with little privacy; a loss of both a sense of purpose and a chance for goal-directed activities; failure to furnish feelings of being needed, loved, and respected; and lack of tactile comfort.

They also talk about the impact of relocation of the elderly in nursing homes. Upon this background, they describe their studies resulting from the placement of dogs in an eight-hundred-bed nursing home which also had apartment buildings and cottages for skilled nursing care of the mentally retarded. They found that the dogs offered positive, nonverbal communication signals. They offered love and tactile reassurance, tactile comfort, and an innocent dependence. Their childlike play was stress-reducing and rejuvenating. The presence of the pets improved morale and created a sense of community. They provided an opportunity for exercise and served as social catalysts. When used in reality therapy, the pets led people toward more responsible, self-reliant behavior.

The Corsons outlined their method of introducing animals. First, they talked about the animals with the residents, then they introduced animals in the presence of or through a staff member. They offered cages of puppies in dormitory wards, dogs in individual dog houses in the cottage settings, and attached kennels with grooming and bathing facilities for the nursing home. The Corsons emphasized the importance of an annual examination by the veterinarian, of allowing the dog to relieve itself before it is taken in to visit with the patients, and of carefully selecting dogs for the purpose intended. They also talked about the necessity of educating the residents, patients, and staff on the care of the animals at the time of their introduction.

The Corsons added some important material to the study of the effects of animals on the institutionalized elderly by formulating an evaluative questionnaire to be used by nurses and by employing videotapes to document the people-pet interactions.

Jules Cass, in his article "Pet Facilitated Therapy in Human Health Care," offers some very specific conditions and circumstances for successful use of pet-facilitated therapy and for failure of or opposition to its use. He emphasizes that the animals in institutions do not offer a potential threat to health. He delineates rules for sanitation and maintenance of the pets and suggests that, for the elderly, small, sedate dogs with quiet temperaments should be chosen.

Boris Levinson (1970a) was one of the first to describe the potential of nursing home pets. He points out the need of the elderly to have someone to love and "lord it over." Pets can restore a sense of identity to the elderly and, he speculates, can cut down the demands placed by the residents on the staff. The pets serve as a love object which the patient can hug and kiss. The pet also restores communion with nature, which is increasingly lost in contemporary society. Caring for a pet can offer a sense of peace and completion and, according to Levinson, can provide an important link with reality.

Carl Brickle, in "The Therapeutic Roles of Cat Mascots with a Hospital-Based Geriatric Population" (1979), looked at the potential use of pets in institutional settings other than a nursing home. He studied pets placed in a day room in a hospital geriatric ward and found that they stimulated patient responsiveness, gave pleasure, enhanced the treatment milieu, and helped staff morale.

SUBJECTS FOR FUTURE RESEARCH

To some extent, reading current literature in the area of animals and the aging is like reading the introduction of a book with blank pages. As the pioneer investigators realize, many studies must yet be conducted to substantiate, in a scientifically credible way, the benefits of pets to the elderly both in and out of institutions. Sam Corson has called for a variety of studies to increase our knowledge in this area. He would like to see controlled studies introducing pets in several comparable institutions. He urges long-term follow-up studies and suggests an intraindividual method with a longitudinal, process-oriented design using each individual as his or her own control. He points out that we need to monitor cardiac and respiratory reactions, electrical skin resistance, and circadian rhythms of the psychophysiologic parameters before and during pet-facilitated psychotherapy. We need long-term studies on the socializing and health maintenance effects of dogs and cats on older people living alone or in family settings in different urban and different socioeconomic strata.

We need to expand the survival studies by Friedmann et al. (1980) and others to a larger number of patients for a longer period of time and include personality assessment recordings and family and other social interactions. We should investigate the extent to which pet-facilitated therapy (PFT) decreases the dosages and/or duration of use of psychotropic drugs. We need data on the extent of which pets are useful to the aged with sensory deficits, and we need to understand whether PFT helps restore individuals to more independent forms of living. Corson also suggests we look at the ways in which pets can serve as catalysts for introducing other positive activities such as gardening and music. And we can investigate the extent to which animals help bridge the generation gap.

Jules Cass points out the very great need for a manual with explicit guidelines for establishing and operating pet-facilitated therapy programs.

In looking at the importance of pets to the institutionalized elderly, we need to undertake well-planned, applied research centering on refining methods of introducing pets into different institutions to maximize positive results. We need to relate institutional characteristics to people-pet matching and resultant effects. Under what conditions do pets contribute positively to the well-being of the institutionalized elderly individuals (resource levels of the individuals, social networks of the institutions)? There is a need for comparative evaluative research on the effects of pet therapy as opposed to, and in conjunction with, other therapeutic modalities considering such factors as criteria, cost-effectiveness, and impact on well-being and health of the residents.

There are many other questions for study. What is the precise cost of maintaining animals of each species in an institutional setting and a home setting? In an institutional setting, who can benefit most from caring for the animals? Is there an increase in the incidence of any diseases when a pet is introduced into an institution? What is the incidence of allergies? How do we deal with people with animal phobias or dislikes in an institutional setting? What benefits, and for whom, are derived from each of the following methods of using pets in institutions: pets introduced in selected areas or under very carefully controlled conditions (as with Brickel and Corson); pets assigned to specific people in a therapy room; pets allowed free range of a facility (except for food areas); nonresident pets brought in for visits? What role can pets play in day care centers for the elderly? Is the success of the pet in meeting the needs of the elderly determined by the strength of a bond with a pet which the person established as a child? Is it related to continuous ownership of a pet? Is it more effective to introduce the same species the person owned before? At what period in a person's life span does possession of an animal companion have the most influence? What different effects are produced by having a dog, cat, bird, or fish? Can lifelong associations or associations after sixty years of age with animals extend life span? What specific procedures should be followed if the elderly are allowed to bring their own pets into nursing homes?

Explorations of the importance of pets to the noninstitutionalized elderly might begin with research on human-animal bonding in natural settings. We could explore the following questions. Is there a critical period for learning how to communicate with and interact with pet companions? When are children most receptive to pet bonds, and can effective learning vehicles be delivered at that time for their long-term benefit? Is access to different types of pets different for various subgroups of society (for example, rural and urban), and if so, how does this affect later social and human-animal bonding? What are the roles of pets in family settings and how do these roles relate to conflict resolution, interpersonal bonding, and teaching of social skills within the family? How does the significance of the human–companion animal and other social bonds vary over the life cycle, the work cycle, and the family cycle in regard to social well-being, mortality, health, and related phenomena?

STRATEGIES

Anyone who reads the popular press realizes that the public interest in programs placing animals with the elderly is at an all-time high. Newspapers and magazines report innumerable programs involving companion animal visitation or placement. In our extensive travels, we have found people in almost every small town or large city who enthusiastically related to us their rewarding experiences using animals to help the elderly. They varied from a Girl Scout who takes her small dog regularly to a nursing home or a couple who successfully placed a cat in a veterans' hospital to well-organized volunteers in humane society or junior league programs. The most memorable vignette involved a distinguished financier who was a board member of a large hospital complex; he would sneak his small dog under his overcoat when he visited his eighty-five-year-old mother who was confined to the hospital. He confided that his mother was not particularly interested in seeing him but she was very excited about seeing the dog.

We also read about existing or pending legislation to enable pet placement. Minnesota has a law allowing residents to bring their pets into institutions. California has adopted a law forbidding discrimination against elderly pet owners in government-subsidized housing. A smiliar law has been proposed nationally.

In spite of the lack of data on pet selection, placement, and benefits, such laws will probably spread and programs will spring up at a phenomenal rate. What should our strategies be to ensure safe, effective programs?

First, we must impress upon the scientific community the importance of undertaking critically needed research. A good example of a negative attitude that must be modified occurred at Washington State University. A social scientist visiting from one of the best known universities in the Midwest was reviewing her data from a research project on the support network in the lives of the elderly. When asked about pets, she indicated that her research group deleted all references to animals or God as irrelevant in their study.

Scientists who already recognize the importance of such research need to convince public and private agencies and individuals of the urgency of funding well-planned research projects. The Dodge Foundation has been a leader in recognizing the importance of such work at the University of Pennsylvania.

We should also offer immediate direction to people who are not research scientists but who want to promote or assist in bringing animals and the elderly together. We can suggest ways to overcome barriers that keep the noninstitutionalized elderly from enjoying an animal companion: provide low-cost care similar to the San Francisco SPCA's Pet-a-Care, encourage pet insurance plans, and investigate subsidies for maintaining medically prescribed animals. Provide short-term, minimal-cost care for animals when the owner is hospitalized. All hospital admission forms could identify such owners in an emergency with three questions: Do you live alone? Do you have animals (kind—number—)? Who should be called to care for them? Recruit volunteers (such as members of youth organiza tions) to exercise animals and transport them to a veterinarian when the owner is unable to do so (or seek a veterinarian who makes house calls). Arrange for foster home placement of the animal after the owner's death so the elderly will not refuse to get animals they need because they are afraid of dying before the animal does. Seek to liberalize no-pet restrictions in low-cost housing units for the elderly, perhaps by offering consultants to assist with problem animals or by suggesting no-pet floors or wings in large units.

In this regard, vote of the majority is not appropriate on "either/or" propositions relative to the issue of pet/no-pet rules in certain retirement units and other housing units for the elderly. The issue is too complex for a "yes" or "no" answer. If a resident has an animal that may cause a problem, a vote of the unit residents could led to expulsion of the resident and pet or euthanizing the animal at great physiological and psychological trauma for the owner. Clearly, there should be responsible action by both parties to avoid such confrontations. In such situations, a consultant on animal behavior should be called in. *Responsible* pet ownership is mandatory, and, with that assured, the resident management should provide a situation that would respect the rights of the animal and its owner as well as the rights of the residents who wish no animal contact.

People in their early sixties might benefit from preretirement counseling on the value of animal companions. Many newly retired people suffer a loss of identity. An animal companion can furnish a degree of continuity to relieve this loss if the animal is obtained before retirement. Some newly retired persons who own a high-quality purebred animal may find breeding and showing the animal a rewarding experience. Others may find that visiting homes for the disabled or the elderly with their well-trained animal is very satisfying.

Our strategies for the institutionalized elderly involve learning from the many existing programs so that we can help beginning programs. We need a central clearing house for specific details on each of these programs. Perhaps the Delta Society can provide a service in contacting each program and compiling the following information: Where are you using animals (size of nursing home, description of hospital ward, etc.)? How did you begin (contact with administration; proposal, selection, and training of volunteers; financing)? How did you select and train the animals involved? How are you evaluating or measuring the benefits? Submit sample data. What problems did you encounter? How were they solved? Describe the exact procedures of a visiting pet program. If the animals are resident animals, are they confined to a few areas, assigned to specific individuals, or kept outside in kennels? What are the future plans for your program? From these and similar questions, we could learn from experience so that others can benefit.

Finally, we need to document even anecdotal accounts of what is happening where pets live with the elderly. Such observations, even though of limited usefulness as scientific data, can nonetheless provide insights into areas in need of more precise studies. Our experiences in the People-Pet Partnership Program have provided us with such observational data. Three are particularly noteworthy.

The first involves a mistake in placement that encouraged us to develop precise selection criteria. The activity director in a local nursing home decided she would like some resident animals and selected gerbils. The placement was a disaster. Several residents beat on the cage and tried to let the gerbils out to stomp on them. We discovered that the residents with farm backgrounds saw them as rats—something to be exterminated. Since that time we have devised profiles and questionnaires (Bustad, 1980a) to enable more effective animal selection and placement.

The second anecdote involves our work with a nursing home that has a pet therapy room containing Handsome, the Persian cat. The health care team at the home meets to decide which resident can derive the greatest benefit from living in the private therapy room. The current resident, Marie, was chosen because she had no family or friends, would not communicate, and remained curled in the fetal position with no interest in living. She also had sores on her legs from continual scratching. When other measures failed, she was moved in with Handsome. Whenever she began to scratch her legs, the cat played with her hands and distracted her. Within a month the sores were healed. She began to watch the cat and to talk with the staff about him. Gradually she invited other residents in to visit with him. Now she converses with strangers as well as the nursing home staff about the cat and other subjects.

The third episode is even more dramatic. A frail, elderly man was brought to the nursing home from the local hospital. He had been discovered in a severely malnourished and confused state in a rural farmhouse, living alone in filth. Once his condition stabilized, he was brought in restraints to the nursing home because he refused to eat. Each day he worked to free himself from the restraints and to remove the feeding tube. The tube was reinserted because he refused to eat. The staff was unable to break this cycle until an aide found the center's three kittens in bed with him. When the cats were removed, he became agitated. A reward system was devised whereby the cats would be returned to him if he ate. He gained forty pounds and interacted with other residents. The cats were the bridge that brought him back to reality. The director of nursing stated that otherwise she believes he would have died.

We are continuing to work with four nursing homes in our area. Once we secure the necessary funding, we hope to assist one nursing home to select and train a mascot dog. We will help another that has had mascot cats for six years devise procedures to allow the frail elderly to bring their own pets when they move into a facility being readied for them. The facility might include dutch doors to enable conversation without letting the pet out and perhaps attached kennels appropriately soundproofed if necessary. The plan also includes remedial measures to correct offensive behavior abnormalities. For a third home that has resident fish, a bird, cat, and dog, we are serving as resource persons in helping to solve problems. The most recent involved getting the dog to stop chasing cars. The fourth home can offer us the opportunity to explore the use of pets in its hospice. (The importance of animal companions for the terminally ill has been shown by Dame Cecily Saunders and associates at St. Christopher's in London.) In three of the homes we will continue our visiting pet program and summer farm days. We will document and share what we learn from these efforts, and we encourage others involved in such activities to do so. By working together, we can increase our knowledge and evaluative techniques with the aim of enabling many more elderly to know the joys that come from having an animal companion—a friend you like who likes you back.

Marcia G. Ory and Evelyn L. Goldberg

26

Pet Possession and Life Satisfaction in Elderly Women

Over the past few decades a considerable body of literature has emerged on predictors of subjective well-being in the elderly. Despite the differences in conceptualization and measurement of subjective well-being, often defined as life satisfaction, happiness, contentment, or morale, most studies report a positive association between measures of psychological well-being and life situation variables such as socioeconomic status, health and physical activity, marital interaction, and social participation (Palmore and Luikart, 1972; Larson, 1978; Speitzer, Snyder, and Larson, 1979–80). Recent research initiatives have given attention to measurement issues and specification of the relative influences of different life situation variables on psychological adjustment (Toseland and Rasch, 1979–80; Medley, 1980; Stones and Kozma, 1980; Elwell and Maltbie-Crannell, 1981). Controlling for the well-documented influence of health and socioeconomic factors, researchers are beginning to examine the role of social interactions more closely. Although positive relationships have been found between measures of subjective well-being and the total number of both informal and formal social activities, current studies emphasize the importance of examining the nature and quality of the social interaction (Brim, 1974; Arling, 1976; Conner, Powers, and Bultena, 1979). The notion of a confidant relationship has been defined and operationalized in the literature with several studies reporting an association between the existence of a confidant relationship and positive health outcomes (Brown, Bhrolchain, and Harris, 1975; Brown, 1980). Although the examination of such life situation variables as health, socioeconomic status, age, race, sex, employment, marital status, transportation, housing, and social activity reveals significant relationships with measures of well-being, the actual individual correlations and proportion of variance attributable to these variables are modest (Larson, 1978). In a review of thirty years of research on subjective well-being among the elderly, Larson estimates that the correlations between major situational life variables range from .0 to .4 and the proportion of variance explained ranges from 0 percent to 16 percent (Larson, 1978). The variables that are the most strongly consistently related are health, socioeconomic factors, and degree of social activity. The fact that the greatest proportion in well-being scores is not explained by the currently examined life situation variables suggests a need for reconceptualization and measurement of existing variables as well as consideration of new variables for explaining subjective well-being of older Americans.

In recent years a separate but related line of research inquiry has emerged which has direct relevance for understanding and predicting psychological well-being in the elderly. Interdisciplinary researchers in veterinary medicine, public health, and behavioral sciences are beginning to explore the physical and psychological correlates of animal-human interactions (Levinson, 1972; Beck, 1980; Savishinsky, 1981). Initial findings positing a therapeutic role of companion animals in the life of chronically ill and aged populations (Brickel, 1979; Brickel, 1980–81; Bustad, 1980a; Corson et al., 1977a) suggest a new variable that should be included in quality of life studies. The basic rationale for examining the importance of pets is that companion animals not only offer a constant and unquestioning source of social contact but that they also serve as a catalyst for social interaction. Although there have been a few well-designed studies (Corson, Corson, and Gwynne, 1975; Mugford and M'Comisky, 1975; Friedmann et al., 1980a), many of the conclusions about the positive benefits of pet ownership and pet-facilitated therapy have been based on studies of small numbers of institutionalized or chronically ill persons. It is valuable to assess the therapeutic benefits of pets in institutionalized populations, but it is also important to study the correlates of pet ownership in community settings where elderly persons reside. Since pet ownership is a relatively modifiable factor, there is a special benefit in including the role of companion animals in studies examining the relative influence of different life situation variables on psychological well-being.

RESEARCH GOALS

The purpose of this study is twofold: first, to examine whether previously reported findings on the relationships between subjective well-being, defined as perceived happiness, and the commonly examined factors of socioeconomic status, health, and physical activity and social interactions are applicable in a community study of married white women aged sixty-five to seventy-five living in a relatively nonurban area; and second, to explore in the same population the nature of the relationship between pet possession and perceived happiness.

In addition to examining the relative influence of the different life situation variables, specific research questions of interest are: whether the presence of a companion animal in the household is related to perceived happiness; whether this relationship is maintained when controlling for other sociodemographic, health, and social interaction factors traditionally associated with happiness; whether the examination of the qualitative aspect of pet possession (degree of attachment) adds to the prediction of happiness in the elderly; and whether the relationship between pet possession and happiness is confounded by other sociodemographic factors.

METHODS

THE SAMPLE

This study is based on data drawn from a five-year prospective community study on factors related to health and well-being in the elderly. The goal of the larger study was to sample all noninstitutionalized married white women aged 65 to 75 listed in a 1975 countywide census and still residing in Washington County, Maryland, in 1979. Washington County, which is located in midwestern Maryland, has a semirural population of approximately 100,000 of which less than 2 percent of noninstitutionalized persons are nonwhite.

Of the 2,121 white married females aged 65 to 75 living in Washington County indentified on the 1975 census, 1,595 were located and considered eligible for study in 1979. In addition to meeting age, marital status, race, and residency criteria, women had to be currently living in a noninstitutionalized setting and deemed well enough to respond to an intensive interview averaging one hour in length. Among those considered eligible for study, 1,144 or 71.7 percent interviews were completed. An analysis of key sociodemographic factors indicated a few significant differences between the 1,144 persons interviewed and the 451 women who were potentially eligible for study but refused to participate in the study or whose interviews were too incomplete for analysis. As in many surveys, participants tended to be of higher socioeconomic status than nonparticipants. An additional nine subjects were dropped from the analysis when it was learned that their husbands were institutionalized.

Although a total of 1,135 women were considered eligible, this study is based on 1,073 respondents for whom complete data on all socioeconmoic, health, and social interaction questionnaire items examined in this study were available. T-test analyses revealed no significant differences (p > .05) on these major variables between the total population of 1,135 eligible women and the 1,073 women analyzed in this study.

THE INDEPENDENT VARIABLES

Home interviews were conducted with 1,073 respondents to obtain information on their demographic characteristics, socioeconomic level, health status and physical activities, and the amount and quality of their social interactions.

Values for age, marital status, racial, and general living situation character-istics were, in large part, predetermined by two concerns: the need to select an appropriate population for studying health and health problems of older, nonin-stitutionalized married women and the realities of the demographic distribution in Washington County. In addition to traditional demographic variables such as age, sex, marital status, race, and geographic residency, most previous studies of subjective well-being in the elderly have included some measure of socioeco-nomic status. Conceptualized as the differential distribution of income, occupa-tion, and education resulting in differential access to resources and prestige as well as the adoption of unique value patterns, socioeconomic status (SES) is hypothesized to be related not only to one's day-to-day morale but also to one's overall evaluation of life satisfaction and contentment (Moynihan, 1968). SES has been traditionally operationalized by individual or composite measures of income, education, and occupational status. Although income, education, and occupational variables were included in the home interviews, there are three difficulties in using any of these measures as good differentiations of SES in this population: first, too many observations of income are missing because 40 percent of the older women interviewed either did not know their family incomes or were reluctant to report this information; second, most women in this age group in this community were primarily homemakers and tended not to have pursued advanced educational training; and third, many of the husbands were already retired or were working reduced hours. Thus the indicator of SES chosen for this study was a measure of the quality of the respondent's housing as reported on the 1975 communitywide census. A housing index that ranged from 0 to 11 was calculated by assigning points for the presence or absence of baths, air conditioning, heating, cooking facilities, and telephones in the respondent's household. (Our records indicate that approximately seventy persons moved between the 1975 census and 1979 home interview. Although there is concern about the accuracy of the 1975 data for these people, we feel the impact will be minimized because they represent only a minority of the respondents. Further, it is our assumption that those who moved are just as likely to have moved into a similar housing situation as a better or worse one.) Representing a measure of the respondent's socioeconomic status, this variable showed acceptable correlations with the separate measure of family income ($p = .000$, $r = .45$); wife's education ($p = .000$, $r = .43$); and husband's occupation ($p = .000$, $r = .57$).

The second major variable category of interest is health status and physical activity. Health factors have been found in previous studies to be the strongest and most consistent predictors of life satisfaction and related constructs (Larson, 1978). Examining both subjective perceptions and objective health status, researchers generally conclude that subjective health perceptions are the more important predictors (Palmore and Luikart, 1972; Larson, 1978). Several measures of health and physical activity are included in the current study. Self-assessed health status was measured by the standard question: "How would you rate your overall health at the present time? Would you say it is excellent, very good, good, fair, or poor?" The degree of physical activity was determined by asking, "In your usual week, including recreation, are you physically: very active, moderately active, slightly active, quite inactive, or bedridden/housebound?"

The number of illnesses or conditions reported by the subject as ever being present were also counted. A measure of the wife's perception of her husband's health was obtained by using the same rating scale as that used for the wife's perception of her own health.

Social interaction factors represent the third major category of predictors of subjective well-being in the elderly to be examined in this study. The presence of supportive social interactions is thought to have a direct impact on psychological well-being as well as a mediating influence on negative life situations and role losses (Lin et al., 1979; Kahn, 1979). Several different concepts and measures of social interactions have been included in this study. The extent of informal social interactions is measured by a count of the number of household members, family, and friends that the respondents usually keep in touch with by telephone or regular visiting. Participation in formal social activities is measured by the number of organizations that the respondents belong to.

The quality of the social interaction is measured by the respondent's perceptions of her interactions with her spouse and other social contacts. The emerging literature on confidant relationships was reviewed to determine relevant criteria for designating a person in the respondent's reported social network as a confidant (McMiller and Ingham, 1976). The husband was considered a confidant if the respondent feels extremely or quite close to him; she is very likely to discuss a personal problem with him; and the husband is very likely to discuss a personal problem with her. A measure of the total number of confidants, excluding the spouse, was determined from responses to the same three criteria applied to the spouse plus the additional requirement of frequent contact or availability as defined by weekly phone contacts or at least three visits a month.

Since contact with companion animals was considered as another form of social interactions and support (Brickel, 1980–81), questions were included about the presence or absence of pets in the household; the quality of pet interactions was measured by degree of attachment rated on a five-point scale ranging from very to not at all attached; and the type of pet was categorized as at least one dog, no cat present; at least one cat, no dog reported; both a cat and dog reported; and an "other" category.

THE DEPENDENT VARIABLE

The dependent variable in this study is the respondent's subjective evaluation of her psychological well-being. Perceived happiness was selected as the construct to indicate subjective well-being in this population. In a review of three different mental health concepts, life satisfaction, happiness, and morale, Stones and Kozma support that happiness is the best construct to represent the mental health concept in psychosocial gerontology (1980). There have been various measurements of these psychological constructs, but no one operationalization has emerged as superior. The similarities between the measures have been viewed as more significant than their differences. When examining the differences between an individual global measure of life satisfaction and a scale composed of a series of related items, Campbell, Converse, and Rodgers conclude that differences between these competing measures are marginal at best. For this study, perceived happiness was assessed by Gurin's measure of overall happiness (Bradburn, 1969). The subject is asked, "Taken altogether, how would you say things are these days. . . . Would you say you were very happy, pretty happy, or not too happy?" The validity of this single item for measuring perceived happiness was supported by its positive correlation with another questionnaire item measuring the frequency with which respondents reported that they enjoyed life ($p = .001$, $r = .57$) and an equally strong negative correlation with the Center for Epidemiologic Study's depression scale ($p = .001$, $r = -.57$).

ANALYSIS OF DATA

The Spearman Rho correlation coefficient was used to examine relationships between independent variables and subjective well-being. Chi square was used for significance testing of contingency tables.

To assess the relative influence of the different demographic, health, and social factors on perceived happiness while holdiing the effects of the other factors constant, a stepwise multiple regression was used. In stepwise regression, the variable that explains the greatest amount of variance unexplained by other variables already in the regression equation will enter at each successive step. Defined as the expected change in the dependent variable with a change in one unit of the independent variable, betas, or standardized regression coefficients, reflect the relative amount of influence each independent variable has on the dependent variable. The F-test is calculated for each specific regression coefficient as well as for the overall test for goodness of fit of the regression equation.

The R₂ value is an indicator of the overall proportion of variance explained by all the variables in the equation.

RESULTS

POPULATION CHARACTERISTICS

The study population is composed of 1,073 white married women aged 65 to to 75 living in Washington County, Maryland, in 1975. They are primarily nonurban residents (65.8 percent), and 58.8 percent have less that twelve years of schooling. Of those reporting income, 70.5 percent have $12,000 or less in annual family income. All households have at least two persons, and a small minority (12.5 percent) have three or more. Within the narrow age range, respondents tend to be younger; 58.2 percent are in the 64 to 65 year range.

Although the very sick and institutionalized were eliminated from the study by the inclusionary criteria, a range of reported health statuses is evident in the population. Dividing themselves into approximate thirds, 37.3 percent of the women consider themselves to be in excellent or very good health; 32.5 percent rate themselves in good health; and the remaining 30.2 percent report themselves in fair or poor health. Most women report being very or moderately active (77.5 percent); 15.8 percent are only slightly active; and 6.5 percent are inactive or nonambulatory. Although, on the whole, perceiving their husbands as slightly less well than themselves, a similiar range emerges for wives' reports of their husbands' health. Excellent or very good health for their husbands was reported by 32.2 percent of the women; 35.6 percent rated their husbands' health as good; and 32.2 percent indicated their husbands to be in fair or poor health. Overall, the respondents perceive themselves to be in a desirable state of happiness. In this study, 42.6 percent perceive themselves as very happy compared to 51.0 percent who report themselves as pretty happy. Only a minority (6.4 percent) evaluate themselves as not too happy.

Because of the nature of the selection criteria, all respondents report having at least one person they talk to or see frequently. The median social network size is 7.74 with 24 percent of the women reporting a social network size of one to five persons; 54.7 percent interacting on a regular basis with 6 to 10 persons; and 20.9 percent reporting 11 or more persons in their social network. More than half of the women (59.7 percent) do not belong to any social organizations; 29 percent participate in one or two organizations; and another 11.2 percent belong to three or more organizations.

Although all of the women interacted with at least one other person, 12.8 percent of the women were considered by study criteria to lack any confidant relationship. Spouses were more likely to serve as confidants than other family members and friends. Whereas 77.9 percent of the women had a spouse who was considered to be a confidant, only 58.2 percent of the women had other family and friends who were considered to be confidants.

Additionally, approximately one third of the women (36.2 percent) had pets. Of the 388 pet owners, most (72.9 percent) reported being very attached to their pets. Small household pets were the most prevalent, with 53.4 percent having dogs without cats, 23.2 percent having cats but no dogs, and 18.6 percent having both a cat and a dog.

SUBJECTIVE WELL-BEING

The first goal of this research was to test the applicability of previously reported predictors of subjective well-being in this population. An intitial bivariate analysis (Table 26.1) reveals that most of the demographic, health, and social factors examined are significantly related to avowed happiness. Greater happiness is associated with higher SES levels, perceptions of healthiness and physical activeness, presence of confidant relationships, and participation in social organizations. Although the relationships are generally significant and in the expected direction, an examination of the Spearman Rho correlation coefficients reveal that the relationships between these predictors and perceived happiness are, for the most part, modest, ranging from .08 to .30.

An examination of the size of the correlations can provide information on the strength of the crude relationships between happiness and traditionally examined demographic, health, and social factors. A small but positive relation-

TABLE 26.1. BIVARIATE RELATIONSHIPS OF DEMOGRAPHIC, HEALTH, AND SOCIAL FACTORS WITH AVOWED HAPPINESS (n = 1,073)

Characteristics	Significance*	Correlation†
Demographic		
Age	ns	—
Household size	ns	—
Socioeconomic status	p = .001	.13
Health and physical activity		
Health perception	p = .001	.30
Perception of husband's health	p = .001	.29
Physical activity	p = .001	.27
Number of health conditions ever present	p = .001	-.13
Marital interaction		
Spouse as confidant	p = .001	.26
Social participation		
Network size (total)	ns	—
Number of relatives	p < .01	-.08
Number of friends	p < .01	+.08
Number of confidants (excluding spouse)	p = .001	.14
Number of organizations	p = .001	.16

*p ≤.05 is considered significant.
†Spearman Rho correlation coefficient.

ship exists between happiness and our SES measure (rs = .13); but no significant relationships were found for age or household size. The lack of a relationship is no doubt due, in part, to our eligibility criteria, which restricted the range of possible living situations and ages. An analysis by the different health factors reveals that the women's perceptions of their own health and physical activeness are more strongly related to happiness than reported health conditions with Spearman Rho values of .30 and .27 for health perceptions versus -.13 for number of health conditions. Second, the wife's perception of her husband's health (rs = .29) is virtually as strongly related to her happiness as is her evaluation of her own health (rs = .30).

The relationships between social interaction factors and happiness indicate the relative importance of the quality of marital interactions (rs = .26). Though still significant, the strength of the relationships for total number of confidants, excluding spouse (rs = .14), and participation in social organizations (rs = .16) are slightly lower.

Previous findings for the relationship between measures of psychological well-being and social network sizes, as measured by counts of family and friends, have been inconsistent. Our data suggest that these previously disparate findings may be the result of the type of social networks examined. Although correlations in the study are very weak, the number of relatives one interacts with tends to be negatively associated with happiness (rs = -.08), while the number of friends one has is positively associated (rs = .08).

POSSESSION AND SUBJECTIVE WELL-BEING

As indicated in Table 26.2, no significant relationship was found between presence of pets in the household and reported happiness. If anything, there is a slight tendency for a higher percentage of persons with household pets to be unhappy, with 8 percent of pet owners versus 5.5 percent of nonowners reporting that they are unhappy.

When separating pet owners who are very attached to their pets from those who are not very attached (Table 26.3), a significant relationship emerges

TABLE 26.2. RELATIONSHIP BETWEEN PET POSSESSION AND HAPPINESS (n = 1,073)

Happiness	Pet Possession	
	Yes (n = 388)	No (n = 685)
Very	41.5% (161)	43.2% (296)
Pretty	50.5% (196)	51.2% (351)
Not too	8.0% (31)	5.5% (38)
	$X^2 = 2.49$	$p = < .30$

TABLE 26.3. RELATIONSHIP BETWEEN QUALITATIVE ASPECTS OF PET POSSESSION AND HAPPINESS (n = 1,073)

Happiness	Quality of Pet Possession		
	Pets, very attached (n = 283)	Pets, not very attached (n = 105)	No pets (n = 685)
Very	45.2% (128)	31.4% (33)	43.2% (296)
Pretty	48.8% (138)	55.2% (58)	51.2% (351)
Not too	6.0% (17)	13.3% (14)	5.5% (38)
	$X^2 = 12.49$	$p = .01$	

between pet ownership characteristics and happiness (x^2 = 12.49, p = .01). Slightly more respondents who have pets and feel very attached to them report the highest levels of happiness as compared to the other two groups, but a closer examination reveals that there is actually little difference between women who are very attached to their pets and those who have no pets in the household (45.2 percent of attached pet owners versus 43.2 percent of nonowners versus 31.4 percent of unattached pet owners report being very happy). The significant differences seem to be attributable to the relative unhappiness of the group of women who are not very attached to their pets. The percentage of unhappy women in this group (13 percent) is more than twice as large as that in the other two groups: 6.0 percent for attached pet owners and 5.5 percent for nonowners. When reported happiness of the 388 pet owners is examined separately, a positive association is shown with degree of pet attachment, which reached the < .01 level of statistical significance.

As an initial test of the hypothesis that the degree of attachment that women feel toward their pets is indicative of their attachments in other social interactions, the association between the women's relationships with their spouses and the qualitative nature of their pet ownership was examined. Pet ownership was categorized in three groups: no pet; not being attached to one's pet; and being attached to one's pet. The data provide partial support for the hypothesis that those women who have pets but are not attached to them are significantly different from the women with no pets or those who are attached to their pets (X^2 = 6.73, p = .03). As indicated in Table 26.4, a greater percentage of women in the pet nonattached group lack a spouse confidant: 31.4 percent of the pet nonattached group, 23.0 percent of pet attached group, and 20.3 percent of no pet group do not have spouse confidant. These differences were statistically significant at the p = .03 level.

The previous bivariate analyses are useful for providing an initial indicator of the nature and strength of the crude relationships between happiness and the

TABLE 26.4. RELATIONSHIP BETWEEN PET FACTORS AND PRESENCE OF SPOUSE CONFIDANT (n = 1,073)

Spouse Confident	Pet Factors		
	No Pet	Pet not attached	Pet very attached
No	20.3%	31.4%	23.0%
	(139)	(33)	(65)
Yes	79.7%	68.6%	77.0%
	(546)	(72)	(218)
	$X^2 = 6.73$	p = .03	

study factors, but it is desirable to employ a multivariate regression technique to assess the relative influence of the different demographic, health, and social factors on perceived happiness, holding the effects of the other factors constant. Using the SPSS regression subprogram, we performed a stepwise multiple regression to rank the variables according to the variance in happiness that they explained. In an initial stepwise multiple regression analysis, eight traditional demographic, health, and social factors plus the dichotomous pet possession factor were regressed on perceived happiness (Table 26.5). Established predictors of happiness such as SES, perceived health factors, presence of confidants, both marital and other, and participation in social organizations all emerged as independent predictors of happiness when adjusting for the effects of the other factors. As with the Spearman Rho correlations described in Table 26.1, the values of the betas are generally low, ranging from .009 to .20, reflecting the small influence that these combined variables have on perceived happiness.

TABLE 26.5. RELATIONSHIP BETWEEN STUDY VARIABLES AND HAPPINESS: PET POSSESSION (n = 1,073)

Variable	Beta (slope)	Significance Test (F)	Cumulative Variance
Self-rated health	.13	14.37*	.099
Spouse confidant	.20	52.36*	.157
Spouse health	.19	43.09*	.187
Physical activity (subject)	.16	26.17*	.212
Organizational activity	.08	8.83*	.220
Other confidants	.07	5.59†	.223
SES (housing)	.06	4.09†	.226
Network size	.04	2.12	.228
Pet possession	.009	.17	.228

$R^2 = .23$ F = 34.85 df = 9/1063 p = < .001
*p < .01
†p < .05

The social participation variables represent the third level of impact variables. Both the amount of organizational activity and the number of total confidants, excluding spouse, have a modest but independent effect on happiness. When controlling for number of confidants, neither the combined network size nor the individual measures of size of friend or relative networks is significantly related to happiness. Even though the potential influences on happiness have been controlled for in this multiple regression analysis, the presence of a pet in the household is still not a significant predictor of happiness.

Just as it is important to examine the quality and quantity of social interactions for human contacts, however, it is important to explore whether an examination of qualitative aspects of pet ownership adds anything to the prediction of happiness when controlling for all the other demographic, health, and social factors. A second multiple regression analysis was performed with the same demographic, health, and social factors but replacing the dichotomous pet ownership variable with a trichotomous dummy variable to represent the qualitative nature of pet ownership. A dummy variable was constructed so that unattached pet owners would serve as the referent category in this analysis. Two comparisons are made, one for very attached pet owners versus nonattached pet owners and the other for nonowners versus unattached pet owners. As shown in Table 26.6, the results for the traditionally examined health and human social interaction variables are generally similar to those presented in Table 26.5. In this analysis, however, the quality of pet ownership is an independent predictor of happiness even after controlling for the effects of the other variables. Although there were still no significant differences between attached pet owners and

TABLE 26.6. RELATIONSHIP BETWEEN STUDY VARIABLES AND HAPPINESS: QUALITATIVE ASPECTS OF PET POSSESSION (n = 1,073)

Variable	Beta (slope)	Significance Test (F)	Cumulative Variance
Self-rated health	.12	14.25*	.099
Spouse confidant	.19	50.22*	.157
Spouse health	.20	45.76*	.187
Physical activity (subject)	.16	27.83*	.212
Organizational activity	.08	8.75*	.221
Other confidants	.06	5.18†	.223
SES (housing)	.05	2.55	.226
Pet quality	—	—	—
Very attached vs. unattached	.15	10.49*	.228
No pet versus unattached	.13	7.80*	.234
Network size	.03	1.56	.235

$R^2 = .24$ F = 32.70 df = 10/1062 p = < .001
*p < .01
†p < .05

TABLE 26.7. RELATIONSHIP BETWEEN SOCIOECONOMIC STATUS AND HAPPINESS (n = 1,073)

Socioeconomic Status	Pet Ownership	
	Yes (n = 388)	No (n = 685)
Low	47.9%	38.2%
	(186)	(262)
High	52.1%	61.8%
	(202)	(423)
	$X^2 = 9.17$	$p = .002$

nonowners, Table 26.6 confirms earlier bivariate findings on the relative unhappiness of the unattached pet owner group. Both being a very attached pet owner and having no pets are significantly related to happiness when compared to the pet unattached category. The relative size of the betas vis-a-vis other variables in the equation (beta = .15 and .13) shows the importance of considering qualitative aspects of pet ownership. A second difference also emerged between the first and second multivariate regression analyses. Whereas SES showed a small significant relationship in the first multiple regression equation (Table 26.5), SES did not emerge as an independent predictor of happiness when the effect of the quality of the pet relationship was controlled for by the inclusion of our pet attachment dummy variable in the second multiple regression equation.

This observation led to the consideration that the relationship between pet ownership and happiness was confounded by socioeconomic factors. To test this hypothesis, the relationship between SES and pet ownership was examined. As shown in Table 26.7, the relationship reaches the p = .002 level of statistical significance. As least in this study, more pet owners (47.9 percent) are of low SES than nonowners (38.2 percent).

Since SES was related to both pet ownership and happiness, a test for interaction was conducted by examining the relationship between pet ownership and happiness controlling for level of SES. As indicated in Figure 26.1, the relationship between pet ownership and happiness is dependent upon the level of SES. Among those with higher SES (SES II), pet ownership is positively associated with happiness while pet ownership is negatively related to happiness among those in the low SES group (SES I). Additional multiple regression analyses confirm the importance of the pet ownership/SES interction term as a significant predictor of subjective well-being (beta = .26, F = 3.99; p < .05). No support was found for the inclusion of a pet/SES interaction in terms of the qualitative nature of pet ownership (p > .05).

FIGURE 26.1.   RELATIONSHIP BETWEEN HAPPINESS AND PET POSSESSION
CONTROLLING FOR SOCIOECONOMIC STATUS: A TEST FOR
INTERACTION (n = 1,073)

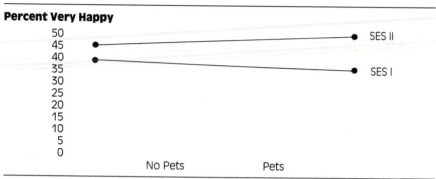

SUMMARY AND DISCUSSION

The previously reported predictors of subjective well-being are generally applicable in this population. One's socioeconomic background, health status, and nature of social interactions are all related to happiness in this elderly population group. When taking all the independent variables together, however, most of the variance in perceived happiness is still unexplained (R^2s in the low twenties). In this respect, our findings are typical of other research on life satisfaction in the elderly (Larson, 1978).

One needs to be cautious in attributing positive attributes to pet possession in a community setting of relatively healthy married persons. The relationship between perceived happiness and pet ownership is complex and needs to be further specified. We reached the following conclusions. First, there was no relationship between the presence of pets in the household and reported happiness. Second, there was a relationship between the qualitative aspects of pet ownership and happiness. Attached pet owners are not different from non-owners, but women who report being unattached to their pets are the most likely to be unhappy. There is evidence that pet attachment is indicative of other social attachments. Third, the relationship between pet ownership and happiness is dependent on SES. Among those with high SES, pet ownership is associated with greater happiness. Among those of lower SES, however, pet ownershipp is associated with unhappiness. We are not sure of the mechanisms by which SES affects this relationship. We can only speculate that the meaning of pet ownership is different for different segments of the population. There is some evidence that pet interactions vary by racial affiliations (Friedmann, Katcher, and Meislich, 1981).

Although this study is one of the first epidemiological investigations of human–companion animal interactions, much more research is needed to understand the meaning of pet possession in the life of the elderly. Because of the cross-sectional nature of this study, it is impossible to determine the causal relationships between the study variables and perceived happiness. We recommend that a longitudinal, prospective study be conducted for a better understanding of the health consequences of pet ownership in the elderly.

In this study there were limited data on characteristics of pet possession or ownership. In future research, more information is needed about the extent and nature of the human–companion animal interactions. Standardized questionnaire items are needed to obtain valid and reliable information that can be used across a variety of different research settings. The findings of this study may have also been limited by the predetermined social characteristics of the study population. The minimal influence of pet ownership in this study may be related to the relatively high level of social integration found in this population of married women living in the community. Additional studies are needed to examine the influence of pet possession in varied living situations.

Susanne S. Robb

27

Health Status Correlates of Pet-Human Association in a Health-Impaired Population

This study was undertaken to extend systematic efforts to identify health status correlates of association with pet animals: the overall study question was whether people who lived with pet animals differed from those who did not live with pet animals in reference to selected psycosocial and physiological attributes. The attributes were locus of control, morale, social resources, perceptions of mental health, and physical health.

The total sample consisted of thirty-seven predominantly male veterans randomly selected from two strata—clients living with pets (sixteen) and clients not living with pets (twenty-one)—who were receiving services from the Hospital Based Home Care Program in a large Veterans Administration Medical Center.

DEFINITIONS

The following operational definitions describe the terms used in this study.
  Identifying and demographic associations: Factors identified in previous

studies as having distinguished pet owners from nonowners such as age and household size.

Instrumental activity of daily living status: The individual's capacity for the performance of a variety of activities necessary in maintaining an independent household, such as using the telephone, shopping, and preparing meals. Defined as the score on the instrumental activity index from the Older Americans Resources and Services (OARS) Multidimensional Functional Assessment Questionnaire (OARSMFAQ) (Duke Uiversity, 1978).

Lives with a pet: Someone who resides in a household that reports currently owning one or more pets. Defined as a person responding yes to the question, "Do you currently own or live with a pet?"

Locus of control: Expectation that control rests internally within the individual or externally in forces within the environment. Defined as the score on Rotter's I-E Scale (Rotter, 1966).

Mental health: Intellectual intactness, the presence or absence of functional psychiatric symptomatology, self-assessed life satisfaction, and the individual's subjective assessment of mental health. Defined as the score on the mental health index from the OARS Multidimensinal Functional Assessment Questionnaire (Duke University, 1978).

Morale: An individual's inner state of satisfaction, of having attained something in life, of fitting in with the environment, and the ability to strive appropriately while accepting the inevitable (Lawton, 1972). Defined as the score on the Philadelphia Geriatric Center Morale Scale (Lawton, 1975).

Physical activity of daily living status: The individual's capacity to take care of bodily functions such as eating, dressing, undressing, and toileting. Defined for this study as the score on the activity of daily living index from the OARS Multidimensional Functional Assessment Questionnaire (Duke University, 1978).

Physical health: The number of visits to a doctor, number of days disability at home, and length of stay in health care institutions; receipt of selected prescription drugs; and presence or absence of selected illnesses and physical handicaps, as well as self-rated health assessment. Defined as the score on the physical health index of the OARS Multidimensional Functional Assessment Questionnaire (Duke University, 1978).

Social resources: The extent, quality, and availability of social interactions. Defined as the score on the social resources index of the OARS Multidimentional Functional Assessment Questionnaire (Duke University, 1978).

SAMPLE

Between October 1980 and May 1981, all clients who lived with pets and a randomly selected sample of people who did not live with pets from the HBHC Program conducted by a large VA Medical Center were invited to participate in the study. Forty-seven randomly selected people who did not live with pets were considered as potential participants in the study before a total sample of 21 was obtained. Reasons for nonparticipation included refusals (12), discharges from the HBHC program (5), and deaths or admissions to a long-term care facility (9). Thirty-one people who lived with pets, all of whom were in the HBHC program between October and April 1981, were considered as subjects before a total sample of 16 people was obtained. Nonparticipation among those who lived with pets was due to refusals (13) and death or admissions to a long-term care facility (2). Despite efforts to learn reasons for refusals, most clients simply said they did not want to be bothered.

All but one of the 37 study participants were male. The age range extended from 20 to 93 with a mean age of 63 years. The pet group had a lower median age of 61 (20 to 93) years compared to 64 (37 to 89) years for the nonpet group. Most participants had either 5 to 8 years of education or had completed high school. Only twelve people had gone beyond high school, two of whom had completed graduate school. Twenty-five respondents were married. Twenty-six were white; the rest were black.

SETTING

The Hospital Based Home Care Program is a specialized medical service administered from a VA Medical Center with resources to provide individual medical, nursing, social, and rehabilitative services to a client within the milieu of his home and family. This program serves clients within a twenty-mile radius of the medical center. The following criteria are used in selecting clients for the HBHC Program (Coordinator HBHC Program, 1979): client lives within 20 miles of the VA Medical Center; client no longer requires inpatient care; client requires follow-up professional care for the conditions(s) for which he or she was hospitalized; the home environment is such that daily care may be provided by members of the family or other, and it is believed that the client will respond to care in the home; client and members of the family (or others) are completely in agreement with the proposed plan.

The program census ranges between 80 and 100 clients with approximately 66 percent aged 65 years or older. Primary diagnoses most frequently identified included chronic destructive pulmonary diseases, diabetes mellitus, cerebral vascular accidents, cancer, and coronary heart disease.

INSTRUMENTS

Specific attributes and their indicators were chosen on the basis of available instruments with established reliability and validity and, when possible, prior use with populations similar to the one selected for this study, that is, predominantly elderly and health-impaired. Locus of control was determined by the I-E Scale (Rotter, 1966). Morale was ascertained by use of the Philadelphia Geriatric Center Morale Scale (PGC Morale Scale) (Lawton, 1972). Indexes from the OARS Multidimensional Functional Assessment Questionnaire (Duke University, 1978) were employed to measure socialization, mental health, instrumental and physical activity of daily living statuses, and physical health.

PROCEDURES

This study was approved by the Human Rights Committee of the VA Medical Center. Potential respondents were visited at home by the principal investigator, who explained that the purpose of the study was to allow nurses to learn more about clients receiving home care with respect to their morale, views about events in life, and ability to care for themselves.

The pet-ownership focus of the study was not disclosed in an effort to avoid biasing responses. Each participant signed a written consent. Interviewers then arranged survey appointments within three weeks after the time the consent form was signed.

All interviews were conducted between October 1980 and May 1981 in single sessions that ranged in length from 35 minutes to 3 hours and 25 minutes with a mean length of 1 hour and 48 minutes. Two trained interviewers completed all the interviews.

Preliminary training sessions were held for interviewers to provide detailed information regarding administration of the questionnaire and to establish an interrater reliability coefficient of 100 percent agreement. Test-retest reliability was evaluated by readministering a subset of twenty-five factual items from OARSMFAQ portions of the questionnaire to nine of the respondents selected as the first and every third respondent thereafter (three individuals declined to be reinterviewed and a fourth could not be contacted before conclusion of the data-collection phase). These follow-up interviews were conducted by telephone by the principal investigator within three to five weeks after the initial interview.

In all, 225 pairs of discrete items were examined comparing first-time responses with second-time responses. The reliability coefficient was 96 percent agreement.

ASSUMPTIONS AND LIMITATIONS

This study was based on the assumptions that morale and locus of control, as well as perceptions about economic resources, pet animals, and other people in general existed within each respondent and were measurable; truthful information could be obtained from each respondent; respondents would understand the questions they were asked; and merely living with a pet animal would permit sufficient association to yield changes in the health status study participants. Limitations associated with this study were that the reliability of information provided by respondents depended upon their memories; the sample sizes were too small to detect any but large differences between the groups; and controls were not imposed for type of pet or extent of pet-human contacts. An additional limitation that in part inspired the study was that a conceptual framework that integrates disparate results of research in the area of animal-human relationships has yet to be developed, although King's (1971, 1981) formulations do serve to tie some of the factors together.

RESULTS

In trying to interpret results from this exploratory study, emphasis was placed on confirming findings derived from earlier studies. Thus results from this study should be considered in conjunction with those from previous empirically based studies.

Box-plots were prepared to summarize and present descriptive statistics for each health status variable according to the two study groups. These results are presented in Figure 27.1. The means and medians were higher for the pet groups than for the no pet group for morale, mental health, and social resources where higher scores represented more favorable status; and lower for locus of control and physical health where lower scores represented more favorable status. Hinges for the box-plots (no pet versus pet) within each health status variable indicated comparable dispersions of scores except for locus of control and social resources. The variance relation for these two variables indicated there were no significant (p < .05) differences between the two groups.

To test for significant differences, two-tailed T-tests were performed for independent groups. Among the health status variables, morale score differences were found to be statistically significant (p = .03), with people who lived with pets demonstrating higher morale than people who did not live with pets. Setting aside the matter of statistical significance, the pet group also fared better than the nonpet group on all other health status variables. That is, people who lived with pets experienced slightly better mental health, a more internal locus of control, more social resources, better physical health, and, as indicated previously, higher morale. These results are reported in Table 27.1.

Exploratory data analysis, conducted to discern possible alternative explanations for pet owners' slightly better health status, indicated that this group was younger (fifty-eight years versus sixty-six years) and perceived itself as having slightly more economic resources (12.8 score versus 12.4 score), although these differences were not statistically significant (p < .05). To examine these relationships further, correlations and scatter-diagrams were computed between each of the health-related variables (morale, locus of control, mental health status, social resources, and physical health status) and age and economic resources, respec-

TABLE 27.1.   MEANS, STANDARD DEVIATIONS, AND SIGNIFICANCE FOR
DIFFERENCES BETWEEN PET AND NO PET GROUPS FOR HEALTH
STATUS VARIABLES

Variables	Pet N = 16		No Pet N = 21		t	df	p
	x	S.D.	x	S.D.			
Mental health*	24.92	5.04	22.62	5.42	1.20	28	.24
Morale*	11.26	3.12	8.78	3.40	2.18	32	.03+
Locus of control††	8.13	3.96	9.87	2.24	-1.52	29	.14
Social resources*	19.08	2.35	18.06	2.21	1.12	25	.26
Physical health††	127.35	36.86	131.88	33.07	-0.36	29	.72

*Higher score optimal.
†Statistically significant p ≤ .05.
††Lower score optimal.

tively, for the pet group and the group that did not live with pets. These
correlations are presented in Table 27.2. Only two correlations proved to be
statistically significant (p < .05); younger people who lived with pets reported
themselves as having more social resources and experiencing better mental
health than did older people. These findings indicated that, on the whole, age
and economic status were not associated with the five health status variables on
which pet owners scored more favorably.

For pet-human relationships, the results reported in Table 27.3, and based
on five-point scales, were as might be expected on the basis of common sense.
The two groups perceived themselves as being equally liked by other people and
shared similar perceptions of how much they liked other people. Significant
differences between the two groups emerged with respect to liking pets (p = .02)
and preferring pets over people (p = .03), with the pet owner preferring pets to
people and liking pets more than did nonowners.

TABLE 27.2.   PEARSON PRODUCT-MOMENT CORRELATIONS BETWEEN HEALTH
STATUS VARIABLES AND AGE AND ECONOMIC RESOURCES

Health-Related Variable	Age		Economic Resources	
	Pet	No Pet	Pet	No Pet
Morale*	-.09	-.19	.34	.13
Locus of control†	.34	-.07	-.44	.14
Mental health*	-.21	-.55††	.45	.00
Social resources*	-.55*	-.30	.48	.09
Physical health†	-.03	-.43	.17	.07

*Higher score optimal
†Lower score optimal.
††p ≤ .05

TABLE 27.3. MEANS, STANDARD DEVIATIONS, AND SIGNIFICANCE FOR DIFFERENCES BETWEEN PET AND NO PET GROUPS FOR RELATIONSHIP VARIABLES

	Pet Group N = 16		No Pet Group N = 21		t or z-test	df	p
	X	S.D.	X	S.D.			
Liked by people	4.00	.84	4.00	.81	0.00	32	1.00
Like people*	4.40	.63	4.30	.73	0.42	33	.67
Like pets*	4.53	.74	3.66	1.27	2.35	34	.02†
Prefer pets or people*	.47	.51	.14	.35	2.18		.05†

*Higher score optimal.
†Statistically significant $p \leq .05$.

Reliabilities of major instruments used in this study were determined using Chrombach's alpha coefficient. These coefficients are reported in Table 27.4. The low value ($r = 66$) for the psychiatric symptomatology schedule may be explained on the basis of multiple psychiatric problems assessed by the instrument. Individual respondents could experience one problem or several and thus fail to answer consistently across a majority of items. The low value ($r = .57$) for Rotter's (1966) I-E Scale is difficult to explain because the scale purports to measure a single factor. Possibly items within the scale have become dated as a result of changing social values and thus no longer function as they once did in relation to each other. For example, the item relating to reasons for war calls for a distinction between wars caused by people not taking enough interest in politics (internal response) versus wars occurring no matter how hard people try to prevent them (external response). Possibly because of the endemic wars in the Middle East, respondents are biased in favor of the external response on the basis of fact rather than their loci of control. Another explanation might be that the length of the instrument and the items, the fact that items were read aloud to

TABLE 27.4. SUMMARY STATISTICS FOR INSTRUMENTS

Instruments	X	S.D.	Chronbach's Alpha Reliability
Philadelphia Geriatric Center Morale Scale	9.88	3.47	.75
Rotter's I-E Scale	9.03	3.26	.57
OARS Psychiatric Symptomatology	5.33	3.05	.66
OARS Short Portable Mental Status Questionnaire	7.40	2.98	.88
OARS Instrumental ADL Scale	6.40	4.41	.89
OARS Physical ADL Scale	4.62	4.09	.88

compensate for respondents' poor vision, and the prevalence of some memory impairments among study participants combined to make option recall difficult for respondents so that they decided arbitrarily rather than on the basis of their beliefs.

DISCUSSION

The findings identify a relationship between having a pet in the home and morale and suggest that people who live with pets may fare better on other indicators of health status than people who do not live with pets. Differences in the magnitude of variables related to health status did not prove to be statistically significant in this study. Additional indication of differences in health status between the two groups is found in the reasons for nonparticipation in the study. People who did not reside with pets were more likely to be lost to the study because of deaths or admissions to long-term care facilities (19 percent), whereas pet owners were more likely to refuse to participate without respect to their health status (42 percent). Previous research has shown a positive association between pet ownership and income (Franti, Kraus, and Borhani, 1974). In this study, clients who lived with pets perceived their financial resources as slightly more adequate than people who did not live with pets, but neither this association nor the younger age of the pet group explained observed health status relationships. observed health status relationships.

Morale is one of several satisfaction-related constructs that has been frequently measured in the study of social-psychological well-being in adulthood (George, 1979). Most of these studies have had as their purpose either definition of the term or identification of related variables. The term "morale" has been variously defined as encompassing the following factors derived from factor analysis of existing scales: agitation, attitude toward own aging, lonely-dissatisfaction (Lawton, 1975), tranquillity, and life progression (Morris, Wolf, and Klerman, 1975). "Morale" is defined by *Webster's Third New International Dictionary* as "an estate of individual psychological well-being based on such factors as a sense of purpose and confidence in the future." Socioeconomic status, health, social integration, and financial satisfaction have been identified as important determinants of morale (Liang et al., 1980). Additionally, morale has been linked to leisure satisfaction (Mancini and Orthner, 1980) and internal locus of control (Fawcett, Stonner, and Zepelin, 1980; Chang, 1980).

One explanation for the relationship observed in this study between association with pets and morale can be found in results of a study that examined the social integration–morale relationship. Liang et al. (1980) found that objective aspects of social integration have only an indirect impact on morale. The subjective meaning of social integration functions as a critical intervening variable, even when other determinants or morale are controlled. Association with pet animals may alter the individual's subjective perception of morale in such a way that regardless of objective indicators such as health impairments, low income, or advancing age, the individual still labels himself as tranquil, not lonely, confident, and so forth.

Further interpretation of the association between morale and living with pet animals is restricted by methodological issues that cloud the meaning and measurement of morale. These issues include failure to distinguish among satisfaction-related constructs such as life satisfaction, happiness, well-being, and morale; inconsistencies in the use of global versus domain-specific measures; and stability of the construct in the face of growth, development, and situational phenomena such as work status, health, and financial resources (George, 1979; Liang et al., 1980). In spite of these issues, morale has been defined as synonymous with depression levels (Morris, Wolf, and Klerman, 1975) and identified as an important indicator of the quality of life (Shaw, 1977; Depner, 1978). Evidence is slowly accumulating to indicate that society no longer regards treatment restricted to biophysiological phenomena and maintenance of ill people in a state where they are merely clean, dry, and fed as adequate. The Veterans Administration has published a guide for appraisal of quality of life factors in long-term client populations (Engquist, Davis, and Bryce, 1979). A lawsuit was brought against a large state-operated psychiatric hospital in western Pennsylvania, in part because of an "oppressive institutional environment, a lack of meaningful treatment, and a regimen of enforced idleness" (Woodville suit, Ask Better Care, 1980). Factors contributing to depression and its sequel have been described in the literature (see, for example, Frances, 1976; Ernst et al., 1978; Solomon, 1981; Rainwater, 1980). Unfortunately, there are few interventions to reverse depression and improve quality of life among people who experience multiple social, economic, and health losses. Thus a relatively low-risk, inexpensive intervention, such as pet animals, that shows promise of having an impact on these problems warrants careful consideration in the context of controlled clinical trials.

Previous psychological studies of pet owners have shown that pet owners tend to feel less well regarded by others and to like their pets better than they like people (Cameron and Mattson, 1972). Brown, Shaw, and Kirkland (1972) concluded, however, that low affection for dogs accompanied low affection for people and, in the case of males, low desire for such affection. Results of this study were consistent with the previous finding that pet owners tend to like pets better than they do people, but otherwise the results contradicted previous findings in that pet owners and nonowners regarded themselves as equally well liked by others and similar in their liking for other people. Pet owners, as might be expected, liked pets to a significantly greater extent than people who did not own pets.

IMPLICATIONS

Although the results of this exploratory study do not warrant a wholesale change in nursing practice, they do support the findings of previous research that indicate close contact with pet animals is associated with superior health status. Thus nurses may find further research in the area of human-animal companionship to be worthwhile. King's conceptual framework suggests that nurses have an obligation to identify factors within the environment that are associated with health status that are closer to the optimum end of the health continuum. Results of this study indicated that living with pet animals was significantly associated with better morale and nonsignificantly associated with better physical health and mental status, more social resources, and a more internal locus of control. The finding of any significant difference in a study with small sample sizes warrants extension of this type of research to increase sample sizes and identify other correlates of pet ownership from the physiologic, psychologic, or sociologic realms. Research is currently being conducted by Robb and associates to determine whether a program to place friendly dogs on a clinical unit in a long-term care facility makes a difference in selected health status variables that include morale. Discovery of important factors and demonstration of beneficial effects is required for decision making by landlords, administrators of prisons, hospitals, and long-term health care facilities and others who must establish rules and regulations governing the presence of animals in congregate living settings.

This study was supported by a research grant from Sigma Theta Tau, National Honor Society of Nursing.

Dan J. Lago, Barbara Knight,
and Cathleen Connell

28

Relationships with Companion Animals among the Rural Elderly

We are cooperating with an independent community organization in conducting a demonstration and longitudinal evaluation of a pet-placement program for community-dwelling elderly persons living in rural central Pennsylvania. This report describes attitudes toward placing pets and experience with pet ownership for a sample of elderly persons. The characteristics of rural elderly owners and their experiences with pets are summarized with an eye to their implications for a placement program.

SAMPLE

The sample was recruited from elderly persons residing in Center County who were likely to be receiving support services. Clients of Senior Citizen centers and members of senior groups were recruited at group meetings following a slide presentation outlining our proposed program. Letters and return postcards were sent to elderly recipients of the Home Health Service inviting them to participate. Brief telephone interviews with interested persons were conducted to assess ownership status and to schedule a detailed personal interview in the individual's home. (The original research design called for sampling equal numbers of current, former, and never owners. The low prevalence of never owners, however, required a decision to interview all interested older persons, resulting in an overrepresentation of former owners.)

Project staff and trained student interviewers conducted all interviews between January and June 1980. The purpose of the study was thoroughly explained before the interview, and each participant signed an informed consent form. Interviews averaged approximately one hour in length. A newsletter survey of widowed women in a nearby county was conducted to gain additional perspective.

MEASURES

The interview protocol included sections on experience with and attitudes toward pets, opinions on pet placement, social activities, physical health, activities of daily living, morale, and basic demographic data. The social activities, health, activities of daily living, and demographic sections were derived from the OARS methodology (Duke University, 1978). The morale items consisted of sixteen questions derived from the Memorial University of Newfoundland Scale of Happiness (MUNSH) (Stones and Kozma, 1980). The items pertaining to pets were taken from the work of Wilbur (1976), Anderson (1975), and unpublished conference proceedings of the Group for the Study of the Human/Companion Animal Bond.

ANALYSIS

Many of the feasibility study questions required simple descriptive data for the entire sample or particular subgroups. Differences between subgroups were analyzed through a series of one-way analyses of variance and by examining differences in the intercorrelation patterns for the Statistical Analysis System (SAS, 1979). Frequency analyses were conducted on responses to individual questions. Comparative analyses were conducted on scaled variables made up of aggregated items. These are defined as follows:

Social activity: Quantitative estimates of group and individual social contacts, phone calls, organization memberships, and size of friendship network.

Social satisfaction: Qualitative estimates of social satisfaction, presence of confidants, and friendliness of neighborhood.

Prostheses: Use of canes, walkers, wheelchairs, hearing aids, artificial limbs, ostomy equipment, and other.

Impairment: Self-ratings of vision, hearing, and health, combined with use of prostheses.

Activities of daily living: Self-rating of ability to use the telephone, prepare meals, do light and heavy housework, go grocery shopping, do strenuous physical exercise, dress, bathe, and climb stairs.

Morale: Sum of sixteen items assessing emotional tone and life satisfaction.

Behavioral intimacy: A weighted combination of owner-animal behaviors self-reported by owners, including talking to pet, stroking, grooming, following, playing, training, disciplining, watching, feeding, sitting together, walking, running, hunting, watching TV together, and riding in the car.

Physical intimacy: Observed physical contact with pet and self-report of where the pet sleeps.

Dominance: Assignment of dominant role to self or pet and decision to neuter animal.

All variables and individual items were scored so that a higher number indicates more of the quantity being assessed. For example, a higher impairment score indicates more serious health problems; a higher activities of daily living score indicates greater functional capability than a low score does.

Analyses reported here focus on basic issues of feasibility of a pet-placement organization. Only preliminary information on the nature of companion animal relationships and their impact in this sample is presented. Missing data for certain individuals cause the sample size for various analyses to fluctuate to a small extent.

RESULTS

FEASIBILITY STUDY

Sample Characteristics   Interviews were completed with 137 persons, 116 women and 21 men. The sample is 41 percent current owners, 54 percent former owners, and only 5 percent never owners. The sample was to be equally divided among ownership categories, but only six never owners volunteered to complete the interview. Table 28.1 provides a descriptive overview of the sample by ownership categories. The average age of the sample was 70.8 years, and although the never owner sample was distributed very differently from the other groups, they were not significantly different in age. Almost 9 percent of the current owners were over age 85. A surprisingly high number of never owners of pets were single, and more former owners had been widowed than were either current or never owners.

Current owners lived in their own home more often than former owners. Seven former owners commented that housing regulations did not permit them to own a pet. Whether or not current owners still lived in their homes mainly

TABLE 28.1. RURAL ELDERLY RELATIONSHIPS WITH COMPANION ANIMALS
SAMPLE DEMOGRAPHIC CHARACTERISTICS

	Current Owners (N=56)		Former Owners (N=72)		Never Owners (N=6)		Total Sample (N=134)	
Age	F	%	F	%	F	%	F	%
45–64	12	21.4	13	18.0	0	0	25	18.6
65–74	23	41.0	33	45.8	4	66.6	60	44.7
75–84	16	28.5	24	33.3	2	33.3	42	31.3
85--94	5	8.9	2	2.7	0	0	7	5.2
Marital Status	N = 56		N = 74		N = 6		N = 136	
Single	5	8.9	4	5.4	2	33.3	11	8.0
Married	23	41.8	20	27.0	2	33.3	46	33.8
Widowed	25	44.6	48	64.8	1	16.6	74	54.4
Divorced	1	1.7	1	1.3	1	16.6	3	2.2
Separated	1	1.7	1	1.3	0	0	2	1.4
Living Arrangements	N = 56		N = 74		N = 6		N = 136	
Own Home	41	73.2	39	52.7	4	66.6	84	61.7
Rent	6	10.7	24	32.4	2	33.3	32	23.5
Public Housing	0	0	5	6.7	0	0	5	3.6
Other	9	16.0	6	8.1	0	0	15	11.0
Locale	N = 55		N = 72		N = 6		N = 133	
Rural	19	34.5	14	19.4	2	33.3	35	26.3
Small Town	29	52.7	44	61.1	3	50.0	76	57.1
Metropolitan	7	12.7	14	19.4	1	16.6	22	16.5
Finances	N = 55		N = 72		N = 6		N = 133	
Excellent	19	34.5	14	19.4	2	33.3	35	26.3
Good	29	52.7	44	61.1	3	50.0	76	51.1
Fair	7	12.7	14	19.4	1	16.6	22	16.5
Poor	0	0	0	0	0	0	0	0

because they owned a pet is not known. Current owners were more likely to live in rural areas and less likely to live in the county's only metropolitan area than were former owners. More than 80 percent of all respondents lived in rural areas or small towns (populations between 250 and 2,500).

The majority of people in all categories appraised their financial situations as excellent or good. Approximately 16 percent indicated that finances were a problem. Current pet owners reported higher satisfaction with their financial situation than did the other groups, although the difference was not statistically significant (p > .16) given the measure used.

Opinions on Pet Placement   An overwhelming majority (90 percent) of the interviewees supported the idea of a program to encourage older persons to have pets (Table 28.2). As anticipated, current owners were the strongest supporters. More former owners disapproved of the idea. A minority of those supporting the idea of a pet-placement program did not approve of a system of financial aid to assist elderly pet owners. They stressed the importance of being able to meet the pets' needs independently, without counting on outside help. But, almost 80 percent agreed that financial assistance should be included in the program's operation.

TABLE 28.2.   RURAL ELDERLY RELATIONSHIPS WITH COMPANION ANIMALS
ATTITUDES TOWARD A PET-PLACEMENT PROGRAM

	Current Owners n=56		Former Owners n=74		Never Owners n=6		Total n = 136	
	F	%	F	%	F	%	F	%
Do you think it is a good idea to encourage older people to have pets?								
Yes	53	94.6	65	87.8	5	83.3	123	90.4
No	1	1.8	7	9.5	1	16.6	9	6.6
Not answered	2	3.6	2	2.7	0	0	4	3.0
Would you favor a program which offered financial support if the owner could not afford the total cost of keeping a pet?								
Yes	46	82.1	58	78.3	4	66.6	108	79.4
No	8	14.2	15	20.3	2	33.3	25	18.3
Not answered	2	3.6	1	1.4	0	0	3	2.3
Would you ever consider getting another pet if your current pet died or because lost? (or) Would you consider getting another pet if you do not presently own one?								
Yes	33	58.9	29	39.7	2	33.3	64	47.4
No	21	37.5	39	53.4	4	66.6	64	47.4
Not answered	2	3.6	5	6.8	0	0	7	5.2
Would you consider getting another pet at the same time you have your current pet?			Not applicable		Not applicable		Not applicable	
Yes	10	17.8						
No	46	82.1						
Not answered	0	0						

Potential demand for pets in this sample was higher than in the newsletter survey group. Twelve interviewees (8.5 percent of the sample) expressed interest in obtaining animals immediately. They were put on a waiting list until a decision on feasibility was reached. Almost half of the sample indicated a willingness to consider owning a pet, with 58.9 percent of current owners saying they plan to continue owning pets after the loss of their present animal. Even two never owners expressed a desire to own pets. A considerable minority of current owners (17.8 percent) indicated interest in acquiring additional pets, becoming multiple pet owners. But 82.2 percent were not willing to add more pets to their households.

Those expressing interest in animals preferred to continue having breeds and species previously owned. Dogs were more likely to be sought than cats (28 to 7). Three persons were interested in birds. There was near universal preference for mature rather than young animals. Females were preferred to males, with the large majority indicating the animal should be neutered.

Respondents were asked to state in their own words what they saw as the major issues confronting such a program and what their requirements for a successful program would be. Table 28.3 provides a tabulation of responses derived from a content analysis of their remarks. They thought that assistance with the responsibility of pet care, the match between owner and pet, the costs of caring for a pet, the owner's housing situation, and guaranteeing the welfare of placed animals were the central issues. Caregiving responsibilities of highest concern were "pet sitting" in times of sickness or travel, assuring that adequate veterinary care could be provided, help with major grooming and training tasks, and exercise of the animal.

Concern over the process of selecting appropriate animals and qualified capable owners and matching the characteristics of each to improve successful placement were mentioned 36 times. The importance of allowing the older person to choose an animal and providing a probationary, get-acquainted period was suggested frequently. The guarantee that the animal could be returned and placed elsewhere in the event of sickness or death of the owner was important to several respondents.

Respondents stressed that prospective owners should consider their financial ability to care adequately for a pet before accepting one. It was commented that some persons could handle day-to-day expenses but could not afford large-scale special services or emergency care. Financial support would be necessary in those cases.

Concern over housing included having enough room for a pet to exercise safely without disturbing others and having adequate living facilities indoors.

A number of persons, primarily former owners, commented on the need to consider housing regulations. This concern was primarily because of the recent opening of a senior citizen high-rise apartment building that forbids pets. (Some spoke of reforming regulations, while others suggested that small pets such as birds might be acceptable in such apartment settings.)

TABLE 28.3. RURAL ELDERLY RELATIONSHIP WITH COMPANION ANIMALS— OPINIONS OF ELDERLY RESPONDENTS' REQUIREMENTS FOR A SUCCESSFUL PET-PLACEMENT PROGRAM

Responsibility of Care	Frequency
Responsibility of pet care	22
Care of animal if sick or traveling	17
Owner needs to have time to care	2
Need to exercise pet	9
Need to train pet	4
Need to give shots, have wormed, neutered	6
Total frequency	60
Owner/Pet Match	
Owner/pet match	14
Health of owner	9
Need to screen owners	5
Health of pet	2
Falling over pet	2
Option to return pet	4
Total frequency	36
Cost of Care	
Housing	
Owner's housing situation	18
Housing regulations	7
Disturb neighbors	3
Total frequency	28
Animal Welfare	
Animal abuse	10
Saving animal's lives	2
Total frequency	12

Spring 1980

Finally, a group of current owners were concerned that animal abuse could occur if the wrong people were given pets or if someone became too ill to care for the pet. They stressed the need to provide follow-up visits to all owners regularly to assure that the animals' needs were being met.

Perception of the Advantages and Disadvantages of Pet Ownership   To add detail to our understanding of the needs of elderly pet owners and the differences between those who continue to own pets and those who stop, all respondents were encouraged to state in their own words up to four advantages and four disadvantages associated with pets. Table 28.4 indicates the summaries of content analyses of their comments. There was a high degree of conformity in the responses of both current and former owners, with several interesting exceptions. Current owners listed more advantages (2.2 versus 1.6) per person than did former owners. Former owners ranked the benefits to children high and stressed

TABLE 28.4. RURAL ELDERLY RELATIONSHIPS WITH COMPANION ANIMALS—
ADVANTAGES AND DISADVANTAGES TO PET OWNERSHIP

Advantages	Current Owners (N = 56)			Former Owners (N = 76)		
	Rank	F	%	Rank	F	%
Companionship/friendship	1	41	73.2	1	45	59.2
House not empty	2	18	32.1	6	8	10.5
Security	3	17	30.3	3	14	18.4
Fun to care for	4	15	26.7	5	9	11.8
Something to love	5	9	16.0	6	8	10.5
Responsibility	6	7	12.5	10	1	1.3
Likes to watch it	6	7	12.5	8	6	7.9
Performs work	8	6	10.7	4	10	13.1
Play with	9	3	5.4	9	5	6.6
Children's benefit	0	0		2	17	22.3
No advantages		1	1.7		3	3.9
Disadvantages						
Interferes with travel	1	22	39.3	1	27	35.5
Care is too much responsibility	2	11	19.6	2	17	22.3
Maintenance costs	3	7	12.5	4	6	7.8
Dirty, shedding hair (cleaning up after)	4	6	10.7	4	6	7.8
Damage to property	4	6	10.7	4	6	7.8
Need to tie up or restrain	6	4	7.1	3	9	11.8
Grief at death	7	3	5.3	7	4	5.2
Housebreaking problems	7	3	5.3	10	1	1.3
Allergies	9	1	1.7	10	1	1.3
Neighbors Disapprove	9	1	1.7	9	3	3.9
Too busy to provide care		0	0	7	4	5.2
No disadvantages		8	14.2		3	3.9

Except for endorsing no advantages or disadvantages, persons could list up to four considerations; therefore, percentages will exceed 100%.

Spring 1980

the utilitarian value of pets as working animals. Current owners were relatively unimpressed by these reasons for ownership, and stressed the personal companionship value of pets. Consistent with the newsletter survey, approximately one third of the owners reported security advantages and approximately 5 percent experienced problematic grief at the death of their pets.

The pattern of disadvantages was essentially consistent across both groups and corroborated priorities of concerns in both the newsletter survey and the respondents' requirements for a successful pet-placement program. Training and behavior problems emerged in more detail, specifically, controlling property damage, restraining the pet, and housebreaking.

The 28 persons owning only dogs indicated a much closer involvement with their pets than did those owning only cats. Fifty percent (14) of the dog owners reported spending 24 hours a day in the company of their pet, including sleeping together. In comparison, only 7 percent (one) of the cat owners reported twenty-four hour companionship. Over 90 percent of the dog owners spent more than 12 hours with the pet as compared to 57 percent for cat owners. Whereas 78 percent of cat owners were satisfied with their pet, 100 percent of dog owners reported satisfaction. The greater closeness of the relationship among dog owners is reflected in their rating of closeness (92 percent versus 57 percent) and in their increased likelihood of getting another pet if this animal should die (64 percent versus 43 percent). The 11 persons owning both dogs and cats showed a pattern of relationship essentially identical to that of dog owners. Two exceptions are that they were more likely to acquire new animals (73 percent), and they spent less money per week on pet care expenses even though they had more animals.

Patterns of cost experienced by elderly current owners provide vital baseline information for the placement program. Table 28.5 summarizes three ranges of expenses for animal care provided on an annual basis. Median food costs per week for dog only owners were $4.30 and $2 for cat only owners. Although there was a wide range in the costs incurred, most owners spent relatively little on their pets. Three-quarters of the current owners claimed no expenses beyond the cost of food. Licensing costs were mentioned by only 9 percent of the current owners.

Unlike people in urban areas, where fecal problems and animal sanitation are major political issues and real burdens in caring for a pet, this sample placed relatively little emphasis on this issue. Those in the more urbanized area of the county mentioned animal sanitation more often.

TABLE 28.5.   RURAL ELDERLY RELATIONSHIPS WITH COMPANION ANIMALS—YEARLY EXPENSES OF PET OWNERSHIP (n = 55)

	Low	Median	High Yearly		Weekly
Food	$26.00 ($.50/Week)	$182.00 ($3.50/Week)	$520.00 $780.00	one animal multiple animals*	$10.00 $15.00
Pet Products	0.00	$6.00 (41 claim none; 74%)	$ 51.00		
Veterinary Care	0.00	$16.00 (41 claim none; 74%)	$200.00		
Grooming Fees	0.00	0.00 (46 claim none; 83%)	$ 50.00		
Boarding Fees	0.00	0.00 (52 claim none; 94.5%)	$ 37.00		
Other Expenses	0.00	0.00 (50 claim none; 91%)	$180.00		
Total	$26.00	$204.00	$1,298.00		

*Owner has 29 animals.

Spring 1980

Similarly, animals in town were more likely to be walked on leads. Almost no rural animals were restrained when outside, although a large majority of the dogs were clearly defined as "house dogs" and did not spend much time unrestrained. Dog owners stressed repeatedly the importance of keeping an animal at home and their ability to prevent the pet from roaming. It is widely known that roaming pets in the rural areas of the county were likely to be killed. Respondents reported such loss of pets, especially cats, although Pennsylvania has laws forbidding the indiscriminate killing of stray pets.

There was inadequate variation among owners on measures of relationship with the pet. Several trends suggest, however, that refinement of the measures of human-animal relationships used would be useful. In general, behavioral intimacy and physical intimacy were higher among dog owners, but certain cat owners were also extremely attached to their pets. Dog owners also reported being dominant more often than did cat owners (71 percent versus 57 percent). Those persons with a single animal reported a closer relationship with it than those with multiple animals, particularly physical intimacy.

Effects of Pet Ownership on the Individual   Pet ownership alone does not seem to be significantly related to differences between the subgroups on measures of social functioning, functional health, and morale for this rural sample (Table 28.6).

Comparisons among current owners on behavioral and physical intimacy produced close to significant relationships, with higher morale scores ($p > .18$,

TABLE 28.6. RURAL ELDERLY RELATIONSHIPS WITH COMPANION ANIMALS— COMPARISON AMONG OWNERSHIP CATEGORIES

		Current Owners n = 56	Former Owners n = 73	Never Owners n = 6	F	PR > F n = 135
Social	X̄ =	24.64	23.60	23.50	.35	.7065
Activity	sd =	7.70	6.63	5.68		
Social	X̄ =	10.16	10.06	10.16	.11	.8969
Satisfaction	sd =	1.00	1.27	1.16		
Prostheses	X̄ =	.74	.81	.75	.90	.9115
	sd =	.82	.90	1.03		
Level of	X̄ =	8.04	8.29	8.83	1.08	.3438
Impairment	sd =	1.38	1.49	1.16		
Activities of	X̄ =	31.21	31.73	30.50	.25	.7755
Daily Living	sd =	5.69	4.92	5.31		
Morale	X̄ =	30.67	30.95	30.51	.30	.7328
	sd =	5.04	4.63	4.82		
Number Lived	X̄ =	.91	.65	.33	.42	.6597
With	sd =	1.11	2.12	.51		

and p > .07 respectively) for both variables. But they accounted for only a small percentage of the variance in morale between the groups (.04) and did not distinguish between the subgroups on the other areas of functioning.

Marital status appeared to be a significant factor in the lives of the current owners, especially in their social functioning. Single or divorced pet owners in particular were likely to be less socially active and to report lower social satisfaction. They were more likely to live alone than were widowed persons. The widowed current owner group could be characterized as having an activity-oriented style of adapting to widowhood. They reported high levels of social activity and social satisfaction and low levels of impairment. They reported more adequate finances than did former owners. Nonetheless, both groups reported high morale and were not noticeably different from each other (p > .99). Table 28.7 shows how the dependent variables were differentially related to morale for current owners and former owners. Despite their high levels of social participation, current owners' social activity was not related to morale.

Only age showed a significant relationship, with higher morale reported at more advanced ages. The social activities of the less active former owner widows were strongly related to their morale. For former owners there was an inverse relationship between morale and the opinion that a pet-placement program is a good idea; those with lower morale were more likely to endorse pet relationships.

TABLE 28.7. RURAL ELDERLY RELATIONSHIPS WITH COMPANION ANIMALS—DIFFERENCES IN MORALE CORRELATIONS FOR WIDOWED CURRENT AND FORMER PET OWNERS

Morale	Social Activity	Social Satisfaction	Impairment	Activities of Daily Life	Prosthesis	Age	Good Idea
Correlation Coefficient	-.0087	.2512	-.2561	-.1649	.1895	.4408	.0525
Probability >H0:Rho=0	.97	.27	.27	.47	.42	.04*	.82
			Former Owners (n = 48)				
	.3545	.2302	-.01718	-.0189	-.0341	-.0872	-.2845
	.01*	.11	.91	.90	.82	.55	.05*

*(p > .05)
Widowed
- Current owners are significantly more socially active.
    (X̄ 22.87 versus 27.52, p < .01)
Widowed
- Current owners report less impairment
    (X̄ 8.37 versus 7.65; p < .07)
Widowed
- Current owners report more adequate finances
    (p < .09)

Former owners who had been widowed seemed to maintain high morale with relatively fewer resources than did the current owners, using adaptive strategies that do not include pet companionship. Those whose morale was lower were more likely to consider a pet as a potential aid in their adaptation.

Among pet owners who simultaneously owned both dogs and cats there were higher than expected levels of impairment compared to those who owned fewer animals, either dogs or cats only ($p > .009$). Further, this group was lower in morale and social satisfaction, although not at significant levels ($p > .21$, $p > .27$, respectively).

Although some pet owners gave evidence of being deeply attached to their animals, the measures of relationship and functional assessments used in this baseline survey failed to detect a major pattern of significant differences among the groups. It is expected that as measures are refined in subsequent waves of the longitudinal study and as individuals are followed over time more significant patterns of differences will emerge.

DISCUSSION

The 8.5 percent of the survey group expressing an interest in obtaining a pet immediately is probably higher than in the population at large, reflecting a self-selection bias after seeing a presentation suggesting the value of animal companions. In the newsletter survey 3 percent expressed a desire for pets.

Those expressing interest were more likely to be widowed, single, or divorced and more likely to have higher levels of health impairment. Although these individuals were most forthright in stating a need, it is felt that a pet-placement program should not be targeted solely to these persons because to do so would unnecessary limit the potential client population. Also, the potential negative effects of the connotation that only impaired persons decide to acquire a pet in later life should be minimized.

The relative priorities placed on different types of pets and the selection process required to assure a good match between person and animal will remain a problem. The two studies conducted in the feasibility process yielded conflicting information in this area. The newsletter survey put great emphasis on cats as an animal favored by current owners, but the survey found a clear trend of less involvement, satisfaction, and closeness among rural elderly cat owners. Both surveys showed a clear preference for female neutered animals. The public relations efforts for a pet-placement project should stress both dogs and cats (and for a much smaller group, birds, caged mammals, and perhaps fish) but the client's preference for a particular type of animal must be understood and adhered to as much as seems consistent with a successful placement and human-animal relationship. Especially in this county, the value and a rationale for owning cats by elderly persons should be a major part of the educative program.

The pattern of multiple ownership also raises issues for placement programs.

A significant minority of current owners would accept multiple animals in placements. Although multiple animal owners seem very strongly attached to having companions, they spend less money on each animal and have higher levels of impairment when compared to single animal households. It seems the most committed pet owners are less likely to surrender ownership, even in the face of serious health problems. Although animals are important to this subgroup, their ability to care adequately for these animals must be called into question in some cases. It is necessary to consider another mode of services to reduce animal ownership to a more manageable, responsible level among a small subgroup of impaired multiple animal owners.

CONCLUSION

The feasibility study process was used in gaining information necessary to initiate a demonstration program of placing pets with community-dwelling elderly persons living in a rural area in central Pennsylvania. The data presented show clear support for this effort and suggest directions for a carefully operated program of modest scope. There was strong interest from between 3 and 8 percent of the elderly in acquiring a pet in the immediate future, and a majority reported being interested in considering owning a pet.

The nature of the attachment bond between owner and animal is much less clear for this sample. Ownership of pets per se is not associated with improved functioning for these rural elderly persons. Preliminary investigation of measures of attachment among pet owners show several interesting statistical trends, but they do not adequately differentiate companionship owners from those less attached to their pet. Given the lack of differences between the current and former owners, it can be concluded that these groups are essentially homogeneous with regard to the major dependent variables used in the baseline stage of this longitudinal evaluation study.

Edward Baker and Michael J. McCulloch

29

Allergy to Pets: Problems for the Allergist and the Pet Owner

During 1978, a survey was conducted among physician allergists to determine their attitudes toward the keeping of pets in households with allergic persons. The reason for the survey was the often reported admission by allergic families in veterinary offices that their physician had insisted they remove their pets and that, although they would not admit it to the doctor, they had no intention of complying. This decision posed problems for clients. Was noncompliance fair to the allergic member of the household? Was it fair to the physician, who in good conscience was trying to improve the health status of his patient? Finally, was it fair to all members of the household, who, in both tangible and intangible ways, were affected during acute allergic episodes? On the other hand, was it fair to the family to insist on pet removal regardless of whether the pet triggered allergic episodes?

With these considerations in mind, allergists were asked to report whether they recommended removal of pets regardless of specific allergic response to the pet, knowing the possible emotional reaction of the patient or family and that there would be a large degree of noncompliance (Baker, 1979).

Of the 170 respondents, 111 permitted pets as long as there were no serious clinical reactions to animals; 55 uniformly insisted on elimination of all pets, a ratio of two to one. Over 50 percent of both groups reported psychological and emotional reactions from patients and families when they insisted that pets be removed. Few, however, reported increases or aggravation of the allergic state if the animal remained. Most allergists tested their patients for animal allergens if regular animal contact was indicated in the history, and the majority of allergists in both groups reported beneficial results with attempted hyposensitization to animal dander. Among the group that did not recommend elimination of pets without evidence of significant allergic problems, the majority were willing to consider hyposensitization to animals as an additional approach to therapy. The group that routinely recommended elimination of pets did not consider hyposensitization to animal danders to be a viable modality, in spite of beneficial effects which they reported.

It became apparent as the results were tabulated that the information obtained would become the basis for future periodic surveys to determine if changes were occurring in both the attitudes and approaches to patient management among practicing allergists.

The deficiencies in the early survey were immediately obvious. No attempt had been made to obtain background information on the responding physicians, such as their age, pet ownership as an adult or child, and institution where allergy training was obtained. To correct these deficiencies, a second questionnaire was prepared and expanded to include not only the information sought in the original survey but additional personal and general information.

Because of the noncompliance of patients perceived by allergists regarding recommendations for removal of pets, a study of allergic families was undertaken (McCulloch, 1979). Twenty-two families with at least one member allergic to pets were interviewed. When asked if they would get rid of these pets if their allergists recommended doing so, 73 percent said no. This finding appeared to verify the allergists' perception that the noncompliance rate was high and reaffirmed the strength of attachment of families to pets. When asked, "How did you react to the recommendation to remove pets?" spontaneous comments included the following: "It would have to be a life or death matter before we would get rid of them." "The children are too attached. We could never do it." "I couldn't get rid of it. It was a present from my husband." "We wouldn't do it. We couldn't put them to sleep, and that is what we would have to do." "I'd give up anything in the house but the dog." "I got rid of our pets once when we had to move. I'd never do it again. It's too hard." "The doctor told me to get rid of the dog, but I can't. I didn't have the heart to tell him we also have a cat." The willingness to maintain pets in spite of severe allergic symptoms and, at times, to lie to the allergist about the number and kind of pets in the household reflected the strength of attachment.

METHODS

We sent 725 questionnaires containing eighteen items to members of the American Academy of Allergy. Of these, 206 (28 percent) were returned.

The first three items on the questionnaire included biographical information, age, place and date of training, and location of practice. Items 4 through 18 contained specific questions regarding experiences with pets, present and past ownership of pets, evidence of allergy in the family, and a group of questions pertaining to clinical recommendations given to allergic patients. The overall response to the questionnaire was better than anticipated, considering that the most recent academy roster available was dated 1979. Numerous comments reflected a "What are you really after?" attitude. Most questions were answered; some were not.

RESULTS OF QUESTIONNAIRE SURVEY

1. Age
2. Institution where training was received. Date and completion of training.
3. Is your practice rural, urban, or suburban?
4. Do you have children living at home?   Yes: *66%*   No: *31%*
5. Are there pets in your household?
    Dog: *66*   Cat: *13*   Dog and Cat: *21*
    Birds: *2*   Other: *11*
6. Do you have a horse?   Yes: *5%*   No: *95%*
7. If you are not a pet owner now, have you owned pets previously?
    Yes: *52%*   No: *11%*   No answer: *37%*
8. Do you believe pets played an important role in your life as a child?
    Yes: *51%*   No: *47%*   No answer: *37%*
    Or currently as an adult?
    Yes: *36%*   No: *44%*   No answer: *20%*
9. Are you or members of your family allergic to animals? Specifically, who?
    Yes: *40%*   No: *58%*   No answer: *2%*
10. When working up an allergic patient, do you routinely test for dog, cat, or other epithelia if the history reveals there is a pet in the household?
    Yes: *98%*   No: *2%*
11. Do you recommend that pets be eliminated from allergic households
    a. in the presence of asthma, regardless of cause?
        Yes: *50%*   No: *47%*   No answer: *2%*
    b. in the presence of rhinitis?
        Yes: *44%*   No: *53%*   No answer: *3%*
    c. even if the patient does not exhibit allergic symptoms to the pet?
        Yes: *34%*   No: *63%*   No answer: *3%*
    d. if the pet owner is a child?
        Yes: *47%*   No: *38%*   No answer: *15%*
    e. if the pet owner is an adult?
        Yes: *45%*   No: *39%*   No answer: *16%*
12. Is this recommendation based on a clinical experience in which you have seen patients who were not allergic to pets at the time of original examination convert to being allergic, or is it based on clinical management recommendations?
    Yes: *55%*   No: *20%*   No answer: *28%*

13. If the allergic person is the child, is he or she consulted before recommendations regarding pets are made?
    Yes: *70%*   **NO:** *25%*   **No answer:** *5%*

14. Do you feel that patients generally tend to follow your instructions to eliminate pets?
    Yes: *38%*   **NO:** *58%*   **No answer:** *4%*

15. Have you observed or received reports of guilt feelings, emotional reactions,
or psychological trauma as the result of the forced elimination of a pet? If yes,
please describe.
    Yes: *43%*   **NO:** *53%*   **No answer:** *4%*

16. If yes, have such emotional reactions resulted in aggravation of the atopic
state or increased incidence or severity of asthma?
    Yes: *11%*   **NO:** *56%*   **No answer:** *33%*

17. Have you found any one species (dog, cat, horse, etc.) more likely to cause
allergic symptoms than any other? (Plese specify.) Any breed (poodle, spaniel,
Siamese, or other.)
    Yes: *72%*   **NO:** *27%*   **No answer:** *1%*
    9 dogs, 172 cats (Siamese, Persian)

18. Where positive reactions to animals have been found have you tried hyposensitization therapy?
    Yes: *72%*   **NO:** *27%*   **No answer:** *3%*
    If yes, have you found that the patient improved with hyposensitization
therapy?
    Yes: *46%*   **NO:** *17%*   **No answer:** *37%*

DISCUSSION

Sixty-six percent of respondents had children at home, and 59 percent had pets
in the household. The vast majority were dog owners. Allergists have similar
patterns of pet ownership to that of the general public (Wilbur, 1976). In that
study, 55 percent of households owned pets, with dog ownership favored two to
one over cat ownership. Forty percent of the allergists had a member of the
family who was allergic. Ninety-eight percent routinely tested for allergy to
animal dander if history indicated a pet in the household. Fifty percent recommended removal of pets in the presence of asthma, regardless of cause, 44
percent in the presence of rhinitis. Thirty-four percent recommended removal of
pets from the household, even in the absence of allergy to the pet. Seventy
percent said that they consult the child pet owner before making recommendations for removal. The belief that patients would not follow instructions to
remove pets was shared by 58 percent. Forty-three percent were aware that
patients had emotional problems as a result of the forced removal of pets. Eleven
percent said that the underlying asthma or allergy was worsened by the emotional
reaction.

Seventy-two percent of respondents believed that certain animal species are
more allergenic. Cats were thought to be the most allergenic, fifteen to one over
dogs. Hyposensitization is tried by 72 percent of allergists, and of those who try
hyposensitization, 46 percent believe that there is clinical improvement.

An interesting discrimination was noted when the allergists who have pets in
their households were compared with those who presently had no pets. Only 23

of 118 (19 percent) pet-owning allergists recommended removal of pets while 30 of 83 (36 percent) of non-pet-owning allergists recommended removal (.001 < p < .01). If the allergist was a pet owner as a child, then similar patterns were observed. Only 23 of 106 allergists (21 percent) who owned pets as a child recommended removal of pets but 30 of 83 allergists (36 percent) who did not own pets as a child recommended removal of pets (.01 < p < .02). Thus prior pet ownership as a child or present pet ownership does affect the rate at which a practicing allergist recommends removal of pets.

It is encouraging that a dialogue usually occurs regarding removal of pets if the pet owner is an allergic child. Allergists appear to appreciate that there is a high rate of noncompliance with their recommendations for pet removal. The nature of people's attachment to their pets suggests that they will resist removal of pets from the household and may not tell the allergist whether they have removed the pet. The best approach seems to be an open dialogue with the allergic family to determine the strength of attachment of each family member and a clinical recommendation that keeps communication lines open. As one patient said, "it probably would be best if there were not pets in the household, but I know that removing them may be hard to consider."

Even if the patients keep their animals when they should not, at least the allergist knows this and can adjust treatment accordingly. In doing so, he can retain rapport with the allergic family. It is doubtful that families who are attached to their pets will remove them without firm evidence by skin test. Recommendations for removal before or after the testing may be disregarded.

It seems essential for the allergist to have increased awareness of the role pets play in family life, the strength of attachment people have to their pets, and feelings of loss that families experience when pets are removed.

Erika Friedmann, Aaron H. Katcher,
and Deborah Meislich

30

When Pet Owners Are Hospitalized: Significance of Companion Animals during Hospitalization

In previous communications we have presented evidence that pets can influence health, play roles in the family that could directly reduce the probability of illness, and decrease the physiological consequences of stress (Friedmann et al., 1980; Katcher and Friedmann, 1980; and Katcher, 1982). Our studies also suggested that the effects of animal ownership may be dependent upon the pet's role in the family. We hypothesize that the more important a pet is in a person's life, the more benefit a person may derive from the pet. In a preliminary investigation of the import of pets in their owners' lives, a questionnaire indexing attachment was developed. Subsequently, 120 dog-owning clients of a veterinary clinic were surveyed. Over 98 percent of the subjects surveyed said that they talked to their pets every day, over 80 percent felt that their pets were family members, over 80 percent talked to their pets as "a person" rather than as "an animal," over 80 percent felt their pets were sensitive to their moods, and 28 percent said that they "confide in" their pets or talk to them about events of the day.

Although pets can provide health benefits to their owners, with pet ownership comes responsibility for the pets' welfare. Responsible adults may delay hospitalization and feel anxiety about the welfare of dependent children and adults during hospitalization. Similarly, pet ownership may present difficulties for the hospitalized or ill pet owner. The current investigation was designed to explore pet-related problems and feelings associated with the pet owner's hospitalization. Ninety-five patients hospitalized under the care of the medical-surgical services of a large university hospital were interviewed. Thirty-six of the 95 patients (38 percent) owned pets: 31 owned dogs and of these, 4 also owned cats; 4 patients owned cats only; and 2 had combinations of birds, cats, horses, and fish. The 36 pet owners owned a total of 56 pets.

Previous studies of pet ownership had indicated a relationship between pet ownership and demographic variables (Friedmann et al., 1980; Katcher et al., 1983; Christensen, 1978; Schneider and Vaida, 1975). Thus the relationship between pet ownership and several demographic variables for this sample was investigated. Age was not significantly related to pet ownership. The mean age of pet owners was 60.4 years and that of nonowners was 59.8 years. Sex also was not related to pet ownership. Pet ownership was significantly less frequent among blacks than among whites (Table 30.1).

The findings in Table 30.1 are consistent with those of several other studies, including our own investigation of coronary heart disease patients. Pet ownership has also been related to income. Although we did not ask participants about their income, the hospital where the patients were interviewed is divided according to medical insurance. Pet ownership among black and white patients was equally distributed on the floors where patients received medical assistance and on those where patients covered by medical insurance are housed.

The admitting diagnoses of the pet owners were noted. None was hospitalized for an elective procedure, ten were having scheduled cardiac catheterizations, and all others were nonscheduled admissions. Diagnoses included coronary heart disease, cardiac arrhythmia, cardiovascular tenosis, cancer, and osteomyelitis.

TABLE 30.1. DISTRIBUTION OF PET OWNERSHIP ACCORDING TO DEMOGRAPHIC CHARACTERISTICS

Characteristic		Pet	No Pet	Total
Sex	Female	18	31	37
	Male	18	28	46
	Total	36	59	95
Race	Black	8	28	36
	White	28	31	59
	Total	36	59	95

$x^2 = 6.01, p < .025$

Each hospitalized pet owner was asked six questions relating to care for their pets during hospitalization, their concerns during hospitalization, and difficulties of hospitalization related directly to pet ownership. Each pet owner was also asked to respond to the ten-question attachment scale (Katcher, 1981). Pet owners were questioned first about who was caring for their pet(s). Of the 56 pets, 41 were being cared for by others in the owner's home. Of the 15 other pets, 4 were being cared for by relatives living elsewhere, 7 by neighbors or friends, and 4 were being boarded at a veterinary or boarding facility (Table 30.2).

On the other hand, 6 percent had some difficulty arranging for care, 33 percent were concerned about their pets' welfare, and 17 percent said their plans for hospitalization were affected by their concerns for their pets. One patient suffering from congestive heart failure had not intended to come to the hospital because she was concerned about her pet, even though she knew she was seriously ill. A friend had visited and insisted that she take her to the hospital. The woman came only after her friend agreed to care for Coco. The hospitalized patients demonstrated concern about and a need for contact with their pets.

Of the 36 owners, 81 percent (29) were receiving news about their pets; 19 (66 percent) received news daily or more frequently through telephone conversations with or visits from the person caring for the pet. Six (21 percent) "talked" to the pet daily on the telephone. When patients who owned pets were asked if they

TABLE 30.2.   CONCERNS OF HOSPITALIZED PET OWNERS ABOUT THEIR PETS (36 Pet Owners Surveyed)

Was difficult to arrange for pet's care during hospitalization	
Not at all	34
A little	1
Moderately	1
Quite a bit	0
Extremely	0
Concerned about pet's welfare	
Not at all	24
A little	5
Moderately	4
Quite a bit	2
Extremely	1
Concerns about pet's welfare affected hospitalization	
Not at all	30
A little	5
Moderately	0
Quite a bit	0
Extremely	1
Is receiving news about the pet	
Yes - 29 No - 7	
Would like pet to visit	
Yes - 14 No - 19	

would like their pets to visit them while they were hospitalized, 39 percent (14) responded affirmatively and 53 percent (19) responded negatively. Negative responses usually expressed concern about the effect of the pet on other hospitalized patients or the danger to the pet, such as that the pet was "too excitable," "would be a problem to other patients," would "certainly make this place liven up," "would jump all over me." Several other patients said their pets would not like to see them sick or they did not want anyone else handling their pets. The previously mentioned demographic characteristics were not significantly related to the distribution of answers to the questions dealing with concerns of hospitalized pet owners.

Each pet owner was asked to respond to the ten-item attachment questionnaire (Table 30.3). Response patterns of these 36 pet owners were remarkably similar to those of the pet owners who responded to the questionnaire in a veterinary clinic waiting room (Katcher, 1981; Katcher et al., 1983). All pet owners talked to their pets, and 86 percent (31) talked to them "often" or "very often"; 75 percent (27) talked to their pets "as a person"; more than 90 percent (33) considered their pets to be members of the family; 89 percent (31) thought their pet was aware of their moods; and 28 percent confided in their pets or talked to them about events of the day. Furthermore, 50 percent of the pet owners had pets sleeping in a bedroom; 25 percent (9) of the patients interviewed said the pet slept in a person's bed; and 25 percent (9) celebrated their pet's birthday. There were no significant differences in the frequency of responses to these questions on the basis of age, sex, or race. Although 64 percent (23) of the respondents had pictures of their pets, 25 percent (2 of 8) of the blacks and 75 percent (21 of 28) of the whites had pictures. Similarly 47 percent of those interviewed (17) kept pictures in albums, displayed, or in their wallets; 1 of 8 blacks and 16 of 28 whites. On both of these points, there was a significant difference between blacks and whites, but there were no significant age or sex differences.

TABLE 30.3. ATTACHMENT INDEX

	Blacks	Whites
Has photographs or paintings of pet	2/8	21/28
Keeps pictures of pet in photo albums, wallet, or displayed	1/8	16/20
Pet sleeps in a bedroom	2/8	16/28
Pet sleeps on a bed	2/8	7/28
Celebrates pet's birthday	2/8	7/28
Talks to pet "often" or "very often"	6/8	25/28
Talks to pet as would to an adult or a child	5/8	22/28
Confides in pet or talks to pet about problems or important events	3/8	7/28
Thinks pet is aware of moods	6/8	26/28
Considers pet a member of family	8/8	25/28

TABLE 30.4. SCORE ON ATTACHMENT SCALE ACCORDING TO DEMOGRAPHIC CHARACTERISTICS

Characteristic		Number of Pet Owners	Average Attachment	S.D.
Sex	Female	18	6.1	2.2
	Male	18	5.7	1.9
Race	Black	8	4.6	2.2
	White	28	6.2	1.9

$t = 1.87, p < .04$

The score on the attachment index was totaled (one point per questions) (Table 30.4). Examination of the relationship between age and sex and attachment revealed no significant differences, although blacks showed significantly lower attachment than did whites. Once the two questions about photographs were eliminated, the race differences disappeared. Thus these questions were responsible for the difference.

These data support previous conclusions that there is a racial difference in pet ownership. Blacks tend to own fewer pets and either are less attached to their pets or express their attachment differently than do whites. Pets may have different roles within these two cultures in the United States.

From the data collected by interviewing hospitalized pet owners we conclude that for some pet owners responsibilities for pets significantly affect willingness to be hospitalized and timing of hospitalization. The pet owners interviewed in this study were hospitalized for nonelective procedures; pets may have a larger effect on elective hospitalization. Further, very few of those interviewed (10) lived alone; more concern would probably be evident in patients whose cohabitants could not care for their pets. This hypothesis gains some support from our data, but additional information is needed for strong conclusions to be drawn.

Even while people are hospitalized for serious illnesses they express concern for and interest in their pets. This interest was demonstrated by patients' frequent contacts with their pets. While alleviating concern about their pets, the act of getting information about pets' welfare necessitates contact with other people. Thus even during hospitalization, pets facilitate interactions between their owners and nonhospitalized friends or relatives.

Considering the impact of pets in people's lives and the feelings of responsibility people have toward their pets, pet ownership should become an important concern of hospital staffs. Dr. Bustad (Bustad and Hines, 1981) emphasized the importance of identifying pet owners and emergency pet caretakers for noninstitutionalized, socially isolated elderly individuals. Hospital social and nursing services are aware of a need for and express concern for dependent children's (or adults') care at the time of hospital admission. Similar attention to the responsibilities of pet owners would also be appropriate. Awareness of pet-related problems by hospital staff would alleviate anxieties of pet owners and thus could improve patients' attitudes toward hospitalization.

Aaron H. Katcher, Erika Friedmann,
Alan M. Beck, and James Lynch

31

Looking, Talking, and Blood Pressure: The Physiological Consequences of Interaction with the Living Environment

Our experiments with looking at animals were an outgrowth of our study of the effects of interaction with dogs on blood pressure (Katcher, 1982). We wanted to separate the effect of tactile and verbal interaction with the animal from the effect of the animal's presence. We set up a simple experimental situation in James Lynch's living room. Neighborhood children who were recruited by his sons were brought into the livin room, where they met the investigator and were introduced to the purpose of the experiment and the recording apparatus. The experimental situation was varied in a very simple way. There were two experimental groups. The first met the experimenter and a dog when they entered the room. They were asked to sit quietly while their blood pressure was recorded and then were asked to read aloud while the recording of blood pressure and heart rate continued. After this first set of observations, the dog left the room and the observations were repeated. The second group faced the experimenter alone for the first set of recordings, and the dog entered before the second set. The children's blood pressure (systolic and diastolic) was signficantly lower, both when the children were silent and when they were reading aloud, when the animal was in the room. The effect of the animal was greater in the first group that met the dog at the start of the experiment. The children did not interact with the dog at all; the animal was part of the visual environment (Friedmann, Katcher, et al., 1983). After observing that the sight of a dog could have a calming effect, we decided to investigate the influence of animals that were not touched and were not considered members of the family but were only visual objects. The most obvious choice for that study was tropical fish.

No one who has stretched out effortlessly watching the life of a coral reef can forget the sensation of joyous, intent wonder at being in the midst of so much variegated, moving beauty. The effortless floating, the repetitive rush of breathing, the weaving about of the bright fish with the visual impact of their color intensified by the silence of their movement, and the undulant motion of seaweed fronds all combine to prduce an envelope of sensation that can take the observer completely outside of himself. He can float with almost no consciousness of self, with no thought, feeling only the intense but peace-giving moving color of the reef. Perhaps because of the effortlessness of floating, perhaps because of the strange combination of rhythmic breathing and silence, perhaps because the sea rocks as well as supports, the intensity of the beauty brings a calm and almost godlike serenity. Some part of the diver's rapture can be captured by gazing into an aquarium. "A man can sit for hours before an aquarium and stare into it a into the flames of an open fire or the rushing waters of a torrent. All conscious thought is happily lost in this state of apparent vacancy, and yet, in these hours of idleness, one learns essential truths about the macrocosm and the microcosm. If I cast into one side of the balance all that I have learned from the books of the library and into the other everything that I have gleaned from the books in running brooks,' how surely would the latter turn the scales" (Lorenz, 1961:16).

To study how contemplation of the life in a home aquarium could influence blood pressure, I established a forty-gallon tank in my office, landscaped the bottom with rocks so that the fish could have some place from which they could emerge into an observer's gaze, and placed living plants about that landscape to offer the eye life in repose. I kept fifteen to twenty fish in the tank. They were all common, relatively inexpensive tropical fish that can be found in almost any pet shop.

The first subjects for our relaxation experiment were a group of students and university employees, all of whom were relatively young and had blood pressures at the low end of the normal range. Subjects in the second group were older, and all had clinical hypertension. The experiment was simple. We brought each volunteer into a laboratory and seated him or her in a comfortable lounge chair with support for the head and arms. We explained the nature of the experiment and wrapped the cuff of an automated blood pressure monitor about the upper arm. The automated equipment measured blood pressure each minute for the rest of the experiment. The first blood pressure readings were always higher than the readings recorded when the subject was resting. These initial readings reflected the subject's uncertainty about the experimental situation. The participants were then asked to read aloud for two minutes so we could obtain a stressed blood pressure level. (As we have described earlier, reading aloud or talking to people always raises blood pressure [Katcher, 1982]). Subjects then watched a blank wall for twenty minutes to permit the blood pressure to fall to a resting level. Then they watched the fish tank for twenty minutes. When they were watching the fish we asked them to fill their minds with the sight of the fish. No other suggestions were given.

The results of the experiment are given in Table 31.1.

The results demonstrated that watching the tropical fish lowered blood pressure to levels below that produced by resting in a chair with no special focus of gaze and produced a state of calm relaxation. The subjects' blood pressure began to fall as they sat quietly in a chair for twenty minutes, doing nothing but watching a wall, and fell again as they watched the fish. The highest blood pressures were recorded when the subjects talked to the experimenters. The changes in blood pressure for the hypertensive subjects were large: over a twenty-five-millimeter change in systolic blood pressure and a sixteen-millimeter change in diastolic blood pressure. This magnitude of change is clinically significant and, more important, the average blood pressure level of the hypertensive group fell to levels within the normal range while watching the fish.

In other experiments we observed that the blood pressure would fall if subjects watched a tank with only plants and no fish. They could still watch the movement of the plants and listen to the bubbling of the filter. Nevertheless, subjects watching an empty tank could not sustain their calm for very long. Before the twenty-minute observation period was over, they became bored and restless, and their blood pressure levels began to rise.

The calm induced by watching fish also reduced the subjects' response to stress. When we asked them to read aloud at the end of the study, the rise in blood pressure with reading was less than half as large as it was at the start of the experiment. Thus after being relaxed they were able to tolerate stress better.

These results could have been obtained by a variety of procedures, some simple, some cumbersome. Sitting quietly in a chair resulted in a fall in blood pressure, but only experimental subjects will sit and face a blank wall for a long

TABLE 31.1. BLOOD PRESSURE RESPONSES TO CONTEMPLATING FISH TANKS

	Initial	Read	Wall	Fish	Read
Hypertensives (n = 15)					
Systolic	143	155	131	123	140
Diastolic	86	91	75	72	83
Normotensives (n = 20)					
Systolic	122	129	118	114	118
Diastolic	69	74	67	63	71

period of time. Biofeedback training produces the same magnitude of change, but it requires specialized electronic equipment. Any of the forms of Eastern meditation will produce a state of relaxation and a fall in blood pressure, but they require long hours of practice and the cultic apparatus of a hairy guru and his adoring followers, or a hairy guru and his slickly franchised and packaged lessons. In contrast, twelve million families have aquariums at home and take considerable pleasure in tending and watching them with no promise of enlightenment, nirvana, eternal health and peace, or a medically certified mind cure.

How do fish relax us? The calming influence of exterior gaze was demonstrated in the laboratory by Lacey (1959). His group studied the physiological response of subjects to different tasks that could be performed in a laboratory. They measured heart rate, blood pressure, and the activity of the sweat glands of the palm. This last measure is a good index of anxiety. They found that, when a subject was required to think, to process data, or to do mental work, the signs of nervous activation increased. Blood pressure and heart rate increased, and the palms secreted more sweat. Subjects became stressed and anxious. The more troublesome the mental work, the more physiological activation. But when the subjects were asked to attend to the external environment, wait for a light to flash, listen to music, or listen to instructions, the heart rate and blood pressure fell and the palms became drier.

These results have been confirmed over and over again. Of course, not all external events reduce stress and anxiety. If subjects watch a bloody movie, filled with gore and mutilation, blood pressure and heart rate go up. Exciting external events cause internal excitement. The stimuli that calm subjects are those that do not threaten but draw the attention outward, interrupt the private dialogue with the self, the constant thought stream of remembrance and recreation of events, the streams of worry and concern. In some ways, these laboratory experiments are self-evident.

We spend an average of four to seven hours a day watching television. Television is recognized to be addicting, to be preferable to play, talk, games, and a variety of social events that the television screen has displaced. Yet we do not think of television as a means of producing relaxation, even though people relax or collapse in front of the set. No one has advocated watching televison as an alternative to meditation, biofeedback, or yoga. Why? It is certainly hypnotic enough. The answer lies, in part, in the technique of television. Television must continually excite and arouse to keep the attention of the viewer on the content of the program. The viewer is expected to set aside his own thoughts, but he is expected to pay attention to the commercial messages and the program content, so he will return to the same content and the same commercial messages day after day, week after week. To capture the viewer's attention for the content, he must not be permitted to lapse into a reverie, as one lapses into a meditative state in front of a fish tank. His attention must be focused on the program by excitement. The techniques of television are excitement and novelty. The camera continually moves, sound changes constantly in volume, scenes shift every few seconds. Sound intensity, violence, motion, color, and sexual arousal are all used to keep the viewer activated and attentive. The technique of television prevents its images from being too relaxing. If you wish to transform the television images into an event more like the tank of tropical fish, try a simple experiment. Find a football, basketball, or hockey game and turn off the sound. With the absence of sound, turn your attention away from the progress of the game and watch the form of events. In a football game, you will see two lines of uniforms forming, opposite one another, moving into and through each other, reforming and repeating the action. It becomes an event that is neutral, repetitive, and calming in the way the motion of fish is calming: a very different experience from the television presentation of football.

Television is designed to fail at the task of bringing complete relaxation. There are, however, more complete means of relaxation that depend upon holding our gaze in the way that fish in a tank hold our gaze. One of the most obvious analogies is the method of hypnosis which depends on fixation of attention on some point, light, or object, while the subject remains quiet and listens to the hypnotist's voice. Everyone remembers at least a few films with "Svengalis" reducing their victims to sleepwalkers by forcing them to stare at a pendulum or a crystal or directly at the hypnotist's eyes. My favorite was Lionel Barrymore, playing Rasputin, charming the tzarevitch out of his hemophilia by swinging a pocket watch in front of his eyes. I can also remember my utter delight, during a hypnosis class I was teaching, when a visiting lecturer put a subject into a deep hypnotic trance within ninety seconds by swinging two crystal chandelier ornaments in front of his eyes, thus joining truth and fiction. To describe the similarity of the two events, the hypnotic induction and quiet gaze at a tank of fish, I quote from a respected text on hypnotic technique:

The Induction of Hypnosis by the Direct Stare: It is all very calm. The patient is brought to a feeling of great trust. "You just let yourself go. It is easy. It is easy and calm and comfortable. Look at me, and you can let yourself go more completely. You let yourself go utterly. Everything lets go. Everything lets go, and your body works automatically. Good, your eyelids get heavy, automatically heavy. Yes they close automatically with the heaviness. It is all through you. Good, your whole body works automatically. . . . "

The use of a bright object to fix the patient's gaze has been used for inducing hypnosis since James Braid first described it and is still probably the most widely used method of induction in medical practice. All manner of items can be used as the bright object: a bead, a crystal pendant, a ring suspended by a cotton thread, or a watch held by its chain. An opthalmoscope light is effective and has the advantage of suggesting a medical rather than a magical procedure. In each case, the bright object is held in front of the patient at a level slightly higher than is comfortable for him. The result is that the upper eyelids are under some strain, they tend to tire, and the suggestions of heaviness of the eyelids become more effective.

The metronome has long been used in the induction of hypnosis as a means of tiring the senses by monotonous auditory stimulation. The type of metronome commonly used by piano teachers is satisfactory. Some therapists use specially designed metronomes in which the pendulum carries a small reflecting mirror. A strong spotlight is directed so that the mirror comes into its beam at the end of each swing of the pendulum. The patient is placed in such a position that the light is intermittently reflected into his eyes. This mechanical aid provides a monotonous sensory stimulation of both eyes and ears, as well as fixing the patient's gaze.

The hypnodisc produces patterns of color and form when it is rapidly revolved in front of the patient and so produces monotonous visual stimulation (Meares, 1961:201–12).

Hypnosis produces a deep state of relaxation from which subjects awake feeling refreshed and relaxed. During hypnotic relaxation, blood pressure and heart rate fall as they do with any other relaxation technique. The unifying dimension between almost all relaxation techniques is the interruption of on-going thought and worrying rumination by focusing attention on some other stimulus. Hypnotic techniques of relaxation use an external stimulus, but the various methods of relaxation that are known as meditation use an internal focus of attention.

The popularity of meditation is a child of young America's infatuation with Eastern religion. The infatuation reflects, in part, the hope for a drugless fix, a way of achieving bliss and freedom from mental pain with no hangover and no letdown. The forms of meditation are almost as numerous as the sonorous names of the gurus associated with each brand. The techniques of meditation are embedded in a matrix of mystical thought about good, evil, mind, and body and the construction of the universe. Because of the combination of techniques for altering behavior with powerful religious symbols, it was difficult to evaluate the claims of various practitioners. The claims that interested physicians stated that meditation offered a way to treat stress and achieve a state of relaxed calm which protected the meditator against the adverse health consequences of anxiety and stress of modern living. One investigator, Herbert Benson (1975), began to ran a series of experiments in which he studied the physiological effects of a single meditative practice, used as a technique, without any religious indoctrination or symbolic associations. He chose the meditative technique of transcendental meditation, because it was the most popular and systematized and had was advocated by a group of activists for the treatment of stress and anxiety. After years of experimentation, Benson convinced himself that the effect of meditation was nonspecific and common to a wide variety of meditative or relaxation techniques. He defined four basic elements of what he called the "relaxation response": the subjective state produced by meditation.

Most accounts of what we now call the Relaxation Response are subjective descriptions of deeply personal unique experiences. However, there appear to be four basic elements underlying the elicitation of the Relaxation Response, regardless of the cultural source.

The first element is a quiet environment. One must "turn off " not only internal stimuli but also external distractions. A quiet room or place of worship may be suitable.

The nature mystics meditated outdoors.

The second element is an object to dwell upon. This object may be a word or sound repetition; gazing at a symbol; concentration on a particular feeling. For example, directing one's attention to the repetition of a syllable will help clear the mind. When distracting thoughts do occur, one can return to this repetition of the syllable to help eliminate other thoughts.

The third element is a passive attitude. It is an emptying of all thoughts and distractions from one's mind. A passive attitude appears to be the most essential factor in eliciting the Relaxation Response. Thoughts, imagery, and feelings may drift into one's awareness. One should not concentrate on these perceptions but allow them to pass on. A person should not be concerned with how well he or she is doing.

The fourth element is a comfortable position. One should be in a comfortable posture that will allow an individual to remain in the same position for at least twenty minutes (Benson, 1975:78–79).

It may be difficult for us to equate something as informal as watching a fish tank with meditation, but we can certainly feel the similarity between the relaxation one feels when sitting quietly before a fish tank and reverie, the dreamy state that one falls into in front of a fire, or while watching the surf pound on the beach or clouds pass in the sky. Reverie is a passive state of mind, while the eye is fixed on the external world, the fire, or clouds, and thoughts pass in and out of the mind of their own accord; they are distant and dreamlike; no attempt is made to make particular thoughts come or to stay their passage out of the mind. Bachelard, in a book with the imposing title *Psychoanalysis of Fire*, talks of reverie before open flames.

The dream proceeds on its way in linear fashion, forgetting its original path as it hastens along. The reverie works in a star pattern. It returns to its center to shoot out new seams. And, as it happens, the reverie in front of the fire, the gentle reverie that is conscious of its well being, is the most naturally centered reverie. It may be counted among those which best hold fast to their object or, if one prefers, to their pretext. Hence this solidity and this homogeneity which give it such a charm that no one can free himself from it. It is so well defined that it has become banal to say, "We love to see a log fire burning in the fireplace." In this case it is a question of the quiet regular controlled fire that is seen when the great log emits tiny flames as it burns. It is a phenomenon both monotonous and brilliant, a really total phenomenon: it speaks and soars, and it sings.

The fire confined to the fireplace was no doubt for man the first object of reverie, the symbol of repose, the invitation to repose. One can hardly conceive of a philosophy of repose that would not include a reverie before a flaming log fire (p. 14).

In Bachelard's description of fire-drawn reverie, we have the same elements, the passive mind, the object of attention, the comfort of warmth, and the unstated but assumed lack of distraction. The description of the fire contains one phrase that distinguishes the natural focus of reverie from meditative or hypnotic techniques. The meditative or hypnotic techniques are monotonous by deliberate intent. Natural events that induce reverie are like the fire, "monotonous and brilliant."

A log fire is the essence of a Heraclitean universe. It is always different yet always the same. The flames change in form from second to second, the logs burn and glow into ashes at a much slower pace, but, in retrospect, one fire is hardly distinguishable from the next, all log fires being the same fire. The beauty of the fire is in the sudden flash of flame or the inconstant form of glowing coals, but these, like the flow of image in reverie, rarely are retained in memory. They pass, and our attention drifts to be caught by another flash which is not clearly distinguishable from the first. The fire offers constant novelty yet is always the same. Natural objects of contemplation, the sights that induce reverie have this property in common: the combination of beauty and monotony, novelty and constancy, sudden beauty, which passes and is indistinguishable from the next flash. The movement of brightly colored fish in a tank or unconfined above a tropical reef, the passing of birds through a forest, the pattern of clouds, all have this dual property of having points of instantaneous beauty that attract our gaze but lapse without notice into an essential constancy. In this sense, the sea, the fire, and the moving patterns of birds or clouds in air are all similar.

Could the clouds, the waves, the fish, or the flame be replaced by mechanical objects: imitation clouds, flames, fish, or waves that moved and flashed colors? Is there something about living objects that has a special attraction for our gaze that cannot be explained by their physical properties, which can be more or less imitated? Instead, do we have to take into account the power of life to be a unique vehicle for symbolic transactions that have a special capacity to move our minds and bodies? The answer is difficult to phrase. If people watch kaleidoscopic machines, they will relax and drift off into reverie. Machines can help one to relax, yet people want to keep living beings about them. They keep fish, not moving models of fish. They want open fires, not electric logs. More of us would rather go to the sea than watch the imitation waves in teetering plastic oblongs that can be bought in any "head shop." I cannot offer any hard evidence that there is something essentially different about looking at life. I can only stop speaking within the rhetorical constraints of science and talk in terms of poetic images. I can only raise the same question raised by Ange Condoret when he observed how the flight of a dove drew Bethsabee out of her inanimate prison and led her out to meet with living. Are our minds moved by living symbols in ways of which we are unaware? Does the living dove bring peace with its flight?

In partial answer I would like to mention the following lines:

> He prayeth well, who loveth well
> Both man and bird and beast.
> He prayeth best, who loveth best
> All things both great and small;

These lines have become part of modern cliche: the sentimentality that can be evoked by the care and love given to animals by veterinarians. Yet in the poem, the mariner is redeemed when he is overcome with love at the sight of living color in the water about his ship, love for the beauty of animals he would never touch or tend in any way. The awakening of love in the albatross-burdened mariner is described in these lines:

> Beyond the shadow of the ship,
> I watched the water-snakes:
> They moved in tracks of shining white,
> And when they reared, the elfish light
> Fell off in hoary flakes.
> Within the shadow of the ship
> I watched their rich attire:
> Blue, glossy green, and velvet black,
> They coiled and swam; and every track
> Was a flash of golden fire.
> O happy living things! no tongue
> Their beauty might declare:
> A spring of love gushed from my heart,
> And I blessed them unaware:

The consequences of that reverie, from that blessing out of awareness, were release from the albatross that fell from his neck and sleep, the "gentle thing."

It is not possible to believe that the ancient mariner could have been redeemed by contemplation of machinery, even as complex as described by Yeats in "Sailing to Byzantium." It is even difficult to entertain such an idea. By moving from a scientific to a poetic frame, I have answered my own question. We are changed in a unique way when we gaze at the living world about us. Life is meant to look at life. I will trust my own humanity, and Coleridge's poetic insight, and do no experiments with plastic waves or mechanical fish.

PART FIVE

The Loss of a
Companion Animal

Introduction

The chapters in the Companion Animals and Human Health section provided impressive evidence that the influence of a companion animal on its owner's health or morale was in part dependent upon the strength of the owner's attachment to the pet. This observation has the inescapable corollary that the loss of a companion animal can be a source of grief for those who benefited most from that animal's presence. Recognition of the possibility of such grief may prevent some from ever owning an animal, but experience with grief is known to dissuade many who have lost an animal from owning one again (Wilbur, 1976). All common species of companion animals have significantly shorter life spans than their human owners, and all fall prey to a wide variety of diseases and accidents that shorten their lives. Therefore pet death is a fact of life—so much so that the experience of the death of a pet is usually cited as one of the "benefits" that children extract from the presence of a pet.

The existence of overt, disabling, and even flamboyant grief after the death of an animal companion was described in Egypt by Herodotus and was known among the more stoic Greeks and Romans. Within modern industrialized societies, mourning of a pet is assumed to be part of normal childhood experience, but there is no consistent expectation for the response of adults. Unlike our feelings about the appropriateness of grief after the death of a human family member, we recognize that there may be extreme variation in the response of adults. Keddie (1977) and Rynearson (1981) have documented existence of grief severe enough to precipitate a depressive psychosis. For some people the definition of a pet as an equivalent to a human family member continues after death of the animal, and interment in a cemetery is used by a relatively small population of pet owners. (There are some four hundred pet cemeteries in the United States, but more than fifteen million pets die each year.) Basic information about grief after the death of a pet can be found in articles by Katcher and Rosenberg (1979), the above-cited publications by Keddie and Rynearson, the chapter by Mary Stewart in this section, and a popular treatise by Neiburg (1981).

The experience of the death of a pet is often made more poignant because the owner and the other family members frequently must participate in the decision to terminate the life of the pet. In their contribution to this section, Michael McCulloch and Leo Bustad document the frequency of euthanasia, which involves more than 3 percent of veterinary patient visits. This figure translates to the death of an estimated two and a half million animals per year, not as a result of malice or neglect but because an owner and veterinarian believe they are doing the best thing for the animal. James Harris examines the response of individual owners to this awesome event. Not surprisingly, he notes that more than half of the owners in this circumstance respond by crying. Harris goes beyond this quantitative analysis and identifies a type of owner that is more prone to experience significant grief at the death of animal. He calls these clients "nonconventional" owners, meaning that they have a deep, somewhat symbiotic relationship with their animal. He advises veterinarians to use a chart identification system to identify such owners so that the staff will be alerted when the death of an animal is imminent. In a complementary piece, James Quackenbush and Lawrence Glickman describe differences between the "average" pet owner and those who were referred to a social work service in a veterinary hospital. Those clients perceived by the staff of the hospital to require help with their reaction to the death of an animal tend to be older, to have owned their animal for a long time, and to have only one animal. There was a relative preponderance of cat owners among the clients referred.

None of the chapters in this part deals with the full range of responses to the loss of a pet, and the reader should guard against the impression that everyone mourns the death of a cat or dog. As noted by Beck (1982) and by John Hoyt in this volume, more than fifteen million dogs and cats are killed in animal shelters around the country yearly, most of them delivered there by owners who wish to give up their pet. The family dog statistically lives a much shorter life than is biologically possible because better than a third of the population is relegated to animal shelters annually where they usually die before the age of two (Beck, 1981c). One of the research challenges of the future is to understand the nature of the bond between people and animals and learn why, for the most part, it is so weak. We need to be studying those who do not mourn as well as those who do. We have no knowledge of how the personal characteristics or the relationship with their animals differs between the population of owners who surrender their animals to shelters and the clients whose animal's final illness is managed by a veterinarian.

The section closes with Mary Stewart's comparison of bereavement after the loss of an animal with the response to the death of a human family member. This section is a complement to the description of the pet as a family member. The frequency with which pets are considered family members or important companions has been documented repeatedly in this volume and elsewhere. This capacity of the animal to act as a significant other has been used to suggest that the animal can act to sustain health, as human family members and companions do. We know that loss of a family member is associated with an increase in illness experience and mortality (Lynch, 1977; Helsing and Szklo, 1981). We do not know as yet if the loss of a pet can be a significant enough event to have a negative effect on the health of elderly pet owners who do not replace their animals.

Michael J. McCulloch and Leo K. Bustad

32

Incidence of Euthanasia and Euthanasia Alternatives in Veterinary Practice

One of the most challenging areas of veterinary practice is the tactful management of the decision to euthanize pet animals. For the pet-owning family, coping with the illness or death of a pet can be extraordinarily difficult. If the pet has held an honored place, grief experienced by the family can be very intense (Brodey, 1973; McCulloch, 1978; Edney, 1979; Katcher, 1979; Bustad, 1980a). Some pet owners are particularly psychologically vulnerable to the illness or death of their pets because of their personality makeup, life change (divorce or recent loss), or illness. When pet owners develop pathological dependence on pets, emotional upset regarding the animals' health can be very difficult for the veterinarian to predict and manage (Rynearson, 1978, 1981; McCulloch, 1979a).

Practitioners who are particularly skilled in handling the decision for euthanasia frequently receive greater appreciation from pet owners than they do for performing complex medical or surgical cures. Letters received from grateful pet owners after euthanasia are far more numerous than after the veterinarian has performed successful medical or surgical therapies (Hopkins, 1981). Veterinarians are frequently placed in the difficult position of mediating among family members who are in conflict about treatment decisions, especially euthanasia. The veterinarian's appreciation of the degree of attachment of various members is important because the decision maker is often not the person who has the strongest attachment (Hopkins, 1978).

Attempts have been made to quantify veterinarians' daily practice activities to determine the amount of time spent in various professional activities (May, Blendon, and McCulloch, 1971). Approximately nine percent was spent in preventive medicine activities. No specific attempt was made to delineate how much time was spent counseling clients regarding euthanasia or its alternatives or dealing with clients' emotional problems.

Veterinarians see more people than pets in the course of their practice. Reports indicate that 1.7 people accompany each pet to the practitioner's office. There are more than 11,000 veterinarians in small animal practice, handling over 55 million pet visits per year. That figure multiplied by 1.7 gives a total of 100 million human contacts per year by the profession. Even if just a small percentage of these involve emotionally upset clients, the actions of the veterinarian can be significant (McCulloch, 1976, 1978). At the time of euthanasia of pet animals, the veterinarian may be the only health professional who can observe and intervene. A previous attempt was made to quantify the amount of time the veterinarian spent with the euthanasia decision (McCulloch, 1979a). Nine practices were surveyed over a three-week period. Each was asked to tabulate the number of inpatient and outpatient contacts and to record the number of euthanasias performed. Contact was defined to each day an animal was seen, whether as an inpatient or outpatient; for example, if an animal was kept in the hospital five days, that meant five contacts. There were 2,715 patient contacts, and 58 euthanasias were performed. The percentage of contacts ending in euthanasia was 2.1. The range in the practices was from .8 to 3.6 percent (.8, 1.4, 2.3, 2.3, 2.3, 2.3, 2.3, 2.9, and 3.6).

The present study was designed to gather similar data on frequency of euthanasia and its alternatives. It was believed that many clients are counseled on euthanasia as an alternative, but the procedure is not done because another course of treatment is elected or the pet owner chooses to have no treatment and takes the animal home. Time spent dealing with actual euthanasia plus the alternatives to euthanasia would be a more accurate reflection of the actual time spent daily in this area.

METHODS

Twenty-three veterinarians in ten practices located in Oregon, Washington, California, and Texas participated in this study. For a four-week period records were kept on the total number of inpatient and outpatient contacts made and the total number of euthanasias performed. The reasons stated for euthanasia were also recorded, similar to the study by Stead (1979). If the reason for euthanasia was the animal's behavior, the practitioners were asked to specify the behavior problem. In addition, each veterinarian was asked to tabulate the number of times euthanasia was discussed as an alternative but not done. They were also asked what specific alternative to euthanasia was elected by the pet owners.

RESULTS

1. Total number of patient contacts, inpatient and outpatient, for FOUR WEEKS
   A. Count each patient contact per day (i.e., if you see the same patient for three days in a row, that is three contacts).
   B. Count each day an inpatient is seen: pet in hospital five days = five contacts.
      Inpatient 2,405
      Outpatient 5,512
      Total 7,917
2. Total number of euthanasias done: 140 1.8%
3. Number of doctors in the practice: 23
4. Is there an animal shelter in your community that performs euthansia?
   Yes__X__   No_____
   The rate of euthanasia was 1.8 percent with a range of .03 percent to 4.1 percent in the ten practices:

.03	1.7
.09	2.2
.09	2.4
1.2	3.8
1.7	4.1

5. Count each time you discussed euthanasia with clients as an alternative to treatment of a patient but did not perform the procedure. Please include:
   A. Palliative treatment (i.e., surgery for removal of tumor) 33
   B. Delays for client emotional well-being (i.e., client too upset to consider euthanasia at this time) 15
   C. Curative treatment (i.e., setting fracture of leg) 6
   D. Client decided on no treatment (took animal home) 7
   E. Client took animal elsewhere for euthanasia 2
      Total: 63

DISCUSSION

The veterinarian can expect to encounter opportunities for discussing euthanasia and euthanasia alternatives in 3 percent of patient contacts. If one calculates 3 percent of the one hundred million human contacts per year by the veterinary profession, the number of pet owner contacts seen in euthanasia counseling is three million. The public health exposure is definite, for even if a small number of those clients have problems coping with euthanasia, the potential value of the veterinarian's actions is evident. Economic considerations may weigh heavily at this time, and the need for the veterinarian's sensitivity about this matter is very apparent.

Three practices did not keep track of euthanasia alternatives because of time constraints. Omitting these from the calculation left 5,178 combined inpatient and outpatient contacts with 63 alternatives to euthanasia discussed, or 1.2 percent. Thus the combined total of euthanasias performed and alternatives to euthanasia discussed was 1.8 plus 1.2 or 3 percent of total patient contacts.

It is important to note that grief is a normal psychological and physiological reaction to loss and can be a healthy expression of loss (Lindemann, 1944). This expression should be encouraged. Recommendation to replace a pet should be delayed to permit a "working through" of loss. For some (15 percent) a pet will not be replaced because the former pet owner cannot handle another loss (Wilbur, 1976).

Facilitating the euthanasia decision or an alternative to euthanasia can be a very important contribution to human mental health. The veterinarian is the only health professional who is present to participate at this crucial time. When comforting is all that can be offered, that may be exactly what is needed.

A questionnaire was filled out for each euthanasia performed. If the reason specified was behavior, the behavior problem was listed.

Species_____

Sex_____

Age _____

Reason for euthanasia: (please check one)

106   1. Clinical (medical, surgical, age—animal's condition warrants euthanasia on humane grounds)

5   2. Behavior problems (if due to behavior problem, please check what the problem behavior was)

12   3. Economic (could not afford treatment, did not want to spend the money)

11   4. Convenience (moving, housing too small, owners died, unwanted animals)

4   5. Stray

2   6. Unstated

Total 140

Behavior Problem List

_____	(1) untrainable	___1___	(5) incontinent/soiling
_____	(2) car chasing	_____	(6) destructive
_____	(3) fighting	___4___	(7) aggressive/biting
_____	(4) wandering	_____	(8) other (please specify)

James Harris

33

A Study of Client Grief Responses to Death or Loss in a Companion Animal Veterinary Practice

Twenty-three years ago, when I was a young veterinarian with a new practice, my client population was younger and my patient population was more pediatric than geriatric. As time progressed, experience, better medical care, improved nutrition, changing client attitudes, and other factors changed this picture. Life expectancies for both humans and companion animals have been extended. My practice now is more balanced between pediatrics and geriatrics in both clients and patients. Few companion animals live past fifteen years. We practitioners of twenty or more years have essentially lost all of the patients we started as infants or acquired during their lives. We have survived them because of our longer expected existence, and we will in all probability survive the patients we serve today. We face and accept as a fact that life is a terminal process. We work with this maxim in daily practice with patients and clients. In providing support, understanding, and social services, one can hope we learn to accept and work with our own mortality.

Some degree of grief inevitably accompanies the death or loss of a companion animal. This phenomenon can be accentuated and occurs more frequently in clients who have unconventional bonds with their companion animals. In recent years Leo Bustad and Michael McCulloch have surveyed the incidence of euthanasia in companion animal practices. In participating in these studies I have been struck both by the relatively high incidence of loss in veterinary practice (2 to 4 percent of contacts) and by the frequency of overt response by clients to this loss. I felt that it would be of value to explore this subject further and to compare loss and grief within conventional and nonconventional human–companion animal bonded clients.

A nonconventional human–companion animal bond may be defined as but not limited to insistence on a special relationship with a companion animal (for example, the companion animal relationship substitutes for a human relationship) or overdependence on a companion animal (Keddie, 1977).

The study period encompassed the three months from May 1, 1981, to July 31, 1981, and included 71.5 working days. My private companion animal veterinary practice was used for the study. It is located in a shopping center business area serving a widespread, hilly, wooded, primarily private single-home, residential neighborhood between the inner city and regional park lands on the east side of the San Francisco Bay area. There is major freeway access and public bus service to the area. Most clients rely on private transportation, few walk, and public transportation is rarely used, even by clients with small species. The practice provides service to avian and exotic species (25 to 30 percent of patients) as well as the usually encountered companion animals. Nonconventional human–companion animal bond clients compose 35 to 40 percent of the clients. The number of contacts and losses were tabulated for the study period. A worksheet was prepared on each loss during the period (see Table 33.1, Worksheet). Additional information was gathered as needed from client information sheets (see Table 33.2, Information Sheet) and through follow-up phone calls.

TABLE 33.1. WORKSHEET

Date _____ No. _____

I. Type of loss (euthanasia, natural death, disease, lost):
2. Client name/Pet's name (for office use only)/Species
2a. Contact phone number
3. Rated a. conventional _____
          b. nonconventional _____
4. Observed stress or grief reaction:
   No _____
   Yes _____ (if yes, brief description of rxn—e.g., crying, anger, withdrawal, etc.)
5. Number of adults in family _____
6. Number of children in family _____ ages? _____
7. Number of animals in family _____ dog, cat, avian, other
8. Returned with another animal:
   No _____
   Yes _____ (species)

372 The Loss of a Companion Animal

TABLE 33.2. INFORMATION SHEET

PATIENT REGISTRATION (Please print clearly).
YOUR NAME & PARTICULARS:
Last _____ First _____ Middle _____
Address _____ City _____ Zip _____
Home phone # _____ Work # _____ Other #_____
Occupation_____
Alternate responsible adult (name) _____ (phone #) _____
Referred by _____
Previous veterinarian_____
Family members: Number of adults _____ Number of children_____
Name, Address & Phone Numbers of Owner, if not you, or of Parent if you
are under 19: _____

PET:
Name _____ Birthdate _____ Age today_____
Breed _____ Color/Markings_____
Gender (sex) _____ spayed [/ castrated [/ Tatooo I.D.# _____
Pet's Function: Companion [/ Breeding [/ Work [/
Your reason(s) for bringing your pet here today is (are): _____
_____

Has your pet had any serious medical problems, allergies, or drug reactions in
the
past? If so, please list them by name with approximate dates: _____
_____

When was your pet last vaccinated against: Canine DHLP _____ Rabies _____
Parvovirus _____ Feline Distemper _____ Feline Respiratory _____
At what hospital(s) was your pet last vaccinated?_____
All clinic fees are to be paid in full when services are performed. This policy helps
control costs--on which we base our fees. Please circle your method of payment:
          CASH   CHECK   VISA   MASTERCHARGE
I am financially responsible for the patient described above and agree to pay all
fees incurred. I understand that any medical or surgical procedure is attended by
some risk and that it is not possible to guarentee the successful outcome of any
such procedure. This agreement is in force indefinitely from this date unless I
notify the clinic in writing to the contrary.
Your signature_____ Date _____
  # _____

The total number of contacts is the sum of outpatient visits plus the number
of additional days each patient was hospitalized. During the study there were
2,510 contacts (an average of 35 contacts per day) and 73 losses (an average of
1.02 losses per day), which represents 2.9 percent of total contacts. The clients
exhibiting conventional and nonconventional bonds are classified in Table 33.3.

TABLE 33.3. CLASSIFICATION OF COMPANION ANIMAL LOSS BY CLIENT BOND

Bond	Number	Percent	Percent of Practice Population
Conventional bond	50	68.5	60–65
Nonconventional bond	23	31.5	35–40
Total	73	100.0	100

TABLE 33.4. CLASSIFICATION OF COMPANION ANIMAL LOSS BY CAUSE

Cause	Number	Percent
Euthanasia	48	66.0
Voluntary placement	1	1.5
Trauma	4	5.5
Disease and natural causes	20	27.0
Missing (lost or stolen)	0	0.0
Total	73	100.0

Euthanasia, disease, and natural causes accounted for 93 percent of the losses in the study. The low incidence of trauma-related loss may be explained by the existence of leash laws for dogs and a great effort by this practice to encourage responsible animal care, housing, and control (Table 33.4).

The twenty-one losses classified as "avian" and "other species" comprise 29 percent of the total. Included in "other species" were turtles (1), cavies (3), hamsters (3), snakes (1), rats (1), rabbits (3), and mice (1). The percentage of these species correlated closely with the number of these patients in the practice (Table 33.5).

TABLE 33.5. CLASSIFICATION OF COMPANION ANIMAL LOSS BY SPECIES

Species	Number	Percent	Percent of Practice
Canine	32	44	70
Feline	20	27	
Avian	8	11	30
Other	13	18	
Total	73	100	100

Outward signs of grief were observed in thirty-seven clients, or 50.7 percent of the group suffering loss of a companion animal (Table 33.6).

TABLE 33.6. INCIDENCE OF OVERT SIGNS OF GRIEF OVER COMPANION ANIMAL LOSS

Group	Number/Group	Number Showing Grief	Percent Showing Grief
Conventional bond	50	20	40.0
Nonconventional bond	23	17	74.0
Total	73	37	50.7

These figures confirm my own and other observers' prestudy impressions. Indeed, nonconventionally bonded clients "put themselves at greater risk from a mental health point of view at the time of loss" (Keddie, 1977:21) than do conventionally bonded clients. Crying is the most frequently observed client grief response and is not uncommon among veterinary staff, who are moved by the loss of a patient and the grief sustained by clients and themselves (Table 33.7).

The composition of the families in this study is tabulated in Table 33.8. Nine "families" consisted of only one adult. Ten families were composed of o ne or more adults. All groups had fewer children (.70 for total group) than the national average (1.01). The average number of animals per family was raised by seven families who had eight or more animal members: one family with 8 animals, one with 11, one with 13, one with 14, one with 18, and two with 25 or more. Of these seven families, four were rated conventional and three nonconventional. Both groups averaged two adults per family. The conventional bonded

TABLE 33.7. GRIEF RESPONSES EXHIBITED BY CLIENTS WHO HAVE SUSTAINED COMPANION ANIMAL LOSS

Response	Number of Total	Percent of Total	Number of Conventional	Percent of Conventional	Number of Nonconventional	Percent of Nonconventional
Crying	30	81	15	75	15	88
Sadness	8	21.6	4	9.2	3	17.6
Hysteria	1	2.7	1	5.0	0	0.0
All responses	*37	–	20	–	17	–

*Thirty-seven clients showed grief response; two of these exhibited more than one response.

TABLE 33.8. COMPOSITION OF FAMILIES SUSTAINING COMPANION ANIMAL LOSS

Composition	Group Conventional	Nonconventional	Total
Total	50	23	73
Total adults	103	47	150
Average Adults per Family	2.06	2.04	2.05
Total Children	42	11	53
Average Children/Family	.84	.48	.70
Families with Children	23	6	29
Percent Families with Children	46.0	26.0	39.7
Number of Animals	144	89	233
Average Number of Animals per Family	2.88	3.87	3.19

TABLE 33.9. CLIENTS RETURNING AFTER A LOSS WITH OTHER ANIMALS FOR SERVICE DURING THE STUDY PERIOD

Group	Number per group	Number of returns	Percent of returns
Conventional	50	16	32.00
Nonconventional	23	8	34.78
Total	73	24	32.88

group had twice the average number of children, and the nonconventional bonded group averaged one more animal per family.

The number of clients returning with other animals during the study period was tabulated, and there were no differences between the groups (Table 33.9).

Previous observations have been that some clients do not return to the same veterinarian after the loss of a companion animal (Harris, 1981). In this study the return rate in each group is almost identical.

The loss cases occurring in this study reflect closely the client and patient populations of the practice. The 2.9 percent loss rate does not reflect the actual practice time expended by both staff and practitioner. Loss-related contacts generally involve twice the amount of time other contacts require. Additional follow-up phone calls and support services may augment this to three times as much time consumed by the practitioner as well as by the support staff. This area of service therefore accounts for a relatively large part of the work week. To use this time most efficiently and to make the effort as successful as possible, a protocol for loss contacts is essential. All members of the companion animal practice staff need to be familiar with this material. The type of loss, the type of bond, makeup of the family, previous history of losses, and choices available for clients for participation and for disposal of remains all need to be considered.

When choices are possible, as in euthanasia, placements, and most losses by disease and natural causes, discussions with clients should be held to make decisions. In contemporary practice, both institutional and private, this job falls mainly on the veterinary practitioner. We as practitioners must rise to the occasion and provide skilled social service.

It has been found most useful in practice to identify the records of noncon-ventional bonded clients' companion animals. Identifying these cases is not difficult. Often the client will state his or her feelings. "Tammy is our child"; "Spot is just like a son (daughter) to us"; "Fluffy was like my own fur and bones" (Harris, 1981); "I bought Nicki the week my husband died eighteen years ago" are just some of the comments made by clients that should be noted. The use of "motherese" and physical overprotection often are clues to the relationship. In these cases the notation "P.A." (Precious Animal) is made on the record card. Since we have a separate medical record file folder for each patient and use color coding (red-striped labels for canines, green-striped labels for felines, plain white labels for other species, and a sequence of colored dots for each year a record is active), we added yellow colored dots to the identification system for nonconventional bonded clients' records. A single yellow dot is placed in the upper right hand corner of the file folder. If the client is overly anxious about the companion animal or requests or requires special or unusual attention, a second yellow dot is placed next to the first. Clients who are highly stressed or exhibit evidence of extremes of behavior receive a third yellow dot. This marking system is very useful to all staff members who have contact with the clients. Scheduling appointments and services, giving advice and information, setting up examination rooms, returning phone calls, handling and examination of patients, planning diagnostics and treatments, and all the other aspects of the contact with client and patient are considered and often tailored to produce a smooth, nonstressful, productive visit for client, patient, staff, and clinician.

We are just scratching the surface of this area of practice. There is much more to explore. It would be useful for a social scientist to interview all of the clients in this study and to do so with clients in any future studies. Only time and funds limit this work. "More demographic information might be considered relative to perceptions, values, attitudes, and feelings of the animal owners" (Bustad, personal correspondence). It would also be appropriate to interview the observers (receptionists, technicians, and clinicians).

Loss is a daily occurrence in veterinary practice; grief accompanies this loss, and overt signs of grief occurred in 50 percent of clients sustaining loss. This incidence was much higher (74 percent) among nonconventional bonded clients. The grief process can be severe and long-lasting in some clients. Veterinary clinician and staff sensitivity and support of clients at the time of loss is an appropriate and needed social service aspect of veterinary medicine.

James Quackenbush and Lawrence Glickman

34

Social Work Services
for Bereaved Pet Owners:
A Retrospective Case Study in a
Veterinary Teaching Hospital

To provide a better clinical description and understanding of the bond between humans and their companion animals, a social work service was designed and implemented at the Veterinary Hospital of the University of Pennsylvania (VHUP) in 1978, following a model for social work in a human medical hospital (Rehr, 1974; Berkman and Rehr, 1973). The program has grown into a full-time service employing one social worker. Certain consistent characteristics of pet owners' difficulties at the VHUP have been identified (Quackenbush, 1981a). The intervention of the social worker has characteristically been short-term, crisis-oriented, and focused on the bereavement accompanying pet loss (Katcher and Rosenberg, 1979).

There is an extensive and growing literature on the concept, nature, and treatment of bereavement following loss of persons (Lindemann, 1944; Parkes, 1972; Gerber, 1969; Averill, 1968; Williams, 1973). The nonanecdotal literature on bereavement from pet loss, however, is virtually nonexistent. Because of this lack of information on pet-related bereavement, we believed it was necessary to begin systematically studying a population of bereaved pet owners, specifically, those whose companion animal had recently died. Such information is important for at least two reasons. First, pet death is not an uncommon event. In the United States alone at least two and a half million cats and dogs die annually as a result of euthanasia. Another large number of pets die as a result of disease or injury (Fogle, 1981a). Second, recent epidemiological studies in human-human bereavement have confirmed that the loss of significant other persons may increase morbidity and mortality in survivors (Helsing and Szklo, 1981). Such effects could also occur as a result of pet loss.

There is justification in hypothesizing that for a certain portion of the pet-owning population pet loss may influence morbidity or mortality in surviving owners. If pet loss could adversely affect owners' health, some of the large number of bereaved pet owners might benefit from professional mental health intervention. We decided it was necessary to examine some specific attributes of the bereaved pet owners in light of the type and quality of the social work service interventions available for those owners.

METHODOLOGY

During the one-year period from July 1, 1980, through June 30, 1981, VHUP veterinarians made 132 referrals that required a social work intervention with the pet owners. All of the cases were reviewed, and 76 cases that involved pet death were selected for systematic analysis. The retrospective case analysis seemed to be the most feasible, efficient way to collect data. Each of the 76 cases was analyzed, and data were abstracted for the following purposes: to describe the basic characteristics of the pets of the bereaved owners and to compare these characteristics to the general VHUP pet population; to survey specific demographic characteristics of bereaved pet owners and to determine what factors appear to be associated with the need for social work intervention, with particular stress on gender, household composition, age, marital status, and life-stress factors occurring within the year preceding the death of the pet; to attempt to identify and categorize the problems the owners faced and to examine the nature and duration of the social work services offered; and to make a limited assessment of the efficacy of the social work service provided at the VHUP.

FINDINGS

CHARACTERISTICS OF PETS OF BEREAVED OWNERS

Of the seventy-six case records sampled, 71 percent involved the death of a dog and 29 percent that of a cat. Although this proportion is slightly different from the general VHUP population (77 percent dogs and 23 percent cats), the difference is not statistically significant ($X_2 = 1.52$; NS). The ratio of cats referred to the social work service to cats brought to the VHUP was .012, and the similar ratio of dogs referred to the social work service to dogs brought to the VHUP was .008. A comparison of these ratios suggests that cat owners are more likely to be referred for bereavement counseling than are dog owners. The pet that died was the only pet for 83 percent of the seventy-six bereaved owners. We have no data on multiple pet ownership for the VHUP client population, but a recent study by Wilbur suggests that in the general population the frequency of pet owners who have only one pet is lower than it is in our sample (Wilbur, 1976).

The age distribution of both the deceased dogs and cats was similar. Almost two thirds (64 percent) of the dogs and 72 percent of the cats were more than seven years old, or the exact inverse of the dog and cat ages typically seen at the VHUP (see Tables 34.1 and 34.2). All of the pets had lived with the owner almost all their lives.

Of the seventy-six pets, 36 percent died in the hospital as a result of euthanasia, 36 percent died in the hospital from illness or injury, and the remaining 29 percent were discharged and died at home. The causes of death were as follows: neoplastic disease, 29 percent; renal disease, 9 percent; behavior problem, 9 percent; cardiac disease, 7 percent; no diagnosis, 13 percent; and other, 33 percent.

The social work service was used by nine departments in the VHUP, with a high of twenty-nine (38 percent) referrals from medicine to two (3 percent) referrals each from radiology and cardiology. Standing faculty made 33 percent of the referrals, residents 33 percent, interns 21 percent, and administrators and

TABLE 34.1. A COMPARISON BY AGE OF FIFTY-FOUR DOGS OF BEREAVED OWNERS AND THE VHUP POPULATION (L978)

Age of Dogs	Social Work Cases		VHUP Population	
	Number	Percent	Number	Percent
> 7	36	64	2,259	35
≤ 7	18	36	4,195	65

$X^2 = 23.67; p < .01$

TABLE 34.2. A COMPARISON BY AGE OF CATS OF BEREAVED OWNERS AND THE VHUP POPULATION (1978)

Age of Cats	Social Work Cases		VHUP Population	
	Number	Percent	Number	Percent
> 7	16	72	490	26
≤ 7	6	28	1,396	74

$X^2 = 23.96; p < .01$

staff the remaining 13 percent. Overall, the data from this sample of referrals to the social work service suggest that a minimum of 1 percent of all pet owners that came to the VHUP are likely to need social work intervention for bereavement as a result of a pet dying.

CHARACTERISTICS OF BEREAVED PET OWNERS

The sex distribution of the seventy-six bereaved pet owners was 71 percent female and 29 percent male. Table 34.3 compares this distribution with nonbereaved pet owners and the general U.S. population. Both pet-owning samples show a higher percentage of females than one might predict.

Table 34.4 shows that there were twice as many widowed females and almost five times as many widowed males as in the general population. Table 34.5 demonstrates that most of the single, bereaved females were under forty years of age, the widowed females fifty years of age or more, and over one half of the males were married. A final age comparison between bereaved VHUP owners and nonbereaved VHUP owners shows a marked difference in the ages of those populations (Table 34.6). The bereaved owners were significantly older ($X^2 = 19.81$; df = 5; p < .01) than the nonbereaved owners. Of the bereaved owners 62 percent were forty years and older, whereas 69 percent of the nonbereaved owners were less than forty years of age.

TABLE 34.3. SEX DISTRIBUTION: A COMPARISON BETWEEN SEVENTY-SIX BEREAVED VHUP OWNERS, ONE HUNDRED VHUP OWNERS, AND THE GENERAL U.S. POPULATION (PERCENT)

	Bereaved Owners	VHUP Owners*	General Population
Male	29	30	47
Female	71	70	53

*Unpublished survey data, VHUP, 1981, Dr. V. Voith, et al.

TABLE 34.4. A COMPARISON BY MARITAL STATUS OF TWENTY-TWO MALE AND FIFTY-FOUR FEMALE BEREAVED PET OWNERS AND THE GENERAL U.S. POPULATION (U.S. Census, 1977) (percent)

	Single	Married	Widowed	Divorced
Male				
Pet owners	22	64	14	0
U.S. population	22	70	3	5
Female				
Pet owners	24	46	26	4
U.S. population	16	65	13	6

TABLE 34.5. A COMPARISON OF AGE GROUP AND MARITAL STATUS BETWEEN NINETEEN BEREAVED MALE OWNERS AND FIFTY-ONE BEREAVED FEMALE OWNERS

	Single		Married		Widowed		Divorced	
	Number	Percent	Number	Percent	Number	Percent	Number	Percent
10–19 years								
Male	0		0		0		0	
Female	3	6	0		0		0	
20–29 years								
Male	2	11	2	11	0		0	
Female	3	6	1	2	0		0	
30–39 years								
Male	0		2	11	0		0	
Female	7	14	7	14	1	2	0	
40–49 years								
Male	2	11	5	26	1	5	0	
Female	0		6	12	0		0	
50–59 years								
Male	0		1	5	2	11	0	
Female	0		4	8	4	8	1	2
60–69 years								
Male	0		2	11	0		0	
Female	0		5	10	7	14	1	2
70+ years								
Male	0		0		0		0	
Female	0		0		1	2	0	

TABLE 34.6. AGE GROUP COMPARISON BETWEEN SEVENTY-TWO BEREAVED PET OWNERS AND NINETY-FIVE NONBEREAVED OWNERS AT VHUP

Age	Bereaved Owners		Nonbereaved Owners*	
	Number	Percent	Number	Percent
20–29	10	14	37	39
30–39	17	24	29	30
40–49	16	22	11	12
50–59	13	18	10	11
60+	16	22	8	8

$X^2 = 19.81$; df $= 5$; p $< .01$
*Unpublished survey data, VHUP, 1981, Dr. V. Voith, et al.

By household type, 60 percent of the bereaved owners either lived by themselves or with a spouse. In comparison, a majority of a sample of one hundred nonbereaved VHUP owners (54 percent) consisted of nuclear families, that is, parent(s) and at least one child, or extended family living situations

TABLE 34.7. A COMPARISON OF HOUSEHOLD TYPE OF SEVENTY-SIX BEREAVED OWNERS AND ONE HUNDRED NONBEREAVED OWNERS AT VHUP

Household Type	Bereaved Owners		Nonbereaved Owners*	
	Number	Percent	Number	Percent
Single person	23	30	11	11
Male/female couple	23	30	35	35
Nuclear family	18	24	30	30
Other	12	16	24	24

$X^2 = 9.85$; df = 4; p < .05
*Unpublished survey data, VHUP, 1981, Dr. V. Voith, et al.

TABLE 34.8. NUMBER OF PERSONS IN THE HOUSEHOLD: A COMPARISON BETWEEN BEREAVED VHUP OWNERS, VHUP OWNERS, AND THE GENERAL PET-OWNING POPULATION

Number of Persons	76 Bereaved VHUP		100 VHUP*		General Population	
	Number	Percent	Number	Percent	Number	Percent
1	23	30	10	10	908	12
2	30	39	47	47	2,460	33
3	12	16	12	12	1,395	19
4	4	5	15	15	1,320	17
5+	7	9	16	16	1,410	19

*Unpublished survey data, VHUP, 1981, Dr. V. Voith, et al.

(Table 34.7). The difference between household type in these two populations was statistically significant ($X^2 = 9.85$; df = 4; p < .05). Table 34.8 indicates the differences between three distinct populations. The trend is toward fewer people in a bereaved household with a statistically significant difference between bereaved and nonbereaved VHUP owners.

REASONS FOR SOCIAL WORK REFERRALS

We believed it was important to understand the reasons why bereaved pet owners were referred to the social work service. We examined the social work referrals from both a veterinarian perspective and a social worker perspective. The reasons veterinarians made referrals to the social work service are as follows: concern about the owner's stress and anxiety, fifty-eight (76 percent); difficulty communicating effectively with the pet owner, eleven (15 percent); and the owner created "problems" for the veterinarian, seven (9 percent).

For those same seventy-six bereaved owners the social worker's perception of the problem, after seeing the owner, were distributed in the following way: difficulty in making a euthanasia decision, forty-six (69 percent); an immediate reaction to the death of a pet, twenty-four (32 percent); prolonged grief, still intense two weeks after the death, four (5 percent); and owner reaction to the medical diagnosis or prognosis, two (3 percent).

As a basis for collecting information on life-stress factors experienced by the bereaved pet owners, we used a classification system developed in 1967 by Holmes and Rahe (1967). The tabulation of those data (see Table 34.9) indicates that the bereaved population of owners had experienced a fairly high frequency of life stress, particularly disease, injury, hospitalization, and death before the loss of the pet. In addition to those specific stress factors we were able to get some idea about how the death of a pet influenced the normal behavioral routines of their owners.

Ninety-three percent of owners experienced some disruption in their daily routine such as changed waking and sleeping patterns and disrupted eating habits. Over half (51 percent) of the bereaved owners significantly reduced their social activities. They remained at home, talked very little with anyone, and chose to spend a great deal of time by themselves. Finally, 45 percent of the bereaved population experienced job-related difficulties. They missed from one to three days of work (sick days or vacation time) or were upset by the insensitivity of work colleagues to their bereavement. Only one of the seventy-six bereaved owners failed to experience problems in at least one of the three categories mentioned above.

TABLE 34.9. LIFE-STRESS FACTORS OF SEVENTY-SIX BEREAVED PET OWNERS OCCURRING WITHIN ONE YEAR BEFORE THE DEATH OF THEIR PETS

Stress Factor	Number	Percent
Serious injury or illness to self	22	29
Serious financial difficulties	15	20
Same injury or illness to pet and self	14	18
Serious injury or illness in the family	14	18
Hospitalization (self)	10	13
Hospitalization (family member)	10	13
Death in family	9	12
Death in another family	9	12
Same injury or illness in pet and family member	8	11
Death of spouse	8	11
Change in residence	6	8
Loss of job	5	7
Birth in the family	3	4
Child(ren) left home	3	4
Job change	2	3
Retirement	2	3
Separation	2	3
Marriage	1	1
Divorce	1	1
Close friend died	1	1

TABLE 34.10. EFFICACY OF SOCIAL WORK SERVICES FOR SEVENTY-SIX BEREAVED OWNERS AT TERMINATION OF INTERVENTION

Final Determination	Number	Percent
Complete resolution	38	50
Partial resolution	22	29
No improvement	6	8
Refused help	6	8
Worse	1	1
Unknown	3	4

The social worker maintained contact for one week or less in 72 percent of the cases. Another 13 percent of the cases required more than one week but less than two weeks of contact. For 8 percent the intervention was from two to four weeks, and in only five instances (7 percent) was there a need for an intervention of four weeks or more. In total, 74 percent of the sample population had two or more contacts, with most of the contacts being a combination of in-person and telephone communications. Finally, as Table 34.10 shows, we took some subjective measures of the efficacy of the social work service; a clinical evaluation was made by the social worker in addition to a follow-up, self-report by the bereaved owner. At the time of the follow-up, approximately two to four weeks after the pet's death, 50 percent of the owners appeared to have appropriately resolved the loss of their pet. Another 29 percent had reached partial resolution and were actively working through the loss by themselves or with the support of friends and family. In ten cases (13 percent) the loss was still causing the owner great difficulty at follow-up; for these persons an outside referral was either recommended or made to provide an option for ongoing help from a mental health professional.

DISCUSSION

Because of the descriptive nature of the data that were collected and analyzed, we are unable to draw any definite, generalized conclusions. We expect to use this information as the first step in isolating factors that may be critical to the understanding of the human bereavement process for deceased companion animals. It allows us to isolate criteria and to ask more specific, sophisticated questions, as well as providing a vehicle through which future research on the subject can take place.

A first factor for consideration relates to cat ownership and bereavement. Cat owners seem to be slightly more inclined toward a social work intervention if their cat dies than are dog owners. Is there something about cats, their owners, and their relationship to one another that makes the owners more susceptible to bereavement difficulties? An equally important consideration is the strong tendency for bereaved pet owners to have a single pet. Perhaps because of the unidimensional focus of both the pet and the owner on one another, the bonding and attachment between them is particularly intense. Therefore, when that bond is broken by the pet's death, the human response to the loss approximates the depth, intensity, and quality of the single-focused relationship. The bereavement process and the accompanying effects of loneliness, aptly presented by Lynch (1977), can be extremely stressful. Another important dimension of the human–companion animal relationship is the age of the animal at death, or, more specifically, the length of time the owner and the pet have been together. The longer a person and a companion animal live together, the more likely it is that their relationship and interdependency will grow stronger and deeper.

The demographic data we collected on the bereaved pet owners show that females were bereaved more frequently than one would predict, but there could be several reasons for this higher frequency. First, perhaps females are more available to bring an animal to the VHUP because they are less likely to be restricted by employment responsibilities. In addition, females may experience bereavement more often bereaved through a mechanism of social default: it is not a generally accepted masculine role to show open concern and sensitivity in public, and it would be even less acceptable for a male openly to display emotion over an animal. This is a classic example of the male-female affective dichotomy of male stoicism and female emotionalism. Affect over the pet tends to become the exclusive territory of females and to be consciously avoided by males. Finally, females may spend more time with a pet by virtue of being home during the day, and more frequent contact promotes greater bonding and attachment. Females may be more frequently bereaved by virtue of their constant opportunities to develop a strong relationship with the "family" pet, therefore the death of the pet is more significant to them.

The apparently high rate of divorce among the bereaved pet owners (23 percent) merits further examination. Helsing and Szklo's human bereavement study confirmed a statistically significant difference in the rate of mortality between married and widowed males. No such difference occurred in a similar population of married and widowed females (1981). The higher mortality occurred in older age cohorts fifty-five to sixty-four years and sixty-five to seventy-four years. All other factors being equal, ownership of a pet by a divorced person may reduce loneliness and the mortality-morbidity risks, but the death of the pet might increase the risk of mortality and/or morbidity. This latter response would be similar to that described by Lynch (1977) in *The Broken Heart: The Medical Consequences of Loneliness*. Lynch links loneliness with physiological, psychological, and socioemotional difficulties. The loss of a companion animal appears to have the potential to create owner response very similar to that experienced with loss and death of human companions.

Almost one quarter of the bereaved owners were at or above retirement age. At that point in life and perhaps even earlier the frequency of social contact tends to diminish through reduced mobility, loss of friends from death, placement and moving, and relationships and companionships becoming less likely to occur and more difficult to sustain. In such cases, one of the roles a pet plays is to facilitate relationships and socialization.

If the human–companion animal bond is the major or at least a major one of a few and dwindling number of attachments for an aging person, the dissolution of that bond by pet death can be stressful. The referral of a high percentage of older pet owners because of bereavement difficulties may be partially a result of the pet's death being the termination of one more of very few remaining social relationships. It may even be the last relationship.

Several other of the descriptive findings reinforce the speculation that loneliness or perhaps fewer home-related relationships are more common among bereaved pet owners than among nonbereaved pet owners. Generally speaking, 43 percent of the nonbereaved pet owners had families consisting of three or more members, whereas 30 percent of bereaved pet owners had three or more persons in the household. Larger families allow for a greater number of relationships and a greater opportunity for various interdependent and mutually supportive attachments. A social network is available to cushion members of a family. They help one another in times of stress. No such extensive support exists in two person–pet or one person–pet families in which the crisis of pet death is more difficult for the owner(s).

Our analysis of reasons for social work referrals basically confirmed our suspicion that veterinary clinicians have developed an intuitive system for determining "normal" owner behavior. Through experience they have come to expect certain owner behavior responses in given clinical situations. Because of this benchmark for "normal owner behavior" they are able to see and sense what they think to be "nonnormal" owner behavior and thus can make a referral to the social work service when needed. The accuracy with which these veterinary personnel were able to make the "normal" versus "nonnormal" distinction is remarkable, at least for the seventy-six cases in this study. In each of these cases the referral resulted in a social work assessment that indicated the bereaved owner could benefit from crisis-oriented, professional mental health intervention. This is not to say that all pet owners whose animals die and who need a social work referral are referred, that everyone referred necessarily needs professional assistance, or that all pet owners who lose animals need professional help. Given the limitations of the program and the state of the art of "expertise" from both a social work and veterinary standpoint, the referral process is most often used appropriately and is effective. These particular referrals were from veterinarians very sensitive to and conscious of the needs of the owners.

The analysis of life-stress factors experienced by the bereaved pet owners suggests a strong tendency for this population of owners to have experienced significant life stresses in the previous year. The most frequent stresses involved medical problems, hospitalization, the loss of significant other persons, or a combination. The pet's death represents an experience similar to the other recent life stresses in the pet owner's life. The owner may associate the pet's death with a recent life-stress factor such as the loss of a spouse if, for example, both pet and person died from neoplastic disease. The owner tends not to understand and deal with the deaths separately, and the resulting response appears to be compounded as the doubly bereaved owner is unable to resolve the two significant losses simultaneously. Also, the pet is perceived, in symbolic terms, to represent a deceased individual because of the relationship both pet and person had before the person died; the death of the pet seems to signify and finalize the death of the person. Thus, the final loss of a person is recognized and experienced through the loss of the pet. The intensity and duration of such a bereavement response seems to be increased because there is also a separate and distinct grief reaction for the loss of the pet. Essentially, the apparent association of life stress factors with pet death might be attributed to similar generalized loss experiences in the recent past. Pet loss may be worthy of consideration as another life-stress factor.

These ideas, however, are purely speculative. We need to know if the frequency of occurrence of life-stress factors in bereaved owners is significantly different from that of all pet owners or if it differs significantly from that of other bereaved pet owners who were not referred to the social work service. Until those comparisons can be made, the information confirms nothing about the relationship between pet death and other life-stress factors. The bereaved owners experienced both cognitive and behavioral changes immediately following the death of their pet. From a behavioral standpoint, their daily living patterns were markedly disrupted. Personal activities were greatly curtailed, and most of the bereaved owners experienced some temporary but classic symptoms of clinical depression such as failing to sleep (insomnia) and failure to eat for several days (Beck, 1972). Probably most interesting is the impact of pet death on the owner's employment responsibilities. Almost one half of the bereaved owners stayed home from work for one to three days or if they did go to work, they felt listless and worked inefficiently and ineffectively. Their failure to work occurred as a result of being too depressed or wanting to avoid working colleagues because of fearing their grief would not be taken seriously. The bereaved owners said they found it emotionally devastating for work associates (or anyone else) to chastise their grief with such statements as "It's only a dog/cat." There was a strong tendency for the bereaved owners to avoid social situations and persons who failed to provide minimal empathy or sensitivity to their feelings.

The analysis of the data about the type, duration, and efficacy of the social work intervention seems to give some initial confirmation of the value and appropriateness of a crisis-oriented, short-term approach. As is emphasized in the crisis intervention literature, the bulk of contact and communication occurred within the first seven days, and much of it took place over the telephone (Parad, Selby, and Quinlan, 1976). The pattern of intervention tended to be an initial contact at the time of crisis, a follow-through contact, usually within forty-eight hours of the crisis, and then a follow-up contact somewhere between two and four weeks from the inception of the crisis. Contact originating from the bereaved owner was encouraged at any point during the intervention to allow for any additional support the owner felt necessary.

At follow-up, half of the owners were back to normal patterns in their daily activities; they were willing and able to socialize with family and friends, and they were going to work on a regular schedule and having no difficulty functioning in the workplace. Approximately another one third of the bereaved owners were actively resolving the loss of the pet. Though they still admitted to slight depression, they were less inclined to socialize, and were able only to "cope" with working, they stated that they felt less grief every day and fully expected to return to "normal." They anticipated being able to talk about and accept the loss of their pet without becoming visibly upset.

For a smaller fraction of the bereaved owners the pet's death was much more problematic. At the time of follow-up these individuals were still emotionally and psychologically paralyzed from the death. Their comments suggest that they had become fixated and unable to move through the denial phase of the grief process (Kubler-Ross, 1969). The owners claimed they could still hear the animal moving about the house, they regularly put out food and water, they had dreams (nightmares) about the pet, and they were displaying obvious signs of deepening clinical depression. All were offered opportunities to begin receiving professional help, and most accepted a referral to an outside source.

SUMMARY

The findings discussed above offer a number of possibilities for better understanding human response to the loss of a companion animal. At best, though, the comments must be considered to be speculative and inconclusive. Ideally, we need to study an equivalent sample population of bereaved owners none of whom were referred for social work service. Comparing common variables between these two populations, such as age, marital status, and life-stress factors, we would get a much clearer picture of "typical" bereaved pet owner characteristics and their significance in contributing the need for professional bereavement care. One product of having such comparisons would be to develop a pet owner profile. With such an instrument we would have a predictive potential and the ability to anticipate high-risk owners and provide ongoing support. Although there is still an active debate as to the effectiveness of bereavement counseling, recent studies in the area of anticipatory grief suggest the predeath phase may be critical for survivors. Traditionally, anticipatory grief has been considered to be a potential coping mechanism for a prospective loss (Lebow, 1976). More recently, Fulton and Gottesman (1980) have studied anticipatory grief in preventive psychiatry as a determinant of the severity of post-mortem grief. They recommend that anticipatory grief be reframed within a psychosocial context. Using a bereaved pet owner profile allows earlier involvement, that is, entering at a predeath phase and ongoing work with the potentially bereaved pet owner. Bereavemnt care could be provided in a preventive as well as a crisis situation.

Finally, we recognize that this population of pets and owners from the VHUP may represent other than typical members of the pet and pet owner population. As a consequence, what can be said about human response to pet loss, based on this initial study, is best limited to this veterinary teaching hospital. We do feel, though, that the factors we have isolated merit further systematic study. The initial findings offer enough evidence to suggest that an "invisible" population with real psychosocial needs is currently being neglected or ignored.

Mary Stewart

35

Loss of a Pet—Loss of a Person:
A Comparative Study of Bereavement

People who develop a close association with a companion animal are aware that as well as enjoying the pleasure of that relationship, they must also be prepared to suffer the pain of the bereavement which follows the death of that animal because most owners, except the very elderly, expect to outlive their pets.

Much work has been published on the nature of the human–companion animal bond, a complex affair involving many factors, such as individual temperament, age, social background, family circumstances, lifestyle, and others (Bustad, 1980a; Fox, 1981; Guttmann, 1981; Freiberger and Levinson, 1980; Katcher, 1981; McDonald, 1981; Rynearson, 1978; Van Leeuwen, 1981; Walster, 1979). Since the nature of the relationship obviously influences the owner's response to the death of the animal, the intensity of the bereavement will vary accordingly. In some cases the owner's distress is so great that it leads to pathological grieving (Keddie, 1977; McCulloch, 1979c; Neiburg, 1981; Rynearson, 1978; Van Leeuwen, 1981). There have been many comments in the literature about the value of animals to children both as companions and as teaching models for life experience (Neiburg, 1981; Whitney, 1981). How do children feel when that animal dies? The death of an animal is often described as being like the death of a member of the family. How does bereavement for a companion animal compare with bereavement for a human? What might be the similarities and the differences? How does the help available compare?

This study was an attempt to answer these questions. The first part was devoted to determining the most significant aspect of pet ownership to children of different ages. The second part was concerned with children's and adult's reactions to the death of their animals, an inquiry that revealed causes of distress as well as sources of comfort. Finally, an attempt was made to compare an animal's death with a human's, from the point of view of events accompanying and following the death, reactions of the bereaved (as well as those of other people involved), and the support available.

METHODOLOGY

The first part of this study was carried out in central Scotland with the help of seventy-five children six to eleven years old from two primary schools (one primary school was semirural, the other urban), and seventy children twelve to fifteen years old from one urban secondary school. From a total of 135 children, 109 had had a dog at some time and 34 had had a cat at some time.

Forty-four had owned some other kind of pet, including budgies, rabbits, fish, hamsters, gerbils, and ponies; many children had two or more species of animal. All the children were asked to write an essay on pets they had, (or had had), indicating both what they liked about the pets (Table 35.1) and how they felt if a pet had died. If they had no pet, they were to mention why not. Although an investigation into the advantages of having a companion animal might appear to be a repetition of a subject already widely covered in the literature, it was considered useful in this case, because the reaction to an animal's death should depend on how the animal was valued in life.

To provide a spontaneous and unbiased method of data collection, the essay was used rather than a questionnaire. Although this method involved obvious limitations in quantification or determining results, much interesting and unexpected material was supplied. During the assessment of the information on the advantages of pet ownership, certain common aspects emerged and were used, rather than any predetermined factors, to provide a basis for the categories described later. The information on childrens' attitudes to animal bereavement was also derived from these essays.

The information on the adults' attitudes to animal bereavement was gathered from personal interviews, correspondence, and again from essays. (The fifty-two adults involved were from a wide variety of backgrounds, the majority from a semirural area in Scotland. Some were students at Glasgow Veterinary School.)

TABLE 35.1. ADVANTAGES OF DOG OWNERSHIP

Age of Respondents Number of Essays	7–8 Years 36		9–11 Years 21		12–15 Years 50	
	Times Mentioned	Percent	Times Mentioned	Percent	Times Mentioned	Percent
Character	9	25	12	57	28	56
Play	1	3	5	24	24	48
Exercise	2	6	5	24	19	38
Responsibility	6	17	4	19	24	48
All above reasons cited	6	17	7	33	26	52
Emotional support	2	6	5	24	22	44
Physical reassurance	1	3	0	0	18	36
Touch	6	17	2	10	11	22
Statement of attachment	5	14	5	25	13	26
Special ties	2	6	3	14	13	26
Appearance	10	27	9	43	10	20

The comparison between human and animal bereavement was attempted by examining both events chronologically, including the anticipation of death if any, then the death itself, the bereavement following, and the aftermath and resolution. The comments on human bereavement are based on both published reports (Furman, 1974; Kubler-Ross, 1969; Lewis, 1961; Parkes, 1972) and anecdotal evidence supplied from correspondence, interviews, and personal experience. Clearly, one cannot draw firm conclusions because individual circumstances are variable; however, it was felt that certain basic aspects recurred with enough regularity to justify their use on a comparative basis in this pilot study.

ANIMAL BEREAVEMENT

REACTIONS OF CHILDREN TO ANIMAL DEATH

Inevitably, many of the children who enjoyed having pets were eventually faced with the death of that pet. Of the sixty-five primary school children, sixty-two had pets and forty-eight wrote of death experiences involving many different species of animal. Of the seventy secondary school children, fifty-six had pets and fourteen mentioned having a pet die. Most of the animals that died were dogs. The wide variety in both pets involved and literacy of the children makes quantification of this small sample impractical, but general trends are noted.

About a third of the children mentioned the death with no comment as to their own emotional reaction; many inferred that the death was very significant to them by the way they emphasized the date or place of the event: "He was knocked down and killed by a car on a Friday afternoon in November." Sadness was mentioned by about two thirds of the children, and it was described in various ways: "I felt terrible." "I felt lonely and started to cry." "I cried and cried and cried until I could cry no more." "I didn't believe it, I didn't know where I was." "I cried all morning at school." Many of the children indicated they got over the loss: "I felt sad when she died, but now I am not so sad." "I was really sad at the time but I got over it." "The whole family was heartbroken, but we got over it." A six-year-old said, "I used to have a rabbit but when I was at school it died I was sad but I feel better now." Three children stated: "I will never forget." One farmer's son mentioned that he was sad when his dog was killed, "but not so sad because we are used to having animals die on the farm." Many indicated that the presence of another animal helped to alleviate the sorrow, and the eventual replacement of the dead animal seemed to be very beneficial: "I got a kitten and now am very happy." "When I heard we could get another dog I was happier."

In all the bereavements that appeared to be unresolved, parents were unwilling to have another animal. Sometimes the reason was that an animal was too much bother or messy in the house, but more often it was "in case it happens again." This reason was reported more often by the older children and appeared to be a source of family arguments. Perhaps replacement was more complex because most of these animals were dogs. When an animal was "put down" because of a behavior or social problem, there were references to anger at the parent(s): "I think people are cruel to kill an animal; they have a right to live just like us." This answer again appeared only in the twelve-to-sixteen-year-old group, as did guilt at "not having looked after it properly." (A ten-year-old wrote, however, "If my dog died I would never forgive myself.") Only one child was comforted by the fact that she had given the animal (a hamster) a good life.

Several of the younger children mentioned being comforted by other people: "Mummy cheered me up." "My sister cheered me up." "Daddy buried my goldfish deep in the ground." One eight-year-old told of her father's gallant rescue of two hamsters from the burning home: "He came out covered in flames, but the hamsters died from smoke in their tummy." When an animal belonging to the younger group died, the event often seemed to be a family affair. None of the older children mentioned humans being helpful with the exception of two, who said, "The vet was kind." (One in this age group said she did not like vets because "they killed your dogs.") Burial was mentioned a few times in different groups, but sometimes it was mentioned as if it were taken for granted as the thing to do: "I will put some flowers on her grave" (not having previously mentioned the burial).

General trends comparing the three age (groups seven to eight, nine to eleven, twelve to fifteen) relating specifically to their attitudes to dog deaths are noted in Table 35.2.

TABLE 35.2. ATTITUDE OF CHILD TO ANIMAL BEREAVEMENT

Age:	7–8 Years		9–11 Years		12–15 Years	
Number of children involved	18		8		10	
Reaction to death	Number	Percent	Number	Percent	Number	Percent
No comment	9	50	2	25	2	20
Sad or very sad	8	44	5	62	8	80
Got over it soon	3	17	4	50	2	20
Comforted by animals	12	67	7	87	4	40
Unresolved	–	–	–	–	5	50

DISCUSSION

Neiburg (1981) views domestic pet loss as the most clinically relevant model for separation and death education. The children in this study who had witnessed more than one animal death implied that the initial experience helped them to cope with subsequent animal deaths. A ten-year-old girl, commenting on the death of her cat, wrote, "I went off to my bedroom and cried and after that I never forgot him." When her next cat was run over, "This time I know how it felt so didn't feel so bad but still felt awful."

It also appeared that the children's reaction to their pet's death was influenced by the investment placed in that animal. If the only pet was a hamster, that hamster's death would be of greater concern than if there were other pets as well, especially dogs. (There may be parallels here with adults who overreact to a dog's death.)

A child can best cope with mourning when he is supported by loved ones, in his struggle with bereavement. This statement was in reference to human death but could also apply to a child's first encounter with the death of a pet. As well as losing the animal, there is the confusing concept of death itself, which is just as final for a goldfish as it is for a human. The father who went to the trouble to bury his daughter's fish created a very different impression on that child than the vet who laughingly made a comment about "fish for dinner" when a daughter's friend brought in a dying goldfish. (That girl never again took an animal to a vet.) There should never be the suggestion of ridicule, and the bereaved should never be made to feel guilty for his grief. There must be a balance between trivialization and overreaction, and parents and vets, in the way they deal with this, have a great influence on subsequent attitudes.

The duration and intensity of mourning related not only to previous experience, investment, and attitudes of others but also the age of the person involved. Young children often expressed profound grief for a very short time and then seemed to adapt quickly to "normal," especially if a new animal was introduced.

On the whole, it took the older children longer to "get over it," but again another animal's presence lessened the grief. The age element is probably a combination of factors all interwoven, including different values and relationships with others.

The tensions and fractured relationships of puberty were often reflected in the essays. Some parents were obviously at a loss as to how to deal with their children's grief and were reluctant to take any chances of "it happening again." This resulted in several children continuing to grieve long after the death of the animal.

REACTION OF ADULTS TO DEATH OF A COMPANION ANIMAL

Most of the fifty-two adults contributing to this study were dog owners. One had a pony, and two felt remarkably involved with their small animals, a guinea pig and a hamster. Data compiled from their comments are presented in Table 35.3. All adults stated that they felt some degree of sadness at the death of their companion animal. About one third said that although they were very upset (and often cried a lot) they were still able to carry on with their normal routine. A smaller number were so distressed that they were temporarily unable to cope with their work. There were reports of anger, hysteria, and one person fainted. Most of this group got "back to normal" fairly soon, though two admitted that even years later they still felt "choked" when remembering the dog. The time factor in "getting over it" varied greatly from a few days to many weeks.

For a few people the bereavement had aspects similar to those often witnessed in human bereavements such as a numbness; a feeling of unreality; disbelief; a sense of amputation; searching for or imagining the presence of the

TABLE 35.3. ATTITUDE OF ADULTS TO ANIMAL BEREAVEMENT

Number of Adults	**52**	**Percent**
Initial Response	Some degree of sadness	100
	Very sad	8
	Very upset but coped	33
	So disturbed temporarily unable to cope	18
	Intense, problematic grieving	10
Concern	Concern about the manner of death	90
	Comforted by good death	39
	Guilt feelings about death	51
Reaction to Vet	Comforted by vet	16
	Upset by vet	14
Helped	Helped by other companion animals	53
	of these, 47% replaced after death	
	8% introduced before death	
	33% already there	
Comforted	Comforted by humans (other than vet)	6
	Comforted by ritual or ceremony (burial)	37

deceased; a loss of interest in surroundings; difficulty in speaking, hearing, sleeping, and eating; aimless activity; depression, guilt, anger, and a feeling that things will never be the same. At the time of the bereavement, none of these people had other companion animals or children.

DISCUSSION

It would seem that being responsible for an animal during its life makes an owner feel responsible for the death as well. There was a great concern (and a lot of worry) on the part of most owners concerning the manner of death, and about half of them carried a considerable amount of self-imposed guilt concerning the death. If the death had been sudden, as from an accident, the owners may have felt that they should have prevented it; if it followed a long illness, the owners sometimes felt that maybe they should have had the dog put down; if the dog had been put down they would feel that maybe they were too hasty in doing so (whatever action they did or did not take could be interpreted as a source of guilt). If the animal had been euthanized as a result of a behavioral disorder or social problem, the burden of guilt was often especially heavy. On the other hand, many felt comforted by the fact that they could influence the course of events in a way that they considered constructive. Some were consoled by knowing that they had allowed the animal to die at home and had not taken it to the vet, and some felt that giving it an easy death by euthanasia, and therefore avoiding suffering, was the best thing they could have done for the animal. Of the bereaved owners who mentioned the vet, some were very comforted by the vet's attitude to both the animal and themselves, but nearly an equal number were distressed or upset by the way the vet handled the situation. They sometimes felt that the vet was disinterested, even callus (for instance, one man stated that he had been extremely upset when the vet asked him to help put his Doberman's body into a plastic garbage bag). Two people blamed the vet for their dog's death.

The presence of other animals did seem to alleviate some of the pain of the bereavement. If there were animals already in the household, the absence of the dead animal would not be felt so acutely—there was still a presence, an animal routine and responsibility. Many bereaved owners "replaced" the dead animal after variable periods of time without any sense of betrayal. Two that had "replaced" dogs immediately felt that the memory of the dead dog made them very critical of the new one.

When death was anticipated, the introduction of a new animal before the death seemed to be helpful. One woman felt that the new pup (introduced three months previously) was all that "got her through." But she was feeling guilty that it may not have been fair to the old dog, and she needed reassuranace on this point. Very few adults mentioned being comforted by people other than the vet. Two mothers mentioned that they were comforted by their children, and one girl felt that her boy friend had made it possible to cope with an extremely traumatic bereavement. He had insisted that she should dig the grave herself and put the dog's body in it (she had been hysterical and then lost consciousness when she heard of the death). She said that the work helped her to face reality. On the gravestone she wrote, "Here Lies Love." Often a gesture of respect and care was helpful, such as making the animal look peaceful and comfortable. This was especially the case when the death followed a distressing illness or an accident. Such a gesture may have been merely wrapping the body in a blanket or garment, but often in rural areas the animal was buried with a grave marker, a stone or a tree. There were no instances of pathological grieving in this study.

COMPARISON BETWEEN LOSS OF A PERSON AND LOSS OF AN ANIMAL

How do some of the main aspects of human bereavement compare with those encountered in companion animal bereavement? An attempt is made to answer this question by considering both situations in chronological order.

GENERAL ANTICIPATION: THEORETICAL

Human   Difficult to conceive of death for self or family.

   Animal   Knowledge of short life span should prepare owner for eventual death of companion animal but often does not.

WHEN DEATH IS FORESEEN: SPECIFIC ANTICIPATION OF IMPENDING DEATH

Human   The potential bereaved person feels a dilemma in face-to-face confrontation and communication with the dying person.

   Animal   No quandary is involved in approach to the animal.

   Human   Discussion with doctor and anticipatory preparation takes place. When possible, the dying person may be involved in discussion, which can be helpful to all involved.

   Animal   Discussion with vet; perhaps postponing euthanasia to allow the owner to adapt to the situation.

   Human   Most of the responsibility for decisions regarding treatment, hospitalization, and other practical aspects are taken by the medical team. The active decision as to termination of life rarely occurs, and then it is not a matter of administration of lethal substances but withdrawal of artificial life-support systems.

   Animal   The owner is often faced with life-and-death decisions. Should euthanasia take place? By whom? When? Where? Who should be present? Some owners make their own decisions; others, less equipped with relevant experience, depend on the vet's advice. Sensitive vets can give owners great reassurance (Antelyes, 1981; Fogle, 1981a; Edney, 1979).

REACTION TO DEATH

In most cases, whether death is anticipated or sudden, the instant when life becomes death is momentous and difficult to conceive.

Human   Often the bereaved is not present at the death.

Animal   Often the owner is present or nearby and aware of its happening, as with euthanasia.

Human   The first reaction on witnessing or hearing of death is often a "crisis reaction" and "earth-stopper." The bereaved feels an initial numbness, perceptions alter, feeling of unreality—"this can't be happening." After sudden death, disbelief may persist for a variable period. The whole body reacts, there are feelings of hollowness and tightness, obstruction in throat, and difficulty in speech.

Animal   Initial "crisis" reaction may be seen in persons who have placed great reliance on the animal. The owner may suffer a similar reaction as to a "normal" human bereavement, with many of the same short-term and long-term reactions. Most animal bereavements are not "earth-stoppers."

Human   Crying often comes later; it is not usually the first reaction.

Animal   Grief reaction with crying and sobbing is often instantaneous.

Intensity of grief is affected by the strength of attachment in both cases.

Human   The bereaved searches for and imagines the presence of the deceased.

Animal   Imagining presence and searching may occur for a short time.

Human   Difficulty in sleeping and eating; aimless activity and depression often occur.

Animal   Marked sleeping and eating problems and depression usually do not occur.

INITIAL REACTION OF OTHERS

Humans   Care and protection of the bereaved is accepted by society as being a communal responsibility. Feeling of involvement by others is considerable. Great sympathy is usually expressed.

Animals   Family or a sensitive veterinary staff may be prepared to offer support, but to do so is not a tradition (Antelyes, 1981; Fogle, 1981a; Edney, 1979; Ryder and Romasco, 1980). Often there may be no help. Others may regard the distress of the bereaved as slightly ridiculous and say, "What a fuss to make over a dog."

ACTIVITIES FOLLOWING DEATH

Human   The body is usually held in funeral parlor or mortuary. The bereaved is not immediately involved in decisions as to the final fate of the body.

Animals   The owner must decide what to do with the body almost immediately, or at least must decide whether the vet is to dispose of it.

Human   The bereaved is not often left alone at this point.

Animal   The bereaved owner often returns home alone to an empty house (Yoxall and Yoxall, 1979).

Human   Activities of daily living are disrupted. The bereaved is given support, with others making decisions. Rituals are important at this time, many people are involved, and there are many things to do. Having a framework of activity is useful and gets all involved through a time of feeling helpless and impotent.

Animal   Even if the bereaved is in a crisis state, normal activities are expected, and sympathy, if there is any, may be mixed with slight impatience (for example, if the bereaved stays off work). There is no framework of special activity.

Human   A funeral is held. Viewing the deceased looking peaceful, especially after a painful or traumatic condition, helps the bereaved accept death.

Animal   Funerals are very unusual in the United Kingdom. Making the dead animal look comfortable (wrapped in a blanket or coat) often is a comfort.

Human   The funeral ceremony may give comfort from the religious point of view. Philosophy of life as well as religion can be a comfort, providing reassurance as to the welfare of the deceased and reassurance as to the meaning or purpose of life.

Animal   In urban areas it may be difficult to make burial arrangements. Some owners get comfort from burying the animal, especially in a favorite spot. There may be a small private ceremony and the planting of a tree or bush. Such activity is not normally done in United Kingdom and most established religions do not offer much comfort, although a few churches do. In the United States there are more pet cemeteries than in United Kingdom).

FEELINGS FOLLOWING DEATH

Human   Participation of others is helpful.

Animal   Participation of others is minimal.

Human and Animal   There is comfort for the end of suffering in terminally ill. There is comfort from knowing an old person or animal had a good life.

Human   There is some comfort when the deceased had an "easy" death, but this is not under the control of the family.

Animal   Comfort can be centered around the death itself in the fact that an owner can ensure that the animal had an easy death, without suffering.

Human   Paradoxically, there may be a certain clarity of perception; trivia appear as such, and there is recognition of a great empathy with all living beings. This feeling can be very precious to the bereaved.

Animal   Clarity does not seem to occur with animal bereavement.

Human   The bereaved may be very lonely, but communication is usually very good (even if mostly one-way from others). Visitors, phone calls, letters, telegrams, and flowers acknowledge the death and offer consolation and support. People are very open; barriers are removed.

Animal   It is a very lonely time. Communication is minimal, but sensitive people may give some support. The bereaved may feel a bit guilty at displaying grief over an animal and may even be an object of slight ridicule to some people. Some vets who are aware of the loneliness reassure, support, and write letters. Barriers with others are up.

Human   The bereaved feels sorrow for the dead person, for potentials not realized (especially when the deceased is young), and for future plans unfulfilled.

Animal   Sorrow for the owner's personal loss is sometimes greater than for the animal's loss of life, unless the animal was very young. Unrealized potential and plans for the future are not very important unless the animal had a special job. Usually a good dog fulfills its potential daily. The present moment, the "nowness" of the relationship, is the most important aspect.

Human   Remorse or guilt are often centered around missed opportunities (especially if there has been a communication failure at some point). There may also be a feeling of partial responsibility for the death.

Animal   As well as sometimes feeling responsible for the cause of the animal's death, the owners often feel guilty about the quality of the death. There is great uncertainty as to whether the right things were done and the right decisions made. This feeling can be allayed by confidence in and reassurance of others, especially the vet.

Human   There may be anger toward doctors, the deceased, self, others, or God.

Animal   There may be anger, most often directed toward the vet, but toward other people as well, even other animals.

AFTER INITIAL PERIOD

Human   Something in life has changed permanently.

   Animal   Life is not usually permanently changed.

   Human   The quality of life has changed, perhaps for a long time.

   Animal   The quality of life has changed temporarily (time varies).

   Human   Sadness for the absence of the person in this life is permanent. A "scar" usually remains.

   Animal   Sadness is usually temporary, even though the bond was very strong. Remembrance of the dead does not usually hurt after a time (a period that may be prolonged in some cases).

AND FINALLY

Human   Often there are great changes in lifestyle, activities, and so on, depending on who has died.

   Animal   Usually there is no great change in lifestyle.

   Human   The bereaved undertakes a life review and reevaluation of priorities.

Animal   Usuallly there is no reevaluation of priorities.

Human   The bereaved recognizes the fact of human suffering, with a resulting empathy with others, and may want to help others as a result of personal experience.

Animal   Empathy with others suffering an animal bereavement may develop but has not been reported.

SOME THOUGHTS ON THE "GAP" LEFT BY THE DEATH

Human   Although the human bond develops with presence, the intensity of the bond is not dependent on continual presence, for example, parents and children living apart except in highly dependent child-parent relationships such as with Mongol children.

Animal   The bond is mostly associated with presence. Animals are usually on the premises or accompanying their owner (obviously, they do not go off to school or work but are there when the humans return). This constant, all-pervading presence makes the gap more obvious when the animal dies.

Human   Roles change with time and circumstances. The bond does not necessarily depend on reinforcement by responsibilities, though sometimes it does.

Animal   The animal is usually completely dependent on the owner, which tends to emphasize the bond.

Human   Most aspects of a beloved person are so unique to that person that "replacement" is impossible. No two people are at all "alike."

Animal   Dogs or other animals are often alike, especially within the same breed or variety, even though there are special qualities about individuals that make them precious.

Human   There are a few general human characteristics (sex or role factors) such as the "boyness" of a son or the "womanness" of a wife that can be compared with the "dogness" of a dog; this is illustrated by statements such as "It's good to have a boy (or woman) around the house."

Animal   A lot of the aspect of a "good" animal, and the reasons people give for valuing that animal, come under the headings listed earlier and can be described as the "dogness" or "catness" of that animal, and in this aspect an animal eventually can be successfully "replaced," although the relationship is not the same. Even the gap left by the death of a special dog can be partially filled (the dogness part) by another well-chosen animal (tactfully introduced).

EXPLANATION: INITIAL REACTION TO THE DEATH

Human   Losing a child (or any other much loved human) may be called an earth-stopper for those involved. Everything else seems to stop. The secure feeling that life is supposed to be "good" (an idea which in the West we sometimes reckon to be one of our inalienable rights) is suddenly swept away.

There is a powerful physical reaction in the body—a state of numbed shock. A great, hollow pain fills the body and mind, making speech an enormous effort. A feeling of disbelief, that it cannot be true, alternates with the horror of the realization that it is true. Later, as the initial shock subsides, friends and family play an important part in supplying support and comfort. Physical presence is good, but phone calls, letters, and telegrams all contribute. It is a time of sharing, sadness for the death, compassion for each person's individual loss, and the acknowledgment of everyone's own vulnerability and fragility—the undeniable impermanence of life. It can be a time of overwhelming communication and love (of course, sometimes it does not happen this way).

Animal   When death comes to the companion animal, the owner may be extremely upset, showing and feeling intense grief, often unable to speak for a while, but not usually going into a real state of shock. I have heard people say that initially they cried more over the death of the dog than they did for their child. It was almost as if the child's death was too huge in significance to be expressed by tears. Although, with the animal death, the basis of one's life structure is not usually threatened, it can be an extremely lonely time, with very little sympathy and support from others. In fact, some people may even suggest that such grief for "just an animal" is unseemly, if not ridiculous. Therefore, unlike a human bereavement which may lead to close communication, the bereaved animal owner may feel completely isolated in his sorrow.

ACTIVITIES FOLLOWING DEATH

Human   Immediately following human death, normal routines are disrupted, nothing seems to be very important or worth doing, and yet the bereaved must cope with the funeral and all the activities that surround it. So this is a busy, painful time, a time of finalizing the loved one's death in the act of either burial or cremation (and later scattering or burial of the ashes). Shock is still there, but sometimes it allows a clarity of vision, a different way of perception, which is immensely valuable. It is a time of reevaluation and of communication and sharing of sorrow.

This is also a testing period of any religious or philosophical beliefs that the bereaved held. If they are strong, they can be a source of great comfort, for reassurance as to the welfare of the dead person, and acceptance of the feeling that somewhere in the scheme of things, there is a reason for that particular life and death, as well as for any suffering that accompanied it.

After that comes the settling of affairs, possessions, and practical matters. Then remains the loneliness, the hollow grief, and the long process of trying to pick up the pieces, to regain lost confidence. There may be guilt when the bereaved feels partially or wholly responsible for the death, but often it is associated with a failure or an imagined failure in communications, of neglected opportunities—"If only I had written a letter—if only I had told her how much I loved her, if only I had spent more time, hadn't been so busy with other things."

This again can be used as a lesson, and a family may become far closer and more loving, realizing that now may be the only time there is. Sometimes there is anger against the deceased, or the doctor, or God, or oneself. The anger may be a protest against one's impotence. There are times of relative peace, then the pain returns with great intensity—the "pangs of grief."

One's life has changed; it will never be the same. There is a knowledge that was not there before (like the eating of the apple in the garden—one has lost one's "innocence"). Somehow one has forged a link with suffering humanity, has seen both sides of the coin, and along with one's own despair, there may also be an expansion of compassion for and understanding of the problems of others.

ACTIVITIES FOLLOWING DEATH: DOG

If an animal has a reason for being hospitalized and ends up dying or being put down there, the whole of the activity on the part of the owner may be as limited as that short conversation on the telephone. On the other hand, when an owner wishes the animal to die at home and wants to be present, there is at least a feeling of participation. As for "disposal of the body," some people feel a real comfort in burying their friend in a favorite part of the garden or a nice place with "the other animals." There are many variations, but it all amounts to the fact that the owner can make decisions on these matters, unless the death is unexpected. Some people will sit up all night with a dying dog so that its last hours will not be lonely. Among the people in the survey, there was a great emphasis on the memories of bereaved owners of the actual death, and any guilt feelings seemed to be centered around decisions that had been made—"Maybe we should have waited longer, given him a little while longer." "If only I had stayed with him when he was dying." "If only we had asked the vet to come to the house." They go on and on. On the other hand, there can be a great deal of consolation from a "good death": "The vet was so kind, she didn't know anything about it." "It was so quick, I didn't even know she'd died." "At least we could make sure that she didn't have to suffer." One said, "We are fortunate that we can assure them a quick, painless death at the kind hands of our vet."

Disposal of the body is often a problem, and here a vet is often much appreciated. The animal may be wrapped in a favorite old blanket or coat; this seems to be the last thing the owner can do for the animal. Then the animal disappears with the vet and that's it! In the country area where part of the survey was carried out, almost all the people who were greatly attached to their dogs had derived comfort from burying them and were often asked to bury animals belonging to town-dwelling friends. So, except for the potential of burial, there is nothing a bereaved owner can do, apart fom wrapping up the body and making it look comfortable. The animal has gone, and life is expected to continue as usual. The quality of life has changed because the animal is often part of that routine; there is a feeling of loss—"the house seems empty." Conventional religion did not appear to be of value for people in this survey. The comfort from the act of burial seemed to stem more from the ritual than from a religious faith. Most of our churches in Great Britain do not provide much reassurance for the animal owner, although there are a few that do.

DISCUSSION ON REPLACEMENT

In the case of human bereavement, replacement as such does not occur, although the presence of another person may help. In most cases of a "normal" animal bereavement a replacement animal can be very successful, if introduced with tact and sensitivity and with respect for the value of the dead animal. The home will then no longer feel empty, and routines will be reestablished because the new animal will require care and nurturing from the owner. Although the new animal will never be the same as the old one, in most cases a good bond will develop with time.

There should be respect for the sorrow of the bereaved owner, who should be allowed to grieve, especially children (Bustad and Hines, 1981). The time scale of replacement is difficult to judge; one child "cried all morning"; one "felt sad for a day and a half"; and that may be recognition enough. There is controversy on this subject. Some workers indicate that replacement should be deferred (Levinson, 1981), whereas others (Bustad, 1981; Holzworth, 1981) suggest that prompt acquisition of another animal may be advisable when children are involved.

This study indicated that prompt "replacement" was beneficial. Even when an animal of great significance died, the resulting desolation of the owner was reduced by the introduction of a suitable animal. The replacement of a child's pet did not seem to "trivialize" the death, as long as it was handled in a sensitive way. Since elderly people may hesitate to replace an animal in case they themselves should take ill or die and leave their animal alone, schemes are now being initiated to alleviate this problem (Bustad, 1981; Walster, 1979).

Therapeutic Uses of Companion Animals

Introduction

This section is primarily devoted to studies of the therapeutic potential of contact with animals: as therapy for children with multiple handicaps, for patients in a mental hospital, and for autistic or disturbed children. The introductory chapter by Michael McCulloch is a comprehensive review of what is known about the psychotherapeutic potential and prosthetic uses of animals. I believe it is useful to separate prosthetic use of animals—seeing eye dogs, hearing ear dogs, and the like—from the use of animals to change the emotional or mental state of someone who has been diagnosed as having a phychiatric disorder. It is possible to specify what a seeing eye dog should do for its owner and to measure the extent to which the animal fulfills his role. Determining the success or failure of psychotherapeutic procedures, on the other hand, is enormously difficult. There is no general agreement that any form of psychotherapy using dogs, horses, or psychiatrists is consistently better than no treatment at all. But separation of the psychotherapeutic from the prosthetic use of animals does not mean to imply that a blind person given the ability to move independently through the help of a guide dog will not experience an improvement in emotional state or even lose such symptoms as depression or anxiety. The chapter by Alysia Zee reminds us that the animal is more than a bit of guidance machinery. The service given the dog by the owner structures a bond between them which has its own value.

The four chapters describing the psychotherapeutic utility of animals are interesting documentations of clinical programs but do not extend our knowledge much beyond the case studies of Samuel and Elizabeth Corson and Boris Levinson. Mary Thompson and her co-workers describe an excellent attempt to provide documentation that contact with animals produces observable changes in the behavior of chronic mental patients. Unfortunately, the sample size was small, and the choice of an instrument factored into a number of scales leaves the reader uncertain about the reality of the changes described. The report does, however, offer a model for studies of the use of companion animals within mental institutions. To be accepted by clinical psychiatrists and psychologists, any study will have to demonstrate that traditional indexes of change or improvement are effected by the intervention with companion animals. One wishes, though, that more ethological observations of patients' behavior would be used to complement the data derived from highly structured psychological indexes. Measures of frequency and latency of social interactions, such as were illustrated by Corson (Corson et al., 1975a), are good examples of behavioral measures with high face validity.

The description of the integration of a horseback riding program into the curriculum of the mentally handicapped presents a very good model for the study of the outcomes of such programs. The obvious enthusiam of both the people who conduct programs with handicapped children and the children shows that these programs need no medical justification. They have enormous value in and of themselves. It would, however, be easier to find funds for such programs if definite psychological or psychophysiological gains could be demonstrated. Natalie Beiber's program needs to be repeated with the imposition of an experimental design studying both children who are engaged in a riding program and children who receive only their regular curriculum with appropriate outcome measures to document both the changes in emotional state and any gains in cognitive or psychomotor abilities.

Two chapters describing therapeutic efforts are case reports of the use of animals as an intervention mechanism with children labeled as autistic. Unfortunately, both presentations were initially accompanied by persuasive film, which cannot be presented in this volume. Ange Condoret was able to demonstrate that a child who had never spoken and had played only with objects, made her first expressions of interest in a living object when a dove took flight in her classroom. Her attention became progressively entrained by living beings, and over the course of months she began playing with other animals, children, and her teacher. Associated with the change in her orientation was a remarkable change in facial expression with increased animation, the appearance of smiling, and the beginning of speech. The film is convincing because the change in the child's behavior was captured on the television tape. The material presented by

Betsy Smith is interesting because of the unusual choice of animal—the bottle-nose dolphin—but there was very little progression in the patients she discussed beyond the initial orientation of the child toward the dolphin, the willingness to interact with the animal, and persistence of the memory of that interaction. The child's social responses did not continue to enlarge, as they did in the case of the child described by Ange Condoret. These case reports are useful, however, because they stimulate the imagination, and perhaps future trials of animal contact with autistic children will provide documentation of progressive changes such as were observed by Condoret. One hopes, however, that autistic children will profit from animals that do not demand the specialized environment required by bottlenose dolphins. If, however, it is the social nature of the animal, the ability of the animal to search out social contact without words, that is the critical variable in the ability of animals to draw the attention of autistic children, then the choice of so social an animal as a dolphin seems less singular than it might at first glance. Where they are residents in city marinas, perhaps some of their time can be made available to children whom they might help.

The other two chapters in this section look at relationships with animals as markers of disturbed family life. James S. Hutton studied families against whom complaints of cruelty to animals had been made and found that the same families were known to a variety of social agencies and had multiple psychiatric and social problems. They also tended to have low incomes and to be highly mobile. Hutton concludes that disturbances in the relationship with animals is a good symptomatic marker for families that are dysfunctional in other spheres of life. The investigation of cruelty to animals might be widened to prevent subsequent cruelty to human beings. The observations of Hutton are in part echoed by the findings of Michael Robin and his co-workers. They studied patterns of animal ownership by high school children and institutionalized delinquents. They did not find any gross difference in significance or frequency of animal ownership, but they did find that the animal had a different position in the family with the delinquent children. These children were less likely to consider the animal to be a family member than were high school children but preferred to see the animal as a special friend or confidant outside of the family. Disturbance in family relationships in families of the delinquents was indexed by the short life span of their pets and the higher frequency with which their animals suffered violent deaths. Thus Hutton and Robin and co-workers, using very different methods, both describe the same coincidence of disrupted family life indexed by a disruption in the relationship with the pet.

Michael J. McCulloch

36

Animal-Facilitated Therapy: Overview and Future Direction

Throughout history, animals have served in many roles to improve the well-being of people. Animals have provided protection, companionship, work, sport, and other benefits. In recent years, there has been considerable interest in the ways animals can be therapeutically used to improve the physical and emotional health of people. These programs are widespread and are directed toward people with specific health problems requiring rehabilitation: the physically handicapped, the deaf, the blind, the emotionally ill, the elderly, and the medically ill. Although some of the programs began over a century ago, strict scientific documentation did not begin until twenty years ago. Unfortunately, many terms have been used to describe the use of animals in therapy (pet-facilitated psychotherapy, pet-facilitated therapy, animal-assisted therapy, pet therapy), which has led to an understandable confusion. Many of these terms suggest a restricted use and do not encompass the full range of therapeutic potential. The term "pet," for example, does not generally include farm animals, which may be part of a residential treatment facility. Animal-facilitated therapy (AFT) therefore becomes the more accurate and broadest term describing therapeutic use of animals. The term "pet therapy" will continue to be used to describe more specialized use of animals.

The relationship that people have with animals has also been described in various ways, leading to similar confusion in terms: pet-owner bond, pet-owner relationship, people-pet bond, human-animal bond. The phrase that has gained some acceptance in recent years is "human–companion animal bond" (Yoxall and Yoxall, 1979). This inclusive label covers all relationships between people and their animal companions, which can encompass farm animals, horses, and animals in the wild as well as animals customarily thought of as pets such as dogs, cats, cage birds, fish, and others.

Although strong sentiment and anecdotal information lead us to believe that relationships with animals can be beneficial in many ways, the actual data are sparse. We are therefore in a paradoxical position. We have to subject various pet therapy programs to rigorous scientific testing even though we believe that these programs work. Many pet therapy activities appear beneficial (such as having pets in nursing homes), but an accurate definition of benefits, mechanisms, hazards, and potential problems has yet to be scientifically defined. In part, this gap in knowledge is the result of the paucity of information on what constitutes normal relationships between people and animals. We have very little knowledge of the basic psychological effects of pet animals on child development, family interaction, and the aged. We are just beginning to understand psychological effects of pets on individuals, and vice versa, and the style of verbal communication and touch between people and pets (Katcher, 1981). We are also becoming more aware of the effects of pet loss on people (Keddie, 1977).

MILESTONES IN ANIMAL-FACILITATED THERAPY

PETS IN INSTITUTIONS

The first recorded use of animals in therapy was at the York Retreat in England, founded in 1792 by the Society of Friends, a Quaker group. William Tuke began this effort in response to the inhumane methods of the lunatic asylums of that day. The basic methods Tuke used were "Christianity and common sense" (Jones, 1955). An essential element of treatment was a positive reinforcement for self-control. The common methods of asylums of that day, punishment and restraint, were not used. Efforts to "normalize" the patients included having them wear their own clothing rather than an institutional uniform. The court areas of the retreat contained gardens and small animals such as rabbits and poultry. A method of getting patients to focus on activities outside of themselves was to encourage them to work in the garden and care for the animals. They were also encouraged to do handiwork, write, and read books (Bustad 1980a). This nonpunitive treatment system, emphasizing acceptance and the natural surroundings of a "living environment," formed the basis of humane treatment standards which are still applicable today.

Bethel in Bielefeld, West Germany, was begun in 1867 as a residential treatment center for epileptics. Pets were an integral part of the center from the beginning, much as in the York Retreat. Bethel now has a capacity of five thousand patients, who are treated for multiple physical and mental handicaps. The animal therapy portion has been expanded to include farm animals and a wild game park. In addition, dogs, cats, horses, and numerous varieties of birds are present in the treatment milieu (Bustad 1980). Caring for animals is an important part of the living enviroment. Unfortunately, no systematic attempt has been made to quantify or record observations of the effects of the animals on the patients and staff.

It was not until 1942 that organized activity in animal-facilitated therapy began in the United States. The Pawling Army Air Force Convalescent Hospital at Pawling, New York, served veterans convalescing from battle injuries or emotional trauma and included a working farm, with livestock, horses, and poultry. The area also included extensive park land, where one encountered animals in a natural setting. Animals were used to divert attention to constructive therapy efforts. Again, no quantitative information was recorded on the effects of the animals on the veterans. The program was later abolished (Bustad, 1980a).

In 1966, Erling Stordahl, a blind musician, established Beitostolen, in Norway, a rehabilitation center for the handicapped. The program is very sports-oriented, with heavy emphasis on physical therapy. Horses and dogs are an active part of the program. Blind persons are taught to ski and to ride horses. Again, no data have been gathered.

Psychologist Boris Levinson was the first to report in detail the therapeutic benefits of contact with pets for children and adults in both inpatient and outpatient settings (Levinson, 1961, 1966, 1968b, 1969a,b, 1972, 1974). Levinson later described the use of pets for children in residential treatment centers for the emotionally disturbed, hospitals for somatic disorders, training schools for the physically handicapped, deaf, blind, and mentally retarded, and schools and classes for the emotionally disturbed (1969a). He believed that pets can function as a "transitional object" so that the child can form a relationship first with the pet, then with the therapist, and later with other people. He advocated the use of pets for cases in which "cuddling, affection, and unconditional acceptance are indicated." He believed in the importance of providing a nonthreatening setting, where the child can be "master of the situation." Specific clinical problems believed to be most responsive to pet therapy were "the young non-verbal child, the inhibited, the autistic, the withdrawn, the obsessive-compulsive, and the culturally disadvantaged." Levinson strongly advocated controlled research study and emphasized the need for strict criteria for selection, training, and therapeutic use of pets. His work has consisted largely of detailed case studies out of which basic principles have been derived. No quantitative data were collected, although he conducted a survey of the Clinical Division of the New York State

Psychological Association in an attempt to determine how widespread the use of pets in therapy was among practicing psychologists. Since not all questions on the survey were answered, definite conclusions were difficult to draw. Fifty of 152 responded that they had used pets, and 25 of 148 respondents said that they were actually using pets in therapy. Fifty-six percent of respondents said that the optimal age for pet therapy was five to fifteen years (1972).

Stimulated by Levinson's work and his appeal for "rigorous research," Samuel and Elizabeth Corson embarked on a program to evaluate the feasibility of pet therapy in a hospital setting. They were aware that the role of a dog named Skeezer as a mascot on a psychiatric ward had been previously reported (Yates, 1973). The primary indication for using pet therapy was refractoriness to other available forms of treatment. Of thirty patients who were withdrawn, self-centered, and uncommunicative, twenty-eight accepted pets as a component of their token system on the psychiatric ward. Observation indicated that the animals served as a catalyst to social interactions. Corson described a "widening circle of warmth and approval" as a result of positive reactions of patients to pets, which included improved relationships with therapists, other staff on the ward, and other patients.

Corson wrote that the essence of pet-facilitated psychotherapy is to introduce a nonthreatening pet to serve as a catalytic vehicle forming adaptive and satisfying social interactions. The patient often relates positively to the pet in nonverbal and tactile interactions. Gradually the circle of social interaction widens to include, first, the therapist who introduced the pet and, later, other patients and medical personnel, with a progressive expansion of positive social interactions outside the hospital. The initial nonverbal forms of interaction are eventually enriched and strengthened with verbal communication and wholesome emotional expressions and warmth (Corson et al., 1975a).

Dogs used were wire-haired fox terriers, border collies, beagles, Labrador retrievers, a German shepherd, and a Husky hybrid. Data accumulated were not conclusive enough to suggest which breed should be matched with which diagnostic category. Videotapes were used and analyzed. It was noted that, when asked questions about the pet, the patient's response time was 1.6 seconds versus 8.4 seconds if asked about other subject areas. The time interval closed as the patient continued to improve. The Corsons believed that the animals promoted a sense of responsibility and a feeling of being needed on the part of the patient. Dogs seemed effective in this role because of "their ability to offer love and tactile reassurance without criticism, and their maintenance of a sort of perpetual infantile dependence, which may stimulate our natural tendency to offer support and protection" (Corson et al., 1975a). Animal-facilitated therapy was used in an adjunctive way with other therapies and was not intended to replace conventional forms of therapy.

Because of financial restraints, the dog colony had to be moved away from Ohio State University but found a welcome at the Castle Nursing Home in Millersburg, Ohio, a facility with some eight hundred residents. Although this was primarily an institution for the aged, there were many younger patients with a variety of mental and physical disabilities. Among the problems encountered in a nursing home are loneliness, depression, boredom, lack of sensory stimulation, and withdrawal. Corson cites eight points that characterize the social structure of a nursing home that tend to reinforce the cycle of "debilitation, social degradation, and dehumanization" (Corson et al., 1977a). They are: a closed social group; low staff-resident ratio with no individual treatment; regimentation with little room for individuality; little privacy; no sense of purpose or goal-directed activity; no reinforcement of positive affective states; minimal socially sustaining tactile contacts; and increasing tactile and social isolation because of sensory deficits.

The Corsons attempted to match residents with appropriate dog companions and recorded the resulting interactions on videotape. The housing units varied from small cottages and apartment buildings to skilled nursing units. Questions were included in the nursing notes so that ten-point scale ratings could be obtained on the patients' physical and emotional well-being, change in personal hygiene or appearance, and social interaction with residents or staff. Similar effects were observed to those noted on the psychiatric unit. The pet-patient interaction gradually widened to include other patients and staff, as was verified by videotape sequences. Physical activity was stimulated, and, in some instances, self-care was improved. No quantitative data were reported because funding limits did not permit such research. The clinical observations were, however, highly encouraging. In some cases, dramatic improvement was noted, as in the case of an elderly man who, after seeing a dog, uttered his first words in twenty years. Although the staff was alert to the possible abuse of the animals, it was not observed to be a problem. The animals were properly immunized and had adequate kennel facilities, so that sanitation was assured. Although dog bites could have presented potential difficulties, they were greatly minimized by the proper selection of the animals and careful supervision of the initial interaction of the animal with the patients.

In 1975, David Lee, a psychiatric social worker at Lima State Hospital for the Criminally Insane at Lima, Ohio, became interested in the work of Levinson and Corson and requested the hospital administration to permit parakeets and tropical fish in the hospital. These had an effect similar to that reported by Corson of catalyzing social interactions between staff and patients and among the patients. The essence of pet therapy at Lima was the incentive system. The patient had to earn the privilege of having his "own" animal through caring for the ward "mascots"—the fish aquarium and gerbils. Once the patient had demonstrated responsible behavior, a request was made and evaluated by the staff. Then an appropriate animal such as a cage bird, rodent (hamster, gerbil, guinea pig), or fish was selected, which the patient had to care for and feed. The patient generally had to work in the hospital greenhouse to raise food to sell or exchange for pet food or sacrifice personal spending allowances. The dramatic effects have been to decrease violence, both patient-to-patient and patient-to-staff, improve morale of staff and patients, and improve the level of trust. Although initially no quantitative data were accumulated, current study is being done, comparing a twenty-eight bed open ward of long-term chronic patients having a pet therapy program and a similar ward without a pet therapy program. Preliminary findings suggest that there are higher incidences of suicide attempts and violent outbursts and higher requirements for medication on the ward without a pet therapy program (Lee, 1981).

There have been some pet therapy failures, such as the program at the California State Prison at San Quentin. Inmates were allowed to keep stray cats, but as the number of cats grew, many inmates complained of the odor. The program was poorly supervised and attention was never directed toward selection criteria or whether the practice should even have been allowed. The cats had been randomly acquired, there were no controls, and the animals became a source of antagonism among inmates. Problems continued to mount, and the cats were finally removed in 1976. Other prisons, however, have successfully integrated pets, including cats. Two minimal security facilities, the California Institution for Women at Frotera, and the California Institution for Men at Chino, have developed programs with cats that have been successful, apparently because of improved supervision (Arkow, 1980).

ANIMAL-FACILITATED THERAPY IN NONINSTITUTIONAL SETTINGS

The vast majority of people live outside of institutions in their own homes, apartments, halfway houses, or other facilities in the community. With increasing pressure to decrease the population of institutions for cost reasons, there are competing forces at work to maintain or increase these facilities (the current legislative climate suggests that a less permissive attitude toward criminal rehabilitation will prevail, putting pressure on the capacity of the present system). Likewise, there is a steady increase in the average age of the population, and life expectancy is enhanced. It is anticipated that the number of people over 65 will increase to 31 million by the year 2000 causing great pressure on the facilities to house and care for them (Bustad, 1980a). The extent to which animals can be used to extend the meaningful independence of the elderly, physically impaired, and mentally ill is an important issue for our society to examine.

Mugford and M'Comisky (1975) studied old-age pensioners (aged 75 to 81 years) living alone in East Yorkshire, England, and placed budgerigars (small Australian parrots) or a houseplant using a design that was balanced for the presence of a television set in the home. A health and morale questionnaire was administered at the start of the experiment and five months after placement.

The presence of budgies made a statistically significant difference when compared to the houseplants on questionnaire items involving physical and psychological health. The author also noted that all twelve of the budgie recipients had formed strong attachments with their animals and that the animals had acted as "social lubricants" in increasing communication and contact with other people.

A study of thirty-one pet-owning outpatients with medical illness and depression examined the perceived influence of pets on their lives and their abilities to cope with their illness (McCulloch, 1981b). True-false questionnaires revealed two distinct groups—fifteen patients claimed to have a primary emotional bond with the pets, and sixteen said that the pet belonged to someone else in the family (Table 36.1).

In spite of this difference, responses of appreciating the pet's affection were surprisingly similar. The pets helped the patients cope with loneliness and isolation, promoted a sense of play, and helped maintain a sense of humor and

TABLE 36.1.   INFLUENCE OF PETS ON OUTPATIENTS

	Patient has Primary bond with pet	Others have Primary bond with pet	Total
	15 patients	16 patients	31
I am my pet's closest companion	15	16	31
Pets have been an important part of my life	14	13	27
Pet is an important source of companionship during illness	13	9	22
Pet made me feel needed	12	9	21
Pet distracted me from worry about problems	12	8	20
Felt more secure with pet around	12	10	22
Pet improved my morale	11	9	20
Pet's affection greatly appreciated	15	14	29
Pet's playfulness improved my spirits	12	11	23
Pet helped me cope with isolation and loneliness	13	13	26
Pet helped me laugh and maintain a sense of humor	15	14	29
Pet's needs stimulated me to be more physically active	15	6	21

laughter. From this study, criteria were suggested for use in prescribing pets for outpatients. Precautions were also given. In prescribing pets for outpatients, the following possible patient characteristics should be considered: chronic illness or disability, depression, positive previous relationship with pets, role reversal, negative dependency, loneliness or isolation, helplessness, low self-esteem, hopelessness, and absence of humor.

Therapeutic horseback riding for the handicapped is a variety of outpatient program directed primarily toward children with physical impairments. The history, development, and utility of such programs are reviewed by Bieber in this section.

Other programs have used animals to improve the lives of handicapped people. Numerous organizations exist to train dogs for the blind. The Seeing Eye Dog program has existed for more than fifty years and has placed more than 7500 dogs in the United States and Canada. Employing German shepherds, golden retrievers, and labrador retrievers, this program places approximately two hundred animals a year. Guide Dogs for the Blind began in 1942 in San Francisco as a program for servicemen blinded in World War II and is using similar methods as the Seeing Eye program. More than thirty-five hundred persons have been enrolled to date. Other programs placing animals include Guiding Eyes for the Blind and Guide Dog Foundation for the Blind in New York and Pilot Dogs Incorporated, in Columbus, Ohio. Major benefits to the visually impaired person appear to be improvement in economic and social independence (Bustad, 1980).

Dogs have also been trained to assist those with hearing impairments. Beginning in 1976, the Minnesota SPCA became aware of an animal that had been trained by its deaf owner to respond to household sounds. Following the owner's death, the dog was turned over to the SPCA. A dog trainer then observed the animal and began training other dogs to perform tasks for hearing-impaired persons. The program was eventually turned over to the American Humane Association, which continues it. At present, more than one hundred dogs have been placed, and each animal is trained specifically for the owner. There is also a Hearing Dog Program operated by the San Francisco SPCA (Bustad, 1980a). Some programs are training animals to augment the independent living skills of disabled persons.

COMMUNITY-ORIENTED PROGRAMS

Efforts are currently under way in some communities to offer comprehensive services, using animals for education in the school system and coordinating animal therapy programs for specific individual and community needs. These programs include therapy efforts for the physically and mentally impaired, the elderly, and those in mental hospitals and prisons. A referral system enables people to obtain specially trained animals. The People-Pet Partnership Program of the Washington State University School of Veterinary Medicine, under the leadership of Dean Leo Bustad and Linda Hines, has been established as a prototype of such a community organization and offers a detailed format on organizational methods and objectives (Hines, 1980; Bustad, 1979). Numerous programs promote pets as therapeutic agents. Many of these are not publicized but provide services to meet specific health needs of people. The Pet-A-Care Program of the San Francisco SPCA provides veterinary services to pets belonging to people over sixty-five who have limited income. A similar program in New York, endowed by the Vincent Astor Foundation, provides free pet care for the elderly poor at the Animal Medical Center. Throughout the United States, programs are being developed for employing animals, including the Pet-Mobile Program in Colorado Springs and the Prescription Pet Program in Minneapolis, Minnesota (Bustad, 1980a). Some involve placement of animals in nursing homes on a full- or part-time basis or placing pets in a person's apartment or home. The humane societies throughout the country are playing an integral part in these programs and continue to provide innovative direction (Arkow, 1980). Little quantitative date are being accumulated on the effect of the endeavors.

ANIMAL-FACILITATED THERAPY MODEL

As described thus far, animal-facilitated therapy programs are extremely varied. There are numerous types of animals available to assist in handling a variety of human problems. The locations and methods of interaction are myriad, and the outcomes are very complicated. These multiple factors can be viewed as a complex set of interrelationships as seen in Figure 36.1. To study the way animals affect people through animal-facilitated therapy, it is necessary to understand the system of interaction between people and pets, the style of interaction, the location, and the outcome. One can then begin testing one model against another with adequate controls.

FIGURE 36.1.   ANIMAL-FACILITATED THERAPY MODEL

Animals	People	Type of Interaction	Location	Outcome
Type	Physically impaired	Individual companion	Institution	Individual (family)
Age	Mentally ill			
Size	Elderly	Part-time Companion	Community	Caregivers
Temperament	Incarcerated	Entertainer		
	Normal individual or family	Mascot		Institution
		Group pet		
		Living environment		Animals

As noted in the many different therapy efforts to date, numerous human problems have been approached through pet therapy. These include treatment of the physically impaired such as the deaf and blind, those with brain injuries or multiple handicaps, and those with chronic medical illnesses. In addition, pets have been used in dealing with certain types of mental illness, including disorders of childhood, psychoses, depression, senility, and various reactive psychiatric problems such as anxiety and depression. Certain pets seem particularly effective with the elderly. Pet therapy has also been used for those incarcerated in penal institutions. Loneliness occurs in many different settings, and, as described, animals can provide necessary companionship. The family can be also studied in this animal-facilitated therapy model because pets appear to serve an important role in family life, even though the exact role in human development, especially child development, is not well understood.

Animals tested in therapy vary considerably according to type, age, size, and temperament and include dogs, cats, caged birds, fish, rodents, horses, farm animals, and many others. Many choices are available, depending on the nature of the human problem and the setting into which the animal is to be placed.

There are at least four types of interaction between people and animals that have been described thus far. First is the "individual companion" or the owned pet, which is placed with an individual on a full-time basis. Examples include programs for the deaf or blind, the elderly in their own homes, those in prison or hospital settings such as Lima State Hospital, and those with chronic illnesses living in the community in halfway houses or their own homes. Second, "part-time companions" include animals that are used on a "loan" basis, being left for periods of time with a person but generally the responsibility of someone else. An example is having pets "visit" an elderly person at home or at a nursing home for several hours a week. Such services are often provided by humane societies or interested volunteer groups. Horses used for therapeutic riding also qualify as part-time companions because they are used for brief periods of time each week and serve many handicapped riders. Pets can be used as "entertainers" in hospital and nursing home settings. "Pet-Mobile" programs often bring young pups or kittens to frolic and play with nursing home residents. They are there for only brief periods of time and then are removed. They are usually maintained as the responsibility of the humane society or a volunteer group (Arkow, 1980). Third is the "mascot," or group pet, who resides in the therapeutic setting, a psychiatric ward, nursing home, halfway house, or prison. These pets provide companionship to all the residents, patients, or inmates, and they are available to everyone, including the treatment staff (Yates, 1973). Finally, animals can be part of a "living environment" such as on a working farm or residential treatment center. Here people may interact with animals who are considered part of the community of living things—plants, livestock, horses, rabbits, poultry, dogs, and cats, as well as birds and animals in the wild. Residential treatment centers such as the York Retreat, Betherl, and Pawling Convalescent Hospital fall in this category. Ironically, many of the mental hospitals and county farms had this system until the laws governing "institutional peonage" virtually eliminated them (Stone, 1975). When states had to reimburse patients a fair wage for labor, the states could no longer afford to maintain the institutions as working farms. The emphasis on mainstreaming patients into the community and closing down custodial institutions also affected this trend. Various interactions can be mixed in the same setting. For example, a nursing home may have a dog "mascot" and permit residents to own caged birds as well; it may also have a visiting pet program that brings litters of pups or kittens in as entertainment.

With proper research, the outcome or effects of an animal-facilitated therapy program can be measured and determined to be positive, negative, or static. Thus effects can be tabulated on the individual (patient, family, inmate) and classified as psychological, social, or physical; on the caregivers (the institutional or community outpatient staff); on the institution; and on the animals themselves.

The numerous benefits to individuals or patients from the programs and studies mentioned above, may be outlined as follows:

PSYCHOLOGICAL BENEFITS
1. Positive affective state (elation)
2. Affiliation
3. Humor
4. Play
5. Self-esteem
6. Need to be needed
7. Independence
8. Increased motivation
9. Education
10. Sense of achievement
11. Stimulus to be active (busy)

SOCIAL BENEFITS
1. Catalyst effect
   "Social Lubricant"
   "Widening circle of warmth"
2. Social cohesion
3. Cooperative play (sports)
4. Increased cooperation with caregivers

PHYSICAL BENEFITS
1. Recovery from illness
2. Coping with illness
3. Neuromuscular rehabilitation
4. ? Life expectancy

Promoting a positive affective state has been claimed by Corson et al., (1975a) and others to be very beneficial. Affiliation, the need to be in close physical proximity to other living things, has been described by several investigators (Corson et al., 1975a; Katcher, 1980; Mugford and M'Comisky, 1975; McCulloch, 1981b). Animals promote humor and a sense of play. They also help improve a person's self-esteem through their trusting dependence. They can also increase a person's independence, physical and economic, as noted with the "seeing eye" and "hearing" dogs. They can increase motivation of handicapped persons to struggle against their impairments, as seen in therapeutic horseback riding. The entire life cycle, activities, and habits of animals are readily observable and make them excellent educational tools (McCulloch, 1978). Children frequently learn about life, death, reproduction, and biological processes by first observing animals. Many people gain a feeling of achievement with pet therapy, whether building a cage for a new pet parakeet at Lima State Hospital or successfully completing a relay race in therapeutic riding. Pet animals stimulate one to be active and busy (feeding, grooming, walking) (Katcher, 1981). The habits of pets can serve as an organizing and an orienting influence (Katcher, 1980).

Social benefits include the catalyst effect, previously described as "social lubricant" or "widening circle of warmth" (Corson et al., 1975a). Pets stimulate social interaction with others and can result in social cohesion, whether in the family of someone with chronic illness or in the milieu of a psychiatric ward. Animals can be part of a sporting activity or cooperative play, such as turtle races and relay races in therapeutic riding. Social benefits also include increased cooperation with the caregivers, especially as noted at Lima State Hospital.

Physical benefits are numerous and include improving the rate of recovery from illness and ability to cope with illness (McCulloch, 1981b). Neuromuscular rehabilitation is especially evident in therapeutic riding (Rosin, 1980). The possible effect on life expectancy has been posed but requires further investigation (Friedman et al., 1980; Katcher, 1981).

Positive effects on caregivers include improved morale (as shown at Lima State Hospital and in nursing homes) because many institutions become decidedly monotonous for the caregivers and staff as well as for patients or inmates. Caregivers share in the humor and play with animals, which helps lighten the atmosphere. Increased staff contact with patients, both verbal and physical, has been noted at Lima State Hospital and in nursing homes. Pets appear to amplify caregiving capacities, possibly by decreasing the level of fear and intimidation or by creating through the pet's "innocent dependence" that "widening circle of warmth."

That the institution can be positively affected by an animal-facilitated therapy program was seen at Lima State Hospital. There were a decreased incidence of crises, reduced patient-to-patient and patient-to-staff violence, and reduced problems with suicide attempts and loss of behavioral control. Improved patient and staff morale can be an important outcome as the overall treatment milieu is enhanced. In general, pet therapy programs are cost-effective when the patients participate through the incentive system in supporting the cost. Humane societies and volunteer groups are frequently willing to donate animals, animal training time, and staff to support animal-facilitated therapy, as seen in numerous nursing home projects throughout the country. Therapeutic riding for the handicapped is the most expensive to maintain on a per patient basis, but the costs are usually underwritten by private sources. The end result of all these benefits for the institution may be an improved community image and a more humane treatment environment.

The animals are also recipients of positive effects which can include companionship and social interaction. For many, such a program gives them a chance for a productive life in surroundings where their companionship is prized. It is obviously a preferable alternative to being euthanized in an animal shelter.

Examination of available literature on AFT programs appears strongly biased toward an advocacy position. Positive effects are lauded and negative effects are usually minimized. There appears to be strong popular sentiment that pet therapy "works" as an effective treatment of human problems.

There is no systematic compilation of pet therapy failures, but there are vague references to what might go wrong. With the vast array of pet therapy efforts, problems are certain to arise. Since much can be learned from pet therapy failures, the lack of such documentation is unfortunate.

Thus negative effects of AFT are summarized from available literature and common sense consideration of possible pitfalls. Problems for the individual can occur if animal selection is inappropriate and animals are mismatched with patient needs (Arkow, 1980; Bustad 1979). If the timing is not right the person's condition can worsen. For example, an animal might be given to a person who is too physically ill to maintain or appreciate it properly. The capacities of an elderly person might be overestimated so that the daily responsibilities required for maintaining an animal on a full-time basis cannot be completed. Good intention is not an adequate substitute for proper research, as seen in the case of a well-meaning husband who brought home a large dog to keep his wife company. She had been lonely and depressed for some time because he did not spend time with her. The dog he brought home was a large guard dog, which terrified her. The end result was that he and the dog became the best of companions and she became more depressed than ever. She wanted more time with her husband, not a pet animal. Pets can be a source of rivalry and competition in group situations, as seen at San Quentin. Patients also can become possessive and try to "adopt" the ward mascot for themselves. Injury can occur in the form of bites or scratches through inappropriate handling by patients, poor animal selection, or inadequate staff supervision. The capacities of some patients with brain injury, mental retardation, senility, or other problems may be such that they do not fully appreciate how they might be provoking or injuring an animal. The pets can appear to "reject" the patients if the attention given is excessive or the expectation is for the pet to sit for long periods of time on the person's lap or at bedside. This problem can also be the result of unrealistic expectations, poor selection, or improper staff supervision. Allergies to feathers and to animal dander, including dog, cat, and horse, occur, although the exact incidence is not known (Ohman,

1978). Patients' history of allergy should be obtained before attempted introduction of pets. Certain diseases are transmissible from animals to man, so proper veterinary examination and adequate sanitation facilities are essential (Bustad, 1980a). Patients with open wounds or low resistance to disease need to be carefully monitored.

For the caregivers, the major negative effects are noncompliance with the animal-facilitated therapy program. If they are not given a proper orientation or are not allowed to participate in the decision and policy-making guidelines for AFT, they may undermine the program. Some staff view AFT as more work and too much hassle. Some simply do not like animals. Of course, they are subject to the same problems with allergy and injury if there is improper selection and inappropriate handling.

For the institution, the negative outcome can take the form of legal liability for patient injury or accident and for animal injury. Legal obstacles may have to be overcome to permit animals to be in the facility at all. In some instances, ordinances permit animals on the premises but restrict housing them. Some states are trying to repeal such statutes, especially restriction of pets in certain housing facilities. Pets have generally been prohibited in federally subsidized housing, especially for the elderly. Noise levels can present difficulties for the patients, the staff, or the neighborhood. Sanitation can be a major problem if there are not adequate kennel facilities. Staff and patient cooperation is vital. Some animals may be inappropriate for settings that are already crowded, as at San Quentin. Disease risk must be weighed, especially if the patient population is vulnerable to infection. Finally, cost can be a factor, although generally minimal. If kennel facilities have to be constructed, cost can increase markedly. Feeding and maintaining horses for therapeutic riding is also costly.

Negative effects on the animals can be injury by the patient as a result of rough or inappropriate handling or injury as the result of fights with other animals. Breeding can be a problem but can be usually handled with adequate spaying and neutering programs for dogs and cats. Secure facilities are needed for some animals so they do not roam off the premises. Basic animal welfare issues need to be respected, including adequate food, shelter, grooming, and access to veterinary services.

RECOMMENDATIONS

Considerable momentum is developing in the adjunctive use of animals in therapy programs all over the world. It is apparent that their evolution and development will continue until research necessary to document benefits and hazards is completed. Recognizing this fact, it is prudent to provide recommendations that synthesize and summarize the known benefits and problems of animal-facilitated therapy to those with existing or planned pet therapy programs. It is also important to pose research questions that delve into comparison of AFT models; therapeutic efficacy; cost-benefit; effects on patient care, staff, and administration; and costs of medical care.

Perform a thorough "system" analysis before beginning, studying the institution, caregivers, or individual family. Carefully review the structure of the institution or family, capabilities and attitudes of the caregivers and the administrative staff, and the specific problems to be addressed by an AFT program.

Proper selection and timing. Tailor the animal(s) to the individual's or institution(s)' needs and capabilities. Carefully match type, age, and temperament of pets for the specific problem to be addressed. Assess the capacities of individuals to respond to animals. Some may be too ill or impaired for pets to have any effect. Also, there must be provisions for caring for the basic needs of the animals.

Define goals and outcome criteria. What are the animals supposed to do: improve staff morale, patient motivation, and patient physical or emotional health, or reduce violence in the treatment setting? Establish methods of evaluating these criteria.

Understand risks and benefits (do no harm). Carefully screen for potential problems, such as inappropriate animal size, untrained animals, inadequate staff for care of pets, and inappropriate handling by impaired patients, which can cause injury to the animals and/or patient. Those with severe cognitive impairments may not be capable of handling pets with care. For example, common sense dictates that it is unwise to place a dog unsupervised in an apartment with an elderly person with known episodes of confusion and memory disturbance.

Conduct proper orientation to all involved. It is essential to "sell" the staff, volunteer group, and family on AFT and to assess the degree of resistance or opposition to the program. Negative attitudes at this level can seriously undermine any therapeutic benefit. It is essential to have the support and cooperation of as many as possible of the involved personnel.

Coordinate "prescription pets" with other therapy modalities. AFT should not displace other therapies. It should be added to those already being used such as physical, occupational, recreational, group, or individual therapy, as well as the necessary forms of drugs and medical treatment. AFT can be a facilitator to patient motivation for other therapies.

Maintain supervision of patients, staff, and animals. Supervision is necessary for the maintenance of a successful program. Continued monitoring of all elements of the interactional network is necessary to assess potential problem areas and maintain the focus of the stated goals and directions. Monitoring safety issues is important, including evidence of animal and patient injury. Awareness of staff attitudes toward the program and avoidance of any open-ended situation with no controls, such as the failed program at San Quentin, is vital.

Evaluate data: cost-benefit, modify, delete, add, improve. Analyze the effects of AFT and refine the program accordingly. Trial and error is a necessary part of any new therapy endeavor. Periodic evaluations are required. Pet therapy failures should be documented. These experiences form an important record for those instances in which AFT may not be useful, or where there has been a system breakdown that is correctable. The strong bias that AFT works must be tempered with objective scientific observation.

Maintain realistic expectations: animal-facilitated therapy is adjunctive. Pets are not a panacea. They serve only as useful adjuncts to existing programs. AFT will not remedy defects in other areas that need special attention, such as relationships between staff and administration, inadequate staff-to-patient ratio, poor overall program design, and negative attitudinal sets of caregivers. Pets should not be expected to execute permanent personality change in the patients. They can, however, help amplify capacities for warmth and empathy, as seen at Lima State Hospital with severe psychopathic criminals, in whom capacities for caring, however constricted, were observed. Permanent character change, however desirable, is not essential for an AFT program to have value. If pet therapy can help reduce the violence in an institution, a more humane treatment environment may result.

RESEARCH QUESTIONS

Many important questions remain for scientific documentation, especially as we begin exploring areas of cost-effectiveness. The following are among the many that need to be addressed:

1. Can animal-facilitated therapy extend meaningful independence of the elderly or the handicapped? How?

2. Can length of hospital stay be reduced with AFT?

3. Can the cost of medical care be reduced?

4. Can violence be reduced in correctional institutions through use of AFT?

5. Can the amount of drugs required for treatment of various medical and psychiatric problems be reduced?

6. What is the most cost-effective AFT model for a given therapy setting?

7. Is one AFT model more effective than another in a given setting?

8. Can staff morale and turnover be affected by the presence of an AFT program?

9. How are the quality and quantity of staff interactions with patients affected by AFT?

10. Can the ability of AFT to produce positive affective states in patients be measured? (How do you measure "a little bit of happiness"?)

11. Under what conditions are animal-facilitated therapy programs not advisable or potentially harmful?

12. How do pets affect normal child and adult development and family life?

Keep in focus that animals are part of normal child, adult, and family development and experience and are not to be exclusively identified with the handicapped. Much of our data base for future use with the impaired will come from the study of normal ineractions between pets and people.

CONCLUSION

In the face of chronic illness, it is difficult for many to maintain dignity and self-worth. For those with a progressive or sudden disability, it is hard to forget "the way I used to be." Unrealistic expectations of improvement serve only to disappoint.

Loss of function is mourned. Creation of humane treatment environments which are comforting and caring can assist rehabilitation and readaptation efforts. The disabled gain a recognition that organs and body parts are not compliant instruments that carry out their owner's intentions. In many cases, the impaired person must accept a life that is irrevocably different. Because of that difference, a new meaning and way of life must be found: to discover the new meaning in life and the dissolution of the old meaning, to accept the difference imposed by the illness, and to maintain one's dignity and worth are *essential* (Feldman, 1974). For persons with congenital impairments, the reality of disability is ever-present, and the struggle for independence and self-respect remains a lifetime endeavor. If pet therapy offers hope for relief of human suffering, it is our professional obligation to explore every available avenue for its use.

Mary Thompson, Robert W. Kennedy, and Sue Igou

37

Pets as Socializing Agents with Chronic Psychiatric Patients: An Initial Study

The use of pets as therapeutic adjuncts in the treatment of the mentally ill and as socializing agents with the elderly has been found overall to have beneficial effects (Brickel, 1979; Corson et al., 1975). Whether pets have been used in institutional individual therapy sessions in individual therapy sessions within an institution, or as socializing agents for the entire ward of an institution, the contact with animals has been generally described as having caused improvement in the patients' interpersonal relationships and self-esteem.

Information is needed in many areas regarding the use of animals within institutions: animal health standards; housing and maintenance issues; the best types of animals to use, that is, which animals elicit the best responses from frail geriatric patients as opposed to middle-aged and younger patients; training and early socialization of animals for use with the disabled; procedures for use of animals in individual or group psychotherapy; legal implications; and so on.

The study reported here with chronic psychiatric patients addressed several issues and attempted to establish procedural guidelines, so that others wishing to implement pet-facilitated therapy may experience less difficulty in so doing.

Most important, it initiated systematic study of generalized behavior change—that which occurs outside the therapy room—as a result of animal contact.

METHOD

SUBJECT

Subjects were selected from a chronic psychiatric unit with 60 patients between the ages of 40 and 60. About 75 percent had diagnoses of schizophrenia, and the rest of severe organic mental disorder. All required close nursing supervision. Half of the patients were housed on a locked end of the ward because of their confusion, acting-out behavior, or socially unacceptable habits.

A total of twenty patients were randomly selected, divided equally between locked and open wards. As patients were chosen, they were screened for desire to participate, allergies to animals, dog or cat phobias, and acting-out tendencies that might result in harm to the patient or the animal. Patients excluded under these criteria were replaced by others, randomly chosen, until ten participants were selected from each ward area.

In compliance with Veterans Administration regulations, all experimental procedures were explained to the subjects and informed consent was obtained. Once selected, subjects were randomly assigned to either the experimental or the control condition.

PROCEDURE

Following group assignment, patients were rated on the Physical and Mental Impairment-of-Function Evaluation (PAMIE) (Gurel, Linn, and Linn, 1972), the Hamilton Rating Scale for Depression (Hamilton, 1960), and the Mini–Mental State Questionnaire (MSQ) (Folstein, Folstein, and McHugh, 1975). The PAMIE was completed by a staff nurse who was familiar with the subjects but blind to experimental questions and group assignment. The Hamilton and the MSQ were administered by a nurse and psychologist who were also blind to subject assignment.

The experimental subjects were exposed to an eighteen-hour group pet-facilitated psychotherapy procedure, conducted in three hour-long sessions each week for six weeks. The procedure was a semistructured exercise which included instruction on pet care (feeding and grooming), petting and handling, sharing attention with other group members, and discussion of feelings about the animal. A different animal was used each week; a wide variety of the staff's pets were employed, including a cat, kittens, dogs, guinea pigs, and a parakeet. In general, there was a progression, with each animal, of therapist "information"-giving, supervised animal handling by each subject, and finally, very loosely supervised handling by subjects individually and collectively. At every step of the procedure, the therapist attempted to stimulate group members to share knowledge of animals, previous experiences with pets, and feelings about the animal being handled. The objective was to create an atmosphere of trust and mutual disclosure in an attempt to stimulate feelings of caring and attachment in patients whose inability to form relationships was a cardinal feature of their disorders.

Control subjects, otherwise assigned to similar group and individual therapies and activities as the experimental subjects, were rated initially and after six weeks and did not participate further in study-related procedures. Because there was a large number of activites for most patients, a "control for attention" was not included.

During the week following termination of the procedures, the subjects were again rated on the PAMIE and MSQ, using the same raters.

INSTRUMENTS

The Physical and Mental Impairment-of-Function Evaluation, or PAMIE, is a seventy-seven-item true-false rating scale, designed for administration by professional or paraprofessional staff. It is a multifunctional assessment device that has been factor analyzed into ten meaningful variables: self-care/dependent, belligerent/irritable, mentally disorganized/confused, anxious/depressed, bedfast/moribund, behaviorally deteriorated, paranoid/suspicious, sensorimotor impaired, withdrawn/apathetic, and ambulatory. Factor scores or individual items can be compared to reveal the most fruitful areas for more controlled research projects. High scores indicate greater impairment of function with a maximum possible score of 55 for the variables used for this study.

The Hamilton Rating Scale for Depression was chosen to provide another, more refined look at affect. Subjects are rated on seventeen variables, with either a three- or five-point scale, by a skilled clinician.

The Mini–Mental State consists of interview questions and is intended to assess the presence and degree of cognitive impairment.

RESULTS

Pretest and posttest scores from the MSQ and PAMIE were statistically analyzed using an analysis of covariance technique. Only the eight PAMIE factors most subject to change were analyzed, omitting the Sensorimotor Impaired and Ambulatory scales. The total score, in this case, was the sum of the eight scales used. Data from the Hamilton Rating Scale for Depression were not analyzed, because very little depression was ratable with this subject population; a mean score of 16.1 (two-rater total) was found on the pretest, out of a possible score of 124, rendering the information obtained essentially meaningless as a change score.

For subjects with an "intermediate" level of impairment (scores between 12 and 33), the overall (total) PAMIE scores showed a statistically significant difference between the experimental and control groups, with $F(1,11) = 4.46$, p

< .05, indicating that the experimental subjects improved, in a global sense, compared with control subjects. There were no significant differences between groups of PAMIE factor scores or for MSQ scores. For all subjects, there were no significant differences on any of the measures. This finding was attributed to three "deviant" subjects in the experimental group, one of whom had very low pre- and posttest scores (2 and 4, respectively), and two of whom had very high scores (40/45, and 40/43, respectively).

DISCUSSION

Perhaps the most important result of this study was the unforeseen subject impairment problem. Although the number of very impaired and very unimpaired subjects was small (n = 3), their lack of change suggests that further work might clarify the issue of which patients will or will not benefit from such a procedure. The other seven subjects had a mean pretest score of 22.9 and a mean posttest score of 16.7; the control subjects had pretest and posttest means of 21.0 and 17.9. These results stand in contrast to the worsening scores of the three subjects in question. Thus such scales may be predictive of success in pet-facilitated psychotherapy programs. More definitive work in this area would, of course, be essential.

That the factor scores did not produce significant change is at least partially explained by the limited number of items in most scales; only three of the factors had as many as ten items. Only one showed changes that approached significance, that being the "self-care/dependent" scale (ten items). It is possible that more ratable items or a scale that allows for more than the "yes-no" responses for the PAMIE would show behavior change more readily.

It is obvious that the retrospective reexamination of the data and the lack of an active control condition weaken the scientific credibility of this research. On the other hand, we have been working in an area in which there are few rigorous studies and no real standards for such research. Perhaps it is remarkable that any significant effects were found, considering the blind rating system and the fact that the measures reflect behaviors only indirectly related to the pet-facilitated therapy.

In summary, this study provides a tantalizing glimpse of the possibilities presented by the use of companion animals in psychotherapy programs for chronic psychiatric patients. A replication is needed, with more participating patients, a longer active treatment program, extended follow-up, and sufficient individual pet contact time for a more definite "bond" to form. Subject groupings by diagnosis and level of impairment would also help clarify the selection issues raised in this study. It is suggested, however, that organized pet contact appears to have effects that are felt beyond the therapy setting. The generalized changes seen with some patients support the hypothesis that relationships with animals can foster healthier interpersonal relations.

Geary Olsen, Robert K. Anderson
Joseph S. Quigley, and Nora Beahl

38

Pet-Facilitated Therapy:
A Study of the Use of Animals in
Health Care Facilities in Minnesota

In February 1979, the Minnesota state legislature passed a law permitting animals on the premises of nursing and boarding care homes subject to reasonable rules and regulations. Since that time, a sizable number of health care facilities are believed to have begun using animals, but no figures were known. At the University of Minnesota School of Public Health, a survey of licensed and certified health care facilities, excluding hospitals, of the state of Minnesota was undertaken in 1981 to ascertain the use of animals in these facilities.

The five major classifications of health care facilities studied were nursing homes, supervised living facilities, boarding care homes, nursing and boarding care homes, and convalescent nursing care units. Nursing homes provided care for aged or infirm persons who require nursing care and related services. Supervised living facilities provided supervision, lodging, counseling, and developmental habilitative or rehabilitative services to persons who were mentally retarded, chemically dependent, adult mentally ill, or physically handicapped. Boarding care homes provided care for aged or infirm persons who required only personal or custodial care. Nursing services were not provided. Convalescent nursing care units were nursing homes operated in conjunction with a hospital where there was direct physical connection between the nursing home and the hospital.

A questionnaire was developed with advice from veterinarians, long-term health care administration educators, state health officials, a psychologist, and a public health nurse. The questionnaire asked the respondents—health care administrators—to identify their facility as falling into one of three categories and to return the questionnaire page with the appropriate indentification. These three categories were Part I (currently using pets); Part II (have used but are not currently using pets); and Part III (have never used pets).

The questionnaire was coded by type of facility, county in which the facility was located, and a number that coincided with an alphabetical listing of health care facilities by counties as printed in the *Directory of Licensed and Certified Health Care Facilities, 1980, of the Minnesota Department of Health*. A presample test was performed on June 9, 1981. The sample respondents mentioned no problems in understanding the style and format of the questionnaire.

A letter was mailed to all health care facility administrators included in the survey on June 10, 1981, which explained the nature of the research and informed the administrators that the questionnaire would arrive in the mail in a few days. The first mailing of the questionnaire with an accompanying letter giving directions was mailed on June 15, 1981. A second letter and questionnaire were mailed on July 10, 1981, to all health care facilities from which questionnaires had not been returned by July 9, 1981. Nonresponding facilities as of July 29, 1981, were contacted by telephone. Two authors of this study questioned the administrators and obtained their responses via telephone.

The questionnaire consisted of a combination of open- and fixed-response questions. The open-response answers by the administrators were categorized by response. Answers to fixed-response questions were tabulated.

The purpose of this questionnaire was to survey health care administrators about the use of animals in their facilities. Many returned questionnaires were answered by assistant administrators, directors of nursing, directors of activity departments, and other administrative assistants. Consequently, the original intent of receiving a response from the health care administrator could not be obtained. Questions pertaining to the administrator should therefore be viewed as a question to a member of the administrative staff.

Analysis of the data was divided into three major areas: total aggregate analysis, intraclassification analysis of health care facilities, and interclassification analysis of health care facilities. Intraclassification analysis consisted of segregating respondents within each type of health care facility into three parts dependent on category of animal use: Parts I, II, and III. Interclassification analysis consisted of comparing the three categories of animal use within each health care facility classification to the corresponding category of another type of health care facility. An example would be comparing the responses received from administrators of nursing homes who currently use animals (Part I) to the responses of administrators of supervised living facilities who also returned Part I.

Statistical significance was calculated using two-tailed student t tests and chi square tests when applicable.

Questionnaires were mailed to 774 health care facilities: 300 nursing homes; 274 supervised living facilities; 59 boarding care homes; 65 nursing and boarding care homes; 68 convalescent nursing care units; and 8 facilities considered as "mixed." All health care facilities in the state of Minnesota except hospitals were included (*Directory of Licensed and Certified Health Care Facilities, 1980, of the Minnesota Department of Health*). The final response was determined from 762 of 774 responding facilities for a response return rate of 98.45 percent. The return rates after the first and second mailings were 67.31 percent and 81.65 percent, respectively. The telephone follow-up brought the final response rate to 98.45 percent.

According to health care facility classification, the response rate was 99.33 percent nursing homes; 97.08 percent supervised living facilities; 100 percent boarding care homes; 100 percent nursing and boarding care homes; and 98.52 percent convalescent nursing care units.

The percentage of questionnaires returned of Part I (currently using animals), Part II (have used but not currently using animals), and Part III (have never used animals) for nursing homes was 56.05 percent, 12.41 percent, and 31.54 percent, respectively. The percent returned of Parts I, II, and III from supervised living facilities was 42.10 percent, 15.80 percent, and 42.10 percent. The percent returned of Parts I, II, and III from boarding care homes was 44.06 percent, 11.88 percent, and 44.06 percent. The percent returned of Parts I, II, and III from nursing and boarding care homes was 60.00 percent, 15.38 percent, and 24.62 percent. The percent returned of Parts I, II, and III from convalescent nursing care units was 32.83 percent, 14.92 percent, and 52.25 percent.

A statistically significant greater percent of nursing homes and nursing and boarding care homes currently used animals than did supervised living facilities, boarding care homes, and convalescent nursing care units ($p < .05$).

An important part of the study was to ascertain the type of animal programs used by health care facilities in Minnesota. Four major programs were identified: nonscheduled visiting animal (such as brought by family, friends, or staff); scheduled visiting animal (such as planned animal programs by humane societies, 4-H clubs, and other organizations); resident animals (owned by health care facility or resident); and animal-facilitated therapy (such as an adjunct to a planned therapy program with individuals or groups of residents).

Of Part I nursing homes, 76.6 percent used nonscheduled visiting animal programs, 62.3 percent used scheduled visiting animal programs, 32.9 percent used resident animals, and 13.8 percent used animal-facilitated therapy programs. The total percent is greater than 100 for each health care facility classification because of multiple responses to types of programs used.

Of Part I supervised living facilities 51.8 percent used nonscheduled visiting animal programs, 17.0 percent used scheduled visiting animal programs, 73.2

percent used resident animal programs, and 7.1 percent used animal-facilitated therapy programs.

From these results it is strikingly apparent that nursing homes are currently using visiting animal programs significantly more (p < .001) than are supervised living facilities. Supervised living facilities, however, are currently using resident animal programs significantly more (p < .001) than are nursing homes. There was no statistically significant difference between Part I nursing homes and Part I supervised living facilities using animal-facilitated therapy programs.

Results from boarding care homes, nursing and boarding care homes, and convalescent nursing care units indicated that these health care facilities were more similar to nursing homes than to supervised living facilities in the type of animal programs currently being used—visiting animal programs more than resident animal programs.

These data suggest that health care facility administrators for the elderly prefer to use visiting animal programs. Administrators of supervised living facilities, which have a much younger resident population (average age thirty-two) compared to nursing home residents (average age eighty-one), prefer to use resident animals.

In comparing the responses from Part II from nursing homes and supervised living facilities results were similar to those found in Part I nursing homes and supervised living facilities. There were 97.3 percent Part II nursing homes using nonscheduled visiting animal programs compared to 64.3 percent Part II supervised living facilities. This finding was significant at the .001 level. There were 78.4 percent Part II nursing homes using scheduled visiting animal programs while no Part II supervised living facilities responded in like fashion. Only 16.2 percent of Part II nursing homes used resident animal programs compared to 90.5 percent of Part II supervised living facilities (p < .001). Unlike their Part I counterparts, there was statistically significant difference (p < .001) between 13.5 percent Part II nursing homes that used animal-facilitated therapy programs versus only 0.4 percent of Part II supervised living facilities.

As for the type of animal-use program Part III (have never used animals) health care facilities would choose if the administrators decided to use animals, of Part III nursing homes 54.3 percent would consider using nonscheduled animal programs, 57.4 percent would use scheduled animal programs, 28.7 percent would use resident animals, and 36.2 percent would use animal-facilitated therapy programs. There was a significant difference (p < .01) between Part I nursing homes currently utilizing visiting animal programs (nonscheduled and scheduled) and Part III nursing homes, which would consider using visiting animal programs. This difference probably reflects the less favorable opinion toward animal use in health care facilities by Part III respondents compared to Part I respondents of nursing homes. Animal-facilitated therapy programs were much more attractive (p < .001) to Part III nursing homes (36.2 percent) than to the 13.8 percent of Part I nursing homes currently using animal-facilitated therapy programs. This difference may reflect the attractiveness of animal-facilitated therapy programs but demonstrates the difficulty of actually attempting to implement such programs. An interesting finding from the responses of Part III supervised living facilities was that only 25.9 percent would consider using resident animal programs compared to the 73.2 percent Part I supervised living facilities that are currently using resident animal programs. Boarding care homes, nursing and boarding care homes, and convalescent nursing care units that returned Part III of the questionnaire preferred visiting animal programs (nonscheduled and scheduled), to resident animal programs.

Of all the health care facilities that returned Part III, 25.4 percent would consider using animal-facilitated therapy programs, but only 10.38 percent of all Part I health care facilities (currently using animals) have animal-facilitated programs. These data again suggest the attractiveness of such a program to nonusers of animal programs and may be a means to introduce such animal programs into health care facilities not using animals. The data are evidence of the need for research in the animal-facilitated therapy area to evaluate the degree of effectiveness of animal therapy.

Although before 1979 Minnesota statutes prohibited animals in nursing homes and boarding care homes, more than 33 percent of the health care facilities currently using animals in Minnesota have done so for more than four years. Minnesota was the first state in the United States to pass such a law. Although the law is relatively new, the practice of allowing animals in health care facilities in Minnesota is not new.

In summary, animal programs are used more in nursing homes than in other health care facilities. Scheduled and nonscheduled visiting animal programs are more prevalent in nursing homes than in supervised living facilities. Resident animal programs are used the most in supervised living facilities. Boarding care homes, nursing and boarding care homes, and convalescent nursing care units are more similar to nursing homes than to supervised living facilities with regard to the types of animal programs used.

We hope the data that we have presented will bring about an understanding that the type of health care facility may play a significant role in determining the appropriateness of animal programs in health care facilities.

Michael Robin, Robert ten Bensel,
Joseph S. Quigley, and Robert K. Anderson

39

Childhood Pets and the Psychosocial Development of Adolescents

Pets can play an important role in the healthy emotional and physical development of the adolescent child. As a source of love, companionship, and responsibility, pets can help smooth the transition from childhood, through adolescence, to young adulthood. Adolescence is widely recognized as a period of rapid change and development. It is characterized by a growing separation and individuation from parents and the emergence of a distinct and separate identity (Erikson, 1968). Adolescence is also recognized as a period of emotional turmoil, when life is confusing and relationships with others are highly volatile. There is a "heightened emotionality" (White and Speisman, 1976), and many adolescents have intense feelings of loneliness or of not being understood. The purpose of this study is to examine the premise that pet animals may be important in the transition through this difficult part of life.

Pets may have a special meaning to children and adolescents who are lonely or needy, emotionally disturbed or delinquent. These young people often have poor self-esteem and have difficulty maintaining relationships. Many disturbed and delinquent youths have suffered from abuse and neglect from their parents or caretakers. As Douglas Kline, an educator at Utah State University, said before a congressional committee in 1979, "The children who come into conflict with the law and ultimately populate our institutions are for the most part victims of physical abuse, neglect, abandonment, and/or sexual molestation before they come into conflict with juvenile authorities and before they are committed to institutional environments." According to Martin and Rodehoffer, the major psychological dynamic in abused children is an identification with their aggression (1980). Abused children respond to their maltreatment by assuming their own "badness," for why would they be abused unless they were at fault?

Abused children are essentially joyless, lonely creatures who have a poor sense of themselves and find relationships with others stressful. During adolescence many of them come into conflict with the law and are institutionalized. We sought to study whether adolescents were attached to their pets and to demonstrate any qualitative differences in those relationships. Most of all, we wanted to know if youths living in special therapeutic institutions had different relationships to their pets than did youths who went to regular public schools.

METHODOLOGY

Our study population included 507 adolescents, 326 boys and 181 girls from five institutions. The age of the youths ranged from 13 to 18 with 16 the average age. The institutions that participated included an urban high school, a suburban high school, an inpatient psychiatric ward for emotionally disturbed youth, and two state training schools for delinquent youth. We did not control for socioeconomic status and racial background, but all the institutions except the suburban school had approximately one-third minority populations.

The study populations were queried by questionnaire. The sample was self-selected because participation was voluntary and anonymous. There were no definite indications that any youth refused to participate, although it is possible that some could have written that they did not have a pet to avoid participating. There is also the possibility that some youths answered questions without fully understanding them. We were surprised, however, that after initially complaining about taking part in yet another survey, most youths enthusiastically went to work after realizing that the survey was about their pets, and most wrote with a great depth of feeling and seriousness.

We purposely used a number of open-ended questions to allow our respondents the greatest possible flexibility. As a result, there was a wide range of answers, which we tried to categorize into themes. If one youth said, "My dog was my best friend" and another youth used a different description, we did not assume that the second youth did not also feel his or her pet was his "best friend." The answers are basically those that first came into the minds of our respondents, given their experiences with their pets and their skills in communicating those experiences. This study is an effort to assess how kids feel and think about their pets and the experience of having a pet.

DATA

Of the total sample population of 507, 463, or 91 percent, had a special pet sometime in their lives. There was very little difference from one group to another, which surprised us. We had suspected, based on a study by Lenoski that showed abusive families were not likely to have pets, that delinquents would be less likely than nondelinquents to have pets (1980). Dogs and cats were the most common pets, and dogs were more common than cats among all groups. An assortment of other pets was cited, including horses, rabbits, snakes, hamsters, gerbils, rats, birds, turtles, and fish. Our respondents indicated that they felt just as strongly about these pets as they did for their dogs and cats.

Of our respondents, 72 percent said they loved their pet very much, 25 percent said they liked their pet, 1 percent said they did not like or dislike it, saying it was just an animal, 1 percent said they did not like it, and 1 percent said they did not know how they felt. Again, there was very little difference from one group to another. Combining the first two responses shows that 97 percent of our respondents either loved their pets very much or liked them. Only 13 out of the 507 youths did not give this response.

We asked the subjects to use their own words to describe how they felt about their pets. Several general themes emerged. The most common was that a pet was a friend, a companion, and, in some cases, "a best friend." Pets are unconditional and "always there" no matter what. They accepted the youths as is and did not expect them to change. Here are a few representative sample quotations:

> Trixie was very special to me. We went on walks together, went to the park and played. She even slept on the edge of my bed. When I was sad, I could cuddle up to her and she wouldn't say anything against me. She just sat there and loved me. [eighteen-year-old urban female]
>
> I loved my cat very much. It was like my best friend when nobody was around. He was like my security blanket. [fifteen-year-old hospitalized female]
>
> My favorite pet was my dog Bell. I loved her very much. I took care of her all the time and never mistreated her. Sometimes she was the only person I could talk to. [eighteen-year-old hospitalized male]

Several youths indicated that their pet was "part of the family." This response was three times more common among youths from regular schools than among delinquents. Among regular school students, 27 percent said their pet was part of the family, but only 8 percent of the delinquents and 6 percent of hospitalized youths said this. This difference may be indicative of the differing roles pets play within the emotional lives of children. For public school students, a pet is usually considered another valued member of the family. For example, "Rusty was one of us. He went everywhere with us—even on camping trips. When he died we all cried" (seventeen-year-old male). For delinquents, a pet frequently becomes the sole love object and a substitute for family love. As an eighteen-year-old delinquent male said, "My kitty was the joy of my life. It never hurt me or made me upset like my parents. She always came to me when she wanted affection." Some youths indicated that they sought out their pets when feeling lonely or bored. Delinquents were three times more likely than nondelinquents to say this. Here are some sample responses:

> A friend when no one else is there to see you through. [seventeen-year-old male delinquent]
>
> I love all my pets but the one I most loved was my dog Teddy. He was the only thing I had since I don't have a family. I took that puppy everywhere I went. He was very smart and he was the only one I could talk to who would listen. [fourteen-year-old female delinquent]
>
> Pets are important especially for kids without brothers and sisters. They can get close to this animal and they both can grow up to love one another. Men have killed for loved animals. I think it is very important, very much so. [fifteen-year-old urban female]

Our data also suggest differences in how delinquents and nondelinquents play with their pets. We got the impression from many delinquent youths that they play with their pets alone, such as the boy who said, "When I grew up there was no other kids to play with so I played with my dog. It was nice to be with her." Whether children play with pets by themselves or whether pets facilitate relationships with other people would be a useful area for further research.

Many youths turned to their pets for emotional support when distressed and in need of comfort. A pet can provide noncritical support to the needy adolescent. As a sixteen-year-old delinquent youth put it, "A pet listens and listens well and it doesn't talk back."

Seventeen percent of all delinquents in our sample indicated that they talked over their troubles with their pets—more than twice the 7 percent of public school students who said they talked to their pets. This point was not explicitly asked for. Several youths indicated that they felt their pets understood their feelings and needs for affection. One sixteen-year-old girl said: "My dog is very special to me. We have had her for seven years now. When I was little I used to go to her and pet her when I was depressed and crying. She seemed to understand. You could tell by the look in her eyes." A sixteen-year-old delinquent boy said: "He was there to talk to anytime I needed him. We were very close. I mean I would talk and he would look at me as though he understood every word I said." These responses are another indication of the significant role pets play in the lives of children, especially lonely or needy ones.

Twenty-six youths, all but four of whom were delinquents, said that their pet, usually a dog, protected them from others. Sometimes they were protected from parents, such as the boy who said, "He was a good hound. My parents couldn't beat me up because he would bite them." The use of pets as protectors could be a sign of macho behavior or it could be a sign of the greater vulnerability of delinquents and their fear of being harmed.

Finally, we asked, "Do you think having a pet is important for a child growing up?" Seventy-eight percent of delinquents and 61 percent of nondelinquents thought having a pet was very important for a child growing up. When we asked youths to explain their answer, three key themes emerged.

The first was that pets are good companions and fun to be around. The second was that having a pet teaches responsibility and how to care for animals. Third, a pet can provide someone to love and be loved by. It was also mentioned that pets teach the meaning of love. When we analyzed our data within these themes, we found that delinquents were much more likely than nondelinquents to emphasize the emotional role of a love object that pets play. Of the delinquent population, 47 percent indicated a pet was important to the growing child because it provided someone to love, 28 percent said it was important because a pet was a good friend, and 25 percent said having a pet was important because it teaches responsiblity. Among hospitalized youths, 61 percent said that having a pet provided something to love, 29 percent said it provided a good friend, and 10 percent said it taught responsibility. Among public school students, 44 percent said that having a pet was important because it taught responsibility, 29 percent said it provided someone to love, and 27 percent said it provided a good friend. These answers are another indication that pets have a special importance to delinquent and disturbed children.

Our data also indicate that delinquents and emotionally disturbed hospital patients are much less likely than students in regular schools still to have their special pet. We do not intend to suggest a causal link between loss of a pet and delinquency, but it is notable that delinquents and hospitalized youths lost their pets frequently and often in violent circumstances. Only 31 percent of the two delinquent populations still had their special pet. Of hospitalized population 29 percent still had their special pet, and of the public school population 49 percent still had their special pet.

The most striking difference between the delinquent and nondelinquent populations was in the number of delinquent youths whose special pet was killed accidentally or on purpose. The two populations of delinquents combined had lost their pet by killing in 34 percent of cases, which is nearly three times the rate for youths in regular schools. The overall rate of losing a pet by killing accidentally or on purpose for public school students was 12 percent. This wide discrepancy could be reflective of the violence and chaos typical of many delinquent families or it could be an indication of a general lack of care for pets and children. Nonetheless, our respondents indicated that they were deeply troubled by their pets' death and were likely to feel anger about it rather than sadness, which is more typical of how kids feel when their pets die of natural processes such as old age and disease. Here are a few reactions to the purposeful killing of pets:

> He was eleven years old and my mother had my little brother and Duke started being grouchy and nipping at people. So my brother-in-law shot him. It really hurt bad, like one of my brothers died, it was really hard to accept. [fifteen-year-old male delinquent]
>
> A cop came up over the curb and ran him over—I hate cops. [sixteen-year-old male delinquent]
>
> My sister was taking it for a walk and this man drove over it, then backed over it and then drove over it again. I was hurt very bad. I hated that man. I cried for two days straight. [fourteen-year-old male delinquent]

Among kids whose pets were killed accidentally rather than purposely, there was generally more sadness than anger.

> It was hit by a car. It made me sad because when he died, I didn't have no one to keep me company anymore. [fourteen-year-old urban female]
>
> Someone came to the house, rang the doorbell, opened the door and the dog ran into the street and got crushed under the back wheels of a school bus. It devastated me more than the death of a person. [seventeen-year-old female delinquent]

It is unclear how much the anger and sadness over their pets' deaths affected their emotional and social development. This is an important topic for research. There are, however, indications that some youth harbor unresolved grief over the death of their pets.

> I was crying for a long time hoping that Shaba would come back. Mom said she would buy another, well I didn't want another. I wanted Shaba. [sixteen-year-old female delinquent]
>
> We had to leave town so we left him with a close friend and later I was told he got hit by a car. Well, I hadn't seen him in a year. After I found out what happened, I was angry because I hadn't found out sooner. And angry at my mom for not letting us keep him and I was and still am very hurt. He was my best friend. [sixteen-year-old female delinquent]
>
> I was talking to our milkman and he was laying under the truck. When the milkman left he ran over Jay Boy, my dog. Right when I saw him get run over I felt I lost a part of my life, ya know. I bummed out royal, man. I cried. I felt it was my fault, ya know. It felt like my brother died. [eighteen-year-old male delinquent]

Several felt vengeful toward the person who killed their pet, such as the boy who said, "I was sad and angry. I said if I ever found out who shot her, I would kill them for sure" [eighteen-year-old hospitalized male].

Suburban and urban youth were more likely than delinquents to lose their pets by the natural processes of old age and disease. Suburban and urban youth also had their pets for longer times than delinquents. The average length of time suburban youth had their special pet was eight years, urban youth seven years, and both delinquent populations three years. Regular school students thus have more opportunities to learn of the natural processes of life and death in less traumatic ways than do delinquents. There was little difference in response from one group to another, however, when a pet died of disease or old age; sadness, depression, or feeling bad were the most common responses

> I was sad that he had to be put to sleep, but I was glad that he didn't die painfully. [fifteen-year-old urban female]
>
> I felt hurt, but she was old and suffered much from arthritis. She went to dog heaven. [sixteen-year-old female delinquent]
>
> My sorrows are very deep for my special pet, but I know she is in someplace where she is treated very well. And I know she is thinking of me because I always think of her. [fifteen-year-old male delinquent]

Only two youths said their pets' deaths did not mean much to them.

Dr. Michael Fox has suggested that the death of a pet can be an opportunity for families to grieve together and a means of bringing family members closer together. Delinquents, however, were much less likely than nondelinquents to talk about their pet's death with parents, siblings, or friends. When pets were killed accidentally or on purpose, 56 percent of delinquents had someone to talk to, whereas 79 percent of students in regular schools had someone to talk to. When pets died of old age and disease, delinquents had someone to talk to in 54 percent of cases, those from public schools in 86 percent of cases. Delinquents clearly have less opportunities to resolve emotional crises or difficulties effectively through talking them through with their family or friends. We were also concerned that there were a few youths who said talking about their grief was useless because it would not bring their pet back, which, of course, is not the purpose of talking of one's grief. There were also signs that youths were offered replacements as a means to assuage grief. Both of these areas would benefit by further research.

CONCLUSION

It is our belief, based on the data presented in this study, that pet animals can be very important to many youths, and that they can play a special role in the lives of disturbed and delinquent youth, for whom pets frequently become a substitute for other human relationships. The pet meets their need for unconditional acceptance and someone to be around who does not make demands or criticize. That a pet would fill this need, of course, gives a sense of the great unmet emotional needs of disturbed and delinquent youth.

We believe that these findings indicate the need for further study of the use of pets to help adolescents resolve their emotional conflicts. So far, most programs that have used pets therapeutically have used the therapist's pet or another pet rather than the child's in the therapeutic relationship. Our data suggest that many youths have deep feelings for their own pets and often have unresolved feelings over the loss of their pets. Future therapeutic work with children could benefit by greater exploration of how children feel about their own pets and the role these pets play in their family lives.

It is also important that future research efforts try to differentiate the types of losses of pets and at what ages they occur. It is not the same emotional experience for a child to lose a pet by accidental or purposeful killing, disease, or old age or to have a pet given away. Moreover, the child's age when these losses occurred is important in how the child is affected by these events. There also needs to be a greater differentiation of the attachments children have for their pets. Our data show that for some youths, pets supplement family love while for others they replace it. There needs to be greater differentiation of the various forms of animal-human attachment if we are truly to understand this relationship.

Finally, we hope this study points out the need for further studies of the role pets play in the lives of children and how this human-animal relationship requires consideration in the formation of social policies and laws pertaining to pet ownership as an integral part of the living environment.

James S. Hutton

40

Animal Abuse as a Diagnostic Approach in Social Work: A Pilot Study

Many people would readily agree that the companion animal is "part" of the family unit. The upsurge of interest in recent years has seemingly concentrated on the beneficial and therapeutic aspects of the human–companion animal bond. A recent article by Dr. Alan Felthous (1980) explores some of the relationships between childhood cruelty to animals and assaultive behavior directed at humans. Most subjects in his "animal cruelty" group had histories compatible with a higher level of aggressiveness against people, along with a significantly higher incidence of paternal neglect and/or abuse than normals. Doreen Hutchinson (1980) cited cases in which the companion animal has not been therapeutic, and she comments pertinently on the family circumstances that contributed to this condition. Roger Mugford (1981) also implies in his work that families sometimes need professional help and guidance to overcome mutual problems with their companion animals.

This study was based on the assumption that the companion animal takes its place as an integral part of the dynamics of family life and could therefore act as a diagnostic indicator of multiple varieties of "abuse" within families.

METHOD

DESIGN

Free-ranging interviews were used to obtain primary data on subjects known to local RSPCA representatives during 1980. Starting with the names and addresses obtained from this primary source, I used a range of secondary sources to gather information about these families (including personal, family, and business networks as well as direct and indirect interviews). The design specifically reflected a desire to keep broadly within the perceived scope of established routines of information gathering within social services departments (that is, cheap, easy, relevant, and confidential). The geographical area covered was coincident with that serviced by one social service department area team. The two sets of data were then analyzed to see if subjects on the RSPCA list were known to local social services and probation officers and whether the descriptions given of the family were similar. Records were then scored for type of abuse identifiable within the family. Other data were noted because this was an exploratory study.

PROCEDURE

RSPCA representatives covering the geographical area of a local authority social services team were asked to give information relating to cases of animal abuse and neglect which had come to their notice during the year 1980. Index cards were supplied with headings for basic information; free-ranging interviews were then necessary, as were some trips to obtain the information to complete the cards; other investigations were also undertaken to establish basics (such as reference to the electoral register for names and addresses and, when necessary, establishing the identity of the individuals concerned, particularly when families had recently moved).

The second stage involved a complex investigation into each of the referrals to see if they were known to the local authority statutory services and if so, how and what was known. This information was obtained through a vast range of local contacts and information-gathering sources as well as via straightforward interviewing, a technique made easier because the author was born and raised in the community. The third stage was to check this information with whatever information was available by discussion with case workers and by referring to files within the probation and social services departments.

RESULTS

From a total of 43 original referrals, 20 were omitted from the study; 6 were not known to either probation or social services departments, 6 were not traceable by the methods employed, and 6 were duplications resulting from the same subjects being referred by more than one reference source. Of the twenty-three families with a history of animal abuse, 82.6 percent (19) were known to social services and 60.8 percent (14) were known to probation. Descriptions of the family in "general" terms appeared similar in 87 percent (20) of the cases seen by both probation and social services. Similarities between the description of family dynamics in social service reports and the referrals for animal abuse occurred in 69.6 percent (16) of cases.

Considering specific forms of abuse, 34.8 percent (8) involved children at risk; 43.4 percent (10) could be broadly classed as inadequate families; 21.7 percent (5) involved physical violence; 21.7 percent (5) concerned neglect; 30.4 percent (7) could not usefully be categorized. Of the cases reported to the RSPCA, 52.1 percent (12) involved dog(s); 21.7 percent (5) cat(s), and 26.1 percent (6) dog(s) and cat(s).

In the sample 91.3 percent (21) of cases had low incomes; 65.2 percent (15) were unemployed; 30.4 percent (7) were single parents; 69.6 percent (15) could have been described as "broken homes." When looking at housing we find only 8.7 percent (2) were owner-occupiers; 65.2 percent (15) were in adequate council or tied accommodation; and 26.1 percent (6) were in substandard housing. Moreover, 56.5 percent (13) of cases referred in this study had moved during the period under investigation.

DISCUSSION

Results from this study appear to suggest that referrals from the RSPCA involving animal abuse could also be families known to the probation and local authority social services departments. In such cases, descriptions given of the family tend to be similar both at a general level and more specifically in the "types" of abuse manifested within the family. This evidence suggests that animal abuse may be symptomatic of similar dynamics within the larger family group.

Any significance of the high mobility of the sample (56.5 percent of referrals) would need a much closer examination than is possible here. It may simply be a quirk of this particular group, or it could indicate that stresses within a family which may result in abuse are increased at times of instability such as are created when a family moves from one home to another.

The analysis of socioeconomic factors indicates the importance of viewing a family not simply as a collection of individuals being subjected only to the dynamics and pressures within that group, but also as an integral part of society, being subjectd to all the sociological pressures of a "total" environment.

As an initial exploration, the study was intended to generate hypotheses for further research. In any further studies it could be useful to: concentrate on specific categories of abuse such as cases involving violence. "Abuse" was never properly defined in this study and included violence, sexual abuse, neglect, and other miscellaneous categories. Larger samples should be taken from different catchment areas. Information from social services and probation should be used without the lengthy process of prior examination of community sources so more time and effort could be concentrated on those who are not known (but perhaps ought to have been known) to the agencies. The perspective of family dynamics should be studied, followed by identification of the role(s) of the companion animal in relation to other participants in the family group.

CONCLUSIONS

This pilot study has been encouraging in that the results tentatively indicate that information obtained from the RSPCA relating to animal abuse could act as an external reflection of similar phenomena within the "family" group. If the results are sound, the study of companion animals in the family might prove to be a useful addition to the diagnostic tools of the so-called "caring" professions such as social work.

My sincere thanks and gratitude to Alisdair Macdonald and Andrew Yoxall for their encouragement and guidance in my first attempt at serious study in this field. Gratitude must also be expressed to the RSPCA, probation, social services, and all the individuals who contributed so willingly to the study. Last, a word of thanks to Peter Messent and Pedigree Petfoods whose unobtrusive support were invaluable.

Natalie Bieber

41

The Integration of a Therapeutic Equestrian Program in the Academic Environment of Children with Physical and Multiple Disabilities

This chapter reports the details of a pilot program conducted in the Village School (Area Cooperative Educational Services), North Haven, Connecticut, during the five-week summer session in 1978. The subjects were the forty-two children, ages six to twenty-one, in the physically handicapped unit of the summer day school.

The intent of the overall program was to combine academic and recreational pursuits. I served as both riding therapist and classroom teacher. The curriculum encompassed cognitive, affective, and psychomotor domains. A horse and a pony were brought to the school once a week. All children were given the opportunity to ride, drive in the pony cart, and otherwise closely interact with the animals. On two other days, the horse was used within the classroom, as the catalyst and theme for academic activities structured and tailored to the individual needs and functional levels of the students, who worked in small groups.

Though riding time was of necessity short because of the ratio of riders to horses, the animal-child interaction elicited responses with positive implications for all but four of the children. Most children were stimulated physically, socially, and intellectually. Results included significant physical benefits, the beginnings of communication in a severely withdrawn, retarded girl, and lively question and answer sessions motivated by the desire to know more about horses.

The purpose of this report is to relate how a therapeutic equestrian program and the resulting interaction between children and horses were used to motivate activities within an academic environment. The intent was to use animal-facilitated therapy (AFT) as a viable option and auxilliary to existing educational programs, an approach that merits consideration by teachers, therapists, and other persons in the helping professions.

REVIEW OF LITERATURE

The horse as a therapeutic agent first appeared in writings in early mythology, beginning with Chiron, the centaur (half man, half horse), known as the first physician and teacher of Aesculapius. Aesculapius is said to have prescribed riding for people with wounds and diseases that would not heal. Medical writers such as Galen in antiquity and others in later times commented favorably about the benefits of riding. In the seventeenth century, Thomas Sydenham, in a treatise on gout, described daily riding to be especially beneficial. In 1735 Quellmatz described therapeutic uses for the horse, and in 1777 Tissot recommended riding for the treatment of symptoms later associated with tuberculosis. In 1870 Chassaigne made a systematic study of the applications of riding to patients with neurological and other disabilities. The work of Mayberry (1978) in researching early medical references was furthered during the summer of 1979 when a seminar was held in Basel, Switzerland, to encourage a systematic search for early reports of horseback riding as medical treatment.

Though it was commonly acknowledged that "the outside of a horse was good for the inside of a man," it was not until 1952 that modern medical authorities began to acknowledge the value of horseback riding as physical therapy, primarily through the efforts of Liz Hartel, a Danish horsewoman. Ms. Hartel, an advanced rider, contracted poliomyelitis. The disease left her confined to a wheelchair with poor prognosis for riding or walking again. Determined to lead a full life, she returned to riding for recreation and as a means to exercise her weakened muscles. In 1952 her equestrial skill enabled her to win the Silver Medal in dressage at the Olympic Games in Helsinki, Finland (Davies, 1967).

Scandinavian physicians and therapists took note of the rehabilitation potential reflected in Liz Hartel's accomplishment, and the novel treatment was tried with other physically handicapped people with positive results (Bodtker, 1974). A letter from Dr. P. E. Paulsen, a neurologist, to Bodtker in 1974 stated: "In my experience based on the study of many patients, riding lessons given by an all-round trained instructor can activate latent mental and physical potential in patients for whom other treatment has not had the same effect" (1974:2).

Hartel's influence was also felt in England, where equestrian interests and pursuits were commonplace. In 1953 Norah Jacques began a therapeutic riding program for spastic children. Through the continued efforts of Jacques and John Davies, who became the foremost practitioner (McCowan, 1972), the first facility for therapeutic equestrian programs became a reality with the establishment of the Riding for the Disabled Trust at Chigwell in 1964 (Davies, 1967). This work spurred the organization of programs throughout the United Kingdom and brought professionalism and standardization to the concept.

In 1967 Davies published the first manual on riding therapy, *The Reins of Life*. His book, written for riding instructors, included information about the beginning and advanced handicapped rider as well as discussion of exercises and games. More important, it stressed that "the value [of riding] is not limited to the physical, which is great enough, but it is equally of value mentally and psychologically" (p. 11).

In North America impetus was supplied by Joseph Bauer in Canada in 1965, Maudie Hunter-Warfel in Pennsylvania in 1967, and Mary Woolverton in Colorado in 1967. My first exposure to therapeutic riding possibilities was through Woolverton, a medical social worker and horsewoman, who organized a program for her clients, mainly amputees returned from Vietnam. These pioneer programs were followed by independent programs conducted by dedicated, enthusiastic horse people and clinicians who volunteered their time and animals.

The founding of the North American Riding for the Handicapped Association (NARHA) in 1969 enabled groups across the continent to have a central body to coordinate efforts and serve as an information center. Then in 1970, with the opening of the Cheff Center at Augusta, Michigan, built and staffed specifically for the purpose of teaching handicapped riders and training practitioners, therapeutic riding became an advertised means for treating or behaviorally managing the physical and mental disabilities of children and adults. Lida McCowan, executive director of the Cheff Center, wrote the manual most widely referred to and circulated at present. *It's Ability That Counts* (1972) offers a good basic overview of the subject and many helpful suggestions for program establishment but contains no objective evidence.

Therapeutic horseback riding does not have a reservoir of research data to justify claims for its efficacy. Clinical observation, anecdotes, and empirical reasoning must, therefore, sustain a rationale for the positive physical and psychological elements ascribed to it. Steps to rectify this situation were taken in September 1979 at the Third International Conference on Riding for the Disabled, which was held at the University of Warwick, Coventry, England. Medically oriented and documented lectures were included in the sessions, which covered a wide range of information on riding therapy. Presently the NARHA is encouraging documented research.

Though literature pertaining to therapeutic equestrian programs is extensive, there are very few references to programs that integrate the general values of the experience into the academic environment of children. Green Chimneys School in Brewster, New York, has long had a residential program for youngsters with special education needs and uses horses and farm animals as an integral part of an educational and therapeutic process (Ross, 1977, 1979, 1980). Winter, in an article "The Influence of Riding on the Learning Disabled" (1975), mentioned a cooperative effort with a classroom teacher who referred the initial students to her program. She further comments that a classroom curriculum and elementary text were devised for use with this group. Clarke (1976) and Bieber (1976) both reported on projects that included integrating the riding experience into the school setting. A therapeutic equestrian program was first introduced to the Village School in 1976 by Cynthia Clarke, then a humane education specialist and coordinator of the Self Improvement through Riding Education (SIRE) for the Humane Society of the United States. The initial program was for a group of students from the ED/LD unit.

SETTING AND SUBJECTS

The Village School is a special education facility that is a part of the Area Cooperative Educational Services (ACES). The school draws its students from many towns and cities near North Haven, Connecticut. The population is made up of children whose special education needs preclude mainstreaming or even attending special classes at their local schools. Many live in regional residential facilities. The school has three main units: PH for the physically handicapped and multiply handicapped, ED/LD for the emotionally disturbed and learning disabled, and DD for those with severe communication disorders or autistic. The students share the building but have few activities together. Depending upon the unique requirements of each group, the school provides academic, therapeutic, and prevocational services.

During the fall of 1976, Clarke, Ann Wright, and I provided therapeutic riding experiences to a sample group of the younger children in the PH unit. The program was unique in that the horses were brought to the school to avoid the logistical problems of transporting disabled children and their wheelchairs to a riding stable. Instead of a regulation riding arena, the animals worked in the playground of a suburban school.

Specially selected horses are the core of every therapeutic riding program. The setting of the Village School program made the choice of horses especially critical. Not only would the animals have to adapt to a large number of riders on and around them in an unfamiliar location, but they would have to ignore the siren and fire engines that might issue from the firehouse nearby. The animals used—Shadow, a Morgan/quarter horse mare, and Leprachaun, a minature Shetland pony gelding—proved to be perfect choices. The horse, a black mare, was fifteen hands, sturdily built so that she could carry two riders (rider plus backrider) if needed, and very smoot-gaited. The pony, a palomino, thirty-two inches at the withers, was small enough to be groomed and handled from a wheelchair, an important consideration, but strong enough to pull a cart with as many as three passengers. The animals were well socialized with one another, other animals, and humans. Both were noteworthy for the aesthetics of their appearance—satin coats and long, luxurious manes—and their impeccable manners. During 1976 and 1977 both animals visited the school approximately twelve times. They were a novel but familiar sight on the playground.

Tack for the program included a standard deep-seat English saddle fitted with safety stirrups and a hand-hold, snaffle bridle with plaited reins, and a bareback pad and neck strap for use when the rider needed a backrider.

The pony was harnessed to a low two-wheeled cart designed to be easily accessible as well as very stable. The many buckles on the harness, saddle, and bridle offered a concrete challenge to fine motor skills.

The subjects involved in the summer school program were 42 children ages 6 to 21 in the physically handicapped unit. Most were multiply handicapped. Of these children, 28 were cerebral palsied, 6 had spina bifida, 1 had muscular dystrophy, and the rest suffered from the effects of strokes or traumatic accidents. Their range of IQ was broad, including those from the severely retarded to above average range of cognitive potential. Most of the children in this group were representative of the many motorically impaired children whose options for recreation are very limited and who spend a major part of their leisure hours in front of a TV set. Television becomes their window on the world, as well as the place where physically attractive people do exciting things. Many of these beautiful people are portrayed in conjunction with horses, either as cowboys or in ways that indicate social status.

It is not uncommon for "normal" children to fantasize and play horse games as they grow up, especially when they are exposed to the real animals. Physically disabled children do not have the mobility to play "cowboys and Indians," but my experiences demonstrated that they shared the interest in doing so. I believed that the therapeutic riding experience would cause many of the children at the Village School to view themselves as members of the select group known as "horse people" and stimulate attention to activities with a horse theme. I assumed that the children would "turn on" to horses in activities appropriate for them.

PROCEDURES

In June 1978, the decision was made to augment the usual summer program at the Village School with an integrated therapeutic equestrian program. Though the focus was recreational rather than strictly academic, I was requested to include unmounted as well as mounted activities. Furthermore, it was suggested that these activities, when possible, should reflect the abilities measured by the subjects on the Illinois Test of Psycholinguistic Abilities (Kirk, 1968). The ITPA measures the ability to receive and understand what is seen and heard; to make associations and understand interrelationships of what is seen and heard; to express oneself by verbal and motor responses; to grasp automatically the whole of a visual or verbal pattern when only part of it is presented; and to remember and repeat visual and auditory sequences of material.

The mounted sessions, held on Fridays when the animals were brought by trailer to the school, provided a short period of time both in the saddle and pony cart for approximately half of the children on an alternating basis. The children participated in the grooming, saddling, and feeding process as well as riding. Six children rode every week; they had been specially designated by the physical therapist because of their physical needs. The limited saddle time and short duration of the program, only five weeks, obviated any realistic expectation of physical change in the children. The program was perceived to be an enriching experience that besides being fun, would serve to motivate in-class sessions. The riding was to be a tool, the horse the "catalyst," and the emphasis basic preacademic and academic skills structured similarly to the ITPA. Format for the mounted sessions followed that described earlier. Some of the students rode independently, some needed a backrider, leader, and side-walkers. All were encouraged to be active participants while riding, as well as to listen to the sounds of the horses' feet on the grassy areas or the concrete areas. The shod hooves of the horse and the unshod ones of the pony were used for many auditory discrimination exercises.

For the unmounted sessions, the students were divided into eight groups based on age and level of cognitive potential. This grouping was done to ensure that activities would be interesting and appropriate as well as individualized. As in the mounted sessions, the number of children served and the length of the school day (five hours) placed strict time constraints on the time allotted to "horsing around." Only three hours per week per child were scheduled and possible during the two days a week I served as the classroom teacher.

As described by Piaget and accepted by educators, all learning proceeds from the concrete to the abstract levels. Thus interaction with the live horse and pony and the opportunity to examine them through the visual, auditory, tactile, kinesthetic and olfactory modalities were promoted to provide a reservoir of concrete information from which the children could draw. Accordingly, lesson plans for the unmounted sessions were designed to incorporate not only the equine theme but also elements of the actual human-animal experience, at a receptive and expressive level appropriate for each group of students.

The following is a list of some of the activities that were provided for various groups of children in class.

1. Obstacle course built in classroom to simulate outdoors. Children not only had to respond to directions for sequence of motion but also had to simulate horse's walk, trot, whoa, and backing movements.
2. Strip down a bridle and saddle and reassemble them. This task required not only fine motor skill but also visual memory. When physical limitations

precluded the mechanical process, I became the hands of the group and followed their directions.

3. Tracing outlines of pictures and a horseshoe. This is a visual-motor exercise.
4. Visual discrimination
    a. Colors of horses, markings on horses.
    b. Differentiate between types of bits.
    c. Breed characteristics—requires sophisticated skills.
    d. Find hidden object in picture.
    e. Bingo game with parts of tack and items associated with horses.
    f. Fill in parts when presented with incomplete diagram of a horse. I did the actual drawing as prompted.
5. Speech and communication
    a. Vocabulary to activate horse. This was practiced mounted and unmounted. The children were told that the animals would not respond properly under saddle unless they were given the correct verbal signals. As the person leading the horse had control at all times, this could be used very affectively and effectively to encourage speech in nonverbal or low-verbal students.
    b. Articulation of bilabial sounds. (b)—brush, bucket, bounce, (trot), back, brown, black; (w)—walk, whoa.
    c. Language cards with pictures of horses or other animals. These encourage recognition of words and serve as a stimuli to language production and signing for nonverbal or low-verbal persons.
    d. Choose subject and allow for discussion period.
6. Reading
    a. Stories with horse themes have been written for readers of all ages and abilities. Many are found in traditional basal or linguistic reading programs.
    b. Phonics games. Find little words in bigger words, names of horses, flash cards.
7. Math
    a. Word problems based on parts of horse.
    b. Compute size of horse as measured by hands (4"). Students were given an opportunity to measure the real horse.
    c. Classification and sorting using grooming tools.
    d. Compute amount of feed based on approximate weight of the horse. Work up whole nutritional program.
8. Social studies and history
    a. Study evolution of the horse, prehistoric to modern.
    b. Study migration of horses across the United States. This was included with a unit about Indians.
    c. How horses compare to people—sizes, uses, colors, body language, anatomy, and reproduction.
9. Laterality and directionality. Used plastic models of horses and riders which

could be positioned and manipulated following instructions. These were also used as an aid in teaching body parts.

The common denominator for all of these materials was subject matter; the applications were varied.

DISCUSSION

The program at the Village School had two distinct but not mutually exclusive purposes: first, to provide an enriching experience for physically and multiply disabled students, and second, to demonstrate that even with limited direct interaction with horses, multiply handicapped children would be motivated to attend to academic activities with a horse theme. It was hypothesized that horses would act as the "catalyst" in the classroom and would both facilitate and enhance cognitive, affective, and motor processes. No attempt was made to measure any qualitative or quantitative gains or to provide a statistical evaluation of the procedures. The overall evaluation of the summer was based on subjective appraisal by the clinical and teaching staff at the Village School plus feedback from the students and their parents. If this seems to be a very weak premise for a research project, it should be understood that it was viewed in the context of research only several months after the summer ended.

The clinical and teaching staff at the Village School were enthusiastic about the horse program from the time of its conception. Orientation and work with the horses at the school preceded the initial session. The physical therapist's and several teachers' previous riding experience was highly advantageous. The situation was further enhanced when the occupational therapist, two teachers, and an aide took lessons. This knowledge and participation assured a rapport and enthusiastic, cooperative effort beyond normal expectation. A contagious "horse fever" seemed to afflict most of the adults connected with the program.

Occasional special horse days were held at the Village School before the summer of 1978. During the spring of 1978, I became a frequent substitute teacher for both the younger and older groups of children in the physically handicapped unit. Thus I was able to gain practical, firsthand knowledge of the traditional aspects of the students' academic environment. The children adjusted well to my change in role from riding therapist to special education teacher. I worked with them in reading, math, language arts, and content course subjects. This experience made possible valuable insights into the individual educational plan (IEP) mandated by Public Law 94-142, Education of the Handicapped Act, for each of the children. The summer program as an integrated element of the academic environment would not have been possible without prior exposure to the strategies and methods already in use.

One final element influenced the follow-up as well as the actual pilot program: Shadow and Leprachaun were my personal pets as well as my co-therapists. My deep affection for them was very obvious to the children and staff at the Village School. The riding therapy program was triadic in concept and involved the horses, especially Shadow, the child who was riding, and myself. The trust I had in the mare and the bond between us dissuaded fearful reactions by the children. Within a short time, several children came to share this special bond. There was almost a Shadow Fan Club. On one occasion Shadow and Leprachaun were invited into the school building and did indeed go inside. As Bodtker stated: "The horse, this living, moving, intelligent and sensitive animal, provides a unique source of encouragement. Patient and pony/horse must be given a chance to get to know each other, trust each other, and preferably become real friends. The pony/horse likes to be responsible for its young rider if it is given time and peace to develop this feeling. In this way contact will be good, both mentally and physically" (1974:4).

There never was any intention of using the ITPA to evaluate changes in the receptive and expressive language of the students. The psycholinguistic model was the suggested framework for lessons and activities and not included for purposes of diagnosis or assessment. It was extremely useful as a means of coordinating the many components of the program, which was holistic in concept.

The holistic model (Clarke, 1976; Wright-Wolcott, 1976; Ross, 1978) seems to be the one with the greatest potential for maximizing the effects of the horse-human interaction. When the carry-over from the mounted experience is extended into the classroom, there is more motivation for academics even when riding teacher and classroom teacher are not the same person (Green, 1976, 1977, 1978). Appropriate material for classroom use is available, though not neatly packaged as having an equine theme. Creativity and the teacher's ability to adapt existing resources are desirable attributes.

RESULTS

Several goals were intrinsic to the Village School summer program whether they were formally stated or not. Similar goals (Link, 1979) were included at Green Chimneys for the horse component of its farm program, although the difference in populations, ED/LD children rather than multiply handicapped, changed the expectations. For instance, it was not realistic to expect mastery of control or riding proficiency when mounted time was so limited, but it was realistic to expect the students to gain self-confidence and self-esteem after riding. The riding sessions were tailored to include a built-in success factor. No child was asked to perform at a level that would spell failure, and it was possible to get the horse to respond to cues given surreptitiously, so that the rider believed he/she was responsible for certain actions when in truth the person leading the horse was.

The results of the program are most easily explained in the context of appropriate goals for an integrated therapeutic equestrian program such as the one here described. These goals include the following: Students will gain self-confidence and self-esteem by assuming control of a horse with proper supervision. Students will enjoy a recreational activity with appropriate behavior. Students will receive the benefits of the exercise and therapy of a challenging outdoor sport. Students' curiosity and awareness of environment will be stimulated through the riding experience and exposure to horses (Link, 1979). Students will experience growth in the development of receptive and expressive language. Students will experience opportunities that will enhance social and emotional adjustment and growth (Link, 1979).

Of the forty-two students participating in the program, all but four reacted positively to a least four of the listed goals. There were no strongly negative reactions. None of the children acted out or exhibited problem behaviors when with me or the horses. For a few children the horse activities seemed to provide little or no enrichment or pleasure. "R," an eighteen-year-old spina bifida girl, showed little enthusiasm for any activities. She was neither more nor less enthusiastic about the horse than about other things. She did, however, love the bingo game. "P" was a seventeen-year-old neurologically impaired boy with autistic mannerisms and predilection for electronic gadgets. Animals did not break through his shell of ritualistic and bizarre behaviors. "B" was a seventeen-year-old boy with a partial metal plate in his skull because of injury. Risk factor contraindicated riding, so he had very limited contact with the animals. "L," a twelve-year-old spina bifida girl, had severe emotional problems, and the animals and I simply could not reach her.

It is difficult to measure the affective influence the horses had on the children or their social and emotional development. Examples of particular reactions will have to suffice.

"C," a nine-year-old spina bifida girl, very small for her age, was terrified of animals. Attempts had been made before June 1978 to get her to accept being near a small dog with negative results. After watching her classmates ride, she rode in the pony cart, brushed the pony, and by the final week of the session happily rode the horse. She proudly spoke of her accomplishment and no longer became hysterical when a dog came near her.

"T" was a fourteen-year-old severe athetoid cerebral palsy boy, quadriplegic, nonverbal, with probable normal intelligence. This child was a prisoner of his body, with no mental or sensory impairment, who was terribly frustrated and unhappy because of his limited options in life. He resided in a ward at the regional center and required complete custodial care. On the horse (with the physical therapist as backrider) his uncontrollable movements subsided, and he was able to gaze down around him rather than always having to look up as when in his wheelchair. He was able to achieve a degree of head and trunk control not possible elsewhere and a personal dignity not demonstrated at other times. More important, he smiled, chuckled, and laughed, which he very rarely did in other settings. During a trip to the store with his classmates, "T" spent his time looking at posters and selected one with a horse for himself. The poster was then hung over his bed at the center.

"M" was a fourteen-year-old, cerebral palsy girl with autistic mannerisms, possible hearing impairment, nonverbal, and very rudimentary signed communication. I had worked with "M" before the summer and had frequently participated in language arts sessions with her and the speech clinician. She displayed no emotion during the time she rode on the horse and in the pony cart. Though she could be volatile and bizarre, she was always passive and flat. After the third week, however, she responded to a language card with a picture of a pony, dog, and cow by pointing appropriately to the pony when asked. This was the first indication that she functioned at a high enough level to use a language board and caused the speech clinician to change her evaluation of "M"'s potential for learning.

"J" was a seventeen-year-old spastic quadriplegic with cerebral palsy and severe contractures. This young man was an adolescent poet who was very aware of his physical appearance and limited options for socialization beyond the school. On the horse, with a backrider, spasticity was reduced and range of movement increased. He was able to exercise a remarkable degree of control over the horse, who seemed unusually sensitive to his reining. After being on the horse for fifteen minutes, he was able to maintain an independent seat for five minutes without backrider support. "J" and two other students with similar physical levels were the ones most interested in reading and hearing about horses. Their questions were challenging, interesting, and insightful. They were very interested in horse reproductive patterns and sex life, subjects that reflected their sheltered environments. They were also very intrigued by the body language of horses, relating it to humans and to many of the nonverbal children in the school.

"D" was a sixteen-year-old retarded, ataxic cerebral palsy boy, nonverbal, with simple signed language. "D" took great delight in greeting me by my signed name, which had elements of the signs for horse and woman combined. He was always very excited when it was his turn to ride or groom the horse; appropriate behavior required great control for him. He was very attentive to instruction when mounted, and the horse gave him a stability physically and emotionally that he was unable to achieve when on the ground. He responded very well to stimulus pictures that included horses; the number of words and ideas he communicated increased.

The cases cited are representative of the quantitative and qualitative changes that were observed by the teaching and clinical staff of the Village School. When the fall academic term began, several teachers continued to draw on the experiences of the summer for their lesson plans. Two field trips were scheduled to enable the students to ride and visit the barn where Shadow and Leprachaun lived. My schedule and commitments at the college precluded my involvement with an ongoing riding program. Another impediment arose because residents of the area near the school reacted adversely to the horses being brought to the school on a regular basis. Neither the horse nor pony ever committed the indiscretion of dropping manure on the playground, though the necessary items for clean-up were part of my equipment.

In January of 1979, Shadow died. My friends on the staff at the Village School sadly reported this event to the children who had ridden her and known her. When I visited there in February, I was inundated with condolences. Perhaps the one that meant the most to me was from "D." He ran over to me excitedly signing my name, then put one arm around me and signed *horse* and *sad*. It is hard to evaluate the impact the riding program had on this severely retarded young man, but he was able to understand the concept of love because of his experience.

Although the results of the integrated summer school program were encouraging, they should not be interpreted as meaning that a therapeutic equestrian program is a necessary adjunct for every program for physically and multiply disabled children. The total integration that was possible at the Village School was the result of unique circumstances, not the least of which was my professional capacity to function as both riding therapist and special education teacher. The freedom I was given in developing the horse component of the summer session was enhanced by the enthusiasm and support of the clinical and teaching staff as a whole. All of this served strongly to reinforce positive attitudes and responses on the part of the students.

The observations and conclusions that emerged from the Village School pilot program strengthen the argument that riding therapy should be viewed as a tool and as an alternative strategy that merits consideration for use in established special education programs. Furthermore, this consideration should extend beyond the obvious recreational and physiotherapeutic components to the motivational, affective, and cognitive domains. The potential for using the horse as a "catalyst" for various academic activities is great; the horse can be a springboard for learning.

Betsy A. Smith

42

Project Inreach:
A Program to Explore
the Ability of Atlantic Bottlenose
Dolphins to Elicit
Communication Responses
from Autistic Children

In the early 1970s, the World Dolphin Foundation established a program called The Dolphin Project at Mashta Island on Key Biscayne. This location provided a one-and-one-half-acre lagoon as a free-swimming environment for a succession of bottlenose dolphins.

In 1972, Dr. Henry Truby, president and director of scientific research of the World Dolphin Foundation, observed that neurologically impaired children appeared to demonstrate exceptional responses to close contact with free-swimming dolphins. During this same year, I noted unique responses from the interaction between a project dolphin, Liberty, and a retarded adult, David. The usually aggressive, unruly adolescent dolphin became exceptionally gentle, patient, and attentive when David entered the water and initiated contact. David, who was usually very cautious near the water and slow to adapt to new stimuli, immediately entered the water, began talking with Liberty, stroking him, and engaging in water play with him.

A series of meetings between Dr. Truby, me, and Nancy Phillips, a consultant to the South Florida Society for Autistic Children, led to the development of Project Inreach in December 1978.

The working hypotheses for this project were, first, the possibility that specialized dolphins and children labeled autistic can elicit unprecedented communicatory demonstrations; second, the possible therapeutic benefit for children, parents, and human service workers; and third, generation of additional study material for serious interspecies programs.

METHODS AND PROCEDURES

The program was made possible by the cooperation of Warren Zeiller, director of the Wometco Miami Seaquarium on Key Biscayne. This facility provided the dolphins, the physical environment, and several of its dolphin-training personnel.

PARTICIPANTS

The three Atlantic bottlenose dolphins (*Tursiops truncatus*, Montagu), Dawn, Holly and Sharkey, are entertainers at the Wometco Seaquarium on Key Biscayne. Dawn has an exceptionally patient and gentle personality. Holly was pregnant during the initial sessions, bore, and then lost her baby dolphin. This event did not appear to interfere with her interactions. Sharkey, the male of the trio, is very gregarious and has an exceptionally energetic disposition.

The South Florida Society for Autistic Children enthusiastically responded to our request for human participants. The investigators (Truby, Smith, and Phillips) established a simple criterion for participation—the parents must understand the purposes of the project and agree that they and their children would have a commitment to the project's goals. The children were to be old enough to have "language" but not demonstrate "speech" as such in their expressive vocabulary. The children should not be frightened by the water or animals.

After an initial session and the withdrawal of some of the parents from the project, a total of eight children between the ages of ten and seventeen and their parents were selected to participate.

The investigating staff consisted of three primary investigators, a parent coordinator, a video crew, dolphin trainers, and students.

PHYSICAL ENVIRONMENT

The basic environment consisted of two connected tanks located in a remote section of the seaquarium grounds. The large tank, some twenty by thirty feet and ten feet deep, is convenient for hand-feeding, touching, and similar human proximity to and contact with dolphins. Connected by run and sluice to the large tank is a circular tank some ten feet in diameter and ten feet deep. The sides of the large tank are rounded on top and smooth to allow humans to reach in painlessly and the dolphins' ready partial emergence.

DATA COLLECTION

Six encounter sessions were held between December 1978 and August 1979. Each session was held on a Sunday or holiday and lasted from four to six hours. The time between sessions varied from one week to one month.

All sessions were tape-recorded and video-recorded by one stationary camera and one hand-held camera. Still photographs were taken as well. The student staffers were constantly moving observers looking for interaction between human and dolphin participants and human-to-human interaction. They would then cue the cameras and microphones to the appropriate activities. The primary investigators moved along the water play activities and were alert for any variance in sound patterns from the children. The parent coordinator was responsible for observing parent reactions and also for the gradual withdrawal of the parents from tank side to an observation deck.

Events of Session One   (Parents involved in all activities.)
1. Casual introduction to the Seaquarium grounds, personnel, other animals, and the tank area.
2. Administration of a questionnaire to parents to obtain basic medical information.
3. Recording of sounds from each dolphin before the arrival of the children.
4. Isolated sound recordings of each child.
5. Video recordings of parents and children in unstructured interaction with each other, the staff, and the physical environment to catalog initial sounds and body language.
6. Initial introduction of the children to the three dolphins.

Events of Session Two   (Parents involved in all activities.)
1. Continued videotaping and tape-recording collection of voice and body movements.
2. The beginning of "water play" with the dolphins, including continuous pouring of buckets of water on the dolphins; splashing by the dolphins and participants; and dolphins sliding over the top of the tank to allow physical contact to occur between parents, children, and dolphins.

Events of Session Three   (Parents involved in all activities.)
1. Continued collection of voice and body movements through videotaping and tape-recording.
2. Continuation of water play activities.
3. Introduction of ball tossing between parents, children, and dolphins.

Dolphins persistently threw balls at the children until several children responded to the parents' and the investigators' coaxing by throwing the ball back into the tank. Two children returned the ball directly to the dolphin, who tossed it back to them several times. Children touched the dolphin at parents' and investigators' coaxing more frequently.

Events of Session Four (By the middle of the session, parents voluntarily removed themselves from the activity area and assumed more of an observers' role.)
1. Continued videotaping and tape-recording of body movements and sounds.
2. Continued water play by children without staff stimulation.
3. Continued ball tossing by all children. Two of the children toss the ball with the three dolphins without any staff coaxing.
4. Constant touching of the three dolphins by all of the children, three children touching without any coaxing.

Events of Session Five
1. Continued collection of voice and body movements.
2. Continued spontaneous water play by children. A cooperative water play activity involving a bucket occurs between two children.
3. Spontaneous touching and ball tossing continue.
4. Actual entrance into the water of the large tank with dolphins in a small tank behind a gate. The entrance into the water was accomplished with great difficulty. A ladder had to be lifted into the tank, and two of the boys were coaxed down the ladder into the water with Dr. Truby. The entrance took three hours. Once in he water, the boys displayed imitative dolphin behavior. They spit water in dolphin fashion, splashed, and responded to the dolphins' clicking behind the gates.
Parents helped with the ladder and offered suggestions to solve the entrance problem, but, except for one parent's needed physical help, they remained in the role of helpful observers.

Events of Session Six
1. Before the arrival of the parents and children, the investigators decided that their discussion about the problems of continuing the program after the physical problems of Session Five could not be immediately solved. They examined several tanks and areas of open access and decided that the lack of a safe entrance and exit area would inhibit any further attempts at contact in the water. The investigators also ruled out sporadic use of alternately changing areas and dolphins.
2. Parents and investigators discussed the physical barriers to continuation of the project.
3. There was continued collection of voice and body movement through videotaping and tape-recording.
4. The children continued the water play.
5. The children continued ball tossing and touching.
This was the last session to date.

Future Sessions Plans are being formulated to allow a resumption of the project in a safer environment on a continuous basis with a small, stable group of participants.

Parent Feedback Sessions The co-investigator and the parent coordinator held two formal meetings to view the videotapes and a series of less formal discussion sessions with the parents.

They separated the sessions into two topic areas: verbal and nonverbal behavior changes in the children and behavioral or "feeling" changes in themselves as parents and the family as a unit.

All parents stated that the sessions were among the "happiest" times they had ever had as a family unit. Several parents expressed a feeling of release of family tensions for weeks after each session. Many reported a feeling of "closeness" and a sense of joy after each encounter.

All parents wanted to continue and were eager to get children into a swimming situation with the dolphins. All expressed a feeling of sadness that the sessions were being halted.

OBSERVATIONS AND CONCLUSIONS

COMMUNICATORY DEMONSTRATIONS

Spectographic Analysis Aside from the human eye and ear, the instrument used to examine the accumulated tapes is a spectograph. Spectograms are being made of all taped encounters of children and dolphins and the consequent human and animal signals.

Verbal and Nonverbal Demonstrations There are several possible alterations in verbal responses that may prove to be significant. In one case, however, there were unquestionable and sustained results.

Michael Williams is an eighteen-year-old who was given the diagnostic label of "a nonverbal autistic child" at the age of six. The label implies that the child does not normally reproduce human sounds.

At the second encounter session with the dolphins, Michael began to make a dolphin clicking sound to get the dolphin Sharkey's attention to participate in the ball-tossing play. Before this day, he had never approximated this signal, as was verified by his parents and his teacher. Michael continued to "click" with the dolphins at all sessions. On the tape, close attention is required to distinguish Michael's "click" from Sharkey's "click," although his "click" is easier to separate from Dawn's and Holly's clicks. To date, when Michael sees an advertisement billboard or a TV commercial with dolphins, he responds by "clicking" at the dolphin image. Six months after the project ended, Michael began furious dolphin clicking in a local drugstore. Mrs. Williams found him clicking at a rubber flotation device shaped and painted like a dolphin.

One year after the project was halted, Michael's class went to the Seaquarium on a field trip. Michael broke away from the group, went to the project areas, and stood outside the locked gate clicking to the dolphins inside. During the fall of 1981, NBC's *Amazing World of Animals* sent a film crew to record Michael's first encounter with the dolphin Sharkey in over a year and a half. Michael began to click as soon as he heard Sharkey's signals in the filming area. He sat on a platform, engaged in water play with Sharkey, and "clicked" with Sharkey for over three hours of a TV crew's demands for retakes. The last verified continuous verbal response from Michael was recorded just weeks ago. The Williamses have a book with a picture of a dolphin in the middle of the text. Since the beginning of the project, after Michael was shown the book once, he has continued, on random occasions, without outside stimulation, to take the book, turn page by page until reaching the picture, and then begin his dolphin clicks. He continues to "click" in response to dolphin images on billboards or TV commercials.

A most important development during the project was the consistent increase of sustained attention span during and after each dolphin-child encounter. The children who before the encounter had a reported attention span of five to ten minutes now had reported sustained attention spans of up to one hour. Michael's behavior can be used to illustrate this observable change. Richard Prager, at the time of the encounter session the teacher of both Michael and another participant child, reported to a *Miami News* reporter on September 3, 1979: "After the first couple of sessions, I noticed that Michael was happier. He was easier to work with, more relaxed, and more enthusiastic in class. Michael bites his finger or smacks his head. But he stopped doing them for a while after the sessions." Michael's attention span continues to be increased when stimulated by the dolphin, exemplified by the filming session. His parents also report an increase in attention span after he views tapes of the dolphins or dolphin advertisements. The best example, of course, is his activity with the book containing the dolphin picture.

Another important documented nonverbal interaction occurred at the fifth encounter session. Michael and another child each wanted to pour water on the dolphins. They each wanted the bucket. They each held a side, lifted it together, and, in a simultaneous and cooperative movement, poured the water into the tank. Neither child had been known to display interactive play activity before. This interaction has not recurred.

THERAPEUTIC BENEFITS

Parents, teachers, and investigators noted the beneficial effect of the encounter sessions on the children. All of them were observed to be more approachable, many were exceptionally calmer, and all seemed to those involved to be "happier." These observations were made for periods of as long as two weeks after each encounter. The parents all continuously express their own sense of joy at what they felt was truly an activity "shared" with the children. All of the parents believed that their lives had been enriched by the encounters and their after-effects.

The investigators experienced the feeling that they had made a positive intrusion into the children's silent world. I believe that the physical activity and constant touching experience by the investigating staff were therapeutic for them as well. Each session left the staff with an optimistic and open attitude for future encounters with these autistic children.

MATERIAL FOR FUTURE STUDY

I believe that in the case of Michael, unprecedented communicatory demonstrations were observed and that the therapeutic benefit for all those involved is well documented. The questions for future study raised by this program, however, are many and varied. Why does man appear to have a unique relationship with the dolphin? Why do dolphins appear to respond so intensely to handicapped people? Why has Michael responded so well yet all of the other similarly diagnosed children responded to an apparently much less significant degree? What triggered the cooperative bucket activity; was it the dolphins or some extraneous variable in the environment? Once it is possible to get the children and the dolphins in free-swimming sessions, will this tactile-aural situation create any major avenues for communicatory attempts by the dolphins or the children?

The author wishes to acknowledge the help of Nancy Phillips, M.S.W., project coordinator; Ms. Shirley Scheckman, B.S.W., parent and child coordinator; Ms. Beth Puckett, M.Ed., media coordinator; Robert Rosen, B.F.A., production assistant; and Helen Scarr, B.S.W. and Gary Van Arman, M.S.W., student participant observers.

Ange Condoret

43

Speech and Companion Animals: Experience with Normal and Disturbed Nursery School Children

Some of the results of this research project on the relationship between children and companion animals in a nursery school were reported previously. The research suggests that a relationship between a child and an animal partner can satisfy essential psychological needs, especially the need to communicate. Thus the presence of an animal partner resulted in modifications of behavior such as new patterns of affective behaviors in angry and violent children and an improved capacity for verbal expression.

METHOD

The experiment was done in the youngest class of a nursery school in Bordeaux, France. The children were between three and a half and five years of age. The animal used in the experiment was a four-year-old half-breed terrier named Polo who belonged to the headmistress. He was a perfectly socialized animal, well adapted to the school environment. He was familiar with the children and their behavior. We also used a cat who lived in the school. He was a submissive cat who let himself be petted and loved by the children without protest.

In the first part of the experiment the dog was introduced into the classroom in the middle of a group of five children who seemed to want to establish a dialogue with the animal rather than engage in active play. They were unlike the rest of the children who played noisily with the animal.

RESULTS

With the help of a speech therapist, the children were categorized in three groups: two children who had difficulties with pronunciation; two children whose language development was retarded; and one autistic child who, at the age of five and a half, had never spoken a single intelligible sound.

Among the first group, who found the pronunciation of some words difficult, the two four-year-old children had problems pronouncing the sound "ch." One of them, however, pronounced the word "le chien" while pointing to Polo during the second week of contact with the animal. The other one pronounced the word "le chat" a few days after the parents adopted a kitten.

Among the second group, there were two children with language retardation (hesitant blocked speech). In the two weeks following the introduction of the animal, they started to structure their sentences better.

Marion was the first to pronounce an excellent welcoming sentence addressed to Polo every morning upon arriving at school. It was a correct sentence with subject, verb, and object, such as, "Polo love me," or, "I love Polo."

ANALYSIS OF RESULTS

The display of emotion which is evoked by the presence of an animal can be considered as a facilitator of speech acquisition. The desire to communicate with animals appears to be one of the motives for acquiring language. There is, at this level, an ambiguity, even a paradox, which should be clarified: the animal, who does not speak, allows the child to speak. This phenomenon can make certain prolix educators or talkative parents wonder.

The child's will to express him/herself can be stimulated by the relationship with an animal. The emotional expression which is often displayed in talk addressed to an animal could also facilitate verbal expression. The path followed seems to be toward language through tenderness. This explanation of the children's change in language ability can be considered to be a working hypothesis for future research.

THE CASE OF BETHSABEE: THE ANIMAL AND THE AUTISTIC CHILD

Bethsabee, a three-and-a-half-year-old girl, was admitted to the youngest class twice a week after her mother won over the headmistress's objections. She was an autistic child, interested only in objects: paper, boxes, blocks. She refused all physical contact. She retreated from all of her classmates. She could not bear to be held by the hand and certainly not to be kissed or hugged. Unlike all of the other children, and in spite of all our urging, she did not show any attraction toward either the cat or the dog that were present in the classroom. Her expression was characterized by oblique and fleeting glances, which never settled on the teacher, the other children, or the animals. She confined her gaze to the objects she manipulated, which she usually carried at eye level with rigid extended arms. This behavior is typical for psychotic children. Her mouth and eyes were always distorted by her incessant grimaces. Sometimes she would utter unintelligible sounds, a clacking of the tongue, a kind of a hiss, and an interdental sound, "ta."

She continued to behave that way for a year, and in that time she paid no attention to any of the animals presented to her, until the day when, fortuitously, a dove, one of the resident animals in the classroom, took flight in front of her. The camera allowed us to record the following changes in her emotional state: for the first time she smiled, and her smile persisted for the duration of the flight (a few seconds); her gaze left the world of objects to follow the flight of the bird; she awkwardly mimicked the motions of flight with her hands; when the dove flew again, she blushed, looked fixedly at the animal, and uttered new sounds, "que-que," as if trying to talk to the bird. Her gaze, the way she was holding her head, and her gestures expressed for the first time a will to communicate with this living, flying being.

With each repeated flight the changes in her emotions and behavior could be observed. During the subsequent sessions she began to desire contact with the dove. First she stroked it, and finally she kissed it. We took the opportunity afforded by these gestures of approach and attempts at tactile contact to present her the dog that she formerly had ignored. After a few tries, she stroked the dog for the first time. Fairly soon, she followed him with her gaze, searched him out, and finally kissed him. The teacher who was in charge of Bethsabee during these experiments with animal intervention seemed to acquire a certain importance for the child. Bethsabee observed the teacher playing with the animal and attempted to reproduce the interaction. At the same time, other improvements were occurring. Bethsabee, who until then ate only porridge or liquids, started to chew on biscuits. She was able to spend a whole weekend with her teacher without insurmountable problems.

The teacher and the child began to weave a relationship in which the child began to show a definite interest in counting songs. Bethsabee's oral expressions, which were formerly onomatopeas, became more refined. She at last started to pronounce "Mommie." She began to make exploratory contacts with human beings. The hand of the teacher became an important object of exploration. A few months later, the child was able to participate in a "ring around the rosie" with the other children and permitted her friends to kiss her. We are continuing to follow her progress.

REFLECTIONS ON THE CASE OF BETHSABEE AND THE DOVE

The failure of Bethsabee to respond to the cat and the dog could have led us to conclude wrongly that animals were not useful in the treatment of this child. Her response to the dove was an unequivocal change in behavior. The flight of the dove permitted Bethsabee to direct her feelings externally with exclamations of joy and vivid facial expressions. The flight of the dove repeatedly provoked the same response from Bethsabee, drawing her out of her indifference, her lethargy, and her state of isolation. This change in behavior generalized rapidly to other animals: a dog and a cat. The generalized changes included attempts to contact the animals through play. These forms of emotional display, which Bethsabee never directed at human beings, were first addressed only to animals. It took her several more weeks before she would show affection to her teacher and some of her classmates.

QUESTIONS RAISED BY THE CASE OF BETHSABEE

Numerous questions are raised by this case. One is the specificity of the animal: why the bird and not another animal? Second, why the flight? How can one define and to what can one link the attractive power of this movement? What is the precise nature of the stimulus? Through what mechanism did the animal reach Bethsabee? Why and how did it motivate Bethsabee to stop isolating herself, to begin communication, and to direct her emotions toward other living beings? How can one explain the generalization of her response from the dove to other animals that were previously ignored and then to humans? How can one explain the appearance of the first word, "Mommie"?

In explaining the results of this research, we take a position similar to Otto Jesperson's, for whom emotion and expressivity constitute the basis of language, for example, the calls of birds, or the gruntings of animals, or the cries and the babblings of babies. True language, according to Jesperson, can be established only when the desire for communication becomes stronger than the desire for expressivity.

In Bethsabee's case, we have a third element: the start of a set of affective gestures which were first addressed to the animal but then turned into a more elaborate communication. It is our hypothesis that animals have the capacity to draw out a set of emotional and verbal behaviors from very young children which facilitate the acquisition of language.

The case of Bethsabee and the bird reminds me of an ancient vedic text retold by Kenneth White: "The first of all teachings consists in meditating endlessly on the bird." Bethsabee has verified this old Hindu formula and has given it a meaning full of practical pedagogy.

(Translated from the French by Anne Menard)

Alyse Zee

44

Guide Dogs and Their Owners: Assistance and Friendship

BACKGROUND OF THE STUDY

In a study done at Arizona State University, two sociologists concluded that blind people who relied on guide dogs to get around had twice as many conversations with strangers as did people using canes. Such findings may begin to suggest and confirm a social benefit of guide dog ownership. In these encounters, guide dogs were acting as catalysts for establishing human contacts.

In his history of The Seeing Eye, Inc., P. Putnam has shared numerous passages from letters written to Seeing Eye acknowledging the significance of a guide dog. People mentioned the exhilaration of walking with a dog, the freedom to relax, and feelings of physical safety and security. One young woman wrote: "A dog would not be guilty of imposing her wishes on me because she thought I was blind and incapable of thinking." As Putnam explains, dogs do not impose their wills on their masters and do not condescend to them; rather, the relationship is one of a profound affection and trust, of a continual interdependence. Putnam elaborates further on the emotional support he derives in the partnership with his own dog, noting that the animal generates and reinforces his human courage to go forward, to reach for goals.

The letter of another writer to the Seeing Eye reiterated this theme. The man emphasized the contagion of his dog's pleasure in a challenge; the animal's enthusiasm and perseverance awakened the blind owner's sense of adventure.

These writings and many additional, haphazard personal accounts steered and sharpened my plans for an illuminating study. Why and how does a guide dog, for individuals who choose to own one, facilitate adjustment to life?

THE STUDY

HYPOTHESIS

People who have owned one guide dog for at least one year will report an enhanced capacity to cope with physical, social, and psychological aspects of visual impairment.

UNDERLYING ASSUMPTION

A relationship with a guide dog will have physical, social, and psychological significance for the visually impaired owner.

DATA COLLECTION

Data were collected through two written questionnaires mailed to forty-four guide dog owners in the Philadelphia and New York areas. Thirty-nine owners responded to the initial survey, and thirty-one responded to the follow-up. In the original, closed-ended questionnaire, questions were designed to elicit descriptive responses, indicating the nature of the bond between individuals and guide dogs. The follow-up questionnaire enabled people to identify problems associated with blindness more concretely. Subjects were presented with a variety of blindness-related problems, extracted from relevant literature (Goffman, 1963, Monbeck, 1973), from my personal experience, and from contact and social work intervention with blind adults. Subjects were asked to strongly agree, mildly agree, feel neutral, mildly disagree, or strongly disagree regarding the potency of each problem in their own lives. Subjects were then asked to explicate elements in the relationship with the dog that helped them deal with problems associated with blindness. They were to designate features in this relationship which accentuated or thwarted their ability to cope with activities and challenges of daily living. In this follow-up questionnaire, subjects were also requested to make explanatory statements or describe an instance or event illustrating specific responses given in the earlier survey. To promote clarity and consistency, their responses were reissued to them to examine and expand.

SUBJECTS

Of the original 39 respondents, 21 were female and 18 male. The majority fell between the ages of 20 and 30, followed by the age group 30 to 40. Of the 39 people, twenty-six owned one guide dog and had owned the dog for at least one year. Of the 31 respondents to the follow-up questionnaire, 24 had owned one dog for at least one year. Twenty-two subjects lived alone; the remaining seventeen lived in households of two or more people.

RESULTS

Answers to the initial survey revealed that a relationship with a guide dog revolves around the person's knowledge of the dog's special needs and capabilities. In ongoing work, dogs must be regulated, systematically rewarded, and corrected in clear and concise patterns. According to these subjects, dogs must also be cared for personally and consistently to reinforce the bond—fed, groomed, exercised, played with, talked to, shown respect, affection, and attention, and calmed and protected from acute stress when upset by demands of the work. In turn, the dog is characterized as devoted, reliable, adaptable, and enthusiastic, displaying loyalty in performance and predictability of behavior. It appears that needs and capabilities of blind individuals and guide dogs can be blended together in a facilitative way if certain behaviors are maintained and exchanged. Recognition of the dog as a family member, plans to keep the dog after it is unable to work, admission of the dog as an aid in one's occupation, and mutual awareness of one another's moods may be additional indicators of bonding and attachment.

Subjects specified some characteristics differentiating the relationship with a guide dog from that with other pets owned. In comparison to pets previously owned, seeing-eye-dog owners felt that their relationship with the guide dog was characterized by more time spent with the animal, more dependence on the dog, more affection for the dog, greater requirement for attention to the dog, more dependence on the owner by the guide dog, more communication with the animal, more attachment of the animal to its owner, and more worry about the health and well-being of the dog.

The information I chose to pursue in the follow-up instrument seemed to reflect people's realization, or at least attribution, of positive gains in attitude and behavior dimensions to the relationship with a guide dog.

In their follow-up answers, people supplied cogent material demonstrating the physical, psychological, and social impact of guide dog ownership. In many reported perceptions, the dog's character or its particular services and functions furnished the owner with some alleviation of certain problems, perhaps allowing these owners to articulate and confront difficulties more openly. The dog seemed to be an impetus for growth and change.

DISCUSSION

Obviously, these results are limited because the sample was small and biased by being voluntary. Some people contacted refused to participate; those who did cooperate doubtless want to appear successful so that inadequacies and problems would not implicate them as failing or irresponsible owners. Some evidence offered concerning reasons for acquiring a guide dog may also contribute to bias in anticipation of, adjustment to, and active shaping of developments and viewpoints.

Yet the sincerity, depth, and consistency of people's revelations constitute at least a nascent understanding of the importance and meaning of the bond between people and guide dogs.

The above findings and the application of some concepts from the social psychology of blindness, need theory, and exchange theory provide basic insight into why and how this fascinating relationship works, or perhaps does not work.

SOCIAL PSYCHOLOGY OF BLINDNESS

Severe visual impairment is a complex phenomenon leading to physical, psychological, and social consequences for the involved individual. Some of these consequences are negative, contributing to a person's insecurity and an uncomfortable social status.

One of the most obvious limitations influencing a person who cannot see is difficulty with orientation and mobility. Some effects of this limitation include discomfort in navigation, infrequent traveling, traveling only short distances, rigidity of destinations, body tension, collision with obstacles, disorientation in old or new environments, distortion of body image, and confusion about one's body in relation to space and direction. Other major restrictions emerge as the blind person attempts to meet requirements of essential reading and writing.

Special equipment and training are necessary to ensure a blind person's mastery of skills connected with adequate mobility and with verbal and nonverbal communication. During and following the process of adjustment and mastery, the person continues to be dependent on others for assistanace. No mobility, communication, or self-care aid can totally replace vision because the world is primarily set up for those who see. This inevitable dependency on another or others may be stressful and difficult for a blind person to accept, presenting him/her with constant decision-making tasks around when, how, and who to ask for help.

Psychological reactions to blindness are as varied as are blind people, but blindness may be a tragedy for newly blinded people and for those who are temporarily frustrated or defeated or who have been overprotected. More than a physical inconvenience, it may be a threat to self-esteem, to one's established identity.

Prison has been used as a metaphor to illustrate the psychological position of blindness (Putnam, 1979). In this state, a blind individual may become rebellious and resentful or withdraw, retreat into self, becoming resigned passively to a perceived loss of freedom. If others in one's vicinity allow or encourage the persistence of such an attitude, blindness can result in a paralyzing effect on the will and on the decision-making capacity.

Socially, blind people may experience barriers in communicating, conversing, and initiating social contacts because they lack vital visual cues, social skills, or basic self-confidence. A blind person may suffer from annoying self-consciousness in groups or in public, related to fears of being ignored, judged negatively, or being unprepared to master any unpredictable situation. Uncomfortable situations may arise because of gaps in the information available to a blind person.

As addressed by Goffman (1963) and illuminated by Monbeck (1973), the blind person carries a social stigma of being different, atypical, customarily classified as inferior or abnormal. Several personal accounts (Chevigny, 1964; Potok, 1980) and other studies (reported below) have indicated some of the negative and inaccurate attitudes, stereotypes, and myths surrounding the phenomenon of blindness. Studies have explicitly demonstrated that there is social devaluation of the blind in the form of attributing false characteristics to blind people and underestimating their actual capabilities.

According to Rusalem (1960), society has singled out blindness as a particularly incapacitating disability and attributed to the blind traits widely different from those of sighted people, such as excessive despondency and melancholy, exceptional prophetic ability, unusual musical interest and talent, and introvertedness. In a study conducted with high school seniors, Gowman (1957) found that in comparison with other acquired disabilities, blindness was overwhelmingly selected as the worst possible handicap, both for self and for prospective mate. Raskin (1956) concluded that the difficulty in attitudes expressed toward the blind derives not from any lack of being liked but from a deficiency of respect.

Siller et al. (1967) propound, as a result of extensive research into the reactions of the nondisabled to the disabled, that when people think about the experience of blindness, they overemphasize the concept of loss. Losses that are imagined by the sighted include loss of qualities that attract others, of most positive personality traits, of independence and psychological normality, and of general ability to function. Such fantasies and perceptions contribute to discomfort, interaction strain, and generalized rejection of blind people, especially as peers and equals.

The blind are thus set apart, and much social policy and legislation still reflects a protective attitude, perpetuating services and programs that tend to isolate and exclude blind people rather than integrate them into the cultural mainstream (Bowe, 1977). Some publicity and fund-raising efforts still continue to appeal to people's fears and sympathies rather than stressing blind people's potential capabilities through appropriate rehabilitation.

People who are congenitally blind or who become blind adventitiously need to learn what blindness means. The various attitudes and patterns of behavior that characterize people who are blind are not inherent in their condition but are acquired through ordinary processes of social learning. There is nothing inherent which requires a blind person to be docile, dependent, or helpless, and yet these qualities may be incorporated by the person because they are so frequently attributed to him. As Scott points out (1969), a part of everyone's socialization experience entails learning attitudes and beliefs about stigmatized people such as the blind. These beliefs and attitudes spell out the effects that blindness is alleged to have upon personality and how a blind person can be differentiated because of these effects. A putative identity for the blind is thus constructed by reference to these beliefs.

A self-concept, or personal identity, is at the heart of one's experience as a socialized human being. A child sees himself as others see him, and conceptions of and expressions toward him as a blind person become guidelines for his feelings and behaviors. Face-to-face interaction with sighted people provides the second context in which the self-concept and social role of a blind person are acquired and defined. Usually, in such encounters, the common-sense convictions and assumptions regarding blindness represent the expectations that others entertain about the blind person's behavior. To the extent that the blind person accepts these imputations, his/her putative identity is sustained and reinforced. Blindness becomes a primary characteristic in the person's assessment of his limitations and abilities.

To return now to the main hypothesis and concern of this study, why do people who have owned one guide dog for at least one year report an enhanced capacity to cope with physical, psychological, and social aspects of visual impairment?

NEED SATISFACTION

The needs of blind people are determined in part by the real limitations imposed by visual impairment as well as by societal attitudes toward blindness and blind people. In the present study, as similarly found in the Sweden study (Adell-Bath, et al., 1979), individuals report perceptions and experiences related to need satisfacton on various levels. Because of elements of complexity, alienation, competition, and the social position of blind people in our society, the guide dog may play a unique and crucial role for some people in the fulfillment of needs, for example:

Physiological: "My dog has enabled me to be much more active and exuberant physically; I have gained confidence and ease in my body and also feel more relaxed and sure when moving around, with or without my dog."

Safety: "My traveling—distances, amount of places, and number of times I go out per week—have increased, so I feel less limited in what I do and where I go. Because I can move faster with the dog, I can get where I'm going sooner with less stress. The dog takes much more responsibility than a cane does."

Belonging: "I feel so lonely sometimes, so left out and kind of overburdened. Tali is the only one I can turn to for comfort. She can't get too much love; just stroking her soft fur and thinking how grateful I am to her for all her dedication cheers me up."

"I have read about and experienced blindness as a social stigma, a negative difference. My dog seems to serve as a link between me and regular people. Some barriers are broken down; they approach me less fearfully, and our mutual love of animals and sometimes dependence on them as companions brings us together. Somehow they think I'll have the insight to understand their attachment to their pets, and I do."

Esteem: "My dog has the basic values I believe in—health, activity, positive outlook, and trust. I feel so proud when I'm with him, in control and able to conquer my environment. I sense that people around me are admiring and awesome, and I like that respect. Sometimes people can be so curious, so invasive with a blind person, and the dog reminds them that I have power too. I am not helpless and deficient; I can manage."

"People seem to have less pity for me because Prince is beautiful, well-trained, and effective. I don't need them or their sympathy; they know I am well taken care of."

Self-Actualization: "I can't explain this fully, but it's like my self-image is more flexible; I'm more spontaneous, more open to experience. Now I'm not in therapy or encounter groups or anything like that, and I believe the explanation is my dog. He's so outgoing, tuned in, full of life. He never knows what to expect next, but he trusts in my ability to take charge of the situation."

"When I got Cinder, I finally generated the energy and the guts to leave my family and get my own apartment."

"When I applied for my first job as a medical typist, some people complained about Duffy, her shedding, etc., but I stood up for her, explaining about the training she had had and her good behavior. I didn't realize before that I could be so outspoken and convincing. The secret of success is belief in yourself and an ability to win others. Duffy and I are a winning duo."

"When I lost my sight, I thought life was over until I got my dog, Patti. My independence and belief in myself have returned. Patti helps me maintain my will power because she never falters or gives up."

"When I lost my sight, I became quite idle and despondent. My dog gave me a reason to live again. My family had been so upset and overprotective, but they respected my need to take care of and have control over my dog. It was my first real independence in months. I had felt so uncomfortable outside with people noticing I couldn't see, but they genuinely admired Angel, and I don't feel ashamed any more."

The kinds of need satisfaction described by subjects and the number of subjects indicating each kind of need satisfaction are listed below in Table 44.1.

Many people's statements and comments, offered to explain the power of the person-dog relationship in enabling the person to overcome obstacles and difficulties, emphasize the blending of the dog and human personalities. There develops a contagion of behaviors, a process of mutual influence. In some instances, the person learns from the dog more about certain qualities such as

TABLE 44.1. SATISFACTION OF PSYCHOLOGICAL NEEDS

Need Satisfaction	Number of Respondents Describing Need Satisfaction
Activity	5
Relaxation	4
Ease of movement	3
Exercise	8
Energy	2
Confidence in body	6
Speed of movement	4
Bodily stamina	6

SATISFACTION OF SAFETY AND SECURITY NEEDS
(defined as self-preservation and freedom from physical danger)

Need Satisfaction	Number of Respondents Describing Need Satisfaction
Physical security	22
Decreased vulnerability	14
Negotiation of weather conditions	7

SATISFACTION OF NEEDS FOR BELONGING AND LOVE
(defined as to be accepted and to give and receive love)

Need Satisfaction	Number of Respondents Describing Need Satisfaction
Dog as supportive and devoted friend	20
Dog serving as link between blind owner and other people	13
Dog as impetus for person to show trust and other feelings	19

SATISFACTION OF ESTEEM NEEDS
(defined as to be firmly based in reality, to have feelings
of confidence, power, and control; to feel useful, to be
recognized by others, to have an effect on others and one's
environment)

Need Satisfaction	Number of Respondents Describing Need Satisfaction
Control over anxiety and other destructive emotions	11
Respect and admiration from others	8
Freedom to be a capable individual	15

SATISFACTION OF NEEDS FOR SELF-ACTUALIZATION
(defined as ability to maximize one's potential,
to become what one is capable of becoming)

Need Satisfaction	Number of Respondents Describing Need Satisfaction
Ability to take risks	10
Assertiveness	7
Self-awareness	20
Tolerance for unexpected events and new situations	6
Sensitivity to other's needs and feelings	4
Sensory awareness	5

courage, playfulness, tolerance, and trust and wants to integrate these characteristics into his/her own approach to living.

These descriptions of the reciprocal influence process suggest another clue to comprehending why and how the person–guide dog relationship works.

INTERCHANGES BETWEEN OWNER AND GUIDE DOG

Blind people value assistance and companionship from other people but dislike constantly asking for help and figuring out how to repay or express appreciation to the other person. Sometimes deference to another person in the form of being dependent or obligated impedes relaxed and spontaneous sociability. Even in ordinary, day-to-day transactions, there may be strain connected with a sighted person's lack of knowledge about blindness or with the blind person's hesitance to be open or inability to supply correct information to the sighted person.

In contrast to another person, the guide dog is always available to the blind owner. There is a one and only dog for each person, eliminating the need to compete or wait for assistance. In interaction with the dog, there is no loss in self-respect, as there sometimes is when taking help from other people, who may be condescending, patronizing, or pitying. Furthermore, what the person gives—how he/she rewards the dog—can and should be steady. An exuberant "good girl," pat on the head, maintenance of physical care, and consistency in giving directions usually sustain a dog's responsiveness. To guarantee a person's devotion is not such a simple task. People, unlike guide dogs, have additional and different needs, responsibilities, and commitments.

With a dog, the person does not have to be preoccupied with impressions, preconceptions, or judgments. Such dominant preoccupations in human relationships can drain energy from work and play. It seems that when the dog-person relationship is harmonious, the reciprocal services provided tend to build an interdependence that balances costs and rewards, needs and power. Such a straightforward, authentic relationship eliminates or at least minimizes common fears of overdependence or rejection. The dog is characterized by ease of acceptance, tireless dedication, and a nonjudgmental attitude. The ability of the dog and person to communicate effectively contributes remarkable stability to the relationship.

This comfort and depth in communication can be explored more thoroughly in the context of Watzlawick's work (1967). In his view of communication as exchange of information and messages, he explains that interaction is punctuated by certain patterns of interchange. If these patterns or sequences of events are understood and agreed upon by both participants in a relationship, a stability of expectations for behavior will ensue and become constant.

Employing Watzlawick's ideas further, the relationship between the person and the guide dog seems to involve complementary interaction, in which dissimilar but fitted behaviors evoke and reinforce each other. Each partner in this special team behaves in a way that presupposes and simultaneously provides a rationale for the behavior of the other.

The analogic mode of communication—defined as all nonverbal communication including posture; gesture; facial expression; voice inflection; sequence, cadence, and rhythm of words—promotes a clear and meaningful exchange between two different species. According to Watzlawick, we depend heavily on analogic communication wherever relationship is a central concern or issue, and the intentions and methods involved in this realm of communication prevent apparent deception. On the other hand, verbal language used exclusively may be vague or confusing, inadequate in cementing relationships.

As the association between person and guide dog solidifies, it cannot be denied or underestimated that the person continues to obtain certain extrinsic rewards such as increased mobility and social contacts which have been discussed elsewhere. Yet the mutual supply of rewards seems to reaffirm and sustain the relationship for itself, making the partnership intrinsically satisfying and at least periodically an end in itself. "We are very attached to each other. When she is not with me, I feel very deprived of someone no matter where I am." In short, the benefits the person derives from this bond seem to be linked to the specific source, the guide dog, that makes them possible.

Inevitably, costs are acknowledged by the person and are experienced by the dog. Yet none of these costs seems to be intense enough to destroy the relationship, to cause the person to choose another alternative such as a cane or one or more sighted companions to replace the dog. In the cases surveyed, the dog did not desert the owner or refuse to work entirely because of debilitating stress. Both parties endured sacrifices and became anchored in the profitable exchange of mutual rewards. Each partner learned and amplified a special repertoire of behaviors that had reinforcing value for the other, so that the pain and ambivalence of dependency were transformed into the stability of a creative, pragmatic, and profound interdependency. What one partner receives from the other necessitates a return, so that giving and receiving are mutually contingent: in this manner, teamwork is strengthened.

IMPLICATIONS FOR FUTURE RESEARCH

The above findings and discussion have delineated how a blind person's relationship with a guide dog, for the person, may contribute to the diminution of problems and certain handicapping effects correlated with blindness. But the guide dog's position—the impact of this relationship on the dog—has not been specified.

It is generally understood and accepted that the domesticated dog is intelligent and social. Its instinct is to belong to a pack: when it lives with people, it requires companionship with them, to be actively together with them in an arrangement where it knows its place, its role. The dog's need for attachment to people is a consequence of its socialization experiences: there are similarities in the dog's and the human's brain development, in limbic and emotional structures, and in the potentiality for various responses to attachment. Voith (1980) examines some of the responses and mechanisms of human-animal attachment.

The guide dog is especially bred and screened for its intelligence, dependability, and loyalty. In addition, it is educated to lead and protect a blind person, frequently in a complicated urban environment, which necessitates a capacity to tolerate noise and confusion, to handle many decisions, to maintain a gentle, patient, and friendly disposition in the midst of crowded or unpleasant conditions. The dog is not completely submissive; it merely obeys commands. The dog and person form a partnership, involving cooperation and the sharing and translation of knowledge and desires during work. When do risks or costs supersede benefits of such a responsible attachment? Do some dogs pay too high a price, in physical or mental health, as a result of work they are expected to do, and what are some factors leading to irremediable debilitation? How can the effects of the initial training process of the dog or dog-person team be separated from subsequent patterns of interaction and exchange between person and dog? In other words, how crucial is the actual training process in shaping the guide dog's behavior and the dog-person team's behavior? Why do some dog-person pairs fail?

Do some blind people rely too exclusively on guide dogs for emotional support so that the dog represents an unnecessary crutch? What might be the roles of trainers, counselors, or veterinarians in preventing a smothering inseparability that depletes the energy of both animal and person for flexibility?

PART SEVEN

Context for Companion Animal Studies

Introduction

Veterinary medicine has a tradition of justifying its existence by claiming that veterinarians have an essential commitment to keeping farm animals healthy and productive. Until recently, companion animal medicine was, at best, a second-class activity within the profession. Within recent years, however, veterinary medicine has begun to admit the centrality of its involvement with companion animals. Perhaps because of the rapid introduction of women into veterinary schools; perhaps because over 70 percent of the bill for veterinary services is for treatment of companion animals; perhaps because the continued growth of factory farming methods forecasts an even greater reduction of the need for agriculture-based veterinary services; or perhaps because of a general humanistic enlightment of the faculty, companion animal studies are finding an increasingly secure place within schools of veterinary medicine. The chapter by William McCulloch and his co-authors describes how one veterinary school developed a curriculum focused on companion animals and the roles they play in their owners' lives. The authors also provide an outline of the professional response growth of the knowledge based in this field.

It is a singular tribute to the caliber of students in veterinary schools that information about the complexities of human behavior in relationship to companion animals attracts their attention. Their curriculum is an extraordinarily dense and difficult one and offers little time for reflection. Yet the second chapter in this section was written by a philosopher who teaches in a veterinary school and has been extraordinarily successful in engaging his students in the consideration of the ethical dilemmas associated with our treatment of animals. He provides an introduction to the ethical and philosophical considerations that must be included in our discussions if we are to be able to have an intelligent dialogue about the position of animals in our lives and the moral constraints on our behavior toward them. Problems like those presented by some of the techniques of factory farming, use of animals in experimentation, mutilation of animals to conform to breed or show standards, sports using animals, and the surrender of no longer wanted companion animals to shelters for destruction cannot be solved or even understood by a scientific analysis alone. Understanding an action requires reaching mutually understood agreements about ethical principles. The framing of relationships in an ethical context is continued in the papers of Robert Shurtleff, a veterinary student, and John Hoyt, the president of the Humane Society of the United States.

The final chapters attempt to place the study of the relationship between people and the living world around them in a context holistic enough to include scientific, historical, ethical, and aesthetic concerns. Aaron Katcher uses the theme of constancy to explore the meaning that dogs and other animals have within our lives. The purpose of the analysis is an attempt to explain why animals might have the ability to sustain our health, but the basis of the analysis could not be limited to the kinds of understanding that can be generated out of experiments or clinical observations alone. Our representations of real animals are always associated with the metaphorical animal, and the interaction of the two demands that anyone seeking to know how we are affected by real animals appreciates the poetic and cosmological uses of the animal metaphor.

The last chapter, which was left unchanged by the editors, is the personal statement of Boris Levinson, who for many years was a lonely pioneer in this field of study. He provides a historical analysis of our life with animals and the problems of developing a new area of knowledge, and he offers a guide for the future. We thought that there was no better way to close this volume than to provide the reader with Dr. Levinson's anticipations of the next.

William F. McCulloch, Archie I. Flowers,
Norman D. Heidelbaugh, and Michael J. McCulloch

45

Teaching About the Human–
Companion Animal Bond
in a Veterinary Curriculum:
People, Process, and Content

The practice of veterinary medicine involves people, animals, and the environment in which they live. The veterinarian is required to make decisions that can
affect the emotional, physical, social, economic, and political well-being of
clients as well as others within the community. The role of veterinary medicine
in society has been changing. It continues to serve a changing and specializing
agriculture but its practitioners are increasingly becoming aware of its role in an
urban society. One aspect of this role is dealing with the human–companion
animal relationship. A report from the American Association of Veterinary
Medical Colleges supports the importance of the human–companion animal
bond: "The health care given to companion animals may be as significant in
terms of the mental and emotional health of individuals in this society as the
protection of the food supply is to their physical well-being"(American Association of Veterinary Medical Colleges Report, 1979).

Because the veterinarian must rely on people to present companion animals
for clinical care, he or she becomes intimately and inescapably involved in issues

that affect the emotional health of the pet owner and the pet owner's family. As a consequence, the veterinarian is frequently confronted with ethical and value decisions that interact with and determine the emotional well-being of his or her clients. Veterinarians are often thrust into roles in which they face decisions for which they may neither be well prepared by veterinary education and experience nor have societal or professional sanction to act (for example, referring a severely disturbed client to a mental health professional). To deal more effectively with clients' emotions and needs as they relate to the psychodynamics of animal ownership, the veterinarian must develop a knowledge base and effective verbal and nonverbal communication skills, including the arts of asking questions, observing, and listening. Those of us who have been in veterinary practice or have used pets as adjunctive therapy in treating chronically ill or depressed human patients have known for years that pets contribute to human mental health and emotional well-being.

We have become increasingly interested in understanding the role that companion animals play in man's mental health. Levinson (1965) and others (Speck, 1964; McCulloch, Dorn, and Blenden, 1970; McCulloch, 1978; Bustad, 1980b; Fox, 1975b; McCulloch and McCulloch, 1981) have emphasized the importance of the veterinarian's role in mental health and the need for more scientific investigation into the psychodynamics of the person-pet relationship. It has become increasingly apparent that we must become knowledgeable about animal and human behavior and needs to deal more effectively with the people-animal interface.

The veterinarian's role in prescribing pets for potential owners has been emphasized (Beaver, 1974; Bustad, 1979). Emphasis has also been placed on the need for pet planning programs with strong multimedia educational efforts involving practicing veterinarians. These programs will have as a goal reducing the impulse buying of pets inappropriate to a given person or family unit (Frederickson, 1975).

Psychiatrists, psychologists, sociologists, social workers, and other health professionals can contribute to the understanding of problems that veterinary clinicians and those in veterinary public health and animal health–related activities face each day with their clients (Ryder and Romasco, 1980; McCulloch and Selby, 1975). To handle potentially emotional and tense situations, the veterinarian must have an understanding that children, geriatric, and other pet owners experiencing excessive life change or emotional crisis present special management problems. The veterinarian must understand the symptoms of grief, depression, anxiety, inappropriate anger, and the effects of change on human health. Dr. T. H. Holmes has studied the role of multiple life changes or events for people and the relationship of such changes to people's vulnerability to illness (1967). The principles found in this study should be extremely helpful for the veterinarian in dealing with clients.

PROFESSIONAL VETERINARY MEDICAL CURRICULUM

We need to increase our communication knowledge and skills in handling both the difficult client (Hart, 1975) and difficult pet (McCulloch, 1975). Although competition for time in veterinary curriculums is keen, the human–companion animal bond area must be given appropriate attention. It has been only within the past ten years, however, that a concerted effort has been made to provide formal lectures and course offerings concerning the human–companion animal bond in veterinary professional and graduate curriculums. The American Veterinary Medical Association's "Essentials of a Veterinary Medical College" indicates that the veterinary professional curriculum must be sufficiently flexible to permit adjustment to the needs of veterinary medicine as a growing and expanding art and science. The professional curriculum should provide adequate instruction in such areas as preventive medicine, public health, and professional and public relations. Students should be supervised for applied training in hospital wards and field service clinics as well as in diagnostic, surgical, and necropsy laboratories. Such training should include diagnosis, treatment, and control of animal disease and veterinary public health. Precisely where the specific areas are taught within the curriculum will vary from one veterinary college to another. Many aspects of the human–companion animal bond have been taught for many years in veterinary curricula, but not under this specific name. The topic has been touched upon in courses in veterinary public health, veterinary economics, physical diagnosis and client relations, practice management, and veterinary ethology.

According to the World Health Organization–Food and Agricultural Organization definition, veterinary public health is that part of public health which uses professional veterinary skills, knowledge, and resources for the protection and improvement of human health. Traditionally, the human and public health aspects of veterinary medicine have been taught by faculties of veterinary public health in our colleges and schools of veterinary medicine in the United States and other countries throughout the world. We will not attempt here to review the present status of teaching of the human–companion animal bond in veterinary colleges in the United States but will concentrate on our own experiences. We hope this information will assist others who are attempting to modify their curricula so as to provide appropriate emphasis on the practitioner's involvement in the human–companion animal bond. The methods and content outlined here represent *a* way of teaching and not necessarily *the* way that would work in all schools and colleges of veterinary medicine. Dr. Leo Bustad and Linda Hines recently reviewed aspects of a lifelong curriculum to promote greater understanding of the human–companion animal bond in a chapter of a book published in June 1981 (Bustad and Hines, 1981). In that chapter they also discussed the professional veterinary curriculum.

The authors' first recollection of the involvement of teaching mental health in the veterinary curriculum was in 1961, when Dr. Donald Blenden of the

University of Missouri engaged a psychiatrist to teach in the veterinary public health curriculum. Although there was only one lecture, it gave veterinary students some insight into mental health problems. One of us participated in a time-function study of small animal practitioners in Missouri (May, Blenden, and McCulloch, 1971) in which about 25 percent of practice time was directly related to public health activities. The mental and emotional health contributions by veterinarians were not studied even though they were felt to be of major significance. We emphasized the importance of objectively discussing the emotional or behavioral interrelationships between the client, family unit, and the pet. In 1970 a proposal of urban extension veterinarians was presented at the annual meeting of the American Veterinary Medical Association as part of a panel on urban health (McCulloch, Dorn, and Blenden, 1970). The urban extension veterinarian would, among other responsibilities, educate the public and promote the potential use of pets for use in child psychotherapy and their beneficial role for the elderly. The first full-time urban extension veterinarian position was established in 1974 at the University of Missouri.

The first competency-based curriculum developed in veterinary medicine was for the specialty area of veterinary public health and preventive medicine. The proceedings of the workshop held at the University of Missouri in 1973 were published by the Pan American Health Organization of the World Health Organization in 1975 (Selby et al., 1975). The curriculum was developed to determine what the student should know, do, and feel about this area of veterinary medicine at the time of graduation. Numerous subject areas were discussed at the workshop, and by an assignment of values, topics were weighted as to importance for inclusion in the curriculum. From these competencies, educational objectives could be developed for evaluation of cognitive and affective domains of learning (Bloom, 1956; Krathwohl, Bloom, and Masia, 1964). Although the terminology of the human–companion animal bond was not specifically used, the following important areas were suggested for inclusion in the veterinary public health and preventive medicine curriculums of the schools and colleges of veterinary medicine in the United States and Canada: noninfectious consequences of animal and human interactions (such as allergies and hypersensitivities, anxieties and psychoses, traumas, and animal bites); animal population control; psychological aspects of animal and human interrelationships (for example, psychotherapy, geriatrics and companion animals, anxieties and phobias, recreational benefits, and child development and basic life processes education); socioeconimic aspects of animal and human interrelationships (for example, cost-benefit analysis, economic impact of animal and zoonotic diseases, socioeconimic implications for professional services); and animal welfare (for example, humane slaughter and euthanasia, humane associations and animal shelters, humane care and treatment, and legal and social implications).

In 1976, Dr. Robert K. Anderson and colleagues published a comprehensive study of the veterinarian's responsibilities as they relate directly to human health (Anderson et al., 1976). Michael McCulloch was a member of the National Advisory Committee and contributed the section "Mental and Emotional Health" as one of the nine human health goals of veterinary medicine. Also during 1976 the Delta concept was initiated in Portland, Oregon, to explore the human–companion animal bond and to study and explain the interrelationships among pets, owners, and members of health and related professions. This concept was reviewed by Dr. Michael J. McCulloch at the symposium held at Texas A&M University in 1976, "Implication of History and Ethics to Medicine—Veterinary and Human." The triangular figure represents the relationship between the veterinarian, the animal owner, and the companion animal (Figure 45.1). The veterinarian is also a part of a larger triangle that involves ethical obligations and responsibilities to the community. Problems he or she must be concerned about include animal control, dog bites, and pet owner responsibility.

A recent symposium, "Veterinary Medical Practice: Pet Loss and Human Emotion," was co-sponsored by the Animal Medical Center of New York City and the Foundation of Thanatology. The published proceedings should be of assistance to faculties of colleges of veterinary medicine. Additionally, in 1981, the American Veterinary Medical Association Executive Board established a Human–Companion Animal Bond Task Force to establish goals for the veterinary profession with respect to teaching, research, service programs, and health benefits as they apply to the human–companion animal bond. The Eighth Symposium on Veterinary Medical Education was held at the University of Tennessee in June of 1982. A $100,000 grant from the National Science Foundation was awarded to Dr. Hyram Kitchen and Dr. William McCulloch to support the symposium, which is entitled "Exploring Values and Ethical Issues in Veterinary Medicine." In addition to bioethics, a major portion of the symposium will be about teaching the human–companion animal bond in veterinary colleges.

FIGURE 45.1.

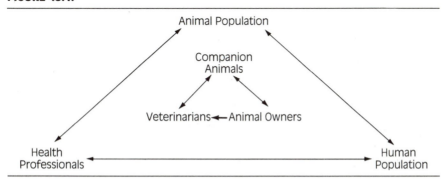

The concept for the Center for Interaction of Animals and Society at the University of Pennsylvania's School of Veterinary Medicine dates from 1977 but officially got under way in 1979 through a grant from the Geraldine R. Dodge Foundation, according to its director, Dr. Alan . This interdisciplinary group has made significant contributions to our understanding of the human–companion animal bond in its few short years of existence. According to Dr. , the center now organizes elective courses in the psychological, political, economic, and general societal aspects of the interaction of animals and society. The interdisciplinary nature of the center has helped to promote significant teaching, research, and continuing education opportunities for veterinarians, veterinary students, and other health professionals.

PRESENT STATUS OF HUMAN–COMPANION ANIMAL BOND PROGRAMS AT TEXAS A&M

TEACHING

Teaching the subject of the human–companion animal bond in the Department of Veterinary Public Health has evolved over the past five years. It received its greatest encouragement following lectures given by Dr. Michael J. McCulloch and Dr. A. F. Hopkins during a symposium held in 1976. Dr. Paul Tallamy, formerly of the department, helped to operationalize these concepts into the veterinary curriculum.

One of the major research-teaching goals of the Department of Veterinary Public Health is "Mental Health Implications of People/Animal Interrelationships: The Veterinarian's Role in Understanding and Dealing Effectively With Human Emotional Responses." Two other areas that focus on public health implications of the human–companion animal bond are animal control, consisting of a multidisciplined approach to reducing adverse public health implications resulting from pet, stray, feral, and exotic animals and epidemiology of acute and chronic diseases (infectious and noninfectious) with emphasis on diseases and disease processes common to humans and animals (such as zoonotic diseases). The College of Veterinary Medicine at Texas A&M University also administers and has major input into a four-year biomedical science degree program. Faculty in the Department of Veterinary Public Health teach several courses. As part of an elective "problems" course, the following human–companion animal bond topics have been offered: psychology of pet ownership; therapeutic uses of animals; death of a pet and human emotions; educational uses of animals; companion animals in nursing/retirement homes; attitudes of pet owners about pets; human dependence on pets; historical perspective on the human–companion animal bond; and relationships of pets, college students, and housing restrictions.

In the professional veterinary curriculum, Dr. William F. McCulloch directs a three-hour credit course on public health to first-year veterinary medical students. One-hour lectures containing material on the human–companion animal bond cover introduction to comparative medicine, recent trends in comparative medicine, the human–companion animal bond, trends and motivations for pet ownership, value dimensions in dealing with client emotions and grief reactions, and the veterinarian and pet-facilitated therapy. The teaching methods involve lectures, films, and handout materials pertinent to each area. A film by Michael J. McCulloch, M.D., *Three Is Company, Not a Crowd*, is used. This film describes the triangular relationship between the veterinarian, the client, and the pet. It was produced at the University of Minnesota College of Veterinary Medicine in cooperation with the Center for Comparative Medicine at Texas A&M University and the former Delta Foundation of Portland, Oregon. Other films used include those about the human–companion animal bond produced by the Delta Group of the Latham Foundation.

In the final year of the professional curriculum, we participate in veterinary public health clerkships as part of a veterinary medicine interdisciplinary course. One of the clerkships is Understanding the Human–Companion Animal Bond: Implications for the Practice of Veterinary Medicine. Objectives include listing and defining the basic attitudes clients have toward dogs and cats as pets; describing the various reasons why people own companion animals; listing the various ways that animals can be used in improving the quality of human life through therapeutic and education programs; developing an appreciation for the need to be sensitive to the intense attachment people may have with their pets, including selected food and exotic animal species; recognizing and appreciating the importance of dealing effectively with client symptoms and signs of grief, depression, anxiety, and inappropriate behavior as related to patient-client associations and recognizing limitations in dealing with certain cases; more effectively dealing with and becoming increasingly sensitive to the emotions of the client or family when their pet dies or is euthanized; and defining the term "thanatology" and briefly discussing its implication for veterinary medicine (for example, stages of a grief reaction).

In each clerkship there are four to seven students per two-hour session. During the introduction each student is asked to discuss past or present pets owned and the reasons for having these particular animals, whether they are large or small. Students are then asked to review reasons people have pets and their uses in selective environments such as prisons, nursing homes, and mental health clinics. Selected newspaper or magazine articles are used as they relate to the goals.

The students develop empathy for the various situations through "role playing" and group discussions. The characterizations of client and doctor portraying four distinct patient-client relationships (elderly couple, newlyweds, young family, parent and teenager) are used to dramatize the significance of environmental factors impinging on the veterinary clinician's suggested resolution of a similar problem. Students then critique each characterization. These examples were taken from Dr. A. F. Hopkins's paper published by the Texas A&M University Press. To add an interdisciplinary dimension to the teaching, other professionals have been invited to attend the two-hour clerkship session. Psychologists, psychiatrists, social workers, biomedical science students, and activity directors for nursing homes have been visiting participants. Through the example of role playing, veterinary students are able to experience sociological and psychological implications of the human–companion animal bond. A further refinement of the role playing by students has been initiated through the use of a televison camera and playback recorder. A live animal is used on an examination table for the student veterinarian and clients in the case study.

Following completion of the office visit, the entire class reviews the verbal and nonverbal communication reactions, commenting about feelings of both veterinarian and client, as well as the role of the animal. A modified version of Dr. Norman Kagan's "Interpersonal Process Recall—A Method of Influencing Human Interaction" is being used (Kagan, 1975). The faculty member plays the part of the inquirer by asking questions about the veterinary student's feelings following client responses. The client describes his or her feelings about the communication skills of the veterinary student. Other colleges of veterinary medicine have used the television playback for several years. We are looking forward to its further refinement in teaching about the human–companion animal bond to veterinary medical students at Texas A&M University.

Another clerkship pertinent to the human–companion animal bond is Animal Control, a two-hour session with from four to seven students. The role of the veterinarian is discussed in reference to animal control, animal bites, humane society role, animal rights issues, and other subjects.

There are clerkships involving zoonotic diseases in private practice and zoonoses of laboratory animals when used as pets. These clerkships have implications for handling emotional problems involving the client-owner and veterinarian. An additional optional two-hour clerkship will involve the same number of students that will visit and then develop criteria for safe use of animals in nursing homes in the Bryan–College Station area. These clerkships allow for active participation by students. Other aspects of the human–companion animal bond are taught in other parts of our curriculum. Dean George C. Shelton teaches a professional orientation course to first-year students. Guest lecturers from the social sciences and humanities participate. Dr. Walter Juliff, Department of Small Animal Medicine and Surgery, teaches physical diagnosis and uses a television playback method to teach students how to answer client telephone calls. Dr. Claudia Barton, Department of Small Animal Medicine and Surgery, presents a one-hour lecture each year about grief reactions by owners whose pets have been diagnosed as having cancer. Dr. Bonnie Beaver, Department of Veterinary Anatomy, teaches two elective classes for senior students. One involves animal behavior and addresses how owner attitudes affect the outcome of treatment. During another animal behavior seminar Dr. Beaver discusses pet owner characteristics, owner attitudes toward pets, and human ideas about animal rights.

Two three-hour graduate courses in the Department of Veterinary Public

Health deal with aspects of the human–companion animal bond. William McCulloch teaches the courses entitled Public Health Concepts, and Animal Diseases and Comparative Medicine. Animal control and humane studies are also included as part of the course material. Individual and community health aspects are discussed. Topical areas include the relationship of animal and child abuse; the veterinarian and other health and helping professions; interdisciplinary nature of people-animal relationships in the areas of research, education, and service; evidence and trends that people are emotionally attached to animals; motives for pet ownership and use; owner attitudes about dogs and cats as pets; proven and potential health values of pet ownership; trends and uses of pets in therapeutic programs for physical and mental health rehabilitation needs; the changing role of pets in society; legal and social aspects of the loss of a pet; death by euthanasia and loss of a pet (thanatology); community health implications of the human–companion animal bond; and animal models used for study of selected human mental and physical health problems.

Problems courses (one to four credits) are offered by graduate students to study the specific problems in the human–companion animal bond area. Graduate students also present seminars on this topic during a one-hour credit course each semester. A representative sample of seminars to be given during the fall semester of 1981 include "Public Health and Behavioral Implications of Obedience Training for Animals," "Geographical Differences in Attitudes about Animals," and "Criteria for Safe Use of Pets in Nursing Homes: Benefits and Concerns." Presently, Dr. McCulloch has seven graduate students, six of whom are working on a master of science or doctor of philosophy degree. Thesis projects are on some aspect of the human–companion animal bond. We also participate in a graduate course, Working with the Elderly, in the Department of Sociology.

RESEARCH

Research has been initiated in several areas. Funds have been received to contrast attitudes about the use of pets in nursing homes for the aged in an urban and a rural area. Other areas of research involve the cooperation of Dr. Claudia Barton, Dr. Bonnie Beaver, and Dr. E. W. Ellett in the College of Veterinary Medicine. Collaborative research efforts are being encouraged among faculty interested in this area from other colleges and departments at Texas A&M University. The Department of Veterinary Public Health initiated the Human/ Companion Animal Bond Interest Group among faculty and students on the Texas A&M University campus in July of 1981. Monthly seminars are given to discuss and learn about teaching, research, and service opportunities in the area of people-animal interrelationships. The newly created Center for Comparative Medicine will also promote increased research and education on the human– companion animal relationship.

CONTINUING EDUCATION AND EXTENSION

As a land-grant university, we are involved in continuing education and extension activites to promote benefits of the human–companion animal bond. Dr. McCulloch has directed postgraduate courses with colleagues Edward R. Ames, Stanley L. Diesch, and Russell J. Martin in the area of pets and human diseases: what's the risk? The first symposium, a problem-oriented case study seminar, was presented at the 1976 annual meeting of the American Medical Association. The audience was primarily family practice physicians, pediatricians, and internal medicine specialists. One of the learning objectives was to write a statement about the importance of companion animals to human health. Physicians were encouraged to be sensitive to the importance of pets to human mental health and to remember to inquire about the role of pets in the social and environmental history of mentally ill children and adults.

Since 1974, Texas A&M University has sponsored an annual five-day animal control conference and workshop. Dr. A. I. Flowers has been instrumental in providing an understanding of people-animal relationships at these conferences. Departmental faculty present talks about human–companion animal bond topics to professional and lay groups, such as the Texas Veterinary Medical Association and Texas Public Health Association, Brazos Valley Humane Society, Brazos Valley Kennel Club, American Veterinary Medical Association, and American Public Health Association.

Articles have been published about benefits of the human–companion animal bond. Dr. McCulloch, with Vicki J. Bailey, and Michael J. McCulloch, M.D., produced an autotutorial slide tape program, "Advances in Knowledge about the Human/Companion Animal Bond," which was first presented at the 1981 Annual Meeting of the American Veterinary Medical Association. Copies are available for purchase.

One objective of the Human/Companion Animal Bond Interest Group at Texas A&M is to provide recent research evidence for supporting the use of pets in educational and therapeutic programs and to develop a speaker's bureau. Our long-range goal is to establish a community-based people-pet partnership program similar to that which was established by Dr. Leo Bustad and Linda Hines at Washington State University.

STUDENTS ARE PEOPLE

We teach students, not courses. We are promoting a more humane and holistic approach to veterinary medical education and its implication for the human–companion animal bond. By a variety of teaching, research, and continuing education programs, all faculty and students are encouraged to attend lectures and seminars. Basically, the process of education involves telling the basic facts, showing by demonstration, and doing the actual task to develop competencies in dealing with both people and animals in a humane and effective manner for the benefit of client, pet, and veterinarian. Indeed, the human–companion animal bond is an old concept with new meaning for veterinary medicine's contribution to animals and society.

THE FUTURE—ENDOWED CHAIR FOR HUMANE STUDIES

One of the recent developments in the Department of Veterinary Public Health, which has been approved in concept by the college's Development Committee (Dr. E. W. Ellett, coordinator), is the launching of a new coordinated program which seeks funds to establish a Chair for Humane Studies. Humane Studies is that part of veterinary public health which concerns the scholarly elucidation of the fundamental motivations and mechanisms of humane activities and the people-animal bond.

Bernard E. Rollin

46

Morality and the Human-Animal Bond

We are only beginning to understand the protean variety of ways in which companion animals contribute to our lives. Once seen as little more than misplaced sentimentality, the pet-human bond is now being understood as a powerful tie, indeed, an unbreakable cable woven evolutionarily out of a variety of strands, each possessing great individual strength. Our tie to these animals is now being explained in surprising ways. We are realizing their value for human physical health, mental health, emotional health, and human social health. They are being recognized as providing a vehicle for facilitating human interaction in such alienating urban environments as New York City. Through these new insights, we are gaining a new and much deeper appreciation of what philosophers call the instrumental value of animals in society, the use value of these creatures for us.

Yet it is important to stress that there is an entirely different part of the story that cannot be overlooked. In addition to the unquestionable instrumental value of pet animals for people, we must also remember that they possess intrinsic value, value that does not derive from their utility for us but is part and parcel of their moral status as living, feeling sentient creatures; creatures whose lives matter to *them*, regardless of whether they do or do not happen to matter to us. And as such, we are bonded to them by something far more awesome—and burdensome—than utility. We are bonded to them by the bonds of morality— bonds that should be stronger than any of the others but have been stretched and weakened by human irresponsibility.

What do we mean by "intrinsic value"? Immanuel Kant, when developing this concept regarding human beings, said that human beings were to be treated "always as ends, never merely as means." Thus if we are to be moral, we must never look at or treat other people simply as tools for furthering our own purposes but rather as beings whose own ends, needs, natures, and dignity need to be respected. In ordinary terms, this is expressed by the idea that it is wrong simply to "use" people without regard for their individual (and general) needs.

A clear example of how this concept cashes out may be gleaned from recent discussions of sexual morality. Many sex theorists hold that no particular sexual act is wrong (or right) in itself. What makes a particular piece of sexual behavior wrong is how one views and treats one's partner. If the other person is seen only as a vehicle for releasing one's own frustrations or for fulfilling one's own needs without regard for the needs or desires of the other, this is wrong. Thus on this view, even marital sex performed in the "normal missionary position" may be immoral if one partner is simply using the other as a release.

Obviously, treating someone as an end in himself does not mean that we cannot use him at all—that would be absurd. We obviously go to dentists because we see them as means to alleviating toothaches; we see plumbers as means of unclogging our drains. The point of saying that all people have intrinsic value is to stress that we must never do anything that ignores the fact that dentists are also human persons, with a moral status worthy of respect and dignity.

But we often forget that animals, and most dramatically, pet or companion animals, also enjoy a moral status, possess intrinsic value, and are legitimate objects of moral concern and attention toward whom our actions must be judged in terms of concepts of right and wrong. This is something we feel intuitively, and which is easily felt and expressed emotionally (as when we grieve for pets).

What is much harder is to give a philosophical and rational articulation of this sense of animal value which to many people seems to be simply sloppy anthropomorphic sentimentality. It is to this task we now turn, for despite its difficulty, it is of great importance to people who work with animals, for they are best suited to press in society for the recognition of the moral status of these animals and to try to make our social practice accord better with our moral intuitions.

Historically, we have ignored these intuitions about the moral status of animals. Perhaps we have repressed them because they make us too uncomfortable about our behavior toward these beings. We would expect that we would have developed an ethic that attempts to come to grips with our relationship with companion animals. But, despite the immense literature on ethics which exists in the West; despite the fact that philosophers have written on all manner of subjects, including the claim that the chair is not there when we are not perceiving it, or that time is unreal, almost nothing has been done on the moral status of animals, dealing with the question of what, if anything, is the relevant difference between people and animals from a moral point of view, and what are our moral duties to other creatures.

I will try to summarize the results of my work in this area, to demonstrate why there are no rational grounds for excluding animals from moral concern, and why animals have moral rights. Let me stress that this theory is meant as a moral ideal, which we cannot live up to instantly in our sociocultural context. But this is true of most moral ideals. Consider "turning the other cheek." Most Christians are incapable of acting that way, but the ideal is still valuable as a mark to aim at and as a yardstick to measure conduct. Without moral theories as ideals, we tend to accept the status quo as normal, inevitable, and acceptable. Given a moral ideal, we try to make that ideal fit our social-cultural reality as far as possible. In my book (Rollins, 1981), I develop the theory in great detail. But I also try to show how current practice regarding animals can be modified to make it much closer to this ideal. Inspiring one to change the status quo is the cash value of moral philosophy.

Let us look at the theory and how it applies to pet animals. To begin, it is necessary to explain the concept of morally relevant differences. If I were suddenly to start punctuating a lecture with a series of right jabs to a nearby gentleman's jaw, you would ask me why I am hitting him. Suppose I said, I am hitting him because he is the only person with a red beard in the room. That would not morally justify my hitting him. Beard color is not morally relevant. On the other hand, if I say I saw him molesting my son before the lecture, that is morally relevant grounds for my hitting him.

The basic question, then, is what morally relevant differences exist between people and animals? There are obviously many differences, but the question is whether they are germane to moral status or whether they are as irrelevant as beard color. Let us look very briefly at some alleged differences between humans and animals in general, before looking at pet animals in particular. These are all differences which have been used to claim that animals are not legitimate objects of moral attention while people are.

1. *Man has an immortal soul.* This is the classic Catholic position. But is it morally relevant? (Let us ignore, for a moment, our obvious inability to know who has a soul and who does not, or even what a soul is.) Does it justify our treating animals as less than humans? No. Cardinal Bellarmine pointed out that, if anything, it cuts the other way. Since animals do not have an immortal soul, they do not get a crack at the afterlife in which wrongs are redressed. So we are actually obliged to threat them better! (Bellarmine allegedly allowed fleas to drink their fill of his blood.)

2. *Man is superior to animals (granted dominion by God; top of the evolutionary ladder)*. So what? Being superior to something does not mean that you can abuse it. In fact, it has nothing at all to do with how you ought to treat that thing. And anyway, how are we superior? Are we stronger? The government is stronger than any of us—does it follow that it is morally entitled to do to individuals as it sees fit? Might does not make right. Perhaps everyone who is drawn to this sort of argument should try the following thought experiment: Imagine a race of extraterrestrials who are smarter and superior in force to humans. Would we consider it morally justifiable for them to deny human rights and to use humans for their own convenience?

From a strict evolutionary point of view, there is no top of the ladder, there is only a branching tree. If there is, it has to do with adaptability and species durability and reproductive success. In that case, the roach and the rat are right on top with us.

Religiously speaking, having dominion does not mean that the other creatures do not have rights. The Old Testament specifically worries about animals. And remember, parents have dominion over children—that does not mean that children have no moral status.

3. *As far as domestic animals and laboratory animals are concerned, man has given them their lives, so these animals can be disposed of as humans see fit*. This is clearly morally irrelevant. We are causally responsible for the lives of our children, yet we cannot morally justifiably treat them as we see fit. We do not feel that slaveowners who bred slaves were morally justified in treating them as chattel, even though they of course had the power to do so. (In the ancient world, one who saved another's life was felt to be responsible for that life forever.)

4. *Animals do not feel pain*. This absurdity goes back to Descartes, who saw them as machines. If someone tells me he cannot *know* for sure that an animal feels pain, I tell him I cannot know for sure that *he* can. I recently debated a physiologist who said that since electrochemical activity in the cerebral cortex of dogs is different from ours, dogs do not feel pain as we do. I pointed out that he does pain research on dogs and extrapolates the results to people and rested my case. The National Society for Medical Research constantly hints at the idea that animals do not feel pain and thereby discredits itself.

5. *Animals cannot reason or speak*. So what? Neither do some humans—infants, children, the senile, the insane, the comatose, the retarded—yet they are moral objects. Second, it is not clear that animals cannot speak. Third, if reason is what makes people moral objects, why do we worry about aspects of their nature which have nothing to do with reason?

Suppose we discover that we can spur the rational activity of college students by wiring their seats and shocking them periodically when their attention wanders. Surely we would not consider this morally permissible. The point is that there are many other factors besides reason which are morally relevant regarding people, factors like pain and pleasure, in which animals share.

6. *Social contract theory* (a version of number 5). This is the idea that morality applies only to individuals who are capable of entering into agreements with one another. For example, I will respect your property on condition that you will respect mine. Only rational beings can enter into such agreements, therefore only rational beings are objects of moral concern, and thus animals are not.

Obviously, this theory refers to agreements in action, mutual adjustment of behavior, rather than to explicit agreements, for none of us have ever verbally agreed to a moral code. What I mean by agreement in action is exemplified by common-law marriage, as recognized by the law. Although there is no explicit marriage contract, there is agreement in action and mutual adjustment and accord of behavior.

But this argument will not work either for a number of reasons. Most relevant here is the fact that pet animals, at least, *do* stand in precisely this relationship to man, behviorally, biologically, and evolutionarily. There is a strong social contract between man and dog. The dog has given up a wild pack nature to live in human society and function as sentinel, guardian, hunting companion, and friend in return for food, care, shelter, and pack leadership on the part of humans. We shall return to this shortly.

But let us sum up. We have seen that none of the alleged differences between man and animal are morally relevant. In a positive vein, we also know that animals possess the same features that we consider morally relevant and significant in humans.

1. They are alive

2. They have needs and interests, physical and behavioral, which matter to them—food, companionship, sex, exercise, avoidance of pain, and so forth. Each animal species has a unique set of interests, genetically programmed, which determines its nature or what I call, following Aristotle, its *telos*.

In human morality, and in our laws, we talk of our moral commitment to the needs of others in terms of their *rights* to certain treatment. When a human need or interest is central to the *nature* of a human being, we try to protect the fulfillment of that need from infringement, except in the case of the gravest social danger. So our Bill of Rights protects human rights growing out of interests we feel are central to human nature—speech, religion, assembly, property, privacy, and so forth.

But animals also have natures and interests central to their natures. And if there is no morally relevant difference between humans and animals, the locic of our morality leads us to the conclusion that animals should have rights! The fundamental rights are obvious. First, animals have the *right to life*, for without life, there is nothing to value. This means, first and foremost, that we should not kill animals for trivial reasons or simply for our convenience. Equally important is the right of the animal to live life in accordance with its nature. This is sometimes even more important than the right to life, as when we feel that morality forces us to euthanize an animal because it cannot live naturally, without pain. Veterinarians realize that to keep a dog "alive" when it cannot move or eat is a monstrous violation of its essential nature. Ironically, this is a favor we do not afford humans, even when they ask for relief! Here, parenthetically, is an area of human morality that can be illuminated by taking animal rights seriously. When we realize that animals are not all that different from people, we might be more prepared to ask ourselves whether it is rational to see what we consider an act of compassion to an animal as a crime against a person. We consider the person who will not euthanize a suffering dog morally culpable; why do we feel differently about persons or societies who refuse to euthanize a person who is begging to die?

In any event, if animals are moral objects, we should not kill them except for morally defensible reasons, and we should not violate their natures. Furthermore, we should grant their claim to moral concern some official, socially sanctioned status in the law, which, after all, exists to protect moral objects.

But if we focus on the pet animal, we realize just how far we are from this rational ideal. As we said earlier, pet animals are vitally integrated into human society in obvious ways and in new ways that are being discovered, such as in the work of Drs. Corson and Katcher and others presented at this conference. The dog has been part of human life for about 12,000 years—the tame wolf has been associated with human society for about 500,000 years. The dog has been shaped by man into a creature that essentially depends on man for its physical existence, satisfaction of its physical needs, behavioral needs, and social nature. Man creates the dog and sustains its existence. If dogs were suddenly turned loose in a world devoid of people, they would be decimated. Aside from the obvious case of chihuahuas, bulldogs, and others who could simply not withstand the elements or who are too small, slow, or clumsy to be successful predators, the vast majority of all dogs would not do well. We know from the case of dogs who have gone feral that they remain on the periphery of human society, living on handouts, garbage, and vulnerable livestock such as poultry and lambs. Without vaccination, overwhelming numbers would succumb to disease.

Man, in turn, relies on the dog to be a guardian of home and family, a warrior and messenger, a sentry, a playmate for and protector of children, a guardian of livestock, a beast of burden, a rescuer of lost people, a puller of carts and sleds, a friend, a hunter, a companion, an exercise mate, a guide for the blind and deaf, a contact with nature for urban man, a way for city dwellers to meet people (cf. the "dog-people" in New York City), a source of friendship and company and solace for the old and lonely, a vehicle for penetrating the frightful shell surrounding the disturbed child, a source of the comfort of touch, and an inexhaustible wellspring of love.

Yet it is man who systematically violates this contract in the most essential ways, callously infringing upon the dog's rights to life and nature.

The violation of the right to life is obvious. Each year, we kill ten to fourteen million healthy dogs in pounds and veterinarians' offices. We kill by barbiturates, decompression, carbon monoxide, shooting, electrocution. Millions more die of disease, starvation, and automobile accidents after they have been turned loose by owners. And the overwhelming majority of animals killed are not feral animals who have never had a home—this population would be reduced to insignificance after a few years of efficient animal control—but animals who have at one point been owned by a person.

Over the past four years, I have worked closely with the people who run the humane society in my home city, as well as managers of human societies and pounds across North America. Highly conscientious people, they have attempted to catalog the reasons why people bring animals in to be euthanized. (Bringing an animal into a humane society or pound is tantamount to bringing it in to be killed. Very few are adopted.) Their results are echoed by veterinarians who are also asked to put animals to sleep for extramedical reasons. People bring animals in to be killed because they are moving and do not want the trouble of traveling with a pet. People kill animals because they are moving to a place where it will be difficult to keep an animal. People kill animals because they are going on vacation and do not want to pay for boarding, and anyway, they can always get another one. People kill animals because their son or daughter is going away to college and cannot take care of it. People kill animals, rather than attempt to place them in other homes, because "the animal could not bear to live without me." People kill animals because they cannot housebreak them, or train them not to jump up on the furniture, or not to chew on it, or not to bark. People kill animals because they have moved or redecorated and the animals no longer match the color scheme. People kill animals because the animals are not mean enough or are too mean. People kill animals because they bark at strangers or do not bark at strangers. People kill animals because the animal is getting old and can no longer jog with them. People kill animals because they feel themselves getting old and are afraid of dying before the animal. People kill animals because the semester is over and Mom and Dad would not appreciate a new dog. People kill animals because they only wanted their children to witness the "miracle of birth," and they have no use for the puppies or kittens. People kill animals because they have heard that when Great Danes get old, they get mean. People kill animals because they are tired of them or because they want a new one. People kill animals because they are no longer puppies and kittens and are no longer cute or are too big. There are clearly legitimate reasons for violating an animal's right to life, but few of the above fall into that category.

Equally intolerable from a moral point of view are our flagrant violations of the pet animals' right to live their lives in accordance with their natures—natures we have shaped. Sometimes these violations are the result of deliberate cruelty, as in the case of the sadistic individual who keeps a dog chained day and night. But most often, these violations grow out of ignorance and stupidity. The average person who acquires a dog or cat is worse than ignorant, worse because such people are invariably infused with outrageously false information.

Consider some of the "common knowledge" about the natures of dogs and cats: Doberman pinscher's brains grow too large for their skulls and they go crazy. Cats suffocate babies. Dogs of the same sex will always fight if put together. A cat will always survive a fall. Big dogs should not be kept in city apartments. Purebred dogs are "better" than mongrels. The way to make a dog mean is to feed him gunpowder. Cats cannot swim. Dogs and cats cannot get along. The way to housebreak a dog is to hit him when he defecates in the house or to rub his nose in the excrement. If a dog is wagging his tail, he is friendly and will not bite. Slapping a dog on the nose is a good method of correction. Slapping a rolled-up newspaper and startling the dog is a good method of correction. Cats cannot be trained. Castration or spaying of an animal removes aggression. And, of course, that time-honored piece of folkwisdom, "You can't teach an old dog new tricks." The above truisms are, of course, false. To put it bluntly, the average person is either ignorant or misinformed about dog and cat behavior, training, biology, nutrition—in short, about the animal's nature.

In some contexts, this ignorance or misinformation is laughable, as when one man informed me that his dog is part bear, or a veterinary student informed me that Dobermans were mean because we had cropped their ears for generations and that this resulted in hereditary ill-temper. ("After all, how would you feel if someone cropped your ears? Pretty mean.") But most often, the net result of this ignorance is a life for the animal wherein its basic nature is abused, thwarted, or ignored. Walk into a parking lot on a hot summer day and see how many dogs are left in closed cars without water or ventilation. ("He's just a small dog; there's plenty of air.") In point of fact, if the temperature inside the car reaches 105 degrees Fahrenheit, not at all unlikely given the greenhouse effect, the dog will suffer permanent brain damage within fifteen minutes.

Or consider the claim that one ought not to keep a large dog in a city apartment, one of the few things that "everyone knows" when they go out to get a dog. Cognizant of that "fact," a family may decide to purchase a small poodle, with unfortunate consequences. The poodle, typically a frenetic, high-strung creature, will be miserable without constant exercise. They would very likely have been better off with a Great Dane, a phlegmatic dog which, despite its size, or perhaps because of it, tends to spend most of its time in a semicataleptic state. (In the case of my Dane, my wife and I would call her periodically just to make sure she was still breathing. Generally, we were lucky to exact one tail-thump in response.)

Veterinarians are an excellent source of information about the animal suffering that is engendered by human ignorance. All too often, a veterinarian is asked to kill a dog, sometimes a puppy but more often an older dog, which is tearing up the house or urinating on the bed. The owners have tried beating, yelling, caging; nothing has worked. They are shocked to learn that the dog, as a social animal, is lonely. Often the older dog has been played with every day for years by children who have now gone off to college. Often the dog has been accustomed to extraordinary attention from his mistress, a divorcee, who suddenly has a new boy friend and has forgotten the dog's needs. Often the dog has been a child substitute for a young couple, who now have a new baby, and the dog is being ignored and is jealous. (Incidentally, these cases illustrate the importance which a knowledge of animal behavior has for veterinarians. Unfortunately, this area is underemphasized in veterinary medical education.)

Veterinarians are called upon almost daily to modify an animal's nature to suit an owner. Consider the case of the house-proud woman who has bought a cute kitten on a whim, oblivious to the fact that kittens climb, scratch things, exercise or "sharpen" their claws on furniture. The "solution": declaw the animal and throw it outside in good weather. Unfortunately, the declawed animal is now devoid of natural defenses and is likely to come home maimed, if at all. Or consider the case of the suburban couple who buys a dog, leaves him outside at night, and then fields complaints from neighbors that the dog barks. The "solution": surgically remove the voicebox—a mutilation called "debarking", which generally does not work, serving only to leave the animal with a grotesque honking noise. The American Kennel Club and similar organizations of dog and cat breed fanciers, are major culprits in perpetuating mutilations and distortions of the animals' *telos*, through the "breed standards" they promulgate and perpetuate in dog and cat shows. If one wishes to win in these shows one must have a Doberman with cropped ears and docked tail; a Great Dane, boxer, Boston bull terrier with cropped ears; a cocker spaniel, old English sheepdog, poodle with docked tails.

In a related area, thoughtless concern with standards which are purely aesthetic or morphological results in perpetuation of genetic defects that cause much suffering in the dog. Concern with a certain shaped face and eye in the collie and Shetland sheepdog has led to a disease called "Collie eye" or "Sheltie eye," which can result in blindness. The breathing difficulties and heart problems of bulldogs are genetically and physiologically linked to the selection for foreshortened faces. There is some evidence that German shepherd aggressiveness, much prized by trainers and the military, is genetically linked to hip dysplasia. The Irish setter has been bred with an exclusive concern for aesthetics to the point of imbecility. (It is sometimes said of these dogs that "they cannot find themselves at the end of a leash.") Manx cats, bred for taillessness, suffer from severe spinal defects. Dachshunds suffer from genetically based spinal diseases that result in paralysis, and they tend to have diabetes and Cushing's syndrome. Dalmations get bladder stones, apparently as a result of genetic linkage with coat color. In Dalmations and Australian shepherds, coat color is linked with hereditary deafness. Siamese cats are bred for cross-eyes. Silver-colored collies suffer from grey collie syndrome, a situation in which their white blood cell count cyclically falls, and they are susceptible to infection. They are also susceptible to digestive, reproductive, skeletal, and ocular problems. Of all dog breeds, boxers have by far the greatest incidence of every sort of cancer. (In fact, more than one hundred diseases of dogs are of genetic origin; that is, they have been perpetuated by irresponsible breeding.) In short, not only do we ignore relevant aspects of our animals' natures, we also systematically destroy these natures through breeding for traits that appeal to us, without regard for the effect of these traits on the animals' lives.

Other examples of our violation of the animals' nature are manifest. Through our own failure to understand and respect the dog, train him properly, and understand his psychology, we tranquilize our pets, cage them in tiny cages for hours, chain them, muzzle them, beat them, use shock collars. Instead of using the dog's natural protectiveness for home and master, we create instant attack dogs through brutal training methods, dogs that bite anything that moves including the owner. Many of these dogs are hairtrigger weapons, primed by stimulus and response and sold to people who know nothing about dogs and who think that by plunking down $2,000 they have bought respect and loyalty. Many of these dogs, especially male dogs trained by men and sold to women, are subsequently destroyed for being "uncontrollable."

Our failure to know anything at all about the dog's biology or behavior results in people buying any dog as long as it is "cute," which in turn results in unscrupulous puppy mills, which turn out inferior animals under appalling conditions for profit. Pet stores often neglect and abuse their animals. Our lack of understanding of the animals' nutritional and biological needs results in myriad medical problems, which arise out of bad diet, overfeeding, and lack of exercise. Our use of animals as extensions of ourselves rather than ends in themselves results in the encouragement of behavior which is unnatural or neurotic— begging, limping for sympathy, whining for attention. Our inability to understand the animal results in an inability to train it, which in turn leads to dogs who chase cars and are killed or maimed in traffic accidents (or engender accidents that harm humans); dogs who chase joggers and are maced; dogs who are euthanized because they nip children. Our failure to confine our animals results in dogs being shot by farmers, run over, becoming pregnant indiscriminately or so young that their development is stunted; overproduction of unwanted animals, problems of damage to lawns and gardens, danger of disease through wholesale deposit of excrement, and worst of all, to pack formation.

We have thus seen that we are far indeed from respecting the fundamental rights of pet animals and that our laws mirror our individual irresponsibility. The laws see pet animals as *private property*; anyone can acquire an animal and usually as many as desired. Only the anticruelty laws "protect" the animals, these are rarely enforced and, in some states, require proof of malicious intent, their point being to weed out sadistic individuals who might harm humans as much as to protect the animals.

We can thus conclude that we are dealing with a morally intolerable situation, all the more so because our legal system and our educational system do nothing to break the cycle. We need to provide laws that protect these creatures, that perhaps make it harder for irresponsible people to own—and destroy—an animal. We must furthermore—and here veterinarians and humane societies are obliged to lead the way—educate people about animal needs and rights. (I discuss all this in great detail in my book.)

We may hope that our awakened concern for the role of companion animals evidenced in the many studies reported in this book will result in greater adherence on our part to the awesome human moral commitment underlying the human-animal bond. Let all of us increase our awareness that care about pet animals is more than just an overflow for draining emotion. It is also a springboard for awakening our moral concern for the millions of creatures who have intrinsic value, whose lives are wasted and twisted at our hands, and yet for whom no tears are shed.

Robert S. Shurtleff

47

In the Patient's Interest:
Toward a New Veterinary Ethic

Ask the average person what is the purpose of veterinary medicine, and the response will be something close to "caring for sick animals." The veterinary profession is in fact far more diverse, versatile, and complex than this popular stereotype would indicate, and nowhere is this diversity more evident than in the area of veterinary ethics. Veterinarians embrace a wide range of ethical views toward animals, views which often conflict with one another.

In this essay I will examine these ethical views, their origins and consequences, and present my argument for a single veterinary ethic that will serve our common interests within the veterinary profession while also benefiting our patients, our clients, and the society at large.

Much controversy exists in the area of veterinary ethics, both within and without the veterinary profession. Those outside the profession attack it for such practices as performing experimental surgery on live animals, contributing to modern factory farming techniques, performing cosmetic surgery on companion animals, and so on. A quick glance at the letters columns of most current veterinary journals will reveal that those within the profession are engaged in often heated arguments with one another over these very same issues.

Meanwhile, our professional organizations have shied away from any consideration of the substantive issues, beyond airing readers' views in the aforementioned letters columns of their journals. Indeed, the "Principles of Veterinary Medical Ethics" published by the American Veterinary Medical Association (AVMA) merely mentions the "relief of animal suffering" as one of three "principal objectives of the veterinary profession," the other two being "to render service to society" and "to conserve our livestock resources" (Journal of the American Veterinary Medical Association, 1979). Aside from this very brief reference, the object of our professional attentions, the patient, is excluded from this consideration of "ethical principles"; the rest of the document is devoted to fees, business practices, personal behavior, and the like.

Why have our professional organizations been so negligent in considering the ethical aspects of our treatment of the patient? One likely reason is that they have recognized the lack of consensus within the profession and have chosen to avoid the inevitable storm of criticism which any pronouncement, however mild, would invite.

What is more important to us here is the fact that this lack of consensus exists. Although we habitually refer to "*the* veterinary profession," in fact veterinary medicine is almost schizophrenic in the variety of tasks it performs. A wildlife veterinarian may work to increase the population of certain animal speciies specifically so that they can be killed by hunters and trappers; a small animal veterinarian works to safeguard the health of individual animals whose sole function is to serve as companions to human beings. A food animal veterinarian chooses a medical treatment for a cow on the basis of whether it will increase or decrease the producer's net profit on the animals; an equine veterinarian will spare no cost to save the life of an old horse whose riding days are long past. Veterinary medicine is a human activity which treats animals as dictated by the needs and demands of other human beings; in many instances the needs or interests of the animal are secondary, if considered at all.

This last point is central to any examination of veterinary ethics because it influences all ethical judgments made by veterinarians. Unlike human medicine, wherein humans treat other humans and serve the interests of the common species of patient and doctor, veterinary medicine is often faced with an unwelcome choice: whether to act in the best interests of the patient, an animal, or whether to ignore the patient's interests and respond to the demands of the client, a fellow human being, who is actually seeking and paying for our services. Dr. Bernard Rollin has called this the fundamental problem of veterinary medicine (Rollin, 1978). Some within the profession would say that the financial consideration silences the issue, that we must submit to the demands of the client because we are engaging in a simple economic transaction in a free-market economy. But Dr. Rollin has pointed to an apt analogy from human medicine: in treating children, the pediatrician is dealing with patients who often cannot represent their own interests, while these services are sought and paid for by a third party, the parents of the child. Still, human medical ethics would certainly put the child's interests over the demands of the parent if the two conflicted (Rollin, 1978).

Yet this central issue remains as an obstacle to any practical consideration of veterinary ethics. Until the profession itself can resolve this dilemma, our ethics will remain fragmented and contradictory, and our professional judgments will constantly be questioned by those who seek our services. The need for a common purpose in veterinary medicine is acute. Without it the prestige of our profession suffers greatly; with it we can address the more basic ethical issues with one voice. What, then, might this common purpose be?

Beneath all of the divergent attitudes in veterinary medicine, there persists some vague notion that the individual animal has some intrinsic value. By virtue of possessing the elusive quality called "life," animals are elevated above the status of mere objects and possess a value beyond that assigned to them by economics alone. As noted earlier, the AVMA has stated that relief of animal suffering is one of the three principal objectives of veterinary medicine. The authors of that document, speaking on behalf of the veterinary profession, recognized that animals can suffer and implied that they deserve to be free from such suffering. Such a view is shared by society in general, as evidenced by the widespread existence of anticruelty laws (Carson, 1972). Why not embrace the following as the fundamental principle of veterinary ethics: our primary obligation as veterinarians is to safeguard the interests of animals, specifically insofar as ensuring their relief from suffering.

This principle can serve quite well as a fundamental veterinary ethic. If we interpret "suffering" to encompass not just physical pain but also such experiences as excessive and prolonged confinement, mutilation or restraint that subverts an animal's ability to fulfill natural drives, and so forth, then our veterinary ethic coincides remarkably well with the beliefs of much of our society as expressed in recent legislation, for example, the Animal Welfare Act in the United States and laws in Germany and Denmark mandating that behavioral needs of farm animals must be considered (Chaloux and Heppner, 1980; McClintic, 1980). Historically, the idea of acting on behalf of animals follows a long tradition in veterinary medicine; in 1863, the United States Veterinary Medical Association, later to become the AVMA, took as its motto *Non Nobis Solum*—"not for us alone" (Crawford, 1976).

If we accept this principle that relieving suffering is our primary obligation in veterinary medicine, then how are we to view instances when the veterinarian causes suffering by his or her actions? Certainly we can accept this if it is in the best interests of the individual animal—for example, vaccinating against disease or performing surgery to correct a traumatic injury. But what of those situations when the animal is made to suffer to serve the interests of mankind or of other animals, the obvious example being the use of animals for scientific research? Having recognized that relief from suffering is the right of the individual animal, we must have a compelling reason to induce suffering when no benefits fall to that particular individual from our actions, and we incur an obligation to take every possible precaution to minimize the suffering of all such animals (Dawkins, 1980). In the area of food animal medicine, this basic ethical principle would not prohibit our participation in these activities, but would obligate us to take a more active role in promoting humane slaughter techniques, efficient but considerate livestock rearing practices, and so forth.

Certainly, there are those who would protest that to take such a position would mean economic suicide in a free marketplace; these objections have been considered by Dr. Michael Fox in a recent article (Fox, 1977). But the other side of the coin is worth noting: in a society that is increasingly concerned for animals and their needs, will not a growing number of clients seek out the veterinarian who reflects these attitudes to the greatest degree, while turning away from the practitioner who apparently lacks this commitment? I believe that embracing such a simple principle as the basis for our professional activity would add to our prestige, our self-respect, and our effectiveness as practitioners.

If we acknowledge that such a common veterinary ethic would be a step forward, it then becomes necessary to consider how to gain its acceptance within the veterinary profession. Certainly, influencing attitudes and beliefs during their formation is the easiest course of action, and it would seem reasonable to assume that most ethical beliefs and attitudes are formed before the completion of the veterinarian's professional education. In this process, two of the major factors shaping their ethical beliefs are the individual student's background and the environment of his or her veterinary education.

In the background of the individual student, certain prejudices can be identified. Students from a rural background are more likely to have been exposed to such practices as livestock rearing, hunting, and trapping that tend to predispose one toward a view of animals as a resource to be consumed or even as a competitor to be eliminated. Students from a more urban background tend to be more familiar with animals in their role as companions or as interesting but nonthreatening exhibits in a zoo or museum. Their concepts of farm animals and wild animals are likely to be colored by stories, films, and television. Of the two groups, one would expect students from rural backgounds to predominate in veterinary colleges; most such schools are affiliated with land-grant (agricultural) universities in predominantly rural states and admit mostly residents of their own states.

The other major force shaping the ethical beliefs of veterinary students is the environment of their veterinary education. A variety of factors interact here, among them the prevailing community attitudes, those of the college's faculty, and the nature of the veterinary curriculum.

First, since most veterinary colleges are affiliated with land-grant universities located in rural or agricultural areas of their respective states, the prevailing local community attitudes toward animals are likely to have a strong consumptive or competitive bias, as noted earlier.

Second, the faculties of the veterinary colleges obviously play a major role in shaping the attitudes of their students. Unfortunately, in many cases their perspectives originate from earlier decades when prevailing attitudes toward animals were somewhat less progressive than today's attitudes. Furthermore, most of them share an interest in research, which often requires the use of animals as experiemental subjects; this interest predisposes some faculty members toward a utilitarian view of animals as a resource to be exploited. These factors no doubt contribute to a tendency I have observed in some faculty members to greet newer, more progressive attitudes toward animals with hostility and resentment.

Third, the veterinary curriculum has traditionally used live animals as a "teaching tool" for two purposes: to practice the skills one must learn to become a veterinarian and to demonstrate concepts in academic courses. Having experienced many such demonstrations, I can attest to the fact that they are often superfluous to one's understanding of the concepts involved. Such routine use of live animals trivializes their value as individuals, and being forced to participate in these exercises inevitably desensitizes the student to some degree toward all animal life. The widespread availability of videotaping equipment makes the annual repetition of these live animal exercises even more unwarranted.

Unfortunately, the one aspect of veterinary education that could counterbalance these influences on a student's attitude toward animals is largely absent. A single course in ethics, dealing with substantive issues and taught by an instructor familiar with the controversies confronting the profession today, would at least expose students to novel ideas or perspectives and increase their sensitivity toward these issues. But austerity in the nation's veterinary colleges has made funds for such "ancillary" courses as ethics all but unavailable. Looking toward the future, we can only hope that those in charge of veterinary education will move toward a reordering of their priorities.

John A. Hoyt

48

The Animal Welfare Perspective

The Humane Society of the United States has for many years initiated and supported many programs that have demonstrated the possibilities and benefits of people-pet bonding: our self-improvement through riding program bringing together disabled children and horses; the CATS program, children and animals together for seniors, bonding not only pets and the elderly but also children and older adults; our use of pets in nursing home facilities; and a variety of less formal programs. Other animal welfare organizations have promoted similar programs throughout the many cities and counties of our nation. We are grateful that many in the medical professions, educators, institutional administrators, and others have joined us in affirming the value of such bonding experiences and are contributing their expertise to help make such experiences of even greater value.

Yet in the midst of our shared enthusiasm and expectations, I would sound a note of caution that should be written in bold print on our several ventures with these bonding experiences. For there stand today in thousands of communitites across our nation monuments to other bonding experiences that have ended in failure—the animal shelters and community pounds. Approximately thirteen and a half million cats and dogs are systematically put to death annually because someone's bonding experience did not work, or was not wanted, or was too costly in money or effort or love. Bonding between humans and animals, like marriage, is a two-way street. The needs and welfare of both parties must be given equal consideration.

Nor is it in the destruction of millions of companion animals that the greatest tragedy for these creatures lies—these are perhaps the fortunate ones—but, rather, in the living who are forced to exist, often for many years, under conditions that result in pain, suffering, and misery.

Over the centuries, man has regarded the nature of animals vis-a-vis himself. He has worshiped some and desecrated others. He has sometimes classified them as things and at other times accepted them as brothers. He has constructively used them and arrogantly abused them. Yet at no time has man so universally respected animals that it could be said they were safe from cruelty and suffering at his hands. It is still so today.

I believe there is an essential quality of being that is as common to animals as to the man-animal. To be sure, animals lack the mystical, metaphysical appropriations surrounding man which have evolved from the historical philosophies and religions, not the least of which is the Judeo-Christian tradition. Yet it is entirely possible that the essence of animal being is just as important as that of man's and, in a nonreligious sense, just as sacred. Man has calculated and defined his own essence and, thus, his own value as a being among beings. That animals have not done likewise, we can only surmise. Or, if they have, they obviously have not discussed it with us. Consequently, it is left to us to define, at least for our own understanding, what is the essence of animal being and what is their inherent value—not in the sense that they are socially and economically valuable to use but to themselves and to life.

Anthony Wayne Smith, former president of the National Parks and Conservation Association, once wrote, "It is the intrinsic value of life to itself that is important; it is irrelevant whether the other forms of life serve man. The other creatures exist not merely to cooperate with man, to serve and be served by him, but for themselves."

Perhaps it is not coincidental that at a time when we are exploring ways and means for using animals to the benefit of human beings in a multitude of circumstances, that is, refining ways in which further to exploit animals for our own benefit, there is a new wave of interest and commitment to affirm the rights of animals. In the extreme, the proponents of animal rights are declaring that animals have a right not to be eaten, not to be used in biomedical experiments and drug testing, and not to be euthanized when deserted and unwanted. Yet apart from these extremes, a larger and ever-growing body of people view man's use of animals as a practice that cannot be taken for granted but must be tempered with compassion, care, and concern.

Those of us within the mainstream of the animal welfare movement support the use of animals in the service of man for purposeful and meaningful ends. But even these uses must seek to guarantee the comfort and well-being of the animal. I could list numerous concerns that will surely be raised by sincere and reasonable people within the animal welfare movement in reference to many of the uses of animals suggested and described in this volume. These must be heard, heeded, and affirmed by all of us who pursue these positive and appropriate uses. For it is of little value that we serve the good on one hand if we do injustice on the other. Yet I am confident that in the further bonding of humans and animals in new and beneficial ways, not only can the lives of humans be enriched and made whole, but those animals which we use can be afforded genuine companionship and care.

Appropriate to this concern is a paragraph from a delightful book entitled *The Outermost House*, by Henry Beston, which though written fifty years ago, is yet a poignant reminder of the need for a feeling and sensitive relationship with our fellow creatures:

> We need another and a wiser and perhaps a more mystical concept of animals. Remote from universal nature, and living by complicated artifice, man in civilization surveys the creature through the glass of his knowledge and sees thereby a feather magnified and the whole image in distortion. We patronize them for their incompleteness, for their tragic fate of having taken form so far below ourselves. And therein we err, and greatly err. For the animal shall not be measured by man. In a world older and more complete than ours they move finished and complete, gifted with extensions of the senses we have lost or never attained, living by voices we shall never hear. They are not brethren, they are not underlings; they are other nations, caught with ourselves in the net of life and time, fellow prisoners of the splendour and travail of the earth (p. 25).

Aaron H. Katcher

49

Man and the Living Environment: An Excursion into Cyclical Time

It is not possible to discuss people and their animal companions without looking at how both are defined in respect to their mutual environment, in part because animals are usually considered as an element of man's environment. In a previous paper (Katcher, 1981), I suggested that we tend to think of both men and animals as beings that are distinct from their environment and can be plucked from it without distortion in for or aberration of function. This habit of thought, which conceptualizes the human or animal subject apart from a habitat, is an outgrowth of the Cartesian definition of animals and the animal part of man as machinery. Thinking of animals and man as clockwork is part of our scientific world-view and is embodied in the Pavlovian and Freudian techniques of studying mental activity by isolating subjects from their environments. It is part of our medical tradition that sees patients in clinics, not homes. It is still with us in the radical definitions of man offere by the modern-day Social Darwinists.

Thus I can quote Richard Dawkins.

> Four thousand million years on, what was to be the fate of the ancient replicators? They did not die out, for they are past masters of the survival arts. But do not look for them floating loose in the sea; they gave up that cavalier freedom long ago. Now they swarm in huge colonies safe *inside gigantic lumbering robots sealed off from the outside world*, communicating with it by tortuous indirect routes, manipulating it by remote control. They are in you and in me; they created us, body and mind; and their preservation is the ultimate rationale for our existence. They have come a long way, those replicators. Now they go by the name of genes, and *we are their survival machines*. (1978:21)

Our view of man, and the medical profession's view of man, is consonant with Dawkins's description of people and animals as survival machinery. It is a successful world-view. Our ability to place man on the moon, or fling him back and forth into space, is a tribute to the technical wisdom of conceptualizing man as potentially independent of any environment. Our science fiction envisions man as an argonaut, surviving in thousands of different environments, usually bringing with him a portable experimental chamber, the capsule of a rocket, or the more commodious quarters of the *Star Ship Enterprise*.

Even our psychosomatic medicine is grounded upon this same concept of man as clockwork to be studied in the shop of the repairman. The insights of psychosomatic medicine are provided by talking to patients isolated in therapeutic chambers or in psychophysical laboratories and by testing patients in consulting rooms, as one might test the component functions of machinery. Disease tends to be related to internal structures like personality and physiological response to experimental stimuli. The significant events of our psychosomatic medicine are internal, and the environment is simply a relatively unorganized source of stimuli, which are reconstructed in the laboratory, not observed directly.

When the environment is incorporated into medical investigation, it exists as a strange kind of statistical or Cartesian space, in which the dimensions are highly abstracted components of both the internal state and the external environment. The relationships between the components of that space are only statistical, and its construction corresponds to no ordering of components in the real world but is built only for the purpose of predicting future events. Thus blood pressure, a psychological test score, weight, marital status, income, a life-change index, and a habit such as cigarette smoking can all be combined to generate a predictive equation, actually a multidimensional space, describing a person's chance of developing disease. This conceptual space reinforces and complements the definition of man as a machine, abstracted from space. The statistical space which is used to study man bears little necessary relationship to the details and realities of transactions within the real, common-sense, three-dimensional, time-continuous world: the world we inhabit.

Thus we have little idea about how the transactions of everyday life, the events of everyday life, or the objects of everyday life influence our health. One hundred years ago it was observed that people who are widowed or divorced have a lower life expectancy than people who are married. Yet only this year has it been learned that remarriage protects men against the lethal effects of the loss of a spouse. We still do not know how marriage preserves life. What goes on day after day between husband and wife that changes the life expectancy of men? Are happy marriages healthier than unhappy ones? We are in a similar state of ignorance about other relationships between environment and disease. Poor women tend to be obese seven times more frequently than more affluent women. Why? The psychosomatic literature of obesity is filled with experimental studies about how people function as eating machines but contains no information telling us how the day-to-day transactions of living poor translate into fat.

How, then, do we connect the real environment, buildings, objects, people, dogs, cats, family, friends, furniture, houses, automobiles, pictures, sculpture, lawns, plants, gardens, wilderness, and parks to our concept of man? How do we return to a physician's eye, similar to the one described by the author of the Hippocratic text, *"Aires, Waters and Places"*? The question is obviously rhetorical, but it must be raised if my description of the intersection between our day-to-day traffic with the living environment and health is to be understood.

I suggest that transactions between people and animals may have an important influence on our sense of well-being and our physical health. This belief was forced upon me when I observed that patients with coronary disease who had a pet enjoyed a better life expectancy than similar patients without pets. This study of survival of patients who were hospitalized in a coronary care unit was a meager initial attempt to open to scrutiny an important area of our social relationships. The chapter by Marcia Ory and Evelyn Goldberg in Part Four of this volume is an important continuation of that effort. The research design they used to study pets and health reflects the complexity of the problem. We can expect that the process of studying the intersection between that social relationship and health will be comfortably long and intricate. I do not expect simple answers. We have known for a long time that marriage and health are interdependent. Yet our knowledge of the way transactions within a marriage relate to health is almost as primitive as our knowledge of human-animal interactions and health.

I propose to explore four descriptive terms for the outcome of transactions between man and animal, and I suggest that these outcomes may be the means through which animals can help preserve our mental and physical equilibrium. These attributes are safety, kinship, intimacy, and constancy. These four descriptive terms are, of course, partially intersecting. Kinship provides only one form of safety. Intimacy is achieved only with a portion of people within or without the family. Constancy may or may not characterize our intimate or family relationships. Each of these terms can be considered as an attribute of an internal mental state. I am going to describe them, however, as outcomes of a series of transactions between people and animals. These transactions can be observed directly and defined objectively. Yet the outcomes of these objective interactions cannot be understood without considering the symbolic meanings packed into concepts like "cat" or "dog." To understand the outcome of a behavioral interaction, it is sometimes necessary to extend the field of observation beyond that interaction and unpack some of the symbolic meanings contained within the iconic animal that always accompanies the flesh and blood animal. I will consider each of these four descriptive terms in turn.

SAFETY

There is no doubt that companion animals make people feel safe in situations characterized by a high degree of novelty. The evidence for this assertion can be simply reviewed. Sebkova observed that subjects left to complete a manifest anxiety scale with the experimenter's dog for company had lower anxiety scores than subjects who completed the test alone. Children brought into a living room of a neighborhood home had lower blood pressures when a dog was present with the experimenter than when the experimenter was there alone. In the same study, the lower blood pressure was observed both when the child was at rest and when he or she was performing a task that provoked performance anxiety: reading aloud. People in a veterinary clinic consulting room have lower blood pressures when they are touching and talking to their pets than when they are talking to the experimenter.

People with animals seem to be more approachable than people without animals. We feel that it is socially permissible to talk to a person with a dog. Our right to talk to strangers walking alone is much more doubtful. The two social triads, person, dog, and stranger or person, child, and stranger, are similar in this respect. One can approach either child or dog without the explicit permission of the owner, and once the child or the animal is approached, one then has the right to talk to the owner. Considering the almost universal proscriptions against touching strangers, it is important to note that one can touch the child or the dog as a means of greeting. These cultural rules were tested by the observations reported by Peter Messent. He observed that when his subjects were walking with their dogs, they were more likely to be talked to and more likely to have longer conversations than when they were walking alone.

The observations of Ann Otney Cain also suggest that people in some families engage in this same triangulation to make contact with each other. They find it easier to establish contact through the animal than to engage in dyadic relationships. One informant at our clinic stated that she was never able to talk to her father directly. The only way she could establish contact was to come and pet the dog, which was almost always at his side. She could then talk to her father about the dog, and only after a dialogue had been established around the dog could they talk directly.

These observations that animals make people safe for people are consonant with our knowledge of the change in meaning that is effected when the image of

a dog is juxtaposed to the image of a person or placed within a human environment. Unless the animal is labeled as vicious or dangerous, a person or a place
coupled with a dog is perceived as safer, more benign, more approachable, and
less dangerous. Political candidates with dogs are more acceptable than candidates without dogs. In the 1980 congressional elections in the United States,
Republican candidates were instructed to have themselves photographed with a
dog.

INTIMACY

In previous publications, I noted that people talk to their animals and delight in
doing so. Moreover, they talked to animals as they talked to other persons.
Smaller numbers of people, about 30 percent of the sample, also said that they
confided in their pets. The fraction of subjects confiding in pets was higher when
children or adolescents were the subject group. People not only speak to animals,
they feel that their pets understand the emotions conveyed by their talk, if not the
words.

We suggested, half in jest, that people attributed to the dog some of the
characteristics of an empathic listener. The dog was nondirective, nonjudgmental, and sensitive to the speaker's emotion. Yet the intimacy that a dog or a cat
can offer goes beyond that provided by the ethical Rogerian analyst, because
people caress their animals when talking to them, and the dialogue with the
animal is an alternation or superimposition of talk and touch. When we think
about the definition of intimacy, one of its hallmarks is the combination of talk
and soft touch. The intimacy passing between people and animals has another
important characteristic: it can be studied in an experimental framework without
apparently distorting the interaction. People are intimate with animals in public,
just as people achieve a feeling of intimacy with children in public situations.
Even more important, this intimacy can be achieved with great rapidity. It has
always been recognized that there is something stereotyped about the emotion
that is evoked from some people by infants and puppies. People asked to pet
strange but friendly dogs rapidly achieve the style of dialogue that I have labeled
as intimacy, and the transactions between stranger and friendly dog look not too
dissimilar from the transactions between owners and beloved pets who have been
with them for years. (I am not implying that it is not possible to differentiate a
friendly dog's behavior toward his owners from his behavior toward strangers but
only that similar transactions characterize both relationships.) Our ability to
observe this behavior has permitted us to define a set of behavioral characteristics
that can be used as a preliminary definition of intimacy.

1. The person directs his or her gaze at the dog and attempts, sometimes by
controlling the head of the dog, to make and hold eye contact.

2. The dog is stroked and talked to simultaneously or alternately.

3. The person's voice becomes softer, sometimes inaudible or poorly audible to the other people in the room. This makes tape-recording the dialogue difficult but clearly differentiates the dialogue with the animal from talk which is meant to include the other people in the room. One subject, conscious that her discourse with the dog was shutting out the experimenters, was impelled to explain what she was saying to the dog. The cadence of the owner's speech changes, and fewer words are uttered per minute. A pseudodialogue is established by alternating questions and silences, and even when questions are not used, phrases are punctuated by a rise in pitch as if a question were being asked. To complete the dialogue the person touches the animal or with some other nonverbal signal solicits a reply from the dog.

4. Blood pressure is lower when the person talks to and touches the dog. than when he addresses a strange observer.

5. There is a change in facial expression, which could be grossly described as a smoothing of the facial features, with the loss of signs of tension and the presence of a fixed smiling.

6. Even when no touch contact is being made, the dog continually orients toward the person and the person toward the dog as if they had eyes only for each other. (The apparent anthropomorphism is deliberate because I believe that it is a good descriptive locution for such intimate behavior.)

I should add that the presence of a dog in an experimental chamber, a veterinary clinic, or a home permits the study of intimacy without sex in the same way that the procedures of Masters and Johnson permitted the study of sex without intimacy.

KINSHIP

The observation that the dog is a kind of kin and best described as a child is not new. This equation is explicit in Plutarch's life of Solon.

> For the soul, having a principle of kindness in itself, and being born to love as well as perceive, think or remember, inclines and fixes upon some stranger when a man has none of his own to embrace. And alien or illegitmate objects insinuate themselves into his affections, as into some estate that lack lawful heirs; and with affection come anxiety and care; insomuch that you may see men that use the strongest language against the marriage-bed and the fruit of it, when some servant's or concubine's child is sick or dies, almost killed with grief, and abjectly lamenting. Some have given way to shameful and desperate sorrow at the loss of a dog or a horse. (Plutarch, Modern Library edition:101–2)

The intimacy that one sees between people and dogs is given concrete expression by placing it in a formal social context. Informants state that the dog is "a member of the family." The following observations indicate that the statement is more than a quaint manner of speech: Over half the respondents surveyed designated the dog as a family member. When given the opportunity to describe it as an animal or human family member, over 48 percent designated the dog as human. This observation has been confirmed by Dr. Victoria Voith in an unpublished survey of subjects in a veterinary clinic and by Dr. Barbara Jones in a survey of adolescents responding to questions about their horses. The respondents tended to identify dogs as children when asked to specify the status of the animal within the family. A substantial number of subjects celebrate the animal's birthday. As Dr. Jay Ruby indicates in this volume, the animal is photographed as children are photographed in the collection of family photographs. Family portraits when taken in a setting about the home tend to include the dog. The dog shares the parental bed and bedroom. The dog is fed and does not feed himself. The animal is permitted to display his anus and genitalia. His excretory functions are a subject of public concern, effort, and direct comment without embarrassment. He is talked to but is not expected to use words. One plays physically with the dog in a peculiar, nondirected way in which the point of the game is to sustain the game, not to keep score or establish a winner or a loser. The manner of speech used toward the dog frequently resembles that used with small children. It is lilting, simplified language of "motherese." If the dog is small enough, whether puppy or adult, it is frequently held in the manner in which infants are held.

Needless to say, even sociologists can tell the difference between the way we treat dogs and the way we treat children, but it is an interesting heuristic exercise to ask what these differences are. The point of the exercise is to learn more about our relationship with dogs and other pets that are treated like family members. In one sense, we know animals have a different status because pets are favored companions for some children who have other children available for play. Most pets in this country live in families with children, indicating that these animals can complement the companionship offered by children and do not necessarily substitute for children.

CONSTANCY

How can a dog or another animal be a source of comfort when people fail? For the purposes of this discourse, one significant difference between human children and animal children can be simply stated: the dog does not become an adult. Since he is not expected to become adult, there is no demand that the dog progress along an axis of intellectual, moral, or social achievement. The dog stays the same. He never grows up, never learns how to talk, or how to care for himself, or how to wear clothes that hide his genitalia. He never learns shame. He remains, to use an elderly metaphor, in the condition of Adam and Eve before the fall, without original sin. He does not have what Mark Twain calls in *The Mysterious Traveler* the moral sense.

The Victorians were able to frame a legal definition of cruelty to animals although they were unwilling to outlaw cruelty to children because punishment rendered to children could always be rationalized as necessary for moral correction and growth. Even the Victorians assumed that the dog was incapable of moral growth, hence cruelty could serve no moral purpose. The dog is then a constant child that always remains subordinate. As I have indicated earlier, the childlike status of mature dogs has been given an organic expression in the configuration of some breeds of dog, for example, the infantile facial conformation of breeds like the pugs or Pekingese. The dog, in being a constant child, like a four-legged Peter Pan, is fixed between culture and nature. The child is between culture and nature but moves inexorably away from his natural origins. The dog stays fixed in his dual role, neither wolf nor person.

The dog is a sign, an icon of constancy. He does not change. The care that a dog receives changes it in no way; it maintains the animal as it is. In turn, the dog does not force us to change. It is an idle fiction to believe that a dog teaches us or our children anything. Information that changes us is imparted with words, and the dog has no words. I am not saying that the dog cannot be a stimulus for learning, just as a picture or a rock strata or a sunset might stimulate interest and motivate learning. That learning, however, is accomplished when the stimulus is translated into words. The dog does not teach a child responsibility; the parents teach a child responsibility using the dog as a stimulus or reward. A dog does not teach a child about death; the dog dies; the child feels sad, and either through discourse or through translation of that experience into words, he learns. The dog may excite, may provide images, which stimulate learning, but the dog teaches nothing, save the simple games that one learns to play with dogs.

The constancy of the animal is the constancy of cyclical time, life in the cycles of day, month, season, lifetime. It is time that existed before our concept of linear history, before time's arrow took flight. It is the time of labor, as Hannah Arendt defines labor, those tasks which must be continually repeated, which leave no lasting artifact, which only sustain, and which fuel consumption. It is the task of the home and the farm.

In a culture devoted to improvement, to hierarchal progress, to getting ahead, to accomplishment, we have a very ambivalent attitude toward labor. At a conscious level, labor, unless it is devoted to the labor of consumption, has little value. It is considered the most degraded kind of work, identified with the activities of unliberated women, prisoners of one kind or another and the least well-paid members of the society. It is an activity from which most people want to escape.

When we escape from labor, however, we have no activities that sustain constancy and guarantee the continuing presence of the familiar. We have no way of sustaining our own constancy. When we devote ourselves to change, novelty, progress, and constant movement, our own sense of self begins to fade for want of consistent reflection from a stable environment. The underside of our worship of change is our fear of change, a fear that may, as I shall indicate, reflect a real danger. One of the many ways we have of assuaging this fear of change is contact with companion animals, with the representations of nature we bring into our immediate environment. The dog sustains our own constancy by the constancy of his behavior. He never changes, never assaults with words. His love is defined as unchanging, always available, quintessentially loyal. Loyalty and persistence are the most outstanding iconic characteristics of the dog, and that loyalty lasts until death or beyond; it is loyalty beyond the capacity of human beings to be loyal. The essential dog story is a story about loyalty.

We tell fables of dogs rescuing people. Yet the probabilities of being rescued from death by a dog are about as great as the probabilites of being killed by a dog, both, considering the number of dogs in this country, infinitesimally small. The fantasy of being rescued by rover or of having one's chidren rescued by Rover is probably an expression of the feeling that the dog protects the family, through its constancy, through the consistency of the love imputed to that unchanging family member.

Is the assertion I have just made about dogs, constancy, and cyclical time testable in any way? At one level it is testable with textual examination and with the projective technique applied to human-animal interaction by Randall Lockwood. He asked people to look at pictures of people with and without animals present and then to attribute characteristics to the people in the scene. He observed changes in the adjectives applied to the people which were dependent upon an animal's presence. This projective test gives one the ability to test experimentally the assumption that animals are associated with constancy and stability.

On a more meaningful level, the ability of the dog to provide constancy can be tested by making the assumption that if the animal acts as an efficacious generator of the feeling of constancy, then those people who have less constancy in their lives would be expected to reap the most emotional and physiological benefits from the presence of the animal. The Holmes and Rahe life-change index has been used successfully to predict illness rates. Their questionnaire was created by listing changes that occur in the life cycle: marriage, death of a family member, birth of a child, a move from one city to another, change in job, vacation, and so on. People were asked to weigh each change for its inherent stressfulness. These weights were then used to generate a life-change score from any given subject's immediate history of change. The subjects with higher life-change scores were more likely to suffer depression, illness, or accident. We should expect that activities providing a sense of constancy and a sense of continuity should protect people from the adverse health effects of change. We would expect, therefore, that pets should protect against the pathogenic effects of life change. Specifically, we would expect that, in the presence of pets and other stabilizing influences, high life-change scores would be associated with less illness, accident, and depression.

High life-change scores are frequently associated with loss of important social relationships. The highest life-change weights are assigned to events that disrupt patterns of intimacy and companionship. The NIH (Youmans and

Yarrow, 1971) study of healthy aged noted that longevity was associated with active, interesting daily activity. It also noted that subjects dropped activities when the people who supported those activities were lost. Pets, then, can have an important role in stabilizing the lives and activity patterns of older people who no longer have friends or family available to support a daily round of activity. People who have looked at the role of pets in the lives of the aged have commented that pets act to "clock" the lives of people who do not have a work or social schedule to pace their lives.

We usually do not take cognizance of the activities that sustain our own identity or our sense of living in a stable if not static environment. We have no life constancy scores. There are no psychological tests that I know of that ask the subject to count the ways in which his world is the same from day to day, season to season, or year to year. We have no means of studying the effect of the ritualistic nature of our behavior which gives continuity and constancy to life from day to day. We recognize the value of constancy in the environment of the child but ignore it for the adult. We overvalue those activities that improve our rank along any number of hierarchical orders, and we tend to devalue or obscure those activities that merely sustain the self. Work is usually conceptualized as a means of achievement rather than a means of providing people with an environment which is stabilized by a set of tasks for eight hours of the day. Yet the dislocations and decrease in health associated with retirement, or even temporary unemployment, evidence the importance of stable work in maintaining our sense of identity. We will not be able to study the way in which animals, and the rest of the living environment, like the gardens people tend, influence health, unless we devote more study to the importance of cyclical activity in sustaining our sense of identity, our emotional and physical equilibrium, and our health.

I have discussed four aspects of our transactions with animals that may shed light on the ability of companion animals to contribute to our health and sense of well-being. The last of these four was the constancy provided by companion animals, a constancy they provide by remaining constant themselves and by engaging us in repetitive cyclical activities that sustain a sense of self. Now, I would like to elaborate on that theme by discussing the two ways in which pets and other parts of the living environment can provide that feeling of constancy. These two ways are in some sense incompatible with each other and are based upon very different habits of thought.

Part of our feeling of intimacy and constancy when with a dog is attributed to the capacity of that animal for overflowing love and loyalty. Constance Parsons rightly said that there was something superhuman about that imputed loyalty, a quality of love that exceeded the capacity of mere humans. Indeed, many commentators on the dog state as both fact and poetry that the dog's love and loyalty exceeds man's.

In the description of the virtues of dog, one recognizes immediately the quality of what psychiatrists call a partial object. In psychoanalytic theory, the prototype for a partial object is the split image of the mother enjoyed by the young infant. It is the supremely satisfying aspect of the mother which is hallucinated by the child in her absence. A partial object is a real being or an entity (like a country or a deity) that is split into a part that is either all good or all bad, with little recognition of the reality that mixes good and bad, helpful and harmful, advantageous and disadvantageous, in everything. Whatever the truth in psychoanalytic theory about infants and their dreams of perfect mothers, the capacity to split the beings to which we are attached into fictions that are either too good or too bad is not limited to infants, nor are the split beings restricted to mothers. Father figures and mother figures can be split into idols and demons, with only one or the other aspect being perceived at any given moment. The love we give to motion picture idols, sports heroes, charismatic political and religious leaders, and animals like lambs, dogs, and dolphins is a love dependent upon that split perception.

Our tendency to create and relate to unreal objects is fostered by the infant's experience with toys and stuffed animals which provides constancy to a child's life in the absence of its mother. Such an object was called a "transitional object" because it permitted the child to effect a transition of affection from the mother to other beings in the environment. Unfortunately, the term "transitional object" suggests too narrow a role for stuffed animals or their successors in the form of the myriad toys and dolls that stock the nursery. All these toys have a common function similar to that of the stuffed animal: they permit the child to be active and engaged and safe without the presence of a parent or without continually interacting with the parent. Both stuffed animals and the rest of the toys and the dolls are animated and personified by the child's play. The child talks to or talks with his toys, animates them, personifies them, names them, and attributes a variety of feelings and behaviors to them. The toys are constant because they do not change their behavior, unless broken, and they permit or suffer great variety of animation or personification.

The dog, which is almost always introduced to the urban child after it has had considerable experience with stuffed animals and toys, has the character of an animated toy. It is personified by the child because the child's models for the animal are the partial images of animals in his stories and the toys and stuffed animals which he animated in the form of partial objects. The tendency of children to make partial objects out of animals, by attributing to them extreme qualities of virtue or vice, is not accidental or trivial. It is supported by almost all of our chidren's literature and apparently is part of the structure of the unconscious. According to Dr. Robert Van De Castle, over 70 percent of children's dreams involve animals, and in these dreams they act out fearful roles that complement the benign love we attribute to such animals as lambs, rabbits, puppies, and kittens in our waking life. Blake was not at all amiss in coupling the lamb and the tiger in the *Songs of Innocence and the Songs of Experience*. Even outside the life of the child, the metaphorical nature of our language has been grounded on animal images. Animal metaphors, which associate animals with single virtues or vices, are an essential part of our literary and mythic heritage.

The tiger and the lamb, the lion and the jackal, still color the way in which we organize our world. Animals, because of their diversity, permit us to give a visible and unequivocal structure to feelings that are hidden behind the common form of mankind.

This way of animating and personifying animals can fail to recognize the existence of the real animal. Moreover, it is frequently an expression of a highly narcissistic attachment, in which the affection and love attributed to the animal is, in reality, affection directed at the self. The animal is perceived as being part of the self, an inseparable companion. The intimacy the person feels in the presence of the animal, and the love the person feels reflected from the animal, is love directed at the self. The animal provides a sense of constancy because it is used as a mirror to reflect love back at the self. These animals are no longer stationed between culture and nature; they are, in fantasy, brought entirely into our own world and linked to the self. Like the self, they are highly individualized, as stuffed animals or security blankets are individualized. The individuality may not be dependent upon the realities of the animal's behaviors but only on what is attributed to the animal. People who love animals in this fashion are more vulnerable to the loss of the animal and can experience intense depression following such loss.

There is, however, another way of being with animals, a way that permits us the same feeling of constancy but recognizes the position of animals between culture and nature. It can recognize the reality of animals without split perception or narcissistic love. It recognizes the identity of the animal with his species in a way that people, who are made individual by their words, their actions, and the memories that other people have of them, cannot be identified with a species but stand unique. When we do not attribute to animals what we wish for ourselves, we can apreciate their own animal reality and see them as both part of our lives and part of nature. This is the kind of relationship with animals that is shared by the farmer, and even by the hunter who is hunting over his own land. (I am thinking here of the fall I spent outside of Chartres, walking over land that had been owned by the same family since the fifteenth century. On that land, near the river, were dolmens, altarlike stones that predated the Roman Empire. The hunters who combed their family land for game that year were following a stable tradition that had persisted for at least the last two thousand years. It was a yearly event like the harvest of grain. The grain and the game were there because the land and its life had been cared for for all of that time.) We have lost the notion that it is possible to love animals and see them die or sacrifice them in their time. Gilles Aillaud, in an insightful article called "Why Look at Animals?" reminds us of the coupling of love and sacrifice: "Animals came from over the horizon. They belonged there and here. Likewise they were mortal and immortal. An animal's blood flowed like human blood, but its species was undying and each lion was Lion, each ox was Ox. Thus—maybe the first existential dualism—was reflected in the treatment of animals. They were subjected and worshipped, bred and sacrificed" (Aillaud, 1981).

How do we learn to see in the continual mutability of living objects the constancy of cyclic change? How do we relearn that the lamb is loved and cared for, though in the end sacrificed, and replaced with another lamb? How do we go beyond the shortsighted error of Lorenz, who described the relationship between man and dog as unnatural and tragic because of the disparity in life span between man and dog. Lorenz failed to learn from the succession of dogs that he loved. Fortunately, desert shepherds learned that in the succession of lambs that were loved, reared, and sacrificed lay the constancy of their existence. That incorporated the equation of love and sacrifice, of individual and succession of individuals, into the central myths of Western civilization. The succession of animals in our lives need not be tragic. It can be another aspect of the simultaneous mutability and constancy in nature that can be seen by man, just as he views the change of the seasons. With a change in vision, and a change in position, man can stand outside of the individual cycle of any one dog and see the repetition of that cycle many times in his own existence. The chance to see stability in the succession of creatures that we love is part of the protective constancy given us by animals. It is a vision that we can have when we stand outside of nature. It is a vision that we attribute to a deity when we include ourselves in nature.

Our way of looking at the world, that is, our myths, should provide us with a vision that sustains our life, just as our interaction with the reality that animates that myth should sustain our lives. Part of the myth that we are reconstructing involves our relationship with the living environment about us. In some real sense, the living environment is a collection of objects which we use and discard. On the other hand, those living things are the ultimate source of the constancy in our life in the face of mutability and change. I am indebted to Northrop Frye for calling my attention to the vision offered by Spenser in the Cantos of Mutability at the end of the *Faerie Queen*.

> Then gin I thinke on that which Nature sayd.
> Of that same time when no more Change shall be,
> But steadfast rest of all things, firmely stayd,
> Upon the pillours of Eternity,
> That is contrayr to Mutabilitie;
> For all that moveth doth in Change delight:
> But thence-forth all shall rest eternally
> With Him that is the God of Sabaoth hight:
> O! that great Sabaoth God, grant me that Sabaths sight.

I would like to suggest that that dual vision, the recognition of the simultaneity of change and constancy, has important consequences for our own lives. It is a vision we can enjoy only when we both pay attention to the symbolic edifice that relates us to the natural world and interact with that world in an intimate and attentive way. These consequences are not merely aesthetic but may be integral to our health and emotional balance. We are, in some sense, struggling to restore that vision, and struggling to assume responsibilities toward the living world. It is a task for the eye which can, in a time of repose, see that Sabaths sight.

James A. Knight

50
Comments on Aaron Katcher's "Excursion into Cyclical Time"

Dr. Katcher, in his research and reporting, has given us an inspiration and a challenge. Every part of the article is worthy of comment. His work is impressive and pragmatic and so clinically relevant that we must ask why such work has not been given greater emphasis in the past or why it is not receiving a greater emphasis today.

Chief Sealth of the Duwamish tribe, state of Washington, wrote in a letter to the president of the United States in 1855: "What is man without animals? If all the animals were gone, men would die from great loneliness of spirit, for whatever happens to the beast also happens to man. All things are connected. Whatever befalls the earth befalls the sons of earth."

This moving statement, not unlike many of the statements of St. Francis of Asissi, points to the deeper, symbolic, even unconscious meaning of animals to the human psyche—a shared heritage, a sense of community that reaches far back in humankind's ancestral past. This heritage may be a source of life for us, of renewal, even of survival of which we only are dimly aware. I strongly support Dr. Katcher's suggestion that "transactions between people and animals may have an important influence on our sense of well-being and our physical health."

In choosing safety, kinship, intimacy, and constancy as the attributes through which animals help in preserving our physical and mental equilibrium, Dr. Katcher has identified universal human needs. These basic needs are not created by society but rather they have become embedded in human nature through evolution. Further, one can postulate that animals and animal symbolism are involved at some level of our awareness in the satisfaction of all four of these basic needs.

Dr. Katcher speaks of a major contribution of Carl Rogers in the identification of empathy and a nondirective strategy. He compares it to the noninterventiveness and empathy of pets, which perhaps make them such good audiences for our words. He goes on to say that we need to explain the general phenomenon, that is, why people find it so important and so satisfying to talk to a pet who does not attend the words being spoken. Maybe that is what people need and want. I could not help thinking of a story about Bob Dylan giving a concert in London. The young people were going wild in response to Dylan. A proper English gentleman turned to one of the young people and asked why they were so turned on by Bob Dylan. The young man replied spontaneously: "Sir, Bob Dylan offers no solutions." There is a message for us in that young man's words.

In the attribute of constancy, one can describe this factor as a search for meaning, a reason to hang on, a kind of lifeline. A woman in the detox unit for drug and alcohol abusers at Charity Hospital of New Orleans told me recently that she had to get well for "Baby." When asked who Baby was, she replied, "My little dog." I asked what Baby meant to her. With a combination of smiles and tears, she said Baby never argued with her, was always happy, usually slept well, and always seemed at home in the world. "She has all the things I want and have never been able to attain." Her pet dog may pull her into sobriety and also serve as a model for a feeling of at-homeness in the universe.

Dr. Katcher states that a task before us is to study the connection between play and comforting touch. Possibly this statement or task suggests a larger issue, such as that raised by the biblical translator who said that the Psalmist's words, "Be still and know that I am God," are better translated, "Be playful and know that I am God."

Dr. Katcher's discussion of constancy is truly insightful in illuminating the constancy of the pet by remaining constant and by engaging the owner in the repetitive cyclical activities that sustain a sense of self. Further, use of the animal as an extension of the self and seeing the animal as part of ourselves and part of nature, as do the farmer and the hunter, both bring the sense of constancy, stability, and permanence in the cyclic dimensions of nature. The loyalty and faithfulness of animals are recurring themes in myth and folklore. The ancient and often repeated proverb gives the same message: "Three faithful friends: an old dog, an old wife, and ready money."

Dr. Katcher suggests that healing may come from the natural environment and that humans may find renewal and restorative power in this environment. Color is an example. There can be no debate as to the psychological benefits of color. Color in nature is a form of psychotherapy, and humans respond favorably to it. Books as old as Edwin S. Babbitt's *The Principles of Light and Color* state that because the color blue lowers blood pressure, it is safe to assume that blue may have possibilities in the treatment of hypertension. Dr. Katcher has compared the comforts of prayer to the comforts of talking to an animal. Maybe both do their part in releasing the inner resources of healing. This is what Hygiea, the goddess of health, is all about. Further, this is the message of Hippocrates when he said, "The natural forces within us are the true healers of disease." These forces, however, must be released.

Since Dr. Katcher's paper has psychoanalytic and existential dimensions, it seems appropriate to look momentarily at our past. We were programmed to cooperate and live with animals. Today, we do not always see nature and animals as friends and partners, and this perceptual failure may be contributing to the widespread sense of alienation in our society.

The first gods of humans were animals, and these animal gods symbolized the elemental forces of nature, such as water, fire, earth, stars, sun, and moon. In general, primitive humans did not consider themselves to be the lords of creation. They knew that in some respects they were inferior to the animals with which they associated, and this view accounts in part for their making gods of them.

In many ways, humans have not changed over the last million years, and at some level of their awareness they still have a need to associate with animals and all that the natural environment encompasses. This is one of the universals of the human psyche, and we see this universality in our dreams, folk tales, drawings, and relationships with animals. The vestiges that humans carry of their physical and psychological past break through at unguarded or strategic moments and are expressed in their symbols and myths.

To understand ourselves, we must understand the meaning of the animal in our conscious and unconscious minds and what influence this meaning had on the development of humankind. To help in this understanding, we should be aware of the abundance of animal symbolism in anthropology, art, mythology, religion, psychoanalysis, fairy tales, and dreams. Children repeatedly dream about animals; and the younger they are the more frequently they dream about them. For example, according to some studies, animals appear in about two-thirds of the dreams of four-year-old children; but by age fifteen, the proportion of animal dreams has decreased to about one in ten.

As has been mentioned, animals played a significant part in human development; therefore, it is not surprising to find animal themes occurring frequently in folklore and fairy tales. Moreover, in these tales many humans learn to speak and to understand the language of animals. Also, the animals have human habits and act and think like human beings. From a psychoanalytic point of view, one can say that animals in fairy tales represent unconscious drives. The oedipal situation, for example, reigns supreme in the fairy tale.

The animal motif, wherever it is found, is usually symbolic of the human's inborn drives and needs. Even the most civilized person must realize the strength of one's instinctual drives and one's powerlessness, at times, in the face of autonomous emotions erupting from the unconscious. The animal demon is a highly expressive symbol for a strong impulse such as rage. The vividness and concreteness of the image enables a person to establish a relationship with it as a representative of overwhelming power within oneself. One fears it and seeks to propitiate, guide, and control it by sacrifice, ritual, and other means.

The profusion of animal symbolism in the religion and art of all times is another indication of how important it is for humans to integrate into their lives the symbol's psychic content of inborn drives or needs and thereby bring about a wholeness of the self.

Suppressed, distorted, or wounded instinctual needs or drives threaten the civilized person. The acceptance of the "animal soul" is the condition for wholeness and a fully lived life. As Carl Jung emphasized: "Primitive man must tame the animal in himself and make it his helpful companion; civilized man must heal the animal in himself and make it his friend." What has been said may give the impression that every animal symbol represents a psychic dimension that is frightening, dangerous, and unfriendly. We know better, for myths, fairy tales, and dreams are often filled with friendly animals.

Animal symbolism in Christianity emphasizes the importance of the human and divine side of the person. Jesus symbolically appears as the Lamb of God or the fish. He is also the serpent exalted on the cross, the lion, and in rarer cases the unicorn. These animal attributes of Jesus indicate that even the Son of Man, as the supreme personification of the human, can no more dispense with his animal nature than he can with his higher, spiritual nature. The animal side, as well as the spiritual side, are both parts of human life. The relationship of these two aspects of the person is symbolized in the Christmas scene of the birth of Jesus in a stable among animals.

Boris M. Levinson

51

The Future of Research into Relationships Between People and Their Animal Companions

In sharp contrast to public attitudes of twenty years ago, the field of animal-human relationships is now respected as a legitimate area of scientific investigation. It is not yet a full-fledged discipline, however, having still to develop a name, a theory, and a methodology of its own. This methodology must make use of both the intuitive and the scientific approaches in order to encompass the full richness of animal-human interaction. Four main areas of investigation would be fruitful at this point: (1) the role of animals in various human cultures and ethnic groups over the centuries; (2) the effect on human personality development of association with animals; (3) human-animal communication; and (4) the therapeutic use of animals in formal psychotherapy, institutional settings, and residential arrangements for handicapped and aged populations.

Although an ambivalent relationship has existed between man and animals since ancient days, we may now be ready to translate into a reality the myth of the golden age when animals and humans lived at peace with each other.

Last year I received an invitation from Dr. Katcher to address the conference on the human–companion animal bond on my "vision of the future of research into relationships between people and their animal companions." I accepted this invitation although puzzled as to what I could say that would be seminal for researchers in this new field of knowledge.

To explain my predicament, it was only twenty years ago, at a meeting of the American Psychological Association, that I first read a paper called "The Dog as 'Co-therapist'" (Levinson, 1961). The reception was lukewarm. Some auditors accepted the ideas, but others met them with ridicule, even inquiring as to whether the dog shared my fees. I became known as the dog's co-therapist.

Obviously, much water has flowed under the bridge since then. As this convention indicates by its very existence, the problems raised in my original paper and in subsequent ones written by distinguished speakers and researchers assembled here today have by now been taken very seriously by society at large. Even the academic world has granted our field recognition by awarding doctorates in the discipline of animal-human relationships. In spite of these promising beginnings and accomplishments, it seems to me that we are not a discipline as yet, one of the reasons being that we do not as yet have a commonly accepted textbook in our area. Some members of this audience ought to sit down posthaste and write such a textbook!

Perhaps there are advantages to this ambiguous status, since our attempts to define our field help us to remain spontaneous and flexible in both methodology and subject matter.

What our new science consists of has not yet been clarified. What are the most salient issues in our area of study? What are the boundaries of our investigations? Where are we now? What world are we in? Whence do we come? Whither are we going?

How, for example, do we account in our research for such factors as the intimate, playful, idiosyncratic interrelations of animal companions and their owners? What are we to do with data that arise spontaneously? How can we measure these? Is it possible that our experimental and statistical studies cancel out these most important interchanges?

It seems to me that the relationship between people and their animal companions, the topic being considered by this meeting, can encompass almost all areas of human behavior. It has to be narrowed down and given a focus. Let us decide what we are trying to do and in what field we are operating. Is it comparative psychology (Denny, 1980; Dewsbury, 1978), ecological psychology (Bronfenbrenner, 1979), environmental psychology (Baum and Singer, 1980; Stokols, 1978), ethology (Barnett, 1981; Fox, 1974a), sociobiology (Barlow, 1980; Wilson, 1975, 1980), or social psychology (Berkowitz, 1980; Goldstein, 1980)?

I believe that our work lies in none of these established disciplines. None of these can encompass all the concerns of our new science. We will have to look for new insights, new definitions, and new boundaries. Above all, we will have to place research in this field in a historical and comparative perspective.

At this point, I would like to offer a tentative definition of our field as the science of "human, companion-animal, environment relationships."

On the one hand, our science's feet touch problems that might well be investigated by rigorous, scientific experimentation, while, on the other hand, its head reaches into the clouds where measurement cannot bring answers and intuition must reign.

After all, science brings us knowledge through the medium of our senses, and this is mighty little. If we forget how much we cannot "know" in this way, we become insensitive to many happenings of great importance in the relationship between man, animal, and the rest of nature. It seems to me, therefore, that in our seeking for new knowledge there are two distinct and yet related paths that we must follow. One is the so-called intuitive (the folk way) of studying the animal, the way used by the artist, poet, writer, plain people for generations; the other is the so-called scientific. Both, in my opinion, are equally valid and equally worthwhile. The intuitive method looks at an animal as a teacher and friend; the scientific method looks at him as an object of curiosity.

INTUITIVE METHOD

People who have worked in this mode have realized consciously or unconsciously that there is only one thread of life going through the universe and that if we break it we may all perish. This living thread connects us to our species, to animals, to all of nature, and perhaps even shows us the way to the future. (One caveat in this approach is that we tend to humanize animals and dehumanize humans.)

I believe that early man was aware of a mysterious something which united him to animals and indeed to all living things. He saw the natural world to which he and animals belonged as the indestructible source of life. Animals were his brothers in nature (Jensen, 1963) from whom he could learn much and through whom he could come to terms somewhat with his own mortality. Our early ancestor regarded animals as rational beings and as partners in life (Giedion, 1962). Even though ferocious, animals were seen as younger companions who, while perhaps not as skilled as he (although some were certainly more skilled in certain ways), were entitled to as much respect and attention as he. In other words, animals were first viewed as equals.

Early man understood that "there is a continuum between animal and man" (Fox, 1974a), and he acted accordingly. There was an understanding of how an animal felt and a corresponding respect for the animal's feelings and drives. Our early ancestors thought of animals as friends, knowing that, like themselves, animals loved, hated, grieved, and were supportive of each other. Early man thought of animals as having intimate thoughts and aspirations and also unseen powers and connections with nature that he did not possess (Tylor, 1958). In this sense, animals were viewed as superior, a source of wisdom and strength. Early man, therefore, began to worship animals as representatives of the natural forces that determined his ultimate destiny. Having learned of his inevitable mortality, perhaps from observing animals in their own life cycles (Desmond, 1979; Jonas, 1976), early man could now alleviate the terrible anxiety which such knowledge aroused in him by believing that he had mediators between himself and nature. Totem animals, for example, could be prayed to and served so that they might intercede with nature on their worshiper's behalf and so provide some protection against extinction in a very dangerous world. Early man saw death as an externally imposed event (fate, killing by an enemy, and the like) and not as a natural end of life which eventually all must reach.

Most likely he saw death not as a deliverance from pain and sorrow but as the gate to a new and frightening life in which the dead person became transformed from a possibly benevolent individual to a malevolent creature who plotted against the living. Primitive man may have experienced mental images of dead companions (Siegel, 1977) and assumed that these were evil spirits. He, therefore, had to dispose of the feared dead body (which taunted him in his dreams) in an honorable fashion so that it would not wish to return to harm him. To pacify the dead person and send him happily on his way into the nether world, help was needed. Man may have turned to animals for guidance in this procedure. Most likely Neanderthal man a hundred thousand years ago noticed that some animals buried their dead while others left their dead unattended, to be eaten by other animals (Desmond, 1979; Siegel, 1980). Two different funeral customs thus evolved in subsequent human cultures—either burial of the dead body, rationalized as a return to mother earth, or exposure of the body to allow it to be eaten by animals. Both ways were seen as means of satisfying the spirits of the dead. Later on, grieving was included as part of the ceremony of disposing of the dead (Desmond, 1979; Jonas, 1976).

But no matter how the body was disposed of, early man believed that the spirit remained alive, unattached, and prone to do evil. This potentially malevolent spirit had to have a guide to the nether world in order to take it out of the human realm. Early man hit upon the happy expedient of using a particular animal, which, as a god, had supreme powers to serve as a psychopomp or guide to the nether world. Animals could now be used as death companions, guides to the nether world, and a preferred means of disposing of the body. The rituals that were evolved to bring about this neutralization of a potentially evil spirit alleviated to a great extent early homo sapiens' death anxiety (Leach, 1961).

Animals, therefore, have fulfilled one of man's deepest needs—the need to feel safe—and have been a symbol of power and nurturance. They have also been an externalization of man's control over his own evil impulses (the "wild" animal with its power to kill becomes the savior that keeps killer man under control). Such a relationship, with its deep unconscious meanings and its elements of empathy and identification, does not lend itself to study merely by objective observation and measurement. There may be an unconscious communication between man and his companion animal of which neither man nor possibly the companion animal is aware until a crisis such as death occurs. The intuitive ties between man and animal require intuitive methods of study, if only to delineate the questions that we might want to try to investigate in more scientific ways, such as how does an animal predict when its master is due to return home? How does it become aware of the death of its master, which may have occurred hundreds of miles away? What is the meaning of an animal mourning for a lost master? How does an animal know when it is about to die? What is the nature of the mourning which an animal does for another animal? We have to learn more about psi trailing, ESP between man and animal companion, and animal hypnosis. These questions presuppose the existence of certain feelings and cognitions on the part of animals (Griffin, 1980). Our certainty that these exist comes from our intuitive knowledge of the animal companions we have lived with, observed, and read about over the ages.

THE SCIENTIFIC METHOD

The second approach, the scientific one, is a method by which we seek to answer some of the questions suggested to us by our intuitive knowledge. It is a method that seeks to systematize our knowledge and reveal the mechanisms that bring animal-human relations under natural law rather than keeping them in the realm of magic, symbolism, and fantasy.

In order to do useful scientific research, we need an adequate theory to generate questions and methods. The results must be very carefully evaluated. The model we should be looking for should allow naturalistic observations and controlled field and laboratory work to validate and supplement each other. We need longitudinal, cross-sectional, as well as experimental studies. We also need replication of studies. We must also remember that there is an interaction, that is, a reciprocal relationship between the companion animal and its master and that each causes effects in the other.

First in our research we must think of our society as a whole, where the relationship between animal companions and their owners are but one cog in a vast and complicated wheel. We must also consider the entire pattern of life of the animal companion and its owner.

Our new science will have to mesh with other sciences, fertilize and be fertilized by them, and perhaps be in the vanguard in demonstrating how methods that have been successful in unlocking the secrets of the inorganic world can be adapted to the complexities of behavior which is meaningful on many levels while yet being nonverbal.

We all know that knowledge is not the result of "methodology." The following or rules, no matter how precise, will not generate new facts. We must, therefore, avoid the temptation of directing the questions of our new discipline into preconceived theoretical and methodological molds. We should also avoid the rigid adoption of postulates that may appear reasonable and valid at the time but which, unless left open to question, can saddle a generation or more of aspiring researchers with restrictions on their creative imaginations.

While I wish to stress most forcefully the need for vigorous research in our field, no matter how we may define the latter, I wish to stress just as forcefully that the nonexperimental, nonreplicable observations made by generations of animal companion owners have contributed immeasurably to the development of our field and indeed may actually have brought it into being.

Scientific research in the field of animal-human relationships, by whatever name we choose to call it, has been quantitatively very meager to date, although there have recently been promising beginnings (Bustad, 1980a; Corson and Corson, 1980; Fogle, 1981a; Katcher, 1977). It has been a stepchild in terms of research interest, financial support, and prestige. When I applied for a research grant to the the NIMH with what knowledgeable professionals in the field of psychotherapy considered to be a very good research design, my application was rejected. This was, as I perceived it, an overt refusal to accept new ideas and an implicit denial of legitimacy to a new field. As is well known, denial of research funds for a new field of inquiry is almost tantamount to a death sentence for that field. Usually, the researcher directs his or her attention to a more lucrative area which at least pays the rent. As you well know, however, research has continued to be carried on in the area of animal-human relationships, although on a piecemeal basis, mostly in the homes of animal companion owners or non-professionals, so that the idea has not died. Most of the research has been of the anecdotal variety carried out by well-meaning professionals and nonprofessionals.

Today, most researchers in our field do not have their primary training in it for the simple reason that no such training as yet exists. This may be because until comparatively recently academicians have viewed interest in animal-human relationships as a childish preoccupation.

We are all aware that young people have always made the greatest contribution to art and science. In my opinion, it is not youth per se that has determined these contributions but the novelty of the situation in which the novice researcher found himself. Unaware that it was impossible to do what he was doing, he did it, providing us with new knowledge and new inventions. Our field presents such a challenge. Unfortunately, this challenge has sometimes been met in very inadequate ways. I have discovered, for example, that a favorite study of investigators into human-animal relationships is the comparison of the personality traits of dog and cat owners with those of nonowners. But this work has been done without specifying in exact terms how such personality traits were to be defined and measured, so that the reliability and validity of the measures used left much to be desired and consequently invalidated the subsequent research involving these measures.

Similarly, sampling techniques were such that the findings could not be generalized to other populations. Important variables of the animal owners such as age, marital status, education, intelligence, and socioeconomic status, if not specified, prevent us from knowing whether the sample studied is representative of more than a particular group.

The characteristics of the companion animals also have to be specified when comparing animal owners with nonowners. We forget that each human and each companion animal is unique. Are we talking about the owner of a Pekingese or a Great Dane? Of a Siamese or an alley cat? Suppose we do secure statistically significant differences between the two groups (owners and nonowners)? We must remember that these are quantitative differences, and we must not forget about the qualitative differences that may exist. We must also think of the situations in which our subjects find themselves. Are they comparable? Are our findings of any practical value in the absence of assurance of comparability between our samples?

In spite of my criticism of the various studies because of the great diversity of instruments and techniques used and the lack of random samples, the mere fact that similar results have appeared in many different studies is significant. This should increase our confidence in our field and in the results obtained, since these have been secured with disparate measures and populations.

What, then, do I see as fruitful avenues for the researcher in the field of companion animal–human relationships? From the vantage point of a participant observer, I see four distinct areas on which we could concentrate, although these are by no means all-inclusive of the questions we need to ask.

These areas are (1) the role of companion animals in various human cultures and ethnic groups from earliest recorded history to the present; (2) the effect of association with animal companions on the development of character, emotions, attitudes, and other traits in humans; (3) human–animal companion communication; and (4) the therapeutic effects of associating with companion animals.

Obviously, all of these research areas are interrelated; if we approach one we cannot help but touch the others. If we discover a new facet in one, we cannot help but see the other problems in a new light. For the sake of brevity and clarity, however, I will limit myself to looking at each of these rubrics separately and leave it to the synthesizers in the field to elucidate their interrelationships.

THE ROLE OF ANIMALS IN HUMAN CULTURES

We are continually being made aware of the mysterious thread that unites all life. W. Horsley Gantt found that the approach of a human to an animal increased the latter's "heart and respiration rate" and that subsequent biocontact such as stroking had a tranquilizing effect on the animal. Gantt hoped to find the modality by which this effect was produced, and he sometimes mused that if he systematically eliminated all the known stimulus modalities he might come upon a special kind of energy. "Is the effect of a person transmitted by the known senses, or is it transmitted through radiation or some kind of as yet unmeasured waves with unknown laws of transmission?" (McGuigan, 1981).

This thread of life has connected animals and humans since time immemorial and has affected the development both of individual human qualities and the nature of the many cultures man has established.

Our relationships with the animal kingdom began in the very distant past, millions of years ago. Our attitudes to our neighbor animals have taken millions of years to develop. By this time they have been codified in our genes. As man *qua* man began to differentiate himself from the animal kingdom, these attitudes remained with him to bother him, confuse and perhaps enlighten him, crystallizing, eventually, in art, literature, and philosophy.

When we look at the history of human art, we notice that in the beginning the animal seemed all-powerful and man a mere fleeting shadow, as in such representations of the natural world as the leaping bison and galloping horses of the caves of Altmira and Lascaux. Later on, man occupied a more important but still subsidiary role, as can be seen in the art of the Egyptians, in which the bodies of the figures were human and the heads were animal. Still later, man became supreme and the animal subordinate, as in the art of ancient Greece, in which the bodies, such as those of the centaurs, were animal and the heads were human (Clark, 1977). In separating himself from animals as he developed symbol-using cultures, man had to repress his longing and veneration of nature (which he was destroying) and to exalt his human reason above the "animalistic" qualites that he shared with the rest of the animal kingdom (for example, such basic drives as hunger and sex).

Medieval and Renaissance paintings depicted animals as man's servants, pets, hunting targets, and status symbols (for example, the nobleman and his mastiff). In tapestries we see the introduction of a mythical animal, the unicorn, a pure white, long-horned, gentle creature which seemed to be an attempt to ennoble sexuality and relate it to Christian mythology (which had already made use of a white dove to represent the "Holy Spirit," the principle of impregnation without carnal contact).

In the art of the twentieth century, both man and beast are disembodied and reduced to abstractions, totally disconnecting man from his own animal nature and his link to the rest of the animal kingdom. This is the triumph of the cerebral, and it is probably not a coincidence that modern man feels closer to the machine than to living creatures and ruthlessly slaughters both men and animals.

Literature, too, has reflected man's changing views of the animal's place in the scheme of things. The Bible assigned to animals the role of teacher: "Who teacheth us more than the beasts of the earth, and maketh us wiser than the fowls of heaven?" (Job 35:11). A Talmudic passage states that "if man had not been taught the laws of propriety, he might have learned them from the animals."

In Greek mythology, Chiron, the centaur who had the legs and body of a horse and the head and brain of a human, ran a school in his cave at Mount Pelion. Chiron was reported to have been an excellent teacher, numbering among his students Achilles, Jason, and Asclepius (Candland, 1980). We know that many preliterate peoples have learned how to take care of their sick and wounded by observing the behavior of animals (Siegel, 1973). These peoples learned about snake-bite treatments and the healing properties of mud and clay through observations of sick animals.

Myths and fairy tales express the basic world-view of a people, often through the behavior ascribed to animals. Ethical values, the struggle between good and evil forces, have often been depicted by use of animals, as in the modern literary myth Moby Dick (Melville, 1952). Freud (1964:9) has reminded us that "animals owe a good deal of their importance in myths and fairy tales to the openness with which they display their genitalia and their sexual functions to the inquisitive little human child."

Research devoted to uncovering, through a study of art, religion, and literature (oral and written), of diverse societies such as pastoral, hunting, tribal, or our own industrialized and technological cultures, as well as different ethnic groups within a society, could help us to determine how man has tried to come to terms with himself as a "reasoning animal" and what has happened to human social relationships as well as human stewardship of natural resources where animals have been elevated or denigrated in relation to man.

ANIMALS AND HUMAN PERSONALITY DEVELOPMENT

In our rapidly changing technological society, with the small nuclear family the "school" in which human relations, love, and empathy are taught, animal companions may have a more important role than they did when the extended family provided more companionship and learning experiences and life, particularly in the rural areas, provided more opportunities for daily contact with animals which were crucial to the economic existence of the family (Levinson, 1972).

I believe that the personality development of an individual who has an animal companion or is surrounded by animals will be somewhat different from that of an individual who does not possess animals (Levinson, 1978). The ownership of a companion animal may aid in the development of adaptive personality traits. Research should be able to determine whether, all other things being equal, adult owners of animal companions show more empathy for fellow human beings than do nonowners. What of those who did or did not have animal companions in their childhood? Are owners of animal companions more comfortable in their sex roles than nonowners? Do animal companions have a different role in the personality development of boys and girls? Is there a different incidence of mental illness such as severe depression and schizophrenia among animal owners and nonowners? Do owners who have experienced the death of an animal companion handle human bereavement more effectively than nonowners? Is there any difference in the way owners treat animal companions when they see the latter as either similar to or different from themselves in personality traits?

Animal ownership may contribute to the establishment of a lifestyle that involves nurturance and companionship with a living creature that can sustain a conviction of life's value even under difficult circumstances. It would be valuable, for example, to investigate the effect of animal companionship on people with terminal illnesses such as cancer. Is there a difference in survival rates between owners and nonowners of animal companions? What of those with chronic illnesses such as diabetes, muscular dystrophy, arthritis, cardiovascular diseases, and the like? Does animal companionship significantly reduce the stress of divorce and widowhood and help in the effective management of these situations?

When a companion animal is introduced into a family, the entire climate of family interaction changes and becomes more complex, thus affecting the development of each individual member and the personality of the family as a unit. Children become "parents" of the animal. The animal becomes a new child to the parents. Research topics in this area might include the following: what influence, if any, does the animal companion in a family have on the incidence of divorce, desertion, child and spouse battering, criminal actions by family members? Does the presence of an animal companion reduce parental stress? How are animals used as child substitutes? Why is it so prevalent to feed zoo animals? Is this done more by animal owners than nonowners? Do family members do this more or less frequently than those who are single?

HUMAN-ANIMAL COMMUNICATION

Men and animals, as we all know, communicate with each other on an intuitive level. We observe humans talking to or petting their animal companions and the latter reciprocating by an appreciative bark or wagging of the tail. Dogs seem to know when their owner has decided to take them for a walk, running expectantly to the door before he has even risen from his chair. We also know that zookeepers understand quite a bit of the moods and behavior of the animals in their charge. Books have been written on the meanings horses try to convey to their owners (Ainslee and Lebetter, 1980).

We know that animals can think (Griffin, 1980). Maybe they do not think the way we do and do not follow human logic. Nevertheless, think they do, and of course they can use language. Again, it is not the same language as we use, although some chimps and gorillas have been taught to manipulate symbols standing for words in our own language (Rumbaugh, 1977). Animals can communicate with each other just as we do (Sebeok, 1977), and as far as I can see, that is what language is all about. Although it is difficult for most of us to accept, the idea that only humans convey meaning has finally been destroyed. We humans can no longer claim language as the greatest distinction between us and the animal kingdom (Schmeck, 1980).

Yet the idea of communicating with animal companions raises ambivalent feelings in most of us. We feel threatened now that our unique position as *primus inter pares* among primates has been challenged by "talking" chimps and gorillas. But we are fascinated by the fact that, like King Solomon, we may be able to communicate with all species. Possibly part of the fascination the animal companion has for us—its inscrutability (because of inability to talk)—will be lost. In communicating with an animal, however, we may yet learn the animal's point of view.

The research into communication between animal and human can be broken down into two overlapping categories: verbal and nonverbal.

As I see it, the important research areas for us to engage in are the areas of nonverbal communication. Here I am adopting, and somewhat expanding, the scheme of Harper, Wiens, and Matarrazo (1978). Under these areas I would include (a) paralanguage and temporal characteristics of speech, (b) facial expressions, (c) kinesic behavior of body movements, (d) visual behavior, (e) proxemics, or the use of space and distance, (f) touch behavior, and (g) chemical sensitivity. We must also include empathy as a form of communication between animal and man, that is, the capacity of a person (or animal) to experience the needs and feelings of others as if they were his own. While for the sake of study we may break these up into separate categories, we must remember that actual communication takes place via many channels simultaneously (Bowlby, 1980; Harlow, 1974; Lynch et al., 1977; Montagu, 1978).

As I see it, the attempts to date to communicate with animal companions have been faulty. They have been limited to certain verbal instructions to our companion animals for purposes of obedience training or even highly skilled "acting" careers in the circus, TV, or movies.

We know that dolphins and whales can communicate with each other through clicks and whistles, sentiments appearing to some human observers to be expressing in this way such feelings as anger, joy, or annoyance (Busnell and Fish, 1980; Lilly, 1978). I believe we have failed to address ourselves to the meanings, that is, the adaptive functions, of the languages of our animal companions. We have tried to teach an animal companion our language, our way of communication, rather than trying to learn his (Terrace, 1979). To give a perhaps farfetched example: what we have done would be tantamount to an anthropologist's visiting a strange tribe and teaching its members his native language. We all realize immediately that this would not be very productive in establishing a relationship with the tribal members or learning about native culture. The same holds true with animals. It is true that we have voluminous records of bird calls, whale songs, and other animal sounds. Unfortunately, however, with a few exceptions, these were collected not to communicate with the animals but as a method of controlling them, of learning about cultural differences between different animal calls, and other reasons.

I believe that bodily states of emotion in animals are universal, and these should be carefully studied as a clue to communicating with them (Peters, 1980).

We should also become aware that in becoming domesticated the animal companion loses some of its ability to engage in nonverbal communication with its own kind (Scott, 1980). This is because a domesticated animal no longer needs to forage for itself or to communicate to a co-specific the location of food or the presence of danger.

Once we solve the problem of understanding the language of the animal companions we are dealing with, they might be able to give us information of benefit to humanity. They might have a store of knowledge which could be useful in medicine, communication, and other fields. For example, they might predict for us such natural phenomena as earthquakes. We may also learn to understand how the animal companion sees his world and us. What does he think of us or of his master? There are many other things, possibly appearing farfetched right now, that we might be able to discover. For example, does our animal companion believe in life after death?

As you will notice, I visualize the animal companion as the coequal of man, distinct, different, and having a variant culture. When we accomplish our task of communicating, I am sure that new horizons and new worlds will open to humankind.

ANIMAL COMPANIONS AS CO-THERAPISTS

When we use animal companions as co-therapists in our attempt to help people resolve emotional problems, we provide the individual with an opportunity to experience a variety of feelings that he may not have recognized in himself. The animal permits the person to see himself or herself as small or big, as father, mother, or child, depending upon his need at that point in his psychological development.

Perhaps this use of animal companions can help us solve the riddle of the way in which therapy works. Many researchers talk about a common element, i.e., the therapeutic factor, in various modes of therapy. Perhaps working with animals as co-therapists will give us the clue to what this common element is. Perhaps animal co-therapists supply the mysterious something that all effective therapies provide. I first mentioned this idea in an article in 1965(a) (p. 698) when I asked: "Do we possibly have in pet·therapy a tool which permits us to examine at great length and under magnification the elusive something which promotes emotional healing?"

In discussing animal companions as co-therapists, we must consider the radical change that has occurred in the way we construe therapeutic services in the last twenty years. We are abandoning the medical model and no longer think of a person who comes to us for help as a patient but as an individual like ourselves who has problems as well as certain strengths and weaknesses.

When we use animals as co-therapists, the patient or client need not feel that he is mentally ill but may consider himself socially maladjusted or socially incompetent and come to recognize that he can do quite a bit to help himself. The model of learned helplessness need not apply to him (Abramson, Seligman, and Teasdale, 1978).

We no longer think that one must be a professional psychotherapist to be able to help. Anyone can help. We now emphasize that paraprofessionals, peer groups, and self-help groups all have much to contribute. The use of animal companions in addition encourages mutual social support and leads to quicker social and emotional adjustment.

We can thus see how the pet therapy movement fits in with this current trend. There is a grass-roots movement in pet therapy. Every day we hear of projects springing up spontaneously all over the country which use animals as aids to help senior citizens, the blind, deaf, crippled, homebound, and others.

The use of a companion animal as a friend is very helpful to a person who is trying to establish competency in coping with his life. Relating to an animal in no way denigrates our client or makes him feel helpless or dependent, as he might if all his attention were focused on the human therapist. He finds the source of good health within himself in association with the animal companion. One factor which I believe has completely escaped research investigation is the fact that the individual who is treated with the help of an animal co-therapist may have an entirely different concept of self than the one who is treated without one.

Increased independence can also be the goal of using animal companions to assist those who have spent much time in congregate living quarters—institutions, nursing homes, prisons—and are trying to learn to live on their own. These might include the aged, partly sighted, deaf, alcoholic, physically handicapped, and mentally retarded.

Animals can be taught to act as "trained" nurses by reacting to any unusual behavior on the part of their charges such as a change in the rhythm of breathing, unusual perspiration, heart palpitation, or excessive fever. With chronically ill, bedridden patients, they can act as twenty-four-hour nurses' aides.

Animal companions can aid the independence of institution-bound people as well, giving them a living creature to be concerned about and take care of to the best of their ability as well as drawing on the animal's strength and intelligence to compensate for their own deficits.

Research is wide open in the area of the therapeutic use of animal companions, whether in formal psychotherapy or as a therapeutic element in the daily environment.

The first broad area involves amassing data about the animals themselves. We must establish criteria for the selection and breeding of animals that are suitable for work with children, the aged, the retarded, and the physically and emotionally handicapped. Animals used as co-therapists in an office setting may need different characteristics from those used in prisons, nursing homes, hospices for the dying, schools for the mentally retarded, and other settings. We might experiment with the use of a wide variety of animals, exploring for each one its particular contribution to therapeutic work.

We must also learn how to train the animal companion to further the goals of therapy or therapeutic living. We must determine the best manner for introducing animals into various settings.

Another area of investigation involves the human therapist–animal co-therapist relationship. What, for example, is the difference in personality between those therapists who can effectively use animals and those who cannot or do not wish to? How can we train people to use animals as co-therapists? How does the use of an animal affect the therapist's attitude toward his patient, for example, if the patient dislikes or mistreats the animal that is so important to the therapist? How does a patient's relating to the animal affect the therapist's self-image and sense of competence? Is the animal experienced as a rival by the human therapist?

Companion animals have proven particularly useful in psychotherapy with children. Here many questions have suggested themselves. For example: what problems best lend themselves to being worked out with the aid of a pet in play therapy? With what types of children, from what types of family? How do the personalities of child, therapist, and animal interact? How does the animal help the child achieve insight or increased maturity? How can a pet at home augment or even substitute for the activity of a therapist? How does the child identify with the animal? How does the therapist make use of the child's nonverbal behavior with the animal? What is the difference between children who can and cannot use animals in their treatment? Is the relationship between the animal and the child similar to the one between the animal and the therapist? What limits should be set on the child in relation to the animal, and how does this affect the treatment? When is the use of an animal co-therapist inadvisable?

Finally, we may explore the nature of therapy itself, especially with therapists who use animals with some patients and not with others. What does the animal introduce into the situation which is therapeutic or, in some cases, not therapeutic? What is a therapist who uses an animal co-therapist conveying to his patient by this action? Do animals make more of a contribution at some stages of therapy than at others? Are there phases of therapy during which the presence of an animal would detract from the therapeutic work?

There are other interesting research problems. How does companion animal therapy compare with current therapies in terms of the change and strengthening of the patient's ego? Does the use of an animal promote better integration and more autonomy? Do transference and countertransference differ in companion animal–treated cases and conventional psychotherapeutic approaches? Research is also needed to discover which companion animal would be helpful to people with specific types of problems.

In conclusion, I would like to suggest that our new science take a close look at the relationships that are currently developing between man and animals. Some of us no longer look upon animals as either domestic or savage, noble or base, but consider them as our partners on earth. Most of us are aware that our humanity depends on how well we relate to animals and to nature as a whole.

And all of us are aware that an ambivalent relationship—really an undeclared war—has existed between man and animal since ancient days. At first, we saw the animal as a god, then as a slave, then as a worker, and now we are beginning to look at him as a companion. Yet we have always dreamed of the mythical golden age when animals and humans lived at peace with each other.

Like all myths, this one described a reality that never existed but expresses the deep longing within human beings to be at peace with others and with themselves. Now I believe that the golden age is approaching in reality. With the gradual disappearance of wild animal life, man-animal peaceful coexistence is approaching in zoos and protected wildlife sanctuaries. It is now our task that the vison of the Prophet Isaiah that "the wolf shall dwell with the lamb, and the leopard shall lie down with the kid" (Isaiah, 2:6) be fulfilled.

Bibliography

Abramson, L. Y.; Seligman, M. E. P.; and Teasdale, J. D. "Learned Helplessness in Humans: Critique and Reformulation." *Journal of Abnormal Psychology* 87(1978):49–74.

Adell-Bath, M.; Krook, A.; Sandqvist, G.; and Skantze, K. *Do We Need Dogs? A Study of Dogs' Social Significance to Man.* Gothenburg: University of Gothenburg, 1979.

"Again the Cry, 'Get a Horse.' " *U. S. News and World Report*, August 27, 1973, pp. 68–69.

Aillaud, G. "Why Look at Animals?" In J. Berger, ed., *About Looking.* New York: Pantheon, 1981.

Ainslee, T., and Ledbetter, B. *The Body Language of Horses.* New York: Morrow, 1980.

Akeret, R. U. *Photoanalysis.* New York: P. H. Wyden, 1973.

Alcock, T. *The Rorschach in Practice.* Philadelphia: Lippincott, 1963.

Allen, R. D. and Westbrook, W. H. "The Pet Paradox." In R. D. Allen and W. H. Westbrook, eds., *The Handbook of Animal Welfare,* pp. 3–14. New York: Garland STPM Press, 1979.

American Association of Veterinary Medical Colleges. *Veterinary Medical Education: An Issue for the 80's.* Knoxville, 1979.

American Horse Show Association. *1980–1981 Rule Book.* New York: American Horse Show Association, 1980.

American Humane Association. *Animal Control Survey.* Denver: American Humane Association, 1972.

———, et al. *Model Dog and Cat Control Ordinance.* American Humane Association, American Veterinary Medical Association, Humane Society of the United States and Pet Food Institute, 1976.

Ames, L. B. "Age Changes in the Rorschach Responses of a Group of Elderly Individuals." *Journal of Genetic Psychology* 96(1960):257–315.

———. "Sleep and Dreams in Childhood." In E. Harms, ed., *Problems of Sleep and Dreams in Children*, pp. 6–29. New York: Pergamon, 1964.

Ames, L. B.; Learned, J.; Metraux, R. W.; and Walker, R. N. *Child Rorschach Responses: Developmental Trends from Two to Ten Years.* New York: Hoeber-Harper, 1952.

Ames, L. B.; Metraux, R. W.; and Walker, R. N. *Adolescent Rorschach Responses.* New York: Hoeber-Harper, 1959.

———. *Rorschach Responses in Old Age.* New York: Hoeber-Harper, 1954.

Amon, R. "Doggone." *The Guardian*, December 31, 1979, p. 8.

Anderson, R. K., et al. *Description of the Responsibilities of Veterinarians as They Relate to Human Health.* Department Health, Education and Welfare. Public Health Service, Bureau of Health Manpower, Contract 321-76-0202, Washington, D.C.: June 1976.

Anderson, R. S., ed. *Pet Animals and Society.* London: Balliere-Tindall, 1975.

Anderson, S., and Gantt, W. H. "The Effect of Person on Cardiac and Motor Responsitivity to Shock in Dogs." *Conditional Reflex* 1(1966):181–89.

Anderson, R., and Olsson, K. "Effects of Bilateral Amygdoloid Lesions in Nervous Dogs." *Journal of Small Animal Practice* 6(1965):301.

Antelyes, J. "Human Emotions and Veterinary Practice." *Journal of the American Veterinary Medical Association* 155(1969):2018–25.

———. "When the Pet Animal Dies—Attitudes and Behavior of the Veterinarian." *Archives of Thanatology* 9, no. 2(1981):8.

Apostoles, E. "Pets: Therapeutic or Anti-Therapeutic." Unpublished seminar paper, University of Maryland, 1972.

Argus Archives. *Unwanted Pets and the Animal Shelter.* New York: Argus Archives Report Series 4(1973):59.

Argyle, M. *Bodily Communication.* London: Methuen, 1975.

Argyle, M., and Dean, J. "Eye-Contact, Distance and Affiliation." *Sociometry* 28(1965):289–304.

Argyle, M., and McHenry, R. "Do Spectacles Really Affect Judgements of Intelligence?" *British Journal of Social and Clinical Psychology* 10(1971):27–29.

Arkow, P. *Pet Therapy: Study of the Use of Companion Animals in Selected Therapies.* Colorado Springs: Humane Society of the Pikes Peak Region, 1980.

Arling, G. "The Elderly Widow and Her Family, Neighbors, and Friends." *Journal of Marriage and the Family* 38(1976):757–68.

Arnold, J. "The High Stepping World of the Saddlebred Horse." *U.S. News and World Report* 133(June 1979):106–9.

Aronson, E., and Mills, J. "The Effect of Severity of Initiation on Liking for a Group." *Journal of Abnormal Psychology* 59(1959):177–81.

Asch, S. E. "Forming Impressions of Personality." *Journal of Abnormal and Social Psychology* 41(1946):258–90.

Associated Press. "Parents of Boy, 2, Slain by Wolf, Sue." *Philadelphia Inquirer*, September 30, 1981, p. 17.

Austen, J. *Sense and Sensibility*. London: Dent, 1906.

Averill, J. R. "Grief: Its Nature and Significance." *Psychological Bulletin* 70, no. 6(1968):721–48.

Azrin, N. H., and Nunn, R. G. "Habit-Reversal: A Method of Eliminating Nervous Habits and Tics." *Behavioral Research and Therapy II*, pp. 619–28, 1973.

Bachelard, G. *The Psychonanalysis of Fire*. Translated by A. C. M. Ross. Boston: Beacon Press, 1956.

Backstrom, C. H., and Hursh, G. D.: *Survey Research*, Chapter II: Evanston: Northwestern University Press, 1963.

Bacon, E. S. "Investigation on Perception and Behavior of the American Black Bear (*Ursus americanus*)." Ph.D. dissertation, University of Tennessee, 1973.

Bailey, M. "Animal Behavior Analysis Applied to Problems of Parks, Zoos and Laboratory." Paper presented at Animal Behavior Society annual meeting, Knoxville, Tennessee, June 22–26, 1981.

Bain, A. "Pony Riding for the Disabled." *Physical Therapy* 51, no. 8(1965):263–65.

Baker, E. "A Veterinarian Looks at the Animal Allergy Problem." *Animal Allergy* 43(1979):214.

Baker, M., ed. *The Design of Human Service Systems*. Wellesley, Mass.: Human Ecology Institute, 1974.

Ballard, P. B. "What Children Like to Draw." *Journal of Experimental Pediatrics* 2(1913):127–29.

Bancroft, R. L. "America's Mayors and Councilmen: Their Problems and Frustrations." *Nation's Cities* 12(April, 1974):14–22, 24.

Bannister, D., and Fransella, F. *Inquiring Man: The Theory of Personal Constructs*. Harmondsworth: Penguin, 1971.

Baptiste, M. E.; Whelan, J. B.; and Frary, R. B. "Visitor Perception of Black Bear Problems at Shenandoah National Park." *Wildlife Society Bulletin* 7, no. 1(1979):25–29.

Barash, D. P. *Sociobiology and Behavior*. New York: Elsevier, 1977.

Barbehenn, K. R. "Notes on the Ecology of Sewer Rats in St. Louis." *Proceedings of the Fourth Vert. Pest Cont.*, pp. 19–22. West Sacramento, Calif., 1970.

Barnes, V. G., and Bray, O. E. "Population Characteristics and Activities of Black Bears in Yellowstone National Park." Fort Collins, Colorado State University, p. 199.

Barlow, G. W., and Silverberg, J., eds. *Sociobiology: Beyond Nature-Nurture*. Boulder, Colo.: Westview, 1980.

Barnett, S. A. *Modern Ethology: The Science of Animal Behavior*. New York: Oxford University Press, 1981.

Basedow, H. "Journal of the Gov't. N.W. Expedition." *Proceedings of the Royal Geographic Society of Australia* 15:1903–04.

Bateson, G., and Mead, M. *Balinese Character*. New York: New York Academy of Sciences, 1941.

Bateson, P. P. G. "Rules and Reciprocity in Behavioural Development." In P. P. G. Bateson, and R. A. Hinde, eds., *Growing Points in Ethology*, pp. 401–21. Cambridge: Cambridge University Press, 1976.

Bauer, J. J.: *Riding for Rehabilitation: A Guide for Handicapped Riders and Their Instructors*. East Toronto: Canadian State and Arts Publications, 1972.

Baum, A., and Singer, J. E., eds. *Advances in Environmental Psychology.* Vol. 2: *Applications of Personal Control.* Hillsdale, N.J.: Erlbaum, 1980.

Beaver, B. "Canine Aggression in Retrospect." *Applied Animal Ethology.* 1983. Forthcoming.

————. *Veterinary Aspects of Feline Behavior.* St. Louis: C. V. Mosby, 1980.

————. "The Veterinarian's Role in Prescribing Pets." *Veterinary Medicine/Small Animal Clinician,* 69(1974):1506–8.

Beck, A. M. "The Animal and the Society." In *Animal Health in the Americas: Proceedings of the First Inter-American Meeting on Animal Health.* Washington, D.C.: WHO/PAHO, 1980.

————. *The Ecology of Stray Dogs: A Study of Free-Ranging Urban Animals.* Baltimore: York Press, 1973.

————. "Ecology of Unwanted and Uncontrolled Pets." *Proceedings of the National Conference on the Ecology of the Surplus Dog and Cat Problem,* pp. 31–39. Chicago: American Veterinary Medical Association, 1974.

————. "The Epidemiology of Animal Bite." *The Compendium on Continuing Education for the Practicing Veterinarian* 3, no. 3(March 1981a):254–55, 257–58.

————. "Guidelines for Planning for Pets in Urban Areas." In B. Fogle, ed., *Interrelations between People and Pets,* pp. 231–40. Springfield, Ill.: Charles C. Thomas, 1981b.

————. "The Impact of the Canine Clean-up Law." *Environment* 21, no.8(1979):28–31.

————. "Population Aspects of Animal Mortality." *Archives of the Foundation of Thanatology* 9(2):1981 (abstract 18).

Beck, A. M.; Loring, H.; and Lockwood, R. "The Ecology of Dog Bite Injury in St. Louis, Missouri." *Public Health Report* 90(May–June 1975):262–67.

Beck, A. T. "The Phenomenon of Depression: A Synthesis." In D. Offer and D. X. Freedman, eds., *Modern Psychiatry and Clinical Research,* pp. 136–58. New York: Basic Books, 1972.

Beeman, L. E., and Pelton, M. R. "Seasonal Foods and Feeding Ecology of Black Bears in the Smoky Mountains." C. J. Martinke and K. L. McArthur, eds., *Bears—Bear Biology and Management,* pp. 141–47. Washington, D.C.: U.S. Government Printing Office, 1980.

Bekoff, M. "The Development of Social Interaction, Play and Meta-Communication in Mammals: An Ethological Perspective." *Quarterly Review of Biology* 47, no.4(1972):412–34.

Bell, B. D., ed. *Contemporary Social Gerontology.* Springfield, Ill.: Charles C. Thomas, 1976.

Bell, L. G. "Paper Sculpting: A Research and Clinical Tool for Describing Families and Other Groups." Unpublished paper, University of Chicago, 1975.

Bellak, L., and Bellak, S. S. *Children's Apperception Test.* Larchmont, N.Y.: C.P.S., Inc., 1949.

————. *The Children's Apperception Test—Supplement* (CAT-S). Larchmont, N.Y.: C.P.S., Inc., 1957.

Bender, L., and Rapoport, J. "Animal Drawings of Children." *American Journal of Orthopsychiatry.* 14(1944):521–27.

Benson, H. *The Relaxation Response.* New York: Morrow, 1975.

Berk, L. S. "Beta Endorphin Response to Exercise Gradation in Athletes and Nonathletes." Paper presented at Conference of the American College of Sports Medicine, Miami, Fla., May 29, 1981.

————. Personal communication. 1982.

Berkman, B. G., and Rehr, H. "Early Social Service Case Finding for Hospitalized Patients: An Experiment." *Social Service Review* 47(June 1973):256-65.

Berkowitz, L. *A Survey of Social Psychology.* 2d ed. New York: Holt, Rinehart and Winston, 1980.

Berndt, R., and Berndt, C. "A Preliminary Report of Fieldwork in the Ooldea Region, Western South Australia." *Oceania* 13(1942).

Berzon, D. R.; Farber, R. E.; Gordon, J., and Kelly, E. B. "Animal Bites in a Large City: A Report on Baltimore, Maryland." *American Journal of Public Health* 62(1972):422–26.

Beston, H. *The Outermost House.* New York, Penguin, 1981.

Bettelheim, B. *The Uses of Enchantment.* New York: Vintage, 1977.

Bieber, N. "Evaluation of the Therapeutic Riding Program at the Little White Schoolhouse." Unpublished manuscript, December 1976.

Bills, R. E. "Animal Pictures for Obtaining Children's Projections." *Journal of Clinical Psychology* 6(1950):291–93.

Blanchard, P. "A Study of Subject Matter and Motivation of Children's Dreams." *Journal of Abnormal-Social Psychology* 21(1926):24–37.

Blau, P. *Exchange and Power in Social Life.* New York: Wiley, 1964.

Blau, T. H. "Quality of Life, Social Indicators, and Criteria of Change." *Professional Psychology* 8, no.4(1977):464–73.

Blenden, D. C.; Dorn, C. R.; Selby, L. A.; and McCulloch, W. F. "Teaching Veterinary Aspects of Public Health in a Segmented Curriculum." *Journal of Medical Education* 48(1973):85–91.

Bloom, B. S., ed. *Taxonomy of Educational Objectives. Handbook I: Cognitive Domain.* New York: David McKay, 1956.

Blum, G. S. "A Guide for the Research Use of the Blacky Pictures." *Journal of Projective Technique* 26(1962):3–29.

————. "A Study of the Psychoanalytic Theory of Psychosexual Development." *Genetic Psychological Monographs* 39(1949):3–99.

Blurton-Jones, N., ed. *Ethological Studies of Child Behaviour.* Cambridge: Cambridge University Press, 1972.

Bochner, R., and Halpern, F. *The Clinical Application of the Rorschach Test.* New York: Grune and Stratton, 1945.

Bodtker, E. *Therapy Riding in Norway for Disabled Children and Young People.* Oslo: Norwegian Association for the Promotion of Therapy Riding for the Disabled, 1974.

Bolwig, N. "Facial Expressions in Primates with Remarks on Parallel Development in Certain Carnivores." *Behaviour* 22(1962):167–92.

Bond, S. *101 Uses For A Dead Cat.* New York: Clarkson N. Potter, 1981.

Booth, G. "Organ Function and Form Perception: Use of the Rorschach Method with Cases of Chronic Arthritis, Parkinsonianism and Arterial Hypertension." *Psychosomatic Medicine* 8(1948):367–85.

Borchelt, P. L. "Aggressive Behavior of Dogs Kept as Companion Animals: Classification and Influence of Sex, Reproductive Status and Breed." *Applied Animal Ethology* 1983. (in press)

Borchelt, P. L., and Voith, V. L. "Diagnosis and Treatment of Separation-Related

Behavior Problems in Dogs." In V. L. Voith and P. L. Borchelt, eds., *The Veterinary Clinics of North America: Small Animal Practice*, vol. 12, pp. 625–35. Philadelphia: W. B. Saunders Co., 1982.

Boss, M. *The Analysis of Dreams*. New York: Philosophical Library, 1958.

Bossard, J. H. S. "The Mental Hygiene of Owning a Dog." *Mental Hygiene* 28(1944):408–13.

Bowe, F. *Handicapping America: Barriers to Disabled People*. New York: Harper & Row, 1977.

Bowen, M. "Family Psychotherapy with a Schizophrenic in the Hospital and Private Practice." In I. Boszormenyi-Nagy and Framo, Jr., eds., *Intensive Family Therapy*. New York: Harper & Row, 1965.

Bowlby, J. *Attachment*. New York: Basic Books, 1969.

————. "Loss: Sadness and Depression." *Attachment and Loss*. Vol. 3. New York: Basic Books, 1980.

————. *Separation: Anxiety and Anger*. New York: Basic Books, 1973.

Boyer, L. B.; Boyer, R.; Kawai, H.; and Klopfer, B. "Apache 'learners' and 'non-learners.'" *Journal of Projective Technique and Personal Assessment* 31(1967):22-29.

Bradburn, N. M. *The Structure of Psychological Well-Being*. Chicago: Aldine, 1969.

Brannigan, C. R., and Humphries, D. A. "Human Non-verbal Behaviour: A Means of Communication." In N. Blurton-Jones, ed., *Ethological Studies of Child Behaviour*, pp. 37–64. Cambridge: Cambridge University Press, 1972.

Breem, V. Physical Therapy Department, University of Pennsylvania Hospital. Personal observation and interview, 1980.

Brehem, H. P. "Organization and Financing of Health Care for the Aged: Future Implications." In S. G. Haynes and M. Feinleib, eds., *Epidemiology of Aging*. Washington, D.C.: U.S. Department of Health and Human Services, 1980.

Breland, K., and Breland, M. "A Field of Applied Animal Psychology." *American Psychologist* 6(1951):202–4.

————. "The Misbehavior of Organisms." *American Psychologist* 16(1961):681–84.

Brick, M. "The Mental Hygiene Value of Children's Art Work." *American Journal of Orthopsychiatry* 14(1944):136–47.

Brickel, C. M. "A Review of the Roles of Pet Animals in Psychotherapy and with the Elderly." *International Journal on Aging and Human Development* 12, no.2(1980–81):119–28.

————. "The Therapeutic Roles of Cat Mascots with a Hospital-Based Geriatric Population: A Staff Survey." *Gerontologist* 19, no. 4(1979):368–72.

Briggs, J. *Never in Anger: Portrait of an Eskimo Family*. Cambridge, Mass.: Harvard University Press, 1970.

Brim, J. "Social Network Correlates of Avowed Happiness." *Journal of Nervous and Mental Disease* 158(1974):432–39.

Brodey, R. "The Pet Animal with Cancer." *Journal of the American Veterinary Medical Association* 162(1973):403.

Bronfenbrenner, U. *The Ecology of Human Development*. Cambridge, Mass.: Harvard University Press, 1979.

Brown, B. "The Impact of Confidants on Adjusting to Stressful Events." Paper presented at the Thirty-Third Annual Gerontological Society of America Meeting, San Diego, November 1980.

Brown, F. A. *Sport from Within.* London: Hutchinson, 1952.

Brown, G.; Bhrolchain, M.; and Harris, T. "Social Class and Psychiatric Disturbance among Women in an Urban Population." *Sociology* 9(1975):225–54.

Brown, L. T.; Shaw, T. G.; and Kirkland, K. D. "Affection for People as a Function of Affection for Dogs." *Psychological Reports* 31(1972):957–58.

Brown, P. *Highland Peoples of New Guinea.* Cambridge: Cambridge University Press, 1978.

Bryan, R. B., and Jansson, M. C. "Perception of Wildlife Hazard in National Park Use." In J. C. Hendee and C. Schoenfield, eds., *Human Dimensions in Wildlife Programs*, pp. 129–43. Seattle, Wash.: People/Natural Resources Research Council, 1973.

Bucke, W. F. "Cyno-Psychoses: Childrens' Thoughts, Reactions, and Feelings Towards Pet Dogs." *Pedagogical Seminar* 10(1903):459–513.

Burghardt, G. M., and Burghardt, L. S. "Notes on Behavioral Development of Two Female Black Bear Cubs: The First Eight Months." In S. Herrero, ed., *Bears: Their Biology and Management.* Morges, Switzerland: IUCN New Series, 23(1972):207–20.

Burghardt, G. M.; Burghardt, L. S.; Hietala, R. O.; and Pelton, M. R. "Knowledge and Attitudes concerning Black Bears by Users of the Great Smoky Mountains National Park." In S. Herrero, ed., *Bears: Their Biology and Management.* Morges, Switzerland: IUCN New Series, 23(1972):255–73.

Burnside, I. M. "Young Old Age through Old Old Age." In I. M. Burnside, P. Ebersole, and H. E. Monea, eds., *Psychosocial Caring throughout the Lifespan.* New York: McGraw-Hill, 1979, pp. 378–624.

Busnell, R. G., and Fish, J. F., eds., *Animal Sonar Systems.* New York: Plenum Press, 1980.

Buss, A. H., and Durkee, A. "The Association of Animals with Familial Figures." *Journal of Projective Technique* 21(1957):366–71.

Bustad, L. K. *Animals, Aging, and the Aged.* Minneapolis: University of Minnesota Press, 1980a.

————. Personal communication, 1981.

————. "Profiling Animals for Therapy." *Western Veterinarian* 17, no.1(1979):2.

————. "The Veterinarian and Animal Facilitated Therapy." *Proceedings of the American Animal Hospital Association, 47th Annual Meeting*, pp. 269–77, 1980b.

Bustad, L. K., and Hines L. H.: "A Curriculum to Promote Greater Understanding of the Human–Companion Animal Bond." In B. Fogle, ed., *Interrelations between People and Pets*, pp. 241–67. Springfield, Ill.: Charles C. Thomas, 1981.

————. Symp. Vet. Med., Practice 4.

Butler, R. N. "Introduction to S. G. Haynes and M. Feinleib, eds., *Epidemiology of Aging.* Washington, D.C.: U.S. Department of Health and Human Services, 1980.

Byrne, D., and Nelson, D. "Attraction as a Linear Function of Proportion of Positive Reinforcements." *Journal of Personality and Social Psychology* 1(1965):661.

Byrne, M. St. C., ed. *The Lisle Letters.* 6 volumes. Chicago: University of Chicago Press, 1981.

Cain, A. O. "A Study of Pets in the Family System." *Research Highlights* Presented to the Georgetown Family Symposium, October 27, 1978.

Camden, C. *The Elizabethan Woman.* Mamaroneck, N.Y.: Paul B. Appel, 1975.

Cameron, P.; Conrad, C.; Kirkpatrick, D. D.; and Bateen, R. J. "Pet Ownership and Sex as Determinants of Stated Affect toward Others and Estimates of Others' Regard of Self." *Psychological Reports* 19(1966):884–86.

Cameron, P., and Mattson, M. "Psychological Correlates of Pet Ownership." *Psychological Reports* 30(1972):286.

Campbell, A.; Converse, P.; and Rodgers, W. *The Quality of American Life.* New York: Russell Sage Foundation, 1976.

Candland, D. K. "Speaking Words and Doing Deeds." *American Psychologist* 35(1980):191–98.

Carding, A. H. "The Significance and Dynamics of Stray Dog Populations with Special Reference to the U.K. and Japan." *Journal of Small Animal Practice* 10, no.7(1969):419–46.

Carson, G. *Men, Beasts and Gods: A History of Cruelty and Kindness to Animals,* p. 217. New York: Charles Scribner & Sons, 1972.

Cass, J. "Pet Facilitated Therapy in Human Health Care." In B. Fogle, ed., *Interrelations between People and Pets,* pp. 124–45. Springfield, Ill.: Charles C. Thomas, 1981.

Cerf, F. "Les animaux de la planche VIII." *Bulletin du Group, France, Rorschach* 9(1957):15–19.

Chalfen, R. "Review of Akeret's *Photoanalysis.*" *Studies in the Anthropology of Visual Communication* 1, no.1(1974):57-60.

—————. "Seven Billion a Year: The Social Construction of the Snapshot." Unpublished manuscript, Philadelphia, Pa., 1977.

Chaloux, P. A., and Heppner, M. B. "History and Development of Federal Animal Welfare Regulations." *International Journal to Study Animal Problems* 1(1980):287–95.

Chang, B. L. "Black and White Elderly: Morale and Perception of Control." *Western Journal of Nursing Research* 2, no.1(1980):371–92.

Chenevix-Trench, C. *A History of Horsemanship.* New York: Doubleday, 1970.

Chevigny, H. *My Eyes Have a Cold Nose.* New Haven: Yale University Press, 1946.

Christensen, A. M. *City of Toronto Pet Survey.* Toronto: Toronto Humane Society, 1978.

Christopherson, R. "From Folk Art to Fine Art." *Urban Life & Culture* 3, no.2(1974):123–58.

Cipriani, L. *The Andaman Islanders.* Translated by D. Taylor Cox. New York: Praeger, 1966.

Clark, K. *Men and Animals.* New York: Williams and Morrow, 1977.

Clarke, C. "Handicapped Riders Make Strides." *Hartford Courant,* June 13, 1976.

Coe, C. L.; Mendoza, S. P.; Smotherman, W. P.; and Levine, S. "Mother-Infant Attachment in the Squirrel Monkey: Adrenal Response to Separation." *Behavioral Biology* 22(1978):256-63.

Coelho, A. M., Jr. "Guardian Behaviour by Baboons Towards Felines." *Laboratory Primate Newsletter* 19(1980):1–10.

Cofer, C. N., and Appley, M. H. *Motivation: Theory and Research.* New York: Wiley, 1967.

Cohen, D. "Zoonoses in Perspective." In R. S. Anderson, ed., *Pet Animals and Society.* London: Balliere-Tindall, 1975.

Colbert, E. H. *Evolution of the Vertebrates.* New York: Wiley, 1955.

Cole, W. *Cat Hater's Handbook: The Ailurophobe's Delight*. New York: Arenel, 1981.

Colette. *The Cat*. Harmondsworth: Penguin, 1958.

Collard, R. R. "Fear of Strangers and Play Behavior in Kittens with Varied Social Experience." *Child Development* 38(1967):877–91.

Collier, J., Jr. *Visual Anthropology*. New York: Holt, Rinehart, & Winston, 1966.

"A Comeuppance for Cats." *Time* 118, no. 12(1981):80.

Condoret, A. *L'animal compagnon de l'enfant*. Paris: Editions Fleurus, 1973.

————. "Pour une biologie du comportement de l'enfant: Sa relation a l'animal familier." *Bulletin de l' Academie Veterinaire de France* 50(1977):481–90.

Conner, K.; Powers, E.; and Bultena, G. "Social Interaction and Life Satisfaction: An Empirical Assessment of Late-Life Patterns." *Journal of Gerontology* 34(1979):116–21.

Cooper, J. E. "Pets in Hospitals." *British Medical Journal* 1(1976):698–700.

Coordinator, HBHC Program. *Hospital Based Home Care Program: Criteria for Selecting Patients; Procedure for Referral*. V.A. Medical Center, Pittsburgh, Pa. December 3, 1979.

Corson, S. A., and Corson, E. O'L. "Companion Animals as Bonding Catalysts in Geriatric Institutions." In B. Fogle, ed., *Interrelations between People and Pets*, pp. 146–74. Springfield, Ill: Charles C. Thomas, 1981.

————. "Pet Animals as Nonverbal Communication Mediators in Psychotherapy in Institutional Settings." In S. A. Corson and E. O'L. Corson, eds., *Ethology and Nonverbal Communication in Mental Health*, pp. 83–110. New York: Pergamon, 1980.

————. "Pets as Mediators of Therapy in Custodial Institutions for the Aged." In J. H. Masserman, ed., *Current Psychiatric Therapies*. New York: Grune and Stratton, 1979.

————. "Pets as Mediators of Therapy." *Current Psychiatric Therapies* 18(1978):195–205.

————. "The Role of Pet Animals as Non-Verbal Communication Links in Mental Health Programs." Paper presented at the American Public Health Association 105th Annual Meeting, Washington, D.C., 1977.

————. "The Socializing Role of Pet Animals in Nursing Homes: An Experiment in Non-Verbal Communication Therapy." In L. Levi, ed., *Society, Stress and Disease*, pp. 1–47. London: Oxford University Press, 1977a.

Corson, S. A. and Corson, E. O'L., eds. *Ethology and Nonverbal Communication in Mental Health*. Oxford: Pergamon, 1980.

Corson, S. A.; Corson, E. O'L.; and Gwynne, P. "Pet-Facilitated Psychotherapy." In R. S. Anderson, ed., *Pet Animals and Society*, pp. 19-36. London: Bailliere-Tindall, 1975a.

Corson, S. A.; Corson, E. O'L.; Gwynne, P.; and Arnold, E. "Pet Dogs as Nonverbal Communication Links in Hospital Psychiatry." *Comprehensive Psychiatry* 18, no.1(1977b):61–72.

————. "Pet-Facilitated Psychotherapy in a Hospital Setting." In H. Masserman, ed., *Current Psychiatric Therapies*, 15:277–86. New York: Grune and Stratton, 1975.

Coulson, J. C. "The Influence of the Pair-Bond and Age on the Breeding Biology of the Kittiwake Gull *Rissa tridactyla*." *Journal of Animal Ecology* 35(1966):269–79.

Craighead, J. J., and Craighead, F. C., Jr. "Grizzly Bear–Man Relationships in Yellowstone National Park." *BioScience* 21, no.16(1971):845–57.

Cranach, M. von; Foppa, K.; Lepennies, W.; and Ploog, D., eds. *Human Ethology: Claims and Limits of a New Discipline.* Cambridge: Cambridge University Press, 1979.

Crawford, L. M. "A Tribute to Alexander Liautard, the Father of the American Veterinary Profession." *Journal of the American Veterinary Medical Association* 169(1976):36.

Crook, J. H. *The Evolution of Human Consciousness.* Oxford: Clarendon Press, 1980.

————. "Social Organization and the Environment: Aspects of Contemporary Social Ethology." *Animal Behaviour* 19(1970):197–209.

Csikszentmihalyi, M. "Play and Intrinsic Rewards." *Journal of Humanistic Psychology* 15, no. 3 (1975):41–63.

Cumming, W. W. "A Bird's Eye Glimpse of Men and Machines." In R. Ulrich, R. Stachnik, and J. Marley, eds., *Control of Human Behavior,* 1:246–56. Glenview, Ill.: Scott, Foresman, 1966.

Curry-Lindahl, K. *Conservation for Survival.* New York: Morrow, 1972.

Cusick, M. K., and Humphrey, G. "The Cost of One Rabid Dog—California." *Morbidity Mortality Weekly Reports* 30, no. 42(1981):527.

Cutting-Baker, H., et al. *Family Folklore.* Washington, D.C.: Smithsonian Institution, 1976.

Damude, D. F., and Campos Terron, J. M. "Evaluation do programas de control de la rabia en zoonas urbanas de las Frontera Norte de Mexico." *Boletin de la Oficina Sanitaria Panamericana* 68(March 1975):2211–57.

Dasmann, R. F. *Wildlife Biology.* New York: Wiley, 1981.

Davids, A., and Talmadge, M. "A Study of Rorschach Signs of Adjustment in Mothers of Institutionalized Emotionally Disturbed Children." *Journal of Projective Technique and Personal Assessment* 27(1963):292–96.

Davies, J. A. *The Reins of Life: An Instructional and Informative Manual on Riding for the Disabled.* London: J. A. Allen, 1967.

Davis, D. E. "The Characteristics of Rat Populations." *Quarterly Review of Biology* 28(1953):373–407.

Dawkins, M. S. *Animal Suffering: The Science of Animal Welfare.* London: Chapman Hall, 1980.

Dawkins, R. *The Selfish Gene.* New York: Oxford University Press, 1978.

Delafield, G. "Self Perception and the Effects of Mobility Training." Ph.D. dissertation, University of Nottingham, 1976.

De Laguna, F. "The Atna of the Copper River, Alaska: The World of Animals and Men." *Folk* 11–12(1969–70):17–26.

Denny, M. R., ed. *Comparative Psychology: An Evolutionary Analysis of Animal Behavior.* New York: Wiley, 1980.

Depner, D. D. "Adult Roles and Subjective Evaluations of Life." Ph.D. dissertation, University of Michigan, 1978. *Dissertation Abstracts International* 39(10)(1979):5131-B. (Order No. 7907057.)

Desmond, A. J. *The Ape's Reflexion.* New York: Dial Press, 1979.

Despert, J. L. "Dreams in Children of Preschool Age." In *The Psychoanalytic Study of the Child* 3–4:141–80. New York: International University Press, 1949.

Dewsbury, D. A. *Comparative Animal Behavior.* New York: McGraw-Hill, 1978.

Dickman, R. L. "Must Nursing Homes Be the End of the Line?" *Hastings Center Report* 11(August 1981):43–44.

"Dixmont Unit, Pace-Setter." *Vital Signs* 16, no.4(1978):1, 7.

Dorn, C. R.; Blenden, D. C.; Selby, L. A.; and McCulloch, W. F. "Veterinary Aspects of Public Health as Part of a Segmented Curriculum: A Progress Report." *Journal of the American Veterinary Medical Association* 161(1972):1502–7.

Douglas, C. "A Symbolic Interpretation of the Bullfight." M.A. thesis, University of Virginia, 1981.

Doyle, M. C. "Rabbit Therapeutic Prescription." *Perspectives in Psychiatric Care* 13(1975):79–82.

Draguns, J. G.; Haley, E. M.; and Phillips, L. "Studies of Rorschach Content: A Review of Research Literature, Part III: Theoretical Formulations." *Journal of Projective Technique and Personality Assessment* 32(1968):16–32.

Duke University Center for the Study of Aging and Human Development. *Multidimensional Functional Assessment: The OARS Methodology.* Durham: Duke University Center for the Study of Aging and Human Development, 1978.

Dulsky, S. G., and Crout, M. H. "Predicting Promotional Potential on the Basis of Psychological Tests." *Personnel Psychology* 3(1950):345–51.

Duncan, S., Jr. "Interaction Units during Speaking Turns in Dyadic, Face-to-Face Conversations." In A. Kendon, R. M. Harris, and M. R. Key, eds., *Organization of Behavior in Face-to-Face Interaction.* The Hague: Mouton, 1975.

Duncan, S., Jr., and Fiske, D. W. *Face-to-Face Interaction: Research, Methods and Theory.* Hillsdale, N.J.: Erlbaum, 1977.

Durrell, G. *Three Singles to Adventure.* Harmondsworth: Penguin, 1964.

Eager, D. C. "Radioisotope Feces Tagging as a Population Estimator of Black Bear (*Ursus americanus*) Density in the Great Smoky Mountains National Park." M.S. thesis, University of Tennessee, 1977.

Edney, A. "Management of Euthanasia in Small Animal Practice." *Journal of the American Animal Hospital Association* 15, no.5(1979):645.

Edwards, E. H., ed. *Encyclopedia of the Horse.* London: Octopus Books, 1977.

Egbert, A. L., and Stokes, A. W. "The Social Behaviour of Brown Bears on an Alaskan Salmon Stream." In M. R. Pelton, J. Lentfer, and G. E. Folk, Jr., eds., *Proceedings of the Third International Conference on Bear Research and Management*, pp. 41–56. Morges, Switzerland: IUCN Series No. 40, Binghamton, N.Y. and Moscow, 1976.

Eisenbud, J. "A Recently Found Carving as a Breast Symbol." *American Anthropologist* 66(1964):141–47.

Eliot, T. S. *Old Possum's Book of Practical Cats.* New York: Harcourt, Brace, Jovanovich, 1968.

Elwell, F., and Maltbie-Crannell, A. "The Impact of Role Loss upon Coping Resources and Life Satisfaction of the Elderly." *Journal of Gerontology* 36(1981):223–32.

Endora, J. "Degradaciones y desvitizasiones en los delincuentes a tranes del test de Rorschach." *Aarchive Crimanle Neuropsiquiatric* 7(1959):167–82.

Engquist, C. L.; Davis, J. E.; and Bryce, R. H. "Can Quality of Life be Evaluated?" *Hospitals* 53, no.22(1979):97, 99–100.

Erikson, E. *Identity: Youth and Crisis.* New York: Norton, 1968.

Ernst, P.; Beran, B.; Safford, F.; and Kleinhauz, M. "Isolation and the Symptoms of Chronic Brain Syndrome." *Gerontologist* 18, no.5(1978):468–74.

Erwitt, E. *Son of a Bitch.* New York: Museum of Modern Art, 1979.

Evang, K. Letter to Elsebet Bodtker, 1974.

Evans-Pritchard, E. E. *The Nuer*. Oxford: Clarendon Press, 1940.

Ewer, R. F. *Ethology of Mammals*. London: Paul Elek, 1968.

Ewers, J. *The Horse in Blackfoot Indian Culture*. Washington, D.C.: Smithsonian Institution Press, 1980.

Exline, R. V., and Winters, L. C. "Affective Relations and Mutual Gaze in Dyads." In S. Tomkins, and C. Izard, eds., *Affect, Cognition and Personality*, pp. 318–51. New York: Springer, 1965.

Fawcett, G.; Stonner, D.; and Zepelin, H. "Locus of Control, Perceived Constraint, and Morale among Institutionalized Aged." *International Journal of Aging and Human Development* 11, no.1(1980):13–23.

Feldman, D. J. "Chronic Disabling Illness: A Holistic View." *Journal of Chronic Diseases* 27(1974):287–91.

Feldmann, B. M. "Why People Own Pets, Pet Owner Psychology and the Delinquent Owner." *Animal Regulation Studies* 1(1977):84–87.

Feldmann, B. M., and Carding, T. H. "Free-Roaming Urban Pets." *Health Services Reports* 88 (December 1973):956–62.

Felthous, A. T. "Companion Animals." In *International Journal to Study Animal Problems* 1, no.6(1980):349.

Festinger, L. A *Theory of Cognitive Dissonance*. Evanston: Row, Peterson, 1957.

Fiedler, L. *Freaks: Myths and Images of the Secret Self*. New York: Simon and Schuster, 1978.

Fine, R. "Use of the Despert Fables (Revised Form) in Diagnostic Work with Children." *Rorschach Research Exchange and Journal of Projective Technique* 11(1948):1–11.

Fisher, T. M. "A Behavioral Problem in Dogs." *Modern Veterinary Practice* 62, no.1(1981):4.

Fogle, B. "Attachment—Euthansia—Grieving." In B. Fogle, ed., *Interrelations between People and Pets*, pp. 331–42. Springfield, Ill.: Charles C. Thomas, 1981a.

————. *Interrelations between People and Pets*. Springfield, Ill.: Charles C. Thomas, 1981b

Folstein, M. F.; Folstein, S. E.; and McHugh, P. R. "Mini-Mental State: A Practical Method of Grading the Cognitive State of Patients for the Clinician." *Journal of Psychiatric Research* 12(1975):189–98.

Ford, M. *The Application of the Rorschach Test to Young Children*. Minneapolis: University of Minnesota Press, 1946.

Foster, J. C., and Anderson, J. E. "Unpleasant Dreams in Childhood." *Child Development* 7(1936):77–84.

Foulkes, D. "Longitudinal Studies of Dreams in Children." In J. D. Masserman, ed., *Dream Dynamics, Science and Psychoanalysis*, 19:48–71. New York: Grune and Stratton, 1971.

————. *A Grammar of Dreams*. New York: Basic Books, 1978.

Foulkes, D.; Pivik, T.; Steadman, H.; Spear, P.; and Symonds, J. "Dreams of the Male Child: An EEG Study." *Journal of Abnormal Psychology* 72(1967):457–67.

Foulkes, D.; Shepard, J.; and Scott, E. "Children's Dreams: Year 3 of a Longitudinal Sleep-Laboratory Study." *NIMH Grant 18315, Final Report, Part I*, 1974. (Unpublished)

Fox, M. W. "Animal Rights and Humane Ethics: A Veterinary Perspective." *California Veterinarian*, July 1977, pp. 21–23.

————. "Behavioral Effects of Rearing Dogs with Cats during the Critical Period of

Socialization." *Behaviour* 35(1969):273–80.

————. *Behaviour of Wolves, Dogs and Related Canids.* New York: Harper & Row, 1971.

————. *Between Animal and Man.* New York: Coward, McCann and Geoghegan, 1976.

————. *Concepts in Ethology.* Minneapolis: University of Minnesota Press, 1974a.

————. "Pet Mutilations and Veterinary Ethics." *International Journal to Study Animal Problems* 1(1980):80.

————. "Pet-Owner Relations." In R. S. Anderson, ed., *Pet Animals and Society.* London: Bailliere-Tindall, 1975a.

————. "Reflex Development and Behavioral Organization." In W. A. Himwich, ed., *Developmental Neurobiology,* pp. 553–80. Springfield, Ill.: Charles C. Thomas, 1970.

————. "Relationships between the Human and Nonhuman Animals." In B. Fogle, ed., *Interrelations between People and Pets,* pp. 23–39. Springfield, Ill.: Charles C. Thomas, 1981.

————. *Understanding Your Cat.* New York: Coward, McCann, and Geoghegan, 1974b.

————. "The Veterinarian: Mercenary, Saint Francis—or Humanist?" *Journal of the American Veterinary Medical Association* 166(1975b):276–79.

Frances, G. M. "Gesellschaft and the Hospital: Is Total Care a Misnomer?" *Advances in Nursing Sciences* 2, no.4(1980):9–13.

————. "Loneliness: Measuring the Abstract." *International Journal of Nursing Studies* 13(1976): 153–60.

Franti, C.; Kraus, J. F.; and Borhani, N. M. "Pet Ownership in a Suburban-Rural Area of California." *Public Health Reports* 89, no.5(1974):473–84.

Franti, C.; Kraus, J. F.; Borhani, N. O.; Johnson, S. L.; and Tucker, S. D. "Pet Ownership in Rural Northern California (El Dorado County)." *Journal of the American Veterinary Medical Association* 176(1980):143.

Frederickson, L. E. "Pet Planning Programs." *Modern Veterinary Practice* 56(1975):93–95.

Freed, E. X. "Normative Data on a Self-Administered Projective Question for Children." *Journal of Projective Technique and Personal Assessment* 29, no.1(1965):3–6.

Freedman, D. G.; King, J. A.; and Elliot, O. "Critical Period in the Social Development of Dogs." *Science* 133(1961):1016–17.

Freiberger, R., and Levinson, B. "Humans and Therapy: Companion Animals in the Family", Symp. Human–Companion Animal Bond. Cambridge, 1980.

Freud, S. "Analysis of a Phobia in a Five-Year-Old Boy" (1909). In P. Rieff, ed., *The Sexual Enlightenment of Children.* New York: Collier Books, 1963.

————. "Analysis of a Phobia in a Five-Year-Old Child." In J. Strachey, ed., *Collected Works,* 10:3–152. Standard ed. London: Hogarth Press, 1964.

————. *The Interpretation of Dreams.* New York: Wiley, 1961.

Friedman, A. S. "Implications of the Home Setting for Family Treatment." In A. S. Friedman, ed., *Psychotherapy for the Whole Family in Home and Clinic,* pp. 240–54. New York: Springer, 1965.

Friedmann, E. "Pet Ownership and Survival after Coronary Heart Disease." Paper presented at the Second Canadian Symposium on Pets and Society, Vancouver, B.C., Canada, May 30–June 1, 1979.

Friedmann, E.; Katcher, A. H.; Lynch, J. J.; and Thomas, S. A. "Animal Companions and One-Year Survival of Patients after Discharge from a Coronary Care Unit." *Public Health Report* 95, no.4(1980a):307–12.
————. "Health Consequences of Animal Ownership." *Archives of the Foundation of Thanatology* 9(2), 1981 (Abstract 20).
————. "Potential Health Benefits of Companion Animals." Paper presented at the Annual Meeting of the American Public Health Association, Detroit, 1980b.
————. "Social Conditions and Blood Pressure: Influence of Animal Companions." *Journal of Nervous and Mental Diseases* 1983, (in press).
Friedmann, E.; Thomas, S. A.; Noctor, M.; and Katcher, A. H. "Pet Ownership and Coronary Heart Disease Patient Survival." Abstract. *Circulation* 58(1978):II–168.
Fromm, E. *The Anatomy of Human Destructiveness*. New York: Holt, Rinehart and Winston, 1973.
Frost & Sullivan. *Pet Care Products---Foods, Health, and Grooming Aids and Pet Accessories*. New York: Frost & Sullivan, 1980.
Fuller, J. L. "Experiential Deprivation and Later Behavior." *Science* 158(1967):1645–52.
Furman, E. A *Child's Parent Dies*. New Haven: Yale University Press, 1974.
Futton, R., and Gottesman, D. J. "Anticipatory Grief: A Psychosocial Concept Reconsidered." *British Journal of Psychiatry* 137(1980):45–54.
Gahagan, L. "Sex Differences in Recall of Stereotyped Dreams, Sleep-Talking and Sleep-Walking." *Journal of Genetic Psychology* 48(1936):227–36.
Garshelis, D. L. "Movement Ecology and Activity Behavior of Black Bears in the Great Smoky Mountains National Park." M.S. thesis, University of Tennessee, 1978.
Geertz, C. *The Interpretation of Culture*. New York: Basic Books, 1973.
Geertz, H., and Geertz, C. "Teknonymy in Bali: Parenthood, Age-Grading and Genealogical Amnesia." In P. Bohannan and J. Middleton, eds., *Marriage, Family and Residence*, pp. 335–76. Garden City: Natural History Press, 1968.
George, L. K. "The Happiness Syndrome: Methodological and Substantive Issues in the Study of Social-Psychological Well-Being in Adulthood." *Gerontologist* 19, no.2(1979):210–16.
Gerber, I. "Bereavement and the Acceptance of Professional Services." *Community Mental Health Journal* 5, no.6(1969):487–95.
Gewirtz, J. L. "On Selecting Attachment and Dependence Indicators." In J. L. Gewirtz, ed., *Attachment and Dependency*, pp. 179–216. Washington, D.C.: Winston, 1972.
Giedion, S. *The Eternal Present*. New York: Pantheon Books, 1962.
Gill, W. S. "Animal Content in the Rorschach." *Journal of Projective Technique and Personality Assessment* 31(1967):49–56.
Glickman, L. T., and Schantz, P. M. "Epidemiology and Pathogenesis of Zoonotic Toxocariasis." *Epidemiologic Reviews* 3(1981):230–80.
Glickman, L. T.; Schantz, P. M.; and Cypress, R. H. "Canine and Human Toxocariasis: Review of Transmission, Pathogenesis, and Clinical Disease." *Journal of the American Veterinary Medical Association* 175(1979):1265–69.
Glosser, J. W.; Hutchinson, L. R.; Rich, A. B.; Huffaker, R. H.; and Parker, R. L. "Rabies in El Paso, Texas, Before and After Institution of a New Rabies Control Program." *Journal of the American Veterinary Medical Association* 157(1970):820–25.
Goldenberg, H. C. "A Resume of Some Make-A-Picture-Story (MAPS) Test Results." *Journal of Projective Technique* 15(1951):79–86.

Goldfarb, W. "The Animal Symbol in the Rorschach Test and an Animal Association Test." *Rorschach Research Exchange* 9(1945):8–22.

Goldman, I. *The Cubeo*. Urbana: University of Illinois Press, 1963.

Goldstein, J. H. *Social Psychology*. New York: Academic Press, 1980.

Goffman, E. *Stigma*. Englewood Cliffs: Prentice-Hall, 1963.

Goodwin, D. "Notes on Feral Pigeons." *Aviculture Magazine* 60(1954):190–312.

Goodwin, R. D. "Trends in the Ownership of Domestic Pets in Great Britain." In R. S. Anderson, ed., *Pet Animals and Society*, pp. 96–102. London: Balliere-Tindall, 1975.

Gordon, K. "Dreams of Orphan Children." *Journal of Delinquency* 8(1924):287–91.

Gowman, A. G. *The War Blind in American Social Structure*. New York: American Foundation for the Blind, 1957.

Green, B., special education teacher, Essex Elementary School, Essex, Conn. Personal communications, 1976, 1977, 1978.

Grey, Z. *Wild Horse Mesa*. New York: Grosset and Dunlap, 1924.

Griffin, D. R. *The Question of Animal Awareness*. 2d ed. New York: Rockefeller University Press, 1980.

Griffith, R. M.; Miyagi, O.; and Tago, A. "The Universality of Typical Dreams: Japanese vs. Americans." *American Anthropologist* 60(1958):1173–79.

Griffiths, A. O. and Brenner, A. "Survey of Cat and Dog Ownership in Champaign County, Ill. (1976)." *Journal of the American Veterinary Medical Association* 170(1977):1333–40.

Gunby, P. "Patient Progressing Well? He May Have a Pet." *Journal of the American Medical Association* 241(1979):438.

Gurel, L.; Linn, M.; and Linn, B. "Physical and Mental Impairment of Function Evaluation in the Aged: The PAMIE Scale." *Journal of Gerontology* 27(1972):83–90.

Gutheil, E. A. *The Handbook of Dream Analysis*. New York: Grove Press, 1960.

Guttmann, G. "The Psychological Determinants of Keeping Pets." In B. Fogle, ed., *Interrelations between People and Pets*, pp. 89–98. Springfield, Ill.: Charles C. Thomas, 1981.

Hadfield, J. A. *Dreams and Nightmares*. Baltimore: Penguin, 1954.

Hall, C., and Domhoff, B. "Aggression in Dreams." *International Journal of Social Psychiatry* 9(1963):259–67.

————. "Friendliness in Dreams." *Journal of Social Psychology* 62(1964):309–14.

Hall, C., and Lindzey, G. *Theories of Personality*. London: Wiley, 1957.

Hall, C., and Van de Castle, R. *The Content Analysis of Dreams*. New York: Appleton-Century-Crofts, 1966.

Hamilton, A. "Aboriginal Man's Best Friend?" *Mankind* 8 (1972).

Hamilton, G., Personal communication.

Hamilton, M. "A Rating Scale for Depression." *Journal of Neurology, Neurosurgery & Psychiatry* 23(1960):56–62.

Hamilton, G., and Robbins, M. "Psychology of the Owner Factor in Animal Behavior." Proceedings of the 48th Annual American Animal Hospital Association Meeting, pp. 3–7. South Bend, 1981.

Hanna, T. L., and Selby, L. A. "Characteristics of the Human and Pet Populations in Animal Bite Incidents Recorded at Two Air Force Bases." *Public Health Report* 96(November–December 1981):580–84.

Harlow, H. F. "The Development of Affectional Patterns in Infant Monkeys." In B. M.

Foss, ed., *Determinants of Infant Behavior*, pp. 3–28. London: Methuen, 1961.

————. *Learning to Love*. New York: Jason Aronsohn, 1974.

Harlow, H. F., and Harlow, M. K. "Social Deprivation in Monkeys." *Scientific American* 207(1962):136–44.

Harlow, H. F.; Harlow, M. K.; and Suomi, S. J. "From Thought to Therapy: Lessons from a Primate Laboratory." *American Scientist* 59(1971):538–49.

Harper, R. G.; Wiens, A. N.; and Matarazzo, J. D. *Nonverbal Communication*. New York: Wiley, 1978.

Harris, D.; Imperato, P. J.; and Oken, B. "Dog Bites—an Unrecognized Epidemic." *Bulletin New York Academy of Medicine* 50(October 1974):981–1000.

Harris, J. M. "The Nonconventional Human–Companion Animal Bond, Death, and the Veterinary Practitioner–Client Relationship." *Archives of the Foundation of Thanatology* 9, no.2(1981).

Harris, M. *Cows, Pigs, Wars and Witches*. New York: Vintage Books, 1975.

Hart, B. L. "Olfactory Tractotomy for Control of Objectionable Urine Marking in Cats." *Journal of the American Veterinary Medical Association* 179(1981):231–34.

————. "The Pet-Owner Relationship: The Difficult Pet." Paper presented at the 112th Annual American Veterinary Medical Association Meeting, July 17, 1975, Anaheim, Calif.

————. "Progestin Therapy for Aggressive Behavior in Male Dogs." *Journal of the American Veterinary Medical Association* 178(1981):1070–71.

Hart, B. L., and Barrett, R. E. "Effects of Castration on Fighting, Roaming, and Urine Spraying in Adult Male Cats." *Journal of the American Veterinary Medical Association* 163(1973):290.

Hart, B. L., and Voith, V. L. "Changes in Urine Spraying, Feeding and Sleeping Behavior of Cats Following Medial Preoptic Anterior Hypothalamic Lesions in Cats." *Brain Research* 145(1978):406–9.

Haworth, M. R. *The Cat: Facts about Fantasy*. New York: Grune and Stratton, 1966.

Hayes, S. Personal Interview Regarding Placement of Companion Dogs with Physically Impaired Individuals. Philadelphia, Pa., 1980.

Heiman, M. "The Relationship between Man and Dog." *Psychoanalytic Quarterly* 25(1956):568–85.

————. "Psychoanalytic Observations on the Relationship of Pet and Man." *Veterinary Medicine/Small Animal Clinician* 90(July 1965):713–18.

Hellman, D. S., and Blackman, N. "Enuresis, Firesetting and Cruelty to Animals: A Triad Predictive of Adult Crime." *American Journal of Psychiatry* 122, no.12(1966):1431–35.

Helsing, K. J., and Szklo, M. "Mortality after Bereavement." *American Journal of Epidemiology* 114(July 1981):41–52.

Helwig, G. Executive Director of the U.S. Pony Clubs, Inc. Personal communication, 1980.

Hemingway, E. *In Our Time*. New York: Charles Scribner and Sons, 1930.

Hemmer, H. "Socialization by Intelligence: Social Behavior in Carnivores as a Function of Relative Brain Size and Environment." *Carnivore* 1, no.1(1978):102–5.

Hendee, J. C., and Schoenfield, C., eds. *Human Dimensions in Wildlife Programs*. Seattle, Wash.: People/Natural Resources Research Council, 1973.

Henriksen, G. *Hunters in the Barrens: The Naskapi on the Edge of the White Man's*

World. St. John's: Institute of Social and Economic Research, Memorial University of Newfoundland, 1973.

Henry, J. *Jungle People: A Kaingang Tribe of the Highlands of Brazil.* New York: Vintage Books, 1964.

Hetherington, E. M., and Parke, R. D. *Child Psychology: A Contemporary Viewpoint.* 2d ed. New York: McGraw-Hill, 1979.

Hinde, R. A. *Towards Understanding Relationships.* London: Academic Press, 1979.

Hinde, R. A., and Spencer-Booth, Y. "Effects of Brief Separations from Mothers on Rhesus Monkeys." *Science* 173(1971):111–18.

Hinde, R. A., and Stevenson-Hinde, J., eds., *Constraints on Learning.* London : Academic Press, 1973.

Hines, L., et al. *The People-Pet Partnership Program.* Alameda, Calif.: Latham Foundation, 1980.

Holmes, T. H., and Rahe, R. H. "The Social Readjustment Rating Scale." *Journal of Psychosomatic Research* 22(1967):213–18.

Holzworth, J. "Easing Grief over Loss of a Pet: Practical Suggestions for Veterinarian and Owner." *Archives of the Foundation of Thanatology* 9, no. 2(1981):(Abstract 15).

Homans, G. *Social Behavior.* New York: Harcourt, Brace and World, 1961.

Hong, K. M.; Bowden, D. M.; and Kogan, K.L. "Telemetered Heart Rate as a Psychophysiological Correlate of Mother-Child Interaction." Paper presented at the Annual Meeting of the American Academy of Child Psychiatry, Houston, 1977.

Hopkins, A. "Ethical Implications in Issues and Decisions in Companion Animal Medicine." In L. McCullough and J. Morris, III, eds., *Implications of History and Ethics to Medicine—Veterinary and Human*, pp. 107–14. College Station, Texas: Texas A&M University Press, 1978.

————. "The Human/Companion Animal Bond—Grief of Loss." Paper presented at Symposium on Veterinary Medical Practice: Pet Loss and Human Emotion, Foundation of Thanatology, New York, 1981.

Hopkins, S. G.; Schubert, T. A.; and Hart, B. L. "Castration of Adult Male Dogs: Effects on Roaming, Aggression, Urine Marking and Mounting." *Journal of the American Veterinary Medical Association* 168(1976):1108.

Hornocker, M. C. "Population Characteristics and Social and Reproductive Behavior of the Grizzly Bear in Yellowstone National Park." M.S. thesis, Montana State University, 1962.

Horseman. Readership Survey Report. Advertising literature. Houston, Texas, 1980.

Hothersall, D., and Tuber, D. S. "Fears in Companion Dogs: Characteristics and Treatment." In J. D. Keehn, ed., *Psychopathology in Animals*, pp. 239–55. New York: Academic Press, 1979.

Hughes, R. *The Shock of the New.* New York: Knopf, 1981.

Huizinga, J. *The Waning of the Middle Ages.* Garden City: Doubleday, 1924.

Hull, R. *Man's Best Friend.* New York: Hippocrene Books, 1972.

Humane Society of the United States. *Responsible Animal Regulation.* Washington, D.C.: 1979.

Hunter-Warfel, M. "Disabled Learn to Ride at Happy Horseman School." *Pennsylvania Horse* 2(1969):4.

Hutchinson, D. "Therapeutic Animals." *Group to Study the Human–Companion Animal Bond Newsletter* 1, no. 4(1980):9-11.

Huxley, L. "A Natural Experiment on the Territorial Instinct." *British Birds* 27(1934):270–77.

Hymes, D. "Introductions: Toward Ethnographies of Communication." In J. Gumperz and D. Hymes, eds., *The Ethnography of Communication, American Anthropologist* 66, no.2, pt.2(1964)1–34.

Insinger, W. "Show Horses." *Town and Country* 135, no.5014(June 1981):120–23, 187–88.

International Union for Conservation of Nature and Natural Resources. *Introduction to the 9th Technical Meeting on Ecology of Man in the Tropical Environment.* Morges, Switzerland: IUCN, 1963.

Jahoda, M.; Deutch, M.; and Cook, S. *Research Methods in Social Relations.* New York: Dryden Press, 1951.

Jelliffe, S. E., and Brink, L. "The Role of Animals in the Unconscious with Some Remarks on Theriomorphic Symbolism as Seen in Ovid." *Psychoanalytical Review* 4(1917):253–71.

Jensen, A. E. *Myth and Cult among Primitive Peoples.* Chicago: University of Chicago Press, 1963.

Joel, W. "The Use of the Make-A-Picture-Story (MAPS) with Disturbed Adolescents." *Rorschach Research Exchange and Journal of Projective Technique* 12(1948):155–64.

Jonas, D. F. "Life, Death, Awareness and Concern: A Progression." In A. Toynbee et al., eds., *Life after Death.* New York: McGraw-Hill, 1976.

Jones, E. *On the Nightmare.* New York: Grove Press, 1959.

Jones, K. *Lunacy, Law and Conscience, 1744–1845.* London: Routledge & Kegan Paul, 1955.

Jonkel, C. J. "North American Bears: The Black, Brown (Grizzly) and Polar Bears." In J. I. Schmidt and D. O. Gilbert, eds., *Big Game of North America: Ecology and Management,* pp. 227–48. Washington, D.C.: Wildlife Management Institute/ Stackpole Books, 1978.

Jouvet, M. "Le comportement onirique." *Pour la science,* November 1979, pp. 136–52.

Jung, C. *The Archetypes and the Collective Unconscious.* New York: Pantheon Books, 1959.

————. *Man and His Symbols.* London: Picador, 1964.

————. *Psychology of the Unconscious.* New York: Moffat, Yard, 1916.

————. *Symbols of Transformation.* Bollingen Series 20. New York: Pantheon Books, 1956.

Kagan, N. *Interpersonal Process Recall—A Method of Influencing Human Interaction.* East Lansing: Michigan State University, 1975.

Kahn, R. "Aging and Social Support." In M. Riley, ed., *Aging from Birth to Death: Interdisciplinary Perspectives.* Boulder, Colo.: Westview, 1979.

Kahn, T. C. "The Kahn Test of Symbol Arrangement: Clinical Manual." *Perceptual Motor Skills* 7(1957):168.

Kahr, M. *Valazquez: The Art of Painting.* New York: Harper & Row, 1976.

Kaplan, H., and Calden, G. "An Elaboration of the 'Projective Question': The Animal Test." *Journal of Clinical Psychology* 23(1967):204.

Kappus, K. D. "Canine Rabies in the United States, 1971–73: A Study of Reported Cases with Reference to Vaccination History." *American Journal of Epidemiology* 103(1976):242–49.

Kasl, S. V.; Ostfeld, A. M.; Brody, G. M.; Snell, L.; and Price, C. A. "Effects of

Involuntary Relocation on the Health and Behavior of the Elderly." In S. G. Haynes and M. Feinleib, eds., *Epidemiology of Aging*. Washington, D.C.: United States Department of Health and Human Services, 1980.

Katcher, A. H. "The Animal in the Family." *Archives of the Foundation of Thanatology* 9, no. 2:1981 (Abstract 19), Foundation of Thanatology, 1983. In press.

————. "Interactions between People and Their Pets: Form and Function." In B. Fogle, ed., *Interrelations between People and Pets*, pp. 41–67. Springfield, Ill.: Charles C. Thomas, 1981.

————. "Potential Health Value of Pet Ownership." *Compendium on Continuing Education for the Small Animal Practitioner* 11, no.2(1980):117–22.

————. "Studies on the Nature of the Bond between People and Companion Animals in Contemporary Urban Society." Paper presented at the symposium from the Group for the Study of the Human-Companion Animal Bond. Dundee, Scotland; March 1979.

————. "Veterinary Medicine and the Study of Human Behavior." A Grant Proposal to H.E.W., Department of Public Health Service, Division of Manpower and Training Programs, Experimental and Special Projects. Washington, D.C., 1978.

Katcher, A. H., and Friedmann, E. "Potential Health Value of Pet Ownership." *Compendium on Continuing Education* II(2)(1981):117–22.

Katcher, A. H., and Rosenburg, M. A. "Euthanasia and the Management of the Clients' Grief." In *Compendium on Continuing Education for the Small Animal Practitioner* 1(December 1979):887–91.

Katcher, A. H.; Friedmann, E.; Goodman, M.; and Goodman, L. "Men, Women, and Dogs." *California Veterinarian*, in press.

Kaufman, I. C. "Mother-Infant Separation in Monkeys: An Experimental Model." In J. P. Scott, and E. Seany, eds., *Separation and Depression: Clinical and Research Aspects*. AAAS No. 94. Washington, D.C.: American Association for the Advancement of Science, 1973.

Kay, J. "Cat Hater's Calendar is Quickly Outdated." *Philadelphia Inquirer*, October 30, 1981, p. 11C.

Keddie, K. G. "Pathological Mourning after the Death of a Domestic Pet." *British Journal of Psychiatry* 131(1977):21–25.

Kellert, S. R. "American Attitudes toward and Knowledge of Animals: An Update." *International Journal to Study Animal Problems* 1, no.2(1980):87–119.

————. "Contemporary Values of Wildlife in American Society." In W. W. Shaw and E. H. Zube, eds., *Wildlife Values*. Fort Collins Center for Assessment of Noncommodity Natural Resource Values, Institutional Series Report. 1(1980):31–60.

————. "Perceptions of Animals in American Society." *Transactions, 41st North American Wildlife and Natural Resources Conference*, Washington, D.C.: The Wild Life Management Institute, 1976.

Kelly, G. A. *The Psychology of Personal Constructs*. Vols. 1 and 2. New York: Norton, 1955.

Kelly, H. H. "The Warm-Cold Variable in First Impressions of Persons." *Journal of Personality* 18(1950):431–39.

Kendon, A. "Some Functions of Gaze Direction in Social Interaction." *Acta Psychologica* 26(1967):22–47.

Kendon, A., and Ferber, A. "A Description of Some Human Greetings." In R. P.

Michael and J. H. Crook, eds., *Comparative Ecology and Behaviour of Primates*, pp. 591–668. New York: Academic Press, 1973.

Kidd, A. H., and Feldmann, B. M. "Pet Ownership and Self-Perceptions of Older People." *Psychological Reports* 48(1981):867–75.

Kilstrup, S., Hearing Dogs, Inc., 5901 E. 89th Ave., Henderson, Colorado 80640. Personal correspondence, 1980.

Kimble, G. A., and Garmezy, N. *Principles of General Psychology.* 2d ed. New York: Ronald Press, 1963.

Kimmins, C. W. *Children's Dreams, an Unexplored Land.* London: Allen & Unwin, 1937.

King, F. W., and King, D. C. "The Projective Assessment of the Female's Sexual Identification, with Special Reference to the Blacky Pictures." *Journal of Projective Technique and Personality Assessment* 28(1964):293–99.

King, I. M. *A Theory for Nursing: Systems, Concepts and Process.* New York: Wiley, 1981.

———. *Toward a Theory for Nursing.* New York: Wiley, 1971.

Kinsey, A. C.; Pomeroy, W. B.; and Martin, C. E. *Sexual Behavior in the Human Male.* Philadelphia: W. B. Saunders, 1948.

Kinsey, A. C.; Pomeroy, W. B.; Martin, C. E.; and Gebhard, P. H. *Sexual Behavior in the Human Female.* Philadelphia: W. B. Saunders, 1953.

Kirk, S. A. *Educating Exceptional Children.* Boston: Houghton Mifflin, 1962.

Klein, R. K., et al. "Transfer from a Coronary Care Unit." *Archives of Internal Medicine* 122(1968):104–8.

Kline, D. Testimony before Senate Subcommittee on Child and Human Development, January 24, 1979.

Kluckhohn, C. *Navaho Witchcraft.* Boston: Beacon Press, 1967.

Knox, T. *Overland through Asia.* Hartford: American Publishing Company, 1870.

Koocher, G., and Simmonds, D. "The Animal and Opposite Drawing Technique: Implications for Personality Assessment." *International Journal of Symbology* 2(1971):9–12.

Kornblatt, A. N., and Schantz, P. M. "Veterinary and Public Health Considerations in Canine Roundworm Control: A Survey of Practicing Veterinarians." *Journal of the American Veterinary Medical Association* 177(1980):1212–15.

Kotkin, A. "The Family Photo Album as a Form of Folklore." *Exposure* 16, no. 1(1978):4–8.

Kottenhoff, H. "Reliability and Validity of the Animal Percentage in Rorschachs." *Acta Psychologica* 22(1964):387–406.

Kramer, E. "The Fables Test." *Journal of Projective Technique and Personality Assessment* 32(1968):530–32.

Kramnick, I. "Children's Literature and Bourgois Ideology: Observations on Culture and Industrial Capitalism in the Later Eighteenth Century." In P. Zagorin, ed., *From Puritanism to the Enlightenment: Essays on British Culture and Politics.* Berkeley and Los Angeles: University of California Press, 1980.

Krathwohl, D. R.; Bloom, B. S.; and Masia, B. B. *Taxonomy of Educational Objectives. Handbook II: Affective Domain.* New York: David McKay, 1964.

Kubler-Ross, E. *On Death and Dying.* New York: Macmillan, 1969.

Kuhn, H. *On the Track of Prehistoric Man.* Translated by Alan Broderick. New York: Random House, 1955.

Kuhn, R. "Uber die Kritische Rorschach-Forschung und einige ihrer Ergebnisse." *Rorschachiana* 8(1963):105–14.

Kummer, H. "Spacing Mechanisms in Social Behavior." In J. F. Eisenberg and W. S. Dillon, eds., *Man and Beast: Comparative Social Behavior*, pp. 221–34. Washington, D.C.: Smithsonian Institution Press, 1971.

Kummer, H.; Gotz, W.; and Angst, W. "Triadic Differentiation: An Inhibitory Process Protecting Pair Bonds in Baboons." *Behaviour* 49(1974):62–87.

Kuo, Z. Y. "Further Study on the Behavior of the Cat toward the Rat." *Journal of Comparative Psychology* 25(1938):1–8.

————. "The Genesis of the Cat's Responses to the Rat." *Journal of Comparative Psychology* 11(1930):1–35.

————. "Studies on the Basic Factors in Animal Fighting: VII. Interspecies Coexistence in Mammals." *Journal of Genetic Psychology* 97(1960):211–25. Lacey, J. I. "Psychophysiological Approaches to the Evaluation of Psychotherapeutic Process and Outcome." In E. A. Rubinstein and M. B. Parloff, eds., *Research in Psychotherapy*. Washington, D.C.: American Psychological Association, 1959.

Lago, D. J. "A Systems Design Methodology for the Development of Individuality Oriented Human Services: The Assessment of Loneliness in Retired Men." *Dissertation Abstracts International* 38, no. 12(1978):5844–B.

La Piere, R. T. "Attitude versus Actions." In M. Fishbein, ed., *Readings in Attitude Theory and Measurement*, pp. 26–31. New York: Wiley, 1967.

Lapras, M. "Modern Psychotrope Therapy in the Dog." *Proceedings of the 6th World Congress, World Small Animal Veterinary Association*. Post Academisch Onderwijs Publikatic, 8:129–30, 177.

Larson, R. "Thirty Years of Research on the Subjective Well-Being of Older Americans." *Journal of Gerontology* 33(1978):109–25.

Laughlin, W. *Aleuts: Survivors of the Bering Land Bridge*. New York: Holt, Rinehart and Winston, 1980.

————. "Hunting: An Integratiing Biobehavior System and its Evolutionary Importancè." In R. Lee and I. DeVore, eds., *Man the Hunter*. Chicago: Aldine, 1968.

Lawrence, R. "Economics of the Horse Industry." Paper presented at the Equine Management Seminar, University of Delaware, Wilmington, Del., October 31, 1981.

Lawton, M. P. "The Dimensions of Morale." In D. P. Kent, R. Kastenbaum, and S. Sherwood, eds., *Research Planning and Action for the Elderly: The Power and the Potential of Social Science*, pp. 122–43. New York: Behavioral Publications, 1972.

Leach, E. R. "Anthropological Aspects of Language: Animal Categories and Verbal Abuse." In E. Lenneberg, ed., *New Directions in the Study of Language*, pp. 23–64. Cambridge, Mass.: M.I.T. Press, 1964.

Leach, M. *God Had a Dog*. New Brunswick, N.J.: Rutgers University Press, 1961.

Lebow, G. H. "Facilitating Adaptation in Anticipatory Mourning." *Social Casework* (July 1976):458–65.

Lee, D. *Hi Ya, Beautiful*. Documentary film on pet therapy at Lima State Hospital, Alameda, Calif.: Latham Foundation, 1978.

————. Interoffice memo, Lima State Hospital, January 24, 1978.

————. Personal communication, 1981.

Leigh, D. "The Psychology of the Pet Owner." *Journal of Small Animal Practice* 7(1966):517–21.

Lenoski, E. G. Personal data. Quoted in R. W. ten Bensel, "Rights of Children: Child Abuse and Neglect." Course syllabus, Minneapolis: School of Public Health, University of Minnesota, 1980.

Lesy, M. "'Mere' Snapshots Considered." *New York Times,* January 16, 1978.

Levin, M. G., and Potapov, L. P. *The Peoples of Siberia.* Chicago: University of Chicago Press, 1964.

Levine, S. "Stimulation in Infancy." *Scientific American* 202(1960):80–86.

Levinson, B. M. "Acute Grief in Animals." *Archives of the Foundation of Thanatology* 9(2)(1981) (Paper 11).

———. "The Dog as 'Co-therapist.'" *Mental Hygiene* 46(1961):59–65.

———. "Household Pets in Residential Schools: Their Therapeutic Potential." *Mental Hygiene* 52(1968):411–14.

———. "Household Pets in Training Schools Serving Delinquent Children." *Psychological Reports* 28(1971):472–75.

———. "Interpersonal Relationships between Pet and Human Being." In M. W. Fox et al., eds., *Abnormal Behavior in Animals.* Philadelphia: W. B. Saunders, 1968b.

———. "Nursing Home Pets: A Psychological Adventure for the Patient." *National Humane Review* 58, no. 4(1970):14–16; 58, no. 5(1970a):6–8.

———. *Pet-Oriented Child Psychotherapy.* Springfield, Ill.: Charles C. Thomas, 1969a.

———. "Pet Psychotherapy: Use of Household Pets in the Treatment of Behavior Disorder in Childhood." *Psychological Reports* 17(1965a):695–98.

———. "Pets and Environment." In R. S. Anderson, ed., *Pet Animals and Society.* London: Bailliere-Tindall, 1975.

———. *Pets and Human Development.* Springfield, Ill.: Charles C. Thomas, 1972.

———. "Pets and Old Age." *Mental Hygiene* 53(1969b):364–68.

———. "Pets and Personality Development." *Psychological Reports* 42(1978):1031–38.

———. "Pets: A Special Technique in Child Psychotherapy." *Mental Hygiene* 48(1964):243–48.

———. "Pets, Child Development, and Mental Illness." *Journal of the American Veterinary Medical Association* 157(1970b):1759–66.

———. "The Veterinarian and Mental Hygiene." *Mental Hygiene* 49(1965):320–23.

Levi-Strauss, C. *The Savage Mind.* Chicago: University of Chicago Press, 1966.

———. *Totemism.* Translated by Rodney Needham. Boston: Beacon Press, 1963.

Levy, S., and Levy, R. A. "Symbolism in Animal Drawings." In E. F. Hammer, ed., *The Clinical Application of Projective Drawings,* pp. 311-43. Springfield, Ill.: Charles. C. Thomas, 1958.

Lewis, C. S. *A Grief Observed.* London: Faber, 1961.

Leyhausen, P. "Dominance and Territoriality as Complemented in Mammalian Social Structure." In A. H. Esser, ed., *Behavior and Environment—The Use of Space by Animals and Men,* pp. 22–33. New York: Plenum Press, 1971.

———. *Cat Behavior.* New York: Garland STPM Press, 1979.

Liang, J.; Dvorkin, L.; Kahaha, E.; and Mazian, F. "Social Integration and Morale: A Re-examination." *Journal of Gerontology* 35, no. 5(1980):746–57.

Lilly, J. C. *Communication between Man and Dolphin.* New York: Crown Publishers, 1978.

Lin, N., et al. "Social Support, Stressful Life Events, and Illness: A Model and an Empirical Test." *Journal of Health and Social Behavior* 20(1979):108–19.

Lindemann, E. "Symptomatology and Management of Acute Grief." *American Journal of Psychiatry* 101(1944):141–48.

Lindner, R. "The Content Analysis of the Rorschach Protocol." In L. E. Abt and L. Bellak, eds., *Projective Psychology*, pp. 75–90. New York: Alfred Knopf, 1952.

Link, M. Riding therapist, Green Chimneys School, Brewster, N.Y. Personal communication, 1979.

Linton, H. "Rorschach Correlates of Response to Suggestion." *Journal of Abnormal Social Psychology* 49(1954):75–83.

Little, L. "The Greyhound Saint, a Review of *Le Saint Levrier: Guinefort, Guerisseur d'Enfants depuis le XIIIe Siecle* by Jean-Claude Schmitt." *New York Review* 28, no.7(1981):26–28.

Lockwood, R., and Beck, A. M. "Dog Bites among Letter Carriers in St. Louis." *Public Health Report* 90(May–June 1975):267–69.

Lohmann, N. "Correlations of Life Satisfaction, Morale and Adjustment Measures." *Journal of Gerontology* 32, no.1(1977):73–75.

London, J. *Great Short Works*. Introduction by Earle Labor. New York: Harper & Row, 1965.

Loney, J. "The Canine Therapist in a Residential Children's Setting: Qualifications, Recruitment Training and Related Matters." *Journal of the American Academy of Child Psychiatry* 10(1971):518–23.

Longrigg, R. "Women in the Hunting Field." In M. Seth-Smith, ed., *The Horse*, pp. 90–93. London: Octopus Books, 1979.

Lorenz, K. Z. "Der Kumpan in der Umwelt des Vogels." *Journal of Ornithology* 83(1935):137–215.

———. *King Solomon's Ring*. London: Methuen, 1952.

———. *Man Meets Dog*. New York: Penguin, 1964.

———. "The Triumph Ceremony of the Grey-Lag Goose." *(Anser anser) Philosophical Transactions of the Royal Society, Series B* 251(1965):477–78.

———. *The Year of the Greylag Goose*. London: Eyre Methuen, 1978.

Lott, D., and Hart, B. "Aggressive Domination of Cattle by Fulani Herdsmen and Its Relation to Aggression in Fulani Culture and Personality." *Ethos* 5, no.2(1977):174–86.

Lumholz, C. *Among Cannibals*. New York: Scribner & Sons, 1889.

Luomala, K. "The Native Dog in the Polynesian System of Values." In S. Diamond, ed., *Culture in History*, pp. 190–240. New York: Columbia University Press, 1960.

Lynch, J. J. *The Broken Heart: The Medical Consequences of Loneliness*. New York: Basic Books, 1977.

Lynch, J. J.; Fregin, G. F.; Mackie, J. B.; and Monroe, R. R. "The Effect of Human Contact on the Heart Activity of the Horse." *Psychophysiology* 11(1974):472–78.

Lynch, J. J., and McCarthy, J. F. "The Effect of Petting on a Classically Conditioned Emotional Response." *Behavior Research Therapy* 5(1967):55–62.

Lynch, J. J.; Thomas, S. A.; Mills, M. E.; Malinow, K.; and Katcher, A. H. "The Effects of Human Contact on Cardiac Arrhythmia in Coronary Care Patients." *Journal of Nervous Mental Disorders* 158(1974):88–98.

Lynch, J. J.; Thomas, S. A.; Paskewitz, D. A.; Katcher, A. H.; and Weir, L.O. "Human Contact and Cardiac Arrhythmia in a Coronary Care Unit." *Psychosomatic Medicine* 39(1977):183–88.

McBride, G. "Theories of Animal Spacing: The Role of Flight, Fight, and Social Distance." In A. H. Esser, ed., *Behavior and Environment: The Use of Space by Animals and Men*, pp. 53–68. New York: Plenum, 1971.

McClellan, C. *The Girl Who Married the Bear*. Ottawa: National Museums of Canada, 1970.

McCleod, C. "Animals in the Nursing Home." *Guide for Activity Directors*. Colorado Springs, 1980 (pamphlet).

McClintic, D. "Animal Welfare: More Pressure Coming." *Journal of Veterinary Medical Education* 7(1980):115.

McCowan, L. *It's Ability That Counts: A Training Manual on Therapeutic Riding for the Handicapped*. Olivet, Mich.: Olivet College Press, 1972.

McCulloch, M. "Contributions to Mental Health." In R. K. Anderson, ed., *A Description of the Responsibilities of Veterinarians as They Relate Directly to Human Health*. Washington, D.C.: Public Health Service, Bureau of Health Manpower. Contract 321-76-0202, 1976.

————. "Coping with Illness and Death of Pets: The Role of the Human Health Care Team." *Archives of the Foundation of Thanatology* 9, no. 2(1981):(Paper 57).

————. "Management of People Allergic to Pets." Paper presented at the American Veterinary Medical Association Annual Meeting, Seattle, Wash., July 1979b.

————. "Pets and Family Health." Paper presented at the American Veterinary Medical Association Annual Meeting, Seattle, Wash., July 1979a.

————. "The Pet as Prothesis: Defining Criteria for the Adjunctive Use of Companion Animals in the Treatment of Medically Ill, Depressed Outpatients." In B. Fogle, ed., *Interrelations between People and Pets*, pp. 101–23. Springfield, Ill.: Charles C. Thomas, 1981b.

————. "The Pet-Owner Relationship: The Difficult Client." Paper presented at the 112th Annual American Veterinary Medical Association Meeting, Anaheim, Calif., July 17, 1975.

————. "The Veterinarian in the Human Health Care System: Issues and Boundaries." In L. McCullough and J. Morris, III, eds., *Implications of History and Ethics to Medicine—Veterinary and Human*, pp. 53–68. College Station, Texas: Texas A&M University Press, 1978.

————. Work reported in D. Brodie, *The Pet-Owner Bond: The Role of the Veterinarian*. Presented at the Dundee Symposium of the Group for the Study of the Human–Companion Animal Bond, March 1979c.

McCulloch, W. F.; Ames, E. R.; Diesch, S. L.; and Martin, R. J. *Pets and Human Diseases: What's the Risk?* The Medical Interview on Animal Related Diseases, 18 Case-Studies and Bibliography. American Medical Association Symposium. 1976.

McCulloch, W. F.; Dorn, C. R.; and Blenden, D. C. "The University and the City: Proposal for Urban Extension Veterinarians." *Journal of the American Veterinary Medical Association* 157(1970):1771–76.

McCulloch, W. F., and McCulloch, M. "The Veterinarian and the Human/Companion Animal Bond." *Veterinary Economics* 22(September 1981):18–22.

McCulloch, W. F., and Selby, L. A. "Attitudes of Professionals toward the Current Teaching of Veterinary Public Health and Preventive Medicine in Schools of Veterinary Medicine." *Pan American Health Organization Scientific Publication* 313(1975):9–26.

McDonald, A. "Mourning After Pets," letter to the editor. *British Journal of Psychiatry* 131(1977):551.

————. "The Pet Dog in the Home: A Study of Interactions." In B. Fogle, ed., *Interrelations between People and Pets*, pp. 195–206. Springfield, Ill.: Charles C. Thomas, 1981.

McGuigan, F. J. Obituary: W. Horsley Gantt (1892–1980). *American Psychologist* 36(1981):417–19.

McKenzie, P. "Are Dogs a Health Menace?" *Journal of Small Animal Practitioners* 18(1977):359–64.

McMiller, P., and Ingham, J. G. "Friends, Confidants and Symptoms." *Social Psychiatry* 11(1976):51–58.

Man, E. H. *On the Aboriginal Inhabitants of the Andaman Islands.* London: Royal Anthropological Institute of Great Britain and Ireland, 1932.

Mancini, J. A., and Orthner, D. K. "Situational Influences on Leisure Satisfaction and Morale in Old Age." *Journal of the American Geriatrics Society* 28, no.10(1980):466–71.

Manning, A. "Animal Learning: Ethological Approaches." In M. R. Rozensweig and E. L. Bennett, eds., *Neural Mechanisms of Learning and Memory*, pp. 147–58. Cambridge, Mass.: M.I.T. Press, 1976.

————. *An Introduction to Animal Behaviour.* 3d ed. London: Edward Arnold, 1979.

Manning, M., and Herrmann, J. "The Relationships of Problem Children in Nursery Schools." In R. Gilmour and S. Duck, eds., *Personal Relationships in Disorder*, pp. 143–66. New York: Academic Press, 1981.

Marks, I. M. "Clinical Phenomena in Search of Laboratory Models." In J. D. Masur and M. E. P. Seligman, eds., *Psychopathology: Experimental Models*, pp. 174–313. San Francisco: W. H. Freeman, 1977.

————. *Living with Fear.* New York: McGraw-Hill, 1978.

Marr, J. S., and Beck, A. M. "Rabies in New York City, with Guidelines for Prophylaxis." *Bulletin New York Academy of Medicine* 52, no.6(1976):606–16.

Martin, H., and Rodeheffer, M. "The Psychological Impact of Abuse on Children." In G. Williams and J. Money, *Traumatic Abuse and Neglect of Children at Home*, pp. 254–62. Baltimore: Johns Hopkins University Press, 1980.

Martin, R. J.; Schnurrenberger, P. R.; and Rose, N. J. "Epidemiology of Rabies Vaccinations of Persons in Illinois, 1967–1968." *Public Health Report* 84(1969):1069–77.

Martinka, C. J. "Preserving the Natural Status of Grizzlies in Glacier National Park." *Wildlife Society Bulletin* 2, no.1(1974):13–17.

Maslow, A. A work discussed in C. Hall and G. Lindzey, *Theories of Personality*. London: Wiley, 1957.

Mason, W. A. "Social Experience and Primate Cognitive Development." In G. M. Burghardt and M. Bekoff, eds., *The Development of Behavior: Evolutionary and Comparative Aspects*, pp. 233–51. New York: Garland Press, 1978.

Mason, W. A., and Berkson, G. "Effects of Maternal Mobility on the Development of Rocking and Other Behaviors in Rhesus Monkeys: A Study with Artificial Mothers." *Developmental Psychobiology* 8(1975):197–211.

Mason, W. A., and Kenney, M. D. "Redirection of Filial Attachments in Rhesus Monkeys: Dogs as Mother Surrogates." *Science* 183(1974):1209–11.

Matthews, L. H. *Man and Wildlife.* London: Croom-Helm, 1975.

May, R. *Love and Will.* New York: Dell, 1974.

May, W.; Blendon, D.; and McCulloch, W. "Public Health Aspects of Small Animal Veterinary Medical Practice." *HSMHA Health Reports* 86, no.10(1971):910.

Mayberry, R. P. "The Mystique of the Horse Is Strong Medicine: Riding as Therapeutic Recreation." *Rehabilitation Literature* 39(June–July 1978):192–96.

Mead, M. *Letters from the Field: 1925–75.* New York: Harper & Row, 1977.

Meares, A. A *System of Medical Hypnosis*. Philadelphia: W. B. Saunders, 1961.

Mech, L. D. *The Wolf: The Ecology and Behaviour of an Endangered Species*. New York: Natural History Press, 1970.

Medley, M. "Life Satisfaction across Four Stages of Adult Life." *International Journal on Aging and Human Development* 11(1980):193–209.

Meggitt, M. "The Association between Australian Aborigines and Dingoes." In A. Leeds and A. Vayda, eds., *Man, Culture, and Animals*, pp. 7–26. Washington, D.C.: American Association for the Advancement of Science, 1965.

————. Personal communication, 1980.

Mehta, G. M. "Use of Domesticated Birds and Animals in a Child Guidance Clinic." *Indian Journal of Social Work* 29, no. 4(1969):400–405.

Meier, G. W. "Infantile Handling and Development in Siamese Kittens." *Journal of Comparative and Physiological Psychology* 54(1961):284–86.

Meier, G. W., and Stuart, J. L. "Effects of Handling on the Physical and Behavioral Development of Siamese Kittens." *Psychological Reports* 5(1959):497–501.

Melville, H. *Moby Dick*. New York: Hendricks House, 1952.

Menninger, K. A. "Totemic Aspects of Contemporary Attitudes Towards Animals." In G. V. Wilbur and W. Muensterberger, eds., *Psychoanalysis and Culture*, pp. 42–74. New York: International Universities Press, 1951.

Merrill, E. H. "Bear Depredations at Backcountry Campgrounds in Glacier National Park." *Wildlife Society Bulletin* 6, no. 3(1978):123–27.

Messent, P. R. "Walking Dogs and the Pet-Owner Bond." *Newsletter of the Society for the Study of the Human–Companion Animal Bond* 2, no. 3(1981).

Messent, P. R., and Serpell, J. A. "An Historical and Biological View of the Pet-Owner Bond." In B. Fogle, ed., *Interrelations between People and Pets*, pp. 5–22. Springfield, Ill.: Charles C. Thomas, 1981.

Milgram, S. "The Image Freezing Machine." *Psychology Today* 10(1977):12.

Modern Veterinary Practice: "Spay Clinics: Boon or Boondoggle?" Staff Report. *Modern Veterinary Practice*, March 1973, pp. 23–29.

————. "Spay Clinics: The Other Side of the Story." Staff Report. *Modern Veterinary Practice*, April 1973, pp. 29–34.

Moelk, M. "The Development of Friendly Approach Behavior in the Cat: A Study of Kitten-Mother Relations and the Cognitive Development of the Kitten from Birth to Eight Weeks." In J. S. Rosenblatt, R. A. Hinde, C. Beer, and M. Musnel, eds., *Advances in the Study of Behavior*, vol. 10. New York: Academic Press, 1979.

Monbeck, M. *The Meaning of Blindness*. Bloomington: Indiana University Press, 1973.

Moniot, D. "Photographs and Their Meaning: An Experimental Study Assessing Cognitive Dimensions Which Viewers of Three Photographic Competence Levels Use in Generating Meaning from Photographs Embedded in Art vs. Documentary Contexts." Ph.D. dissertation, Temple University, 1979.

Monks of New Skete. *How to Be Your Dog's Best Friend*. Boston: Little Brown, 1978.

Montagu, A. "Time, Morphology and Neoteny in the Evolution of Man." In M. F. Ashley Montagu, ed., *Culture and the Evolution of Man*, pp. 324–42. New York: Oxford University Press, 1962.

————. *Touching*. New York: Harper & Row, 1978.

————. *Touching: The Human Significance of the Skin*. New York: Columbia University Press, 1971.

Morgan, W. "Snapshot Anniversary." *Popular Photography*, October 1974, pp. 28, 127.

Morris, D. *The Naked Ape*. New York: McGraw-Hill, 1967.

Morris, J. N.; Wolf, R. S.; and Klerman, L. V. "Common Themes among Morale and Depression Scales." *Journal of Gerontology* 30, no.2(1975):209–15.

Morrow, S. *The Second Official I Hate Cats Book*. New York: Holt, Rinehart and Winston, 1981.

Moyer, K. E. "Kinds of Aggression and Their Physiological Basis." *Communication and Behavioral Biology* A(2):65-87.

Moynihan, D. *On Understanding Poverty*. New York: Basic Books, 1968.

Mugford, R. A. "Dog Behaviour: Living with a Neurotic Dog—Part 2." *Veterinary Practice* 16, no.2(1981):7–8.

————. "Problem Dogs and Problem Owners: The Behavior Specialist as an Adjunct to Veterinary Practice." In B. Fogle, ed., *Interrelations between People and Pets*, pp. 295–317. Springfield, Ill.: Charles C. Thomas, 1981.

————. "The Social Significance of Pet Ownership." In S. A. Corson and E. O'L. Corson, eds., *Ethology and Non-verbal Communication in Mental Health*, pp. 111–22. Oxford: Pergamon, 1980.

Mugford, R. A. and M'Comisky, J. G. "Some Recent Work on the Psychotherapeutic Value of Caged Birds with Old People." In R. S. Anderson, ed., *Pet Animals and Society*. London: Bailliere-Tindall, 1975.

Murphree, O. D.; Peters, J. E.; and Dykman, R. A. "Effect of Petting on Nervous, Stable and Crossbred Pointer Dogs." *Conditional Reflex* 2(1969):273–76.

Musello, C. "Home Mode Photography: A Study of Visual Interaction and Communication in Everyday Life." Master's thesis, Annenberg School of Communications, University of Pennsylvania, 1977.

Neiburg, H. A. "Domestic Pet Loss as a Model for Subsequent Human Loss and Bereavement." *Archives of the Foundation of Thanatology*, Abstracts 54 (1981).

————. "Pathologic Grief in Response to Pet Loss." *Archives of the Foundation of Thanatology* Abstracts 7 (1981).

Neiburg, H. A., and Fischer, A. *Pet Loss*. New York: Harper & Row, 1982.

Nelson, B. *The Sulidae, Gannets and Boobies*. London: Oxford University Press, 1978.

"A Newsweek Poll." *Newsweek*, March 23, 1981, p. 47.

Nowell, I. *The Dog Crisis*. New York: St. Martin's Press, 1978.

Ohman, J. "Allergy in Man Caused by Exposure to Mammals." *Journal of the American Veterinary Medical Association* 172(1978):1403.

Okoniewski, L. A. "The Psychological Aspects of Man-Animal Relationships." Master's thesis. Hahnemann Medical College, 1978.

Ordish, L. S. "Motivating Factors in Animal Welfare Workers." Workshop presentation at the International Conference on the Human/Companion Animal Bond, Philadelphia, Pa., October 1981.

Orlowitz, L. "The Content Analysis of Adolescent Dreams." Unpublished manuscript, 1971.

Orr, M. *Le test de Rorschach et l'imago maternelle*. Paris: Groupement Francais du Rorschach, 1958.

Orwell, G. *Animal Farm*. New York: Harcourt, Brace, 1946.

Otto, D. M., and Purvis, M. J. "Recreational Horse Ownership in Minnesota: A Case Study of Anoka County." Department of Agriculture and Applied Economics, Economic Report 78-4. Minneapolis: University of Minnesota, Institute of Agriculture, Forestry and Home Economics, 1978.

Oxford Universal Dictionary on Historical Principles. Oxford: Clarendon Press, 1955.

Palmore, E., and Luikart, C. "Health and Social Factors Related to Life Satisfaction." *Journal of Health and Social Behavior* 13(1972):68–80.

Papez, J. E. *Comparative Neurology.* New York: Crowell, 1929.

Parad H.; Selby, L.; and Quinlan, Jr. "Crisis Intervention with Families and Groups." In R. W. Roberts and H. Northen, eds., *Theories of Social Work with Groups,* pp. 304–30. New York: Columbia University Press, 1976.

Parkes, C. M. *Bereavement.* Harmondsworth: Penguin, 1972.

————. "Bereavement Counselling: Does It Work?" *British Medical Journal* 281, no.6232(1980):3–6.

————. *Bereavement: Studies of Grief in Adult Life.* New York: International Universities Press, 1972.

Parrish, H. M.; Clack, F. B.; Brobst, D.; and Mock, J. F. "Epidemiology of Dog Bite." *Public Health Report* 74(1959):891–903.

Pedigree Petfoods. *Pets and the British.* Leicestershire: Pedigree Petfoods' Education Centre, 1980.

Peele, S. *Love and Addiction.* New York: Taplinger, 1975.

Pelton, M. R., and Marcum, L. C. "The Potential Use of Radio-Isotopes for Determining Densities of Black Bear and Other Carnivores." *Proceedings of the Symposium on Predators, 55th Annual Meeting of the Society of Mammalogists,* pp. 221–36. Missoula, Mont.: Morges, Switzerland, IUCN.

Pelton, M. R.; Scott, C. D.; and Burghardt, G. M. "Attitudes and Opinions of Persons Experiencing Property Damage and/or Injury by Black Bears in the Great Smoky Mountains National Park." In M. R. Pelton, J. Lentfer, and G. E. Folk, Jr., eds., *Third International Conference on Bear Research and Management,* pp. 157–68. Binghamton, N.Y., and Moscow. Morges, Switzerland: [IUCN Series Rep. 40, 1976.

Perin, C. "Dogs as Symbols in Human Development." In B. Fogle, ed., *Interrelations between People and Pets,* pp. 68–88. Springfield, Ill.: Charles C. Thomas, 1981.

Peters, R. *Mammalian Communication: A Behavioral Analysis of Meaning.* Monterey, Calif.: Brooks, Cole, 1980.

Petulla, J. M. "Historic Values Affecting Wildlife in American Society." In W. W. Shaw and E. H. Zube, eds., *Wildlife Values,* pp. 23–30. Fort Collins: Center for Assessment of Noncommodity Natural Resource Values, Institutional Series Report No. 1, 1980.

Phares, E. J. "Internal-External Control as a Determinant of the Amount of Social Influence Exerted." *Journal of Personality and Social Psychology* 2, no.5(1965):642–47.

Phillips, L., and Smith, J. G. *Rorschach Interpretation: Advanced Techniques.* New York: Grune and Stratton, 1953.

Piotrowski, Z. A. *Perceptanalysis.* New York: Macmillan, 1957.

Pitcher, E. G., and Prelinger, E. *Children Tell Stories: An Analysis of Fantasy.* New York: International Universities Press, 1963.

Plutarch. Dryden translation, revised by A. H. Clougy. New York: Modern Library, 1956, pp. 101–2.

Pope, A. "Shedding Light on the 'Rage Syndrome' in Springer Spaniels." *Kennel Review* 1981, pp. 64, 68, 70.

"Popularity of Horseback Riding Continues to Grow." *California Horse Review* 17, no.1(1980):124.

Potok, A. *Ordinary Daylight.* New York: Holt, Rinehart, and Winston, 1980.

Power, E. *Medieval People.* Garden City: Doubleday, 1954.

"Principles of Veterinary Medical Ethics." *Journal of the American Veterinary Medical Association* 174(1979):31.

Proceedings of the First Canadian Symposium on Pets and Society: An Emerging Municiple Issue. Toronto, Ontario, June 23–25, Ottawa, 1976. Ontario: Canadian Veterinary Medical Association, 1976.

Proceedings of the National Conference on Dog and Cat Control. Denver, Colorado, February 3–5, 1976. Chicago: American Veterinary Medical Association, 1976.

Proceedings of the National Conference on Ecology of the Surplus Dog and Cat Problem. Chicago, Ill., May 21–23, Chicago: American Veterinary Medical Association, 1974.

Proceedings of the Second Canadian Symposium on Pets and Society. Vancouver, Canada, May 30–June 1, 1979. Toronto, Ontario: Dr. Ballard's Pet Food Division, Standard Brands Food Company, 1979.

Pruitt, C. H. "Social Behavior of Young Captive Black Bears." Ph.D. dissertation, University of Tennessee, 1974.

Purvis, M. J., and Otto, D. M. "Household Demand for Pet Food and the Ownership of Cats and Dogs: An Analysis of a Neglected Component of U.S. Food Use." Staff paper, pp. 76–83. Department of Agriculture and Applied Economics, University of Minnesota, St. Paul, 1976.

Putnam, P. *Love in the Lead.* New York: Putnam, 1979.

Quackenbush, J. E. "Pets, Owners, Problems and the Veterinarian: Applied Social Work in a Veterinary Teaching Hospital." *The Compendium on Continuing Education for the Small Animal Practitioner* 3, no.9(1981a):764–70.

———. "Social Work in a Veterinary Hospital: A Response to Owner Grief Reactions." *Archives of the Foundation of Thanatology* 9(2)(1981), Abstract 56.

"Quarter Horse: Most Popular Breed." *Quarter Horse Journal*, February 1978, pp. 154–62.

Quinn, K. "Dogs for Therapy." *Pure-Bred Dogs American Kennel Gazette*, September 1979, pp. 38–41.

Rainwater, A. J. "Elderly Loneliness and Its Relation to Residential Care." *Journal of Gerontological Nursing* 10, no.6(1980):593–99.

Rappaport, R., and Rappaport, R. N. *Leisure and the Family Life Cycle.* Boston: Routledge & Kegan Paul, 1975.

Rappaport, E. A. "Zoophily and Zooerasty." *Psychoanalytical Quarterly* 37(1968):565–87.

Rappaport, R. *Pigs for the Ancestors.* New Haven: Yale University Press, 1968.

Raskin, N. J. *The Attitudes of Sighted People toward Blindness.* National Psychological Research Council on Blindness, 1956.

Redding, R. W., and Walker, T. L. "Electroconvulsive Therapy to Control Aggression in Dogs." *Modern Veterinary Practice* 57(1976): 595–97.

Rehr, H., ed. *Medicine and Social Work: An Exploration in Interprofessionalism.* New York: Prodist, 1974.

Reis, H., and Nezlek, J. "Physical Attractiveness in Social Interaction." *Journal of Personality and Social Psychology* 38(1980):604–17.

Reite, M; Short, R.; Kaufman, I. C.; Synes, A. J.; and Pauley, J. D. "Heart Rate and Body Temperature in Separated Monkey Infants." *Biological Psychiatry* 13(1978):91–105.

Reznikoff, C. *Holocaust*. Los Angeles: Black Sparrow Press, 1975.

Rheingold, H., and Eckermen, C. "Familiar Social and Nonsocial Stimuli and the Kitten's Response to a Strange Environment." *Developmental Psychobiology* 4 (1971):71–89.

Rice, B. *The Other End of the Leash*. Boston: Little, Brown, 1968.

Rice, S.; Brown, L.; and Caldwell, H. S. "Animals and Psychotherapy: A Survey." *Journal of Community Psychology* 1(1973):323–26.

Riesman, D.; Glazer, and Denny, R. *The Lonely Crowd*. New Haven: Yale University Press, 1950.

Ripley, S. D., and Lovejoy, T. E. "Threatened and Endangered Species." In H. P. Brokaw, ed., *Wildlife in America*, pp. 365–78. Washington, D.C.: U.S. Government Printing Office, 1978.

Robb, S. S. "Residents' Use of Leisure: Report of a Pilot Study." Pittsburgh, Pa.: Veterans Administration Medical Center, April 1978.

————. "Resources in the Environment of the Aged." In A. G. Yurick, S. S. Robb, B. E. Spier, and N. J. Ebert, eds., *The Aged Person and the Nursing Process*. New York: Appleton-Century-Crofts, 1980.

Robb, S. S.; Boyd, M.; and Pristash, C. L. "A Wine Bottle, Plant and a Puppy." *Journal of Gerontological Nursing* 6, no. 12(1980):721–28.

Robinson, K. D. "Therapeutic Interaction: A Means of Crisis Intervention with Newly Institutionalized Elderly Persons." *Nursing Clinics of North America* 9(1974):89–96.

Rogers, L. L. "Movement Patterns and Social Organization of Black Bear in Minnesota." Ph.D. dissertation, University of Minnesota, 1977.

Rollin, B. E. "Moral Philosophy and Veterinary Education." Unpublished manuscript.

————. "Updating Veterinary Medical Ethics." *Journal of the American Veterinary Medical Association* 173(1978):1016.

————. *Animal Rights and Human Morality*. Buffalo: Prometheus, 1981.

Rosenblatt, R. C. "Behavior in Public Places: Comparison of Couples Accompanied and Unaccompanied by Children." *Journal of Marriage and the Family* 36(1974):750–55.

Rosenthal, S. R. Personal communication, 1982.

————. "Risk Exercise (RE)." *Polo '67*, reprinted in *The Corinthian*, September 1968, pp. 10–12.

————. "Risk Exercise (RE)." *Stress* 1, no. 2(1980):37–40.

————. "Risk Exercise and the Physically Handicapped." *Rehabilitation Literature* 36, no. 5(1975):144–49.

Rosin, P. "Horseback Riding for the Handicapped: A Discussion of the Benefits." Paper presented to the Fourteenth World Congress Rehabilitation International, June 1980.

Ross, S., executive director of the Green Chimneys School, Brewster, N.Y. Personal conversations, 1977, 1978, 1979, 1980.

Rotter, J. B. "Generalized Expectancies for Internal Versus External Control of Reinforcement." *Psychological Monographs* 80(1), Whole No. 609(1966): 1–28.

Rubin, H. D., and Beck, A. M. "Ecological Behavior of Free-Ranging Urban Dogs." *Applied Animal Ethology* 8(1982):161–68.

Rubin, Z. "Liking and Loving." In Z. Rubin, ed., *Doing Unto Others*. Englewood Cliffs: Prentice-Hall, 1974.

Ruby, J. "In a Pic's Eye: Interpretive Strategies for Deriving Significance and Meaning from Photographs." *Afterimage* 3, no. 9(1976).

————. "Is an Ethnographic Film a Filmic Ethnography?" *Studies in the Anthropology of Visual Communication* 2, no.2(1975).

Rumbaugh, D. M., ed. *Language Learning by a Chimpanzee: The Lana Project*. New York: Academic Press, 1977.

Rusalem, H. "Environmental Supports of Public Attitudes toward the Blind." *New Outlook* 54(1960):277–88.

Ryder, E. L., and Romasco, M. "Establishing a Social Work Service in a Veterinary Hospital." In B. Fogle, ed., *Interrelations between People and Pets*, pp. 209–20. Springfield, Ill.: Charles C. Thomas, 1981.

————. "Social Work Service in a Veterinary Teaching Hospital." *Compendium on Continuing Education for the Practicing Veterinarian* 2(March 1980):215–20.

Rynearson, E. K. "Humans and Pets and Attachment." *British Journal of Psychiatry* 133(1978):550–55.

————. "Pathologic Attachment between Human and Pet: The Veterinarian's Nightmare." Paper presented to the Symposium on Veterinary Medical Practice: Pet Loss and Human Emotion. New York: Foundation of Thanatology, 1981.

Salmon, I. M., and Salmon, P. W. *Who Owns Who?: Psychological Research into the Human-Pet Bond in Australia*. Melbourne: Pet Care Information and Advisory Service, 1981.

Salmon, P. W. *Personal Psychology of Change in Management*. University of Melbourne, 1981.

————. *A Psychological Investigation of Farm Management Education*. University of Melbourne, 1980.

Salmon, P. W., and Bock, I. M. *Rural Community Attitudes toward Land Use in the Geelong Region*. Melbourne: University of Melbourne, 1978.

Sapolsky, A. "An Effort at Studying Rorschach Content Symbolism: The Frog Response." *Journal of Consulting Psychology* 28(1964):469–72.

Sarason, E. K. "The Discriminatory Value of the Rorschach Test between Two Etiologically Different, Mentally Defective Groups." Ph.D. dissertation, Clark University, 1950.

Sarton, M. *Journal of Solitude*. New York: Norton, 1977.

SAS Institute. *SAS Users Guide: The Statistical Analysis System*. Cary, N.C.: SAS Institute, 1979.

Savishinsky, J. "The Child Is Father to the Dog: Canines and Personality Processes in an Arctic Community." *Human Development* 17, no.6(1974b):460–66.

————. "The Dog and the Hare." In A. Clark, ed., *Proceedings of the Northern Athapaskan Conference*, vol. 2. Ottawa: National Museums of Canada, 1975.

————. *The Trail of the Hare: Life and Stress in an Arctic Community*. New York: Gordon and Breach, 1974a.

Schaller, G. B., and Lowther, G. R. "The Relevance of Carnivore Behavior to the Study of Early Hominids." *Southwestern Journal of Anthropology* 25, no.4(1969):307–41.

Schantz, P. M., and Glickman, L. T. "Current Concepts in Parasitology: Toxocaral Visceral Larva Migrans." *New England Journal of Medicine* 298, no.8(1978):436–39.

Scheuerman, M. L. "An Exploratory Study of the Functions of Canine Pets in Families." Master's thesis, Rutgers, The State University of New Jersey, 1973.

Schmeck, H. M., Jr. "Survey in Africa Finds Monkeys Using 'Rudimentary' Language." *New York Times*, November 28, 1980, pp. 1A & 22A.

Schneider, R., and Vaida, M. L. "Survey of Canine and Feline Populations: Alameda and Contra Costa Counties, California, 1970." *Journal of the American Veterinary Medical Association* 166(1975):481–86.

Schnell, A. M. "Uber Gespenstertraume bei Schulkindern." *Psychiat. Neurol. Med. Psychol.* 7(1955):10–18, 33–42.

Schwabe, C. *Cattle, Priests and Progress in Medicine*. Wesley W. Spink Lectures on Comparative Medicine, Vol. 4. Minneapolis: University of Minnesota Press, 1978.

Schwartz, A. A., and Rosenberg, I. "Observations on the Significance of Animal Drawings." *American Journal of Orthopsychiatry* 25(1955)729–46.

Scott, J. P. "Critical Periods in Behavioral Development." *Science* 138(1962):949–57.

————. "The Domestic Dog: A Case of Multiple Identities." In M. A. Roy, ed., *Species Identity and Attachment*. New York: Garland STPM Press, 1980.

————. "Evolution and Domestication of the Dog." In T. H. Dubzhansky, M. K. Hecht, and W. Steere, eds., *Evolutionary Biology*, 2:243–75. New York: Appleton-Century-Crofts, 1968.

————. "Nonverbal Communication in the Process of Social Attachment." In S. A. Corson et al., eds., *Ethology and Nonverbal Communication in Mental Health*, pp. 135–41. New York: Pergamon, 1980.

Scott, J. P., and Fuller, J. L. *Genetics and the Social Behavior of the Dog*. Chicago: University of Chicago Press, 1965.

Scott, J. P., and Marston, M. V. "Critical Periods Affecting Normal and Maladjustive Social Behavior in Puppies." *Journal of Genetic Psychology* 77(1950):25–60.

Scott, J. P.; Stewart, J. M.; and DeGhett, V. J. "Separation in Infant Dogs: Emotional Response and Motivational Consequences." In J. P. Scott and E. Senay, eds., *Separation and Depression: Clinical and Research Aspects*, no. 94. Washington, D.C.: American Association for the Advancement of Science, 1973.

Scott, R. *The Making of Blind Men*. New York: Russell Sage Foundation, 1969.

Searles, H. F. *The Nonhuman Environment*. New York: International Universities Press, 1960.

Sebeok, T. A., ed. *How Animals Communicate*. Bloomington: Indiana University Press, 1977.

Sebkova, J. Senior Thesis, Department of Psychology, University of Lancaster, Lancaster, England, 1978.

Seiler, C.; Cullen, J. S.; Zimmerman, J.; and Reite, M. "Cardiac Arrythmias in Infant Pigtail Monkeys Following Maternal Separation." *Psychophysiology* 16, no.2(1979):130–35.

Seitz, P. F. D. "Infantile Experience and Adult Behavior in Animal Subjects: [II. Age of Separation from the Mother and Adult Behavior in the Cat." *Psychosomatic Medicine* 21(1959):353–78.

Selby, A. A.; Anderson, R. K.; Blenden, D. C.; Dorn, C. R; Hubbard, H. B.; and McCulloch, W. F. "A Competency-Based Curriculum for Veterinary Public Health and Preventive Medicine." *Pan American Health Organization Scientific Publication No. 313*, 1975.

Selected Papers, Third International Conference on Riding for the Disabled. Warwickshire, England: Riding for the Disabled Association, 1979.

Self, M. C. *The American Horse Show*. New York: A. S. Barnes, 1958.

Seligman, M. E. P., and Hager, J. L., eds. *Biological Boundaries of Learning*. New York: Appleton-Century-Crofts, 1972.

Selltiz, C.; Wrightsman, L.; and Cook, S. *Research Methods in Social Relations*. New York: Holt, Rinehart and Winston, 1976.

Serpell, J. A. "Duets, Greetings and Triumph Ceremonies: Analogous Displays in the Parrot Genus Trichoglossus." *Zeitschrift fur Tierpsychologie* 55(1981):268–83.

Sevenster, P. "Incompatability of Response and Reward." In R. A. Hinde and J. Stevenson-Hinde, eds., *Constraints on Learning*, pp. 265–83. London: Academic Press, 1973.

Shanas, E. "Living in Families: Cross National Research on the Family Life of Old People." In G. Maddox, I. C. Siegler, and D. Blazer, eds., *Families and Older Persons: Policy, Research, and Practice*. Durham, N.C.: Duke University Center for the Study of Aging and Human Development, 1980.

Shaw, A. "Defining the Quality of Life." *Hastings Center Reports* 7, no.5(1977):11.

Sheridan, J. P. "Dogs, Cats, and Other Pets." *Practitioner* 215(1975):172–77.

Sherman, E., and Newman, E. S. "The Meaning of Cherished Personal Possessions for the Elderly." *Journal of Aging and Human Development* 8, no.2(1977–78):181–92.

Shneidman, E. S. *The Make-A-Picture-Story Test*. New York: Psychological Corporation, 1949.

————. "The MAPS Test with Children." In A. I. Rabin, and M. R. Haworth, eds., *Projective Techniques with Children*, pp. 130–48. New York: Grune and Stratton, 1960.

Siegel, A. "Reaching Severely Withdrawn through Pet Therapy." *American Journal of Psychiatry* 118(1962):1045–46.

Siegel, J. S. "Recent and Prospective Demographic Trends for the Elderly Population and Some Implications for Health Care." In S. G. Haynes and M. Feinleib, eds., *Epidemiology of Aging*. Washington, D.C.: U.S. Department of Health and Human Services, 1980.

Siegel, R. K. "An Ethologic Search for Self-Administration of Hallucinogens." *International Journal of the Addictions* 8(1973):373–93.

————. "Normal Hallucinations of Imaginary Companions." *McLean Hospital Journal* 2, no.2(1977):66–80.

————. "The Psychology of Life after Death." *American Psychologist* 35(1980):911–31.

Siller, J.; Chipman, A.; Ferguson, L.; and Vann, D. *Attitudes of the Nondisabled toward Physically Disabled*. New York: New York University School of Education, 1967.

Singer, F. J., and Bratton, S. P. "Black Bear Management in the Great Smoky Mountains National Park." *United States Department of Interior, National Park Service, Great Smoky Mountain National Park Management Report* 13(1977):32.

Singer, M. "Pygmies and Their Dogs: A Note on Culturally Constituted Defense Mechanisms." *Ethos* 6, no.4(1978):270–77.

Simons, F. *Eat Not This Flesh: Food Avoidances in the Old World*. Madison: University of Wisconsin Press, 1961.

Skipper, J., et al. "Physical Disability among Married Women." In Stubbins, Jr., *Social and Psychological Aspects of Physical Disability*. Baltimore: University Park Press, 1977.

Skinner, B. F. "Pigeons in a Pelican." *American Psychologist* 15(1960):28–37.

Smith, W. J. *The Behavior of Communication: An Ethological Approach*. Cambridge, Mass.: Harvard University Press, 1977.

Smotherman, W. P.; Hunt, L. E.; McGinnis, L. M.; and Levine, S. "Mother-Infant Separation in Group-Living Rhesus Macaques: A Hormonal Analysis." *Developmental Psychobiology* 12, no.3(1979):211–17.

Solomon, K. "The Depressed Patient: Social Antecedents of Psychopathology in the

Elderly." *Journal of the American Geriatrics Society* 29, no.1(1981):14–18.

Sontag, S. *On Photography.* New York: Dell, 1977.

Speck, R. V. "Mental Health Problems Involving the Family, the Pet, and the Veterinarian." *Journal of the American Veterinary Medical Association* 145(1964):150–54.

————. "The Transfer of Illness Phenomenon in Schizophrenic Families." In A. S. Friedman, ed., *Psychotherapy for the Whole Family in Home and Clinic.* New York: Springer, 1965.

Speitzer, E.; Snyder, E.; and Larson, D. "The Relative Effects of Health and Income on Life Satisfaction." *International Journal on Aging and Human Development* 10(1979–80):283.

Spenser, E. *Faerie Queen.* London: Macmillan, 1886.

Spier, B. E. "The Nursing Process as Applied to the Developmental Tasks of the Aged." In A. G. Yurick, S. S. Robb, B. E. Spier, and N. J. Ebert, eds., *The Aged Person and the Nursing Process.* New York: Appleton-Century-Crofts, 1980.

St. Expury, A. *The Little Prince.*

Starkey, M. *The Devil in Massachusetts.* New York: Time-Life Books, 1963.

Starr, M., and Huck, J. "Man vs. Coyote in L.A." *Newsweek,* October 26, 1981, p. 35.

Stead, A. "Euthanasia in the Cat and Dog." Report to British Small Animal Veterinary Association, 1979.

Steele, J. H. "The Epidemiology and Control of Rabies." *Scandinavian Journal of Infectious Diseases* 5(1973):299–312.

Steinhart, P. "Essay: The Need to Feed." *Audubon* 82, no.2(1980):126–27.

Stekel, W. *The Interpretation of Dreams.* New York: Liveright, 1943.

Steward, J. *Theory of Culture Change.* Urbana: University of Illinois Press, 1955.

Stokols, D. "Environmental Psychology." *Annual Review of Psychology* 29(1978):253–95.

Stone, A. "Institutional Peonage." In *Mental Health and Law: A System in Transition,* pp. 109–17. Washington, D.C.: U.S. Department of Health, Education and Welfare. Public Health Service, 1975.

Stones, M., and Kozma, A. "Issues Relating to the Usage and Conceptualization of Mental Health Constructs Employed by Gerontologists." *International Journal on Aging and Human Development* 11(1980):269–81.

Stonorov, D., and Stokes, A. W. "Social Behavior of the Alaska Brown Bear." In S. Herrero, ed., *Bears: Their Biology and Management.* Morges, Switzerland: IUCN New Series No. 23:232–42, 1972.

Strathern, M. *Women In-Between.* London: Seminar Press, 1972.

"Study on the Economic Impact of Horse Shows." *Quarter Horse Journal,* May 1980, pp. 170–73.

Styron, W. *Sophie's Choice.* New York: Bantam Books, 1980.

Sue, H. "Hare Indians and Their World." Ph.D. dissertation. Bryn Mawr College, 1964.

Suomi, S. J. "Factors Affecting Responses to Social Isolation in Rhesus Monkeys." In G. Serban and A. Kling, eds., *Animal Models in Human Psychobiology,* pp. 9–26. New York: Plenum, 1976.

Swanson, G. A. "Wildlife on Public Lands." In H. P. Brokaw, ed., *Wildlife in America,* pp. 428–41. Washington, D.C.: U.S. Government Printing Office, 1978.

Szasz, K. *Petishism: Pets and Their People in the Western World.* New York: Holt, Rinehart and Winston, 1969.

Tanner, A. *Bringing Home Animals: Religious Ideology and Mode of Production of the Mistassini Cree Hunters.* St. John's: St. John's Institute of Social and Economic Research, Memorial University of Newfoundland, 1979.

Tate-Eagar, J. and Pelton, M. R. "Panhandler Black Bears in the Great Smoky Mountains National Park." Contract report to the National Park Service, Southeast Regional Office, Atlanta, Ga., 1979.

Tate, J. "Aggression in Human-Bear Interactions: The Influence of Setting." *Proceedings of the Second Conference on Scientific Research in the National Parks.* San Francisco, 1979.

Tate, J., and Pelton, M. R. "Human-Bear Interactions in the Great Smoky Mountains National Park." *Proceedings of the Fifth International Conference on Bear Research and Management.* Madison (in press).

Taulbee, E. S., and Stenmark, D. E. "The Blacky Pictures Test: A Comprehensive Annotated and Indexed Bibliography (1949–1967)." *Journal of Projective Technique and Personality Assessment* 32(1968):105–37.

Taylor, B. *Stubbs.* London: Phaidon, 1975.

Terrace, H. S. *Nim: A Chimpanzee Who Learned Sign Language.* New York: Knopf, 1979.

Thomas, K. J.; Murphree, O. D.; and Newton, J. E. "The Effect of Person on Nervous and Stable Pointer Dogs." *Conditional Reflex* 5(1972):74–81.

Thompson, S. *Motif-Index of Folk-Literature.* Rev. ed. 6 volumes. Bloomington: Indiana University Press, 1955.

Thornton. G. R. "The Effect upon Judgements of Personality Traits of Varying a Single Factor in a Photograph." *Journal of Social Psychology* 18(1943):127–48.

Thurber, J. *Thurber's Dogs.* New York: Simon and Schuster, 1963.

Tinbergen, E. and Tinbergen, N. "The Aetiology of Childhood Autism: A Criticism of the Tinbergens' Theory: A Rejoinder." *Psychological Medicine* 6(1976):545–49.

————. "Early Childhood Autism: An Ethological Approach." *Zeitschrift fur Tierpsychologie* 10(1972):1–53.

Tinbergen, N. "Comparative Studies on the Behaviour of Gulls (Laridae): A Progress Report." *Behaviour* 15(1959):1–70.

Todd, A. "Public Relations, Public Education, and Wildlife Management." *Wildlife Society Bulletin* 8, no.1:55-60.

Toseland, R., and Rasch, J. "Correlates of Life Satisfaction: An Aid Analysis." *International Journal on Aging and Human Development* 10(1979–80):203–11.

Town and Country. Numerous articles about the thoroughbred horse industry. July 1981.

Townsend, J. "The Relationship between Rorschach Signs of Aggression and Behavioral Aggression in Emotionally Disturbed Boys." *Journal of Projective Technique and Personality Assessment* 31(1967):13–21.

Truby, H.; Smith, B.; Phillips, N. "Project Inreach: Can Bottlenose Dolphins Elicit Unprecedented Communication Responses from Children Labelled Language-Impaired, Retarded, or Autistic?" Paper prepared in conjunction with a videotape production and slide demonstration for presentation at the annual meeting of the Society for Applied Anthropology, Denver, Colo., March 21, 1980.

Tuber, D. S.; Hothersall, D.; and Peters, M. F. "On the Expression of Emotion and the Treatment of Fear." In V. L. Voith, P. L. Borchelt, eds., *The Veterinary Clinics of North America: Small Animal Practice: Animal Behavior,* vol. 12, pp. 607–23. Philadelphia: W. B. Saunders.

Tuber, D. S.; Hothersall, D.; and Voith, V. L. "Animal Clinical Psychology: A Modest Proposal." *American Psychologist* 29(1974):762–66.

Tylor, E. B. *Religion and Primitive Culture.* Vol. 2. New York: Harper and Brothers, 1958.

U.S. Department of Interior, National Park Service. *Environmental Assessment of the*

Alternatives for the General Management Plan, Great Smoky Mountain Park. Gatlinburg, Tenn., 1976. Unpublished report.

Vance, M. E. "The Significance of Animals in Dreams." M.A. thesis, Western Reserve University, 1956.

Van Leeuwen, J. "A Child Psychiatrist's Perspective on Children and Their Companion Animals: Animals and Child Development." In B. Fogle, ed., *Interrelations between People and Pets*, pp. 175–94. Springfield, Ill.: Charles C. Thomas, 1981.

Verhave, T. "The Pigeon as a Quality-Control Inspector." *American Psychologist* 21(1966):109–15.

Vines, G. "Wolves in Dogs' Clothing." *New Scientist* 91, no.1270(1981):648–52.

Vladeck, B. E. *Unloving Care: The Nursing Home Tragedy.* New York: Basic Books, 1980.

Voith, V. L. "Attachment between People and Their Pets: Behavior Problems of Pets that Arise from the Relationship between Pets and People." In B. Fogle, ed., *Interrelations Between People and Pets*, pp. 271–94. Springfield, Ill.: Charles C. Thomas, 1981.

————. "Attachment of Owners to Pets Despite Behavior Problems of the Animal: A Review of 100 Cases Seen at the Animal Behavior Clinic, Veterinary Hospital, University of Pennsylvania." 1981. Submitted for publication, Journal American Veterinary Medical Association.

————. "Behavior Problems." In S. J. Ettinger, ed., *Textbook of Veterinary Internal Medicine*, Vol. 1, pp. 208–27. Philadelphia: W. B. Saunders, 1983.

————. "Behavioral Problems." In E. A. Chandler et al., eds., *Canine Medicine and Therapeutics, British Small Animal Veterinary Association Textbook of Canine Medicine*, pp. 395–424. London: Blackwell Scientific Publications, 1979.

————. "Diagnosis and Treatment of Aggressive Behavior Problems in Dogs." *American Animal Hospital Association's 47th Annual Meeting Proceedings*, South Bend, Ind.: 1980.

————. "Intermale Aggression in Dogs." *Modern Veterinary Practice*, March 1980, pp. 256–58.

————. "Multiple Approaches to Treating Behavior Problems." *Modern Veterinary Practice*, August 1979, pp. 651–54.

————. "Profile of 100 Animal Behavior Cases." *Modern Veterinary Practice*, May 1981, pp. 394–96.

————. "What is Attachment?" Unpublished manuscript, University of Pennsylvania School of Veterinary Medicine, 1980.

von Bertalanffy, L. *General System Theory.* New York: George Braziller, 1968.

Waehner, T. S. "Interpretation of Spontaneous Drawings and Paintings." *Genetic Psychology Monographs* 33(1946):3–72.

Walster, D. *Proceedings of the Meeting of Group for the Study of Human-Companion Animal Bond.* Dundee, Scotland, March 23–25, 1979.

Watzlawick, P. *Pragmatics of Human Communication.* New York: Norton, 1967.

Wenzel, B. M. "Tactile Stimulation as Reinforcement for Cats and Its Relation to Early Feeding Experience." *Psychological Reports* 5(1959):297–300.

White, K., and Speisman, J. *Adolescence.* Monterey, Calif.: Brooks/Cole, 1976.

White, S. A. "Narrative of an Expedition into the North-Western Regions of South Australia." *Transactions of the Royal Society of South Australia* 139, 1915.

Whitney, G. D. *Archives of Foundation of Thanatology* (1981):36.

WHO *Expert Committee on Rabies. World Health Organization Technical Report Series.* No. 523. Geneva: World Health Organization, 1973.

Wilbur, R. "Pets, Pet Ownership and Animal Control, Social and Psychological Attitudes 1975." Proceedings of the National Conference on Dog and Cat Control. February 3–5, Denver, Chicago: American Veterinary Medical Association, 1976.

Williams, J. E. "Crisis Intervention among the Bereaved: A Mental Health Consultation Program for Clergy." In G. A. Specter, W. L. Claiborn, eds., *Crisis Intervention*, pp. 138–57. New York: Behavioral Publications, 1973.

Wilson, E. O. *Sociobiology*. Cambridge, Mass.: Harvard University Press, 1975.

Wilson, M.; Warren, J. M.; and Abbott, L. "Infantile Stimulation, Activity, and Learning by Cats." *Child Development* 36(1965):843–53.

Winkler, W. G. "Human Deaths Induced by Dog Bite, United States, 1974–1975." *Public Health Report* 92(1977):425–29.

Winnicott, D. W. "Transitional Objects and Transitional Phenomena." *International Journal of Psychoanalysis* 24(1953):88–97.

Winter, N. H. "The Influence of Riding on the Learning Disabled." *North American Riding Handicapped Association News* 3, no.2(1975):5–7.

Wolanin, M. O. "The Cinderella Effect: An Administrative Challenge." *Concern* 3, no.3(1977):8–12.

Wolfman, A. *The 1973–74 Wolfman Report on the Photographic Industry in the United States*. New York: 1974.

Wolpe, J. *The Practice of Behavior Therapy*. New York: Pergamon, 1969.

————. *Psychotherapy Reciprocal Inhibition*. Stanford, Calif.: Stanford University Press, 1958.

Wood, B. S.; Mason, W. A.; and Kenney, M. D. "Contrasts in Visual Responsiveness and Emotional Arousal between Rhesus Monkeys Raised with Living and Those Raised with Inanimate Substitute Mothers." *Journal of Comparative and Physiological Psychology* 93(1979):368–77.

"Woodville Suit Asks Better Care." *Pittsburgh Post Gazette*, December 9, 1980, p. 1.

Woolf, V. *Flush: A Biography*. New York: Harcourt Brace, 1933.

Woolverton, M., medical social worker, Fitzsimmons Army Hospital, Aurora, Colo. Personal conversations.

World Wildlife Fund. Declaration of First International Congress on Nature and Man. Amsterdam, World Wildlife Fund, 1967.

Wormser, J. V. "The World of the Black Bear." Philadelphia: Lippincott, 1966.

Worth, D., and Beck, A. M. "Multiple Ownership of Animals in New York City." *Transactions & Studies College of Physicians Philadelphia* 3, no.4(1981):280–300.

Worth, S. "Film as Non-Art." *American Scholar* 35(1966):322–34.

————. *Studying Visual Communication*. L. Gross, ed. Philadelphia: University of Pennsylvania Press, 1981.

Worth, S., and Adair, J. *Through Navaho Eyes*. Bloomington: Indiana University Press, 1972.

Wright-Wolcott, A. riding therapist. Lower Connecticut Valley Educational Riding Association, Lyme, Conn. Personal conversations, 1976, 1977.

Wundt, W. *Grundzuge der physiologischen Psychologie*. Leipzig, 1874.

Yates, W. *Skeezer: Dog with a Mission*. Irvington-on-Hudson, N.Y.: Harvey House, 1973.

Yoder, A. *Animal Analogy in Shakespeare's Character Portrayal*. New York: King's (Columbia University Press), 1947.

Youmans, E. G., and Yarrow, M. "Aging and Social Adaptation: A Longitudinal Study of Healthy Elderly Men." In S. Granik, R. D. Patterson, eds., *Human Aging II: An Eleven Year Follow-Up Biomedical and Behavioral Study*. DHEW Publication

Number (HSM) 70-9037, Washington, D.C.: U.S. Government Printing Office, 1971:95–104.

Yoxall, A., and Yoxall, D. Proceedings of the Meeting of Group for the Study of Human–Companion Animal Bond. Dundeee, Scotland, March 23-25, 1979.

Yurick, A. G. "Sensory Experiences of the Elderly Person." In A. G. Yurick, S. S. Robb, B. E. Spier, N. J. Ebert, eds., *The Aged Person and the Nursing Process*. New York: Appleton-Century-Crofts, 1980.

Zeuner, F. A *History of Domesticated Animals*. New York: Harper & Row, 1963.

Zunin, L., and Zunin, N. *Contact: The First Four Minutes*. Los Angeles, Nash, 1972.

Proceedings of the
International Conference on
the Human–Companion Animal Bond

· The University of Pennsylvania
Philadelphia

October 5, 6, 7, 1981

Host
The Center for the Interaction of Animals and Society
School of Veterinary Medicine, University of Pennsylvania
The Conference and the work of the Center have been supported by grants from:
    The Geraldine R. Dodge Foundation
    The National Institutes of Mental Health

Sponsors

The Center for the Interaction of Animals and Society
The Delta Society
The Latham Foundation

Cosponsors

American Animal Hospital Association
American Psychiatric Association
American Veterinary Medical Association
British Small Animal Veterinary Association
British Veterinary Association
The Humane Society of the United States

Program Committee

Aaron Honori Katcher, M.D., Chairman
Alan M. Beck, Sc.D.
Leo K. Bustad, Ph.D., D.V.M.
Bruce Fogle, D.V.M., M.R.C.V.S.
Alton Hopkins, D.V.M.
Meredith Lloyd-Evans, M.A., Vet.M.B., M.R.C.V.S.
Michael J. McCulloch, M.D.
Peter R. Messent D.Phil.

Conference Administration

Frances Paone, Administrator
Barbara Dixon, Assistant

Major Support for the Conference Was Provided by:

Pet Food Institute
The Gaines Dog Care Center
Allen Products Co., Inc.
American Pet Products Manufacturers Association, Inc.
Kal Kan Foods, Inc.
Pet Industry Joint Advisory Council
Docktor Pet Centers, Inc.

Contributors Were:

Alabama Veterinary Medical Assoc., Ms. Stephanie Amey, Animal Welfare League of Arlington, Va., Bayshore Animal Hospital, Beecham Laboratories, Community Animal Control Magazine, Mrs. Jill Cooper, Bernice B. Gorden, The Greater Akron Canton Professional Dog Groomers Assn., International Association of Pet Cemeteries, Felicia D. Lovelett, Martin's Feed Mills, Richard Meen, Dr. Joseph Millar, Morris Animal Foundation, National Groomers Association, New York State Veterinary Medical Society, Oregon Veterinary Medical Association, Gerald M. Ormon, DVM, Paw Prints Country Estate Burial, Valerie Penstone, Professional Groomers Association, Inc., Elizabeth Randolph, Richard Manufacturing Co., Riverside Humane Society, A. H. Robbins Co., Sylvia B. Salk, D.V.M., E. R. Squibb & Sons, Inc., Summer County Humane Society, Ermengarde Sweeney, Florence Webster.